GUINNESS WORLD RECORDS

★ ABOUT THIS BOOK

This year's typeface is a slightly condensed version of Frutiger, a san serif font designed in 1976 by one of the world's most famous type designers, Adrian Frutiger (Switzerland, b. 1928). The face was created for signage in Charles de Gaulle Airport (Paris, France); not quite as round as Frutiger's other famous creation, Univers, this font – and its **various weights** – can be read clearly from many angles.

Creating this year's cover has been a long and challenging process. The design incorporates two different kinds of very thin silver foil – holographic (providing the vertical "pillars-of-light" effect) and lens (providing the reflective globe in the center). This combination of foils makes its debut with this edition of the book, and, in all, we'll get through around 508 miles (818 km) of it – enough to line the route from London to Paris and back!

New international editions this year include Hungarian and Arabic – so we now publish in over 100 countries! Our list of languages for 2007 reads: American English, Arabic, Brazilian Portuguese, Chinese, Croatian, Czech, Danish, Dutch, English, Estonian, Finnish, French, German, Greek, Hebrew, Hungarian, Icelandic, Italian, Japanese, Latvian, Norwegian, Portuguese, Russian, Slovakian, Spanish, and Swedish!

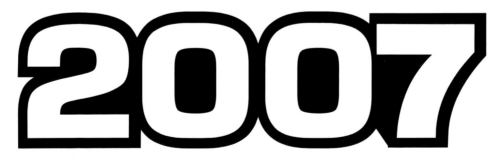

2007

Dedicated to Ann Collins
1956–2005

British Library Cataloging-in-Publication Data: a catalog record for this book is available from the British Library

ISBN
ISBN-13 9781904994121
ISBN-10 1904994121

For a complete list of credits and acknowledgments, turn to p.286

If you wish to make a record claim, find out how on p.7. Please ALWAYS contact us <u>before</u> making a record attempt

A selection of the exclusive interviews featured in this book can be read in their unedited form at www.guinnessworld records.com/2007

Check the website regularly for record-breaking news as it happens, plus exclusive video footage of record attempts. You also can sign up for the official Guinness World Records newsletter, *Off the Record.*

© 2006 Guinness World Records Ltd, a HIT Entertainment Ltd company

EDITOR-IN-CHIEF
Craig Glenday

DEPUTY EDITOR
Ben Way

EDITORIAL TEAM
Rob Dimery, Carla Masson, Marcus Hardy, Anna Amari-Parker

PROOFREADERS
Gary Werner, Antonia Cunningham

DESIGN CONCEPT AND CREATION
Keren Turner, Lisa Garner at Itonic Design Ltd, Brighton, UK (www.itonicdesign.com)

COVER DESIGN
Ron Callow at Design 23

VICE PRESIDENT, PUBLISHING
Patricia Langton

PRODUCTION EXECUTIVE
Jane Boatfield

PRINTING AND BINDING
Printer Industria Gráfica
Barcelona, Spain

TECHNICAL CONSULTANTS
Esteve Font Canadell, Roger Hawkins, Salvador Pujol Miralles

COLOR ORIGINATION
Resmiye Kahraman at Colour Systems, London, UK

COVER FOIL
Developed and supplied by Spectratek Technologies, Inc., USA

HEAD OF PICTURE DESK
Michael Whitty

PICTURE EDITOR
Laura Jackson

PICTURE RESEARCH TEAM
Jo Gibb
Beverley Hadfield
Maureen Kane
Caroline Thomas

ORIGINAL PHOTOGRAPHY
Drew Gardner
Paul Hughes
Ranald Mackechnie

ARTISTS
Ian Bull
Ken Harrison
Graham Rawle

SENIOR CONSULTANTS
Earth, Science & Technology: David Hawksett
Life on Earth: Dr. Karl Shuker (zoo & wild animals);
Elizabeth Lucas, Kew Gardens (plants);
Dr. Shaun Opperman (pets)
Human Body: Dr. Eleanor Clarke (medicine, anatomy);
Robert Young (gerontology)
Engineering: Hein Le Roux; Michael Flynn
Weapons & warfare: Chris Bishop
Entertainment: Thomasina Gibson
Computer Games: Walter Day (Twin Galaxies)
Music: Dave McAleer; *British Hit Singles & Albums*
Sports & Games: Christian Marais; David Fischer (US sports)
General: Stuart Claxton, Kim Lacey

HEAD OF RECORDS MANAGEMENT
Marco Frigatti

RECORDS MANAGEMENT TEAM
Andrea Bánfi
Scott Christie
Amarilis Espinoza
Laura Hughes
Amanda Sprague
Alessandra Stanimirov
Sophie Whiting

RECORDS ASSISTANTS
Sarah Wagner, Matthew White

ACCREDITATION
Guinness World Records Limited has a very thorough accreditation system for records verification. However, while every effort is made to ensure accuracy, Guinness World Records Limited cannot be held responsible for any errors contained in this work. Feedback from our readers on any point of accuracy is always welcomed.

ABBREVIATIONS & MEASUREMENTS
Guinness World Records Limited uses both metric and imperial measurements. The sole exceptions are for some scientific data where metric measurements only are universally accepted, and for some sports data. Where a specific date is given, the exchange rate is calculated according to the currency values that were in operation at the time. Where only a year date is given, the exchange rate is calculated from December of that year. 'One billion' is taken to mean one thousand million. 'GDR' (the German Democratic Republic) refers to the East German state, which unified with West Germany in 1990. The abbreviation is used for sports records broken before 1990. The USSR (Union of Soviet Socialist Republics) split into a number of parts in 1991, the largest of these being Russia. The CIS (Commonwealth of Independent States) replaced it and the abbreviation is used mainly for sports records broken at the 1992 Olympic Games.

Guinness World Records Limited does not claim to own any right, title, or interest in the trademarks of others reproduced in this book.

GENERAL WARNING
Attempting to break records or set new records can be dangerous. Appropriate advice should be taken first and all record attempts are undertaken at the participant's risk. In no circumstances will Guinness World Records Limited have any liability for death or injury suffered in any record attempt. Guinness World Records Limited has complete discretion over whether or not to include any particular records in the book. Being a Guinness World Record holder does not guarantee you a place in the book.

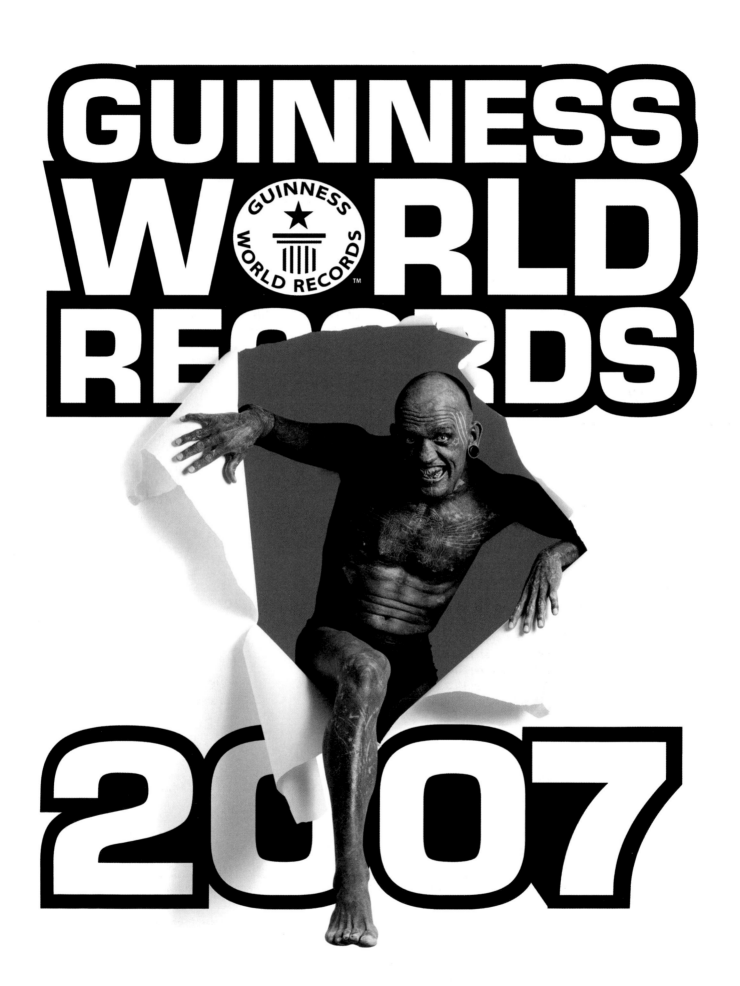

GUINNESS WORLD RECORDS 2007

CONTENTS

Fun Facts!
You'll find more than just records in this year's book... Look out for fascinating snippets of trivia that add depth to the records

? DID YOU KNOW?
The United Nations predicts that there will be almost 2.5 million "entertainment and leisure" robots in homes in 2007, compared the 137,000 that there ...ently. By th...

Actual size
Where possible, we've tried to show you record holders at the same size you'd encounter them in the real world. Check out the world's **largest wasp** (p.36)!

Color coding
Each chapter is color-coded for easy reference, and colored **crossheads** help to organize records in a logical and informative way

Annotation
Full-color photography throughout is enriched with extra facts and figures

Moveable joints
with 31 degrees of freedom

ACTUAL SIZE

★ BRAND-NEW RECORDS ARE INDICATED BY A RED STAR, IN BOTH THE TEXT AND RECORD HEADINGS

★ BROKEN OR **UPDATED RECORDS** ARE INDICATED BY A YELLOW STAR, IN BOTH THE TEXT AND RECORD HEADINGS

MOVIES

★ MOST POWERFUL ACTOR

★ HIGHEST ANNUAL EARNINGS BY AN ACTRESS

★ HIGHEST AVERAGE BOX-OFFICE GROSS (ACTOR)

★ MOST POWERFUL ACTRESS

★ MOST CONSECUTIVE $100-MILLION-GROSSING MOVIES (ACTOR)

★ HIGHEST GROSSING STUDIO

HIGHEST ANNUAL EARNINGS – FILM PRODUCER

★ HIGHEST AVERAGE BOX-OFFICE GROSS BY (ACTRESS)

★ MOST CONSECUTIVE $100-MILLION-GROSSING MOVIES (ACTRESS)

★ HIGHEST ANNUAL EARNINGS BY AN ACTOR

★ HIGHEST GROSSING NOVELIST AT THE MOVIES

MOST "BEST ACTRESS" NOMINATIONS FOR AN ACTOR IN THE SAME FILM

AT THE OSCARS

★ MOST NOMINATIONS FOR BEST ORIGINAL SCREENPLAY

★ LOWEST AGGREGATE AGE FOR BEST ACTOR AND ACTRESS NOMINEES

MOST "BEST DIRECTOR" OSCARS WON BY AN ACTOR IN THE SAME FILM

HIGHEST SALARY PER FILM FOR AN ACTRESS

★ NEW RECORD
★ UPDATED RECORD

NARROWEST WAIST

★ MOST FLEXIBLE MAN

FARTHEST EYEBALL POPPER

LONGEST TOENAILS

ACTUAL SIZE

SHORTEST MAN

ACTUAL SIZE

★ LONGEST EAR HAIR

STRETCHIEST SKIN

★ NEW RECORD
★ UPDATED RECORD

Exclusive interviews
Look out for face-to-face Q&As with the likes of Harry Potter star **Daniel Radcliffe** (p.185), the new Doctor Who **David Tennant** (p.178), the greatest living adventurer **Sir Ranulph Fiennes** (p.220), cosmonaut **Sergei Krikalev** (p.143), and airline sickbag collector **Niek Vermeulen** (p.104)!

Giant foldout features
Huge gatefold pages bring the records to life. See the world's **smallest man** at actual size (p.55), catch up on **celebrity gossip** (p.160), and meet some inspirational **soccer legends** (p.167)

Incredible images
Specially commissioned full-color photographs let you see Guinness World Record holders in their full glory!

GATEFOLD FEATURES IN THIS YEAR'S BOOK:

Hall of Fame. Meet our best-loved multiple-record holders and collect tips from them on how you, too, can be a record breaker. **p.52**

Extreme Bodies. Marvel at the human form's capacity to be squeezed, stretched, and grown into all kinds of bizarre shapes and sizes. **p.55**

Human Anatomy. Take a look inside yourself and witness the complex workings of your body. **p.59**

Sshhh! Celebrity News. Get the low-down on Tinseltown's biggest earners and their best-kept secrets. **p.160**

Natural Born Killers. Get up close and personal with the world's most frightening flesh-eaters and man-killers! **p.163**

Soccer Legends. Meet the stars of the beautiful game and admire their incredible achievements. **p.167**

INTRODUCTION

65,000 CLAIMS PROCESSED... 2,244 NEW RECORDS APPROVED... 36 COCKROACHES EATEN... 1 MAN TATTOOED HEAD TO TOE... IT CAN MEAN ONLY ONE THING – IT'S THE LATEST EDITION OF *GUINNESS WORLD RECORDS*!

*Head of US Research Stuart Claxton presents Michael "Wild Thing" Wilson (USA) of the Harlem Globetrotters with his Guinness World Records certificate. The 6-ft 6-in (1.98-m) Wilson achieved a slamdunk of 12 ft (3.6 m) – the **highest slamdunk** ever made – in front of 8,286 fans during the NBA All-Star Jam Session in Houston, Texas, in February 2006. Find more basketball-related records on p.230.*

Yes, welcome to the 2007 edition of the world's most popular book. And first off, a very big thank you to everyone who took part in our first ever **Guinness World Records Day** on November 9 last year.

The aim was to celebrate the anniversary of the day on which **Guinness World Records** became a record breaker in its own right – when it took the title of world's best-selling copyright book – with a few record attempts in a handful of countries. In the end, however, we found ourselves hosting dozens of attempts everywhere from Finland to Johannesburg, and from New York to New Zealand. Find out more on p.8 and p.9.

I'm excited to reveal that at least two of our classic, long-standing records – namely, the world's **tallest person** and the ★ **most tattooed person** – have both been broken this year, and we were pleased to welcome both holders – China's **Xi Shun** and Australia's

Lucky Diamond Rich – to our London offices.

We were also very honored to welcome home one of America's – if not the world's – greatest adventurers, **Steve Fossett**. GWR Science Consultant David Hawksett and I were among the first on the runway to say hello to Steve after the **longest solo human flight** in history (see p.81). Thanks are due to Sir Richard Branson, Virgin, and Watermark Events Management for making this fantastic event happen.

In the **Arts & Media** section (pp.170–193), we can reveal a whole host of celebrity record holders new to Guinness World Records. So, welcome aboard **Johnny Depp**, **Jennifer Lopez**, **Natalie Portman**, **Drew Barrymore**, **Orlando Bloom**, **Jada Pinkett Smith**, **Will Ferrell**, **Robert Rodriquez**, and **Reese Witherspoon** and congratulations on entering the record books.

INTRODUCING... THE WORLD'S NEW TALLEST MAN

Guinness World Records Editor Craig Glenday presents Xi Shun (China) with his official certificate. Xi Shun (on the right, of course) left his native China for the first time ever this year to visit the London offices of GWR. At 7 ft 8.95 in (2.361 m) tall, the goatherder from Inner Mongolia just beats the previous record... by less than a centimeter!

★ THE MAGIC OF ➡ HARRY POTTER... TWICE!

Harry Potter fans are in for a double treat this edition. Firstly, GWR's Laura Plunkett paid a visit to the studio where Jim Dale records the voices for the Harry Potter audiobooks. Read our exclusive interview with Jim on p.177. Then, our TV Consultant Thomasina Gibson bumped into the on-screen Harry, Daniel Radcliffe, on the set of the latest movie – find out what it's like to be the face of Harry Potter on p.185.

★MEET GWR AT THE X GAMES ⬈

Here's skateboarder Danny Way catching air as he practices for a Guinness World Record **highest bomb-drop** attempt at the Hard Rock Hotel-Casino in Las Vegas on April 6, 2006. GWR has a close relationship with the X Games – see p.264, and look out for our record-breaking area at the Games each year.

Meanwhile, regular favorites such as **Tom Hanks**, **George Lucas**, and **Woody Allen** continue to break records. Read about these and other famous faces on pp.184–185 and in our exciting new **Celebrity Secrets** foldout (p.160).

We've continued to secure interviews with your favorite record holders. If you're a fan of *Doctor Who* or the Harry Potter movies, we've got a special treat for you: hear what the new Doctor has to say about his role in the ★**longest-running sci-fi series**, and how Daniel Radcliffe feels about starring in the world's ★**fastest-selling DVD**.

And I'd like to welcome aboard a new US Sports Consultant, **David Fischer**, onto the records research team. Sports fans will relish the fantastic input we'd had from David, and I'm sure you'll agree our Sports section is better than ever this year. Thanks for all your help, David.

As ever, it's the public who have proved themselves the true stars of the book. Our world-famous records database lists achievements by people from all walks of life, from Alabama (★**largest bubblegum bubble blown**) to Wyoming (**tallest active geyser**), and from everywhere in between, from New York and the ★**fastest modeling-balloon dog** to New Mexico and the **highest man-made temperature**.

Over the past year, the database has grown by another 2,244 new or updated records, so thank you to every one of the 65,000 people who've submitted crazy, awe-inspiring, courageous claims this year. America has once again proved itself top of the list for contributions – the ★**ugliest dogs** (p.259), the ★**most flexible man** (p.56), the ★**tallest mohawk** (p.73), and almost every record on the **Computer Games** pages (pp.152–155) are among the

office favorites this year. (Thanks for the majority of the computer games records go to another fantastic new consultant, **Walter Day** of **Twin Galaxies**. His contribution has been invaluable.)

If your record has been approved but not included in this book, I apologize – there are only so many records that we can squeeze into one book... But check out our website: you might have made it online!

Finally, I'm pleased to say that plans for Guinness World Records Day 2007 are underway, so get practicing your yodeling, chopsticking, pogosticking, or whatever it is you do best – you just might make it into next year's book.

Craig Glenday

Editor-in-Chief

★ NEW RECORD
☆ UPDATED RECORD

GET YOUR NAME INTO *THE* RECORD BOOK

These guys did – on May 16, 2006, the stars and crew of *The Da Vinci Code* (USA, 2006) traveled by train from London, UK, to Cannes, France: the ★**longest nonstop international train journey**. Eurostar Chairman Guillaume Pépy (right) and director Ron Howard are presented with their certificates by GWR's Sam Knights (far left) and the Mayor of Cannes. Remember, record breaking is free, and limited only by your imagination... well, that and our strict guidelines!

!	**2007'S TOP TEN NEW WEIRDEST RECORDS...**

1. *Largest knitted sculpture* (p.173)
2. *First robot trumpeter* (p.157)
3. *Most kicks to the head* (p.91)
4. *Largest coconut ensemble* (p.87)
5. *Most people dressed as gorillas* (p.87)
6. *Largest forehead inflation* (p.72)
7. *Ugliest dogs* (p.259)
8. *Longest full-body burn (no oxygen)* (p.74)
9. *Largest collection of back scratchers* (p.105)
10. *First face transplant* (p.68)

HOW TO BE A WORLD-CLASS RECORD BREAKER

As ever, it's free to break or set a Guinness World Record – all you need to do is **get in touch with us before** you make your record attempt.

The easiest way to do this is by using the online application at **www.guinnessworldrecords.com**

Tell us as much as you can about what you want to try to break or set and we'll get back to you in about six weeks with a decision. If we like your idea, **we'll send you all the rules** and guidelines you'll need to follow to make your attempt.

If you want a *faster service*, there is a premium *Fast Track* option – for a fee, we can process your application within three days. **Whichever option you choose, good luck!**

GUINNESS WORLD RECORDS DAY

Back in November 1974, the *Guinness World Records* book made history in its own right by becoming the biggest-selling copyright book of all time. To celebrate this anniversary, we decided to organize the first ever Guinness World Records Day on November 9, 2005 – a day on which the whole world was encouraged to get involved and break a record.

The event was so successful that we'll be holding an annual international Guinness World Records Day every November 9, so look out on the website – www.guinnessworldrecords.com/gwrday – for how you can get involved!

★ FIREMAN'S CARRY – FASTEST MILE

The fastest mile covered carrying another person on one's shoulders is 15 min 11.87 sec by Ashrita Furman (USA) on November 9, 2005, at Liberty State Park, New Jersey, USA, for Guinness World Records Day.

MOST HEADS SHAVED IN 24 HOURS

A total of 23,069 heads were completely shaved in 24 hours at several different locations around South Africa to set a Guinness World Record for the CANSA Shavathon.

★ MOST PUSH-UPS ON THE BACK OF THE HANDS IN ONE MINUTE

Steve Bugdale (UK) completed 100 push-ups using the back of his hands in one minute on ITV's *Des and Mel* show, filmed at The London Studios, UK, on November 9, 2005.

★ FASTEST TIME TO DRINK A PINT OF MILKSHAKE

The world record for the fastest time to drink a 1-pint (500-ml) milkshake through a straw is 9.8 seconds by Osi Anyanwu (UK) on the *The Paul O'Grady Show* at The London Studios, UK, on November 9, 2005.

★ FASTEST TIME TO PEEL AND EAT A LEMON

The world record for the fastest time to peel and eat a lemon is 46.53 seconds by Robert Mark Burns (UK) on ITV's *The Paul O'Grady Show* at The London Studios, UK, on November 9, 2005.

★ LONGEST DISTANCE COVERED ON A WATERSLIDE IN 24 HOURS

A team of 10 employees covered 472.413 miles (760.276 km) in 24 hours on a 242-ft 9-in (74-m) waterslide at Bremer Bäder in Bremen, Germany, to celebrate Guinness World Records Day.

★ LONGEST SINGING MARATHON BY AN INDIVIDUAL

The longest continuous singing marathon by an individual is 54 hr 41 min by Hartmut Timm (Germany) in Waren, Müritz, Germany, on November 8–10, 2005.

★ LONGEST CARTOON STRIP

A cartoon strip created by a team of 35 Disney artists (all Italy) and entitled *Ciccio e il compleanno sottosopra* (*Ciccio and the Topsy-Turvy Birthday*) measured 795 ft 5 in (242.45 m) long and 3 ft (90 cm) high in Lucca, Italy. The cartoon was completed in a record time of 8 hr 30 min.

★ LONGEST TANDEM BUNGEE JUMP

Grant Denyer (Australia, right) and A. J. Hackett (New Zealand) bungee jumped from a helicopter 984 ft (300 m) above the water near Bondi Beach, New South Wales, Australia, to celebrate Guinness World Records Day. The cord stretched to 820 ft (250 m) during the attempt.

★ FASTEST CARROT CHOPPING

In one minute, chef James Martin (UK, pictured with certificate, next to host Ainsley Harriott) peeled and chopped 18.1 oz (515 g) of washed carrots on BBC 2's *Ready Steady Cook* to mark Guinness World Records Day 2005.

LARGEST UNDERPANTS ⬆

The world's largest pair of underpants measured 47 ft 3 in (14.4 m) wide and 34 ft 5 in (10.4 m) high and were made by Bolton anti-poverty campaigners Pants to Poverty. They were displayed and measured in Bolton town square, Bolton, UK, on November 9, 2005.

★ NEW RECORD
⭐ UPDATED RECORD

★ MOST KISSES IN A MINUTE

Grant Denyer (Australia) was kissed by 62 different people in one minute on the set of the *Sunrise* TV show in Sydney, Australia, to celebrate Guinness World Records Day.

★ MOST SOCKS WORN ON ONE FOOT

On November 9, 2005, in Auckland, New Zealand, Alastair Galpin (New Zealand) wore 70 socks on one foot. At a similar event in Auckland, on July 18, 2005, he set a record for the ★ **most finger snaps in one minute**, with 119.

★ FASTEST PERSON WITH A PRICING GUN

The world record for the most books priced in a minute is 24 by Charlene Tilton (USA) on ITV's *Paul O'Grady Show*, The London Studios, UK, on November 9, 2005. Charlene is more famous for her role as Lucy Ewing Cooper in the late 1970s/1980s TV soap opera *Dallas*.

★ LARGEST COLLECTION OF VERSIONS OF ONE SONG

The largest collection of different versions of the same song is 1,384 interpretations of "My Funny Valentine," originally by Richard Rodgers and Lorenz Hart, in a collection held by J. Gerardo Barbosa Lima Filho (Brazil). The collection was verified on November 9, 2005.

★ LARGEST MOTORIZED SUPERMARKET CART

The largest motorized shopping cart measures 9 ft 10 in (3 m) long, 11 ft 6 in (3.5 m) tall and 5 ft 11 in (1.8 m) wide. It was made by Edd China (UK) and displayed at the Asda store, Watford, UK, on November 9, 2005.

★ LARGEST NEWSPAPER ➡

The largest single copy of a newspaper was an edition of *The Sun* (UK) measuring 9 ft 10.5 in x 8 ft 3 in (3.01 x 2.51 m) made by Victory Design Ltd in Clowne, Chesterfield, UK, for the inaugural Guinness World Records Day on November 9, 2005.

AROUND THE WORLD

GUINNESS WORLD RECORDS ADJUDICATORS HAVE TRAVELED THE GLOBE TO BRING YOU THIS YEAR'S BOOK. HERE'S JUST A SMALL SAMPLE OF THE PLACES WE'VE BEEN IN THE LAST FEW MONTHS...

FLORIDA, USA–BOURNEMOUTH, UK: LONGEST NONSTOP FLIGHT
American adventurer Steve Fossett (pictured, left) set off from Kennedy Space Center on February 8, 2006, onboard the *Virgin Atlantic Global Flyer*. He flew 26,389.3 miles (42,469.4 km), and landed 76 hr 45 min later in Bournemouth, Dorset, UK, on February 11, 2006! GWR Editor Craig Glenday and Science Consultant David Hawksett joined the welcoming party and were among the first to congratulate him on his epic journey.

LONDON, UK, CHANNEL 4: THE PAUL O'GRADY SHOW
Over the past 12 months, GWR's Sam Knights (right) and Amarilis Espinoza (second left) have appeared on this TV show adjudicating record attempts by celebrities such as Charlene Tilton (yes, *Dallas*'s "Poison Dwarf," center), the boxer Amir Khan, and host Paul himself!

LAS VEGAS, USA: LARGEST BUFFET
American comedian Kathy Griffin (pictured, right) and GWR's Nadine Causey oversaw the world's largest buffet in the home of excess, Las Vegas, in March 2006. With 500 dishes to get through, it was just as well the event was sponsored by Alka-Seltzer...!

MEXICO CITY, MEXICO: LARGEST SOCCER SHIRT
GWR's Michael Whitty presided over the measuring of a giant soccer shirt in the Azteca Stadium in Mexico City, on May 10, 2006. Its length of 168 ft (51.32 m) – enough to cover the Statue of Liberty – secured it a place in the record books!

COUNTY CAVAN, IRELAND: FASTEST TURKEY PLUCKER
In December 2005, we were honored to travel to County Cavan to photograph Vincent Pilkington (pictured, center), the world's fastest turkey plucker. He set his record back in 1980, but he showed Editor Craig Glenday and Picture Editor Laura Jackson (wearing hats) that he was still top of his game...

LAS VEGAS, USA: GWR PINBALL CHALLENGE
Another trip to Vegas, in April 2006, saw GWR computer games consultant Walter Day (pictured, below) hosting the first ever Guinness World Records pinball tournament. Walter and his judges from Twin Galaxies ensured that only the very best players made it into this year's book. Find out more on p.152.

ST. MICHAEL, BARBADOS: WORLD RECORDS FESTIVAL
No fewer than five Guinness World Records were set or broken at the first annual World Records Festival in Barbados. Attending for GWR was Scott Christie, who witnessed, among other things, the fastest pizza eating and fastest bicycle wheelie!

BOGOTÁ, COLOMBIA: LARGEST PARADE OF WILLYS VEHICLES
GWR's Amarilis Espinoza (second left) received a warm welcome – and was able to put her language skills to good use – in Bogotá, when she adjudicated at this enormous parade of Willys (it's pronounced WILL-is) automobiles in February 2006.

MOSCOW, RUSSIA: LARGEST SINGLE POURING OF CONCRETE
A very cold editor, Craig Glenday (second left), was invited by the Mirax Group to the foundations of what will become Europe's tallest building for the world's **largest pouring of concrete** back in February 2006. A total of 494,400 ft³ (14,000 m³) of concrete was finally poured – despite what seemed like record-breaking cold weather!

CHIFENG, INNER MONGOLIA: TALLEST MAN
We didn't even realize *Inner* Mongolia existed until we heard about a very tall man living there. And indeed, Xi Shun proved to be exactly that – a record-breaking 7 ft 8.9 in (2.361 m) – when we had him measured in his hometown of Chifeng.

ROTTERDAM, NETHERLANDS: MOST PEOPLE DRESSED AS CELL PHONES
If you were passing through Rotterdam on March 18, 2006, and saw 150 cell phones running through the streets, don't worry – you weren't hallucinating… it was a Guinness World Records attempt!

HONG KONG, CHINA: WORLD'S LARGEST PERMANENT LIGHT AND SOUND SHOW
November 2005 saw Head of Records Marco Frigatti (above, left) head for Hong Kong to present a certificate to members of Hong Kong's Tourism Commission. Every night, 33 buildings in the city's Victoria Harbour light up accompanied by music, producing the world's **largest permanent light and sound show**.

AROUND THE WORLD: SHELL GAS ECONOMY CHALLENGE
The red line you see snaking around the world is the route taken by John and Helen Taylor (below) on their record-breaking circumnavigation. They drove around the world on a new Shell gas formula… and did so on just 24 tankfuls!

MILAN, ITALY: LO SHOW DEI RECORD
A brand-new Guinness World Records TV special aired across Italy in January 2006, showcasing the likes of the hairiest family (left) and GWR favorite Garry Turner (above, left) of stretchiest-skin fame.

SYDNEY, AUSTRALIA: GUINNESS WORLD RECORDS
Grant Denyer, assisted by GWR's Chris Sheedy, hosted a fantastic original TV series that saw dozens of records smashed throughout 2005.

JOHANNESBURG, SOUTH AFRICA: LARGEST CANNED FOOD MOSAIC
Evan Williams (with certificate) adjudicated at his first-ever Guinness World Record in South Africa in March 2006. It was National Volunteers Week, and Evan approved the creation of the largest can mosaic!

★ **NEW RECORD**
☆ **UPDATED RECORD**

PLANET EARTH

CONTENTS

LARGEST LAND GORGE

The Grand Canyon, created over millions of years by the Colorado River in north-central Arizona, USA, extends from Marble Gorge to the Grand Wash Cliffs over a distance of 277 miles (446 km). It attains a depth of 1 mile (1.6 km) – more than four times the height of the Empire State Building – while its width ranges from 0.25 to 18 miles (0.5 to 29 km). This means that at its widest point, it is only around 3 miles (5 km) less than the shortest distance between England and France.

EARTH

TALLEST GRANITE MONOLITH

At 3,593 ft (1,095 m), El Capitan in Yosemite National Park, California, USA, is the tallest granite monolith in the world. The plutonic granite rocks here formed around 102 million years ago.

★ HARDEST OXIDE

Stishovite has a KH of 33 (or a Mohs hardness of 7.5–8) – the fourth hardest known substance. It is a high-pressure modification of SiO_2 (quartz) and can be formed by asteroid and meteorite impacts. KH stands for "Knoop Hardness" and is based on how deep a diamond stylus can cut into a substance under a given pressure.

PRE-HISTORY

★ LARGEST SEA TO DRY UP

Around 5.9 million years ago, geological processes closed the marine passage between the Atlantic Ocean and the Mediterranean Sea. This led to the Mediterranean Sea completely or almost completely drying out over a period of perhaps several tens of thousands of years. As the water evaporated and rained down over the rest of the world, this would have led to a decrease in the average salinity of the world's oceans, and possibly helped to start an ice age. Around 5.4 million years ago, the barrier at the current Straits of Gibraltar broke, and the Mediterranean Sea reflooded. Today, the Mediterranean Sea covers an area of around 965,000 miles^2 (2.5 million km^2).

OLDEST EARTH FRAGMENTS

A tiny crystal of zircon discovered in Australia is the oldest recorded fragment of the Earth. At between 4.3 and 4.4 billion years old, this tiny sample is 100 million years older than any previous discovery, challenging the theory that the Earth's surface was once an ocean of molten magma.

LONGEST ICE AGE

Geological evidence suggests that the Earth endured several severe ice ages early in its history. The longest and most severe was between 2.3 and 2.4 billion years ago, and lasted around 70 million years. During this period, the entire Earth was probably covered in ice, to a depth of around 0.6 mile (1 km).

OLDEST ROCK

The greatest reported age for any scientifically dated rock is 3.962 billion years, in the case of the Acasta gneisses found in May 1984. The rocks were discovered around 200 miles (320 km) north of Yellowknife, Northwest Territories, Canada, by Dr. Samuel Bowring (USA) during a geology mapping project.

LARGEST CONTINENT EVER

Around 250 million years ago, all of today's continents were joined together as one "supercontinent," Pangea (meaning "all lands" in Greek). Pangea began to slowly break apart around 180 million years ago owing to plate tectonics, a process that eventually led to the land masses of today.

Evidence for the existence of Pangea becomes apparent when you recognize that the coastlines of Africa and South America seem to fit together like two pieces of a jigsaw puzzle.

Today, Asia is the **largest continent** in the world, covering an area of around 17,388,686 miles^2 (45,036,492 km^2). Africa ranks second, with a land area of 11,715,721 miles^2 (30,343,578 km^2).

LARGEST GEODE
This cluster of crystals is part of the largest geode. Find out where it is – and what it is – on p.16.

RELATIVE HARDNESS OF MATERIALS

Mohs' scale is the standard means for comparing the hardness of solids, especially minerals. It is named after the German mineralogist Friedrich Mohs.

1. Talc (right) – easily scratched by the fingernail
2. Gypsum – just scratched by the fingernail
3. Calcite – scratches and is scratched by a copper coin
4. Fluorite – not scratched by a copper coin and does not scratch glass
5. Apatite – just scratches glass and is easily scratched by a knife
6. Orthoclase – easily scratches glass and is just scratched by a file
7. Quartz – not scratched by a file
8. Topaz
9. Corundum
10. Diamond (right)

★ LARGEST GLACIAL ERRATIC

The largest erratic boulder so far identified is "Big Rock," near Okotoks, Alberta, Canada. Around 134 ft (41 m) long by 59 ft (18 m) wide by 29 ft (9 m) high, and weighing around 36.3 million lb (16,500 tonnes), this quartzite block was carried by the movement of a glacier (see box, right) around 300 miles (480 km) from the Athabasca Valley, near Jasper, Alberta, 18,000–10,000 years ago.

RAREST ELEMENT
Astatine is the rarest element in the Earth's crust, with around 0.9 oz (25 g) occurring naturally.

★ NEW RECORD
UPDATED RECORD

★ SOFTEST AND HARDEST MINERALS
Mohs' scale of hardness uses talc as its starting point, with a value of 1. Because of its softness and perfect cleavage in one direction (like the graphite in pencils), talc makes a great lubricant in situations where it will not be put under too much stress, as in body powders. The **hardest mineral** is diamond, with a value of 10 on Mohs' scale (see table above).

? DID YOU KNOW?

A glacial erratic is a large boulder of a type of rock that is different from the rocks surrounding it. In the last ice age, which ended approximately 10,000 years ago, such boulders were carried from their place of origin by advancing glaciers. The glaciers picked up the rocks, carried them along, then deposited them on the ground upon melting.

★ FIRST IDENTIFIED IMPACT CRATER
The Barringer Meteorite Crater (also known as Meteor Crater) in Arizona, USA, is a hole in the ground approximately 0.7 mile (1.2 km) wide and 570 ft (173 m) deep. Geologists now believe the iron meteorite that produced it, some 49,000 years ago, exploded with a force equivalent to 2.5 megatons of TNT – more than 150 Hiroshima bombs.

ELEMENTS & MINERALS

MOST COMMON ELEMENTS
Hydrogen is the **most common element in both the Universe** (over 90%) **and the Solar System** (70.68%). Iron is the **most common element on Earth**, accounting for 36% of the mass, while molecular nitrogen (N_2) is the **most common element in the atmosphere** at 78.08% by volume or 75.52% by mass.

LARGEST SINGLE CRYSTAL ON EARTH
The Earth's inner core is a sphere that is mostly made up of iron and measures around 1,517 miles (2,442 km) across. At around 9,000–11,000°F (5,000–6,000°C), it is solid rather than liquid, due to the huge pressures within the Earth's interior.

This gigantic hot ball of iron is about three-quarters the size of the Moon, and has a mass of around 100 million million million tonnes.

Many geologists now believe that this huge iron ball is actually a single crystal. This is owing to differences in the behavior of seismic waves passing through it in different directions.

★ LARGEST SALT FLATS

The Salar de Uyuni – a flat expanse of salt in Bolivia – covers an area of around 4,600 miles² (12,000 km²), and contains an estimated 10 billion tonnes of salt. It is situated at an altitude of 11,975 ft (3,650 m) above sea level.

EARTH

LARGEST FORESTS

The world's **largest forested areas** are the vast coniferous forests of northern Russia, lying between Lat. 55°N and the Arctic Circle. The total wooded area covers 1.5 million miles² (4 million km²).

By way of comparison, **the largest area of tropical forest** is the Amazonian rainforest (left), which covers approximately 2.5 million miles² (6.5 million km²).

MOUNTAINS

HIGHEST MOUNTAIN

Mount Everest, in the Himalayas, Nepal, is 29,035 ft (8,850 m) high, and its peak is the highest point in the world. It was first conquered in 1953 by Sherpa Tenzing Norgay (Nepal) and Sir Edmund Hillary (New Zealand).

TALLEST MOUNTAIN

Mauna Kea (White Mountain) on the island of Hawaii, USA, is the world's tallest mountain. Measured from its submarine base in the Hawaiian Trough to its top, it has a height of 33,480 ft (10,205 m), of which 13,796 ft (4,205 m) is above sea level.

★ OLDEST NATIONAL PARK

Yellowstone National Park, USA, was the first area to be designated a national park anywhere in the world. It was given its status in 1872 by US president Ulysses S. Grant, who declared that it would always be "dedicated and set apart as a public park or pleasuring ground for the benefit and enjoyment of the people."

The park covers 3,470 miles² (8,980 km²), mostly in the state of Wyoming. Its geysers (pictured below) are one of its most distinctive features. Yellowstone contains the **tallest active geyser** – Steamboat Geyser, the maximum height of which ranges from 197 to 377 ft (60 to 115 m).

★ LARGEST LAVA LAKE

The shield volcano Mount Nyiragongo, in the Democratic Republic of Congo, contains an active lava lake in its crater some 820 ft (250 m) across.

The volcano has erupted at least 34 times since 1882.

★ LONGEST ICE TONGUE

The Drygalski Ice Tongue is a floating extension of the David Glacier, Ross Dependency, Antarctica. It extends around 40 miles (65 km) into the McMurdo Sound in the Ross Sea and has an average width of 3 miles (5 km). It was discovered in 1902 by Robert Falcon Scott (UK) and is believed to be at least 4,000 years old.

LARGEST GEODE

The world's largest geode (a rock cavity filled with minerals) is near Almería, Spain, and was discovered by the geologist Javier Garcia-Guinea (Spain) in May 2000. It forms a mineral-lined cave 26 ft (8 m) long, 6 ft (1.8 m) wide, and 6 ft (1.8 m) high and was probably formed about 6 million years ago. Most geodes are small enough to fit in the palm of a human hand.

★ MOST FORESTED COUNTRY (OVERALL AREA)

In 2005, Brazil had an estimated forest cover of 1,844,400 miles² (4,776,000 km²), or 57.2% of the country's overall area.

A total of 95.7% of the Cook Islands were covered in forest as of 2000, making them the **most forested country in terms of percentage covered**.

LARGEST FORESTATION PROJECT

The "Green Great Wall," a 2,783-mile (4,480-km) belt of forest, is being created in northwest China in order to combat the encroaching threats of desertification and overfarming.

The project was initiated in 1978, and is set to last until 2050 when 137,400 miles² (356,000 km²) of land will be afforested. It is currently being coordinated by the State Forestry Administration of China.

★ TALLEST MOUNTAIN FACE

The Rupal face of Nanga Parbat in the western Himalayas, Pakistan, is a single rise of some 16,000 ft (5,000 m) from the valley floor to the summit (the precise figure varies according to where the measurement is taken from). The mountain itself, with a summit at 26,656 ft (8,125 m), is the eighth highest mountain in the world and the highest mountain in Pakistan.

GREATEST MOUNTAIN RANGE

The Himalayas contain 96 of the 109 peaks in the world that are more than 24,000 ft (7,315 m).

LONGEST MOUNTAIN RANGE

The Andes, in South America, are 4,700 miles (7,600 km) long, span seven countries, and include some of the highest mountains on Earth. Over 50 of the Andean peaks are in excess of 20,000 ft (6,000 m) high. Along most of its extent, the range is around 186 miles (300 km) in width.

DEEP EARTH

★ LONGEST EARTHQUAKE FAULT RUPTURE

The Great Sumatra-Andaman earthquake of December 26, 2004, was the longest earthquake fault rupture ever measured.

The rupture occurred along approximately 745–800 miles (1,200–1,300 km) of the curving boundary between the Indo-Australian Plate and the southeastern part of the Eurasian Plate.

In places, the displacement of ocean floor along the fault was as much as 50 ft (15 m).

★ DEEPEST EARTHQUAKE OBSERVATORY

The San Andreas Fault Observatory at Depth (SAFOD) is a project with the aim of installing scientific detectors right at the heart of the active fault line that passes through California, USA.

Although the project was not due for completion until 2007, the drilling phase reached its target depth of 10,081 ft (3,072 m) in August 2005, having drilled through the Pacific Plate and the North American Plate.

★ LARGEST ▪▶ WATERFALL EVER

Around 18,000 years ago, a huge glacier dammed a river in North America, near the present-day city of Missoula, Montana, trapping a body of water some 500 miles^3 (2,000 km^3) in volume. Eventually the water broke through and the lake emptied.

As the water drained away, some flowed over what is now known as Dry Falls, resulting in a waterfall measuring around 3.5 miles (5.6 km) long by 380 ft (115 m) high.

★ DEEPEST DEPRESSION

The bedrock of the Bentley Sub-Glacial Trench, Antarctica, at 8,326 ft (2,538 m) below sea level, is the deepest known depression that is not on the ocean floor.

DEEPEST PENETRATION INTO THE EARTH'S CRUST

A geological exploratory borehole near Zapolyarny, on the Kola peninsula of Arctic Russia, which began on May 24, 1970, had reached an unprecedented depth of 40,226 ft (12,261 m) by 1983, when work stopped owing to lack of funds.

◀▪▪ LARGEST DEFORESTATION

Between 1990 and 2000, Brazil cleared an average of 8,596 miles^2 (22,264 km^2) every year (a surface area approximately equivalent to that of El Salvador).

Between 1994 and 1995, deforestation rates in Brazil rose to about 11,200 miles^2 (29,000 km^2) annually – the **greatest increase in the rate of deforestation ever recorded**.

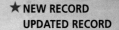

★ NEW RECORD
UPDATED RECORD

DEEPEST VALLEY

The Yarlung Zangbo Valley in Tibet is, on average, 16,400 ft (5,000 m) deep. Its deepest point has been measured at 17,657 ft (5,382 m).

LARGEST LIQUID BODY ON EARTH

The largest liquid body on Earth is its outer core. The inner core is solid iron/nickel, with a radius of around 758 miles (1,221 km). This is surrounded by the liquid outer core, with a thickness of 1,403 miles (2,259 km). The outer core has a total volume of around 6.07 x 10^{21} ft^3 (1.719 x 10^{20} m^3). It represents 29.3% of Earth's mass and 16% of its volume.

UNDERGROUND

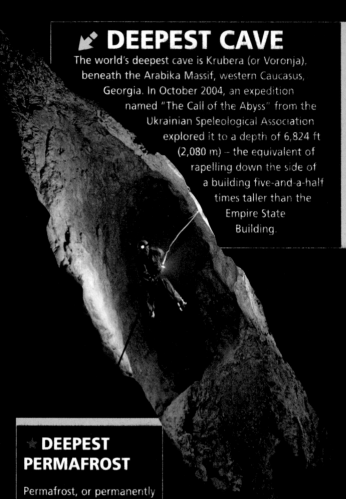

⚑ DEEPEST CAVE

The world's deepest cave is Krubera (or Voronja), beneath the Arabika Massif, western Caucasus, Georgia. In October 2004, an expedition named "The Call of the Abyss" from the Ukrainian Speleological Association explored it to a depth of 6,824 ft (2,080 m) – the equivalent of rapelling down the side of a building five-and-a-half times taller than the Empire State Building.

★ DEEPEST PERMAFROST

Permafrost, or permanently frozen ground, accounts for around 15% of the Earth's land surface and occurs in China, Canada, Alaska, and Siberia. The deepest permafrost occurs in Siberia, where the ground is constantly frozen to a depth of around 3,200 ft (1,000 m). The picture below shows plants frozen in ice, from the Museum of Permafrost, Igarka, Russia.

★ TALLEST NATURAL CAVE COLUMN

The tallest cave column measures 201 ft 8 in (61.5 m) in height – 21 ft 4 in (6.5 m) taller than the Tower of Pisa – and is located in a cave at Tham Sao Hin, Thailand. It has been formed by a natural process whereby a stalactite, descending from the roof of a cave, has met and joined together with a stalagmite rising in the opposite direction from the floor.

★ TALLEST STALAGMITE

The tallest stalagmite in the world is reported to measure an incredible 230 ft (70 m) in height – several yards taller than Nelson's Column in Trafalgar Square, London, UK. It is located in Zhi Jin Cave, Zhejiang province, China.

★ TALLEST UNDERWATER STALACTITE

Known locally as Tunich Ha, the world's largest underwater stalactite measures 42 ft (12.8 m) and is located in a cave formation called Sistema Chac Mol in Mexico. The stalactite has been formed as saltwater from the nearby Caribbean Sea has penetrated the limestone in the region and mixed with freshwater already present.

LONGEST STALACTITE

The longest free-hanging stalactite in the world is 92 ft (28 m) long and can be found in the Gruta do Janelao, in Minas Gerais, Brazil.

★ LARGEST CAVE OPENING

The entrance to Cathedral Caverns in Grant, Alabama, USA, measures 126 ft (38 m) wide and 25 ft (7 m) high – so large, you could fit a blue whale in sideways without touching the sides! Approximately 4,000 ft (1,220 m) long, Cathedral Caverns was originally known as the Bat Cave until it was developed into a tourist attraction in 1955.

★ LONGEST VERTICAL DROP

The Lukina Jama Cave in Croatia has a total depth of 4,566 ft (1,392 m) However, the cave is only 3,536 ft (1,078 m) long. The greatest single vertical drop inside the cave measures 1,692 ft (516 m).

LONGEST UNDERWATER CAVE TRAVERSE

The longest underwater traverse in a cave covered a distance of 10,000 ft (3,050 m) from King Pot to Keld Head, North Yorkshire, UK. It was achieved by Geoff Yeadon and Geoff Crossley (both UK) on August 3, 1991.

★ FLOWSTONE CASCADE WITH THE GREATEST VERTICAL EXTENT

Flowstone cascades are sheet-like deposits of calcite that are formed as limestone-saturated water runs down cave walls and floors, leaving deposits that build up over lengthy periods of time. The flowstone cascade with the greatest vertical extent is 492 ft (150 m) in length and is located in the Neverland to Dead Sea Lechuguilla Cave in New Mexico, USA

LARGEST GLACIAL GROTTO

The largest artificial cave inside a glacier measures 59,200 ft (5,500 m) – twice the size of a hot air balloon It is located inside the Fee Glacier in Switzerland and was built by the Swiss glaciologist Benedikt Schnyder

EISPAVILLON 3500 M.ü.M

Kazumura's lava formations
Among the many lava formations in the Kazumura Cave are these large lava stalactites, formed just 350–500 years ago

LARGEST
CAVE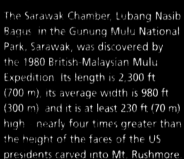

The Sarawak Chamber, Lubang Nasib Bagus, in the Gunung Mulu National Park, Sarawak, was discovered by the 1980 British-Malaysian Mulu Expedition. Its length is 2,300 ft (700 m), its average width is 980 ft (300 m), and it is at least 230 ft (70 m) high – nearly four times greater than the height of the faces of the US presidents carved into Mt. Rushmore.

✸ DEEPEST DESCENT INTO AN ICE CAVE
In 1998, the glacier explorer Janot Lamberton (France) descended to a depth of 662 ft (202 m) in a cave in a glacier in Greenland. The cave had been formed by a river of meltwater during the Arctic summer.

✸ LONGEST CONTINUOUS FLOWSTONE CASCADE
The "Snowy River" passage in Fort Stanton Cave, New Mexico, USA,

is the longest continuous calcite formation yet mapped, covering more than 1.8 miles (3 km). The flowstone is so easily damaged by human contact that the cave is closed to all but a few scientists.

DEEPEST FRESHWATER CAVE SCUBA DIVE
On August 23, 1996, Nuno Gomes (South Africa) scuba dived to a depth of 927 ft 2 in (282.6 m) at the Boesmansgat Cave, Northern Cape, South Africa. Essentially a very deep sink-hole, the cave at the surface resembles a small lake with vertical sides.

Verna van Schaik (South Africa) dived to a depth of 725 ft (221 m) in the Boesmansgat Cave, Northern Cape, South Africa, on October 25, 2004, the **deepest freshwater cave scuba dive by a woman**. The dive lasted 5 hr 34 min, of which only 12 minutes were spent descending.

✸ LARGEST NATURAL LAVA CAVE
The **deepest** and **longest lava cave** – an open tube inside a lava flow – is Kazumura Cave, on Hawaii, USA (see above). It is 36.9 miles (59.3 km) long and descends 3,605 ft (1,099 m) down the eastern flank of Kilauea Volcano.

UNDERGROUND MUSICAL INSTRUMENT
Stalactites covering 3.5 acres (1.4 ha) of a cavern have been harnessed to produce musical tones when struck with rubber-tipped mallets linked to a keyboard. The Great Stalacpipe Organ, located in the Luray Caverns of Shenandoah Valley, Virginia, USA, is a three-year project by Leland W. Sprinkle (USA), a mathematician and electronics scientist.

LARGEST CRATER FROM AN UNDERGROUND NUCLEAR EXPLOSION
A 104-kiloton nuclear device was detonated at the Semipalatinsk Test Site, Kazakhstan, 583 ft (178 m) beneath the dry bed of the Chagan River on January 15, 1965, leaving a crater 1,338 ft (408 m) wide with a maximum depth of 328 ft (100 m). A major lake later formed behind the 65–114-ft (20–35-m) lip of the crater, which was then cut through with earth-moving equipment to allow it to be used as a reservoir.

✸ DEEPEST LIVE RADIO BROADCAST UNDERGROUND

The deepest live radio broadcast was performed by CBC Radio Points North (Canada), 7,680 ft (2,340 m) underground in Creighton Mine, Sudbury, Ontario, Canada, on May 24, 2005.

✸ NEW RECORD
★ UPDATED RECORD

LARGEST DISCOVERY
OF BURIED COINS ➡
The largest deliberately buried hoard of coins ever found was the so-called Brussels hoard of 1908. This find contained approximately 150,000 coins, including those minted by the English King Henry III (1216–72), possibly to fund his soldiers fighting in the Crusades.

DYNAMIC EARTH

CROSS-SECTION OF ANDEAN SUBDUCTION ZONE

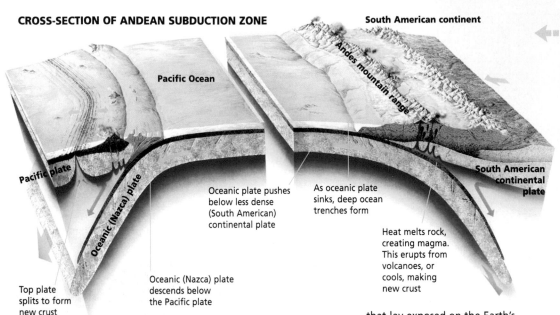

South American continent

Pacific Ocean

Andes mountain range

Pacific plate

Oceanic (Nazca) plate

Oceanic plate pushes below less dense (South American) continental plate

As oceanic plate sinks, deep ocean trenches form

South American continental plate

Heat melts rock, creating magma. This erupts from volcanoes, or cools, making new crust

Top plate splits to form new crust

Oceanic (Nazca) plate descends below the Pacific plate

★ NEW RECORD
☆ UPDATED RECORD

☆ COSTLIEST YEAR FOR NATURAL DISASTERS

According to reinsurers Swiss Re, 2005 was the costliest year in history for natural disasters.

A combination of the damage wreaked by the Asian tsunami of December 26, 2004, and an unusually active hurricane season, along with other disasters such as floods, meant that the total economic loss for 2005 reached a total of $225 billion.

LONGEST DAY ON EARTH

The tidal bulges in the Earth's oceans, caused by the gravitational effect of the Moon, are gradually transferring momentum from the Earth's rotation to the Moon's orbit. As a result, the Earth's rotation is slowing at a rate of around 0.02 seconds per century and each day is fractionally longer than the day before. Therefore, the longest day on Earth is always today.

FASTEST-MOVING LAND MASS

Owing to convection currents in the Earth's mantle, all of the continental plates move slowly in relation to each other. The greatest movement occurs near Samoa at the Tonga microplate, which is moving into the Pacific at a rate of 9.4 in (24 cm) per year.

LONGEST-BURNING FIRE

A burning coal seam in New South Wales, Australia, beneath Mount Wingen, is believed to have started around 5,000 years ago when lightning struck part of the coal seam that lay exposed on the Earth's surface. Today, the fire is burning around 100 ft (30 m) underground, as it has slowly eaten away at the seam. Until 1866, the seam was believed to be a volcano.

FASTEST-RISING MOUNTAIN

Nanga Parbet, in Pakistan, is growing at a rate of 0.27 in (7 mm) per year. The mountain is part of the Himalayan Plateau, formed when India began colliding with the Eurasian continental plate between 30 and 50 million years ago.

EARTHQUAKES

★ LONGEST EARTHQUAKE

The Sumatra-Andaman Islands earthquake in the Indian Ocean, on December 26, 2004, was the longest ever recorded. Its duration, monitored by seismometers all over the world, was measured at between 500 and 600 seconds. It had an earthquake magnitude of between 9.1 and 9.3 on the Richter Scale.

★ LONGEST SUBDUCTION ZONE

The Earth's crust is made up of different tectonic (or lithospheric) plates. The term "subduction" is used to describe the movement of one plate sinking beneath another.

The Andean Subduction Zone runs for some 4,350 miles (7,000 km) along the western coast of South America and is the world's longest destructive tectonic plate boundary.

HIGHEST DEATH TOLL FROM AN EARTHQUAKE

The earthquake that struck the Shaanxi, Shanxi, and Henan provinces, China, on February 2, 1556, is believed to have killed around 830,000 people.

VOLCANOES

LONGEST CONTINUOUSLY ERUPTING VOLCANO

Mt. Stromboli, in the Tyrrhenian Sea off the coast of Italy, has been undergoing continuous volcanic eruptions since at least the 7th century BC, when its activity was recorded by Greek colonists. Its regular mild explosions of gas and lava – usually several each hour – have led to it becoming known as the "Lighthouse of the Mediterranean."

HIGHEST VOLCANO

Cerro Aconcagua, a 22,834-ft-high (6,960-m) snow-clad peak in the Andes, is the highest volcano; it is not active.

★ WORST CYCLONE DISASTER – DAMAGE TOLL

According to reinsurers Swiss Re, Hurricane Katrina, which devastated the coast of Louisiana, USA, on August 29, 2005, caused damage in the region of $45 billion. It was the first category-5 hurricane of the 2005 hurricane season.

Pictured above is the city of New Orleans, Louisiana, which experienced widespread destruction.

ACTIVE VOLCANOES

The **largest active volcano** is Mauna Loa, Hawaii, USA, a broad, gentle dome 75 miles (120 km) long and 31 miles (50 km) wide (above sea level). Mauna Loa has a volume of 10,200 miles³ (42,500 km³), of which 84.2% is below sea level. Its lava flows occupy more than 1,980 miles² (5,125 km²) of the island.

The world's **most active volcano** is Kilauea, in Hawaii, USA, which has erupted continuously since 1983. It discharges lava at a rate of 176 ft³ (5 m³) per second.

The Ojos del Salado on the border between Chile and Argentina is the world's **highest active volcano**, at 22,595 ft (6,887 m) high.

YOUNGEST VOLCANO

Paricutin, in Mexico, is a volcanic cone that erupted from a corn field on February 20, 1943, and was volcanically active until 1953. Most of the activity occurred in the first year, during which the volcanic cone grew to a height of 1,100 ft (336 m). Paricutin offered geologists a rare chance to witness the birth, evolution, and death of a volcano.

FASTEST LAVA FLOW

Nyiragongo, in the Democratic Republic of Congo, erupted on January 10, 1977. The resulting lava, which burst through fissures on the volcano's flank, traveled at speeds of up to 40 mph (60 km/h).

HIGHEST VOLCANIC ERUPTION IN THE SOLAR SYSTEM

On August 6, 2001, NASA's *Galileo* spacecraft performed a close flyby of Jupiter's volcanically active satellite, Io. Mission scientists later realized that the spacecraft had passed through the top of a 310-mile-high (500-km) volcanic plume.

LIEUTENANT MIKE SILAH

Lt. Mike Silah, a P-3 pilot, saw Hurricane Katrina close up when he flew a number of missions into the storm in the week before she hit New Orleans. He talked to *Guinness World Records* about the experience... We had been flying into Katrina, monitoring her during the week leading up to her making landfall. The day before landfall we had already made a number of flights, so had seen her develop over time, but we were amazed at how much she had intensified.

The day before Katrina made landfall on the Gulf Coast, you took a series of images capturing her eyewall... Apart from monitoring storms, we often carry a camera to take our own photos. The flights offer a unique vantage point over some spectacular sights. It's not always possible to describe and having a photograph helps.

What did you think when you saw the size of the hurricane? We started to become alarmed. On Sunday before landfall we knew that the die had been cast in terms of the eventual outcome. We found ourselves comparing her to Hurricane Camille, a massive storm of the 1960s, that is still etched on many people's minds.

You must have known what was likely to happen once the storm achieved landfall? We just hoped that the work we had been doing would give enough time for people to evacuate. I have a great affinity for the city of New Orleans and I knew that what I was seeing would change people's lives.

How did it feel when you were in the eye of the storm? Inside the storm was as beautiful a day as you'll ever see. Katrina was a beautifully constructed storm with a clear eye. She was spectacular.

? DID YOU KNOW?

Volcanic eruptions eject huge amounts of sulfur dioxide gas (SO_2). This combines with water to form a "mist" of sulfuric acid in the stratosphere, blocking sunlight from reaching the Earth's surface and causing temperatures to fall.

*The cataclysmic eruption of the Tambora volcano in Indonesia in 1815 caused average global temperatures to drop by up to 5°F (3°C), the **greatest recorded climactic impact of volcanic eruption**. It led to 1816 becoming known as "the year without summer."*

DESERTS

SIZE

LARGEST DESERT

At its maximum, the Sahara in north Africa stretches 3,200 miles (5,150 km) from east to west. From north to south, its extent varies from 800 to 1,400 miles (1,280 to 2,250 km). The total area covered is approximately 3,500,000 miles^2 (9,100,000 km^2).

The ★ **smallest desert** is the Atacama in Chile, which covers 70,000 miles^2 (180,000 km^2).

★ LARGEST OASIS

The Nile Valley and Delta is the most extensive oasis on Earth, covering approximately 8,500 miles^2 (22,000 km^2). The ancient Egyptians were the first people to use the word "oasis" (meaning "dwelling place"), and without the Nile River – the world's **longest river** at 4,160 miles (6,695 km) – the whole of Egypt would be desert.

★ WETTEST DESERT

The Sonora Desert, Arizona, USA – where daytime temperatures may exceed 104°F (40°C) in summer – receives 4.7–11.8 in (120–300 mm) of rain annually. This desert is unusual in that it experiences two wet seasons – one from December to March and a second from July to September.

? DID YOU KNOW?

In general, any place that receives less than 8 in (200 mm) of rain a year (where the rate of water evaporation is greater than the amount of rainfall) can be called a desert, regardless of whether it is hot or cold.

TEMPERATURE

EXTREME HIGHS

On September 13, 1922, a temperature of 136°F (58°C) in the shade was recorded at Al 'Aziziyah in the Sahara, Libya, the **highest temperature recorded**.

Based on readings taken from 1960 to 1966, the average temperature at Dallol, Ethiopia, was 94°F (34°C).

In Death Valley, California, USA, temperatures in excess of 120°F (49°C) were recorded on 43 consecutive days, from July 6 to August 17, 1917.

At Marble Bar, Western Australia, 160 consecutive days with maximum temperatures of 100°F (37.8°C) or higher were recorded from October 31, 1923 to April 27, 1924, although the maximum temperature measured was 120.5°F (49.2°C).

★ COLDEST HOT DESERT

In the Gobi Desert, Central Asia, winter temperatures can drop below -4°F (-20°C). As temperatures can reach around 104°F (40°C), the Gobi can be classed as both a hot and cold desert.

★ COLDEST DESERT

The McMurdo Dry Valleys, Antarctica, receive less than 4 in (100 mm) of precipitation per year and have a mean annual temperature of -4°F (-20°C). Despite the inhospitable conditions, this polar desert supports life in the form of algae, nematode worms, phytoplankton, and bacteria.

DRIEST PLACE

For the period between 1964 and 2001, the average annual rainfall at the meteorological station in Quillagua, in the Atacama Desert, Chile, was just 0.02 in (0.5 mm). This discovery was made during the making of the documentary series *Going to Extremes*, by Keo Films, in 2001.

★ NEW RECORD
UPDATED RECORD

★ CONTINENT MOST AFFECTED BY DESERTIFICATION

Desertification – the transformation of arable land to desert – has a number of natural causes, such as climate variation and soil erosion. Human activities – including overintensive farming, deforestation, and even the migration of refugees during wartime – can also give rise to conditions that make desertification possible.

The situation is at its worst in Africa, where two-thirds of the continent has been reduced to desert or dryland.

★ HIGHEST SAND DUNES

Sand dunes in the Saharan sand sea of Isaouane-n-Tifernine in east central Algeria have a wavelength of 3 miles (5 km) and attain a height of 1,525 ft (465 m) – more than enough to cover the Empire State Building entirely.

LARGEST SAND ISLAND

Fraser Island, a World Heritage Site off the coast of Queensland, Australia, is effectively a sand dune 74 miles (120 km) long and 18 miles (30 km) at its widest, covering an area of approximately 402,750 acres (163,000 ha). It is the only known place in the world where rainforests thrive on top of sand dunes.

MISCELLANEOUS

★ HIGHEST AND LOWEST DESERTS

The People's Republic of China contains both the highest desert – the Qaidam Depression, which is 8,530 ft (2,600 m) above sea level – and the lowest desert – the Turpan Depression, which is 492 ft (150 m) below sea level.

★ SANDIEST DESERT

The Arabian Desert covers 1 million miles^2 (2.6 million km^2), one-third of which is covered in sand.

TALLEST WILD CACTUS

A cardon (*Pachycereus pringlei*) found in the Sonora Desert, Baja California, Mexico, in April 1995, measured 63 ft (19.2 m) – nearly the combined height of four giraffes.

LONGEST DROUGHT

The Atacama Desert, in northern Chile, experiences virtually no rain, although several times a century a squall may strike a small area of it.

★ MOST HEAT-TOLERANT ANIMAL (LAND BASED)

The scavenger ant *Cataglyphis bicolor* lives in the Sahara Desert, where it forages at temperatures of more than 131°F (55°C). It moves rapidly on its foraging trips, thereby reducing exposure to the heat of the sun, and rests occasionally on stalks of vegetation, where the temperature is lower. The ant's long legs raise its body by around 0.15 in (4 mm), a height at which the temperature is a few degrees cooler than the surface of the desert.

MOST DESTRUCTIVE INSECT

The desert locusts (*Schistocerca gregaria*) from the dry and semi-arid regions of Africa, the Middle East, and western Asia are only 1.8–2.4 in (4.5–6 cm) long, but can eat their own weight in food every day.

Certain weather conditions induce unimaginable numbers of desert locusts to gather in huge swarms that devour almost all vegetation in their path. In a single day, a "small" swarm of about 50 million locusts can eat food that would sustain 500 people for a year.

MAJOR DESERTS

NAME	AREA (MILES^2)	AREA (KM^2)	LOCATION
Sahara Desert	3,500,000	9,100,000	Algeria, Chad, Libya, Mali, Mauritania, Niger
Arabian Desert	1,000,000	2,600,000	Arabian Peninsula (including Iraq, Jordan, Kuwait, Oman, Qatar, Saudi Arabia, UAE, Yemen)
Australian Desert	600,000	1,550,000	Australia
Gobi Desert	400,000	1,040,000	Mongolia and China (Inner Mongolia)
Kalahari Desert	200,000	520,000	Botswana, Namibia, South Africa
Takla Makan	125,000	320,000	Xinjiang, China
Namib Desert	120,000	310,000	Namibia
Sonora Desert	120,000	310,000	Arizona and California, USA, and Mexico
Kara Kum Desert	105,000	270,000	Turkmenistan
Somali Desert	100,000	260,000	Somalia
Thar Desert	100,000	260,000	North-western India and Pakistan
Atacama Desert	70,000	180,000	Northern Chile

RIVERS & LAKES

★ DEEPEST EXPOSED DEPRESSION ⇒

The shore surrounding the Dead Sea, lying on the border between Israel and Jordan, is 1,312 ft (400 m) below sea level. The deepest point on the bed of this salty lake is 2,388 ft (728 m) below sea level.

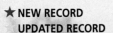

★ NEW RECORD
UPDATED RECORD

★ LARGEST PINK LAKE

Retba Lake, better known as Lac Rose (Pink Lake), measures around 1 x 3 miles (1.5 x 5 km) at low water. The shallow lagoon is located 18 miles (30 km) north of Dakar, Senegal – famous as the last leg in the Paris–Dakar Rally. Its color is the result of the presence of micro-organisms and a strong concentration of minerals.

LAKES

LARGEST LAKE

The largest inland sea or lake in the world is the Caspian Sea (in Azerbaijan, Russia, Kazakhstan, Turkmenistan, and Iran). It is 760 miles (1,225 km) long, with an area of 143,550 miles² (371,800 km²). Of the total area, some 55,280 miles² (143,200 km²) – 38.5% – is in Iran. Its maximum depth is 3,362 ft (1,025 m), and the surface is around 93 ft (28 m) below sea level.

LARGEST FRESHWATER LAKE

Lake Superior, on the border between Canada and the USA, is the world's **largest freshwater lake by area**. It covers 31,700 miles² (82,100 km²) – larger than Belgium and Switzerland combined! The **largest freshwater lake by volume** is Lake Baikal in Siberia, Russia, with an estimated volume of 5,500 miles³ (23,000 km³).

DEEPEST LAKE

Lake Baikal in the southern part of eastern Siberia, Russia, is the deepest lake in the world. In 1974, the lake's Olkhon Crevice was measured by the Hydrographic Service of the Soviet Pacific Navy and found to be 5,371 ft (1,637 m) deep – the average depth of the Grand Canyon and capable of accommodating a stack of three Taipei 101s (the world's **tallest building**) with 373 ft (113 m) to spare.

LARGEST RESERVOIR

The **largest artificial lake by surface area** is Lake Volta in Ghana, formed by the Akosombo dam and completed in 1965. By 1969, the lake had filled to an area of 3,275 miles² (8,482 km²) – large enough to accommodate Manhattan island, New York, USA, nearly 145 times over!

The **largest reservoir by volume** is the Bratskoye reservoir on the Angara River in Russia, with a volume of 40.6 miles³ (169.3 km³) and an area of 2,112 miles² (5,470 km²). It was completed in 1967.

LARGEST UNDERGROUND LAKE

The largest known underground lake is that in the Drachenhauchloch (Dragon's Breath) cave near Grootfontein, Namibia, discovered in 1986. When surveyed in April 1991, the surface area was found to be 6.44 acres (2.61 ha). The surface of the lake is some 217 ft (66 m) underground, and it has a depth of 276 ft (84 m).

SALTIEST LAKE

Don Juan Pond in Wright Valley, Antarctica, is so salty – the salt by weight is 40.2% – that it remains liquid even at temperatures as low as -63.4°F (-53°C). To re-create this in your average bathtub at home, you would need to add over 22 lb (10 kg) of salt.

DEADLIEST LAKE

The lake responsible for the most deaths – other than by drowning – is Lake Nyos in Cameroon, West Africa, where toxic gases have claimed nearly 2,000 lives in recent decades. On one night in August 1986, between 1,600 and 1,800 people and countless animals were killed by a natural release of carbon dioxide gas.

HIGHEST COMMERCIALLY NAVIGABLE LAKE

Lake Titicaca, which lies in the Altiplano on the Andean border between Peru and Bolivia, is situated at an altitude of 12,500 ft (3,810 m) above sea level. Its surface area covers approximately 3,200 miles² (8,300 km²) and the average depth is between 460 and 590 ft (140 and 180 m) – deep enough for the safe passage of commercial vessels.

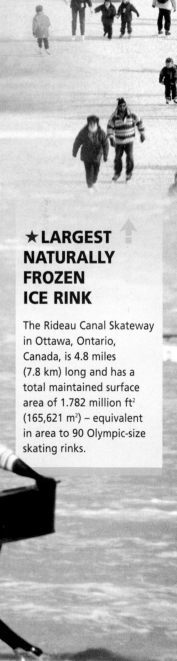

LARGEST RIVER TO DRY UP

The Yellow River (Huang He) is China's second longest river. In 1997 and 1998, the Yellow River ran completely dry along its lower section for more than 140 days in each year, threatening the fall harvests. For several months a year, the 3,390-mile-long (5,460-km) river now dries up in Henan province, some 250 miles (400 km) before it reaches the sea. The problem is the result of below-average rainfall, increased irrigation, and the industrial demands of a growing population.

★ LARGEST MAN-MADE REED ISLANDS

The Uros Islands in Lake Titicaca (Peru/Bolivia) are made from mats of reeds tied together, and are constantly under construction as they rot away over a three-month period. The largest of the islands is Taquile Island, which is around 0.6 mile (1 km) wide and 4.3 miles (7 km) long.

GREATEST WATERFALL ANNUAL FLOW

On the basis of the average annual flow, the greatest waterfall in the world is the Boyoma Falls in the Democratic Republic of the Congo (former Zaire), at 600,000 ft³/sec (17,000 m³/sec).

The flow of the Guaira (Salto das Sete Quedas) on the Alto Paraná River between Brazil and Paraguay had on occasions reached a rate of around 1,750,000 ft³/sec (50,000 m³/sec). However, the closing of the Itaipú dam gates in 1982 ended this claim to fame.

HIGHEST WATERFALL

The Salto Angel in Venezuela, on a branch of the Carrao River, an upper tributary of the Caroni River, is the highest waterfall (as opposed to vaporized "bridal veil") in the world. It has a total drop of 3,212 ft (979 m), with the longest single drop being 2,648 ft (807 m). The Angel Falls were named after the American pilot Jimmie Angel, who recorded them in his logbook on November 16, 1933.

GREATEST RIVER FLOW

The greatest flow of any river in the world is that of the Amazon, which discharges an average of around 7,100,000 ft³/sec (200,000 m³/sec) into the Atlantic Ocean, increasing to more than 12,000,000 ft³/sec (340,000 m³/sec) in full flood. The lower 900 miles (1,450 km) average 55 ft (17 m) in depth, but the river has a maximum depth of 407 ft (124 m). The flow of the Amazon is 60 times greater than that of the Nile.

LARGEST HOT SPRING

The largest boiling river issues from alkaline hot springs at Deildartunguhver, north of Reykjavik, Iceland, at a rate of 65 gallons (245 liters) of boiling water per second.

LONGEST RIVER

The Nile is credited as the longest river in the world. Its main source is Lake Victoria in east central Africa. From its farthest stream, in Burundi, it extends 4,160 miles (6,695 km) in length. By way of comparison, the Amazon is 4,007 miles (6,448 km) long.

★ WIDEST RIVER

While not in flood, the main stretches (i.e. excluding the tidal reaches, where an estuary/delta can be much wider) of the Amazon River in South America can reach widths of up to 7 miles (11 km) at its widest points.

RIVERS

★ LONGEST ESTUARY

The world's longest estuary (body of water where a river meets the sea) is that of the Ob in the north of Russia, at 550 miles (885 km). It is up to 50 miles (80 km) wide, and is also the ★ widest river to freeze solid.

LARGEST BASIN

The largest river basin in the world is that drained by the Amazon, which covers about 2,720,000 miles² (7,045,000 km²) – an area almost the size of Australia. It has countless tributaries, including the Madeira, which at 2,100 miles (3,380 km) is the longest tributary in the world, surpassed in length by just 17 rivers.

★ LARGEST NATURALLY FROZEN ICE RINK

The Rideau Canal Skateway in Ottawa, Ontario, Canada, is 4.8 miles (7.8 km) long and has a total maintained surface area of 1.782 million ft² (165,621 m²) – equivalent in area to 90 Olympic-size skating rinks.

SEAS & OCEANS

★ DEEPEST
BLUE HOLE ⇒

Dean's Blue Hole is a 249-ft-wide (76-m) vertical shaft that sinks for 663 ft (202 m) on the Atlantic edge of The Bahamas. It contains 38.8 million ft³ (1.1 million m³) of water and is the second-largest water-filled cavern on the planet. Blue holes are found at or just below sea level, and were once dry caves or shafts that filled with seawater as the ice-caps melted and the water levels rose following the last ice age.

★ **NEW RECORD**
☆ **UPDATED RECORD**

★ REMOTEST SPOT
FROM LAND

The world's most distant point from land is a spot in the South Pacific that is 1,600 miles (2,575 km) from the nearest points of land, namely Pitcairn Island, Ducie Island, and Peter I Island. Centered on this spot is a circle of water with an area of 8,041,200 miles² (20,826,800 km²) – much larger than Russia, the world's **largest country**.

★ FLATTEST PLACE
ON EARTH

Abyssal plains are vast expanses of flat, featureless terrain found in the deepest parts of the ocean. They cover approximately 40% of the ocean floor at depths of 13,000–16,400 ft (4,000–5,000 m). The uniform flatness is caused by the accumulation of sediments, up to 3 miles (5 km) thick in places, which overlie the basaltic rocks of the oceanic crust.

★ SHALLOWEST SEA

The Sea of Azov, which is a northern part of the Black Sea, has a maximum depth of 42 ft (13 m). It measures around 14,500 miles² (37,600 km²) in area.

DEEPEST POINT
IN THE OCEAN

In 1951, HM Survey Ship *Challenger* pinpointed the deepest area of the ocean as a part of the Mariana Trench in the Pacific Ocean. On January 23, 1960, the manned US Navy bathyscaphe *Trieste* descended to the bottom, and on March 24, 1995, the unmanned Japanese probe *Kaiko* recorded a depth of 35,797 ft (10,911 m), the most accurate ever measured. If Mount Everest was dropped into the Mariana Trench, it would disappear 6,560 ft (2,000 m) below the surface of the seabed.

★ BRIGHTEST
BIOLUMINESCENT BAY

Mosquito Bay, on the island of Vieques in Puerto Rico, USA, contains up to 700,000 tiny dinoflagellates per gallon of water (150,000 per liter). When agitated, these microscopic organisms (*Pyrodinium bahamense*, meaning "whirling fire") flash a blue-green light for about one-tenth of a second. Mosquito Bay's narrow mouth prevents the dinoflagellates from being washed out to sea.

HIGHEST OCEAN
TEMPERATURE

The highest temperature recorded in an ocean is 759°F (404°C), measured above a hydrothermal vent some 300 miles (480 km) off the American West Coast in 1985. The record temperature was measured by a US research submarine examining these largely unexplored ocean features.

MAJOR SEAS

NAME	AREA (MILES²)	AREA (KM²)	DEPTH (FT)	DEPTH (M)
South China*	1,148,500	2,974,600	4,000	1,200
Caribbean Sea	1,063,000	2,753,000	8,000	2,400
Mediterranean Sea	966,750	2,503,800	4,875	1,485
Bering Sea	875,750	2,268,180	4,700	1,400
Gulf of Mexico	595,750	1,542,985	5,000	1,500
Sea of Okhotsk	589,800	1,527,570	2,750	840
East China Sea	482,300	1,249,150	600	180
Hudson Bay	475,800	1,232,300	400	120
Sea of Japan	389,000	1,007,500	4,500	1,370
Andaman Sea	308,000	797,700	2,850	865
North Sea	222,125	575,300	300	90
Black Sea	178,370	461,980	3,600	1,100
Red Sea	169,000	437,700	1,610	490
Baltic Sea	163,000	422,160	190	55
Persian Gulf**	92,200	238,790	80	24
Gulf of St. Lawrence	91,800	237,760	400	120
Gulf of California	62,900	161,950	2,660	810
English Channel	34,700	89,900	177	54
Irish Sea	34,200	88,550	197	60
Bass Strait	28,950	75,000	230	70

The Malayan Sea, which embraces the South China Sea and the Straits of Malacca (3,144,900 miles²; 8,142,900 km²), is not now an entity accepted by the International Hydrographic Bureau
**Also referred to as the Arabian Gulf or, popularly, "the Gulf"*

LARGEST BAY ⇒

Measured by shoreline length, the largest bay in the world is Hudson Bay, Canada, with a shoreline of 7,623 miles (12,268 km) and an area of 476,000 miles² (1,233,000 km²). Measured by area, the Bay of Bengal, in the Indian Ocean, is larger, at 839,000 miles² (2,173,000 km²).

★ LARGEST ICEBERG

As of April 2005, the world's largest iceberg is B15-A in the Ross Sea off Antarctica. Measuring around 75 x 12 miles (120 x 20 km), with an area of around 960 miles² (2,500 km²), it is the largest remaining section of the B15 iceberg, which calved from the Ross Ice Shelf in March 2000. B15-A began to break up in October 2005, but remains closely monitored by Antarctic scientists.

★ LONGEST FJORD

The Nordvest Fjord arm of Scoresby Sund in eastern Greenland extends inland 195 miles (313 km) from the sea. Scoresby Sund is named after the Scottish whaling captain William Scoresby Jr., who, in 1822, was the first to sail into it.

LARGEST...

★ MEROMICTIC BASIN

With an area of approximately 196,000 miles² (508,000 km²) and a maximum depth of 7,365 ft (2,245 m), the Black Sea is the world's largest meromictic lake – a body of water characterized by layers of water at different densities. These layers do not mix, as there is little movement of the water. Trapped in the lower layer is toxic hydrogen sulphide that, if released by an earthquake, could kill thousands of people.

★ PANCAKE ICE

Sea ice covers 7% of the world's oceans, and is found mostly in the polar regions. In very cold places, such as the Weddell Sea in Antarctica, the ice can last for two, three, or more summers. When this occurs, sections of pancake ice form – large, rounded areas of ice that can range from 1 ft to 10 ft (30 cm to 3 m) in diameter and may grow up to 15 in (40 cm) thick.

MARINE ANIMAL STRUCTURE

The largest marine structure ever built by living creatures is the Great Barrier Reef, off Queensland, Australia, covering an area of 80,000 miles² (207,000 km²). It is actually composed of thousands of separate reefs made up of countless billions of dead and living stony corals (order Madreporaria or Scleractinia). Over 350 species of coral are found there, and its accretion is estimated to have taken 600 million years.

At 1,260 miles (2,027 km), it is also the world's **longest reef**.

★ OCEAN LANDFILL SITE

The North Pacific Central Gyre is a vast vortex of slow, high-pressure, clockwise-revolving ocean water that naturally concentrates floating litter in its center.

In 2002, environmental studies revealed that the center of the Gyre contains around 13 lb (6 kg) of waste plastic for every 2.2 lb (1 kg) of natural plankton.

MOST DANGEROUS SEA URCHIN

The flower sea urchin (*Toxopneustes pileolus*) is the world's most dangerous. Toxin from the spines and pedicellaria (small pincer-like organs) causes severe pain, respiratory problems, and paralysis.

ACTUAL SIZE

? DID YOU KNOW?

*The Pacific Ocean is the **largest ocean** in the world. It represents 45.9% of the world's oceans and covers an area of 64,186,000 miles² (166,241,700 km²). Its average depth is 12,925 ft (3,940 m).*

WEATHER

WORST DAMAGE TOLL FROM A HAIL STORM

In July 1984, a massive hail storm in Munich, Germany, wrought damage on trees, buildings, and vehicles, leading to insurance losses of $500 million. The final bill – which included losses to the economy caused by damage to uninsured buildings and public property – was estimated at $1 billion.

★ NEW RECORD
★ UPDATED RECORD

★ COLDEST LIQUID WATER DROPLETS

On August 13, 1999, Dr. Daniel Rosenfeld (Israel) and Dr. William Woodley (USA) reported tiny water droplets in clouds over West Texas, USA, that remained liquid for several minutes at temperatures down to -35.5°F (-37.5°C).

Colder droplets have been reported, but these 17-micron-wide droplets are the coldest ever seen that remained stable for several minutes. The density of the droplets was measured at 0.01 oz per ft³ (1.8 g per m³).

★ WARMEST YEAR ON RECORD

According to scientists at the Met Office, UK, 2005 was the warmest year in the northern hemisphere since records began in the 1860s.

The average temperature over the year for this region was 1.17°F (0.65°C) more than the average temperature between 1961 and 1991.

The 1990s was the **warmest decade** on record; the six warmest years on record were all in the 1990s.

FASTEST WIND SPEED (NOT SURFACE SPEED)

Using instrumentation known as the "Doppler on Wheels," scientists at the University of Oklahoma, USA, recorded a 302 +/-20 mph (486 +/-32 km/h) wind speed associated with a large tornado near Bridge Creek, Oklahoma, USA, on May 3, 1999.

The previous record was measured using a portable 3-mm Doppler radar, which registered a 286-mph (460-km/h) wind speed associated with a tornado near Red Rock, Oklahoma, USA, on April 26, 1991.

STORMY WEATHER

MOST POWERFUL SHORT-TERM NATURAL CLIMATE CHANGE

The El Niño Southern Oscillation occurs as a result of cyclic warming of the eastern and central Pacific Ocean. Apart from the seasonal effects of the Earth moving around the Sun, it is the most powerful short-term natural climate change on Earth.

The entire cycle of El Niño and La Niña (its cooler counterpart, characterized by unusually cold ocean temperatures) lasts between three and seven years. It causes unusual weather conditions all around the world, which were particularly dramatic in the 1982/83 and 1997/98 hurricane seasons.

★ TROPICAL CYCLONES

The spinning motion of a cyclone is brought about by the Coriolis effect, caused by the Earth's rotation.

At the absolute center, in a region usually around 20–40 miles (30–65 km) across, is the "eye," where conditions are tranquil – the ★ **calmest place in a tropical cyclone**. The eye is like a huge funnel in which air is drawn up from the ground and then spirals outward at the top, at an altitude of approximately 50,000 ft (15,000 m).

Just beyond the eye is the "eye wall" – a complete circle of storm clouds, often in a towering vertical structure, whirling around the eye. This represents the ★ **most violent place in a tropical cyclone**. It is here that the highest winds and strongest rainfall occur. Often in cyclones with wind speeds of over 110 mph (177 km/h), a second eye wall will form further out than the first.

★ MOST COWS KILLED BY LIGHTNING

A total of 68 Jersey cows were sheltering under a tree on Warwick Marks's (Australia, pictured) farm near Dorrigo, New South Wales, Australia, on October 31, 2005, The tree was hit by lightning and the electricity spread out into the surrounding soil, killing the animals.

★ STRONGEST
HURRICANE

The category-5 Hurricane Wilma, which occurred during October 2005, was the strongest hurricane since records began in 1851.

A hurricane hunter plane measured a barometric pressure in the eye of just 882 millibars – the lowest ever recorded for a hurricane. Wind speeds in Wilma's eye wall reached a staggering 165 mph (270 km/h).

LARGEST MEASURED TORNADO

On May 3, 1999, near Mulhall, north Oklahoma, USA, a tornado was measured with a diameter of 5,250 ft (1,600 m), using the University of Oklahoma's "Doppler on Wheels" mobile weather observatory, by Professor Joshua Wurman (USA).

The diameter is the distance between the rotational wind speed maxima. Wind velocities in the center are zero, but increase further out until they reach a maximum, then fall off again.

MOST TORNADOES IN 24 HOURS

On April 3–4, 1974, 148 tornadoes swept through the Southern and Midwestern US states, a region known as "Tornado Alley."

LONGEST LIGHTNING FLASH

At any one time, around 100 bolts of lightning hit the Earth every second. Typically, the length of these bolts is around 5.6 miles (9 km). In 1956, meteorologist Myron Ligda (USA) observed and recorded a lightning flash, using radar, that covered a horizontal distance inside clouds of 93 miles (149 km).

MOST LIGHTNING STRIKES SURVIVED

The only man in the world to be struck by lightning seven times was park ranger Roy C. Sullivan, the "human lightning conductor" of Virginia, USA. A single lightning strike is made up of several hundred million volts (with peak current in the order of 20,000 amps). Sullivan sustained the strikes between 1942 and 1977.

MOST TREES DESTROYED BY STORMS

A total of 270,000,000 trees were felled or split by storms in France on December 26–27, 1999.

SNOW & ICE

LARGEST SNOWFLAKE

It is reported that on January 28, 1887, at Fort Keogh, Montana, USA, ranch owner Matt Coleman (USA) measured a snowflake that was 15 in (38 cm) wide and 8 in (20 cm) thick, which he later described as being "larger than milk pans" in *Monthly Weather Review Magazine*.

WORST DAMAGE TOLL FROM AN ICE STORM

The most damaging ice storm ever took place in the first week of January 1998 in eastern Canada and adjoining parts of the USA. The storm began on January 6 and shut down airports and trains, blocked highways, and cut off power to 3 million people, almost 40% of Quebec's population.

Freezing rain over five days coated power lines with 4 in (10 cm) of ice, more weight than they could carry. The bill for damage was estimated to be $650 million.

GREATEST SNOWFALL

The **greatest snowfall recorded in a single day** was 76 in (1,930 mm) at Silver Lake, Colorado, USA, on April 14–15, 1921. A total of 1,224.5 in (31,102 mm) of snow fell at Paradise, Mt. Rainier, Washington, USA, from February 19, 1971 to February 18, 1972, the **greatest snowfall over a 12-month period**. The **greatest depth of snow on the ground** measured 451 in (11,460 mm) at Tamarac, California, USA, in March 1911.

? DID YOU KNOW?

*The UK experiences **more tornadoes by area than anywhere else in the world**. In an average year, one tornado is reported for each 2,856 miles² (7,397 km²).*

RECORD-BREAKING RAINFALL

Greatest annual rainfall
467 in (11,873 mm) in one year
Mawsynram, Meghalaya, India

Greatest monthly rainfall
366 in (9,300 mm) in July 1861
Cherrapunji, Meghalaya, India

Greatest rainfall in 24 hours
73 in (1,870 mm) on
March 15–16, 1952
Cilaos, Reunion, Indian Ocean

Most intense rainfall
1.5 in (38.1 mm) in one minute
November 26, 1970
Basse Terre, Guadeloupe

TROPICAL STORMS – WORST YEARS

YEAR	TROPICAL STORMS	HURRICANES	TOTAL TROPICAL CYCLONES
★ 2005	12	14	26
1933	11	10	21
1995	8	11	19
1887	8	11	19
1969	6	12	18
1936	9	7	16
2003	9	7	16
2004	6	9	15
2001	6	9	15
2000	7	8	15

Statistics from 1851 to present.
Source: National Hurricane Center

LIFE ON EARTH

CONTENTS

★ MOST NORTHERLY PRIMATES

Japanese macaques (*Macaca fuscata*) live near Nagano (36°40N, 138°10E) in the mountainous Jigokudani area of Honshu, Japan. Humans aside, they are the northernmost population of primates. Also known as snow monkeys, they survive the 5°F (-15°C) winters by warming themselves in the hot volcanic springwater. The water temperatures can reach 109°F (43°C), so the snow monkeys test the water with a few tentative splashes before easing themselves in. They leave the water before nightfall, giving themselves time to dry off – otherwise, they risk freezing to death.

EXTRAORDINARY PLANTS

←LARGEST BLOSSOMING PLANT

The largest known blossoming plant is a Chinese wisteria (*Wisteria sinensis*), similar to the one pictured, which was planted at Sierra Madre, California, USA, in 1892. By 1994 it had grown to cover an area of 1 acre (0.4 ha) and weighed 48,500 lb (22 tonnes), with branches measuring 500 ft (152 m) long. During the five-week blossoming period, the wisteria produces an estimated 1.5 million blossoms.

? DID YOU KNOW?

Biologists generally divide the living world into five kingdoms:

- **Monera**: *bacteria and simple single-celled organisms with no nucleus (prokaryotic)*

- **Protoctista**: *more complex single-celled organisms containing a nucleus (eukaryotic)*

- **Fungi**: *eukaryotic organisms that lack chlorophyll and reproduce by spreading spores*

- **Plantae** *(plants): multi-cellular organisms that contain chlorophyll and obtain energy from photosynthesis*

- **Animalia** *(animals): complex, multicellular organisms that feed by ingesting food into a specialized internal cavity*

★ NEW RECORD
☆ UPDATED RECORD

LARGEST AREA COVERED BY FLOATING FERNS

The largest recorded area of water covered entirely by the same fern, red *Azolla japonica*, measured 104,284 ft^2 (9,685 m^2) – enough to blanket over 35 tennis courts – when measured in 2000. The fern was floating on the Furukawa-Sawanoike pond in Kasuga Town, Japan.

TALLEST FERN

The tallest fern in the world is the tree fern *Cyathea australis,* which can grow to a height of 80ft (24 m) and has fronds up to 10 ft (3 m) long.

SPECIES WITH THE MOST CHROMOSOMES

The organism with the highest number of chromosomes recorded to date is the adder's tongue fern, *Ophioglossum reticulatum*, which has an estimated 1,440 (or 720 pairs). Humans have just 23 pairs.

SLOWEST-FLOWERING PLANT

The slowest-flowering plant is the rare *Puya raimondii*, discovered at an altitude of 12,992 ft (3,960 m) in Bolivia in 1870. The flower cluster emerges after about 80–150 years. After it has blossomed, the plant then dies. However, one planted near sea level at the University of California's Botanical Garden, Berkeley, USA, in 1958 grew to 24 ft 11 in (7.6 m) and bloomed as early as August 1986 after only 28 years.

SMELLIEST PLANT

Also known as the "corpse flower," the *Amorphophallus titanum* or titan arum is the smelliest plant on Earth. When it blooms, it releases an extremely bad smell, comparable to that of rotten flesh, which can be smelled from a distance of 0.5 miles (0.8 km). A native of the Sumatran rainforests, very few have ever flowered in Europe or the USA since first being discovered in 1878.

HIGHEST PLANTS

The greatest confirmed altitude at which any flowering plant has been discovered is 21,000 ft (6,400 m) on Mt. Kamet (25,446 ft; 7,756 m) in the Himalayas by N. D. Jayal (India) in 1955. Two plants were discovered at this altitude: *Ermania himalayensis* and *Ranunculus lobatus*.

★FASTEST ⬇ ENTRAPMENT BY A PLANT

On land, the clamshell-like leaves of the Venus flytrap (*Dionaea muscipula*) shut in one-tenth of a second (100 milliseconds) from the moment they are stimulated, typically by insects moving on the leaves (see below). Underwater, the hinged trapdoor of the bladderwort (*Utricularia vulgaris*) captures its victim in less than 1/500th of a second, making it the ★ **fastest underwater plant entrapment**.

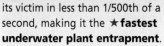

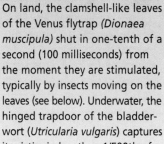

MOST TREES PLANTED IN A DAY BY AN INDIVIDUAL

Ken Chaplin (Canada) planted 15,170 red pine seedlings in one day near Prince Albert, Saskatchewan, Canada, on June 30, 2001.

MOST TREES PLANTED IN...

1 hour	13,125	Geelong Landcare Network, Victoria, Australia	Aug. 18, 2005
1 day	80,244	Nagapattinam District, Tamil Nadu, India	Dec. 4, 2002
1 day*	15,170	Ken Chaplin (Canada), Saskatchewan, Canada	Jun. 30, 2001
3 days	107,781	Tree Council, throughout UK and Ireland	Nov. 24–25, 2000
1 week	125,256	Sahara Lake City, Amby Valley, India	Jun. 5, 1998
★ Simultaneously	134,083	Kelowna City, British Columbia, Canada	May 5, 2005

* Individual record

★ RAREST PLANT

The world's rarest plant is arguably *Encephalartos woodii*, a cycad (evergreen cone bearer), of which only one specimen has ever been found growing wild. Discovered in 1895 by John Medley Wood (South Africa) in the Ngoya forest of KwaZulu-Natal, South Africa, this specimen has long since disappeared and the species now exists only in botanical gardens.

★ LONGEST ROOT

The longest root system is that of a single winter rye plant (*Secale cereale*), which has been shown to produce 387 miles (622.8 km) of roots in 1.8 ft³ (0.05 m³) of earth.

★ FIRST PHOTOSYNTHESIS

Chemical evidence in ancient rocks from Greenland suggests that photosynthesis was occurring on Earth 3.7 billion years ago – around a billion years earlier than previously believed. The analysis was carried out by scientists from the University of Copenhagen, Denmark, and published in *Earth and Planetary Science Letters* journal in December 2003.

★ LARGEST UNDIVIDED LEAF

The largest undivided leaf is that of *Alocasia macrorrhiza*, from Sabah, Malaysia. A specimen found in 1966 was 9 ft 11 in (3.02 m) long, 6 ft 3.5 in (1.92 m) wide, and had a surface area of 34.12 ft² (3.17 m²).

LARGEST LEAF

The largest leaves of any plant are those of the raffia palm (*Raphia farinifera* or *R. ruffia*) of the Mascarene Islands in the Indian Ocean, and the Amazonian bamboo palm (*R. taedigera*) of South America and Africa, of which the leaf blades can measure 65 ft 7 in (20 m) long, with petioles (the stalk that attaches a leaf to a stem) measuring 13 ft (4 m).

CARNIVOROUS PLANTS – LARGEST PREY

Of all the carnivorous plants, the ones that digest the largest prey belong to the Nepenthaceae family (genus *Nepenthes*). Both the *Nepenthes rajah* and *N. rafflesiana* have been known to eat large frogs, birds, and even rats. These species are commonly found in the rainforests of Asia, in particular Borneo, Indonesia, and Malaysia.

DEEPEST PLANT

Mark and Diane Littler (both USA) found algae at a depth of 882 ft (269 m) off San Salvador Island, The Bahamas, in October 1984. These maroon-colored plants survived although 99.9995% of sunlight was filtered out.

★ FASTEST-OPENING FLOWER

It takes less than 0.5 milliseconds for the petals of the bunchberry dogwood (*Cornus canadensis*) to open and the pollen to be released.

MOST POISONOUS PLANT

Based on the amount it takes to kill a human, the most poisonous plant is the castor bean (*Ricinus communis*). The poison – ricin – is 6,000 times more poisonous than cyanide and an amazing 12,000 times more poisonous than rattlesnake venom.

LARGEST SINGLE FLOWER

The mottled orange-brown and white parasitic plant *Rafflesia arnoldii* has the largest of all flowers. Native to Southeast Asia, they measure up to 3 ft (91 cm) across and weigh up to 24 lb (11 kg). Their petals are 0.75 in (1.9 cm) thick.

LOW LIFE

← LARGEST JELLYFISH

Most jellyfish have a bell or body diameter ranging from 0.8 to 15.8 in (2 to 40 cm), but some species grow considerably larger. The largest is the Arctic giant jellyfish (*Cyanea capillata arctica*). An Arctic giant that washed up in Massachusetts Bay, USA, in 1870 had a bell diameter of 7 ft 6 in (2.28 m) and tentacles stretching 120 ft (36.5 m). This particular jellyfish is also known as the Arctic lion's mane and is a predator that hunts its prey. Its favorite food is fish, plankton, and other jellyfish.

LARGEST PARASITES

The broad or fish tapeworm *Diphyllobothrium latum* (below) inhabits the small intestine of fish and sometimes humans. On average, it attains a length of 30–40 ft (9–12 m) – the length of a school bus – but some have been known to reach 60 ft (18 m).

Another human parasite, the pork tapeworm *Taenia solium*, sometimes exceeds 20 ft (6.09 m); and the beef tapeworm *Taeniarhynchus saginatus* can reach ⬇ up to 50 ft (15.24 m). ↘

MOST HEAT-TOLERANT ORGANISM (WATER BASED)

Strain 121 is a microbe belonging to the ancient group of bacteria-like organisms called archaeans – a group entirely to themselves, neither animal, nor plant, nor fungus, nor bacteria. This organism can survive temperatures of 250°F (121°C).

LONGEST ANIMAL

Although they superficially resemble true jellyfish and are distantly related to them, siphonophores are very different, special creatures. Each individual is actually a colony or super-organism – each part of its body is a distinct, highly specialized organism or zooid in its own right, adapted anatomically to fulfill a specific function (such as floating, stinging, feeding, or reproducing). In other words, each of its tentacles is a separate organism, as is each of its reproductive organs, each of its bells, and so on. One species of siphonophore, *Praya dubia*, is the longest

animal in the world, measuring 100–160 ft (30–50 m). At the head it has large paired, transparent swimming bells that produce a blue bioluminescent glow, and trailing behind is a long stem made up of units called cormidia, which it pulls through the water. Its thin tentacles can deliver a powerful sting.

★ MOST VENOMOUS JELLYFISH

The beautiful but deadly Flecker's sea wasp or box jellyfish (*Chironex fleckeri*) has a cardiotoxic venom that has caused the deaths of at least 70 people off the coast of Australia in the past century. If left untreated, some victims die within four minutes. One effective defense is women's pantyhose: Queensland lifeguards once wore oversized versions during surfing tournaments as the stinging cells cannot penetrate this material!

PARASITES

MOST BENEFICIAL PARASITE TO HUMANS

The saliva of the medicinal leech *Hirudo medicinalis* contains substances that will anesthetize a wound area, dilate the blood vessels to increase blood flow, and prevent blood from clotting. In 1991, a team of Canadian surgeons led by Dr. Dean Vistnes took advantage of the anticoagulants in leech saliva to drain away blood and prevent it from clotting during an operation to reattach a patient's scalp.

A lifespan of 27 years has been reliably recorded for *Hirudo medicinalis*, making it the **longest-living parasite**.

SMALLEST PARASITE

Pneumocystis carinii is 0.02–0.03 in (0.5–1 mm) long – no bigger than a period. It inhabits the human lungs and can cause pneumonia.

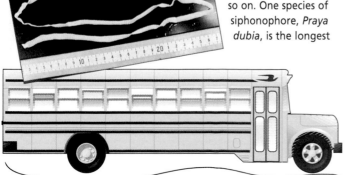

LARGEST → PARASITIC PROTOZOANS IN HUMANS

Balantidium coli (circled), which sometimes lives in the large intestine of humans, measures 0.003 x 0.002 in (0.08 x 0.06 mm).

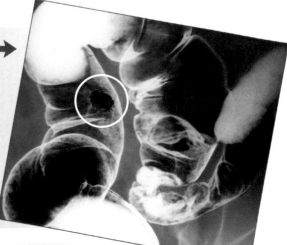

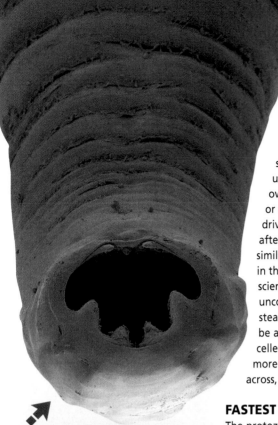

skin irritation, weight loss, and inexplicable bouts of memory loss. In some cases, the men were unable to remember their own telephone numbers, or even where they were driving to, but all recovered after three months. When similar cases were reported in the North Sea in 1997, scientific investigations uncovered the memory-stealing culprit. It proved to be a species of tiny single-celled dinoflagellate, no more than 0.0007 in (0.02 mm) across, called *Pfiesteria piscicida*.

MOST BLOODTHIRSTY PARASITE

The indistinguishable eggs of the hookworms *Ancylostoma duodenale* (pictured) and *Necator americanus* are found in the feces of 1.3 billion people. In severe cases, the lining of the gut is so thickly covered with worms that it looks like the pile of a carpet. The bleeding that results from their feeding adds up to a total of 2.6 million gal (10 million liters) of blood worldwide every day.

PROTOZOANS

★ SMALLEST ORGANISM TO CAUSE AMNESIA IN HUMANS

In 1996, fishermen on the Pocomoke River and estuaries close by in Chesapeake Bay, Maryland, USA, began suffering from an unexpected set of maladies, including headaches,

FASTEST REPRODUCTION

The protozoan *Glaucoma*, which reproduces by binary fission, divides as frequently as every three hours. In the course of a day it could become a great-great-great-great-great-great grandparent and the progenitor of 512 descendants.

SPONGES

BEST ANIMAL REGENERATION

The sponges (Porifera) have the most remarkable powers of regeneration of any animal. If they lose a segment of their body, it grows right back. If a sponge is forced through a fine-meshed silk gauze, the separate fragments can re-form into a sponge.

DEEPEST SPONGE

The deepest sponges have been recovered from depths of 29,000 ft (8,840 m) – as deep as Everest is high. They belong to the family Cladorhizidae.

WORMS

★ LONGEST WORM SPECIES

The bootlace worm (*Lineus longissimus*), a species of nemertean or ribbon worm, inhabits the shallow waters of the North Sea. In 1864, following a severe storm in St. Andrews, Scotland, UK, a record-breaking specimen washed ashore and was found to measure more than 180 ft (55 m) long.

★ FIRST ANIMAL TO BE GENETICALLY SEQUENCED

Caenorhabditis elegans, a 0.03-in-long (1-mm) soil-dwelling non-parasitic nematode worm, is the first species of multicellular animal whose entire genome (genetic code) has been sequenced. Although its full-size adult body consists of only 959 cells (humans have trillions), it has 100 million genetic bases comprising at least 18,000 genes. More than 50% of known human genes correspond with versions possessed by *C. elegans*. Dr. Sydney Brenner (South Africa) initiated the worm genome project in the 1960s at the Medical Research Council's Laboratory of Molecular Biology in Cambridgeshire, UK, and began the sequencing in 1990.

MOST FERTILE PARASITE

One female *Ascaris lumbricoides* roundworm can produce up to 200,000 eggs every day of her adult life, and has a total reproductive capacity of 26 million eggs. The eggs are highly resistant to all kinds of environmental conditions, which contributes to the widespread distribution of the species. These large worms, often up to 17 in (45 cm) in length, inhabit the intestines. It is the **most ubiquitous parasite in humans** with an estimated one billion people infected worldwide.

★ NEW RECORD
✩ UPDATED RECORD

★ MOST SIGNIFICANT NEW PARASITE ➡

A microscopic ectoparasite known as *Symbion pandora* was discovered in 1995. Its discovery is significant for two reasons. First, its unusual location – it was found on the bristles surrounding the mouth of the Norway lobster (*Nephrops norvegicus*), pictured right. Secondly, it could not be classified in any existing species or phylum category. (There are over 1.5 million known species in the world, all classified into around 35 phyla.) *Symbion pandora* was so unusual that it could not be classified into any of these existing phyla and therefore a new one called Cycliophora was created.

INSECTS & ARACHNIDS

Most resistant insect
The green peach aphid (*Myzus persicae*) – which varies in color from green to pale yellow to pink – has been documented as being resistant to 71 different chemical pesticides!

HEAVIEST SPIDER

Female bird-eating spiders (family Theraphosidae) are more heavily built than males, and in February 1985 Charles J. Seiderman (USA) captured a female example near Paramaribo, Surinam, which weighed a record peak 4.3 oz (122.2 g) before its death from moulting problems in January 1986. Other measurements included a maximum leg span of 10.5 in (26.7 cm), a total body length of 4 in (10.2 cm), and fangs measuring 1 in (2.5 cm) long.

HEAVIEST SCORPION

The large black West African species *Pandinus imperator* can weigh up to 2 oz (60 g) and measure between 5 and 7 in (13 and 18 cm) in length – the same as the average hand length of a human adult.

ACTUAL SIZE

INSECTS

★ LARGEST SPECIES OF BEE

Female king bees (*Chalicodoma pluto*) can attain a total length of 1.5 in (3.9 cm). This species – found only in the Molucca Islands of Indonesia – was first discovered in 1859 by naturalist Alfred Russel Wallace (UK), after which no specimen was recorded until February 1981, when two enormous females were seen by entomologist Dr. Adam Messer (USA).

★ MOST VENOMOUS CENTIPEDE

The venom from *Scolopendra subspinipes*, which inhabits the Solomon Islands, is so potent that human victims have been known to plunge their bitten hands into boiling water to mask the excruciating pain.

LONGEST PARASITIC FASTS

The common bedbug (*Cimex lectularius*), which feeds upon human blood, is famously able to survive without feeding for more than a year. However, the soft tick (*Ornithodoros turicata*), which spreads a bacterium of the order Spirochaetales that causes relapsing fever, can survive for periods of up to five years without food.

LARGEST BUTTERFLY

Queen Alexandra's birdwing (*Ornithoptera alexandrae*), which is native to Papua New Guinea, has a wingspan in female specimens in excess of 11 in (28 cm). The insect is so big (the size of a domestic pigeon) that tribesmen bring it down from the high tree canopies where it usually flies by shooting it with a

ACTUAL SIZE

★ LARGEST SPECIES OF WASP

The Asian giant hornet (*Vespa mandarinia*) – native to the mountains of Japan – can grow to be 2.2 in (5.5 cm) long, with a wingspan of approximately 3 in (7.6 cm). The stinger is about 0.25 in (0.6 cm) long and can inject a venom so powerful that it dissolves human tissue.

bow and arrow. The first specimen obtained by scientists was brought down using a shotgun!

★ LARGEST EARWIG SANCTUARY

The first – and only – earwig sanctuary is inside the Great Cave at Niah in Sarawak, northern Borneo. The species protected is the hairy earwig (*Arixenia esau*); the insects live in a single block of timber, which was fenced off in the early 1960s by Sarawack Museum curator Dr. Tom Harrisson (UK), thus creating the sanctuary.

FASTEST MOVING INSECT

Large tropical cockroaches of the order Dictyoptera can run with a speed of 3.3 mph (5.4 km/h), or 50 body lengths per second. The **fastest flying insect** is the Australian dragonfly (*Austrophlebia costalis*), which flies at 24 mph (39 km/h), rising to 36 mph (58 km/h) over short bursts.

★ MOST ACUTE SENSE OF SMELL

The male emperor moth (*Eudia pavonia*) can detect the sex attractant of the virgin female at a range of 6.8 miles (11 km). The female carries less than 0.0001 mg of scent – since identified as a higher alcohol ($C_{16}H_{29}OH$) – but the chemoreceptors on the male moth's antennae are so sensitive that they can detect a single molecule of scent.

★ MOST FREQUENT SEX

Australia's male scaly cricket (*Ornebius aperta*) can copulate more than 50 times in 3–4 hours, all with the same female.

ARACHNIDS

LARGEST TICKS

Hard ticks, members of the suborder Ixodida, are eight-legged parasites that inject paralyzing neurotoxins into their hosts and suck their blood, expanding to 1.4 in (30 mm) – the size of a walnut – to accommodate the volume of blood they require.

MOST VENOMOUS SCORPION

The Tunisian fat-tailed scorpion (*Androctonus australis*) is responsible for 80% of stings and 90% of deaths from scorpion stings in North Africa.

DEEPEST-LIVING SCORPION

The scorpion *Alacran tartarus* has been found in caves more than 2,600 ft (800 m) below the Earth's surface – approximately equal to twice the height of the Empire State Building in New York City, USA.

★ LARGEST VENOM GLANDS

Each of the venom glands of the spider *Phoneutria nigriventer* measures up to 0.4 in (10.2 mm) long and 0.1 in (2.7 mm) in diameter. Moreover, each gland can contain up to 0.000044 oz (1.35 mg) of venom, which is sufficient to kill 225 mice. *P. nigriventer* is South America's largest – and also probably most aggressive – species of spider.

NOISIEST SPIDERS

The male European buzzing spider (*Anyphaena accentuata*) vibrates its abdomen rapidly against the surface of a leaf, producing a buzzing sound as part of courtship behavior. This is audible to the human ear, but cannot be heard by the female spider. She can only detect the sound through vibrations.

The male of the American species *Lycosa gulosa*, once known as the purring spider, is equally audible. It taps its palps and abdomen on dry leaves to produce a purring sound.

MOST VENOMOUS SPIDER

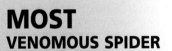

The Brazilian wandering spiders of the genus *Phoneutria*, and particularly the Brazilian huntsman *P. fera*, have the most active neurotoxic venom of any living spider. The venom is so potent that only 0.00000021 oz (0.006 mg) is sufficient to kill a mouse. *Phoneutria* are usually dark in color and have a body-and-leg spread of approximately 6.75 in (17 cm). These large and highly aggressive creatures often enter human dwellings and hide in clothing or shoes. When disturbed, they bite furiously several times, and hundreds of accidents involving these species are reported annually. Fortunately, an effective antivenom is available.

STRONGEST SPIDER WEB

The American spider *Achaearenea tepidariorum* has the strongest known spider web. In one recorded instance, its web was strong enough to ensnare a small mouse, which was completely lifted off the ground and supported by it.

The extremely tough webs created by spiders of the genus *Nephila* can also catch small birds and are even capable of slowing down the passage of mammals up to the size of humans.

Spiders of the tropical African species *N. senegalenis* have a special garbage line in their web, in which the sucked-out remains of small birds have been found.

LARGEST CONTINUOUS AREA OF SPIDER WEBS

Members of the Indian genus *Stegodyphus* build huge three-dimensional interwoven and overlapping webs that have been known to cover vegetation in a continuous silken mass for several miles.

★ SMALLEST ANIMAL USED IN DETECTING LAND MINES

The smallest animal currently being trained potentially to detect land mines is the honeybee (*Apis mellifera*), which measures 0.5 in (12 mm) long. In August 2003, researchers from the University of Montana, in cooperation with Sandia National Laboratories, S&K Electronics, and Montana State University (all USA), noted a 98% success rate in tests observing the insects hovering in response to chemicals leaking into the air from buried explosives (pictured above).

Smallest spider
A male *Patu marplesi* (family Symphytognathidae) of Western Samoa measured a record adult size of just 0.017 in (0.43 mm).

★ NEW RECORD
★ UPDATED RECORD

CRUSTACEANS & MOLLUSCS

CRUSTACEANS

HIGHEST DENSITY OF CRABS

An estimated 120 million red crabs (*Gecarcoidea natalis*) live exclusively on the 52-mile² (135-km²) Christmas Island in the Indian Ocean – a density of approximately one crab per square meter for the whole island. Every year (from around November until Christmas, appropriately enough), millions of the crabs swarm out of their burrows to mate and spawn at the coast.

★ MOST DRAMATIC CRUSTACEAN TRANSFORMATION

Although the larva of the copepod crustacean *Sacculina carcini* is free-swimming and closely resembles those of other copepod species, the adult bears no resemblance to any other type of crustacean. On becoming an adult, the larva loses its limbs, gut, and segmentation, and its body dramatically transforms into a shapeless sac-like structure. This pierces the body of a crab and then sends out root-like branches that permeate the crab's body and limbs.

Bearing this bizarre parasitic copepod's amorphous body on its own undersurface, the crab is now said to be "sacculinized," and often undergoes a degree of sex reversal – owing to the modification of its gonads and/or release of inhibiting compounds by the now strangely plant-like *Sacculina*.

MOST LIGHT-SENSITIVE EYES

The animal that has eyes with the highest light-collecting ability is the ostracod *Gigantocypris*, which has an f-number (the focal ratio of an optical system) of 0.25. By way of comparison, humans have an f-number of around 2.55 and a camera lens has an f-number of 1.8.

LARGEST CRUSTACEAN (LENGTH)

The Japanese spider crab (*Macrocheira kaempferi*), found off the southeastern coast of Japan, has an average body size of 10 x 12 in (25 x 30 cm) and an average leg span of 6–9 ft (2–3 m). The largest specimen ever found had a leg span of 12 ft 1 in (3.69 m) and weighed 41 lb (18.6 kg).

HEAVIEST MARINE CRUSTACEAN

The heaviest marine crustacean is the American or North Atlantic lobster (*Homarus americanus*). On February 11, 1977, a specimen weighing 44 lb 6 oz (20.14 kg) and measuring 3 ft 6 in (1.06 m) – from the end of the tail fan to the tip of the largest claw – was caught off the coast of Nova Scotia, Canada.

OLDEST PENIS

The oldest known fossilized penis dates back around 100 million years. It belongs to a crustacean called an ostracod found in Brazil, which measures just 0.039 in (1 mm) across. The discovery was announced in September 2002 at the British Association for the Advancement of Science Festival in Leicester, UK.

★ STRONGEST ANIMAL PUNCH

The peacock mantis shrimp (*Odontodactylus scyllarus*), a species of stomatopod, flails its club-shaped front leg at peak speeds of 75 ft/sec (23 m/sec) to shatter the shells of its prey. The force of the blow is over a hundred times the mantis shrimp's body weight. Stomatopods also have the ★ **most sophisticated eyes** of any animal on Earth – some species have more than 10 pigments sensitive to different wavelengths of light, compared with only three pigments in human eyes.

GREATEST DIFFERENCE IN SIZE BETWEEN PREDATOR AND PREY

Blue whales (*Balaenoptera musculus*) are the **largest mammals** on Earth, measuring an average of 80 ft (25 m) long. They feed on krill (euphausiids), tiny shrimp-like creatures of the zooplankton, about 2 in (50 mm) in length.

★ DEEPEST
OCTOPUS

The dumbo octopus (*Grimpoteuthis*) lives at depths of up to 5,000 ft (1,500 m), close to the ocean floor. Its body, roughly 8 in (20 cm) long, is soft, semi-gelatinous, and capable of resisting the great pressure found at this depth. It swims by moving its fins, pulsing its webbed arms, or pushing water through a funnel for jet propulsion.

MOLLUSCS

★ FIRST CAPTURE OF A LIVING GIANT SQUID

The *Architeuthis dux* is commonly known as the giant squid. Specimens have measured up to 60 ft (18 m) in length and 2,000 lb (900 kg) in weight. In March 2002, an international scientific team led by marine biologist Steve O'Shea (New Zealand) announced that it had caught seven juvenile specimens of the famously elusive giant squid – measuring 0.35–0.05 in (9–13 mm) – off the coast of New Zealand. These did not survive long in captivity, and no adult has ever been captured and maintained alive.

On September 30, 2004, Japanese researchers photographed a 26-ft-long (8-m) giant squid that had become entangled on bait in waters nearly 0.6 mile (1 km) deep, off the Ogasawara Islands, Japan. This is the ★ **first sighting of an adult giant squid in its natural habitat**.

★ MOST VENOMOUS GASTROPODS

The most venomous gastropods are cone shells of the genus *Conus* that can deliver a fast-acting neurotoxic venom. Several of these species are venomous enough to kill humans, but the geographer cone (*Conus geographus*) of the Indo-Pacific Ocean is one of the most dangerous.

★ RAREST SEASHELL

The rarest seashell in the world is the white-toothed cowry (*Cypraea leucodon*). It is known from just two specimens, the second of which turned up in 1960, and is thus the most coveted species among conchologists. Its only recorded locality is the Philippines' Sulu Sea.

LARGEST PEARL

The Pearl of Lao-tze (also called the Pearl of Allah) was found at Palawan, Philippines, on May 7, 1934, in the shell of a giant clam. It weighs 14 lb 1 oz (6.3 kg) and is 9.4 in (24 cm) long and 5.5 in (14 cm) in diameter.

FASTEST LAND SNAIL

The fastest-moving species of land snail is the common garden snail (*Helix aspera*). On February 20, 1990, a specimen named Verne completed a 12-in (31-cm) course at West Middle School in Plymouth, Michigan, USA, in 2 min 13 sec at 0.09 in/sec (0.23 cm/sec). To put this into perspective, the snail-racing equivalent of a four-minute mile would be roughly an eight-day mile.

SLOWEST GROWTH RATE

The slowest growth rate in the animal kingdom is that of the deep-sea clam *Tindaria callistiformis*, which takes about 100 years to reach a length of 0.3 in (8 mm).

MOST PARASITIZED HOST SPECIES

Stagnicola emarginata, a species of freshwater snail from the Great Lakes of the USA and Canada, is a host for the larvae of at least 35 species of parasitic fluke (flatworms). It transmits parasites that cause swimmer's itch.

! **X-REF**

The flower sea urchin has a harmless enough name, but it's actually one of world's most deadly marine creatures. Find out more on p.27.

★ NEW RECORD
★ UPDATED RECORD

LARGEST EYE

The Atlantic giant squid (*Architeuthis dux*) has the largest eye of any animal – living or extinct. It is also the **largest of all invertebrates**.

It has been estimated that a specimen found in 1878 in Thimble Tickle Bay, Newfoundland, Canada, had eyes 16 in (40 cm) in diameter – almost the width of an open *Guinness World Records* book! Its body was 20 ft (6 m) long and one tentacle measured 35 ft (10 m).

FISH

HEAVIEST BONY FISH ⬆

The ocean sunfish (*Mola mola*), which has been recorded weighing 4,400 lb (2 tonnes) and measuring 10 ft (3 m) from fin tip to fin tip, is the heaviest bony fish in the ocean. The **heaviest cartilaginous fish** is the whale shark (see entry for *Largest fish*).

★ MOST FERTILE FISH ⬆

Found in Australian waters, the ocean sunfish (*Mola mola*) is the most fertile of all living fish. The ovaries of one female contained 300 million eggs, each measuring about 0.05 in (1.27 mm) in diameter.

★ NEW RECORD
☆ UPDATED RECORD

★ SMALLEST SEAHORSE ⬈

An adult pygmy seahorse (*Hippocampus denise*) is typically just 0.63 in (16 mm) long – smaller than an average human thumbnail. It is

ACTUAL SIZE

the smallest seahorse and is almost as tiny as the world's smallest fishes. A master of camouflage, this new species lives among deep corals and was discovered in 2003 in the delicate corals of the Flores Sea, off the coast of Indonesia, by a marine biologist working for Project Seahorse.

★ FISH WITH THE MOST EYES

The six-eyed spookfish (*Bathylychnops exilis*), which inhabits depths of 300–3,000 ft (90–900 m) in the northeastern Pacific, has not only a pair of large, principal eyes, but also a second, smaller pair, known as secondary globes, positioned within the lower half of the principal eyes and pointing downward. Each of these globes possesses its own lens and retina, and may help to increase the spookfish's sensitivity to light in its shadowy surroundings. Moreover, located behind the secondary globes is a third pair of eyes, which lack retinas but divert incoming light into the fish's large principal eyes.

★ MOST ENERGETIC ANIMAL BRAIN

The brain of the the African elephant-trunk fish (*Gnathonomus petersi*) accounts for 3.1% of its body mass, and uses more than 50% of the oxygen that its body takes in. By contrast, the human brain uses a mere 20% of the oxygen that the body takes in.

☆ SHORTEST LIFE SPAN FOR A VERTEBRATE

In 2005, researchers at James Cook University, Queensland, Australia, revealed that the coral-reef pygmy goby (*Eviota sigillata*) lives for a maximum of just 59 days.

FIRST MODERN-DAY SPECIES OF LAND-LIVING FISH

Formally known as *Phreatobius walkeri* and not brought to scientific attention until the mid-1980s, this small red worm-like species of trichomycterid catfish from Brazil lives a fully terrestrial existence among leaf litter on riverbanks. When placed in water, it will swiftly jump back out again.

FASTEST FISH

The cosmopolitan sailfish (*Istiophorus platypterus*) is considered to be the fastest species of fish over short distances, although practical difficulties make measurements extremely difficult to secure. In a series of speed trials carried out at the Long Key Fishing Camp, Florida, USA, one sailfish took out 300 ft (91 m) of line in 3 seconds, which is equivalent to a velocity of 68 mph (109 km/h). By way of comparison, a cheetah – the **fastest mammal on land over short distances** – can reach a speed of 60 mph (96 km/h).

★ FEWEST EGGS PRODUCED BY A FISH

The mouth-brooding cichlid *Tropheus moorii* of Lake Tanganyika, east Africa, produces seven eggs or fewer during normal reproduction. As each egg is released, the female takes it into her mouth, where it is fertilized by the male and incubated for up to 30 days.

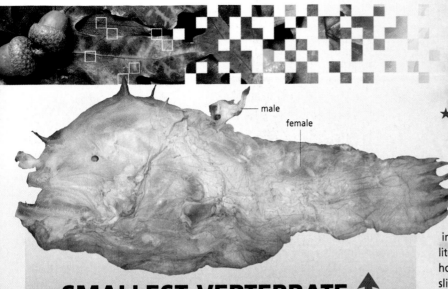

male

female

SMALLEST VERTEBRATE ⬆

According to research published by Theodore W. Pietsch of the University of Washington, Washington State, USA, on August 25, 2005, a sexually mature male *Photocorynus spiniceps*, collected from a depth of 4,675 ft (1,425 m) in the Philippine Sea, measured just 0.24 in (6.2 mm) long. Interestingly, this species of anglerfish reproduces through sexual parasitism: the male permanently attaches itself to the larger female – who, on average, is 1.8 in (46 mm) – by biting her belly, sides, or back (see above), and gradually becoming part of her, thereby effectively turning her into an hermaphrodite.

LARGEST FISH

The largest scientifically recorded example of the rare plankton-feeding whale shark (*Rhincodon typus*) measured 41 ft 6 in (12.65 m) long and 23 ft (7 m) around the thickest part of the body, and weighed about 33,000–46,300 lb (15–21 tonnes). It was captured off Baba Island, near Karachi, Pakistan, on November 11, 1949.

LARGEST FISH EGG

The egg of a whale shark (*Rhincodon typus*) found by a shrimp trawler in the Gulf of Mexico on June 29, 1953, measured 12 x 5.5 x 3.5 in (30.5 x 14 x 8.9 cm). It contained a live embryo measuring 13.8 in (35 cm) long.

LARGEST FRESHWATER FISH

The Mekong giant catfish (*Pangasius gigas*) of the Mekong River basin, and *P. sanitwongse* of the Chao Phraya River basin, both in Southeast Asia, are reputed to attain a length of 10 ft (3 m) and weigh 660 lb (300 kg).

The **smallest freshwater fish** is the pygmy gobi (*Pandaka pygmaea*) of Luzon in the Philippines, the males measuring just 0.28–0.38 in (7.5–9.9 mm) long.

LARGEST PREDATORY FISH

The rare great white shark (*Carcharodon carcharias*) averages 14–15 ft (4.3–4.6 m) in length, and generally weigh 1,150–1,700 lb (520–770 kg). There are many claims of huge specimens up to 33 ft (10 m) in length and, although few have been properly authenticated, there is plenty of circumstantial evidence to suggest that some great whites grow to more than 20 ft (6 m) in length.

★LARGEST SNEEZING FISH

The only species of fish that can sneeze is the hagfish or slime eel (*Myxine glutinosa*), a primitive species of jawless fish or agnathan. It bores inside other fishes – living, dying, or dead – and eats their internal organs until they are literally hollow. It then slips out of the hole by secreting vast amounts of a slime-like lubricant. To prevent itself from suffocating in this substance, it literally sneezes the slime out of its primitive respiratory slits.

★ LARGEST PREHISTORIC FISH

Paleontologists have yet to discover prehistoric fish larger than living species, but modern estimates suggest that the largest in prehistoric times was the megalodon shark *Carcharocles megalodon,* which lived 50–4.5 million years ago. Recent studies suggest that it attained a maximum length of 45 ft (13.7 m) – the size of a school bus – although this has been a subject of debate since the first fossil teeth were found in the early 19th century.

★SMALLEST COMMERCIAL FISH

The now endangered sinarapan (*Mistichthys luzonensis*) is a goby found only in Lake Buhi, Luzon, Philippines. Males are 0.39–0.51 in (10–13 mm) long, and a dried 1-lb (454-g) fish cake would contain about 70,000 of them!

FISH WITH THE GREATEST ➡ SENSE OF SMELL

Sharks have a better sense of smell – and more highly developed scent organs – than any other fish. Well known for detecting prey from great distances, they can detect one part of blood in 100 million parts of water.

AMPHIBIANS & REPTILES

ACTUAL SIZE

SMALLEST NEWT

The Mexican lungless salamander (*Bolitoglossa mexicana*) attains a length of about 1 in (2.54 cm), including the tail, when fully grown.

? DID YOU KNOW?

• An amphibian is a smooth-skinned, cold-blooded vertebrate that belongs to the class Amphibia. It can live both on land and in water. Its young are usually born as aquatic larvae, with gills.

• A reptile, class Reptilia, is a cold-blooded vertebrate, usually with a hard skin of scales or plates. Its young hatch from eggs covered by a leathery shell.

AMPHIBIANS

LARGEST AMPHIBIAN

The Chinese giant salamander (*Andrias davidianus*), which lives in mountain streams in northeastern, central, and southern China, averages 3 ft 9 in (1.14 m) in length and weighs 55–66 lb (25–30 kg). One record-breaking specimen from the Hunan province measured 5 ft 11 in (1.8 m) in length and weighed 143 lb (65 kg).

For the **smallest amphibian**, see *Largest frog* box below.

RAREST AMPHIBIAN

The golden toad (*Bufo periglenes*) is found in a small area (less than 4 miles^2; 10 km^2) contained in the Monteverde Cloud Forest Preserve in the Cordillera de Tilaran, near Monteverde, Provincia de Puntarenas, Costa Rica. Its numbers have mysteriously plummeted in little over a decade, with the last recorded sighting of one specimen between 1988 and 1989. Although some herpetologists have written off this species as extinct, it is officially classified as critically endangered.

★ LARGEST CAECILIAN

Caecilians are rarely seen, limbless amphibians that are frequently mistaken for earthworms on first sight, but can be distinguished by their very large mouths. The largest is Thompson's caecilian (*Caecilia thompsoni*), from Colombia, which grows up to approximately 5 ft (1.5 m) long and attains a width of up to 1.2 in (3 cm).

★ FURRIEST FROG

Male specimens of the hairy frog (*Trichobatrachus robustus*) of West Africa are unique in exhibiting a profuse covering of apparent hair on their hind limbs during the breeding season. Closer observation, however, reveals that this "hair" is actually a mass of tiny skin filaments, richly supplied with blood vessels. Scientists believe that the frog uses these as accessory respiratory aids, like gills, absorbing oxygen directly from surrounding water where it lives, thereby supplementing the amount of oxygen taken in by its lungs, which are poorly developed in this species.

MOST POISONOUS FROG

The golden poison-dart frog (*Phyllobates terribilis*) of South and Central America is only 1.5–2 in (4–5 cm) long but secretes enough toxin to provide a lethal dose to 10 adult humans or 20,000 lab mice. Scientists have to wear thick protective gloves when they pick it up, in case they have cuts or scratches on their hands.

★ FARTHEST GLIDING AMPHIBIAN

Certain species of flying frogs are able to glide up to 50 ft (15 m) using the extensive webbing on their feet to sustain their flight. Pictured above is the Costa Rican flying frog (*Agalychnis spurrelli*).

REPTILES

SHORTEST SNAKE

The world's shortest snake is the very rare thread snake (*Leptotyphlops bilineata*), known only from Martinique, Barbados, and St. Lucia. The longest known specimen measured 4.25 in (10.8 cm), and had such a matchstick-thin body that it could have entered the hole left in a standard pencil after the lead has been removed.

The **shortest venomous snake** is the namaqua or spotted dwarf adder (*Bitis schneideri*) of Namibia, which has an average length of 8 in (200 mm).

← LARGEST FROG

An African goliath frog (*Conraua goliath*) captured in April 1889 on the Sanaga River, Cameroon, had a snout-to-vent length of 14.5 in (36.8 cm), an overall length of 34.5 in (87.6 cm) with its legs extended, and weighed 8 lb 1 oz (3.6 kg). The average length for this species is 11.8 in (30 cm), about the average size of a rabbit. The **smallest frog**, and the **smallest known amphibian**, is *Eleutherodactylus limbatus* of Cuba, which is 0.3–0.5 in (8.5–12 mm) long from snout-to-vent when fully grown.

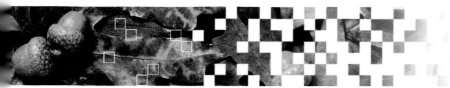

← MOST RESTRICTED
AMPHIBIAN DEVELOPMENT

Certain newts and salamanders fail to develop into "normal" adults, although they do become sexually mature and can reproduce (a condition known as "neotony"). The best known example is the axolotl (*Ambystoma mexicanum*) or "water monster" of Mexico, which looks like a giant tadpole measuring up to 9.8 in (25 cm) long. It can metamorphose into the terrestrial adult form – such as when its water source dries up – but normally breeds in its immature, aquatic form.

(1.7 m) and is found across east central Australia. In a single strike, this snake can inject 0.002 oz (60 mg) of venom, sufficient to kill a small marsupial in seconds, but also more than enough to kill several human adults.

MOST VENOMOUS
MARINE SNAKE

The Belcher's sea snake (*Hydrophis belcheri*), found around Ashmore Reef in the Timor Sea off northwest Australia, has a myotoxic venom many times more poisonous than the venom of any land snake. The common beaked sea snake (*Enhydrina schistosa*) is probably equally as venomous as *Hydrophis belcheri* but is more dangerous as it is more common, more widely distributed, and more aggressive.

? DID YOU KNOW?

• *When some species of salamander lose an eye, limb, or tail, the missing pieces may regenerate – often in a different color and shape.*

• *In some forests in North America, there are so many salamanders that their total mass may exceed that of all mammals and birds in the forest combined.*

★ NEW RECORD
UPDATED RECORD

OLDEST VOMIT

In 2002, a team of palaeontologists led by Professor Peter Doyle (UK) announced their discovery of the 160 million-year-old fossilized vomit of an ichthyosaur – a large, fish-like marine reptile – in a quarry in Peterborough, UK.

★ RAREST LIZARD

The Jamaican iguana (*Cyclura collei*) is a critically endangered species only rediscovered in 1990. With no more than 100 adult specimens existing, it is clinging to survival in southern Jamaica's remote Hellshire Hills.

★ RAREST CROCODILIAN

There are fewer than 200 Chinese alligators (*Alligator sinensis*) living in the wild, making it one of the most endangered species on Earth. Found in the lower parts of the Yangtze River in wetland habitats, the species can grow to 6.5 ft (2 m) and weigh 88 lb (40 kg).

MOST VENOMOUS LAND SNAKE

The most venomous land snake is the small-scaled snake (*Oxyuranus microlepidotus*), which measures 5 ft 7 in

LARGEST LIZARD ➡

Found on the Indonesian islands of Komodo, Rintja, Padar, and Flores, the Komodo dragon (*Varanus komodoensis*) – a.k.a. the Komodo monitor or ora – averages 7 ft 5 in (2.25 m) in length and weighs about 130 lb (60 kg). The largest accurately measured specimen was a male displayed at St. Louis Zoological Gardens, Missouri, USA, in 1937. It measured 10 ft 2 in (3.1 m) long and weighed 365 lb (166 kg).

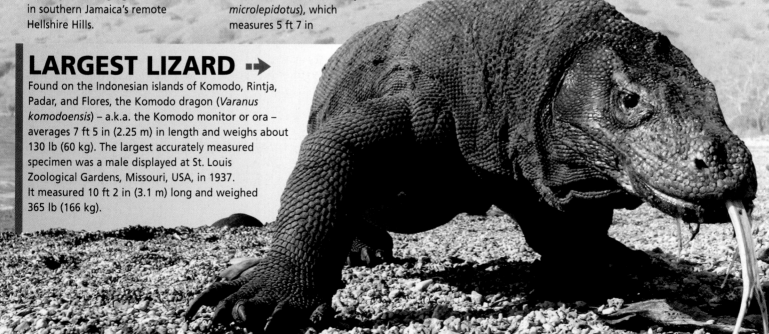

★ BIRDWATCHING: ➡ FASTEST TIME TO SPOT ALL BIRD FAMILIES

Derek Scott and Harry Howard (both UK) have together spotted all the bird families of the world in exactly one year from January 1, 1998 to December 31, 1998. Their extensive itinerary covered 28 countries and an incredible 12,000 miles (19,312 km). In total, the "twitchers" sighted 2,726 different types of bird.

ACTUAL SIZE

SMALLEST BIRD

The smallest bird is the bee hummingbird (*Mellisuga helenae*) of Cuba and the Isle of Youth. Males measure 2.24 in (57 mm) in total length, half of which is taken up by the bill and tail, and weigh 0.056 oz (1.6 g). Females are slightly larger.

The hummingbird also has the **fastest wing beat**. During courtship, the ruby-throated hummingbird (*Archilochus colubris*) can produce a wing-beat rate of 200 beats per second, as opposed to the normal 90 beats per second produced by all other hummingbirds.

★ NEW RECORD
★ UPDATED RECORD

★ KEENEST SENSE OF SMELL

Few birds have a highly developed sense of smell. However, the black-footed albatross (*Diomedea nigripes*), native to the North Pacific, can be attracted by the smell of bacon fat poured into the ocean surface at least 18 miles (30 km) away.

★ MOST ABUNDANT BIRD EVER

The most abundant bird ever was the passenger pigeon (*Ectopistes migratorius*) of North America. It is impossible to provide an exact count of specimens, but even conservative estimates of its total population at its peak indicate that during the early 19th century there may have been as many as 10 billion birds. Their flocks darkened the skies when in flight, took up to three days to pass overhead, and a single flock could contain more than two billion birds.

Not surprisingly, they were popular targets for sportsmen – so popular that their relentless persecution ultimately achieved the seemingly impossible. In 1914, the very last known passenger pigeon, an adult female called Martha, died in Cincinnati Zoo (USA).

★ MOST BIRDS RINGED

The Icelandic Institute of Natural History has been operating the Icelandic Bird Ringing Scheme since its establishment in 1932. Between 1953 and February 1997, Óskar J. Sigurósson (Iceland), a lighthouse keeper at Stórhöfôi in the Westmann Islands, had ringed 65,243 birds.

★ OLDEST WILD BIRD

The oldest recorded age for a bird in the wild is 50 years for a Manx shearwater (*Puffinus puffinus*), a small seabird. It was first ringed in 1957 (when it was five years old) and then again in 1961, 1977, and finally in 2002. It was captured on Bardsey, an island off the Lleyn Peninsula, North Wales, UK, on April 3, 2002.

★ GREATEST MIMIC

The marsh warbler (*Acrocephalus palustris*) is capable of imitating the songs of up to 80 other species of birds, most of them African birds heard in the warbler's winter home. Song is necessary for mate attraction and selection as well as being an important means of marking territory.

★ FIRST FEATHERED ANIMAL

In June 2000, scientists announced that a 220-million-year-old fossilized creature named *Longisquama insignis* – an early species of reptile – had appendages on its back that were hollow and similar to the feathers of birds seen today. This creature probably used its primitive feathers to glide between trees 75 million years before the first birds evolved.

LONGEST ⬇ BILL

The longest bill is that of the Australian pelican (*Pelecanus conspicillatus*) and is 13–18.5 in (34–47 cm) long.

The **longest beak in relation to overall body length** is that of the sword-billed hummingbird (*Ensifera ensifera*), which lives in the Andes between Venezuela and Bolivia. The beak measures 4 in (10.2 cm) – making it longer than the bird's actual body if the tail is excluded.

ACTUAL SIZE

★ MOST BLOODTHIRSTY BIRD

The sharp-beaked ground finch or vampire finch (*Geospiza difficilis*) of Wolf Island in the Galapagos Islands normally eats seeds, but since 1964 scientists have observed this species pecking large seabirds called boobies and drinking the blood that seeps from the wound.

★ LONGEST COCK-CROW

The longest cock-crow ever recorded was one of 23.6 seconds by a rooster named Tugaru-Ono-94 in Ueda City, Nagano, Japan, on May 8, 1995.

★ LARGEST EGG RELATIVE TO BODY SIZE

The brown kiwi (*Apteryx australis*) of New Zealand lays the largest eggs relative to body size. One female kiwi weighing 3.7 lb (1.7 kg) laid an egg weighing 14.3 oz (406 g), which is almost one-quarter of her total body mass, and weights of up to 18 oz (510 g) have been reliably reported for other kiwi eggs.

★ LARGEST WINGSPAN EVER

The greatest wingspan of any known bird belonged to the South American teratorn (*Argentavis magnificens*), a superficially vulture-like species that lived 6–8 million years ago. Fossil remains found in Buenos Aires, Argentina, give an estimated spread of 25 ft (7.6 m).

★ LEADING BIRDWATCHER

The world's leading birdwatcher was Phoebe Snetsinger (USA), who passed away in 1999. She saw 8,040 of the 9,700 known species (representing over 82% of the world's species), all of the world's families on the official list, and well over 90% of the genera during her years of birdwatching, which started in 1965.

LOWEST TEMPERATURE ENDURED

The breeding emperor penguin (*Aptenodytes forsteri*) can endure an average temperature of -4°F (-20°C) on the Antarctic sea ice, where the wind speed can vary from 16 to 47 mph (25 to 75 km/h).

LARGEST VOCABULARY

Camille Jordan (USA) was the proud owner of a budgerigar named Puck, who knew an estimated 1,728 words before its death in 1994.

MOST POISONOUS BIRD

The hooded pitohui (*Pitohui dichrous*) from Papua New Guinea is one of a small number of poisonous birds in the world. It was discovered in 1990 and has puzzled scientists as its feathers and skin contain the powerful poison homobatrachotoxin, the same one secreted by the dart frogs of South America.

Like many other poisonous animals, this bird also emits a bad smell and advertises its dangerousness with bright colors. The venom affects the nerves of the victim but scientists have not yet discovered how the species produces it.

LARGEST BIRD

The largest living bird is the North African ostrich (*Struthio camelus camelus*). Male examples of this flightless (ratite) sub-species have been recorded up to 9 ft (2.75 m) tall and weighing 345 lb (156 kg).

The ostrich also lays the **largest egg**. The heaviest on record weighed 5.47 lb (2.48 kg) and was laid at a farm owned by Luk Schelfhout (Netherlands) in Deerlijk, Belgium, on June 3, 2004. The shell, although only 0.06 in (1.5 mm) thick, can support the weight of an adult person.

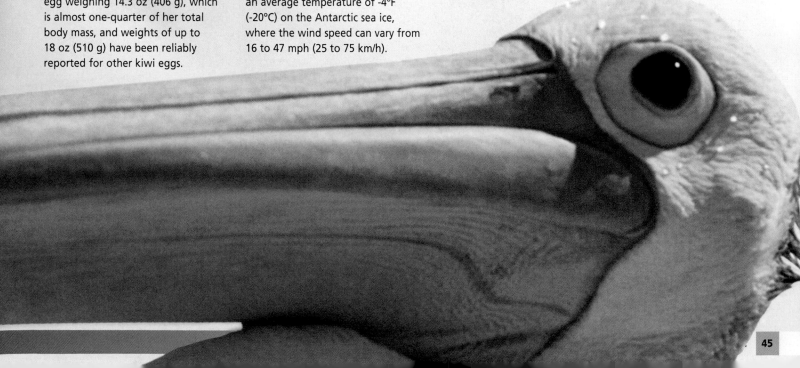

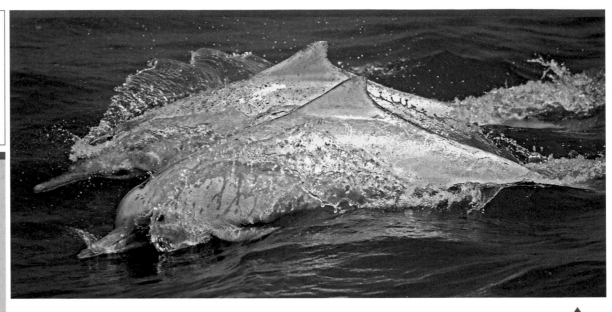

★ SMALLEST BEAR SPECIES

The Malayan sun bear (*Ursus malayanus*) of subtropical, southeast Asia is the smallest species of bear. Named after the golden crescent patch that appears on the chest of the otherwise black bear, an adult male typically measures 4 ft 6 in (1.4 m) long with a shoulder height of 28 in (72 cm). Being excellent climbers, sun bears skillfully use their long tongue and claws to gather fruit or dig for honey and grubs.

CARNIVORA

★ MOST RECENTLY IDENTIFIED CARNIVORE

In December 2005, environmental researchers hoped to capture a new species of carnivore on Borneo, the first such discovery on the island since that of the Borneo ferret-badger in 1895. The animal looks like a cross between a cat and a fox and is believed to be carnivorous. Photographed in the mountainous rainforests of the Kayan Mentarang National Park in 2003, it was kept unpublished as research continued. Likely to be a viverrid (the family which includes the civets), this potential new species has not yet been confirmed.

★ RAREST WILD DOG

The Ethiopian wolf (*Canis simiensis*) is the rarest species of wild dog, and may also be the rarest carnivore of any type in Africa, with fewer than 450 specimens alive. The species is very vulnerable to the threat of rabies, which has been a major reason for the decreasing numbers.

MAMMAL WITH THE MOST NAMES

In the English language alone, the puma (*Puma concolor*) has more than 40 names, including cougar, red tiger, mountain lion, catamount, and Florida panther. Pumas live in both North and South America – this wide distribution is probably the reason why so many common names have developed.

MOST FEARLESS MAMMAL

The ratel or honey badger (*Mellivora capensis*) will defend itself against animals of any size. Its skin is so tough that it is impervious to the stings of bees, the quills of porcupines, and the bites of most snakes. It is also so loose that if the creature is held by the scruff of the neck by a hyena or leopard, it can turn inside its skin and bite the attacker until it is released.

★ SMELLIEST MAMMAL

The striped skunk (*Mephitis mephitis*), a member of the mustelid family, ejects a truly bad-smelling liquid from its anal glands when threatened. This defensive secretion

★ MOST BRIGHTLY COLORED DOLPHIN

The bright pink skin of the Chinese pink dolphin (*Sousa chinensis chinensis*), a subspecies of the Indo-Pacific hump-backed dolphin, is not due to pigmentation, but results from the numerous blood vessels just beneath the surface of its skin. The blood vessels help to regulate its body temperature during exertion by dilating to release heat. When newly born, however, the Chinese pink dolphin is black, changing to gray as a youngster, and ultimately to pink as it matures.

contains seven major volatile and stench-filled components. Two of these substances, both sulfur-containing thiols, are responsible for the secretion's strongly repellent odor, and are known respectively as (E)-2-butene-1-thiol and 3-methyl-1-butanethiol. They are so powerful that they can be detected by humans at a concentration of 10 parts per billion – an incredibly low dilution that is about equivalent to mixing a teaspoonful with the water from an Olympic-sized swimming pool!

★ LONGEST AQUATIC MUSTELID

The South American giant otter or saro (*Pteronura brasiliensis*) has a head-and-body length of 34–55 in (86–140 cm) and a tail length of 13–40 in (33–100 cm).

★ LARGEST WEASEL ⬆

The largest terrestrial member of the mustelid or weasel family is the wolverine (*Gulo gulo*) with a height of 15 in (38 cm) and length of 40 in (100 cm). An adult male typically weighs 26–30 lb (12–14 kg) and an adult female 17–22 lb (8–10 kg). The largest male ever recorded by The Wolverine Foundation, USA, weighed 55 lb (25 kg).

★ MOST HYDROPHOBIC SEAL

A seal pup found washed up on a beach in South Shields, Tyne and Wear, UK, in November 1999 developed hydrophobia after being separated from its mother during a storm and sustaining injuries caused by hitting the rocky beach. After its recovery at the Sea Life Centre, Scarborough, UK, it refused to go back to the water, getting highly stressed even when being sprayed with water. This unlikely phobia was never cured and the seal never re-accustomed to water during her lifetime.

CETACEA

★ NEWEST CETACEAN

The most recently recognized species of cetacean is the Australian snubfin dolphin (*Orcaella heinsohni*), formally reclassified as a separate species in its own right in 2005. For many years, this shy, tri-colored dolphin, with a very rounded jutting brow and a very small stubby dorsal fin, had been sighted regularly in the shallow waters off the Great Barrier Reef, Australia. But until DNA and other studies confirmed its distinct status, it had always been classified as belonging to the same species as the Irrawaddy dolphin.

★ RAREST CETACEAN

Longman's beaked whale (*Indopacetus pacificus*) was for many years known from only two skulls, but by 2003 at least seven specimens had been obtained (three in South Africa and one in Japan). Until then, its external appearance – light gray in color and up to 24 ft 7 in (7.5 m) in length, with a long snout – was known only from various brief sightings in tropical seas.

RAREST MARINE MAMMAL

Of the cetaceans that are fully known, the baiji, or Yangtze River dolphin (*Lipotes vexillifer*), has an estimated population of only a few dozen in the whole world. The numbers are still falling owing to competition with fisheries, accidental capture in nets, habitat destruction, and pollution.

LARGEST MAMMAL

The blue whale (*Balaenoptera musculus*) has an average length of 80 ft (24 m) and can weigh up to 352,000 lb (160 tonnes).

This animal also has the **slowest heartbeat of any warm-blooded animal** with between four and eight beats per minute. (By comparison the average adult human heart beats at 70 beats per minute.)

Blue whales also have the **largest heart of any animal** on the planet – so big that you could swim through the aorta! Their heartbeat can be heard up to 19 miles (32 km) away underwater.

SMALLEST CETACEAN

There are two contenders for the smallest cetacean: Hector's dolphin (*Cephalorhynchus hectori*) and vaquita (*Phocoena sinus*), both of which are 3 ft 11 in (1.2 m) long.

★ LONGEST ⬆ WHALE TOOTH

The longest whale tooth is the single (or very rarely paired) spiraled ivory tusk of the male narwhal (*Monodon monoceros*). When found washed up with dead narwhals, it was once thought to be the horn of the mythical unicorn. Narwhal tusks attain an average length of about 6 ft 6 in (2 m) but can occasionally exceed 9 ft 10 in (3 m), and weigh up to 22 lb (10 kg), with a maximum girth of approximately 9 in (23 cm).

★ NEW RECORD
★ UPDATED RECORD

★ MOST ABUNDANT SEAL

The most abundant seal in the world is the crabeater seal (*Lobodon carcinophagus*), whose total Antarctic population is estimated to be well in excess of 10 million, and possibly as high as 35 million.

MAMMALS

LARGEST

KANGAROO

The male red kangaroo (*Macropus rufus*) of central, southern, and eastern Australia measures up to 5 ft 11 in (1.8 m) tall when standing, and up to 9 ft 4 in (2.85 m) in length (including the tail). It can weigh up to 200 lb (90 kg) in exceptional cases.

INSECTIVORA

★ LARGEST INSECTIVORE

The world's largest species of insectivore is the moon rat (*Echinosorex gymnurus*), an odd name as it is neither a rat nor from the Moon! Inhabiting Borneo, Malaysia, Sumatra, Thailand, and Myanmar, it is a giant relative of the hedgehog, but has thick fur instead of spikes, and is known as a gymnure ("naked tail"). It has a head-and-body length of 10–18 in (26–46 cm), and a tail length of 6–10 in (17–25 cm). It weighs 2–4 lb (1–2 kg), with females being slightly larger than males.

[?] DID YOU KNOW?

*Aye-ayes (see **Largest nocturnal primate**) have a skeletal, dexterous middle finger. They use it to tap on tree bark and listen for any reverberations that reveal edible insect larvae. They then make a hole in the trunk and use their finger to hook out the larvae.*

★ MOST DANGEROUS INSECTIVORES

The solenodon is a harmless-looking, small, rat-like Caribbean mammal with a long cartilaginous snout. There are two species – the Haitian solenodon (*Solenodon paradoxus*) and the very rare Cuban solenodon (*S. cubanus*) – both of which measure approximately 11 in (28 cm) long. The solenodon's saliva is toxic to prey and potentially dangerous to humans.

LARGEST ➡
KOALA LITTER

The largest koala litter is a pair of identical twins called Euca and Lyptus who were born on April 10–11, 1999, in Queensland, Australia. They are the first known koala twins and the first to be identified as such using DNA fingerprinting, by Leigh Slater of the Koala Study Program, University of Queensland, Australia, on November 25, 1999. Koala twins are especially rare because the size of the mother's pouch means she cannot normally care for both offspring and so only one would usually survive.

LAGOMORPHIA

★ LARGEST LAGOMORPH

The largest lagomorph – the order that includes rabbits and hares – is the Alaskan or tundra hare (*Lepus othus*), native to western and southwestern Alaska's tundra. It has a head-and-body length of 20–24 in (50–60 cm) and weighs 7–14 lb (3–6 kg).

HIGHEST-LIVING MAMMAL

The large-eared pika (*Ochtona macrotis*) lives at elevations of up to 20,100 ft (6,130 m) in high-altitude mountain ranges in Asia.

LARGEST ⬆
NOCTURNAL PRIMATE

The aye-aye (*Daubentonia madagascariensis*) of Madagascar has a body length of 16 in (40 cm), a tail length of 20 in (50 cm), and weighs approximately 6 lb (2.75 kg). These solitary animals spend up to 80% of the night foraging for food in tree canopies, and most of the day sleeping in tree nests.

MARSUPIALIA

HEAVIEST MARSUPIAL EVER

Diprotodon optatum lived in Australia during the Pleistocene era, between 1.6 million and 40,000 years ago. Research by Stephen Wroe (Australia) on a complete skeleton of this creature produced an estimated mass of around 6,170 lb (2.8 tonnes) for an average-sized 10-ft-long (3-m), 6-ft 6-in-tall (2-m) adult.

★ FIRST KNOWN SKIN-BREATHING MAMMAL

When first born, the Julia Creek dunnart (*Sminthopsis douglasi*), a tiny species of Australian marsupial mouse, is so small – only 0.15 in (4 mm) long – that its muscles are too weak to inflate its lungs. McGill University (Australia) physiologist Dr. Jacopo Mortola (Canada) discovered that it absorbs oxygen directly through its skin, a process that continues until it leaves its mother's pouch, by which time it is large enough to inflate its lungs.

←LONGEST PRIMATE NOSE

The proboscis monkey (*Nasalis larvatus*), found only on the island of Borneo, has a droopy nose up to 7 in (17.5 cm) long in elderly male specimens. Often large enough to hang over the mouth, it becomes red and swollen when the monkey is in danger or excited, and acts as a resonator when it makes its characteristic honking warning sound.

PRIMATA

★ NEWEST MONKEY

The kipunji mangabey (*Lophocebus kipunji*) was discovered in Tanzania by two separate research teams during 2003, one team working in Ndundulu Forest Reserve in the Udzungwa Mountains, and the other hundreds of miles away on Mount Rungwe and in the adjacent Kitulo National Park. The shy, tree-dwelling monkey that both teams encountered was approximately 35 in (90 m) long, with long brownish fur, a black face and paws, a long tail, an off-white belly, a distinctive crest, and bushy whiskers that gave its head an almost triangular shape, plus a very unusual (for mangabeys) low-pitched, honking bark-like cry.

Although this monkey was totally unknown to science, the local people knew it well, and called it "kipunji" – hence its Latin name, given to it when it was officially described by science in 2005. It is the first new African monkey to have been discovered for over 20 years.

★ LARGEST PRIMATE EVER

Gigantopithecus blacki was an enormous ape that lived alongside humans for a million years in southeast Asia before becoming extinct 100,000 years ago for reasons that are still unclear. Its fossilized 1-in-wide (2.5-cm) teeth and huge jawbones suggest that this veritable King Kong stood 9 ft 10 in (3 m) tall, and weighed approximately 3,480 lb (1,580 kg).

★ LARGEST LEMUR

The largest living species of lemur is the indri (*Indri indri*). It has a total length of 25–28 in (64–72 cm), of which its head and body account for 23–26 in (60–67 cm), as it is virtually tailless – the only such lemur alive today. This predominantly daytime tree-dweller weighs 13–16 lb (6–7.5 kg) and inhabits the central-eastern and northeastern rainforests of Madagascar, from sea level to around 4,920 ft (1,500 m).

★ MOST SOUTHERLY NON-HUMAN PRIMATES

The chacma baboons (*Papio ursinus*) inhabit the Cape Peninsula, South Africa, at a latitude of 34°S.

★ SMALLEST MONKEY ↑

Pygmy marmosets (*Callithrix pygmaea*), found in the Upper Amazon and the evergreen forests of Peru, Ecuador, Colombia, Bolivia, and Brazil, weigh only 0.53 oz (15 g) at birth and grow to an average adult weight of just 4.2 oz (120 g). They measure, on average, 5.3 in (13.6 cm) excluding the tail, which is usually longer than the body. Despite its size, the pygmy marmoset can leap up to 16 ft 5 in (5 m) into the air!

★ NEW RECORD
★ UPDATED RECORD

SMALLEST MARSUPIAL

The long-tailed planigale (*Planigale ingrami*), also known as the flat-skulled marsupial mouse, is about 2 in (5 cm) in length.

FASTEST MARSUPIALS

The highest speed recorded for a marsupial is 40 mph (64 km/h) for a mature female eastern gray kangaroo (*Macropus giganteus*). The highest sustained speed is 35 mph (56 km/h), recorded for a male red kangaroo, which died from its exertions after being paced for 1 mile (1.6 km).

LONGEST KANGAROO JUMP

During a chase in New South Wales, Australia, in January 1951, a female red kangaroo made a series of bounds including one measuring 42 ft (12.8 m).

★ LARGEST MONKEY →

The male mandrill (*Mandrillus sphinx*) or man-ape of equatorial West Africa has an average head and body length of 24–30 in (61–76 cm) and a tail length of 2–3 in (5–7 cm). Adult males weigh an average of 55 lb (25 kg), although specimens weighing up to 120 lb (54 kg) and measuring 20 in (50 cm) to the shoulder have been recorded. The mandrill is also one of the most colorful mammals, recognized by its vivid-blue rump, red-striped face, and yellow beard.

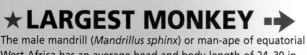

MAMMALS

OLDEST MAMMALS

The **oldest land mammal** (excluding man, *Homo sapiens*) is the Asian elephant (*Elephas maximus*). There are a number of claims of animals reaching 80 years or more, but the greatest verified age is 86 years for a bull elephant named Lin Wang, who died on February 26, 2003, at Taipei Zoo, Taiwan.

Certain whale species are believed to live even longer, although little is known about this. The fin whale (*Balaenoptera physalus*) is probably the **longest living**, with a maximum lifespan estimated at 90–100 years.

PROBOSCIDEA

LARGEST MAMMAL ON LAND

The adult male African elephant (*Loxodonta africana*) typically stands 9 ft 10 in–12 ft (3–3.5 m) at the shoulder and weighs 8,800 lb–15,400 lb (4–7 tonnes).

★ LARGEST ELEPHANT RELOCATION PROJECT

The world's largest elephant relocation project was carried out in August 1993 by the wildlife charity Care For The Wild International (CFTWI). Organized and overseen by CFTWI chairman and wildlife vet Dr. Bill Jordan, CFTWI managing director Chris Jordan (both UK), and wildlife management expert Clem Coetsee (Zimbabwe), more than 500 elephants in whole family groups were transported some 155 miles (250 km) across Zimbabwe, from Gonarezhou National Park to the Save Valley Conservancy, in order to avoid being culled.

RODENTIA

★ LOWEST BODY TEMPERATURE IN A MAMMAL

The body temperature of the Arctic ground squirrel (*Spermophilus parryii*) of Alaska and northwest Canada drops to 26°F (-3°C) when in a state of suspended animation during its eight-month hibernation period in the Arctic winter (also the **longest hibernation by a rodent**). Its normal body temperature in the summer is 98°F (37°C).

★ MOST BLOODTHIRSTY UNGULATES

On the Inner Hebridean island of Rhum, UK, the vegetation is deficient in certain minerals, such as calcium and phosphorus. In order to obtain these important dietary requirements, the herds of red deer (*Cervus elaphus*) living there attack the fledglings of ground-nesting seabirds, particularly Manx shearwaters (*Puffinus puffinus*), and bite their heads off, killing the birds. The deer then chew on their bones, thereby obtaining the necessary calcium and phosphorus.

★ LARGEST PREHISTORIC RODENT

Phoberomys pattersoni ("Patterson's mouse of fear"), a swamp-dwelling species that lived 6–8 million years ago in what is today Venezuela, was as big as a buffalo. Weighing around 1,500 lb (700 kg), it resembled a gigantic guinea pig with huge teeth. Using its powerful tail, it balanced on its hind legs looking for predators (such as giant crocodiles, marsupial saber-tooth cats, and flesh-eating terror birds or phorusrhacids). Its fossils were first discovered in 2003.

OLDEST RODENT

A Sumatran porcupine (*Hystrix brachyura*) lived to the age of 27 years 3 months in the National Zoological Park, Washington D.C., USA.

SMALLEST ANTELOPE

The royal antelope (*Neotragus pygmaeus*) of western Africa stands 10–12 in (25–31 cm) tall at the shoulder and weighs 7–8 lb (3–3.6 kg), the size of a brown hare (*Lepus europaeus*).

LONGEST MAMMAL'S TONGUE (PROPORTIONATELY)

With an average head-and-body length of 3–6 ft (1–2 m), the giant anteater (*Myrmecophaga tridactyla*) has a tongue typically measuring 23 in (60 cm) long – the longest for a mammal proportionate to body size. The **longest mammal tongue** of all is that of the blue whale, which can weigh up to 8,800 lb (4 tonnes).

SLOWEST MAMMAL

The three-toed sloth (*Bradypus tridactylus*) of tropical South America has an average ground speed of 6–8 ft (1.8–2.4 m) per minute (0.07–0.1 mph; 0.1–0.16 km/h), but in the trees it can accelerate to 15 ft (4.6 m) per minute (0.17 mph; 0.27 km/h).

SLEEPIEST MAMMAL

Some sloths (Bradypodidae and Megalonychidae), opossums (Didelphidae), and armadillos (Dasypodidae) spend up to 80 percent of their lives sleeping or dozing. The least active of all mammals are probably the three species of three-toed tree sloths of the genus *Bradypus* (pictured).

★ NEW RECORD
☆ UPDATED RECORD

ANIMAL MOST LIKELY TO PROCREATE QUADRUPLETS ↑

A close relative of the anteater, the nine-banded armadillo (*Dasypus novemcinctus*) is the only mammal known to bear identical quadruplets routinely. They develop from the same egg and share a single placenta in the womb, and so have the same sex.

UNGULATES

★ SMALLEST UNGULATE

The lesser Malay mouse deer (*Tragulus javanicus*) has a body length of 17–22 in (42–55 cm), a shoulder height of 8–10 in (20–25 cm), and a body weight of 3–5 lb 8 oz (1.5–2.5 kg). Primarily nocturnal, the lesser Malay mouse deer is rarely seen.

LONGEST TERRESTRIAL ANIMAL MIGRATION

Grant's caribou (*Rangifer tarandus*) of Alaska and the Yukon Territory of North America travels up to 3,000 miles (4,800 km) per year, the farthest distance traveled by a migratory land animal.

MOST HORNS

The male four-horned antelope (*Tetracerus quadricornis*), which lives in India and Nepal, is the only mammal with four horns. The pair at the foremost part of the forehead are often poorly developed but average 0.5–2 in (2–5 cm) in length. The second pair (just in front of the ears) are slightly longer at 3–4.5 in (8–12 cm).

★ MOST UNCLASSIFIABLE MAMMAL

The African aardvark (*Orycteropus afer*) is so peculiar anatomically that it cannot be classified with any other living species of mammal, and is therefore placed within a whole order of mammals – Tubulidentata ("tube-teeth") – all to itself.

HALL OF FAME

There is a certain kind of record holder who is unique to the *Guinness World Records* experience. They may not be Olympians or recognizable household names, and they rarely receive sponsorship from big-name brands. Their collection of talents, however, makes them unique in their particular fields. *Guinness World Records* is nothing without the dedication, passion, mental strength, generosity, and sense of humor of these inspiring characters. So, here is a small selection of people who epitomize what it is to be a Guinness World Record holder. This is a thank-you to them all for their continuing support...

SURESH JOACHIM (AUSTRALIA), 19 CURRENT RECORDS

Why did you start breaking records?
In 1991, my uncle brought home a copy of the *Guinness World Records* book. I started turning the pages and realized that everyone in it was famous for having done something special. I thought to myself, "I want to use celebrity to help others, especially in raising social awareness about children growing up in conflict areas."

What was your first Guinness World Record?
Running for 1,000 consecutive hours in 1996. Since then, I've been averaging two records every month and have officially held 26 world records.

Have you ever had any serious injuries?
During my first attempt at setting the record for the longest time/distance spent carrying a 10-lb (4.5-kg) brick, I fainted after about 24 hours, having nearly lost a pint of blood from my exertions. I did succeed the second time around though!

What's the secret of your success?
A steady mind, my family, and God.

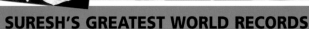

SURESH'S GREATEST WORLD RECORDS

ATTEMPT	RECORD	DATE
Distance on foot per hr (1,000 consecutive hrs)	2.17 miles (3.49 km)	Aug.–Sep. 1996
Bridegroom with the most ushers	47	Sep. 6, 2003
Longest escalator ride (145 hr 57 min)	140 miles (225 km)	May 25–31, 1998
Longest solo dance marathon	100 hours	Feb 16–20, 2005
Greatest distance moonwalked (24 hr)	30.6 miles (49.2 km)	Jan. 11, 2006
Longest duration on one foot (above)	76 hr 40 min	May 22–25, 1997
Greatest distance with 10-lb (4.5-kg) brick	78.71 miles (126.68 km)	Dec. 11, 1999
Longest continuous crawl	35.18 miles (56.62 km)	May 8–19, 2001
Longest solo drumming kit marathon	84 hr	Feb. 1–4, 2004
Longest wedding bouquet	197 ft 1 in (60.09 m)	Sep. 6, 2003

PETER DOWDESWELL (UK), 7 CURRENT RECORDS

Why did you start breaking Guinness World Records?
I didn't set out wanting to become a record holder. I was sort of conned into it when I attended a fund-raising event in Northhamptonshire and drank a yard of ale [3 pints; 1.42 liters] in record time. From that day onward, I began to see setting records as an opportunity to raise money for handicapped children.
I could perform at charity events and bring in the funds necessary for all kinds of useful equipment – wheelchairs, scooters, even beds.

What was your first Guinness World Record?
I drank the yard of ale in five seconds at the Earls Barton carnival in 1975. Out of the other 50 participants who also entered the competition, only

two managed to finish without spilling a drop!

What training do you do?
I don't follow any fitness plan but I do like to go for walks around the wonderful countryside near where I live. I also enjoy a seafood diet, especially cod.

Have you ever had any injuries?
Never – what is strange, though, is that the alcohol has never gone to my head while setting these records!

What's the secret of your success?
Dedication and mental strength.

Any advice for those who want to follow in your footsteps?
Ensure that a doctor is always on standby!

PETER'S GREATEST WORLD RECORDS

ATTEMPT	RECORD	DATE
Fastest time to drink 1 pint of stout	2.1 sec	Jan. 24, 2001
Fastest time to drink 1 pint of beer upside down	3 sec	Feb. 16, 1998
Fastest time to eat a three-course meal *(rested)*	45 sec	May 13, 1999
Fastest time to eat soft-boiled eggs *(rested)*	38 in 1 min 15 sec	May 28, 1984
Fastest time to drink a yard (3 pints; 1.42 liters) of ale	5 sec	May 4, 1975
Most hotdogs and buns eaten in 3 minutes	4	Jul. 27, 2001

Rested = a record no longer monitored by Guinness World Records

PADDY DOYLE (UK), 13 CURRENT RECORDS

Why did you start breaking records?
I picked up a copy of *Guinness World Records* when I left the army and looked up the push-up records. There were very few and they were held mostly by Japanese men. I beat them and it just snowballed from there. I've had 32 entries and re-entries since 1990.

What was your first Guinness World Record?
I broke the 24-hour push-up record with 37,350 repetitions.

What training do you do?
I train for two hours in the morning and evening, and do running, boxing training, martial arts, weight-lifting, cycling, and swimming.

What advice would you give to those who want to follow in your footsteps?
Success is all in the mind – if you put your mind to it, you can achieve anything but you need humility to be a real success.

PADDY'S GREATEST WORLD RECORDS

ATTEMPT	RECORD	DATE
Most consecutive martial arts bouts	131	May 6, 2000
Most one-arm push-ups in 5 hours	8,794	Feb. 12, 1996
Fastest physical fitness challenge	18 hr 56 min 9 sec	Feb. 16, 2005
Most martial arts punches in 1 minute	470	Aug. 13, 2005
Most squat thrusts in 1 hr	3,743	May 4, 1998
Most full contact kicks in 1 hour	2,805	Nov. 7, 2004
Most push-ups in 1 year	1,500,230	Oct 1988–89
1-mile march with 40 lb (18.1 kg) bergen	5 min 35 sec	Mar. 7, 1993

GEORGES' GREATEST WORLD RECORDS

ATTEMPT	RECORD	DATE
Fastest 10 m (32.8 ft) with table and mouth weight	7.5 sec	Jul. 28, 2004
Most phone books ripped (spine) in 2 min	28	Jul. 21, 2003
Most 100-kg (221-lb) lifts with teeth in 1 min	24	Aug. 22, 2005
Highest beer-barrel lift using teeth (barrel weighing 30 lb 14 oz; 14 kg)	124 ft (38 m)	Mar. 6, 2005
Fastest hot-water-bottle burst (pictured)	52.68 sec	Dec. 6, 2000

★ NEW RECORD
☆ UPDATED RECORD

GEORGES CHRISTEN (LUXEMBOURG), 5 CURRENT RECORDS

Why did you start breaking records?
Ever since I was a kid, I've been intrigued by strength and fitness challenges. When my brother brought home a copy of *Guinness World Records*, I noticed there was only one record holder from Luxembourg. I wanted to be the second.

What was your first Guinness World Record?
I bent 250 iron nails that were 7.9 in (20 cm) in length and 0.3 in (0.7 cm) thick in 72 minutes and 55 seconds.

What training do you do?
I do regular weight-lifting exercises using dumbbells and kettlebells and I am currently training for two feats: stopping a racing car in its tracks with my hands and lifting a car engine using only my teeth.

Have you ever had any serious injuries?
I've had a few minor accidents but nothing too serious.

What's the secret of your success?
I'm not a particularly tall or heavy guy – 5.8 ft (1.79 m) in height and 192 lb (87 kg) in weight – so I must really enjoy what I do otherwise there would be no point.

What advice would you give to those who want to follow in your footsteps?
I would strongly recommend training in a progressive manner, over time, and also being realistic about what your body can do.

EXTREME BODIES

LONGEST FINGERNAILS ■➡

Lee Redmond (USA) has grown the fingernails of both her hands to reach a total length of 24 ft 7 in (7.51 m). She has been growing her nails for 24 years and treats them daily with warm olive oil and nail hardener.

Lee lives a very active life, despite her fingernails, although she does attract a few "unusual" admirers: she was once offered money to have her nails nibbled, the prospective buyer suggesting that he buy by the inch! Even the prospect of the bathroom is undaunting to Lee. When asked how she "goes," she replies: "Carefully!"

NARROWEST WAIST

Inspired by her love of Victorian clothing, Cathie Jung (USA) – who stands at 5 ft 8 in (1.72 m) – has "trained" her waist to an incredible 15 in (38.1 cm) when corsetted and 21 in (53.3 cm) uncorsetted.

| 2 in (5.08 cm) ★Longest eyelash (Daniel Williams, USA) | 3.7 in (9.5 cm) Longest tongue (Stephen Taylor, UK) | 6 in (15.2 cm) Longest toenails (see above) | 6 in (15.2 cm) Lowest limbo dance (King Limbo, USA) | 7. L (T |

ASHRITA FURMAN (USA), 39 CURRENT RECORDS

Why did you start breaking records?
Ever since I was a kid, I've wanted to get into *Guinness World Records*. I was deeply fascinated by the challenge of being the best in the world at something. If the record's a little unusual or silly, so much the better!

What was your first Guinness World Record?
My first official record was for continuous jumping jacks. The old record stood at 20,000 jumps and I managed to do 7,000 more for a grand total of 27,000.

What training do you do?
I try to keep in shape by going to the gym and exercising on a regular basis. Each week, I make sure that I do a bit of weight training, work out with a Swiss ball, and generally do as many sit-ups as it takes before my abdominals start killing me!

Have you ever had any serious injuries?
Luckily, I've never sustained any serious accidents during my attempts. Some people speculate that a few screws came loose while I was setting my somersault record years ago. I enjoy doing crazy things so they may be right and they can certainly keep on believing it!

What's the secret of your success?
Meditation is key. I'm not a natural athlete, but through the power of meditation, I'm able to channel energy and push my body beyond its physical limits of endurance to achieve fantastic results.

What advice would you give to those who want to follow in your footsteps?
Remember to have fun! Find an event that you love doing, then practice, practice, practice, and never give up.

ASHRITA'S GREATEST WORLD RECORDS

ATTEMPT	RECORD	DATE
Pogostick jump up CN tower (1,899 steps)	57 min 51 sec	Jul. 23, 1999
Fastest 100 m on a spacehopper	30.2 sec	Nov. 16, 2004
Largest hula hoop spun (diameter)	16 ft (4.8 m)	Sep. 24, 2005
Fastest stilt walker over 5 miles (8 km)	39 min 56 sec	Dec. 17, 2004
Most consecutive forward rolls in 1 mile	19 min 11 sec	Nov. 25, 2000
Fastest mile...		
balancing pool cue on finger	7 min 16 sec	Sep. 14, 2005
milk-bottle-balancing (pictured)	7 min 47 sec	Feb. 12 2004
★egg and spoon race	10 min 45 sec	Mar. 28 2006
on a hopper ball	15 min 3 sec	Jan. 19, 2005
★fireman's carry	15 min 11 sec	Nov, 9, 2005
crawling	29 min 30 sec	Feb. 17, 2006
hopping	27 min 51 sec	Feb. 1, 2006
lunging	30 min 50 sec	Oct. 27, 2002

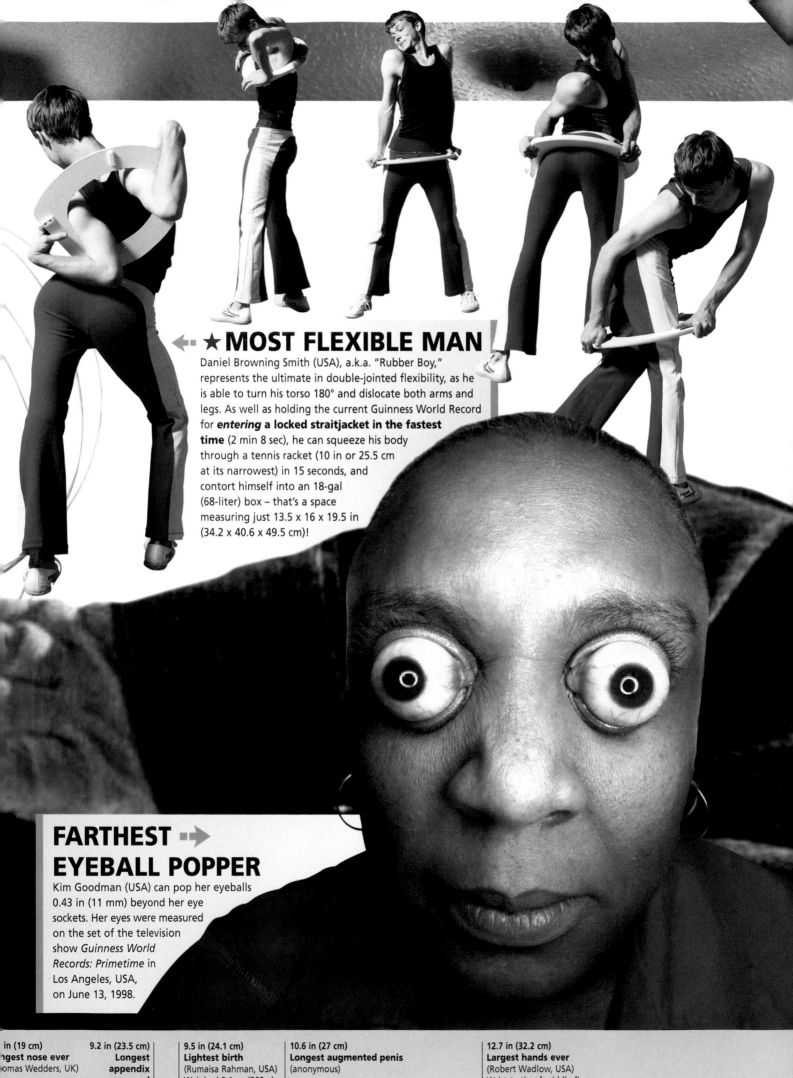

←★ MOST FLEXIBLE MAN

Daniel Browning Smith (USA), a.k.a. "Rubber Boy," represents the ultimate in double-jointed flexibility, as he is able to turn his torso 180° and dislocate both arms and legs. As well as holding the current Guinness World Record for **entering a locked straitjacket in the fastest time** (2 min 8 sec), he can squeeze his body through a tennis racket (10 in or 25.5 cm at its narrowest) in 15 seconds, and contort himself into an 18-gal (68-liter) box – that's a space measuring just 13.5 x 16 x 19.5 in (34.2 x 40.6 x 49.5 cm)!

FARTHEST ⇨ EYEBALL POPPER

Kim Goodman (USA) can pop her eyeballs 0.43 in (11 mm) beyond her eye sockets. Her eyes were measured on the set of the television show *Guinness World Records: Primetime* in Los Angeles, USA, on June 13, 1998.

| in (19 cm) ngest nose ever omas Wedders, UK) | 9.2 in (23.5 cm) **Longest appendix removed** (anonymous) | 9.5 in (24.1 cm) **Lightest birth** (Rumaisa Rahman, USA) Weighed 9.1 oz (260 g) | 10.6 in (27 cm) **Longest augmented penis** (anonymous) | 12.7 in (32.2 cm) **Largest hands ever** (Robert Wadlow, USA) Wrist to tip of middle finger |

HUMAN ANATOMY

THE INCREDIBLE HUMAN BODY

Congratulations – you are the owner of one of the most extraordinary pieces of engineering on Earth! The human body has evolved into a highly adaptable tool, one that has been essential in ensuring the survival of mankind.

It's capable of quick bursts of speed (Jamaica's Asafa Powell ran the **fastest 100 m** in just 9.77 seconds) but also sustained effort – Paul Tergat (Kenya) completed the **fastest marathon** in a time of 2 hr 4 min 55 sec. And it's strong, too: David Huxley (Australia) pulled a 412,000-lb (187-tonne) Boeing 747 a distance of 298 ft 6 in (91 m) in 1 min 27.7 sec – the **heaviest aircraft pulled.** Our bodies are resilient as well – stunt rider Evel Knievel (USA) broke bones in his body 433 times during his career, the **most bones broken in a lifetime.**

So to celebrate our wonderful bodies, we've highlighted more record-breakers that get under your skin – literally.

LONGEST MEMORY OF A CELL

As successive generations of the lymphocyte (a type of white blood cell that is part of the body's immune defense system) are produced during one's life, they never forget an enemy.

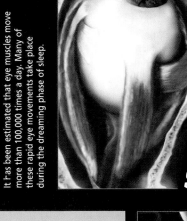

STRONGEST MUSCLE

The masseter is a paired muscle (one on each side of the mouth) responsible for the action of biting.

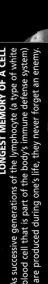

ACTUAL SIZE

SMALLEST JOINT

Not surprisingly, the smallest joint is between the smallest bone, the stapes, and the incus bone in the ear.

SMALLEST MUSCLE

The stapedius muscle, which controls the stapes bone, is less than 0.05 in (0.127 cm) long.

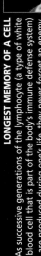

ACTUAL SIZE

MOST ACTIVE MUSCLE

It has been estimated that eye muscles move more than 100,000 times a day. Many of these rapid eye movements take place during the dreaming phase of sleep.

▶ MOST COMMON BLOOD GROUP

Blood group O is common to 46% of the global population. However, in some countries – for example, Norway – group A predominates.

The **rarest blood group** in the world is a type of Bombay blood (subtype h-h) found so far only in a Czechoslovak nurse, in 1961, and in a brother (Rh positive) and sister (Rh negative) named Jalbert in Massachusetts, USA, and reported in February 1968.

MOST MOBILE JOINT

The shoulder joint, a ball-and-socket joint with a shallow cup, is the most mobile of all the joints in the human skeleton. It is held in position by muscle rather than the shapes of the bones and is the easiest joint to dislocate.

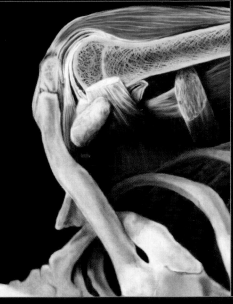

← LONGEST EAR HAIR

Radhakant Bajpai (India) has hair sprouting from the center of his outer ears (middle of the pinna) that measures 5.19 in (13.2 cm) at its longest point.

"Making it into *Guinness World Records* is indeed a special occasion for me and my family," said Radhakant. "God has been very kind to me."

STRETCHIEST SKIN

Garry Turner (UK) is able to stretch his skin to a maximum distension length of 6.25 in (15.8 cm) because of a condition called Ehlers-Danlos Syndrome. With this condition, the collagen that strengthens the skin and determines its elasticity becomes defective, resulting in a loosening of the skin and "hypermobility" of the joints.

★ **NEW RECORD**
⭑ **UPDATED RECORD**

25.5 in (65 cm)
(Younis Edwan, Jordan)
ge Bester, South Africa)

25.5 in (67 cm)
Lightest person
(Lucia Xarate, Mexico)
4.7 lb (2.13 kg)

30 in (76 cm)
Longest and **Heaviest baby at birth**
(born to Anna Bates, UK)
23 lb 12 oz (108 kg)

31.9 in (81 cm)
Shortest supporting actor
(Verne Troyer, USA)

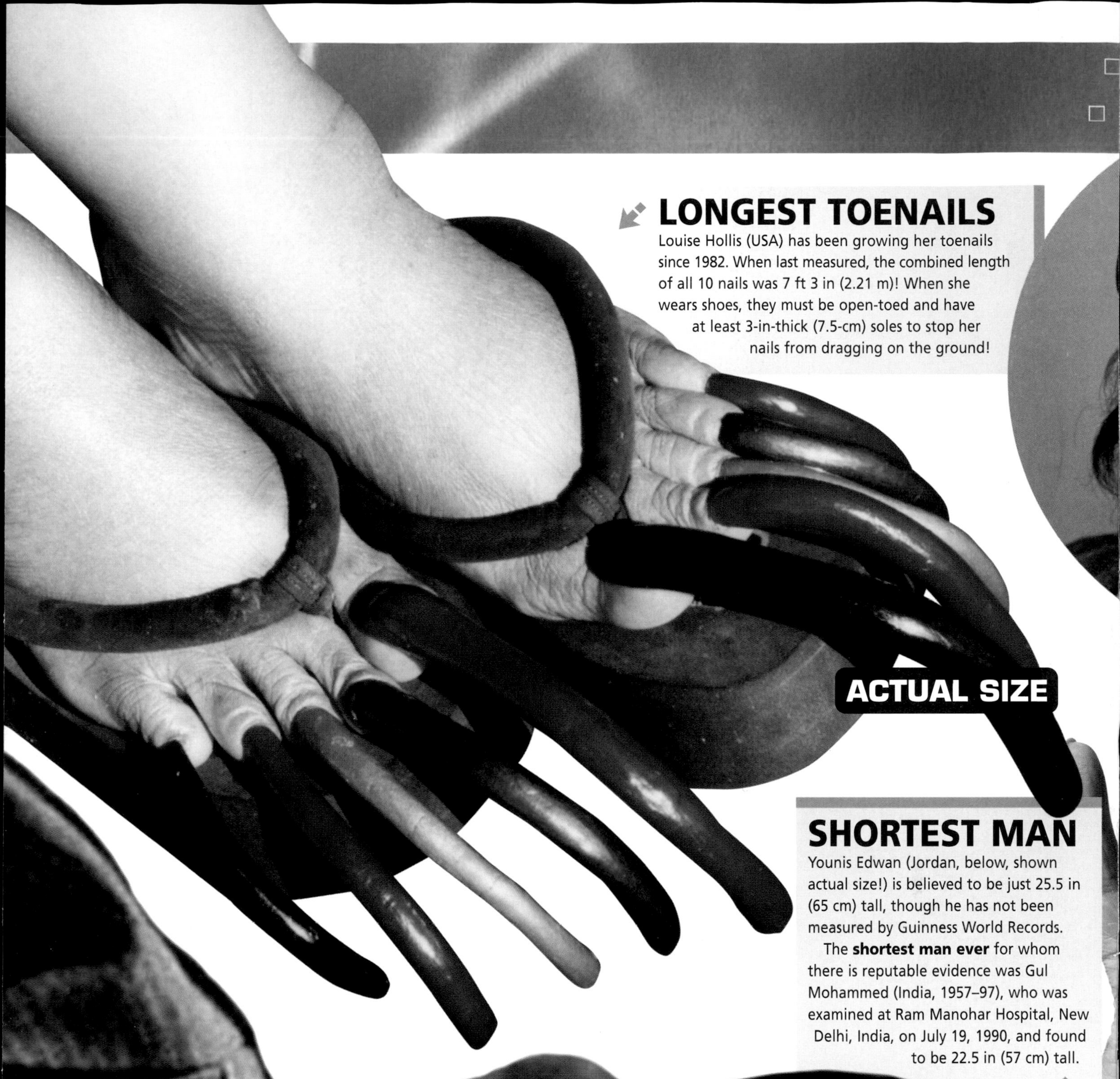

LONGEST TOENAILS

Louise Hollis (USA) has been growing her toenails since 1982. When last measured, the combined length of all 10 nails was 7 ft 3 in (2.21 m)! When she wears shoes, they must be open-toed and have at least 3-in-thick (7.5-cm) soles to stop her nails from dragging on the ground!

ACTUAL SIZE

SHORTEST MAN

Younis Edwan (Jordan, below, shown actual size!) is believed to be just 25.5 in (65 cm) tall, though he has not been measured by Guinness World Records.

The **shortest man ever** for whom there is reputable evidence was Gul Mohammed (India, 1957–97), who was examined at Ram Manohar Hospital, New Delhi, India, on July 19, 1990, and found to be 22.5 in (57 cm) tall.

ACTUAL SIZE

18.75 in (47 cm)	18.75 in (47 cm)	22.5 in (57 cm)	
Largest feet ever	**Smallest living horse**	**Shortest man ever**	**Shortest living man**
(Robert Wadlow, USA)	(Black Beauty, USA)	(Gul Mohammed, India)	& **Shortest living woman** (Ma

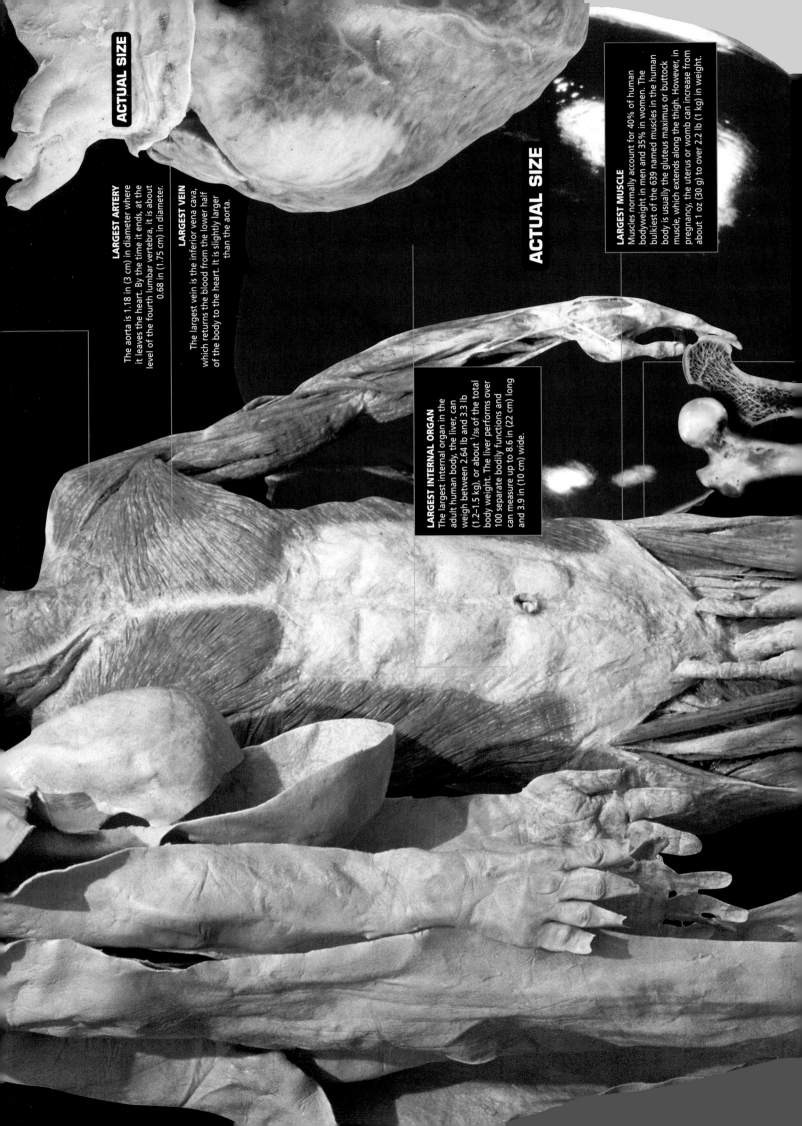

LARGEST ARTERY

The aorta is 1.18 in (3 cm) in diameter where it leaves the heart. By the time it ends, at the level of the fourth lumbar vertebra, it is about 0.68 in (1.75 cm) in diameter.

LARGEST VEIN

The largest vein is the inferior vena cava, which returns the blood from the lower half of the body to the heart. It is slightly larger than the aorta.

LARGEST MUSCLE

Muscles normally account for 40% of human bodyweight in men and 35% in women. The bulkiest of the 639 named muscles in the human body is usually the gluteus maximus or buttock muscle, which extends along the thigh. However, in pregnancy, the uterus or womb can increase from about 1 oz (30 g) to over 2.2 lb (1 kg) in weight.

LARGEST INTERNAL ORGAN

The largest internal organ in the adult human body, the liver, can weigh between 2.64 lb and 3.3 lb (1.2–1.5 kg), or about 1/36 of the total body weight. The liver performs over 100 separate bodily functions and can measure up to 8.6 in (22 cm) long and 3.9 in (10 cm) wide.

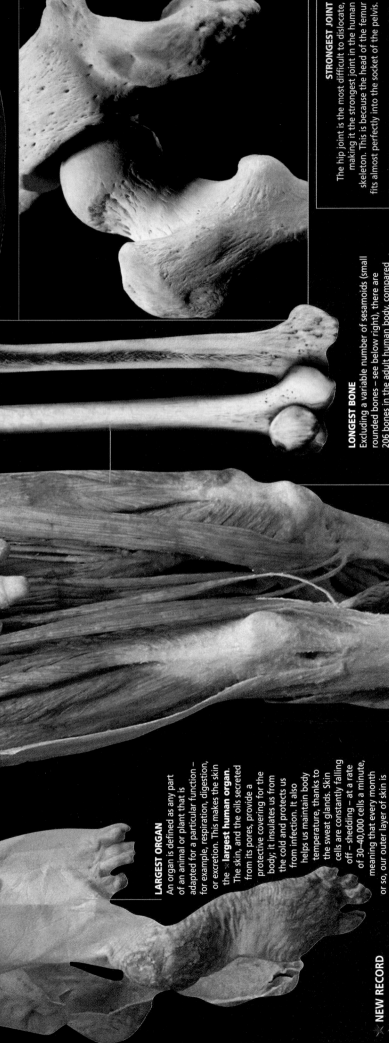

STRONGEST JOINT

The hip joint is the most difficult to dislocate, making it the strongest joint in the human skeleton. This is because the head of the femur fits almost perfectly into the socket of the pelvis.

LONGEST BONE

Excluding a variable number of sesamoids (small rounded bones – see below right), there are 206 bones in the adult human body, compared with about 300 for children (as they grow, some bones fuse together). The thigh bone, or femur, is the longest. It generally constitutes 27.5% of a person's stature, and may be 19.75 in (50 cm) long in a man measuring 6 ft (180 cm) tall. The longest recorded bone was a femur measuring 2 ft 6 in (76 cm), which belonged to Constantine, a German giant.

LARGEST SESAMOID BONE

Sesamoid bones are named after the ovoid seeds of the sesame plant, and most are only a few millimeters in diameter. The largest sesamoid bone in the body is the patella or knee cap. Sesamoids are usually embedded in tendons close to joints or where the tendons angle sharply around bone. Their function is to take compression when a tendon is going around a joint, as when a human being kneels.

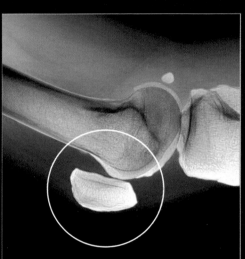

LARGEST ORGAN

An organ is defined as any part of an animal or plant that is adapted for a particular function – for example, respiration, digestion, or excretion. This makes the skin the **largest human organ.** The skin, and the oils secreted from its pores, provide a protective covering for the body; it insulates us from the cold and protects us from infection. It also helps us maintain body temperature, thanks to the sweat glands. Skin cells are constantly falling off – shedding – at a rate of 30–40,000 cells a minute, meaning that every month or so, our outer layer of skin is completely replenished.

LONGEST CELL

Motor neurons are approximately 4 ft 3 in (1.3 m) long; they have cell bodies (gray matter) in the lower spinal cord with axons (white matter) that carry nerve impulses from the spinal cord down to the big toe. The cell systems that carry certain sensations (vibration and positional sense) back from the big toe to the brain are even longer. Their uninterrupted length, from the toe and up the posterior part of the spinal cord to the medulla of the brain, is effectively equal to the height of the body.

HUMAN BODY

CONTENTS

★TALLEST LIVING MAN

Xi Shun (China, b. 1951) measured a record-breaking 7 ft 8.95 in (2.36 m) when examined on January 15, 2005, at Chifeng City Hospital, Inner Mongolia, China. In September 2005, Xi Shun made his first ever trip outside China when he visited the London offices of *Guinness World Records*.

BIRTH & LIFE

⚠ X-REF

Old age need not stand in the way of achieving a Guinness World Record. Can you guess the age of the oldest person to have run a marathon on each continent? Find out for yourself on p.101.

★ NEW RECORD
☆ UPDATED RECORD

MOST CHILDREN TO SURVIVE A SINGLE BIRTH

There have been three known cases of seven children surviving birth.

Bobbie McCaughey (USA) gave birth to four boys and three girls on November 19, 1997.

Four boys and three girls were born eight weeks premature on January 14, 1998, to Hasna Mohammed Humair (Saudi Arabia).

Lastly, six girls and two boys were born to Nikem Chukwu (USA) at St. Luke's Hospital, Houston, Texas, USA. The first was born on December 8, 1998, the remaining seven (pictured below) 12 days afterwards. The lightest baby later died.

BIRTH

★ LARGEST GATHERING OF TEST-TUBE BABIES

A total of 579 children born as a result of artificial insemination gathered at the Iscare IVF Assisted Reproduction Center, Prague, Czech Republic, on September 6, 2003.

LONGEST INTERVAL BETWEEN BIRTH OF TWINS

Peggy Lynn (USA) gave birth to a baby girl, Hanna, on November 11, 1995, but she did not deliver the other twin, Eric, until February 2, 1996, 84 days later, at the Geisinger Medical Center, Danville, Pennsylvania, USA.

SHORTEST INTERVAL BETWEEN BIRTHS IN SEPARATE CONFINEMENTS

Jayne Bleackley (New Zealand) gave birth to Joseph Robert on September 3, 1999, and Annie Jessica Joyce on March 30, 2000, an interval of 208 days.

◄ ★ OLDEST MOTHER

Adriana Emilia Iliescu (Romania, b. May 31, 1938) was 66 years 230 days old when she gave birth by Caesarean section to her daughter Eliza Maria Bogdana at the Clinical Hospital of Obstetrics and Gynaecology, Bucharest, Romania, on January 16, 2005.

★ MOST SIBLINGS BORN ON LEAP DAY

The three children of the Henriksen family (Norway) – Heidi (b. 1960), Olav (b. 1964), and Lief-Martin (b. 1968) – all celebrate their birthdays infrequently, as they fall on Leap Day – February 29.

★ OLDEST MOTHER TO HAVE TWINS

Donna Maas (USA, b. November 28, 1946) gave birth to twin boys on September 9, 2004, at the age of 57 years 286 days. The twins, Matthew and Michael, were delivered by Caesarean section at Northridge Hospital Medical Center, Northridge, California, USA.

YOUNGEST GREAT-GREAT-GREAT GRANDMOTHER

The youngest person to learn that their great-granddaughter had become a grandmother was Harriet Holmes (Canada; b. January 17, 1899), who was aged 88 years 50 days when she became a great-great-great-grandmother to Brian Bursey on March 8, 1987.

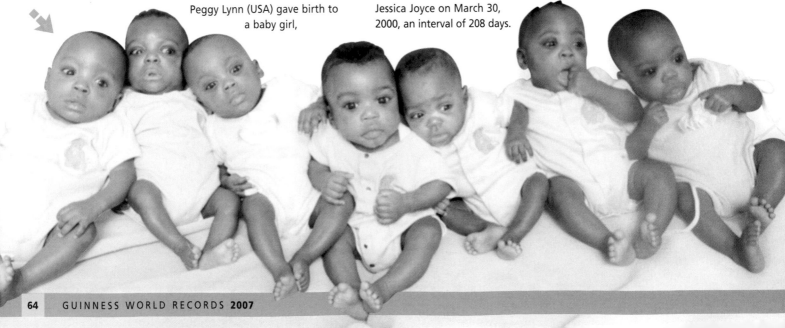

HEAVIEST BIRTH

Anna Bates (née Swan, Canada), who measured 7 ft 5.5 in (2.27 m), gave birth to a boy weighing 23 lb 12 oz (10.8 kg) at her home in Seville, Ohio, USA, on January 19, 1879, but the baby died 11 hours later.

The heaviest baby born was a boy weighing 22 lb 8 oz (10.2 kg), to Carmelina Fedele (Italy) at Aversa, Italy, in September 1955.

FAMILY LIFE

YOUNGEST BRIDES

Of the 38,820 marriages that took place in Tajikistan in 1994, 49.6% of the brides were aged 19 or under (compared with 4.7% aged 30 or over).

In 1997, 18% of the 51,526 grooms who married in Guatemala were aged 19 or under, making them the world's **youngest bridegrooms**.

★LONGEST MARRIAGE FOR A LIVING COUPLE

John Rocchio (USA, b. Giovanni, November 24, 1903) and his wife Amelia (née Antonelli, USA, b. October 10, 1905) were married on February 10, 1923, in Rhode Island, USA, and celebrated their 83rd wedding anniversary on February 10, 2006.

★LARGEST FAMILY REUNION

A total of 2,369 members of the Busse family converged on Grayslake, Illinois, USA, on June 28, 1998, to celebrate the 150th anniversary of Friedrich and Johanna Busse's arrival in the USA from Germany.

★MOST TWINS IN THE SAME ACADEMIC YEAR AT ONE SCHOOL

Eight sets of twins from different families were registered in the same academic year at one school. Timothy and Gabrielle Lynch, Amy and Anna Lam, Cerina and Krystal Kelly, Samantha and Savannah Fuller, Monquel and Elijah Faison, Jess and Jamison Caskinette, Brittany and Brooke Hobart, and Brier and Brody Riggs (all USA) entered the sixth grade of the 2004/05 academic year at Indian River Middle School, Philadelphia, New York, USA.

★MOST SIBLINGS TO HAVE CELEBRATED THEIR GOLDEN WEDDING ANNIVERSARY

Between February 5, 1974 and June 11, 1999, all 12 siblings of the Wade family celebrated their golden wedding anniversaries.

★MOST SIBLINGS TO MARRY THE SIBLINGS OF ANOTHER FAMILY

All five daughters of Narandra Nath and Taramoni Roy married five brothers – the sons of Trarpoda Karmaker and Khana Rani Roy (all Bangladesh) – between 1977 and 1996.

LONGEST FAMILY TREE

The lineage of K'ung Ch'iu or Confucius (551–479 BC) can be traced back farther than that of any other family. His great-great-great-great grandfather Kung Chia is known from the 8th century BC. Kung Chia has a total of 86 lineal descendants.

ACTUAL SIZE

LIGHTEST BIRTH

The lowest birth weight recorded for a surviving infant, of which there is definite evidence, is 9.17 oz (260 g) in the case of Rumaisa Rahman (USA), who was born at Loyola University Medical Center, Maywood, Illinois, USA, on September 19, 2004, at 25 weeks 6 days gestation.

←·· ★LARGEST GAP BETWEEN TEST-TUBE BIRTHS

Laina Beasley (USA) was conceived in a test tube along with her siblings Jeffrey and Carleigh. She was then kept in suspended animation for nearly 13 years, as a two-celled embryo, before her birth on May 13, 2005. From left to right: Jeffrey (brother), Debbie (mother), Laina, Kent (father), and Carleigh (sister).

AGING & LONGEVITY

OLDEST → LIVING CONJOINED TWINS (MALE)

Ronnie and Donnie Galyon (USA, b. October 25, 1951) are the oldest living conjoined male twins. Joined at the waist, they traveled in side shows, carnivals, and circuses for 36 years, but retired in 1991. As of May 8, 2006, they were 54 years old. They are pictured here on their third birthday.

oldest authenticated twins. Kin died of heart failure on January 23, 2000, at the age of 107 years 175 days.

The **oldest male twins ever** authenticated were Glen and Dale Moyer (USA), both of whom reached 105 years. Born on June 20, 1895, they became the oldest living twins on January 23, 2000. Dale is a retired farmer and is 20 minutes older than Glen, a retired teacher. Glen passed away on April 16, 2001, at the age of 105 years 9 months 26 days.

LIVING TWINS (FEMALE)

Identical sisters Della Vecchione Darmo and Marie Vecchione DiLoreto (both USA) were born on October 12, 1907. They became the oldest living female twins on May 26, 2004 aged 96 years 227 days.

LIVING TWINS (MALE AND FEMALE)

Louisa Dunn and Fred Adams (UK) were born on March 9, 1907. They became the oldest living fraternal twins in November 1999 aged 92 years 199 days.

CONJOINED TWINS (MALE)

Giacomo and Giovanni Battista Tocci were born in northern Italy on October 4, 1877, and lived to be 63 years old. The twins were separate above the waist, but shared a pelvis, abdomen, and two legs. They died in 1940.

TRIPLETS

Faith, Hope, and Charity Cardwell (all USA) were born on May 18, 1899, at Elm Mott, Texas, USA. Faith died on October 2, 1994, aged 95 years 137 days.

LIVING TRIPLETS

Minna Dora Blöcker, Luise Amalie Stefener, and Bertholdine Alwine Bernecker (all Germany) were born on January 31, 1914. All three celebrated their 91st birthday in 2005.

QUADRUPLETS

The Ottman quadruplets of Munich, Germany – Adolf, Anne-Marie, Emma, and Elisabeth – were born on May 5, 1912. All four quads lived to the age of 79.

OLDEST...

WOMAN

The greatest fully authenticated age to which any human has ever lived is 122 years 164 days by Jeanne Louise Calment (France). Born on February 21, 1875, to Nicolas (1837–1931) and Marguerite (neé Gilles 1838–1924), Jeanne died at a nursing home in Arles, southern France, on August 4, 1997.

TWINS

Kin Narita and Gin Kanie (Japan, b. August 1, 1892), whose names mean Gold and Silver, were the

★ OLDEST LIVING WOMAN

Maria Esther de Capovilla (Ecuador) became the oldest living woman on December 8, 2005, aged 116 years 85 days. She was born on September 14, 1889 – at which time the famous artist Vincent van Gogh was still alive.

◄·· OLDEST LIVING WOMAN WITH DOWN'S SYNDROME

Nancy Siddoway (USA, b. August 18, 1937) became the oldest living person with Down's syndrome on June 21, 2005, aged 67 years 307 days. She currently resides in West Jordan, Utah, USA, and is pictured here at her 65th birthday.

Keith Roberts (South Africa, b. June 6, 1953) is the **oldest living man with Down's syndrome**. He was 52 years 16 days old as of June 22, 2005.

★ NEW RECORD
☆ UPDATED RECORD

← OLDEST MAN

Shigechiyo Izumi (Japan) of Isen on Tokunoshima, an island 820 miles (1,320 km) southwest of Tokyo, Japan, lived to be 120 years 237 days old. He was born in Isen on June 29, 1865, and was recorded as a six-year-old in Japan's first census of 1871. He died at 12:15 GMT on February 21, 1986, after developing pneumonia.

PEOPLE TO GROW TEETH

Mark Tora (UK, b. May 25, 1938) had a lower right third molar tooth erupt at the age of 61 in February 2000, making him the **oldest person to grow a new tooth**.

The **oldest person to grow a wisdom tooth** is Timotheus Louw (South Africa, b. June 27, 1922). On January 29, 2003, an X-ray photo revealed that he was growing a wisdom tooth in his top left gum at the age of 80 years 216 days.

☆ OLDEST LIVING MAN ↙

Emiliano Mercado del Toro (Puerto Rico) – born in Cabo Rojo, Puerto Rico, on August 21, 1891 – became the oldest fully authenticated man in the world on January 17, 2005, aged 113 years 149 days. Emiliano is also the **oldest living veteran**, having been called up in 1918 by the US Army. A non-combat veteran, he had trained for two months when World War I ended on November 11, 1918. Inset is his discharge letter.

MOTHER TO HAVE QUADRUPLETS

On April 18, 1998, Merryl Thelma Fudel (Australia) gave birth to three girls and one boy at Sharp Memorial Hospital, San Diego, California, USA, aged 55 years 286 days. One baby died at birth as a result of respiratory failure.

ADOPTIVE PARENT

Frances Ensor Benedict (USA, b. May 11, 1918) was aged 83 years 329 days when she legally adopted Jo Anne Benedict Walker (USA) on April 5, 2002, in Putnam County, Tennessee, USA.

Jo Anne was 65 years 224 days old at the time, making her the **oldest adoptee**.

PERSON WITH DOWN'S SYNDROME

According to a number of medical reports, a Down's syndrome sufferer known only as Mrs. K, from Illinois, USA, died aged 83 after developing complications from a broken hip.

PATIENT

James Henry Brett Jr. (USA, 1849–1961) was aged 111 years 105 days when he underwent a hip operation on November 7, 1960.

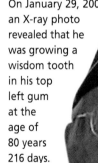

WORLD'S OLDEST LIVING PEOPLE

NAME	NATIONALITY	AGE	DATE OF BIRTH
Maria Esther de Capovilla (f)	Ecuador	116	Sep. 14, 1889
Elizabeth "Lizzie" Bolden (f)	USA	115	Aug. 15, 1890
Emiliano Mercado del Toro (m)	Puerto Rico	114	Aug. 21, 1891
Julie Winnefred Bertrand (f)	Canada	114	Sep. 16, 1891
Camille Loiseau (f)	France	114	Feb. 13, 1892
Emma Tillman (f)	USA	113	Nov. 22, 1892
Yone Minagawa (f)	Japan	113	Jan. 4, 1893
Moses Hardy (m)	USA	113	Jan. 6, 1893
Edna Parker (f)	USA	113	Apr. 20, 1893
Maria de Jesus (f)	Portugal	112	Sep. 10, 1893
Giulia Sani-Casagli (f)	Italy	112	Sep. 15, 1893
Naka Morii (f)	Japan	112	Sep. 27, 1893
Mary Margaret Smith (f)	USA	112	Oct. 7, 1893
Helen Stetter (f)	USA	112	Nov. 18, 1893
Florence Homan (f)	USA	112	Nov. 18, 1893

Source: Gerontology Research Group (www.grg.org)   *f = female, m = male*

MEDICAL MARVELS

LARGEST
FOREIGN OBJECT LEFT IN A PATIENT

Meena Purohit (India) underwent a Caesarean section to deliver her daughter on July 1, 1989, during which surgeons left a pair of artery forceps measuring 13 in (33.02 cm) long, in her abdomen. The forceps remained undiscovered until doctors carried out an exploratory laparotomy on September 3, 1993.

← --

ACTUAL SIZE

! **X-REF**

Thanks to advances in medical science, a deadly disease that killed two million people annually up to the 1960s has now been eradicated. Which disease was it? Find out on p.71.

★ FIRST ⇒
SUCCESSFUL PARTIAL FACE TRANSPLANT

Isabelle Dinoire (France) underwent the first partial face transplant at Amiens University Hospital, France, on November 27, 2005. Isabella was severely disfigured after her pet dog chewed off her nose, lips and chin in May 2005. Her new face came from a multi-organ-donor suicide victim from Lille, France, and the operation was led by Professor Jean-Michel Dubernard (France), who carried out the **first hand transplant** in 1998.

YOUNGEST TRANSPLANT PATIENT

On November 8, 1996, one-hour-old Cheyenne Pyle (USA) received a donor heart at Jackson Children's Hospital in Miami, Florida, USA.

OLDEST SURGICAL PROCEDURE

Trepanation, the process of removing bone from the skull's cranial vault, is the oldest surgical procedure. The earliest definite evidence of trepanation was found on the skeleton of a 50-year-old man in a 7,000-year-old burial site in Ensisheim, France.

HIGHEST PERCENTAGE OF BODY BURNS SURVIVED

David Chapman (UK) survived burns of 90% to his body after a canister exploded and drenched him with gasoline while he was filling his moped on July 2, 1996. During a subsequent operation, surgeons spent 36 hours removing dead tissue from David's body.

★ FIRST SUCCESSFUL FULL-FACE REPLANT ⇒

In 1994, leading microsurgeon Dr. Abraham Thomas (India) performed the world's first full-face replant operation on nine-year-old Sandeep Kaur (India), whose face and scalp was ripped off when one of her pigtails became caught in a threshing machine. The operation was a success and, in 2005, 20-year-old Sandeep was studying to be a nurse.

FIRST TRANSPLANTEE TO GIVE BIRTH

Johanna Rempel (Canada) gave birth to a baby boy, Kerry Melvin Ross, weighing 7 lb 12 oz (3.5 kg) at Winnipeg General Hospital, Manitoba, Canada, on September 7, 1967. She had received a donor kidney in December 1960.

MOST...

★ BLOOD DONATED

Maurice Creswick (South Africa) had donated 353 pints of blood as of April 21, 2006. Having donated blood since his 18th birthday in 1944, he has given the equivalent of 52.9 gal (423.7 pints) to date.

This achievement also gives him the record for the ★ **oldest regular blood donor**.

OPERATIONS

From July 22, 1954 to the end of 1994, Charles Jensen (USA) underwent 970 operations to remove tumors associated with basal cell naevus syndrome, the **greatest number of major operations endured**.

Dr. Robert B. McClure (Canada) carried out 20,423 major operations in 1924–78, the **most major operations performed**.

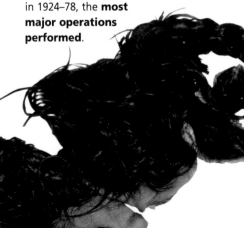

ACTUAL SIZE

⭐ LONGEST- ⬆ SURVIVING
ARTIFICIAL HEART TRANSPLANT PATIENT

Peter Houghton (UK) was implanted with a Jarvik 2000 heart pump at the John Radcliffe Hospital, Oxford, UK, on June 20, 2000 after suffering from severe heart failure. Since the operation was carried out, the left ventricular assist device has worked continuously supporting his heart. He broke the previous artificial heart transplant duration record after 1,513 days on August 11, 2004.

ORGAN TRANSPLANTS

Dr. Andreas Tzakis (USA) transplanted seven organs – a liver, pancreas, stomach, large and small intestines, and two kidneys – into a 10-month-old Italian girl during 16 hours of surgery at Jackson Children's Hospital in Miami, Florida, USA, on March 23, 1997. This represents the **greatest number of organs transplanted in a single operation**.

Daniel Canal (USA) received his third set of four new organs in June 1998 at the age of 13 – the **most**

organs transplanted into one **person**. He was given a new stomach, liver, pancreas, and small intestine at Jackson Children's Hospital, Miami, USA, for the third time in a little over a month.

ARTIFICIAL JOINTS

Long-term arthritis sufferer Anne Davison (UK) had 12 major joints (both shoulders, elbows, wrists, hips, knees, and ankles) and three knuckles replaced by the age of 47.

Charles N. Wedde (USA), who has rheumatoid arthritis, had 12 major joints replaced from 1979 to 1995.

BEE STINGS REMOVED

Johannes Relleke survived 2,443 bee stings at the Kamativi tin mine, Gwaii River, Wankie District, Zimbabwe (then Rhodesia), on January 28, 1962. Each sting was removed and counted.

LONGEST...

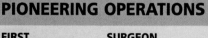

COMA

Elaine Esposito (USA) entered a coma following an appendectomy on August 6, 1941, when she was six years old. She died on November 25, 1978, aged 43 years 357 days, having been comatose for 37 years 111 days.

LARGEST OBJECT ⇢ TO BE REMOVED FROM A HUMAN SKULL

Doctors worked throughout the night to remove an 8-in (20.32-cm) knife (similar to the one pictured) that had been plunged into the head of a 41-year-old victim in the USA, on April 25, 1998. Astonishingly, the victim was able to speak and function normally the very next day.

MEDICAL OPERATION

From February 4 to 8, 1951, in Chicago, Illinois, USA, Gertrude Levandowski (USA) underwent a 96-hour operation to remove an ovarian cyst.

SURVIVAL WITHOUT A PULSE

Julie Mills (UK) survived three days without a pulse in her vascular system after suffering severe heart failure and viral myocarditis on August 14, 1998. Cardiac surgeons at the John Radcliffe Hospital, Oxford, UK, used a non-pulsatile blood pump (AB180) to support her for a week, during which time her heart recovered and the pump was removed.

⭐ TIME TO SURVIVE WITH ONE LUNG

ACTUAL SIZE

Bruce Geiling (USA, b. June 7, 1923) lost his right lung to cancer on April 10, 1969, and was still leading a healthy life on August 14, 2004.

Wolfgang Muller (Canada) underwent a single-lung transplant at Toronto General Hospital, Ontario, Canada, on September 15, 1987, and became the **longest-surviving single-lung transplant recipient** on July 19, 2004, at 16 years 307 days.

SURVIVOR OF A PORCINE AORTIC VALVE REPLACEMENT – LIVING

Harry Driver (UK, b. October 9, 1930) received a (pig's) aortic valve replacement on April 12, 1978, under surgeon Dr. John Keates (UK). It functioned for 25 years 238 days until it was replaced by another on March 16, 2004 by Dr. Philip Kay (UK).

As of April 21, 2006, Driver was also the ⭐ **oldest survivor of a porcine aortic valve replacement**, at the age of 75 yr 194 days.

PIONEERING OPERATIONS

FIRST...	SURGEON	PATIENT	DATE
General anesthetic – diethyl ether ($C_2H_5)_2O$	Dr. C. W. Long (USA)	James Venable (USA)	Mar. 30, 1842
Kidney transplant	R. H. Lawler (USA)	(Unnamed)	Jun. 17, 1950
Heart transplant	Prof. C. N. Barnard (South Africa)	Louis Washkansky (South Africa)	Dec. 3, 1967
Heart-lung transplant	Dr. B. Reitz (USA)	(Unnamed)	1981
Artificial heart recipient	Dr. W. C. DeVries (USA)	Barney Clark (USA)	Dec. 1–2, 1982
Heart-lung-liver transplant	J. Wallwork (UK) Prof. Sir R. Calne (UK)	Davina Thompson (UK)	Dec. 17, 1986
Bionic arm	Team of five bioengineers	Campbell Aird (UK)	1993
Double-arm transplant	Prof. J.-M. Dubernard (France)	(Unnamed)	Jan. 2000
Artificial eye	(Eye developed by William Dobelle, USA)	Jeremiah Teehan (USA)	Announced Jan. 17, 2000

⭐ NEW RECORD
⭐ UPDATED RECORD

DISEASE & MEDICINE

ACTUAL SIZE

MOST GALLSTONES
REMOVED FROM A PATIENT
In August 1987, a total of 23,530 gallstones were removed from an unnamed 85-year-old woman, after she complained of severe abdominal pain, by K. Whittle Martin (UK) at Worthing Hospital, UK.

The ★ **youngest person to have gallstones** is Brandon Brunette-Seguin (Canada), who was first diagnosed at the age of 6 years 194 days at Grand River Hospital (Canada) on December 10, 1996. The stones were not removed.

★LONGEST ➡ HOSPITAL GURNEY DURATION
Tony Collins (UK) spent 77 hr 30 min on a hospital gurney in a corridor at Princess Margaret Hospital, Swindon, Wiltshire, UK, from February 24 to 27, 2001, before he was finally admitted to a ward. Tony, a diabetic, was suffering with a virus.

DISEASE

LEADING CAUSE OF DEATH
In industrialized countries, diseases of the heart and blood vessels (cardiovascular disease) account for over 50% of deaths. Heart attacks and strokes are the most common of these, generally owing to atheroma (degeneration of the arterial walls). The **highest level of cardiovascular disease** is in Northern Ireland, UK, where over 300 men in every 100,000 have experienced related symptoms.

★ FASTEST-GROWING DISEASE
The Human Immunodeficiency Virus (HIV) saw an increase in 2005 of approximately 4.9 million new cases,

taking the estimated total number of people living with HIV to 40.3 million.

★ YEAR WITH THE MOST AIDS-RELATED DEATHS
According to the *AIDS Epidemic Update 2005* annual report by the United Nations Program on HIV/AIDS and the World Health Organization (WHO), 2005 was the year in which the most AIDS-related deaths occurred. A total of 3.1 million deaths in 2005 were related to Acquired Immune Deficiency Syndrome (AIDS). Out of this figure, 570,000 of the victims were under 15 years old and 2.4 million were in sub-Saharan Africa. The number of AIDS-related deaths since official monitoring began is 23.1 million.

MOST PREVALENT ALLERGIC DISEASE
Bronchial asthma affects up to 150 million people globally; deaths from the condition reach 180,000 each year. Worldwide, it is estimated that the economic costs associated with the disease exceed those of tuberculosis and HIV/AIDS combined.

DEADLIEST DISEASE
Based on estimates from the *United Nations Health Report 2004*, the disease that kills the most people is ischemic heart disease, responsible for an estimated 7.2 million deaths (or 12.6% of the total) in 2004.

MOST URGENT HEALTH PROBLEM
The WHO estimates that by 2020 tobacco-related illness, including heart disease, cancer, and respiratory disorders, will be the world's leading killer, responsible for more deaths than AIDS, tuberculosis, road traffic accidents, murder, and suicide combined.

★ MOST BONE MARROW ⬅ DONORS (24 HOURS)
On July 16, 2005, 250 people registered for bone marrow donation at an event held in Pembrokeshire, UK, in memory of acute myeloid leukemia sufferer Adam Evans-Thomas (UK, 1969–2004). Adam spent the last 10 years of his life raising awareness of the treatment of cancer. Among those pictured is his mother, Chris (third from right).

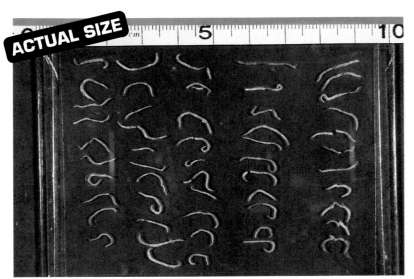

ACTUAL SIZE

MOST ⬆
WORMS REMOVED FROM A HUMAN STOMACH

A 58-year-old woman from Shizuoka, Japan, was admitted to Isogaki Gastroenterosurgical Clinic in May 1990. She complained of severe gastric pain and nausea brought on by eating sashimi (raw fish). Doctors discovered 56 white, thread-like worms (above) in her stomach, and removed them during a 90-minute operation. The worms measured up to 0.67 in (17.27 mm) in length and were later identified as the larvae of *Anisakis simplex*.

LARGEST CHOLERA OUTBREAK

According to the WHO *Report on Infectious Diseases 1999*, over 500,000 people became infected with cholera in Latin America in 1991.

TREATMENTS

★ MOST CORONARY STENT IMPLANTS

From August 8, 2000 to January 31, 2005, Emil Lohen (USA) had a total of 31 coronary stents implanted. The most at any one time has been six in an operation on September 13, 2002, at Lenox Hill, New York City, USA.

LARGEST PRESENT-DAY WAR HOSPITAL

Founded in 1987 with a total of just 40 beds, the International Committee of the Red Cross (ICRC) Hospital in Lopiding, Kenya, now has 560 beds. It has treated approximately 17,000 victims of the civil war in neighboring Sudan to date, supplying 1,500 with artificial limbs.

LONGEST STAY IN HOSPITAL

Martha Nelson (USA) was admitted to the Columbus State Institute for the Feeble-Minded in Ohio, USA, in 1875. She died in January 1975 at the age of 103 years 6 months in the Orient State Institution, Ohio, after spending more than 99 years in hospitals.

MOST PILLS TAKEN

The highest recorded total of pills swallowed under medical care by a patient is 565,939 between June 9, 1967, and June 19, 1988, by C. H. A. Kilner (Zimbabwe).

FIRST ORAL CONTRACEPTIVE

Carl Djerassi (USA) developed the modern contraceptive pill as a researcher working for Syntex Laboratories in Mexico City in 1951.

MOST ➡
LEPROSY PATIENTS TREATED

The Avadhoot Bhagwan Ram Kushta Seva Ashram Hospital in Parao, India, has treated more leprosy patients than any other hospital. The total number of registered patients since 1961 has been 99,045 with full leprosy and 147,503 with partial leprosy – all of whom were fully cured.

MOST LEPERS CURED

In the 15 years between 1983 and 1998, almost 10 million people were cured of leprosy.

★ MOST VACCINATIONS GIVEN IN A DAY

A total of 2,480 flu shots were administered by the Florida Hospital Centra Care at the Osceola Heritage Stadium in Kissimmee, Florida, USA, on December 3, 2004.

MOST SUCCESSFUL IMMUNIZATION

The WHO declared the world free of smallpox from January 1, 1980. Smallpox caused around 2 million deaths per year in the 1960s, but was eradicated by the availability of one type of vaccine effective against all forms of the disease.

MOST CEREBRAL ANEURYSMS PERFORMED

Neurosurgeon Hirotoshi Sano (Japan) of the Department of Neurosurgery at Fujita Health University, Toyoake, Aichi, Japan, performed 2,100 aneurysm operations between July 6, 1972 and April 2, 2001.

★ NEW RECORD
★ UPDATED RECORD

MOST ⬆
COMPULSIVE SWALLOWER

An extreme case of compulsive swallowing involved a woman with mental health problems, "Mrs H." (Canada), who complained of a "slight abdominal pain." She was found to have 2,533 objects, including 947 bent pins, in her stomach. These were surgically removed in June 1927 at the Ontario Hospital, Canada.

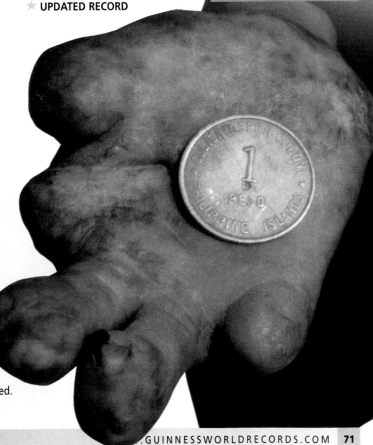

BODY ♥ BEAUTIFUL

★ NEW RECORD
UPDATED RECORD

TATTOOS

MOST TATTOOED WOMAN
Strip artiste Krystyne Kolorful (Canada) spent 10 years having up to 95% of her body tattooed in order to secure a unique look for her dance act.

LONGEST TATTOO SESSION
Glen Keizer (Australia) underwent a grueling 42 hr 10 min of tattooing by artist Paul Blackhall (Australia) at Outta Limits Tattoo and Body Piercing Studio, Dubbo, New South Wales, Australia, between September 16 and 18, 2005.

★ LARGEST FOREHEAD INFLATION

Body and performance artist Jerome Abramovitch's (USA) signature work is forehead-inflation – a means of face and forehead modification using saline injections. Injecting the 8 fl oz (250 ml) of saline takes up to four hours – and a further 24 hours is required for the saline to disperse. He occasionally injects his cheeks with an additional 5 fl oz (150 ml). *Guinness World Records* recommends that you do not try this at home.

PIERCINGS

MOST PIERCED MAN
Luis Antonio Agüero, from Havana, Cuba, sports 230 piercings on his head and body. His face alone carries over 175 rings. Agüero assists the upkeep of his family by charging a nominal fee for photographs.

MOST PIERCINGS WITH 18-GAUGE SURGICAL NEEDLES
Benjamin Drucker (USA) had 745 18-gauge (0.5-in; 1.2-cm) surgical needles inserted into his body by Nate Adams (USA) in 2 hr 21 min at Ix Body Piercing of Taos, New Mexico, USA, on July 12, 2003.

MOST TATTOOED MAN

The ultimate in multilayered tattooing is represented by the chainsaw-juggling, unicycling, sword-swallowing Lucky Diamond Rich (Australia, b. New Zealand), who has spent over 1,000 hours having his body modified by hundreds of tattoo artists. He began by having a full collection of colorful designs from around the world tattooed over his entire body. Lucky next opted for a 100% covering of black ink, including eyelids, the delicate skin between the toes, down into the ears, and even his gums. He is now being tattooed with white designs on top of the black, and colored designs on top of the white!

MAKEOVERS

MOST COSMETIC MAKEOVERS (24 HR)
Sidonia Massie Hutagalung (Indonesia) – a makeup artist for Professional Artist Cosmetics Martha Tilaar – performed 96 cosmetic makeovers in 24 hours at the Kelapa Gading Mall in Jakarta, Indonesia, on May 22–23, 2005.

MOST BIKINI WAXES (4 HR)
Lareesa Guttery (Australia) gave 262 clients a bikini wax in four hours at the Every Woman's Expo 2004 in Burswood Dome, Perth, Australia, on June 12, 2004.

MOST LEG WAXES (1 HR)
Sue Ismiel (Australia) waxed 32 pairs of legs in one hour on the set of *Guinness World Records* at Seven Network Studios, Sydney, New South Wales, Australia, on May 8, 2005.

MOST HAIRCUTS (1 DAY)
Christian Petrillo (Italy) cut and styled 250 different heads of washed hair on June 18–19, 2004, at Nicostyle Hair Salon, Hamburg, Germany.

★ MOST EXPENSIVE HAIRCUT
The Couture Cut by celebrity hairdresser Lee Stafford (UK) will set you back a cool £1,000 ($1,751) for a visit to his salon, or £2,000 ($3,502) for a visit by Stafford to a venue of your choice. Included in the price are champagne, truffles, and chocolate-dipped strawberries, plus a follow-up session six weeks later.

COUNTRY WITH THE MOST ESTHETIC PLASTIC SURGERY PROCEDURES

According to the International Society of Esthetic Plastic Surgery, the USA continues to hold the top spot in the esthetic surgery league, with 76,091 procedures – or nearly 13% of the world's esthetic operations – carried out in 2004.

★ COUNTRY WITH THE YOUNGEST ESTHETIC SURGERY PATIENTS

In Spain, a record 40.19% of patients undergoing esthetic surgery are under the age of 21. The ★**country with the oldest esthetic surgery patients** is India, where 54.43% of those treated are over 50 years old.

MOST POPULAR NONSURGICAL ESTHETIC PROCEDURE

According to a survey carried out in 42 countries by members of the International Society of Esthetic Plastic Surgery, the most popular nonsurgical procedure performed in 2004 was Botox injections. This represented a total of 13.74% of all esthetic plastic surgery carried out in that year.

MOST PIERCINGS IN ONE SESSION

Kam Ma (UK) received a total of 1,015 new titanium body piercings without the aid of an anesthetic. All piercings were executed by Charlie Wilson (UK) in one continuous session lasting 7 hr 55 min on March 4, 2006, at Sunderland Body Art, Sunderland, Tyne and Wear, UK.

★TALLEST MOHICAN

Aaron Studham (USA) boasts a Mohican – or Mohawk – that reached 21 in (53 cm) when measured in Leominster, Massachusetts, USA, on September 11, 2005. The secret to its huge size, says Studham, is a thorough wash every day.

PLASTIC SURGERY

MOST GENDER REASSIGNMENT SURGERY

Fulvia Celica Siguas Sandoval (Peru) has had 64 surgical operations since December 1979 to complete gender reassignment. Of these, over 25 have been to her face and neck, with other alterations including ear reductions, transformations to her legs, and arm liposuction. Fulvia – a transsexual TV clairvoyant – hit the headlines back in 1998 when she registered as a mayoral candidate in Lima, Peru.

SURGEON TO PERFORM THE MOST GENDER-REASSIGNMENT OPERATIONS

Surgeon Stanley Biber (USA), who died in 2006, performed sex change operations for over 30 years in Trinidad, Colorado, USA – the "Sex Change Capital of the World." The former pre-Olympic weightlifter conducted over 5,000 operations – mostly male-to-female procedures, but also about 300 female-to-male ops. He also carried out at least three "reversals" before ending his surgery career in 2003 at the age of 80. At one point, Biber had performed two-thirds of the world's sex changes.

MOST PLASTIC SURGERY

Cindy Jackson (USA) has spent $99,600 on 47 cosmetic procedures, including nine full-scale surgical operations, since 1988. These have included three full facelifts, two nose operations, two eye lifts, liposuction, knees, waist, abdomen, thigh, and jawline surgery, lip and cheek implants, chemical peels, and semi-permanent makeup.

HUMAN ACHIEVEMENTS

CONTENTS

LONGEST FULL-BODY BURN
(WITHOUT OXYGEN)

Ted A. Batchelor (USA), a professional stuntman who has been performing fire stunts since 1976, endured a full-body burn without oxygen supplies for 2 min 38 sec on an island at Ledges Quarry Park, Nelson, Ohio, USA, on July 17, 2004.

EXPLORATION

★ YOUNGEST PERSON TO CLIMB EVEREST

Ming Kipa Sherpa (Nepal, below right) reached the summit of Mount Everest on May 22, 2003, at the age of 15. She made the climb with her brother Mingma Gyula Sherpa and sister Lakpa Sherpa (below left).

All three were climbing in support of a Romanian expedition.

MOUNTAINS

★ FASTEST ASCENT OF ALL 14 PEAKS ABOVE 25,000 FT

Jerzy "Jurek" Kukuczka (Poland) climbed the 14 peaks above 25,000 ft (8,000 m) in 7 years 11 months 16 days between October 4, 1979, when he ascended Lhotse (27,890 ft; 8,501 m) on the Nepal–Tibet border, and September 18, 1987, when he climbed Shisha Pangma (26,286 ft; 8,012 m) in Tibet.

In mountaineering circles, the "8,000ers" are regarded as the ultimate challenge and seen as more prestigious than the "seven summits."

★ FIRST PERSON TO COMPLETE THE "EXPLORERS' GRAND SLAM"

Young-Seok Park (South Korea) reached the North Pole on foot on April 30, 2005, becoming the first person to achieve the "explorers' grand slam." This involves climbing the highest peaks on all seven continents (the "seven summits"), the 14 peaks over 25,000 ft (8,000 m), and reaching the North and South poles on foot. His quest began when he reached the peak of Mount Everest on May 16, 1993.

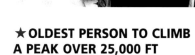

★ OLDEST PERSON TO CLIMB A PEAK OVER 25,000 FT

The oldest person to have climbed one of the 14 peaks over 25,000 ft is Toshiko Uchida (Japan), who reached the summit of Cho Oyu – which, at 26,906 ft (8,201 m) is the world's sixth tallest mountain – on October 1, 2002, at the age of 71.

★ MOST ASCENTS OF EVEREST BY A WOMAN

Lakpa Sherpa (Nepal, pictured far left) successfully reached the summit of Mount Everest for the fifth time on June 2, 2005. She made the climb with her husband, George Demarescu (USA), who was himself completing his seventh ascent of the **world's highest mountain**.

POLAR REGIONS

★ LARGEST POLAR/ ANTARCTIC EXPEDITION

The US Navy's "Operation Highjump," a survey and mapping expedition carried out in Antarctica in the summer of 1946–47, involved 13 ships, including the aircraft carrier *Philippine Sea*, around 25 aircraft and approximately 4,700 men.

★ FIRST AIRPLANE FLIGHT IN ANTARCTICA

The first heavier-than-air flight on the Antarctic continent was made on November 16, 1928, by Sir Hubert Wilkins (Australia) and Carl Ben Eielson (USA) in a Lockheed Vega aircraft.

YOUNGEST ⬆ PERSON TO VISIT BOTH POLES

Jonathan Silverman (USA, b. June 13, 1990, pictured right) reached the North Pole on July 25, 1999, and the South Pole on January 10, 2002, by the age of 11 years 211 days. He reached the North Pole as part of a tourist expedition on the Russian icebreaker *Yamal*, and the South Pole on another tourist expedition, landing at the pole by aircraft from Chile.

FIRST POLAR TREKS

At 11 a.m. on December 14, 1911, a Norwegian party of five men led by Captain Roald Engebereth Gravning Amundsen (Norway) became the first people to reach the South Pole, after a 53-day march with dogsleds from the Bay of Whales.

The Arctic explorer Robert Peary (USA) is regarded as the **first person to have reached the North Pole**. He set off from Cape Columbia, Ellesmere Island, Canada, on March 1, 1909, with his close associate Matt Henson (USA). On April 6, Peary made observations indicating that he had reached his destination.

Dr. Albert Paddock Crary (USA) reached the North Pole in a Dakota aircraft on May 3, 1952. On February 12, 1961, he arrived at the South Pole by Sno-Cat on a scientific traverse party from the McMurdo Station, making him the **first person to visit both poles**.

DEEPEST
MANNED OCEAN DESCENT

Dr. Jacques Piccard (Switzerland) and Lt. Donald Walsh (USA) piloted the Swiss-built US Navy bathyscaphe *Trieste* to a depth of 35,797 ft (10,911 m) in the Challenger Deep section of the Mariana Trench on January 23, 1960. Challenger Deep is thought to be the deepest point on Earth and is situated 250 miles (400 km) southwest of Guam in the Pacific Ocean.

DEEPEST UNDERWATER
SALVAGE WITH DIVERS

The deepest salvage operation with divers was on the wreck of HM cruiser *Edinburgh*, which had sunk on May 2, 1942, in the Barents Sea off northern Norway, inside the Arctic Circle, in 803 ft (245 m) of water.

Over a period of 31 days (from September 7 to October 7, 1981), 12 divers worked on the wreck in pairs. A total of 460 gold ingots were recovered.

★ FIRST
FLIGHT
OVER THE
SOUTH POLE

Pioneering aviator Richard Byrd (USA) made the first flight over the South Pole on November 29, 1929.

The round trip to and from the expedition's base camp on the Ross Ice Shelf took 19 hours.

★ FASTEST
ASCENT OF
MOUNT
KILIMANJARO

Sean Burch (USA) ran the 21 miles (34 km) from the base to the summit of Mount Kilimanjaro (altitude 19,340 ft; 5,895 m) in 5 hr 28 min 48 sec on June 7, 2005, the fastest anyone has climbed Africa's highest peak.

The journey takes typical climbers four to five days, owing to the need to acclimatize to the increasing altitude. Burch, a well-known fitness guru in the USA, acclimatized for eight days by running around a crater at 18,503 ft (5,640 m), which is roughly the height of Everest base camp.

★ FIRST
PERSON TO CLIMB ALL
PEAKS OVER 25,000 FT

Reinhold Messner (Italy) became the first person to climb the world's 14 peaks over 25,000 ft (8,000 m) when he summited Lhotse (27,890 ft; 8,501 m) on the Nepal–Tibet border on October 16, 1986. His quest began in June 1970. By the second half of 2005, only 12 people had ever achieved this feat – an indication of how demanding it is.

FIRST PERSON TO
WALK TO BOTH POLES

Robert Swan (UK) led the three-man *In the Footsteps of Scott* expedition, which reached the South Pole on January 11, 1986; three years later, he headed the eight-man *Icewalk* expedition, which arrived at the North Pole on May 14, 1989.

OLDEST PERSON
TO VISIT BOTH POLES

Major Will Lacy (UK, b. July 7, 1907) went to the North Pole on April 9, 1990, at the age of 82, and the South Pole on December 20, 1991, at the age of 84. On both trips he arrived and left by light aircraft.

LONGEST
POLAR SLED JOURNEY

Six members of the International Trans-Antarctica Expedition sledded a distance of some 3,750 miles (6,040 km) in 220 days from July 27, 1989 (at Seal Nunataks)

to March 3, 1990 (at Mirnyy). The expedition was accompanied by a team of 40 dogs (the sleds of more modern expeditions are pulled by parafoils), but several of them were flown out from one of the staging posts for a period of rest before returning to the journey.

FIRST SURFACE POLE-TO-
POLE CIRCUMNAVIGATION

Sir Ranulph Fiennes and Charles Burton (both UK) of the British Trans-Globe Expedition traveled south from Greenwich, London, UK, on September 2, 1979, crossed the South Pole on December 15, 1980, the North Pole on April 10, 1982, and returned to Greenwich on August 29, 1982, after a 35,000-mile (56,000-km) journey.

UNDERWATER

★ DEEPEST
SEAWATER SCUBA DIVE

Nuno Gomes (South Africa) dived to a depth of 1,044 ft (318.25 m) in the Red Sea off Dahab, Egypt, on June 10, 2005.

★ LONGEST TIME SPENT
LIVING UNDERWATER

Richard Presley (USA) spent 69 days 19 min in a module underwater at a lagoon in Key Largo, Florida, USA, from May 6 to July 14, 1992.

The test was carried out as part of a mission called *Project Atlantis*, devised to explore the effects of living under the sea.

★ NEW RECORD
UPDATED RECORD

EPIC JOURNEYS

★ LONGEST ➡ JOURNEY
BY A SOLAR-POWERED ELECTRIC VEHICLE

The Midnight Sun solar car team from the University of Waterloo in Ontario, Canada, traveled a distance of 9,364 miles (15,070 km) through Canada and the United States, departing from the University of Waterloo on August 7 and finishing at Parliament Hill in Ottawa, Canada, on September 15, 2004. The race team managed to double the mileage of the previous record holders.

★ NEW RECORD
★ UPDATED RECORD

LONGEST LAWNMOWER RIDE

Gary Hatter (USA) traveled a record 14,594.5 miles (23,487.5 km) in 260 consecutive days on his lawnmower. He started in Portland, Maine, USA, on May 31, 2000, and passed through all 48 contiguous US states as well as Canada and Mexico before arriving in Daytona Beach, Florida, USA, on February 14, 2001.

Hatter rode an $11,500 stock Kubota BX2200-60 at a top speed of 9 mph (14.5 km/h), wearing out four sets of front and three sets of rear tires. He completed the journey to raise money for surgery to treat a back injury.

LAND

★ MOST CONQUESTS OF MOUNT EVEREST
Apa Sherpa (Nepal) reached the summit of Mount Everest for the 15th time on May 31, 2005.

FASTEST SEVEN SUMMITS
Andrew Salter (UK) completed the seven-summit ascent in 288 days, between May 16, 2000, when he conquered Everest, Nepal (Asia), and February 27, 2001, when he climbed Aconcagua, Argentina (South America).

Joanne Gambi (UK) achieved the ★fastest seven-summit ascent by a woman. She climbed the highest peak on each continent in 799 days, starting at Mt. McKinley, Alaska, USA (North America), on June 12, 2003, and ending at Puncak Jaya, Indonesia (Australasia), on August 19, 2005.

GREATEST DISTANCE TRAVELED BY RAIL IN 24 HR
On September 3–4, 1992, Norma and Jonathan Carter (UK) traveled (not duplicating any of the journey) by train for 1,766.3 miles (2,842.5 km).

★ FASTEST SPEED IN THE WORLD SOLAR CHALLENGE
Nuna 3 completed the 1,877-mile (3,021-km) 2005 World Solar Challenge race across Australia in 29 hr 11 min at an average speed of 63.84 mph (102.75 km/h).

Nuna 3's builders, the Nuon team from the University of Delft in the Netherlands, left Darwin, Northern Territories, Australia, on September 25 and arrived in Adelaide, South Australia, on September 28, 2005. The World Solar Challenge race takes place every two years. It was devised by Hans Thorstrup (Denmark) and first held in 1987.

TRUE CIRCUMNAVIGATIONS BY BICYCLE
Steven Strange (UK) cycled around the world in 276 days 19 hr 15 min from May 9, 2004 to February 13, 2005, the ★fastest true circumnavigation by bicycle. He cycled 18,424 miles (29,651 km) and traveled more than 24,917 miles (40,100 km). His journey started and finished in Vancouver, Canada, and covered North America, Europe, India, the Far East, Australia, and New Zealand.

The ★youngest person to complete a true circumnavigation by bicycle is Philip White (UK), who achieved his feat aged 24 years 125 days between June 19, 2004 and April 24, 2005. His journey started and ended in Trafalgar Square, London, UK.

★ LOWEST FUEL CONSUMPTION

On January 17, 2006, John and Helen Taylor (UK and Australia, respectively) embarked upon the Shell Fuel Economy Challenge, aiming to drive around the world on as little fuel as possible. The couple drove an unmodified Volkswagen Golf FSI fueled by a new Shell gasoline formulation. They covered a minimum distance of 18,000 miles (28,970 km) in 78 days, using just 344 gal (1,303 litres) of gasoline. This works out at an astonishingly low fuel consumption rate of 22.2 km per litre (52.6 miles per gal).

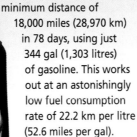

★ FARTHEST MOTORCYCLE RIDE (TEAM)

As of May 2005, Simon and Monika Newbound (UK) had covered over 104,887 miles (168,800 km) on separate motorcycles. They started in Dublin, Ireland, on May 12, 2002.

LONGEST SOLO MOTORCYCLE RIDE BY A WOMAN

Benka Pulko (Slovenia) traveled 111,856 miles (180,016 km) on her solo motorcycle journey through 69 countries and seven continents, which started in Ptuj, Slovenia, on June 19, 1997 and ended at the same location 2,000 days later on December 10, 2002.

FASTEST CIRCUMNAVIGATION BY CAR

The record for the first and fastest man and woman to have circumnavigated the Earth by car covering six continents under the rules applicable in 1989 and 1991 embracing more than an equator's length of driving (24,901 road miles; 40,075 km) is held by Saloo Choudhury and his wife Neena Choudhury (both India).

The journey took 69 days 19 hrs 5 min from September 9 to November 17, 1989. The couple drove a 1989 Hindustan "Contessa Classic" starting and finishing in Delhi, India.

★ LONGEST JOURNEY BY TRACTOR

Vasilii Hazkevich (Russia) covered 13,172 miles (21,199 km) on an unmodified tractor from April 25 to August 6, 2005, starting and finishing in Vladimir, Russia.

LONGEST WIND-POWERED LAND JOURNEY

Robert Torline (USA) traveled 2,119 miles (3,410 km) – from Brownsville, Texas, USA, to Maida, North Dakota, USA – on his wind-powered *Streetsailor* from April 29 to June 16, 2001.

★ LONGEST ONGOING PILGRIMAGE

The greatest distance claimed for an "around-the-world" pilgrimage is 37,015 miles (59,571 km) by Arthur Blessitt (USA), covered in 37 years since December 25, 1969. He has visited all seven continents, including Antarctica, having crossed 305 "nations, island groups and territories," while carrying a 12-ft-tall (3.7-m) wooden cross and preaching from the Bible along the way.

★ FASTEST SURFACE JOURNEY TO THE NORTH POLE

Starting on March 21, 2005, and arriving on April 26, an expedition consisting of Tom Avery (UK), Matty McNair (Canada), Andrew Gerber (South Africa), George Wells (UK), Hugh Dale-Harris (Canada), and a team of 16 husky dogs reached the North Pole in 36 days 22 hr 11 min. They left from Cape Columbia on Ellesmere Island in Arctic Canada and were attempting to re-create, as closely as possible, the disputed 1909 expedition of explorer Robert Peary (USA).

EPIC JOURNEYS

★FASTEST PISTON-POWERED HELICOPTER SPEED OVER A CLOSED CIRCUIT OF 100 KM

Roger André Eilertsen (Norway) achieved a speed of 140 mph (225.41 km/h) over a closed circuit of 62.13 miles (100 km) in Oslo, Norway, on November 13, 2005, flying a Robinson RH-44 helicopter. Roger set four other Fédération Aéronautique Internationale (FAI) world records on this day, bringing his total to seven.

★ **NEW RECORD**
★ **UPDATED RECORD**

! X-REF

What's the farthest distance covered on a single, nonstop commercial aircraft flight? The one-off journey took place in 2005. Find out more on p.201.

SEA

★ FASTEST CROSSING OF THE ENGLISH CHANNEL BY SINGLE CANOE (KAYAK)

Ian Tordoff (UK) paddled a kayak across the English Channel in a time of 3 hr 21 min between Folkestone, Kent, UK, and Wisant, France, on May 18, 2005.

★ FASTEST UNSUPPORTED ROW AROUND THE BRITISH MAINLAND

Lt. William de Laszlo, Lt. Ben Jesty, Sgt. James Bastin, and William Turnage (all UK) rowed around the British mainland in 26 days 21 hr 14 min from June 7 to July 4, 2005. They did not touch land or receive any physical assistance during the journey, which was over 2,000 miles (3,200 km) long, starting and finishing at Tower Bridge in London, UK.

★ FASTEST POWERBOAT CIRCUMNAVIGATION OF THE BRITISH MAINLAND

The fastest circumnavigation of mainland Britain (not including Ireland) took 27 hr 10 min at an average speed of 53.5 knots

(61.6 mph; 99.1 km/h) and was accomplished by Neil McGrigor, Tony Jenvey, Jeremy Watts, and John Guille (all UK) in *Bradstone Challenger*, a Bladerunner 51 powerboat. The 1,691-mile (2,721-km) journey started in Southampton on August 11, 2005, and finished there the following day.

FASTEST SOLO ROW ACROSS PACIFIC (EAST–WEST)

Jim Shekhdar (UK) rowed across the Pacific Ocean in 273 days 13 hr 12 min, beginning from Ilo in Peru on June 29, 2000, and ending near Brisbane, Australia, on March 30, 2001. He made the estimated 9,100-mile (14,650-km) journey without any support in his 33-ft (10-m) custom-built boat *Le Shark*.

★ FASTEST SOLO ROW ACROSS THE ATLANTIC (EAST–WEST)

The fastest solo row across the Atlantic, as recognized by the Ocean Rowing Society, is by Emmanuel Coindre (France), who made the 2,891-nautical-mile (5,354-km) journey between Playa Santiago, La Gomera, Canary Islands, and Port St. Charles, Barbados, in 42 days 14 hr 31 min, from January 7 to February 19, 2004.

★ OLDEST PERSON TO SAIL AROUND THE WORLD (SOLO AND NONSTOP)

Minoru Saito (Japan) was 71 years old when he completed a nonstop solo circumnavigation of the world in his 50-ft (15-m) yacht *Shuten-doji II* on June 6, 2005, becoming the oldest person to sail around the world. His 233-day journey, which started and finished near the Japanese port of Misaki, covered around 31,000 miles (50,000 km).

FASTEST TIME TO SAIL AROUND THE WORLD (SOLO)

Ellen MacArthur (UK) sailed solo and nonstop around the world in 71 days 14 hr

18 min 33 sec from November 28, 2004 to February 7, 2005, in the trimaran *B&Q*. She started off at Ushant, France, rounded the Cape of Good Hope in South Africa, sailed south of Australia, and rounded Cape Horn in Argentina before heading back up to Ushant.

FASTEST TIME TO SAIL AROUND THE WORLD (CREW)

A crew of 14, captained by Bruno Peyron (France), sailed around the world from Ushant, France, in 50 days 16 hr 20 min 4 sec in the maxi catamaran *Orange II* from January 24 to March 16, 2005.

★ FIRST WOMAN TO SAIL AROUND THE WORLD (SOLO AND NONSTOP)

Kay Cottee (Australia) left Sydney, Australia, on November 29,1987, in her 36-ft (11-m) yacht *First Lady* and returned there 189 days later.

★ GREATEST DISTANCE BY KAYAK IN 24 HOURS (FLOWING WATER)

Ultra-endurance multisport champion Ian Adamson (USA) paddled a kayak down the Yukon River, Canada, for 261.6 miles (421 km). The record was set over 24 hours on June 20–21, 2004.

★ LONGEST NONSTOP FLIGHT (ANY AIRCRAFT)

The longest nonstop flight by any aircraft was achieved by Steve Fossett (USA) who flew 26,389.3 miles (42,469.4 km) in the Virgin Atlantic *GlobalFlyer*. Fossett took off from the Kennedy Space Center in Florida, USA, on February 8, 2006, and landed 76 hr 45 min later in Bournemouth, Dorset, UK, on February 11, 2006.

He beat the previous record, held by the *Breitling Orbiter 3* balloon, by 102.8 miles (165.4 km) and with only 200 lb (90 kg) of fuel remaining from an initial load of 18,100 lb (8,210 kg).

★ YOUNGEST PERSON TO ROW THE ATLANTIC

Oliver Hicks (UK, b. December 3, 1981) crossed the Atlantic from west to east solo and unsupported between May 27 and September 28, 2005, aged 23 years 299 days. He rowed from Atlantic Highlands, New Jersey, USA, to St. Mary's, Isles of Scilly, UK, in 123 days 22 hr 8 min to become the ★ **first person to row from the USA to the UK solo and unsupported**, and also the ★ **youngest person to row any ocean solo and unsupported**. He is pictured right with Sir Richard Branson (UK).

AIR

★ LONGEST AIRSHIP FLIGHT

The longest ever nonstop flight by an airship, both in terms of distance covered and duration, was one of 3,967 miles (6,384.5 km) made by Hugo Eckener (Germany) piloting the *Graf Zeppelin* in November 1928. This historic flight lasted 71 hours and was made over the Atlantic between Lakehurst, New Jersey, USA, and Freidrichshafen, Germany.

★ HIGHEST ALTITUDE FLIGHT IN AN AIRSHIP

The greatest ever altitude reached by an airship (FAI-approved) is 21,699 ft (6,614 m) by David Hempleman-Adams (UK). He achieved the record flying a Boland Rover A-2 over Rosedale, Alberta, Canada, on December 13, 2004.

★ FIRST NONSTOP FLIGHT ACROSS THE ATLANTIC

The first ever nonstop flight across the Atlantic Ocean was made by John William Alcock and Arthur Whitten Brown (both UK). They took off in a Vickers Vimy biplane from St. John's, Newfoundland, Canada, on June 14, 1919, and

landed near Clifden, Ireland, some 16 hr 12 min later. Both men received knighthoods.

FASTEST HELICOPTER CIRCUMNAVIGATION (WEST–EAST)

Simon Oliphant-Hope (UK) flew eastbound around the world in a time of 17 days 14 hr 2 min 27 sec at an average speed of 55.2 mph (88.9 km/h) in an MD 500E single-engined helicopter. His journey took place from June 3 to 21, 2004, with his start and finishing point at Shoreham, West Sussex, UK.

★ HIGHEST HELICOPTER LANDING

On May 14, 2005, Didier Delsalle (France) took off and landed at an altitude of 29,035 ft (8,850 m) in a Eurocopter AS 350 B3 at the summit of Mt. Everest. The very thin air at such altitudes makes it extremely difficult for helicopters to stay airborne.

★ FIRST SOLO AERIAL CIRCUMNAVIGATION

Wiley Post (USA) made the first solo flight around the world from July 15 to 22, 1933, in a Lockheed Vega called *Winnie Mae*. He covered 15,596 miles (25,110 km) in just 7 days 18 hr 49 min. The plane was equipped with new technology of the day such as an automatic pilot.

★ LONGEST JOURNEY BY POWERED PARAGLIDER

From June 18 to July 12, 2004, Bob Holloway (USA) traveled 2,580 miles (4,150 km) from Astoria, Oregon, to Washington, Missouri, USA, in a powered paraglider.

? DID YOU KNOW?

*The **first person to circumnavigate the world under sail, solo, and without stopping**, was Robin Knox-Johnston (UK). He departed from Falmouth, Cornwall, UK, on June 14, 1968, as a participant in the* Sunday Times *Golden Globe Race, and by the time he returned – on April 22, 1969 – he was the only remaining competitor.*

FASTEST SOLO OCEAN ROWERS

OCEAN	NAME	BOAT	START	RECORD
Atlantic (E–W)	Emmanuel Coindre (France)	*Lady Bird*	07/01/04	42d 14h 31m
Atlantic (W–E)	Emmanuel Coindre (France)	*Lady Bird*	07/09/04	62d 19h 48m
Pacific (E–W)	Jim Shekhdar (UK)	*Le Shark*	06/29/00	273d 13h 12m
Mid Pacific (E–W)*	Maud Fontenoy (France)	*Oceor*	01/12/05	72 days
Indian (E–W)	Pavel Rezvoy (Ukraine)	*Ukraine*	11/13/05	57 days

*From Callao, Lima, Peru, to Hiva Oa, Marquesas Islands, French Polynesia

YOUNGEST SOLO OCEAN ROWERS

Atlantic (W–E)	Oliver Hicks (UK)	*Miss Olive*	05/27/05	23 years old
Atlantic (E–W)	Samson Knight (UK)	*Pacific Pete*	01/20/04	23 years old
Pacific (W–E)	Gerard d'Aboville (France)	*Sector*	07/11/91	45 years old
Pacific (E–W)	Peter Bird (UK)	*Hele-on-Britannia*	08/23/82	34 years old
Mid Pacific (E–W)	Patrick Quesnel (USA)	*Hawaiiki*	07/14/76	27 years old
Indian (E–W)	Simon Chalk (UK)	*True Spirit*	02/27/03	30 years old

STRENGTH & STAMINA

★ **NEW RECORD**
★ **UPDATED RECORD**

★ CAR-PUSHING (INDIVIDUAL) – FASTEST MILE

Julian Adams (UK) pushed a van weighing 4,145 lb (1,880 kg) a distance of 1 mile (1.6 km) in 50 min 14 sec at Bruntingthorpe Aerodrome, Leicestershire, UK, on October 3, 2004.

★ LONGEST RODEO RIDE

Nigel Medley (Australia) rode a mechanical bull for 2 min 15 sec in Taylors Arm, New South Wales, Australia, on August 13, 2005.

★ HIGHEST BEER-BARREL LIFT WITH TEETH

On March 6, 2005, in Boxhorn, Luxembourg, Georges Christen (Luxembourg) held in his teeth a rope tied to a 30-lb (14-kg) barrel filled with 105 pints (13 gal) of beer (a total weight of 141 lb or 64 kg), then lifted the barrel to a height of 124 ft (38 m) with the use of a crane.

★ HEAVIEST RIGHT-HAND DEADLIFT – BAR

Hermann Goerner (Germany) officially carried out a right-handed deadlift of 663 lb 8 oz (301 kg)

★ GREATEST WEIGHT SUPPORTED ON THE SHOULDERS

Franz Müllner (Austria) supported an average of 1,144 lb (519 kg) on his shoulders for 30 seconds while a 4,409-lb (2,000-kg) helicopter landed on a frame that he was partially supporting on his back. The record was achieved on the set of *Guinness World Records: Die größten Weltrekorde* on September 24, 2005.

on October 29, 1920, in Leipzig, Germany, using a Berg Olympic revolving bar. He unofficially lifted a 727 lb 8 oz (330-kg) bar with his right hand on October 8, 1920, also in Leipzig.

★ HIGHEST BEER-KEG TOSS

Juha Rasanen (Finland) threw a 27 lb 1 oz (12.3-kg) beer keg over a 23-ft 3-in (7.1-m) bar on the set of *L'Été De Tous Les Records* in Benodet, France, on August 26, 2005.

★ HEAVIEST WEIGHT LIFTED WITH LITTLE FINGERS

On October 19, 2005, Barry Anderson (UK) lifted a 138 lb 12 oz (63-kg) bar with his little fingers at the Open International Grip Championships in Norwood, Massachusetts, USA.

He also holds the record for the **heaviest deadlift with the little finger** at 197 lb 8 oz (89.6 kg).

★ MOST ➡ POWERFUL LUNGS

The inflation of a standard meteorological balloon weighing 2.2 lb (1 kg) to a diameter of 8 ft (2.44 m) against time was achieved by Manjit Singh (UK) in 42 minutes at Rushley Pavilion Centre, Leicester, UK, on September 16, 1998.

FARTHEST...

★ DISTANCE TO PUSH A CAR IN 24 HOURS (PAIR)

Rob Kmet and Adam Zeglen (both Canada) pushed a 2,600-lb (1,180-kg) Dodge SX 2.0 a distance of 43.67 miles (70.28 km) around a 1-mile (1.6-km) oval race track at Gimli Motorsports Park in Gimli, Manitoba, Canada, on September 2–3, 2005.

★ DISTANCE TO THROW A PERSON

Juha Rasanen (Finland) threw a person weighing 132 lb (60 kg) a distance of 12 ft 8 in (3.87 m) on to a pre-marked mattress on the set of *Lo Show Dei Record* in Milan, Italy, on January 5, 2006.

★ DISTANCE TRAVELED ON A HAND-CRANKED CYCLE IN 24 HOURS

Didier Simons (Belgium) covered 255.93 miles (411.88 km) on a hand-cranked cycle in 24 hours around a circuit at Hannut, Belgium, on August 27–28, 2004.

FASTEST...

★ MILE (CRAWLING)

Christopher Holl (UK) crawled 1 mile (1.6 km) in 37 min 33 sec at Kettering Athletics Track, Northamptonshire, UK, on December 11, 2004.

★ PIANO-LIFT STAIR CLIMB

On December 5, 2001, José Angel Aria Villanueva (Spain) climbed a 15-step staircase spanning 8 ft 2 in (2.5 m), carrying a piano stool, then returned to carry up a 385-lb (175-kg) piano – all in 1 min 6.35 sec – before sitting down to play the piano for three minutes on the set of *El Show De Los Récords*, Madrid, Spain.

★ TIME TO BREAK 16 CONCRETE BLOCKS ON BODY

On June 19, 2005, Neal Hardy (Australia) piled 16 concrete blocks on his chest and had them broken with a sledgehammer by Patrick Bellchambers (Australia) in 11.57 seconds on the set of *Guinness World Records* at Seven Network Studios, Sydney, New South Wales, Australia.

★ BODY-VERTICAL ONE-HAND HOP – 10 M

On August 12, 2005, Rodolfo Reyes (Germany) completed a body-vertical one-hand hop over 32 ft 9 in (10 m) in 14.8 seconds at Flensburg, Germany.

★ COAL-BAG CARRYING

David Jones (UK) carried a 110-lb (50-kg) bag over the 3,321-ft 9-in (1,012.5-m) course at the annual Coal Carrying Championship Race, Gawthorpe, West Yorkshire, UK, in a time of 4 min 6 sec on April 1, 1991.

The record for the ★ **fastest time for a woman to carry a coal bag** in the same race is held by Viki Gibson (UK), who carried a 44-lb (20-kg) bag over the course in 4 min 48 sec on March 28, 2005.

MOST...

★ ANVIL LIFTS IN 90 SECONDS

Alain Bidart (France) performed 88 anvil (weighing at least 39 lb 9 oz; 18 kg) lifts in 90 seconds in Soulac, France, on August 17, 2005.

★ TELEPHONE DIRECTORIES TORN TOP TO BOTTOM IN THREE MINUTES

Ed Shelton (USA) ripped 55 telephone directories from top to bottom – each with 1,044 numbered pages – in three minutes at the Waste Management of America Recycling Facility in Reno, Nevada, USA, on November 18, 2005.

★ CHIN-UPS IN 12 HOURS

Stephen Hyland (UK) performed 2,222 chin-ups in Stoneleigh, Surrey, UK, on November 9, 2005.

★ 220-LB STONE LIFTS IN ONE MINUTE (FORCE BASQUE)

Jose Jamon Izeta (Spain) carried out 22 lifts of a 220-lb (100-kg) stone in one minute on the set of *L'Été De Tous Les Records* in Soulac, France, on August 16, 2005.

★ HEAVIEST ➡ WEIGHT HUNG FROM A SWALLOWED SWORD

Matthew Henshaw (Australia) swallowed a 15.9-in-long (40.5-cm) sword and then held a sack of potatoes weighing 44 lb 4 oz (20.1 kg) attached to the handle of the sword for five seconds at the studios of *Guinness World Records*, Sydney, Australia, on April 16, 2005.

★ FASTEST ⬆ CROSSING OF THE ENGLISH CHANNEL ON A PADDLEBOARD

A paddleboard is a long, narrow board that the rider can lie, kneel, or stand on, as with a conventional surfboard. On September 11, 2005, Pete Craske and James Cracknell (both UK) took 5 hr 26 min to paddle their boards across the English Channel.

MARATHONS

★ CLUB ⬇ DJ SET

Damion Houchen, a.k.a. DJ Genix (UK), played a mixing session that lasted for a total of 84 hours at Beavers Bar in Hinckley, Leicestershire, UK, from February 16 to 19, 2005.

SINGING ⇢ MARATHONS

Hartmut Timm (Germany, right) sang for 54 hr 41 min in Müritz, Germany, from November 8 to 10, 2005, setting a record for the ★ **longest singing marathon**. Comunidade Evangélica Luterana Da Paz (Brazil) sang for 36 hours at the Campus Chapel, ULBRA, Canoas, Brazil, on July 3–4, 2004, the ★ **longest singing marathon (team)**. The Durg-Bhilai Lifecraft Singers choral group (India) sang for 31 hr 45 min at the Kalamandir Civic Center, Bhilai, Chhattisgarh, India, the ★ **longest singing marathon by a group**, on February 5–6, 2005.

★ ARCHERY SESSION

Eight archers carried out a 24-hour archery session at Bogenschießanlage am Sägewerk, Traunreut, Germany, on July 24–25, 2004.

★ BASEBALL

A game of baseball lasting 25 hours was played at Beckwith Recreational Complex, Mississippi Mills, Ontario, Canada, on October 18–19, 2003. The White team played the Gray team through 68 innings with a final score of 99–86 to the Gray team.

★ BASKETBALL

Titans Basketball Club played a basketball marathon that lasted 40 hr 3 min at the Galway-Mayo Institute of Technology, Galway, Ireland, on September 23–24, 2005.

★ WHEELCHAIR BASKETBALL

Staff and students at the University of Omaha, Nebraska, USA, played for 26 hr 3 min on September 24–25, 2004.

★ CHURCH-ORGAN PLAYING

Matthew Penn (UK) played a church organ for 33 hr 5 min at the Holy Trinity Church, Stratford-upon-Avon, Warwickshire, UK, from March 31 to April 1, 2005.

★ CONCERT BY A GROUP

A concert by the Arsuz Hi-Jazz Band (Turkey) lasted 44 hr 20 min in Arsuz, Hatay, Turkey, on August 18–20, 2005.

★ CONTINUOUS CRAWL

The longest continuous voluntary crawl (progression with one or the other knee in unbroken contact with the ground) is 35.18 miles (56.62 km) by Suresh Joachim (Australia), who completed over 2,500 laps of a circuit 66 ft (20.1 m) in circumference outside the Queen Victoria Building, Sydney, New South Wales, Australia, on May 18–19, 2001.

★ DANCE SESSION

Suresh Joachim (Australia) performed a dance marathon lasting 100 hours at the Dixie Outlet Mall, Mississauga, Ontario, Canada. The performance lasted from February 16 to 20, 2005.

★ LONGEST ⬇ SOFTBALL MARATHON

The longest game of softball lasted 95 hr 23 min and took place at Ed Janiszewski Park, Dollard-des-Ormeaux, Quebec, Canada, from June 29 to July 3, 2005. After 417 complete innings the final score was Delmar 774, Renmark 729.

This game of softball was a charity match for Montreal Children's Hospital and the Starlight Children's Foundation of Canada.

★ LONGEST ↑ RADIO DJ MARATHON

Marko Potrc (Slovenia) carried out a radio DJ marathon that lasted a total of 122 hours on the Radio Center station in Maribor, Slovenia, from November 21 to 26, 2004.

★ DEBATE

The Rostrum Clubs of Tasmania, with members of the Tasmanian community (725 people in all), debated the motion "Tasmania's greatest asset is its people" for 29 days 4 hr 3 min and 20 sec from November 2 to December 1, 1996. The debate took place on the lawns of Parliament House, Hobart, Tasmania, Australia.

★ DRUM KIT SESSION (TEAM)

Fourteen drummers played for 52 hr 15 min at the Nexus Music Academy, Coventry, West Midlands, UK, from May 17 to 19, 2005.

★ ELVIS-STYLE SINGING

Thomas "Curtis" Gäthje (Germany) performed an Elvis Presley singing marathon that lasted for a total time of 43 hr 11 min 11 sec at Modehaus Böttcher, Heide, Germany, from June 24 to 26, 2004.

★ SOCCER

The Tyson and Snickers teams played football for 26 hr 24 min at the Ingram FC Complex, Centerton, Arkansas, USA, on August 19–20, 2005.

★ GUITAR PLAYING

Brian Engelhart (USA) played guitar for 44 hours at Mo Doggie's Bar and Grill, Fenton, Michigan, USA, from June 14 to 16, 2005.

★ GROUP DRUM ROLL

A drum roll lasting 12 hr 49 min 33 sec was played by eight students at Lake Orion High School, Michigan, USA, on January 15, 2005.

★ HANDBELL RINGING

Joe Defries (Canada) played the handbells for 28 hr 50 min 21 sec at the Penticton Convention Center, Penticton, British Columbia, Canada, on July 25–26, 2005.

★ INDOOR HOCKEY

Members of Mandel Bloomfield AZA played a game of indoor (or floor) hockey for 24 hours at the Talmud Torah School, Edmonton, Alberta, Canada, on February 28–29, 2004.

★ LECTURE

Narayanam Siva Sankar (India) talked on the subject of the "Fundamentals of Hindi Grammar" for 72 hr 9 min, from November 28 to December 1, 2004, at the Sree Bharathi Residential School, Eluru, Andhra Pradesh, India.

★ LESSON

David Specchio and 30 pupils (all China) from English First in Shanghai, China, took part in a lesson about the English language that lasted 72 hours, from September 9 to 12, 2005.

★ RAPPING

DO (a.k.a. Duane Gibson, Canada) rapped continuously for 8 hr 45 min at Dark Knights Nationals Car Show, Toronto, Ontario, Canada, on July 5, 2003.

★ READING ALOUD (TEAM)

A team of four – Linda Bagnal, Emily Churchman, Angela Furney, and Shirley Horn (all USA) – read aloud continuously for 110 hr 4 min at the Barnes & Noble bookstore in Wilmington, North Carolina, USA, from October 17 to 21, 2005.

★ SITAR

Shambhu Das (Canada) played sitar for 24 hours at the University of Toronto, Ontario, Canada, on October 8–9, 2004.

★ SKIING

Nick Willey (Australia) skiied non-stop for 202 hr 1 min at Thredbo, New South Wales, Australia, from September 2 to 10, 2005.

★ LONGEST WAKEBOARDING MARATHON

Ian Taylor (UK) wakeboarded behind a cable tow at Whitecap Leisure on Willen Lake, Milton Keynes, Buckinghamshire, UK, for 6 hr 17 min on September 1, 2004.

★ NEW RECORD
★ UPDATED RECORD

★ LONGEST HAND DRUM MARATHON

Kuzhalmannam Ramakrishnan (India) played a hand drum for 101 hours in Cannanore, Kerala, India, from May 25 to 29, 2005.

MASS PARTICIPATION

⭐ LARGEST FREEFALL FORMATION (PARACHUTING)

A freefall formation consisting of 400 skydivers from 31 countries was formed at an altitude of 24,000 ft (7,300 m) over Udonthani, Thailand, on February 8, 2006. The event was organized by World Team '06 and formed part of the Thailand Royal Sky Celebration, supported by the Royal Thai Air Force and performed in honor of the Thai royal family.

⭐ COUPLES KISSING SIMULTANEOUSLY

A record 5,875 couples kissed at an event organized by Színes Bulvár Lap and SuperGroup Ltd on the Elisabeth Bridge, Budapest, Hungary, on June 25, 2005.

LARGEST...

⭐ CUSTARD-PIE FIGHT (MOST PEOPLE)

Two groups share this record. On October 7, 1998, 50 people – including the band Electrasy – threw 4,400 pies in three minutes for the band's video of their single "Best Friend's Girl," released on November 9, 1998. The video was filmed in London, UK.

On August 27, 2005, 50 pupils from the Craigdhu Primary School, Glasgow, UK, threw 1,000 pies as part of The Saturday Show (BBC).

⭐ GATHERING OF PEOPLE DRESSED AS CELL PHONES

Organized by The Phone House Company, Rotterdam, Netherlands, a group of 150 students gathered

⭐ LARGEST UNDERWATER WEDDING

On March 26, 2005, 208 divers in full scuba gear submerged themselves in Bakersfield, California, USA, to witness the marriage between Stuart J. Rex and Misty Kuykendall (both USA, below).

On Valentine's Day 2001, 34 couples from 22 countries exchanged their wedding vows at a depth of 32 ft (10 m) off the coast of Kradan Island, southern Thailand, creating the record for the **most couples married underwater** (right).

FASTEST...

⭐ TIME TO LAY DOWN A MILE OF PENNIES

The fastest time to lay down a mile of pennies is 2 hr 26 min 7 sec. The feat was achieved by representatives of the Willow Canyon Elementary School in Sandy, Utah, USA, on March 11, 2004.

⭐ BANDAGE RELAY

A total of 215 arm slings were applied in one hour by children from St. Fagan's Church in Wales Primary School, along with trainers from St. John Cymru Wales, in Cardiff, UK, on July 7, 2005.

⭐ TIME TO POP 1,000 BALLOONS

Without using any sharp objects, a team from the advertising agency Claydon Heeley Jones Mason (UK) took 27.12 seconds to burst 1,000 balloons at Harrow School, Middlesex, UK, on August 18, 2005.

MOST...

PEOPLE STUFFED INTO A NEW MINI

On August 20, 2004, 21 people squeezed into a standard new Mini Cooper at the Galea Music Club in Athens, Greece.

HUGS IN ONE HOUR

Marianne Harjula (Finland) hugged 612 people in one hour in Tuuri, Finland, on September 4, 2004.

TOP 10 SINGLE-VENUE RECORD ATTEMPTS

RECORD*	PARTICIPANTS	LOCATION	DATE
Largest walk	77,500	Singapore	May 21, 2000
Trash collection	74,206	Japan	Oct. 3, 2004
Simultaneous marriage	35,000 couples	South Korea	Aug. 25, 1995
Aerobics class	48,188	Philippines	Feb. 16, 2003
Human logo	34,309	Portugal	Jul. 24, 1999
Martial-arts display	30,648	China	Apr. 10, 2004
Human rainbow	30,365	Philippines	Sep. 18, 2004
Breakfast	27,854	Germany	May 29, 2005
Artwork	25,297	USA	Jun. 14, 1998
Bubble-blowing	23,680	UK	May 16, 1999

*Only those events at which the final head count has been verified

★ MARACAS ENSEMBLE

A maracas ensemble consisting of 407 people – led by Happy Mondays star Bez (UK) – shook their maracas for the launch of the XFM radio station in Manchester, UK, on March 15, 2006.

★ LOCOMOTION DANCE

A locomotion dance involving 673 participants took place at an event organized by the HBOS (Halifax and Bank of Scotland) Foundation at the Corn Exchange, Leeds, UK, on November 23, 2005.

★ GAME OF TELEPHONE (A.K.A. "CHINESE WHISPERS")

A record 814 students and their parents from Somerville Elementary School, Ridgewood, New Jersey, USA, took part in a game of Chinese whispers (a.k.a. "Telephone") on April 15, 2005.

★ DANCE BY COUPLES

A total of 422 couples danced an Austrian *Klatschpolka* for five minutes at an event arranged by Life Radio in Linz, Austria, on November 24, 2005.

★ SIMULTANEOUS FLYING-DISC THROW

The most people to simultaneously throw flying discs is 853 at an event held at Bethel College, North Newton, Kansas, USA, on October 1, 2005.

★ MOST CURLY WURLYS STRETCHED IN ONE VENUE

On October 30, 2005, at the Renaissance Hotel in Heathrow, UK, 126 members of the "Get Amanda Back In Town" (GABIT) fan club – a group dedicated to *Stargate SG-1* star Amanda Tapping (UK) – each stretched a Curly Wurly candy bar. The aim of the record is to stretch the chocolate-caramel lattice as far as possible in three minutes.

★ LARGEST AUDIENCE FOR A COMEDIAN

UK comedian Lee Evans performed at the MEN Arena, Manchester, UK, on December 19, 2005, to an audience of 10,108. The size of the audience was calculated by the number of tickets sold at the venue's box office.

★ MOST PEOPLE WEARING BALLOON HATS

A record 1,491 people donned balloon hats at an event organized by Sentosa Leisure Group at Siloso Beach, Sentosa Island, Singapore, on June 4, 2005.

together dressed as cell phones on March 18, 2006. The Phone House was celebrating the opening of its 150th shop, located in Rotterdam.

★ DANCE CLASS

Darrin Henson (UK) led a dance class involving 242 participants at the Trafford Centre, Manchester, UK, on August 20, 2005.

★ AQUA-AEROBICS DISPLAY

On November 14, 2005, an aqua-aerobics display comprising 247 participants took place at Vannkanten Waterworld in Loddefjord, Bergen, Norway.

★ LION-DANCE DISPLAY

The Singapore National Wushu Federation set a new Guinness World Record by organizing a lion dance display consisting of 328 lions. The dance took place at the Jurong East Sports Complex in Singapore on January 23, 2005.

★ GATHERING OF DANCING DRAGONS

The largest gathering of dancing dragons involved 40 dragons – each operated by 10 dancers – and took place at the Taman Jurong Community Club in Taman Jurong, Singapore, on March 5, 2005.

★ NEW RECORD
★ UPDATED RECORD

MASS PARTICIPATION

★ **NEW RECORD**
☆ **UPDATED RECORD**

☆ LARGEST HUMAN NATIONAL FLAG

On February 5, 2006, a total of 13,254 fans attending the Scotland vs. France Six Nations rugby match in the East Stadium of Murrayfield Rugby Club in Edinburgh, UK, formed the Saltire (the Scottish national flag). The achievement clearly inspired the Scottish players, who went on to defeat France 20–16.

★ TABLE FOOTBALL TOURNAMENT
In all, 884 participants took part in a table football tournament at the Olympic Stadium in Berlin, Germany, on December 9, 2005.

★ GAME OF "SIMON SAYS"
A game of "Simon Says" involving 1,169 participants was staged at Victoria Park, Glasgow, UK, on April 22, 2006.

★ COMPUTER CLASS
On January 15, 2006, 1,135 students at the Shandong Lanxiang School in Jinan City, Shandong province, China, took part in a computer lesson.

☆ WATER-PISTOL FIGHT
The largest water-pistol fight involved 1,173 participants at Loyola Marymount University, Los Angeles, California, USA, on April 28, 2005.

★ GOLF-BALL STRIKE
The greatest number of golf balls hit simultaneously at multiple venues is 1,453. They were struck at 13 different golf courses during events organized to celebrate the National University of Singapore's 100th anniversary on February 19, 2006. The challenge drew a total of 1,710 golfers – 257 of whom failed to drive the ball 100 yd (300 ft; 91 m), or to keep the shot between a marked area of 60°.

★ COCONUT ENSEMBLE
The largest number of people gathered in one location playing coconuts – that is, banging the two halves together – at the same time is 1,789 outside the Shubert Theater in New York City, USA, to the tune of Monty Python's "Always Look on the Bright Side of Life" to celebrate the one-year anniversary of the Broadway show Spamalot on March 22, 2006.

☆ MACARENA DANCE
A record 1,829 people simultaneously danced the Macarena on the set of L'Été De Tous Les Records in Benodet, France, on August 26, 2005.

← ★ LARGEST FIRST-AID LESSON
The largest first-aid lesson involved 408 participants. It was organized by the Bavarian Red Cross and took place at the DJK Neustadt Football Stadium, Neustadt, Germany, on May 29, 2005.

★ CPR TRAINING SESSION
The largest cardiopulmonary resuscitation (CPR) training session involved 2,152 participants and was organized by the San Diego/Imperial Counties Chapter of the American Red Cross in San Diego, California, USA, on March 5, 2005.

☆ HAKA
In all, 2,200 participants performed a Haka – a Maori ceremonial dance – in Federation Square, Melbourne, Australia, on September 3, 2005.

☆ WATER-BALLOON FIGHT
On March 23, 2006, 2,849 participants threw 55,000 water balloons at Coogee Beach, Australia, to mark the launch of the Xbox 360 console.

☆ CUSTARD-PIE FIGHT (MOST PIES)
The largest custard-pie fight – in terms of number of pies thrown, as opposed to number of participants – involved 3,320 pies thrown by two teams of 10 in three minutes at Bolton Arena, Bolton, UK, on August 29, 2005.

☆ HEART FORMATION
A total of 3,600 participants formed the shape of a heart at an event organized by the Hungarian National Blood Transfusion Service in Budapest, Hungary, on August 14, 2005.

★ LARGEST SAME NAME GATHERING (FIRST NAME) ⬆

On February 10, 2005, a total of 1,096 men named Mohammed congregated at Creek Park, Dubai, United Arab Emirates, as part of the Dubai Shopping Festival.

★ PILLOW FIGHT

A pillow fight between 3,648 people took place at the University of Albany, New York, USA, on April 17, 2005.

★ WHOOPEE-CUSHION SIT

The largest simultaneous whoopee-cushion sit featured a total of 5,983 participants and was staged at the Catalyst Conference in Atlanta, Georgia, USA, on October 6, 2005.

★ IRISH DANCE

On September 10, 2005, 7,664 dancers took to the streets for an Irish dance organized by the City of Cork council in Cork, Ireland.

★ HORSE PARADE

A horse parade involving 8,125 horses and their riders took place in Santa Catarina, Brazil, on August 27, 2005, at an event organized by Abracamp (Brazil).

★ EASTER-EGG HUNT

The largest Easter-egg hunt consisted of 301,000 eggs that were searched for by 5,189 children and 4,834 adults – totaling 10,023 people – at Stone Mountain Park, Georgia, USA, for the release of *Peter Cottontail: The Movie* on April 9, 2006.

★ TOAST

The most people performing a toast at one venue is 10,079, set at the Oodori Parade Zone, Sapporo, Hokkaido, Japan, on June 7, 2003.

★ HORO DANCE

The largest *horo* – a Bulgarian circle dance often set in an asymmetrical meter such as 25/16 – involved 11,961 participants and took place in Sofia, Bulgaria, on May 2, 2005.

★ TIN-CAN MOSAIC

In March 2006, during National Volunteers Week in Johannesburg, South Africa, a mosaic comprising 41,064 cans of food was laid by health insurance company Discovery (South Africa).

★ TEA PARTY

The largest simultaneous tea party was arranged by The Cancer Council (Australia) and involved 280,246 participants at 6,062 locations across Australia on May 26, 2005.

ANNUAL GATHERING OF WOMEN

In February or March each year, more than 1 million women gather at the Attukal Bhagavathy Temple in Thiruvananthapuram, Kerala, India, for the "Pongala" offering. The women, from all religions and communities in Kerala, gather with their cooking pots to perform a ritual for the health and prosperity of their families. In February 1997, 1.5 million women attended the festival, the event's largest-ever gathering.

★ GAY FESTIVAL

On May 29, 2005, the annual MiX Brasil: Festival of Sexual Diversity in São Paulo, Brazil, attracted a crowd of 1.8 million people.

★ CARNIVAL

Rio de Janeiro's street carnival in March attracts around 2 million people each day. In 2004, the carnival attracted a record 400,000 foreign visitors, 2,600 of whom were thought to be from the *Queen Mary 2* ship.

HUMAN CHAIN

On December 11, 2004, over 5 million people formed a human chain that reached 652 miles (1,050 km) long from Teknaf to Tentulia, Bangladesh.

★ LARGEST GATHERING OF PEOPLE DRESSED AS GORILLAS ⬆

On your marks... get set... Go... rilla! In London, UK, on September 25, 2005, 637 participants took part in the Great Gorilla Fun Run to raise money for The Dian Fossey Gorilla Fund.

! X-REF

*The **largest anti-war rally** drew a crowd of 3 million people to which European city? You'll find the answer on p.118.*

118

JUST A MINUTE...

★ 180° BICYCLE JUMPS

Kenny Belaey (Belgium) managed 26 180° bicycle jumps in a minute on the set of *L'Été De Tous Les Records* in Cabourg, France, on August 4, 2005.

★ APPLES BOBBED

James Cracknell (UK) bobbed five apples in one minute on ITV's *The Paul O'Grady Show* at the London Studios, UK, on March 23, 2005.

! X-REF

Want to get your name in the record books? You can start by checking out these 60-second marvels... Can you do any better? **Contact us first** *for guidelines – find out how on p.7 – then grab a stopwatch and see for yourself.*

★ NEW RECORD
★ UPDATED RECORD

★ APPLES CUT IN THE AIR BY SWORD

Using a samurai sword, Kenneth Lee (USA) sliced 21 apples in the air in one minute at the Way of the Tiger Karate Do Academy in New Jersey, USA, on May 30, 2004.

COCKROACHES EATEN ➡

Ken Edwards (UK) ate 36 cockroaches in one minute on the set of *The Big Breakfast* (Channel 4, UK) on March 5, 2001. Ken's technique is to pop the roach – which, according to Guinness World Records rules, must be the fully grown Madagascar hissing variety – into his mouth and crush its head with his back teeth. "This stops them wriggling and scratching my gullet on the way down!" says the former rat-catcher.

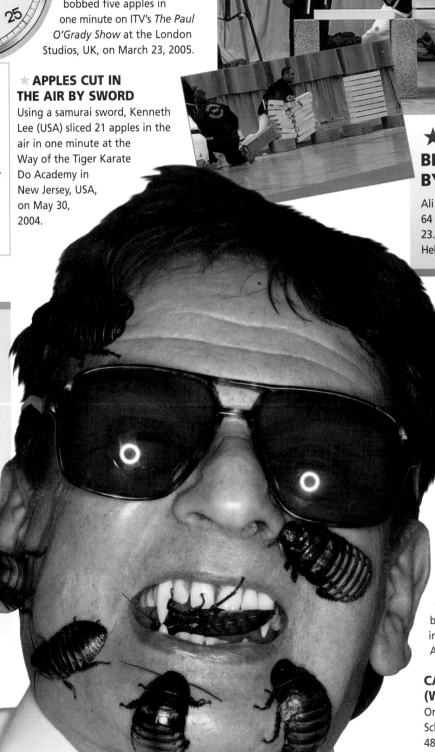

★ CONCRETE ⬆ BLOCKS BROKEN BY HAND

Ali Chehade (Sweden) smashed 64 blocks, each measuring 2.7 x 23.6 x 7.8 in (7 x 60 x 20 cm), in Helsingborg, Sweden, on May 30, 2004.

BEER BOTTLES OPENED WITH TEETH

Jose Ivan Hernandez (USA) removed 56 beer bottle caps with his teeth in 60 seconds at the television studios of *Ricki Lake*, New York City, USA, on December 5, 2001.

★ BRAS UNHOOKED

Using one hand only, Rick Canzler (Australia) unhooked 42 bras through one layer of clothing in a minute on the set of *Guinness World Records* in Sydney, New South Wales, Australia, on June 19, 2005.

★ BULLWHIP CRACKS

Chris Camp (USA) cracked a bullwhip 222 times in a minute in Springfield, Illinois, USA, on April 29, 2005.

CARTWHEELS (WITH HANDS)

On November 1, 1997, Brianna Schroeder (USA) performed 48 complete cartwheels at the GymCarolina Gymnastics Academy in Raleigh, North Carolina, USA.

★ SOCCER BALL TOUCHES WITH HEAD

The most touches of a soccer ball in one minute, using only the head to keep the ball in the air, is 319 by Erick Hernández (Cuba) at La Giraldilla, Havana, Cuba, on December 11, 2004. He is pictured here with Cuban leader Fidel Castro.

★ CARTWHEELS (WITHOUT HANDS)

Pierre-Henri Toubas (France) performed 37 cartwheels without using his hands in one minute on the set of *L'Été De Tous Les Records* in Soulac, France, on August 15, 2005.

★ CHIN-UPS

Robert Natoli (USA) performed a total of 40 chin-ups in one minute in Oswego, New York, USA, on February 4, 2006.

★ ELASTIC BANDS
STRETCHED OVER THE FACE ➡

On a visit to the London, UK, offices of Guinness World Records in December 2005, Matthew Winn (UK) set a new world record by stretching 44 regular elastic bands over his head, one at a time, in just one minute. To qualify for this record, the unstretched elastic bands must be no longer than 4 in (10 cm).

★ COIN ROLLS

De'vo vom Schattenreich (Belgium) passed a half-dollar coin around the fingers of his right hand a total of 45 times in one minute in Ulmen, Germany, on November 19, 2005.

★ CUSTARD PIES THROWN (TWO PEOPLE)

Vince Nickel (thrower) and Rob Hart (receiver, both UK) threw and caught 12 custard pies on the set of *The Paul O'Grady Show* at the London Studios, UK, on March 30, 2005.

★ DRUMBEATS (HANDS)

George Urosevic (Australia) hit 1,168 single-stroke beats in a minute in Sydney, New South Wales, Australia, on June 26, 2005.

★ MARTIAL-ARTS PUNCHES

Paddy Doyle (UK) recorded 470 martial-arts punches in one minute at the Tummelum Festival in Flensburg, Germany, on August 13, 2005.

★ NAILS HAMMERED INTO WOOD

British TV DIY expert Andy Kane (UK) – a.k.a. "Handy Andy" – hammered 10 nails, each 6-in (15.24-cm) long, into a wooden block in one minute at the *Blue Peter* TV studios in London, UK, on July 25, 2005.

★ POGOSTICK ROPE JUMPS

Ashrita Furman (USA) performed 173 rope skips on his pogostick in one minute at Angkor Wat – the world's **largest religious temple** – in Cambodia on September 6, 2005.

★ SELF-INFLICTED KICKS TO THE HEAD

J. B. Destiny (USA) kicked himself in the forehead a total of 57 times in one minute in Tucson, Arizona, USA, on September 3, 2005.

★ SQUAT THRUSTS

Stuart Burrell (UK) did 23 squat thrusts in one minute at Georges Gym, Rayleigh, Essex, UK, on February 8, 2005.

IN JUST ONE MINUTE...

- light travels 11,184,678 miles (18 million km)

- 150 acres (60 ha) of rainforest – an area larger than the Vatican City – is cut down

- the crew of *Apollo 10* traveled 413 miles (665 km), the **highest speed ever achieved by humans** (May 1969)

- the heart of a clam beats twice, that of a blue whale beats between four and eight times, and a hummingbird's beats more than 1,200 times

- 50,000 text messages are sent globally

- the Earth rotates one-quarter of a degree, traveling the equivalent of 17.27 miles (27.8 km) at the equator

- 112 people die and 260 babies are born worldwide, increasing the world's population by a total of 148 people a minute

- 150 foreign tourists visit France, 31 of them arriving in Paris, the **city that attracts the most visitors in the world**

- a tiny midge of the genus *Forcipomyia* beats its wings 62,760 times

- Nicole Kidman (Australia) earned $928,800 for acting in a television advertisement for Chanel No.5 perfume

- Leonardo D'Andrea (Italy) smashed 36 watermelons, using only his head, while appearing on *Lo Show Dei Record* in Milan, Italy, on January 5, 2006

- 192 bicycles and 78 cars are manufactured around the world

- animal waste produces 121 billion lb (55 million tonnes) of methane

- 133 crimes are reported around the world

IN A DAY...

★ NEW RECORD
☆ UPDATED RECORD

☆ GREATEST DISTANCE RIDING A WATERSLIDE

A team of 10 employees – Jochen Ralle, Thomas Anker, Nils Engelmann, Anders Filipsson, Torsten Kamp, Marcel Kuzyk, Mario Lawendel, Jan-Berendt Stuut, Time Oetjen, and Frank Bahlmann (all Germany) – covered 472.413 miles (760.276 km) in 24 hours on a 242-ft 9-in (74-m) waterslide in Bremen, Germany, on November 11–12, 2005 to mark GWR day.

★ LARGEST FOOD DRIVE BY A NON-CHARITABLE GROUP

A food drive organized by Thunder in the Valley (USA) collected 156,889 lb 5 oz (71,163.8 kg) of food within a 24-hour period starting on September 9, 2005, in Bechtelsville, Pennsylvania, USA.

GREATEST...

☆ DISTANCE ON A SNOWMOBILE – TEAM

Nathan Hudye and Nolan Nykolaishen (both Canada) traveled 2,040.95 miles (3,284.59 km) by snowmobile on a closed circuit at Madge Lake, Saskatchewan, Canada, in 24 hours on March 4–5, 2005.

★ DISTANCE ON A 50-CC SCOOTER

Mark "Brownie" Brown (Australia) traveled 576.6 miles (928 km) on a two-stroke Yamaha Aerox in 24 hours at the Grand Prix Training Centre, South Morang, Victoria, Australia, on August 23–24, 2005.

←■ ★ FASTEST-SELLING FICTION BOOK

Harry Potter and the Half-Blood Prince, the sixth novel in J. K. Rowling's (UK) Harry Potter series, sold 6.9 million copies in the first 24 hours (or 287,564 books per hour), following its release in the USA on July 16, 2005. The novel follows Harry in his sixth year at Hogwarts School of Witchcraft and Wizardry. The previous holder of this record was the fourth book in the series, *Harry Potter and the Goblet of Fire*.

★ DISTANCE TO PUSH A SHOPPING CART – TEAM

On July 23, 2005, a team of 12 staff members (all Germany) from the company EDEKA Südbayern took turns to push a shopping cart for 24 hours around a 1,423-ft-long (434-m) track at Munich Airport, Germany. They covered a distance of 183 miles (294.5 km) at an average speed of 7.6 mph (12.2 km/h)!

DISTANCE WALKING BACKWARD

Anthony Thornton (USA) walked 95.4 miles (153.5 km) backward in Minneapolis, Minnesota, USA, from December 31, 1988, to January 1, 1989. His average speed was 3.9 mph (6.4 km/h).

DISTANCE ON A STATIC CYCLE (SPINNER) – TEAM

The greatest distance traveled on a static cycle (or spinner) in 24 hours by a team of six is 486.5 miles (783 km) by Sybille Bick-Gerberding, Kathrin Brinkmann, Anne von der Ecken, Gerd Hoppe, Julia Matus and Matthais Theile (all Germany) at Drei Fit Fitness and Sauna in Quakenbrueck, Germany, on November 6–7, 2004.

DISTANCE ON A UNICYCLE

Ken Looi (New Zealand) covered 235.3 miles (378.7 km) on his unicycle in a 24-hour period at Basin Reserve Cricket Ground, Wellington, New Zealand, on February 5–6, 2005.

★ HEIGHT ACHIEVED CLIMBING STAIRS

The greatest vertical height ascended by climbing stairs is 49,212 ft 6 in (15,000 m) – over one and a half times the height of Mount Everest – by Kurt Hess (Switzerland), who climbed the 147-ft (45-m) Esterli Tower in Lenzburg, Switzerland, and descended by foot 333 times on October 8–9, 2004. Only the height ascended counts toward the total, but in order to qualify, all ascents and descents must be made by foot.

★ MOST CONCERTS
PERFORMED ⬆

Adam Tas (a.k.a. Francois van der Merwe, pictured), accompanied by musicians Jaco van Deventer and Daniel Roos (all South Africa), played 41 gigs in 24 hours at venues in and around Pretoria, South Africa, on May 5–6, 2005.

The **most concerts by a brass band in 24 hours** is 16 by the Brassband Immanuel Eemsmond, which performed 16 concerts in Uithuizermeeden, the Netherlands, on September 28–29, 2001.

★ FARTHEST DISTANCE IN A MONOHULL IN 24 HOURS ⬇

Skippered by Sebastien Josse (France) during the second leg of the Volvo Ocean Race in the Southern Ocean, on January 11, 2006, *ABN Amro Two* traveled 562.9 nautical miles (647.8 miles; 1,042.6 km) in 24 hours at an average speed of 23.45 knots.

MOST...

★ CONSECUTIVE HAIRCUTS
On June 18–19, 2004, Christian Petrillo (Italy) cut and styled 250 heads of hair in Hamburg, Germany.

★ SKIPS
Isabel Bush (USA) skipped a record 151,036 jumps of a rope in 24 hours in Juneau, Alaska, USA, on July 20–21, 2005. She averaged 104 skips every minute for the entire day.

BUNGEE JUMPERS
On October 26, 2000, 505 people bungee-jumped at A. J. Hackett Bungy in Cairns, Queensland, Australia. That is one jump every 2 min 51 sec!

The **most bungee jumps by an individual in 24 hours** is 101 by Bill Boshoff (South Africa) at Bloukrans River Bridge, South Africa, on May 10, 2002. He jumped for just 14 hr 23 min.

★ HUGS
Brett Sharp (USA) hugged 4,135 different people in 24 hours, starting on July 4, 2005, at the Salem Fair, Salem, Virginia, USA.

PASSENGERS ON AN UNDEGROUND (METRO) RAILWAY

The Moscow Metro in Russia carries 8 to 9 million passengers each day, making it the world's busiest metropolitan railway system.

PARACHUTE JUMPS

Jay Stokes (USA) made an amazing 534 successful parachute jumps in a 24-hour period on November 11–12, 2003, above Lake Elsinore, California, USA. Stokes endured 10 hours of rain during the record attempt, which involved making one jump every two-and-a-half minutes! Each jump was made from an altitude of around 2,100 ft (640 m).

★ SIT-UPS (ABDOMINAL FRAME)

Jack Zatorski (USA) completed 130,200 sit-ups using an abdominal frame in 24 hours at Accelerated Physical Therapy, Fort Lauderdale, USA, on September 24–25, 2005.

★ PARTICIPANTS IN A SWIMMING RELAY

The record for the most participants to swim one lap each in a 24-hour swimming relay is 2,889. It was set at the Santa Maria da Feira municipal swimming pool, Portugal, on June 3–4, 2005.

★ PARTICIPANTS IN A TRACK RELAY

The most participants to carry a baton 100 m (328 ft) each in a 24-hour-long relay is 801. This was achieved at Stanney High School Sports College track, Ellesmere Port, Cheshire, UK, on April 28, 2005.

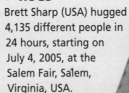

DON'T TRY THIS AT HOME

★ **NEW RECORD**
UPDATED RECORD

MOST SWORDS SWALLOWED AT ONCE BY A FEMALE

Natasha Veruschka (USA, below) swallowed 13 swords, each at least 15 in (38 cm) long, in Wilkes-Barre, Pennsylvania, USA, on September 3, 2004.

Matt Henshaw (USA) swallowed 14 swords on April 6, 2000, in Perth, Australia, the **most swords swallowed by a male**. They were exactly 1.5 in (4 cm) wide and 23.1 in (58.9 cm) long and weighed 9 lb 14 oz (4.5 kg).

LONGEST...

TIME LIVING WITH SCORPIONS

Kanchana Ketkaew (Thailand) lived in a glass room measuring 129 ft^2 (12 m^2), containing 3,000 scorpions, for 32 days from September 21 to October 23, 2002, at Royal Garden Plaza, Pattaya, Thailand. She was stung nine times over this period.

Dean Sheldon was able to hold a scorpion measuring 7 in (17.78 cm) in his mouth for a total of 18 seconds on the set of *Guinness World Records: Primetime* on December 21, 2000, giving him the record for the **largest scorpion held in the mouth**.

★ FIRE WALK

Scott Bell (UK) walked 250 ft (76.2 m) over embers with a temperature of 1,009–1,114°F (543–601°C) at Belah Primary School, Carlisle, UK, on January 28, 2006.

SURVIVAL WITHOUT FOOD

Doctors estimate that a well-nourished individual can survive for 30 days or more on a diet of just sugar and water without any serious medical consequences. The longest period for which anyone has gone without solid food is 382 days in the case of Angus Barbieri of Fife, UK. To achieve this feat, he lived on tea, coffee, water, soda water, and vitamins in Maryfield Hospital, Dundee, UK, from June 1965 to July 1966. As a result of this "diet," his weight fell from 472 lb (214 kg) to 178 lb (80.74 kg).

MOST SCORPIONS EATEN

The most live scorpions eaten in a lifetime by a human is about 35,000 by Rene Alvarenga a.k.a. "El Comealacranes" ("scorpion eater") of Intipucá, El Salvador. He catches 20–30 of them a day with his bare hands and eats them alive.

SURVIVAL WITHOUT FOOD AND WATER

Eighteen-year-old Andreas Mihavecz (Austria) was put into a holding cell on April 1, 1979, in Höchst, Austria. The police then forgot about him. On April 18, 18 days later, he was discovered close to death.

TUNNEL OF FIRE MOTORCYCLE RIDE

Stephen Brown (UK) rode a motorcycle through a tunnel of fire 167 ft (51 m) long at Knockhill Racing Circuit, near Dunfermline, Fife, UK, on August 7, 2003.

MOST LIVE ▾ RATTLESNAKES HELD IN MOUTH

"Snakeman" Jackie Bibby (USA) held eight 2-ft 6-in-long (75-cm) western diamondback rattlesnakes in his mouth for 12.5 seconds – without any assistance – at the Guinness World Records Experience in Orlando, Florida, USA, on May 19, 2001. Jackie has handled snakes all his life – he even married his third wife in a pit of 300 rattlesnakes!

MOST COCKROACHES IN A COFFIN
"Jungle" John LaMedica (USA) lay in a Plexiglas coffin and had 20,050 giant Madagascan hissing cockroaches (*Gromphadorhina portentosa*) poured over him on August 12, 1999.

MOST BEES IN THE MOUTH
Dr. Norman Gary (USA) held 109 honeybees in his closed mouth for 10 seconds on October 20, 1998, in Los Angeles, California, USA.

ENDURANCE RIDE ON THE WALL OF DEATH
The longest duration for which an individual has ridden a motorcycle on a so-called "wall of death" is held by Martin Blume (Germany). He rode the wall for 7 hr 13 sec in Berlin, Germany, on April 16, 1983.

BANZAI SKYDIVE
The "sport" of banzai skydiving involves throwing a parachute out of a plane at nearly 10,000 ft (3,000 m) and then jumping after it – the aim being to catch up with it, strap it on and deploy the parachute before hitting the ground! To date, the longest time between jump and deploy is 50 seconds by Yasuhiro Kubo (Japan) on September 2, 2000, over Davis, California, USA.

★ TIME TO HOLD BREATH
Tom Sietas (Germany) held his breath for 14 min 12 sec under 10 ft (3.05 m) of water in Milan, Italy, on January 5, 2006. By way of preparation, Tom hyperventilated with oxygen for 30 minutes before his watery descent.

MOST...

CRASH-TEST COLLISIONS ENDURED
By February 2003, W. R. "Rusty" Haight (USA) had endured 718 collisions in cars as a "human crash-test dummy." The record came about during the course of his work as a traffic-collision reconstructionist.

★ EXPLOSIVES (SQUIBS) DETONATED ON A PERSON
Will Purcell, David Hill, David Beavis, Phil Fravel, and Mike Hudson (all USA) safety-rigged a wetsuit with 160 movie squibs – the type that normally contains fake blood. The wetsuit was then donned by stunt enthusiast Mike Daugherty (USA) and the squibs were detonated. The stunt took place at EUE Screen Gems Studios in North Carolina, USA, on April 11, 2005. In all, 157 squibs were exploded.

★ ARROWS CAUGHT
Standing 26 ft (8 m) from two archers, Anthony Kelly (Australia) caught 34 arrows by hand in two minutes on the set of *Lo Show Dei Record* in Milan, Italy, on January 5, 2006.

STEPS TUMBLED DOWN
Stuntman Martin Shenton (UK) carried out a pre-planned fall down 109 concrete steps outside Ashton Memorial, Lancaster, UK, on November 1, 1998.

FLAMING TORCHES EATEN
Antti Karvinen (Finland) put out 36 torches with his mouth in one minute on October 9, 2000. The torches were handed to him by two assistants from a rack of 40 on the set of *Guinness World Records* in Helsinki, Finland.

DEADLY MAGIC TRICK
At least 12 people (eight magicians and four bystanders) have been killed during the famous bullet-catching trick, in which at least one gun loaded with a marked bullet is fired at a magician, who appears to catch the bullet in his teeth. Even though the feat involves illusionary elements, it is fraught with danger. The best-known bullet-catching death was that of Chung Ling Soo (USA, b. William Elsworth Robinson), a world-famous magician who was shot on stage at the Wood Green Empire, in London, UK, on March 23, 1918.

[?] DID YOU KNOW?
Stephan Kovaltchuk (Ukraine) spent 57 years in the attic of his home in Montchintsi, Ukraine. He originally went into hiding to avoid the Nazis, finally emerging at the age of 75 in September 1999 when his sister died.

★ MOST CHAINSAW-JUGGLING CATCHES
Since this record was last published, it has been beaten twice. On January 24, 2003, Chad Taylor (USA, pictured) – juggling three running chainsaws – made a total of 78 catches on the set of *Mitä Ihmettä*, Tampere, Finland. On September 23, 2005, Aaron Gregg (Canada) juggled three running chainsaws and made 86 catches in Portland, Oregon, USA.

DO TRY THIS AT HOME

? WANT TO BE A RECORD BREAKER?

If you want your name in the record books, but don't know which record you want to break, look around your home for inspiration. On these pages are a collection of records that use everyday objects, such as clothespins, paper, playing cards, and drinking straws. For a full set of guidelines for all the records on this spread, visit **www. guinnessworldrecords. com/trythisathome**.

★ **NEW RECORD**
★ **UPDATED RECORD**

MOST SMARTIES EATEN WITH CHOPSTICKS IN THREE MINUTES

Using chopsticks, Kathryn Ratcliffe (UK) ate 170 Smarties (similar to M&Ms) in three minutes at the *Guinness World Records 2005 Roadshow* at The Trafford Centre, Manchester, UK, on November 27, 2004. Kathryn first claimed the record for this category in 2002, but has improved her score every year since.

MOST RICE GRAINS EATEN WITH CHOPSTICKS IN THREE MINUTES

On November 7, 2000, using just a pair of chopsticks, Tae Wah Gooding (South Korea) ate 64 grains of rice – one by one – in three minutes at Peterborough Regional College, Peterborough, UK.

★ MOST JELL-O EATEN WITH CHOPSTICKS IN ONE MINUTE

The most jell-o eaten in one minute – using only a set of chopsticks – is 1.58 oz (45 g) by Noelle Ike (USA) at the launch of the *So You Want to be a Record-Breaker?* book on *Fox & Friends* in New York City, USA, on June 9, 2005.

FASTEST BALLOON DOG MADE BEHIND BACK

With his arms behind his back, Craig "Blink" Keith (UK) made a balloon poodle using a single 260Q modeling balloon in a time of 9.6 seconds at the offices of *Guinness World Records*, London, UK, on May 25, 2004.

★ LARGEST M&M MOSAIC

Maurice Bennett (New Zealand) used 5,040 M&Ms – in six different colors – to create a portrait of Eminem (a.k.a. Marshall Mathers III, USA). The portrait was submitted to the Color My World Competition, organized by the maker of M&Ms. The trickiest part of the process was self-control: "At times, I couldn't help myself from eating the M&Ms that were supposed to be part of the work!"

★ FASTEST QUILT DRESSING

Liz Barker (UK) took just 1 min 13 sec to stuff a double quilt into its cover at BBC Television Centre, London, UK, on July 25, 2005.

LONGEST TIME TO SPIN A FRYING PAN ON THE FINGER

Anders Björklund (Sweden) was able to spin a regular 12-in-wide (30-cm) aluminum frying pan on his finger for 14 minutes on the set of *Guinness Rekord TV* in Stockholm, Sweden, on November 29, 2001.

FASTEST WINDOW CLEANERS

In the highly regulated discipline of competitive window-cleaning, two British names currently shine out above all others: Terry Burrows and Janine Guiseley.

Terry cleaned three standard 45 x 45 in (114.3 x 114.3 cm) office windows using a 12-in-long (30-cm) squeegee and 19 pints (2.4 gal) of water in a time of 9.24 seconds at the NEC, Birmingham, UK, on March 2, 2005. Janine achieved the same feat in 25.38 seconds at the Holiday Inn Hotel, Newcastle-upon-Tyne, UK, on April 23, 2005, securing the women's world record.

Both events were supervised by the National Federation of Master Window & General Cleaners (UK).

← FASTEST SANDWICH MADE BY FEET

Using just his feet, Rob Williams (USA) made a bologna, cheese, and lettuce sandwich – complete with olives on cocktail sticks – in 1 min 57 sec on the set of *Guinness World Records: Primetime* on November 10, 2000. He also removed all ingredients from their packaging using just his feet.

TIGHTEST FRYING-PAN ROLL

The tightest roll that a 12-in (30-cm) aluminum frying pan has been reduced to in 30 seconds – using bare hands only – had a circumference of 9.25 in (23.5 cm). This feat has been accomplished by two men. Craig Pumphrey (USA) set the record in Los Angeles, California, USA, on October 16, 1999, followed by Ralf Ber (Austria) in Munich, Germany, on January 26, 2001.

MOST CLOTHESPINS CLIPPED TO THE FACE

Garry Turner (UK) clipped 159 wooden clothespins to his face in Manchester, UK, on November 27, 2004.

★ MOST CLOTHESPINS HELD IN THE HAND

The most clothespins a person has picked off a washing line and held in a single hand is 22, a feat achieved by Elliott Howes (UK) in Newbury, Berkshire, UK, on July 9, 2005. He was able to maneuver the pins and prevent them from dropping without touching any part of his body other than his nominated hand.

MOST STRAWS STUFFED IN THE MOUTH

Marco Hort (Switzerland) stuffed 258 drinking straws in his mouth and successfully held them there for 10 seconds on April 22, 2005, at Belp, Bern, Switzerland.

FARTHEST THROW OF A PLAYING CARD

The magician Rick Smith Jr. (USA) threw a single playing card a distance of 216 ft 4 in (65.96 m) at the Cleveland State Convocation Center, Ohio, USA, on March 21, 2002.

MOST EGGS HELD IN THE HAND

Daniel Miller (UK) managed to hold 11 eggs in one hand on April 6, 2006, at Hexham Middle School, Northumberland, UK. The feat was witnessed by assistant principal Mrs. Rossiter.

TALLEST SUGAR-CUBE TOWER

Mat Hand (UK) built a sugar-cube tower 57.2 in (145.5 cm) tall on June 19, 2003, in Berlin, Germany. It contained 1,194 individual sugar cubes.

LONGEST DISTANCE FLOWN BY PAPER AIRPLANE

Stephen Krieger (USA) flew a paper plane a distance of 207 ft 4 in (63.19 m) in a hangar near Moses Lake, Washington, USA, on September 6, 2003. The plane was constructed of a single sheet of 8½ x 11 paper and a length of standard Scotch™ tape 1.18 in (30 mm) long and 0.98 in (25 mm) wide.

FASTEST BED-MAKING BY A TEAM OF TWO

The team record for making a bed with one blanket, two sheets, an undersheet, an uncased pillow, one pillowcase, one counterpane, and hospital corners is 14 seconds by Sister Sharon Stringer and Nurse Michelle Benkel (both UK) at Canary Wharf, London, UK, on November 26, 1993.

! YOU WILL NEED

To try these records, find:
- *Spoons (16)*
- *Playing cards*
- *Modeling balloons (5)*
- *Smarties (200)*
- *Chopsticks (2)*
- *Rice grains (65)*
- *Jelly (1.76 oz; 50g)*
- *Bucket of soapy water (19 pints; 2.4 gal) and a squeegee*
- *Clothespins (160)*
- *8½ x 11 paper and Scotch™ tape*
- *Drinking straws (259)*
- *Frying pan (1, 12 in; 30 cm wide)*
- *Quilt and its cover (1)*
- *Eggs (12)*

★ MOST SPOONS BALANCED ON THE FACE

Tim Johnston (USA) was able to balance 15 stainless-steel spoons on his face (one on each ear, two on each cheek, three on his chin, two on his lips, one on his nose, and three on his forehead) and hold them for 30 seconds at Havens High School, Piedmont, California, USA, on May 28, 2004.

EARLY STARTERS

★ YOUNGEST PERSON TO VISIT THE WRECK OF *TITANIC*

On August 4, 2005, while he was an 8th grade honor student in Florida, USA, Sebastian Harris (USA, b. September 19, 1991) dived to the wreck of RMS *Titanic* aboard the submarine *Mir 1* at the age of 13 years 10 months and 15 days. For his record-breaking feat – commemorated by an engraved plaque placed at the site of the wreck (inset) – Sebastian has been made a full member of the Explorers Club.

★ YOUNGEST DOUBLE TOPPERS

McFly (all UK) – from left to right, Harry Judd (b. December 23, 1985), Tom Fletcher (b. July 17, 1985), Danny Jones (b. March 12, 1986), and Dougie Poynter (b. November 30, 1987) – are the youngest group to top the UK album charts twice. *Room on the 3rd Floor* debuted at No.1 on July 5, 2004, and *Wonderland* reached No.1 on September 10, 2005.

YOUNGEST...

★ ANIMAL TRAINER

The youngest legally licensed animal trainer is Carl Ralph Scott Norman (UK, a.k.a. Captain Carl), who was born on March 23, 1968, and was licensed to train animals under the Performing Animals (Regulation) Act, 1925 (UK), on March 13, 1970, aged just 1 year 355 days.

MONARCHS

The youngest monarchs in the world were a king of France and a king of Spain who became sovereigns from the moment of their birth. Jean (John) I of France was the posthumous son of Louis X and succeeded to the throne at birth on November 14,

1316, although he died five days later. Alfonso XIII of Spain was the posthumous son of Alfonso XII and succeeded at him birth on May 17, 1886.

★ GAMEKEEPER

Robert Mandry (UK, b. January 1, 1994) led his first professional shoot on his family's estate – Holdshott Farm in Hampshire, UK – on November 9, 2005, at the age of just 11 years 312 days. Robert led three further shoots during that season (October 2005–February 1, 2006), all following the retirement of his predecessor, Colin Parsons (UK). Robert dedicates most weekends and after-school evenings to gamekeeping, including rearing birds, controlling vermin, and preparing for the next season's shoots.

★ YOUNGEST CLIFF DIVER

In December 2005, at the age of 12, Iris Alvarez (Mexico, b. June 19, 1993) became the youngest person to dive 59 ft (18 m) off La Quebrada Rock in Acapulco, Mexico. A person diving from the top of the 100-ft-high (30-m) cliff will hit the water at over 56 mph (90 km/h)!

POLITICAL PRISONER

Thaint Wunna Khin (Myanmar), a three-year-old girl, was one of 19 "anti-government rallyists" – including her mother – arrested in July 1999 in Pegu, Myanmar.

★ RADIO HOST

Eight-year-old Kimberley Perez (USA, b. February 20, 1998) hosts a show every Saturday on KLAX 97.9 La Raza FM in Los Angeles, California, USA.

PERSON EQUIPPED WITH A PAIR OF BIONIC ARMS

Kyle Barton (UK) was just eight years old when he was equipped with a second bionic arm by Dr. Dipak Datta at the Northern General Hospital, Sheffield, UK, in February 2002. Kyle's legs and arms were removed after he contracted meningitis in 1998. His first arm was attached in 2001.

YOUNGEST SPORTSMEN AND SPORTSWOMEN

NAME	DISCIPLINE	AGE
Nick Stoekenbroek (Netherlands)	Darts	12 years
Fu Mingxia (China)	Platform-diving World Champion	12 years 141 days
Kim Yun-Mi (South Korea)	Olympic gold medalist (skating)	13 years 85 days
Souleymane Mamam (Togo)	World Cup football	13 years 310 days
Hasan Raza (Pakistan)	Test cricket	14 years 227 days
Martina Hingis (Switzerland)	Wimbledon champion (female)	15 years 282 days
Joseph Henry Nuxhall (USA)	Major League Baseball	15 years 314 days
★ Chia-Ching Wu (Taiwan)	Pool World Champion	16 years 121 days
Jamieson Finlay (GB)	Rugby union	17 years 36 days
Boris Becker (West Germany)	Wimbledon champion (male)	17 years 227 days
Gavin Gordon (Ireland)	Rugby league	17 years 229 days
Bill Sutherley (UK)	Heavyweight boxing champion	18 years 11 days
Jermaine O'Neal (USA)	Basketball (NBA)	18 years 53 days
Sergio Garcia (Spain)	Ryder Cup	19 years 229 days
Henri Cornet (France)	Tour de France winner	19 years 350 days
Kyle Busch (USA)	NASCAR driver	20 years 125 days
Stephen Hendry (UK)	Snooker World Champion	21 years 106 days

LICENSED STOCKBROKER

The youngest licensed stockbroker in the world is Jason A. Earle of Princeton, New Jersey, USA. He passed the stockbroker exam (Series 7) administered by the National Association of Securities Dealers on October 25, 1993, aged 17 years 206 days.

★ PERSON TO SKI ON EVERY CONTINENT

Timothy Turner Hayes (USA) started skiing at the age of four at the ski resort in Stratton, Vermont, USA. Aged 11, he skied in Europe (Courmayer, Italy); at 12, he skied in Australia (Thredbo); and, at 13, he skied in both Africa (Oukaimeden) and South America (Chile). Lastly, at 14, he finished visiting all continents (excluding Antarctica) by skiing in Asia (Nagano, Japan).

★ YOUNGEST CHESS GRAND MASTER

The youngest individual to qualify as an International Grand Master is Sergey Karjakin (Ukraine, b. January 12, 1990), who did so on August 12, 2002, aged 12 years 212 days.

★ NEW RECORD
UPDATED RECORD

GUERRILLA LEADERS

On January 24, 2000, a renegade ethnic militia from Myanmar called "God's Army," led by Luther and Johnny Htoo, 12-year-old twins said to possess "mystical powers," took a total of 700 people hostage for 24 hours at a hospital in Ratchaburi, Thailand.

HOLE-IN-ONE GOLFER (MALE)

Christian Carpenter (USA, b. June 6, 1995) scored a hole-in-one aged 4 years 195 days at the Mountain View Golf Club, Hickory, North Carolina, USA, on December 18, 1999.

The **youngest female golfer to score a hole-in-one** is Katy Langley (UK), aged 9 years 136 days, at the par-3 first at Forest Pines Beeches golf course, Broughton, Lincolnshire, UK, on August 9, 2005.

★ CAVE DIVER

Tony DeRosa Jr. (a.k.a. "Cave Kid", USA), born in 1983, embarked upon his first cave dive at the Carwash Cenote, near Akumal, Mexico. Tony was just 14 years old when he plunged into the dark depths of the Chamber of the Ancients, a cave that extends nearly 90 ft (27.4 m) underwater.

ELECTED POPE

Pope Benedict IX (Italy) served three terms as pope: 1032–44; April to May 1045; and November 8, 1047 to July 17, 1048. It is believed that he was aged only 11 or 12 years old when he began his first papal term.

MOVIE DIRECTOR

The youngest director of a professionally made feature-length movie is Sydney Ling (Netherlands, b. November 20, 1959) who directed *Lex the Wonderdog* (Netherlands, 1973), a canine detection thriller, when he was 13 years old.

YOUNGEST ➡
X GAMES ATHLETE

Takeshi Yasutoko (Japan, b. June 25, 1986) was 11 years 360 days old when he made his X Games debut on June 20, 1998, in Aggressive In-Line Skate Vert.

GOLDEN OLDIES

OLDEST...

★ LAWN BOWLS PLAYER

Leslie Brittan (b. March 17, 1905) from Blackheath, London, UK, has been a life-long bowler and was club president of Woolwich and Plumstead Bowling Club in his centennial year.

★ PROFESSIONAL CHORUS LINE

The combined age of the 10 dancers from the touring chorus line of The Tivoli Lovelies, based in Melbourne, Victoria, Australia, was 746 years 147 days as of October 12, 2004. The original Tivoli Theater toured Australia, entertaining crowds with performances by jugglers, fire eaters, and dancers.

PROFESSIONAL PIANIST

The Romanian pianist Cella Delavrancea (1887–1991) gave her last public recital, with six encores, aged 103 – making her the oldest-ever professional piano player.

★ ACTIVE COMMERCIAL PILOT

Reginald Thomas Weaver (South Africa, b. October 12, 1932) became a qualified commercial pilot in 1957. As of March 2006, the 73-year-old continues to fly and has completed over 6,500 hours of flight to date.

★ HANG-GLIDER PILOT

As of 2005, Neal Goss Jr. (USA, b. October 26, 1920) was an active hang-glider pilot, flying several times each month.

BRIDE

Minnie Munro (Australia), aged 102, married Dudley Reid, 83 – a man who, as some have pointed out, is technically young enough to be her son – on May 31, 1991. The marriage took place at Point Clare, New South Wales, Australia.

★ PERSON TO RECEIVE A UNIVERSITY VARSITY LETTER

Morton Cohn (USA) is the oldest person ever to receive a university varsity letter, at the age of 78 years 8 days on July 28, 2001. He received the accolade 52 years after excelling at playing golf for the University of Michigan, USA.

★ MAN TO FLY IN ZERO GRAVITY

On April 10, 2005, Ugo Sansonetti (Italy, b. January 10, 1919) flew on the "SpaceLand" zero gravity experimental flight – on board a Boeing 727 especially modified for the flight – at the age of 86 years 90 days. The event took place in Fort Lauderdale, Florida, USA.

The **oldest woman to fly in zero gravity** is Dorothy Simpson (USA, b. November 27, 1924), who participated in a zero-gravity flight on an Ilyushin IL-76 aircraft, aged 79 years 237 days, on July 22, 2004. The flight, which took off from Zhukovsky Airbase, near Moscow, Russia, was organized by Space Adventures (USA).

PROFESSIONAL INLINE SKATER (WOMEN)

Donna Vano (USA, b. June 3, 1953) has been competing as a professional inline skater since 1991. She also competes in skateboarding and snowboarding events.

★ TABLE TENNIS PLAYER

The oldest table tennis player is Arthur Sweeney (UK, b. December 1, 1916), who is still playing for the Ravenshead Rebels in the Mansfield and District Table Tennis League, Nottinghamshire, UK, aged 89.

★ HEART SURGERY PATIENT

On June 10, 1993, Herbert Carrington (USA, b. October 17, 1898) received a Medtronic Hancock II tissue valve, aged 94 years 129 days. The valve was still working on June 15, 2005, when he was aged 106 years 134 days.

★ ARTIST AT NO.1 ON UK ALBUM CHART

The oldest artist to top the UK chart with a newly recorded album is Tom Jones (UK, b. June 7, 1940), who was 60 when *Reload* (released September 27, 1999) went to the top of the charts in June 2000.

WOMAN TO REACH THE SUMMIT OF MOUNT EVEREST

Tamae Watanabe (Japan, b. November 21, 1938) reached the top of Mount Everest at the age of 63 years 177 days at 9:55 a.m. on May 16, 2002, thereby becoming the oldest woman to do so.

★ SOLO PARACHUTE JUMP

Milburn Hart (USA) made a solo parachute jump near Bremerton National Airport, Washington, USA, on February 18, 2005, at the age of 96 years 63 days.

★ REGULAR ➡ NEWSPAPER COLUMNIST

Jack Tucker (USA, b. April 25, 1914) has written a theater column for the *West County Weekly* newspaper in Richmond, California, USA, since May 1994.

The record for the **oldest solo parachute jump (female)** is held by Sylvia Brett (UK), who was 80 years 166 days old when she parachuted over Cranfield, Bedfordshire, UK, on August 23, 1986.

★ PERSON TO COMPLETE A MARATHON ON EACH CONTINENT

Over a period of nearly 10 years, Margaret Hagerty (USA) completed a marathon on all seven continents. Her attempt started on November 5, 1995, when she was aged 72 years 225 days, and ended on July 4, 2004, by which time she was aged 81 years 101 days old.

CONTESTANTS TO TAKE PART IN A BEAUTY PAGEANT

To enter the Ms. Senior America pageant (founded in 1971) you must be a woman who is 60 years of age or older – one who has reached the "Age of Elegance."

OLDEST GOLF COMPETITOR AT A MAJOR EVENT

Ed Alofs (Netherlands, b. February 13, 1902) competed in the 1997 Compaq World Putting Championships in Orlando, Florida, USA, from November 29 to December 1, 1997, at the age of 95 years 289 days.

OLDEST ASTRONAUTS

The oldest astronaut is John Glenn Jr. (USA), who was 77 years 103 days old when he was launched into space as part of the crew of *STS-95 Discovery* on October 29, 1998. The mission lasted 11 days, returning to Earth on November 7, 1998.

The **oldest woman in space** to date is Shannon Lucid (USA, b. January 14, 1943), who was aged 53 years 67 days when she launched with the rest of the crew of the space shuttle mission *STS 76 Atlantis* on March 22, 1996; the shuttle landed nine days later on March 31, 1996. Shannon Lucid is also the first and only woman to have made five spaceflights.

★ HOCKEY PLAYER

Julie Jones (UK, b. July 13, 1934) is the oldest regular county league field hockey player in the world. She played the complete 2004/05 season for the Yeovil & Sherbourne (UK) 3rd XI in the Channel 2A West Clubs' Women's Hockey League, in Dorset, UK, aged 70.

★ NEW RECORD
★ UPDATED RECORD

MEMORY CHALLENGE

HOW MANY OBJECTS CAN YOU MEMORIZE?

The current Guinness World Record for **most random objects memorized** is 200 by Jayasimha Ravirala (India), who recalled the items in the order that they were read to him at the Sri Thyagaraya Gana Sabha in Hyderabad, India, on December 28, 2005.

Think you can challenge Jayasimha? To help you get started, we've collected together 100 objects. Get a friend to read out, say, 10 random items and try to recall them in the same order. Then try with 20, then 30, and so on, until you become good at it. Then, perhaps, you could apply for the *real* record! Find out how on p.7. Good luck!

COLLECTIONS

NIEK VERMEULEN

Niek Vermeulen (left), a retired 70-year-old Dutch consultant and seasoned worldwide traveler, holds the record for the largest collection of vomit bags. Spanning more than 20 years, it now numbers 5,034 items.

Why collect vomit bags?
Each bag is unique, with the company's printed name and logo on it. Those with souvenir stickers, stamps, or handwritten names fail to become part of my hoard.

Where do you get them from?
My regular visits to the Far East mean that I'm frequently in and out of airports, so I make sure to pick up different vomit bags from airlines and aviation companies while in transit. There have been contributions from other sources as well, because it's been physically impossible for me to be a passenger on almost 1,000 different airlines!

Is there much competition?
In the 1970s, we were very few, but more people started collecting in countries like Holland, Germany, and the USA. There are now well over 200 collectors worldwide.

Do you have a favorite item?
A vomit bag from Finnaviation displaying a barfing reindeer, another from the Swiss airline Tell Air, and a very rare KLM piece pre-dating World War II.

Have you ever been sick while flying?
No... never but I did pick up the "full" bags from a plane twice and had to wash my hands immediately afterwards! If I was ever sick, my friends would tell me to put what I had around me to good use.

★ BOTTLED WATER LABELS
Lorenzo Pescini (Italy) has a collection of 6,701 bottled water labels from 95 countries and 1,327 different springs. He has been collecting since 1992.

★ PENGUINS
Benjamin Binkau (Germany) began his penguin collection with the stuffed toy that he received for his 1st birthday; 15 years later, he now owns 1,289 items. His favorite is a large cuddly toy called Königspinguin.

★ GIRAFFES
Susa Forster from Breitenfelde, Germany, has 2,443 giraffe-related items in her collection, which she started in 1974.

★ OWLS
Dianne Turner of Maine, USA, owns a collection of owls that comprises 18,055 items.

★ SICK-BAGS
Since the 1970s, Niek Vermeulen (Netherlands) has collected 5,034 airline vomit bags from around 1,000 airline companies.

★ CLOTHING TAGS
Tao Chun Lin (China) has amassed a collection of 102,005 clothing tags since the 1970s.

★ BANKNOTES

Since 1985, Sanjay Relan (India) has collected 221 banknotes from 221 different countries. Sanjay also has the ★ **largest collection of coins (most countries)**, with 235 coins from 235 different countries.

★ KEY CHAINS

Emilio Arenas Florin of Colonia, Uruguay, owns 25,630 unduplicated key chains. He began his collection in 1955.

★ COFFEE POTS

Irma Goth (Germany) began collecting coffee pots some 20 years ago, and now owns 3,028 unique items.

★ WHISKEY BOTTLES

Alfredo Gonçalves of Lisbon, Portugal, has collected 10,500 unduplicated whiskey bottles in all different shapes and colors. His collection is open to the public at his shop "Whisky & Co." in Lisbon, Portugal.

★ MENUS

Harley Spiller (USA) has accumulated 5,006 Chinese-food menus from 80 countries and all 50 US states since 1981.

★ ANTIQUE CAMERAS (STILLS PHOTOGRAPHY)

Dilish Parekh of Mumbai, India, has a collection of 4,425 antique cameras that he has amassed since 1977.

★ ERASERS

Petra Engels (Germany) has collected an incredible 19,571 non-duplicate erasers from 112 different countries since 1981. The erasers are displayed in 22 glass showcases at Petra's home.

★ MICKEY MOUSE MEMORABILIA

Janet Esteves (USA) has amassed a collection of 2,143 different Mickey Mouse items since 1960.

★ RUBBER DUCKS

Charlotte Lee (USA) began her record-breaking collection when she bought a pack of three rubber ducks for her bathroom back in 1996. The following week she bought another three to keep them company, and friends who saw these were so amused that they began to give her ducks as gifts. As of April 3, 2006, Charlotte's collection numbers 2,583 ducks, all displayed in glass showcases throughout her home.

BRAND-NEW COLLECTIONS FOR 2007

COLLECTION	COUNT	HOLDER	BEGAN
★ Back scratchers	518	Manfred S. Rothstein (USA)	1970s
★ Belt buckles	1,642	Chester Lindgren (Canada)	1974
★ Board games	868	Linda Ivey (USA)	1992
★ Bowling stickers	17,455	Cedric Brown (UK)	1980s
★ Clocks	921	Ulrich Kriescher (Germany)	1970s
★ Lions	1,515	Reinhard Stöckl (Austria)	1998
★ Masks	4,300	Gerold Weschenmoser (Germany)	1957
★ Monkeys	5,680	Wang Lingxian (China)	1970
★ Playing cards	1,800	Lee Donelson (USA)	1990
★ Radios	625	M. Prakash (India)	1970s
★ Rosaries	1,020	Jamal Sleeq (Kuwait)	1980s
★ Sea floats	174	Theo Henry Vandeligt (Australia)	1970s
★ Soccer balls	861	Roberto A. Fuglini (Argentina)	1995
★ Snow globes	904	Wendy Suen (China)	2002
★ Teddy bears	4,109	Jackie Miley	2002
★ Unicorns	2,719	Suzy Bralliar (USA)	1980s

★ NEW RECORD
★ UPDATED RECORD

SOCIETY

CONTENTS

FASTEST TURKEY PLUCKER

Vincent Pilkington of Cootehill, Co. Cavan, Ireland, plucked a turkey in 1 min 30 sec on RTE television in Dublin on November 17, 1980. He also holds the record for killing and plucking 100 turkeys in 7 hr 32 min on December 15, 1978.

ANCIENT WORLD

OLDEST
ICE BODY

In September 1991, two hikers discovered the mummified remains of a Neolithic man in a melting glacier in the Tyrolean Alps on the Italian-Austrian border, 5,300 years after he had died. Analysis of "Ötzi" and his belongings has given archaeologists a new insight into the technology and culture of Central Europe some 5,000 years ago.

★ NEW RECORD
UPDATED RECORD

⬅ OLDEST
PLAYABLE INSTRUMENT

In 1999, a team of archaeologists led by Juzhong Zhang (China) uncovered six complete 9,000-year-old Chinese bone flutes and managed to play a tune on the best-preserved one. This flute, which is 8.6 in (22 cm) long, has seven holes and is made from the leg bone of a red crowned crane. The instruments were discovered at Jiahu, the site of an ancient farming village on the Yellow River flood plain, China.

EARLY CIVILIZATIONS

★ OLDEST STAR MAP

A tiny section of mammoth tusk found in a cave in the Ach Valley, Germany, in 1979, is believed to be between 32,500 and 38,000 years old. It features a carving of a figure whose limbs are placed in the same shape as the stars in the constellation of Orion. The ivory tablet is 1.5 x 0.5 x 0.1 in (38 x 14 x 4 mm) in size and was created by the Aurignacian people, about whom little is known. It is also one of the oldest known representations of a human.

A series of carvings on a rock at Knowth, Ireland, has been identified as the ★ **oldest Moon map** found to date. It is thought to have been carved around 5,000 years ago.

GREATEST FLOOD

Approximately 18,000 years ago, a Siberian lake about 75 miles (120 km) long ruptured, causing the greatest freshwater flood in history. The discovery of this event, in 1993, suggests a catastrophic flood 1,600 ft (490 m) deep and traveling at a speed of 100 mph (160 km/h).

★ OLDEST LOVE POEM

Archaeologists have dated a love poem written on a clay tablet to the time of the Sumerians, who invented writing ca. 3500 BC. It was given the rather unromantic name of "Istanbul #2461" and is thought to have been recited by a bride of the Sumerian king Shu-Sin, who ruled between 2037 and 2029 BC. It begins:

Bridegroom, dear to my heart,
Goodly is your beauty, honeysweet,
Lion, dear to my heart,
Goodly is your beauty, honeysweet.

FIRST RAILROAD

Track-guided vehicles were used by the Babylonians (ca. 2200 BC) and ancient Greeks. The earliest record of railroads as we know them today is an illustration of wagons running on wooden rails in a mine at Leberthal, Alsace, France, ca. AD 1550.

★ OLDEST BELL

The tintinnabulum found in the Babylonian Palace of Nimrod in 1849 by Austen (later Sir) Henry Layard (UK) dates from ca. 1100 BC.

★ FIRST
WINEMAKERS

The earliest documented evidence proving that grapes were cultivated to make wine dates to 6000 BC in Mesopotamia (modern-day Iraq). However, it was the ancient Egyptians (below), in 3000 BC, who first recorded the process of winemaking (enology).

LONGEST ANCIENT CANAL

The Grand Canal of China from Beijing to Hangzhou was begun in 540 BC and not completed until 1327, by which time it extended (including canalized river sections) for 1,107 miles (1,781 km).

LARGEST PYRAMID

The largest pyramid – and the **largest monument ever constructed** – is the Quetzalcóatl Pyramid at Cholula de Rivadavia, 63 miles (101 km) southeast of Mexico City. It is 177 ft (54 m) tall and its base covers an area of nearly 45 acres (18.2 ha).

The total volume of the pyramid has been estimated at 116.5 million ft³ (3.3 million m³), compared with the current volume of 84.7 million ft³ (2.4 million m³) for the Pyramid of Khufu or Cheops in Egypt. Archaeologists have dated this pre-Columbian pyramid as far back as 800 BC.

BELL JAR
An air-tight jar in which the cake is now stored.

TOPPING
The cake is covered in a paste made from sesame seeds.

FILLING
Sandwiched between the sesame toppings is a filling of honey and, possibly, milk.

MOLDS
The cake was cooked in two tight copper molds that fit perfectly together. When the cake cools, a vacuum is formed.

★ OLDEST PIECE OF CAKE

The Alimentarium Food Museum in Vevey, Switzerland, has as one of its exhibits the world's oldest cake. The 4,200-year-old confectionery was sealed and vacuum-packed in the grave of Pepionkh, who lived in ancient Egypt ca. 2200 BC. The cake, which measures 4.25 in (11 cm) in diameter, has sesame on the outside and honey inside, and was possibly made with milk.

★ OLDEST ZERO

The figure zero, or "0," was first used by the Babylonians ca. 300 BC, as a placeholder – as with the "0" in "10" or "100." The oldest known reference to zero as a numerical value to signify "nothing" was by the Indian mathematician and astronomer Brahmagupta, in his great work of AD 628, the *Brahmasphutasiddhanta*.

SEVEN WONDERS OF THE ANCIENT WORLD

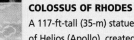

TEMPLE OF ARTEMIS
The Temple of Artemis (Diana) was built ca. 350 BC at Ephesus, Turkey, but was destroyed by the Goths in AD 262.

COLOSSUS OF RHODES
A 117-ft-tall (35-m) statue of Helios (Apollo), created ca. 292–280 BC, once bestrode the entrance to Rhodes harbor. It collapsed during an earthquake in 224 BC.

MAUSOLEUM
The tomb of King Mausolus of Caria stood at Halicarnassus, now Bodrum, Turkey. It was constructed ca. 325 BC.

PHAROS LIGHTHOUSE
The earliest lighthouse was built ca. 270 BC on the island of Pharos, off the coast of Egypt, and stood 400 ft (122 m) tall. It fell during an earthquake in AD 1375.

HANGING GARDENS
No trace now remains of the Hanging Gardens of Semiramis, in Babylon, modern-day Iraq. They were constructed ca. 600 BC.

STATUE OF ZEUS
The sculptor Phidias created a 40-ft-tall (12-m) marble, gold, and ivory statue of Zeus (Jupiter) at Olympia, Greece, ca. 450 BC. It was later moved to Istanbul, where it was destroyed in a fire.

PYRAMIDS
The pyramids of Giza, in Egypt, were built by three 4th-Dynasty Egyptian pharaohs. The great pyramid (the "Horizon of Khufu") was built ca. 2550 BC and was originally 481 ft (146.6 m) tall.

! X-REF

To learn about the Seven Wonders of the Modern World, turn to p.197.

ANCIENT WORLD

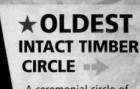

★OLDEST MAYAN ROYAL TOMB

The tomb of a Mayan king discovered in 2001 at a site in San Bartolo, Guatemala, dates to *ca.* 150 BC. A mural discovered in San Bartolo in the same year has been dated to *ca.* 100 BC, making it the ★oldest Mayan mural (above). It tells the story of creation and gives insights into the Maya's view of kingship. (A detail of the mural has been used as the background to these pages.)

? DID YOU KNOW?

On May 3, 2002, scientists announced the discovery of the fossilized remains of *Archaefructus sinensis, the* **oldest known flowering plant,** *in a slab of stone in northeast China. It is at least 125 million years old.*

★OLDEST INTACT TIMBER CIRCLE ➡

A ceremonial circle of oak posts with a central stump was discovered on the Norfolk coast (UK) in 1998. Known as "Seahenge," this 22-ft 2-in-diameter (6.78-m) Bronze Age structure was built from trees felled in the spring or early summer of 2049 BC. It is also the only intact ancient timber circle in the world.

ANCIENT EGYPT

★OLDEST HIEROGLYPHS

Hieroglyphs unearthed in 1999 in Abydos, 300 miles (483 km) south of Cairo, Egypt, have been dated to between 3400 BC and 3200 BC. The ivory tags and clay seal impressions were used to label containers.

★FIRST SIGNED PEACE TREATY

A peace treaty signed by the Egyptian pharaoh Ramses II (also known as Ramses the Great) and Hattusilis III, king of the Hittites, has been dated to 1271 BC. In the treaty, both parties ended years of warring between Egypt and Hatti (in present-day Turkey) and formed a mutual alliance in the event of

foreign or domestic aggression. A copy of the document remains in the Karnak Temple at Luxor; the treaty was originally recorded on silver tablets.

OLDEST MATHEMATICAL PUZZLES

When transcribed, a 3,650-year-old Egyptian scroll known as the Rhind Papyrus was found to contain various mathematical and lateral-thinking puzzles. The most durable problem is the riddle better known today as *Going to St. Ives*:

As I was going to St. Ives,
I met a man with seven wives.
Every wife had seven sacks, and
every sack had seven cats.

Every cat had seven kits.
Kits, cats, sacks, and wives, how
many were going to St. Ives?

The answer, of course, is one!

OLDEST MUMMY

The oldest complete mummy is that of Wati, a court musician of *ca.* 2400 BC from the tomb of Nefer in Saqqâra, Egypt, which was found in 1944.

★OLDEST OBELISK IN SITU

A raised obelisk at Heliopolis, near Cairo, Egypt, has remained in place since it was erected by Senusret I *ca.* 1750 BC to mark 30 years of his rule.

FIRST OLYMPIC GAMES

The ancient Olympic Games – so called because they were originally held on the plains of Olympia in Greece – can be accurately traced back to July 776 BC, when Coroibos, a cook from Elis, won the foot race (such a competition is depicted on the vase, pictured left, which dates from the 5th century BC). The games attracted famous competitors, such as Socrates, Pythagoras, Aristotle, and Hippocrates. Events included running, discus, javelin, shot-put, jumping, wrestling, boxing, pankration (an early form of martial art of which Plato was a double winner), and equestrian disciplines.

The ancient Games were terminated by an order issued in Milan in AD 393 by Theodosius I "the Great," emperor of Rome, who banned such "pagan cults." At the instigation of Pierre de Fredi, baron de Couberti, the modern Olympics were inaugurated in Athens on April 6, 1896.

The first Winter Olympics were held in Chamonix, France, in 1924 and were held the same year as the Summer Games – which take place every four years – until 1992. Since then, the International Olympic Committee (IOC) has made the decision to alternate the Winter and Summer Games every two years.

MOST VALUABLE GLASS

The Constable-Maxwell cage-cup – a Roman glass cage-cup made *ca.* AD 300, and measuring 7 in (17 cm) in diameter and 4 in (10 cm) in height – sold at Sotheby's, London, UK, for £520,000 ($1,078,480) on June 4, 1979. The buyer was Robin Symes (UK) of the British Rail Pension Fund. The cage-cup is so called because the body and base of the vessel are completely surrounded by a delicate network, or "cage," of glass.

LONGEST REIGN

Phiops II (also known as Pepi II or Neferkare) was a 6th-Dynasty pharaoh who ruled from *ca.* 2281 BC, when he was six years old, for 94 years.

OLDEST WILL

The oldest written will dates from 2061 BC and is that of Nek'ure, the son of the Egyptian pharaoh Khafre. The will was carved onto the walls of his tomb and indicated that he would bequeath 14 towns, two estates, and other property to his wife, another woman, and three children.

FIRST ASSASSINATION ATTEMPT

The earliest recorded assassination attempt was that made against the pharaoh of the Middle Kingdom of Egypt, Amenemhat I, *ca.* 2000 BC.

FIRST ALPHABET

The oldest known example of an alphabet – that is, a writing system in which a small number of symbols is used to represent single sounds rather than concepts – dates back to *ca.* 1900 BC. It was found carved into limestone in Wadi el-Hol near Luxor in Egypt by Egyptologist John Darnell (USA) in the early 1990s.

OLDEST HORSE STABLES

The world's oldest horse stables were established by the Egyptian pharaoh Ramses II (1304–1237 BC) to breed horses for war, hunting, and recreation. They were discovered in early 1999 by a joint German-Egyptian archaeological team headed by Edgar Pusch (Germany) in the ancient city of Piramesse, Nile Delta, Egypt.

OLDEST CONTAGIOUS DISEASE

Cases of leprosy were described in ancient Egypt as early as 1350 BC. *Tuberculosis schistosomiasi*, an infectious disease of the lungs, has also been seen in Egyptian mummies from the 20th Dynasty (1250–1000 BC).

MOST VALUABLE JEWELRY BOX

A Cartier jeweled vanity case, set with a fragment of ancient Egyptian steel, was sold at Christie's, New York City, USA, for $189,000 on November 17, 1993.

GREEKS

FIRST DICTIONARY

The writer of the first dictionary is thought to be the ancient Greek philosopher Protagoras of Abdera, who in the 5th century BC compiled a glossary of difficult words encountered in the writings of Homer.

GREATEST ANCIENT NAVAL BATTLE

At the Battle of Salamis, Greece, in September 480 BC, there were an estimated 800 vessels in the defeated Persian fleet and 380 in the victorious fleet of the Athenians and their allies. It is possible that 200,000 men took part in the confrontation.

★ NEW RECORD
UPDATED RECORD

★ TALLEST STUPA

The Jetavanarama dagoba in the ancient city of Anuradhapura, Sri Lanka, is the largest Buddhist brick monument. It is around 400 ft (120 m) tall.

★ FIRST KNOWN MAYAN WRITING

In 2001, archaeologists found a section of Mayan writing thought to date back to 300–200 BC at a site in the city of San Bartolo, Guatemala. This discovery suggests that writing developed within the Mayan civilization at a rate far more similar to that of other Mesoamerican cultures than was previously believed.

MODERN WORLD

THE WORLD'S TOP 10 MOST SPOKEN (FIRST) LANGUAGES ARE:

1. Mandarin Chinese (915 million speakers)
2. English (354 million)
3. Spanish (325 million)
4. Hindi (300 million)
5. Arabic (272 million)
6. Bengali (194 million)
7. Portuguese (170 million)
8. Russian (164 million)
9. Japanese (125 million)
10. German (108 million)

★ NEW RECORD
★ UPDATED RECORD

COUNTRY OF ORIGIN FOR MOST REFUGEES

The country with the most people seeking asylum elsewhere is Afghanistan. According to provisional figures from the United Nations High Commission for Refugees (UNHCR) for the end of 2003, 2.1 million Afghans applied for political asylum in 74 countries. This represents 22% of the total global refugee population.

★ YOUNGEST MAYOR

The youngest mayor is high-school student Michael Sessions (USA), who was elected on November 8, 2005, and sworn in as mayor of Hillsdale, Michigan, USA, at the age of 18 years 61 days on November 21, 2005, following his victory over the incumbent, Douglas Ingles (USA).

★ LARGEST ANNUAL TRADE DEFICIT

The USA has the largest trade deficit in the world. For the first 11 months of 2005, it totaled $661.8 billion, with a predicted annual total of $700 billion for 2005.

★ NEWEST CAPITAL

On November 3, 1998, President Ruslan Aushev of Ingushetia inaugurated the new capital of the republic, a member of the Russian Federation. The capital, Magas (literally "Sun City"), initially comprised no more than a multi-million-dollar presidential palace and an equally expensive square with government headquarters. The project was heavily criticized.

★ HIGHEST PERSONAL MAJORITY

The highest-ever personal majority for any politician was 4,726,112 in the case of Boris Nikolayevich Yeltsin (Russia), the people's deputy candidate for Moscow, in the parliamentary elections held in the Soviet Union on March 26, 1989. Yeltsin (later president of the Russian Federation) received 5,118,745 votes out of the 5,722,937 cast; his closest rival obtained 392,633 votes.

LOWEST CAR OWNERSHIP

Africa's war-torn Somalia and the former Soviet republic of Tajikistan jointly have the world's lowest rate of car ownership, with 0.1 cars per 1,000 people, or one car per 10,000 people. By contrast, Luxembourg has 576 cars per 1,000, or one for every 1.7 people. The USA (8th in the world) has one car for every 2.05 people (or 476 per 1,000).

★ GREATEST ↑
POLITICAL INSTABILITY

El Salvador (above) has averaged one government every 18 months since it obtained its independence in 1821. Syria had 17 governments in the space of just 33 months between March 1949 and December 1951, thus averaging a change every other month. And since it became a sovereign country in 1825, Bolivia has had a record 191 attempted coups, of which 23 have been successful.

COUNTRY ↓
WITH THE MOST DEBT PER CAPITA

Qatar borrows excessively against the country's oil reserves, and in 1999 owed $12 billion, which is the equivalent of approximately $15,000 per citizen.

★ LOWEST COST OF LIVING

According to the worldwide cost of living survey done by *The Economist*'s Intelligence Unit, the capital of Iran, Tehran, was the world's cheapest city in December 2005. The ★ **highest cost of living** in December 2005 was in Oslo, Norway – beating Japanese cities for the first time since 1991.

★ LARGEST NATIONAL DEBT

The USA had a national debt of $8.2 trillion as of February 2006. This debt is sustainable because of the size and strength of the US economy; it represents 65% of the USA's Gross Domestic Product (GDP).

LARGEST POLITICAL CONSTITUENCY (BY AREA)

The Kalgoorlie Australian federal parliamentary constituency in Western Australia covers more than 1,000,000 miles^2 (2,600,000 km^2), an area greater than the whole of Western Europe. The constituency measures 1,400 miles (2,250 km)

FIRST ➡
FEMALE PM

Sirimavo Bandaranaike became prime minister of Sri Lanka on July 21, 1960, and served until 1964; she returned to rule between 1970 and 1977, and again from 1994 to 2000.

FIRST ➡
FEMALE PRESIDENT

María Estela Martínez de Perón became president of Argentina upon her husband's death on June 29, 1974; she was deposed in a military coup on March 24, 1976.

from north to south and 1,000 miles (1,600 km) from east to west and covers the whole state of Western Australia except for the Perth urban area in the southwest.

★ LARGEST POLITICAL PARTY MEMBERSHIP

The Chinese Communist Party, established on July 1, 1921, in Shanghai, claims a membership of 69 million as of 2004 – roughly 5% of the population.

HIGHEST AND LOWEST LIFE EXPECTANCY

Average life expectancy in Andorra is 83.5 years; in Mozambique, it is just 31.3 years.

★ MOST
EXPENSIVE INAUGURATION

The inauguration of George W. Bush (pictured with his wife, Laura) for his second term as president of the United States of America on January 20, 2005, was the most costly ever. Estimated spending for the three-day event was $40 million.

CONSUMPTION

The figures stated here are the amounts eaten, drunk, smoked, or chewed per person per year – so, taking the example of bovine meat, the amount eaten is equivalent to every single person in Argentina devouring 124 lb (56.3 kg) each year.

However, this does not mean that Argentina consumed the most meat overall – this record is held by the USA (where 26.5 billion lb, or 12 million tonnes, of meat were eaten in 2005). But per capita, this works out at just 97 lb (44 kg) per annum.

★ BOVINE MEAT (BEEF & VEAL)
Argentina
124 lb (56.3 kg)
This equates to over 4 billion lb (2 million tonnes) of bovine meat.

★ BEER/LAGER
Czech Republic
332 pints (41.5 gal)

★ BREAD
Turkey
440 lb (200 kg)
This is the equivalent of the average human eating his or her body weight in bread every 100 days!

★ VODKA
Russia
38 pints (4.8 gal)
Taking into account children and non-drinkers, this figure is the equivalent of 80% of adult Russian men drinking 220 bottles of vodka per year.

★ CIGARETTES
China
1.69 trillion cigarettes sold.
One out of every three cigarettes smoked today is smoked in China.

? DID YOU KNOW?

Argentina has the ★**highest food consumption**. Each citizen consumes 183% of the UN Food and Agriculture Organization (FAO) minimum daily recommendation.

Tajikistan, where only 5–6% of the land is arable, has the ★**lowest food consumption**. Each Tajikistani citizen consumes just 55% of the FAO minimum daily requirement.

★ SUGAR
Belize
138 lb (62.6 kg)

★ ALCOHOL
Luxembourg
26.6 pints (3.3 gal)
This intake is based on the amount of pure (100%) alcohol consumed within wine, beer, and spirits.

★ APPLES
Moldova
156 lb 4.9 oz (70.9 kg)
Assuming a weight of 5.2 oz (150 g) per apple, this equates to 472 apples consumed per person.

★ CHEESE
Greece
60 lb 9 oz (27.5 kg)
In total, 643.7 million lb (292,000 tonnes) of cheese was eaten in Greece in 2005 – the equivalent of 20 Leaning Towers of Pisa!

★ FROZEN FOOD
Norway
78 lb 6 oz (35.6 kg)

★ CHEWING GUM
Andorra
2 lb (900 g)

★ WINE

Luxembourg
168 pints
(21 gal)

By contrast, the smallest measurable wine consumer is Egypt, where the average yearly wine consumption amounts to about two tablespoons.

★ BREAKFAST CEREAL

Sweden
22 lb 14 oz (10.4 kg)

? DID YOU KNOW?

*The **oldest cultivated plant for food** is the Abyssinian banana (Ensete ventricosum). Historians suggest that the hunter-gatherers of ancient Ethiopia learned to use this plant as food between 4,000 and 7,000 years ago.*

★ BAKED BEANS

United Kingdom
11 lb 10 oz (5.3 kg)

In contrast, the USA consumes just 2 lb 13 oz (1.3 kg) of baked beans per capita

★ ICE CREAM

Australia
35 pints
(4.4 gal)

★ CHOCOLATE

Switzerland
25 lb 6 oz (11.5 kg)

This is the equivalent of each person eating 230 bars weighing 1.75 oz (50 g) per year.

★ HONEY

Central African Republic
6 lb 9.7 oz (3 kg)

★ TEA

Ireland
5 lb 14 oz (2.6 kg)

This equates to approximately 1,184 cups per person in one year.

★ SPIRITS

Russia
13.1 pints
(1.6 gal)

★ CONFECTIONERY

United Kingdom
35 lb (15.9 kg)

★ COFFEE

Sweden
13 lb 12 oz (6.3 kg)

The banana (musa sapientum) is the most consumed fruit in the world. It is the 4th most important staple food worldwide and therefith most important agricultural product after wheat, sugar, coffee and cocoa. The Brits eat 140 million bananas every week!

★ NEW RECORD
★ UPDATED RECORD

DISASTERS

WORST ⬇ AIR-SHOW DISASTER

A total of 78 people were killed and over 100 injured at Sknyliv Air Base near L'viv, Ukraine, on July 27, 2002, when a Sukhoi Su-27 "Flanker" fighter jet crashed into a crowd of spectators during an aerobatics demonstration. The aircraft lost power during a maneuver, clipping trees before hitting a stationary object and exploding into the crowd.

WORST...

AIRSHIP DISASTER

The worst-ever airship disaster occurred on April 3, 1933, when the US Navy airship *Akron* ripped apart in a storm off the coast of New Jersey, USA, resulting in 73 deaths.

COAL-MINING DISASTER

On April 26, 1942, 1,549 people were killed by an enormous coal-dust explosion at Honkeiko (Benxihu) Colliery, China.

DAM-BURST DISASTER

In August 1975, the Banqiao and Shimantan dams burst and flooded Henan province, China, killing 230,000 people. The tragedy was caused by a combination of geological problems and inherent structural weaknesses.

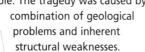

ACCIDENTAL EXPLOSION ON BOARD A SHIP

On December 6, 1917, the French freighter *Mont Blanc*, packed with 11 million lb (5,000 tonnes) of explosives and combustibles, collided with another ship in Halifax Harbour, Nova Scotia, Canada, killing 1,635 people and creating a blast that could be felt more than 60 miles (95 km) away.

DISASTER CAUSED BY A MASS PANIC

Approximately 4,000 people were killed on June 6, 1941, at an air-raid shelter in Chongqing, China. The crowd was leaving the shelter after an air-raid when the warning siren sounded again. The deaths were due to suffocation and trampling as people panicked and tried to return to the shelter.

WORST ⬆ ELEVATOR DISASTER

On May 10, 1995, a gold mine elevator at Vaal Reefs, South Africa, fell 1,600 ft (490 m), killing a total of 105 people. The accident was caused by a locomotive entering the wrong tunnel and plunging down a shaft, where it landed on top of the elevator.

AVIATION DISASTER

The worst-ever air disaster took place on March 27, 1977, when two Boeing 747s (Pan Am and KLM) collided on the runway at Tenerife, Canary Islands, killing 583 people.

FAMINE

Between 1959 and 1961, approximately 40 million people died throughout China. This figure represents an astonishing 1 in 15 of the population at that time.

★ WORST TUNNEL FIRE

On November 12, 2000, at least 155 skiers lost their lives in a tunnel fire on the Kaprun railroad, which was built to take passengers up the Kitzsteinhorn Glacier in the Austrian Alps. The fire was caused by a blocked heating ventilator in the driver's cab, which led to the ignition of leaking hydraulic oil.

FERRY DISASTER

The ferry *Doña Paz*, sailing from Tacloban to Manila, Philippines, collided with the tanker *Vector* in the early hours of December 21, 1987. Both vessels sank within minutes. Officially, the *Doña Paz* had around 1,550 passengers on board, but its owner, Sulpicio Lines, later put the total number of fatalities at 4,375, based on interviews with survivors and relatives of passengers.

FIRE DISASTER

During the sacking of the city of Moscow, Russia, in May 1571, fires were started by the invading Tartars (Mongolians). As a result, up to 200,000 Muscovites were reported to have perished.

FIREWORKS DISASTER

Approximately 800 people were killed as a result of an accident during a fireworks display beside the river Seine in Paris, France, on May 16, 1770. The display was to celebrate the marriage of Louis, the Dauphin of France.

RIOT

In March 1947, around 1,400 people died in the riots In Taiwan that ensued after the arrest of a woman for selling contraband cigarettes.

GOLD-MINING DISASTER

On September 16, 1986, about 176 people were killed in Kinross gold mine, Mpumalanga, South Africa.

HELICOPTER DISASTER

The worst-ever disaster involving a single helicopter occurred on December 14, 1992, when a Russian military helicopter carrying 61 refugees, including women and children, was shot down near Lata, Georgia, killing all on board.

INDUSTRIAL CHEMICAL DISASTER

In the early hours of December 3, 1984, a toxic cloud of methyl isocyanate (MIC) gas enveloped a settlement around the Union Carbide Corporation's pesticide plant in Bhopal, Madhya Pradesh, India. Some sources have suggested there may have been up to 20,000 fatalities, and more than 100,000 people still suffer from medical complications brought about by the disaster.

WORST PEACETIME SEA DISASTERS

NAME OF SHIP	DATE	DEATH TOLL
Doña Paz	1987	4,375
Kiangya	1948	3,920
Joola	2003	1,863
Sultana	1865	1,650 (est.)
Titanic	1912	1,503

INDUSTRIAL EXPLOSION

On June 1, 1974, an explosion at a chemical plant in Flixborough, Lincolnshire, UK, killed 55 people and injured 75. The cause was probably the leaking of around 110,000 lb (50 tonnes) of cyclohexane gas from a pipe. This caused an explosion equivalent to 35,000 lb (16 tonnes) of TNT. As a result of the explosion, over 1,800 houses situated nearby also reported blast damages.

LIGHTNING STRIKE

A total of 81 people on board a Boeing 707 jet airliner died when the plane was struck by lightning near Elkton, Maryland, USA, on December 8, 1963.

ROAD ACCIDENT

About 176 people died when a gasoline tanker exploded inside the Salang Tunnel, Afghanistan, on November 3, 1982.

★ NEW RECORD
★ UPDATED RECORD

HIGHEST ROAD-TRAFFIC FATALITY RATES

Mauritius has the **highest mortality rate caused by road-traffic injury**, with 43.9 fatalities per 100,000 people in 2000, according to the World Health Organization's (WHO) *World Report on Road Traffic Injury Prevention, 1992–2002.*

The country with the **most road deaths** is the USA, with 44,249 in 1999 (as reported in the same document).

LARGEST PARADE OF CANADIAN MILITARY PATTERN (CMP) TRUCKS

A total of 34 Canadian Military Pattern (CMP) trucks took part in a parade at Bangerang Park, Corowa, New South Wales, Australia, on March 16, 2002 – the largest known gathering of these vehicles since World War II.

★ OLDEST EX-SERVICEMAN

The longest surviving soldier on record is Antonio Todde (Italy) who served during World War I. Born on January 22, 1889, he died on January 4, 2002, aged 112 years 346 days, surpassing the previous record held by John B. Salling (USA) of the US Confederate Army by 41 days.

AIR WARFARE

★ LONGEST-RANGE AIR ATTACKS

Two USAF B-52H bombers launched cruise missiles at targets in Iraq on September 2, 1996, as part of a 16,000-mile (25,750-km), 34-hour round trip from Andersen Air Force Base, Guam.

BLOODIEST WARS

By far the costliest war in terms of human life was World War II (1939–45), in which the total number of fatalities, including battle deaths and civilians of all countries, is estimated to have been 56.4 million, assuming 26.6 million Soviet fatalities and 7.8 million Chinese civilian deaths.

LARGEST CHARIOT BATTLE

The Battle of Kadesh (Qadesh) in 1299 BC, on the Orontes River in modern-day Syria, involved around 5,000 chariots. Egyptian pharaoh Ramses II sought to recapture Kadesh with 2,000 chariots and 16,000 infantry from the Hittite army under Muwatallis, who commanded an infantry of 20,000 with 3,000 chariots. Both sides claimed a victory, with peace finally secured in a treaty of 1283 BC.

LONGEST CONTINUOUS INTERNATIONAL CONFLICT

The longest war that could be described as continuous was the Thirty Years' War between various European countries from 1618 to 1648. As a result of the conflict, the map of Europe underwent radical changes.

★ LARGEST ARMY

The country that has the largest armed forces is China. According to 2005 estimates, the number of people available for military service was 342,956,265, of which 281,240,272 were fit for active duty. The People's Liberation Army makes up the majority, but the figure also includes the People's Armed Police Force (for internal security) which is considered by China to be an "armed force."

LARGEST ANTI-WAR RALLY

On February 15, 2003, anti-war rallies took place around the world. The largest occurred in Rome, Italy, where a crowd of 3 million gathered to protest about the USA's threat to invade Iraq. Police figures report that millions more demonstrated in nearly 600 cities worldwide.

LONGEST IRREGULAR WAR

The so-called Hundred Years' War between England and France, which lasted from 1337 to 1453 (116 years), was actually an irregular succession of wars rather than a single conflict.

SHORTEST WAR

The shortest war was between Britain and Zanzibar (now part of Tanzania), which lasted from 9 a.m. to 9:45 a.m. on August 27, 1896. Three British warships sealed the victory.

★ LARGEST AIR FORCE (BY NUMBER OF AIRCRAFT)

The largest air force, in terms of number of aircraft, is the United States Air Force (USAF), with a total of 6,042 as of September 2005. This includes 182 bombers and 2,506 fighter and attack aircraft.

★ NEW RECORD
☆ UPDATED RECORD

! X-REF

Do you know when the first atomic bomb was used in battle? And what the greatest death toll from an atomic raid was? You'll find the answers on p.202.

BIGGEST CAUSES OF GENOCIDE IN THE 20TH CENTURY

COUNTRY	DEAD	REASON & DATE
China	30,000,000	Rape of Nanking (1937), Mao's "Great Leap Forward" (1958–61), "Cultural Revolution", 1966–69
USSR	20,000,000	Stalin's foreign and domestic policies, 1920–50s
Germany	11,400,000	Nazi extermination of "undesirables," 1930–40s (top right)
Japan	10,000,000	Sino-Japanese War, 1930–40s (center right)
Pakistan	3,010,000	Persecution of Bengali people, 1970s
Sudan	2,850,000	State-sanctioned mass murders, 1990s
Nigeria	2,000,000	Persecution of Ogoni people, 1990s
Afghanistan	1,800,000	Soviet invasion of Afghanistan, 1970–80s
Cambodia	1,700,000	Civilians murdered by Khmer Rouge, 1970s
Indonesia	1,200,000	Mass murder of East Timorese civilians, 1970–90s
Rwanda	1,020,000	Ethnic cleansing of Tutsi minority, 1990s (below)

Source: Barbara Harff, Strassler Family Center for Holocaust and Genocide Studies

★ OLDEST FIGHTER PILOT

Uri Gil (Israel, b. April 9, 1943), a brigadier-general in the Israeli Air Force, was an active fighter pilot from 1964 until his last flight in an F-16 jet on June 20, 2003, at the age of 60 years 72 days.

MOST PRODUCED WORLD WAR II FIGHTER

More than 36,000 Ilyushin Il-2 "Sturmovik" ground-attack aircraft are said to have been produced in Russia before, during, and immediately after World War II, making this one of the most numerous combat aircraft of all time. The fighter's heavy armor and solid build earned it the nickname "flying tank".

MARINE WARFARE

FIRST NUCLEAR SUBMARINE

The world's first nuclear-powered submarine was USS *Nautilus*, launched in Groton, Connecticut, USA, on January 21, 1954. Built by General Dynamics Electric Boat, *Nautilus* was 324 ft (98 m) long with a beam of 88 ft (26 m).

★ FASTEST SHIP-BUILDING

Complete ships of over 22 million lb (10,000 tonnes) deadweight were built in record time at Kaiser's Yard, Portland, Oregon, USA, during the World War II Liberty ship-building program. In 1942, No. 440, named *Robert E. Peary*, had her keel laid on November 8, was launched on November 12, and was operational after 4 days 15.5 hr on November 15.

LARGEST STEALTH SHIP

The Swedish Visby-class corvette is approximately 236 ft (72 m) long and has a displacement of 1.32 million lb (600 tonnes). Developed by the Kockums shipyard, the carbon fiber vessel is far lighter than a conventional ship of its size and features the large, flat surfaces commonly used in aircraft to provide low radar visibility.

WORST DEATH TOLL FROM A SINGLE SHIP DISASTER

A total of 7,700 people died when the German liner *Wilhelm Gustloff* (57 million lb; 25,893 tonnes) was torpedoed off Danzig by a Soviet S-13 submarine on January 30, 1945.

★ LARGEST NAVY

The United States Navy is the world's largest in terms of manpower. In early 2006 there were 356,283 uniformed personnel on active duty, supported by 175,581 civilian employees.

The **navy with the largest number of ships** is also the United States Navy, which, in early 2006, had 281 deployable battle-force ships (including submarines) on active duty.

LARGEST DEATH TOLL FROM A CHEMICAL WEAPONS ATTACK

An estimated 4,000 people died in the worst single chemical weapons attack. The victims perished when President Saddam Hussein of Iraq attacked members of his country's Kurdish minority at Halabja, Iraq, in March 1988. The attack was ostensibly punishment for the support that the Kurds had given to Iran in the Iran–Iraq War of 1980–88.

ESPIONAGE

★ FIRST PHOTO-OPTICAL SPY SATELLITES

Project CORONA (est. 1959) was the first known use of "spy" or "reconnaissance" satellites to gather intelligence. The project was established to provide photographic surveillance of Russia and China, and was funded by the CIA and the US Air Force. The satellites were designed to eject canisters (or "buckets") of exposed film, which would parachute down for collection by specially adapted aircraft.

HIGHEST-RESOLUTION SATELLITE IMAGES

The best commercially available satellite images are those taken by DigitalGlobe's QuickBird Satellite. Launched on October 18, 2001, QuickBird can take black-and-white images of the Earth at a resolution of 24 in (61 cm) per pixel, and multispectral images at 8 ft (2.44 m) per pixel.

★ HIGHEST-RANKED AMERICAN SPY

Retired Army Reserve Colonel George Trofimoff (USA) is the highest-ranking American in uniform to be charged with espionage. On June 14, 2001, he was found guilty of spying for the USSR and Russia while serving as the civilian chief of the US Army Element of the Nuremburg Joint Interrogation Center (Germany) between 1969 and 1994. He was sentenced to life imprisonment on September 28, 2001.

SMALLEST SPY PLANE

The palm-sized Black Widow was developed by Aerovironment of Monrovia, California, USA, for possible reconnaissance use by ground combat troops. It has a wingspan of 6 in (15.24 cm), weighs just 2.8 oz (80 g), and carries a tiny color video camera weighing 0.07 oz (2 g).

★ SHORTEST SPY

The smallest recorded spy was the Frenchman Richebourg (1768–1858), who measured just 1 ft 11 in (58 cm) as an adult. Officially, Richebourg was employed as a butler by the Duchess of Orleans, mother of King Louis-Philippe, but he was called upon to act as a secret agent during the French Revolution (1789–1799), dispatching messages into and out of Paris while disguised as an infant and carried by his "nurse."

★ LARGEST INCREASE IN PHISHING

"Phishing" is a means of identity theft using fake emails or websites to obtain details such as bank account numbers and other personal details from the public. According to the Anti Phishing Working Group, phishing grew by a record 42% in January 2005, from 8,829 phishing emails sent in December 2004 to 12,845 by the end of January.

The number of phishing websites also increased from 1,740 to 2,560, almost a doubling of figures from October 2004.

★ DEADLIEST LIPSTICK GUN

The "Kiss of Death" lipstick pistol, designed for use by Soviet KGB agents during the Cold War, could fire a single – fatal – 4.5-mm shot.

★ LARGEST MILITARY TROJAN HORSE THEFT

In November 2004, a gang of Chinese hackers were suspected of using a "Trojan horse" (see facing page) to steal sensitive data from various high-level US military and government establishments. Targets included the US Army's Aviation and Missile Command in Alabama, Information Systems Engineering Command in Arizona, the Defense Information Systems Agency, the Naval Ocean System Center in San Diego, and the Space and Missile Defense Acquisition Center in Alabama. Secret plans for NASA's Mars Reconnaissance Orbiter (pictured) were among the stolen files. The thefts continue to this day.

★LARGEST CIVILIAN TROJAN HORSE THEFT

In May 2005, Israeli police uncovered a large industrial spying ring believed to have used "Trojan horse" software – in the form of a business proposal on CD sent to targeted companies – to steal "tens of thousands" of documents from leading Israeli businesses, including the major utilities and TV companies.

In March 2006, Ruth and Michael Haephrati (both Israel) – a married couple – were sentenced to four and two years respectively for writing and selling the Trojan horse, and were also ordered to pay victims 2 million new shekels ($427,000).

MOST WIDELY DEPLOYED MILITARY UAV

By early 2004, the *Predator* unmanned aerial vehicle (UAV), manufactured by General Atomics Aeronautical Systems, had logged more than 65,000 flight hours, of which more than half were in combat zones such as Iraq, Kosovo, and Afghanistan. The 100th example of the aircraft, which has a wingspan of 48 ft 7 in (14.8 m) and a flight endurance time of more than 40 hours, was delivered to the US military in February 2004.

★MOST POWERFUL CELL-PHONE GUN

In October 2000, during a raid on a drugs dealer on the Croatia-Slovenia border, police seized ten .22-caliber pistols disguised as cell phones. Each gun, tellingly branded as MOKTEL, could

fire a (close-range) lethal round of four bullets if numbers 5, 6, 7, and 8 were pressed. In another incident, Dutch police also recovered cell-phone guns, plus pistols so small they were disguised as keyrings.

★LARGEST MARINE MAMMAL MILITARY DIVISION

The US Navy's Marine Mammal Program of San Diego, California, USA, established in 1960, had 75 Bottlenose dolphins (*Tursiops truncatus*) and 20 California sea lions (*Zalophus californianus californianus*) all trained for deployment, as of April 2003.

★LARGEST COLLECTION OF ESPIONAGE-RELATED ITEMS

H. Keith Melton (USA), a military and intelligence historian and author, owns more than 7,000 items of spying equipment, such as papers, cameras, concealment devices, and various other items of espionage gadgetry. He also boasts over 6,500 books and 30,000 photographs. So secret is the collection that we cannot reveal where it is located!

★GREATEST RANGE FOR A WIRELESS PEN CAMERA

The pocket clip on Swann's (USA) wireless PenCam contains a color camera and a microphone disguised as a logo. The transmission of the signal to a handheld receiver – which can be connected to a TV or VCR – is wireless and effective to about 260 ft (80 m).

MOST DEFENSIVE FEATURES ON A TRUCK

The US Army's SMARTRUCK III, based on a standard Ford F-350, has more than 10 James Bond-style defensive features, including Kevlar armor, run-flat tires, a fire-suppression system, and a remote-controlled .50-caliber

machine gun with sniper-detection. Also on board are anti-missile missiles, side flares, smoke and tear-gas launchers, and a "telemmersion" system for high-resolution situation awareness.

★LARGEST INTELLIGENCE AGENCY

The National Security Agency (NSA) is the largest and most secretive institution of its kind. Often known as the "No Such Agency," its mission is to gather data on international economic, military, and diplomatic situations. An estimated 38,000 people work at the HQ in Washington, D.C., USA, with an annual budget of more than $40 billion.

According to author and NSA expert James Bamford (USA), each of its dozen largest global listening posts picks up more than 2 million communications – including emails, phone calls, and faxes – every hour.

★ NEW RECORD
⋆ UPDATED RECORD

CRIME & PUNISHMENT

MOST ➡
STOLEN PAINTING

The famous Rembrandt painting called *Jacob III de Cheyn* (1632) has been stolen (and recovered) from museum galleries no less than four times – making the pocket-sized portrait the world's most stolen picture. It has been returned anonymously each time and, as a result, no one has ever been charged with theft. The painting is so well known that thieves would find it virtually impossible to sell.

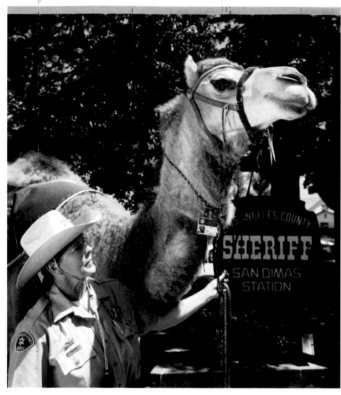

HIGHEST-RANKING LAW-ENFORCEMENT CAMEL

A camel named Bert was accepted as Reserve Deputy Sheriff for the Los Angeles County Sheriff's Department, San Dimas, California, USA, on April 5, 2003. Bert regularly goes on patrol with his handler Nancy Fite (USA).

MOST PROLIFIC MURDERER IN A SINGLE DAY

In a drunken rampage lasting just eight hours on April 26–27, 1982, policeman Wou Bom-kon (South Korea), aged 27, killed 57 people and wounded 35 with 176 rounds of rifle ammunition and hand grenades in the Kyong Sang-Namdo province of South Korea. He subsequently blew himself up.

MOST PROLIFIC SERIAL KILLER

Pedro López (Colombia), who raped and killed young girls in Colombia, Peru, and Ecuador in the late 1970s, eventually confessed to 300 such murders. Charged on 57 counts of murder in Ecuador, the "Monster of the Andes" was sentenced to life imprisonment in 1980.

★ MOST SCENT-DEPENDENT ROBBERIES

Seiichi Shirota (Japan) has been linked to more than 200 robberies worth ¥60 million ($510,000) because of his nose for crime. Shirota selected potential female victims by sniffing at the mailboxes of their homes to identify whether their perfume scent suggested they might be wealthy and likely to own luxury goods. He would also check for male underwear hung on laundry lines, to confirm that the potential victim lived alone.

LARGEST WHITE-COLLAR CRIME

In February 1997, copper trader Yasuo Hamanaka (Japan) pleaded guilty to fraud and forgery in connection with illicit trading that cost the Japanese company Sumitomo an estimated $2.6 billion over a 10-year period of unauthorized transactions.

★ MOST AND LEAST CORRUPT COUNTRIES

The record for the world's **most corrupt country** is shared by Bangladesh and Chad, according to Transparency International's Corruption Perceptions Index (2005). This index compares the misuse of public office for private gain in more than 150 countries, as perceived by business and country analysts (resident and non-resident).

According to the same index in 2005, the ★ **least corrupt country** was Iceland.

IN COURT

★ FASTEST REAL-TIME COURT REPORTER

Mark Kislingbury of Houston, Texas, USA, is the National Court Reporters Association speed and real-time champion, achieving 360 words per minute with 92.23% accuracy, at the NCRA 2004 summer convention on July 30, 2004.

★ FASTEST-GROWING ➡ CRIMINAL GANG

The Mara Salvatrucha (MS-13) gang based in Los Angeles, California, USA, has grown faster than all others in recent times. Formed by migrants fleeing civil war in El Salvador during the 1980s, it is involved in drug- and weapon-trafficking as well as murder. Membership is estimated at 700,000 worldwide, including 8,000–10,000 members in the USA. Members are recognizable by their Gothic-style MS-13 tattoos.

WORLDWIDE CRIME STATISTICS

MOST CRIMES (OVERALL)	HOLDER	NUMBER OF CRIMES
Kidnappings*	Colombia	5,181
Murders	India	37,170
Rapes	United States	89,110
Robberies	Spain	497,262
Frauds	Germany	895,758
Car thefts	United States	1,147,300
Burglaries	United States	2,099,700
Total crimes	United States	23,677,800
Total crime victims (as % of population)**	Australia	30.1%

MOST CRIMES	HOLDER	CRIMES PER 1,000 PEOPLE
Kidnappings	Colombia	0.120617
Murders	Colombia	0.617847
Rapes	South Africa	1.19538
Car thefts	Australia	6.92354
Frauds	Germany	10.8668
Robberies	Spain	12.3265
Burglaries	Australia	21.7454
Total crimes	Dominica	113.822

Except where indicated, source is Seventh United Nations Survey of Crime Trends and Operations of Criminal Justice Systems, covering the period 1998–2000 (United Nations Office on Drugs and Crime, Center for International Crime Prevention)
*SOURCE: Hiscox Group
**SOURCE: UNICRI (United Nations Interregional Crime and Justice Research Institute) 2002. Correspondence on data on crime victims. March. Turin

★ LARGEST DEATH ROW POPULATION

The USA has the largest death row population in the world, with 3,373 inmates awaiting execution as of January 1, 2006. On December 2, 2005, Kenneth Lee Boyd (USA, pictured), who had been imprisoned for murders committed in 1988, became the 1,000th person to be executed since the death penalty was reintroduced in 1977.

LONGEST HEARING

The longest civil case heard before a jury is *Kemner vs Monsanto Co.*, concerning an alleged toxic chemical spill in Sturgeon, Missouri, USA, in 1979. The trial started on February 6, 1984, at St. Clair County Court House, Belleville, Illinois, USA, before Circuit Judge Richard P. Goldenhersh, and ended on October 22, 1987.

MOST SUCCESSFUL LAWYER

Sir Lionel Luckhoo (Guyana), senior partner of Luckhoo and Luckhoo of Georgetown, Guyana, succeeded in securing 245 successive murder-charge acquittals between 1940 and 1985.

$1 billion

★LARGEST ROBBERY BY A STATESMAN
Amount that Qusay Saddam Hussein – the second son of former Iraqi president Saddam Hussein – stole from Iraq's Central Bank in March 2003, just prior to the US-led invasion.

£292 million ($435 million)

LARGEST ROBBERY BY A MUGGER
Value of Treasury bills and certificates of deposit stolen by a mugger who attacked a money-brokers messenger in the City of London, UK, on May 2, 1990.

$100 million

LARGEST JEWEL ROBBERY
Estimated loss from the largest-ever gem theft in a raid on the Antwerp Diamond Center, Belgium, on February 15–16, 2003.

£53,116,760 ($92,515,054)

LARGEST CASH ROBBERY
Amount stolen on February 22, 2006, from a money depot in Kent, UK. Securitas' insurers subsequently offered a reward of £2 million ($3.5 million) – one of the largest rewards ever offered in UK criminal history.

(£9–22 million) $20–50 million

LARGEST SAFE-DEPOSIT BOX ROBBERY
Estimated amount stolen from safe-deposit boxes in the vaults of the British Bank of the Middle East in Beirut, Lebanon, on January 22, 1976.

£2,631,784 ($7,369,784)

LARGEST TRAIN ROBBERY
Amount taken from a UK General Post Office mail train on August 8, 1963. Around 120 mailbags, containing banknotes, were stolen. Only £343,448 ($961,757) was recovered.

★ NEW RECORD
☆ UPDATED RECORD

WEALTH

MOST EXPENSIVE SKIN BEAUTY TREATMENT

The Botaenica Dual-Mud Kit by Bergdorf Goodman (USA) costs $845 for two 7-oz (28-g) mud masks.

★ MOST EXPENSIVE RESIDENCE

Updown Court in Windlesham, Surrey, UK, is currently valued at $122.2 million. It has 103 rooms and five swimming pools. Features include a squash court, bowling alley, heated marble driveway, and 24-carat-gold leafing on the study's mosaic floor. The underground garage has room for eight limousines.

★ MOST VALUABLE SOAP

Artist Gianni Motti (Italy) has made a bar of soap from body fat removed from former Italian Prime Minister Silvio Berlusconi. It is on display in a gallery in Basel, Switzerland, but can be purchased for $17,506. The artist, who has called his creation *Mani Pulite* ("Clean Hands"), claims to have received the fat from an unnamed employee at a plastic surgery clinic in Lugano, Switzerland, where Berlusconi underwent cosmetic procedures.

★ HIGHEST PRICE PAID FOR A RACE HORSE

The highest price paid for a thoroughbred at public auction is $16 million for a two-year-old colt – unnamed at the time – who had yet to even race. The colt was bought at an auction held at Calder Race Course, Florida, USA, on February 28, 2006.

LARGEST PRIVATE ROLLS-ROYCE FLEET

Sultan Hassanal Bolkiah of Brunei is believed to have the biggest private collection of Rolls-Royce cars. The fleet has been estimated to consist of 150 vehicles, and he is reported to own a further 1,998 luxury cars.

★ MOST EXPENSIVE CHOCOLATE

Amedei Porcelana is priced at $90 per 1 lb (450 g). It is the first chocolate in the world made from cocoa beans of a single variety, Porcelana, which are a translucent white color. Around 20,000 packs are produced annually by the Italian chocolatier, Amedei.

★ RICHEST LIVING PERSON

William H. Gates III (USA), chairman and chief software architect of the Microsoft Corporation, is the richest person in the world according to *Forbes* magazine, which estimated his wealth at $50.1 billion in March 2005.

RICHEST PERSON EVER

John D. Rockefeller was worth $900 million in 1913, $189.6 billion in today's terms. He made his fortune in oil and became a philanthropist in later life.

ACTUAL SIZE

← ★MOST EXPENSIVE TOAST

A toasted sandwich said to bear an image of the Virgin Mary sold for $28,000 on eBay in November 2004. Having noticed the image on her snack, Diane Duyser (USA) sealed it, kept it for 10 years as a lucky charm, then sold it to Canadian online casino Goldenpalace.com.

★ RICHEST DEAD CELEBRITY

In 2005, 29 years after he died of a heart attack, Elvis Presley earned $45 million. Approximately $15 million is made annually in admission fees to his estate, with the balance coming from sales of Presley-related products.

★ MOST EXPENSIVE CAVIAR

The most expensive of all caviar – and the world's **most expensive food** – is "Almas," from the Iranian Beluga fish. Just 2 lb 3 oz (1 kg) of this "black gold" regularly sells for $34,500. Almas is produced from the eggs of a rare albino sturgeon between 60 and 100 years old, found in the Caspian Sea.

MOST EXPENSIVE PRODUCTION CAR

The Mercedes Benz CLK/LM cost $1,547,620 when launched in 1997. It has a top speed of 198 mph (320 km/h) and can travel from 0 to 62 mph (100 km/h) in just 3.8 seconds.

MOST EXPENSIVE PAIR OF JEANS

The world's most expensive pair of jeans – commercially available, in accordance with Guinness World Records stipulations – are Escada's Couture Swarovski Crystal Jeans, which can be purchased from Neiman Marcus Stores across the United States for a mere $10,000! The embroidered, designer-denim pairs of jeans are studded with Swarovski crystals.

WEALTHIEST UNIVERSITY

In 2005, the endowment of Harvard University in Cambridge, Massachusetts, USA, totaled $22 billion. This figure is larger than the annual operating budgets of 142 countries, including Cuba, Jordan, and Lithuania.

★ NEW RECORD
★ UPDATED RECORD

2005'S HIGHEST EARNERS

SPEAKER	Bill Clinton (USA) $6 m	
CHEF, TV	Jamie Oliver (UK) $8.9 m	
CHEF	Wolfgang Puck (Austria) $12 m	
BROADCASTER	Katie Couric (USA) $13 m	
SUPERMODEL	Gisele Bundchen (Brazil) $15.2 m	
TENNIS PLAYER	Maria Sharapova (Russia) $18.2 m	
SOCCER PLAYER	David Beckham (UK) $32.5 m	
BASKETBALL PLAYER	Shaquille O'Neal (USA) $33.4 m	
TALENT SHOW JUDGE, TV	Simon Cowell (UK) $34 m	
BOXER	Oscar de la Hoya (USA) $38 m	
SINGER (FEMALE)	Madonna Ciccone (USA) $50 m	
MAGICIAN	David Copperfield (USA) $57 m	
CHILDREN'S AUTHOR	J. K. Rowling (UK) $59.1 m	
RACE CAR DRIVER	Michael Schumacher (Germany) $60 m	
AUTHOR	Dan Brown (USA) $76.5 m	
GOLFER	Tiger Woods (USA) $87 m	
TALK SHOW HOST	Oprah Winfrey (USA) $225 m	
CEO	Terry S. Semel (USA) $230.6 m	
FILM PRODUCER	George Lucas (USA) $290 m	
WOMAN	Liliane Bettencourt (France) $16 bn	
MAN	Bill Gates (USA) $50.1 bn	

ACTUAL SIZE

SMALLEST RABBIT BREEDS

The Polish and Netherland dwarf both weigh in at 2–2.5 lb (0.9–1.1 kg). Pictured is Sniffles, a Netherland dwarf who, until 2005, held the record for the **oldest living rabbit**.

★ NEW RECORD
☆ UPDATED RECORD

ACTUAL SIZE

RABBITS

★ HIGHEST RABBIT JUMP

On June 28, 1997, Mimrelunds Tösen, a rabbit owned by Tine Hygom (Denmark), cleared 39.2 in (99.5 cm) in Herning, Denmark.

LONGEST EARS ON A RABBIT

Nipper's Geronimo, an English lop owned by Waymon and Margaret Nipper (USA), measured 31 in (79 cm) in a complete span on November 1, 2003, at the American Rabbit Breeders Association National Show in Wichita, Kansas, USA.

OLDEST RABBIT EVER

Flopsy, a wild rabbit caught on August 6, 1964, died 18 years 10 months 3 weeks later at the home of L. B. Walker (Australia).

DOGS

★ FASTEST TIME TO POP 100 BALLOONS BY A DOG

The fastest time to pop 100 balloons by a dog is 53.74 seconds by Anastasia (a four-year-old Jack Russell terrier) owned by Doree Sitterly (USA) on Animal Planet's *Guinness World Records: Amazing Animals* in Los Angeles, California, USA, on September 24, 2005.

★ LONGEST FLYING DISC THROW CAUGHT BY A DOG

On October 12, 1994, in Pasadena, California, USA, a flying disc thrown by Mark Molnar (USA) was caught by his dog Cheyenne-Ashley Whippet 390 ft (118.9 m) away.

★ LARGEST DOG "STAY"

"Super Sit," organized by the RSPCA at the Wag and Bone Show, Windsor Great Park, UK, on August 6, 2005, was a simultaneous dog stay involving a record 627 dogs.

★ MOST DOGS WALKED SIMULTANEOUSLY (SOLO)

The most dogs simultaneously walked by an individual is 22 by John Garcia (USA) representing Best Friends Animal Society. The walk took place in Kanab, Utah, USA, and lasted 14 min 18 sec on August 11, 2005.

★ FASTEST 10-OBSTACLE AGILITY COURSE (TEAM)

The fastest time for a team of four dogs to complete a 10-obstacle agility course in relay is 1 min 2 sec and was set by France's Delphine Boucher (Narla), Daniel Jubault (Uguette), Eric Gravoil (Lady), and Adeline Boisnartel (Rusty) on the set of *L'Été De Tous Les Records* in La Tranche Sur Mer, France, on July 28, 2005.

LONGEST DOMESTIC GOAT HORNS

Uncle Sam the goat has a pair of horns that measured 52 in (132 cm) – about three times the length of this open book – from tip to tip on April 16, 2004. Sam is owned by William and Vivian Wentling of Rothsville, Pennsylvania, USA.

SMALLEST DOGS

The **smallest living dog in terms of *height*** is Danka Kordak Slovakia, a Chihuahua that measured 5.4 in (13.8 cm) tall and 7.4 in (18.8 cm) long on May 30, 2004, and is owned by Ing. Igor Kvetko (Slovakia).

Heaven Sent Brandy, a Chihuahua who lives with her owner, Paulette Keller in Florida, USA, is the **smallest dog in terms of *length***, measuring 6 in (15.2 cm) from the nose to the tip of the tail on January 31, 2005.

The **smallest dog ever** was a dwarf Yorkshire terrier who stood 2.8 in (7.11 cm) tall and measured 3.75 in (9.5 cm) from nose to tail.

← LARGEST RABBIT

The **largest breed of domestic rabbit** is the Flemish giant, which can weigh 16 lb 8 oz–17 lb 10 oz (7.5–8 kg) and have a toe-to-toe length when fully stretched of 36 in (91 cm). Weights of up to 24 lb 14 oz (11.3 kg) have been known, but *Guinness World Records* does not ratify pet records based on weight, to avoid force-feeding.

★ LONGEST WHISKERS

The longest whisker on a cat measure 7.5 in (19 cm) and belong to Fullmoon's Miss American Pie (a.k.a. Missi), a Maine coon cat who lives with her owner, Kaija Kyllönen in Iisvesi, Finland. The record-breaking whisker was measured on December 22, 2005.

CATS

SMALLEST CATS

The **smallest living cat** in terms of height and length is Itse Bitse, who measured 3.75 in (9.52 cm) high and 15 in (38.1 cm) from tip to tip on November 24, 2003. The Himalayan/Siamese mix is owned by Mayo and Dea Whitton (USA).

The **smallest cat ever** was a male blue point Himalayan-Persian named Tinker Toy that measured only 2.75 in (7 cm) tall and 7.5 in (19 cm) long when fully grown. He was owned by Katrina and Scott Forbes (USA).

★ OLDEST CAT EVER

Creme Puff (b. August 3, 1967) lived until August 6, 2005 – an amazing 38 years and 3 days! She lived in Austin, Texas, USA, with her owner, Jake Perry – who was also owner of the previous record holder, Grandpa Rex Allen.

MOST PROLIFIC CAT

A tabby named Dusty from Bonham, Texas, USA, produced 420 kittens during her breeding life. She gave birth to her last litter (a single kitten) on June 12, 1952.

CAT WITH THE MOST TOES

Jake, a ginger tabby who lives with Michelle and Paul Contant in Ontario, Canada, has 28 toes – seven on each paw – as counted in September 2002.

MISCELLANEOUS

★ LONGEST GOLDFISH

A goldfish (*Carassius auratus*) owned by Joris Gijsbers (Netherlands) measured 18.7 in (47.4 cm) from snout to tail-fin end on March 24, 2003, in Hapert, the Netherlands.

★ OLDEST LIVING PONY

Sugar Puff, an Exmoor–Shetland cross owned by S. Botting (UK) of West Sussex, was born in 1951.

★ HIGHEST JUMP BY A PYGMY MINIATURE HORSE

Lovebug, a pygmy miniature horse owned by Krystal Cole (USA), jumped 24 in (61 cm) on the set of Animal Planet's *Guinness World Records: Amazing Animals* on September 24, 2005, in California, USA.

★ LONGEST DIVE BY A PIG

Miss Piggy, owned by Tom Vandeleur (Australia), jumped 10 ft 10 in (3.31 m) into a pool at the Royal Darwin Show, Northern Territory, Australia, on July 22, 2005, for the TV show *Guinness World Records*.

LARGEST LITTERS

ANIMAL	LITTER	DATE
Mouse	34	Feb. 12, 1982
Hamster	26	Feb. 28, 1974
Dog	24	Nov. 29, 2004
Rabbit	24	1978
	24	May 1999
Cat	19	Aug. 7, 1970
Guinea pig	17	Aug. 17, 1992
Ferret	15	1981
Gerbil	14	1960s
Cattle	5	Mar. 18, 2005

★ TALLEST DOG

The tallest dog living is Gibson, a harlequin Great Dane who measured 42.2 in (107 cm) tall on August 31, 2004. A therapy dog, he is owned by Sandy Hall of Grass Valley, California, USA.

◀ LONGEST CAT

Verismo's Leonetti Reserve Red – a.k.a. Leo – measured 48 in (122 cm) from his nose to the tip of his tail on March 10, 2002. Leo, a Maine coon cat, lives with his owners, Frieda Ireland and Carroll Damron, in Chicago, Illinois, USA. The mammoth moggie, whose favorite food is blue cheese, has paws so big they can fit into a size-2 child's shoe!

GARDEN GIANTS

★ LONGEST-RUNNING HORTICULTURAL SHOW

The Philadelphia Flower Show has been hosted annually by the Pennsylvania Horticultural Society in Philadelphia, Pennsylvania, USA, since June 6, 1829. The only years in which the show has not been held were 1918 and 1943–46, owing to US involvement in World War I and II.

LARGEST GARLIC FESTIVAL

The three-day summer Gilroy Garlic Festival in Gilroy, California, USA, attracts 130,000 people. Visitors can sample garlic-flavored food ranging from meat to ice cream.

★ LARGEST ORANGE

Grown in the garden of Patrick and Joanne Fiedler (both USA) in Fresno, California, USA, the largest orange by circumference measured 23 in (58.4 cm) around its widest point on May 15, 2005.

★ HEAVIEST PUMMELO

The pummelo (*Citrus grandis osbeck*) is a fruit native to southeastern Asia. Seiji Sonoda (Japan) presented one weighing 10 lb 11 oz (4.86 kg) at the Banpeiyu competition, Yatsushiro, Kumamoto, Japan, on January 28, 2005.

★ LONGEST ASPARAGUS

On October 2, 2004, the world's longest asparagus, measuring 138.5 in (351.7 cm), was presented by Harry and Carson Willemse (both Canada) at the Port Elgin Pumpkinfest, Ontario, Canada.

★ LONGEST GOURD

Grown by Grant McGregor (Canada), the longest gourd measured 9 ft 6.75 in (2.91 m) on October 2, 2004, when it was presented and measured at the Port Elgin Pumpkinfest, Ontario, Canada.

HEAVIEST FRUITS AND VEGETABLES

FRUIT/VEGETABLE	WEIGHT	NAME	DATE
★ Apple	4 lb 1 oz (1.84 kg)	Chisato Iwasaki (Japan)	2005
Avocado	4 lb 6 oz (1.99 kg)	Anthony Llanos (Australia)	1992
Beet	51 lb 9 oz (23.4 kg)	Ian Neale (UK)	2001
★ Blueberry	0.24 oz (7 g)	Brian Carlick (UK)	2005
Broccoli	35 lb (15.87 kg)	John & Mary Evans (USA)	1993
Brussels sprout	18 lb 3 oz (8.3 kg)	Bernard Lavery (UK)	1992
Cabbage	124 lb (56.24 kg)	Bernard Lavery (UK)	1989
Cabbage (red)	42 lb (19.05 kg)	R. Straw (UK)	1925
Cantaloupe	64 lb 13 oz (29.4 kg)	Scott & Mardie Robb (USA)	2004
Carrot	18 lb 13 oz (8.61 kg)	John Evans (USA)	1998
Cauliflower	54 lb 3 oz (24.6 kg)	Alan Hattersley (UK)	1999
Celery	63 lb 4 oz (28.7 kg)	Scott & Mardie Robb (USA)	2003
Cherry	0.76 oz (21.69 g)	Gerardo Maggipinto (Italy)	2003
Zucchini	64 lb 8 oz (29.25 kg)	Bernard Lavery (UK)	1990
Cucumber	27 lb 5 oz (12.4 kg)	Alfred J. Cobb (UK)	2003
Garlic head	2 lb 10 oz (1.19 kg)	Robert Kirkpatrick (USA)	1985
Gooseberry	2 oz (61.04 g)	K. Archer (UK)	1993
Gourd	94 lb 5 oz (42.8 kg)	Robert Weber (Australia)	2001
Grapefruit	6 lb 12 oz (3.06 kg)	Debbie Hazelton (Australia)	1995
Jackfruit	76 lb 4 oz (34.6 kg)	George & Margaret Schattauer (USA)	2003
Kale	42 lb 6 oz (19.2 kg)	Scott Robb (USA)	2001
Kohlrabi	63 lb 15 oz (29 kg)	Dave Iles (UK)	2004
Leek	17 lb 13 oz (8.1 kg)	Fred Charlton (UK)	2002
Lemon	11 lb 9 oz (5.26 kg)	Aharon Shemoel (Israel)	2003
★ Mango	5 lb 7 oz (2.46 kg)	Colleen Porter (USA)	2005
★ Marrow squash	136 lb (62 kg)	Mark Baggs (UK)	2005
Nectarine	12 oz (360 g)	Tony Slattery (New Zealand)	1998
Onion	15 lb 15 oz (7.24 kg)	Mel Ednie (UK)	1994
★ Parsnip	10 lb 8 oz (4.78 kg)	Colin Moore (UK)	1980
Peach	25 oz (725 g)	Paul Friday (USA)	2002
Pear	4 lb 8 oz (2.1 kg)	Warren Yeoman (Australia)	1999
Pineapple	17 lb 12 oz (8.06 kg)	E. Kamuk (Papua New Guinea)	1994
Pomegranate	2 lb 3 oz (1.04 kg)	Katherine Murphey (USA)	2001
Potato	7 lb 11 oz (3.5 kg)	K. Sloane (UK)	1994
Potato (sweet)	81 lb 9 oz (37 kg)	Manuel Pérez Pérez (Spain)	2004
★ Pummelo	10 lb 11 oz (4.86 kg)	Seiji Sonoda (Japan)	2005
★ Pumpkin	1,469 lb (666.32 kg)	Larry Checkon (USA)	2005
Quince orange	5 lb 2 oz (2.34 kg)	Edward Harold McKinney (USA)	2002
Radish	68 lb 9 oz (31.1 kg)	Manabu Ono (Japan)	2003
Rhubarb	5 lb 14 oz (2.67 kg)	E. Stone (UK)	1985
Rockmelon	23 lb 2 oz (10.5 kg)	Ned Katich (Australia)	1982
Squash	962 lb (436 kg)	Steve Hoult (Canada)	1997
Strawberry	8 oz (231 g)	G. Anderson (UK)	1983
Rutabaga	75 lb 12 oz (34.35 kg)	Scott & Mardie Robb (USA)	1999
Tomato	7 lb 12 oz (3.51 kg)	G. Graham (USA)	1986
Turnip	39 lb 3 oz (17.7 kg)	Scott & Mardie Robb (USA)	2004
★ Watermelon	268 lb 12 oz (121.93 kg)	Lloyd Bright (USA)	2005

★ HEAVIEST MANGO

The world's heaviest mango weighed in at 5 lb 7 oz (2.46 kg). It was from a variety known as Keitt and was presented by Colleen Porter of Kailua-Kona, Hawaii, USA, in October 2005.

★ LARGEST FOOD FIGHT

Each year, on the last Wednesday in August, the town of Buñol, near Valencia, Spain, holds its tomato festival, La Tomatina. In 2004, 38,000 people threw about 275,500 lb (125 tonnes) of tomatoes at each other. By the time the food fight is over, everything and everyone is saturated with tomato paste. Rivers of tomato juice up to 12 in (30 cm) deep run through the town until fire engines come in to hose it all away.

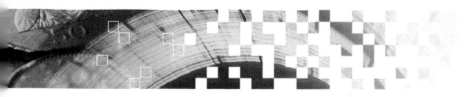

LARGEST FRUIT PIE

Members of the Oliver Rotary Club, British Columbia, Canada, baked a cherry pie weighing 37,721 lb (17.11 tonnes) on July 14, 1990.

LARGEST FRUIT SALAD

The world's largest fruit salad, weighing 8,866 lb (4.02 tonnes), was made by La Florida and displayed in the main square, La Merced, Chanchamayo, Peru, on July 27, 2003.

LONGEST ZUCCHINI

The world's longest zucchini measured 7 ft 2 in (2.2 m) on October 17, 2003, and was grown by Klaus Schoenemann (Germany) in his garden in Hagen, Germany.

★ TALLEST SUGAR CANE

The tallest sugar cane (*Saccharum officinarum*) measured 31 ft (9.5 m) on February 21, 2005, and grows in the garden of M. Venkatesh Gowda (India) in Mysore, Karnataka, India.

★ TALLEST BLUEBONNET

Discovered by Margaret Lipscomb and Arthur Bullis Cash (both USA) in Big Bend National Park, Texas, USA, the tallest bluebonnet flower (*Lupinus harvardii*) measured 65 in (164.5 cm) tall on March 27, 2005.

TALLEST PLANTS

PLANT	HEIGHT	NAME	DATE
Amaranthus	15 ft 1 in (4.61 m)	David Brenner (USA)	2004
Eggplant/Brinjal	18 ft (5.5 m)	Abdul Masfoor (India)	1998
Bean plant	46 ft 3 in (14.1 m)	Staton Rorie (USA)	2003
Brussels sprout	9 ft 3 in (2.8 m)	Patrice & Steve Allison (USA)	2001
Cactus (homegrown)	270 ft (1.3 m)	Pandit S. Munji (India)	2004
Celery	9 ft (2.74 m)	John Priednieks (UK)	1998
Chrysanthemum	14 ft 3 in (4.34 m)	Bernard Lavery (UK)	1995
Coleus	8 ft 4 in (2.5 m)	Nancy Lee Spilove (USA)	2004
Collard greens	9 ft 2 in (2.79 m)	Reggie Kirkman (USA)	1999
Cosmos	12 ft 3 in (3.75 m)	Cosmos Executive Committee, Okayama, Japan	2003
Cotton	25 ft 5 in (7.74 m)	D. M. Williams (USA)	2004
Daffodil	5 ft 1 in (1.55 m)	M. Lowe (UK)	1979
Dandelion	3 ft 3 in (100 cm)	Ragnar Gille & Marcus Hamring (Sweden)	2001
★ Fuchsia (climbing)	37 ft 5 in (11.4 m)	Reinhard Biehler (Germany)	2005
Herba cistanches	5 ft 8 in (1.75 m)	BOC Hong Kong Baptist University, Hong Kong, China	2003
Papaya tree	44 ft (13.4 m)	Prasanta Mal (India)	2003
Parsley	4 ft 7 in (1.39 m)	Danielle, Gabrielle & Michelle Kassatly (all USA)	2003
Pepper	16 ft (4.87 m)	Laura Liang (USA)	1999
Periwinkle	7 ft 2 in (2.19 m)	Arvind, Rekha, Ashish & Rashmi Nema (all India)	2003
Petunia	19 ft 1 in (5.8 m)	Bernard Lavery (UK)	1994
★ Rosebush (self-supported)	13 ft 3 in (4.03 m)	Paul & Sharon Palumbo (USA)	2005
Rose (climbing)	91 ft (27.7 m)	Anne & Charles Grant (USA)	2004
★ Sugar cane	31 ft (9.5 m)	M. Venkatesh Gowda (India)	2005
Sunflower	25 ft 5 in (7.76 m)	M. Heijms (Netherlands)	1986
Sweet corn (maize)	31 ft (9.4 m)	D. Radda (USA)	1946
★ Bluebonnet	5 ft 6 in (164.5 cm)	Margaret Lipscome & Arthur Cash (USA)	2005
Tomato	65 ft (19.8 m)	Nutriculture Ltd, Lancashire, UK	2000
Umbrella	27 ft (8.22 m)	Konstantinos Xylakis & Sara Guterbock (USA)	2002
Zinnia	12 ft 6 in (3.81 m)	Everett Wallace & Melody Wagner (USA)	2004

ACTUAL SIZE

★ HEAVIEST BLUEBERRY

Cultivated by Brian Carlick of Aldeburgh, Suffolk, UK, in September 2005, the world's heaviest blueberry weighed in at 0.24 oz (7 g).

★ HEAVIEST PUMPKIN

A pumpkin weighing 1,469 lb (666 kg) was presented by Larry Checkon (USA) at the Pennsylvania Giant Pumpkin Growers Association Weigh-off, Pennsylvania, USA, on October 1, 2005.

← HEAVIEST BEET

The heaviest ever beet weighed 51 lb 9 oz (23.4 kg) and was presented by Ian Neale (UK) at the National Giant Vegetable Championship in Shepton Mallet, Somerset, UK, on September 7, 2001.

★ NEW RECORD
★ UPDATED RECORD

FOOD & DRINK

★ NEW RECORD
★ UPDATED RECORD

LARGEST...

★ BAGEL
A bagel weighing 868 lb (393 kg) was made by Brueggers Bagels (USA) and displayed at the New York State Fair, Geddes, New York, USA, on August 27, 2004.

★ BREAKFAST
For the 40th anniversary of Nutella chocolate spread (Ferrero, Germany), a breakfast was cooked for 27,854 people in Gelsenkirchen, Germany, on May 29, 2005.

★ BOX OF CHOCOLATE BARS
Kit Kat (Nestlé, Middle East) made a box of chocolate bars weighing 3,748 lb (1,700 kg) for the Sweet Surprises Festival held at BurJuman Shopping Center, Dubai, United Arab Emirates, on June 30, 2005.

★ CINNAMON ROLL
A cinnamon roll weighing 246 lb (111.8 kg) – the weight of two female adults – was made by the House of Bread in Mill Creek, Washington, USA, on October 15, 2005.

★ DONER KEBAB
A doner kebab weighing 910 lb (413 kg) was made by the Maroosh Lebanese Café at the Applause Festival in Albury, New South Wales, Australia, on October 23, 2004.

★ MOST EXPENSIVE SANDWICH
The McDonald sandwich – named after its creator Scott McDonald (UK), a chef at Selfridges department store in London, UK – is a 2,500-calorie offering that retails for £85 ($147).

Sandwiched between two pieces of 24-hour fermented sourdough bread is Wagyu beef (from Japanese cattle that are hand-massaged and fed on a diet of beer and classical music), fresh lobe foie gras, black truffle mayonnaise, brie de meaux, arugula leaves dressed in avocado oil, red pepper and mustard confit, and English plum tomatoes.

★ DUMPLING
Made in Metro City, Hong Kong, on May 21, 2005, the largest rice dumpling was prepared by Ocean Empire Food Shop (Holdings) Ltd and weighed 1,322 lb (600 kg).

★ FOCACCIA BREAD
A focaccia loaf weighing 6,172 lb (2,800 kg) was made by Pietro Catucci and Antonio Latte (Italy) in Mottola, Taranto, Italy, on August 6, 2005.

★ FISH MARKET
Tsukiji – part of the Tokyo Central Market in Japan – is the world's largest fish market, importing over 450 varieties of marine products from 60 countries. In 2003, staff handled an incredible 1.3 billion lb (615,400 tonnes) of produce.

★ ICE CREAM BOAT
Made by Hemglass Sverige AB (Sweden), the largest ice cream boat weighed 1,910 lb (866.5 kg) and was displayed in Stockholm, Sweden, on April 18, 2004.

★ MUSSELS DISH
A *mouclade* made from 4,400 lb (2 tonnes) of mussels, 485 lb (220 kg) of onions, 154 lb (70 kg) of carrots, 110 lb (50 kg) of garlic, 11 lb (5 kg) of parsley, 42.3 pints (5.28 gal) of olive oil, and 359.2 pints (44.9 gal) of wine was unveiled on the set of *L'Été De Tous Les Records* in St Pierre Sur Mer, France, on September 5, 2003.

★ LARGEST BUCKET OF POPCORN
CINEBOX's (Spain) bucket of popcorn had an incredible 1,695 ft³ (48 m³) of volume. The box was filled with popcorn over eight hours at an event held in Salt Gerona, Spain, on September 15, 2005. The ★ **largest popcorn ball** weighed 3,100 lb (1,406 kg) and was made by 40 volunteers at the Noble Popcorn Farm, Iowa, USA, on June 12, 2004.

★ SANDWICH
Wild Woody's Chill and Grill in Roseville, Michigan, USA, made a giant corned beef and mustard sandwich weighing 5,440 lb (2.467 tonnes) on March 17, 2005. It was 18.1 in (5.34 m) thick and 12 ft (3.6 m) wide.

★ TOM YUNG KUNG
Thailand's Ministry of Commerce, Department of Industrial Promotion, and Tourism Authority made the world's largest *tom yung kung*, a type of highly spiced Thai soup, at Patty Beach, Chonburi, Thailand, on November 18, 1999. When finished, the final serving of soup measured 10,567 pints (1,320.86 gal) – enough to fill over 60 bathtubs!

★ LARGEST SEAFOOD STICK

Created by the Pacific Fish Processing Co., Ltd., at its factory in Songkhla province, Thailand, on March 23, 2005, the largest seafood stick ever made weighed 110.34 lb (50.05 kg).

LONGEST...

★ CAKE

A cake measuring 8,737 ft 2 in (2,663.11 m) was baked by the Reach for a Dream Foundation in Johannesburg, South Africa, on July 7, 2005.

★ SALAMI

The world's longest salami measures 1,853 ft 3 in (564.88 m) – longer than the largest sand dunes found in the Sahara Desert, which measure up to 1,526 ft (465 m). The salami was created in Varallo, Vericelli, Italy, on August 14, 2005, and the record-breaking feat was organized by the town's mayor in association with the salami-producing company Salumificio Manuelli.

★ HOT DOG

The world's longest hot dog measured 57 ft 4 in (17.5 m). The bun was made by Conshohocken Bakery while the sausage was provided by Berks Meat Packing (both USA). The huge dog was made for the Annual Corvettes for Kids fundraiser at Fogesville, Pennsylvania, USA, in August 2005.

★ CURLY WURLY STRETCH

The farthest a Curly Wurly candy bar has been stretched in three minutes – under strictly controlled conditions – is 5 ft (1.53 m) by Kyle Dartnell-Steinberg (UK/USA) at the Guinness World Records office in London, UK, on December 22, 2005.

★ SPRING ROLL

Made by members of the Roll for Relief Campaign at Cornell University, Ithaca, New York, USA, on April 30, 2005, the longest spring roll ever made measured 1,428 ft 4 in (435.36 m).

★ SUSHI ROLL

A giant sushi roll, measuring 5,987 ft (1,825 m) was made by participants at the Saga Genki Matsuri in Yoshinogari, Saga, Japan, on October 20, 2002.

LARGEST FOODS EVER

LARGEST FOOD (BY WEIGHT)	HOLDER	WEIGHT
Birthday cake	EarthGrains Bakery and residents of Fort Payne (USA)	128,238 lb (58.1 tonnes)
King Cake (Rosca de Reyes)	10,000 visitors to the Acapulco "Day of the Three Kings" Festival (Mexico)	59,260 lb (26.8 tonnes)
Cheese	Agropur (Canada)	57,518 lb (26.0 tonnes)
Ice cream sundae	Palm Dairies Ltd (Canada)	54,917 lb (24.9 tonnes)
Pecan pie	El Paso Diablos Baseball Club (USA)	41,586 lb (18.8 tonnes)
Fruit pie	Oliver Rotary Club (Canada)	37,721 lb (17.1 tonnes)
Pizza	Norwood Hypermarket (South Africa)	26,883 lb (12.1 tonnes)
Spanish omelette	Representatives at Swatch (Japan)	24,339 lb (11.0 tonnes)
Meat pie	Catering students from the Stratford-upon-Avon College (UK)	23,237 lb (10.5 tonnes)
Curry (see recipe top right)	Abdul Salam, Eastern Eye Restaurant (UK)	22,707 lb (10.3 tonnes)

LARGEST BUBBLEGUM BUBBLE BLOWN (UNASSISTED)

Chad Fell (USA) blew a bubblegum bubble with a diameter of 20 in (50.8 cm) – without using his hands to steady or stretch the bubble – at the Double Springs High School, Winston County, Alabama, USA, on April 24, 2004. The secret of his success, says Chad, is blowing with three pieces of Dubble Bubble gum.

FOOD & DRINK

★ FASTEST TIME TO EAT A RAW ONION

Brian Duffield (UK) ate a raw onion in 1 min 29 sec on the set of *Lo Show Dei Record* in Milan, Italy, on January 5, 2006.

★ NEW RECORD
★ UPDATED RECORD

[?] DID YOU KNOW?

The Scoville Scale measures the amount of capsaicin in a pepper (i.e. the chemical that makes it hot). It was devised by pharmacist Wilbur Scoville (USA) in 1912. Sweet bell peppers have a value of 0; pure capsaicin has a value of 16 million.

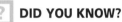

FOOD

★ FASTEST TIME TO EAT THREE SODA CRACKERS

Ambrose Mendy (UK) devoured three soda crackers in 34.78 sec at the studios of LBC Radio, London, UK, on May 9, 2005.

★ FASTEST TIME TO EAT THREE MINCE PIES

David Cole (UK) ate three mince pies in 1 min 26 sec live on ITV's *The Paul O'Grady Show* at the ITV Studios in London, UK, on December 20, 2005.

★ FASTEST TIME TO MAKE ONE LITER OF ICE CREAM

Peter Barham (UK) made one liter of ice cream in 18.78 seconds at the Hinds Head Hotel in Bray, Maidenhead, UK, on June 21, 2005.

★ MOST FLAVORS OF ICE CREAM DISPLAYED

UPA Gelatieri Padova (Italy) displayed 521 flavors of ice cream together at the 500 Tastes of Solidarity Event in Padua, Italy, on March 28, 2004.

★ MOST TABASCO SAUCE DRUNK IN 30 SECONDS

Andrew Hajinikitas (Australia) drank 4.2 fl oz (120 ml) of Tabasco sauce in 30 seconds, in Sydney, New South Wales, Australia, on May 8, 2005.

HIGHEST PANCAKE TOSS

Aldo Zilli (Italy) tossed a pancake 11 ft (3.35 m) high on ITV's *This Morning* television show in London, UK, on February 28, 2006.

★ HOTTEST CHILI POWDER

The "16 Million Reserve," created by Blair Lazar (USA), is the hottest chili powder commercially available. It measures 16 million Scoville units – the maximum figure on the "hotness" scale, and therefore effectively pure capsaicin (see box above) – and is available to purchase for $199.95. The spice is sold as a powder that is added to the cooking ingredients.

★ TALLEST CREPE STACK

A stack of 980 crepes, measuring 27.5 in (70 cm) in height, was made on the set of *L'Été De Tous Les Records*, Benodet, France, on August 1, 2003.

★ TALLEST POPPADOM STACK

A stack of poppadoms measuring 40.1 in (102 cm) high was made by a team from Magneticnorth – Kate Bowen, Chris Conlan, Chris Johnstone, and Jay Roche (all UK) – at a charity event at the Great John Street Hotel, Manchester, UK, on October 14, 2005.

★ MOST EXPENSIVE SOUP

A bowl of "Buddha Jumps Over the Wall" soup – containing shark's fin, abalone, Japanese flower mushroom, sea cucumber, dried scallops, chicken, huan ham, pork, and ginseng – costs £108 ($190) at Kai Mayfair in London, UK. The dish has to be pre-ordered five days in advance.

★ MOST CHILI PEPPERS EATEN IN ONE MINUTE

This fiery record was broken twice in 2005, first on April 7 by TV host Mark S. Allen (USA, above), who ate 11 jalapeño chili peppers in a minute. But taking home the chili crown was Stuart Ross (Australia), who ate 15 in Templestowe, Melbourne, Victoria, Australia, on November 20, 2005.

DRINKS

★ STRONGEST BEER

Sam Adams Utopias, brewed by the Boston Beer Company, Massachusetts, USA, had an alcohol volume of 25% when tested on August 2, 2005.

ACTUAL SIZE

★ LARGEST
WHISKY MENU

As of September 2005, Forbes Robertson (UK), owner of the Millionayr Casino in Ayr, Scotland, UK, had 800 varieties of whisky available for sale to the public at his premises. The 800 bottles represent the 800 years since the founding of Ayr.

MOST EXPENSIVE SINGLE PURCHASE OF WHISKY

On November 16, 2000, Norman Shelley (UK) bought 76 bottles of The Macallan malt whisky at a value of £231,417.90 ($341,154). The collection includes old, rare, and unusual Macallan malts, the oldest dating as far back as 1856.

★ MOST EXPENSIVE COCKTAIL

Although not currently available, the Lord Bowmore cocktail – sold at the Park Lane Hilton, London, UK – was the most costly cocktail ever, at £799 ($1,431). It contained 1.75 fl oz (50 ml) of 40-year-old Bowmore malt whisky and 0.5 fl oz (15 ml) of pure, dark melted chocolate.

The Ritz Side Car at the Paris Ritz's Hemingway Bar, France, is currently the world's most expensive cocktail, with a price tag of €400 ($528).

★ LARGEST COCKTAIL MENU

As of August 12, 2005, Pench's Club Cocktail Bar in Varna, Bulgaria, featured 1,227 different cocktails on its drinks menu.

★ LARGEST BEER MENU

As of January 9, 2004, the Delírium Café in Brussels, Belgium, sold a record 2,004 different beer varieties.

★ LARGEST SHERRY MENU

The Sherry Club in Tokyo, Japan, stocked 227 varieties of sherry as of November 3, 2005.

★ SMALLEST BREWERY

The Bragdy Gwynant in Capel Bangor, Aberystwyth, Wales, UK, has a brewing capacity of 86.4 pints (11 gal) per batch. It supplies exclusively to the adjacent Tynllidiart Arms pub.

LARGEST WINE CELLAR (NUMBER OF BOTTLES)

The cellars of the Milestii Mici wine-making plant in Moldova contain over 1.5 million bottles of wine. The bottles are stored in 34 miles (55 km) of underground galleries excavated in lime-mining operations. The first bottle was stored in 1968.

NOTE: For food and drink records to qualify for a Guinness World Record, they must be commercially available.

★ MOST
EXPENSIVE CUP OF TEA

A rare Chinese green tea called Tieguanyin costs $3,000 per 2.2 lb (1 kg) – which works out at around $15 for a single cup!

In January 2005, PG Tips (Unilever UK Foods) commissioned the world's **most expensive teabag** – a pyramid teabag encrusted with 280 diamonds (pictured) and valued at $13,100.

★ FASTEST
TIME TO EAT A 12-INCH PIZZA

Nyron Weekes (Barbados) ate a 12-in (30.5-cm) pizza in 2 min 58.47 sec on March 25, 2006. At this rate, it would take Nyron over 63 hours to eat the world's **largest pizza**, which measured 122 ft 8 in (37.4 m) and weighed 26,883 lb (12.19 tonnes) on December 8, 1990!

HOBBIES & PASTIMES

! X-REF

Why would more than 600 people get dressed up as gorillas and then go for a run? For the answer, turn to p.89.

★ **NEW RECORD**
☆ **UPDATED RECORD**

★ LONGEST ➡ DISTANCE
ON INLINE SKATES

Mauro Guenci (Italy) covered 24 miles (38.6 km) on inline skates in one hour on a road circuit at Senigallia, Ancona, Italy, on June 11, 2005.

A year before this, at the same Italian circuit, Mauro also set the 24-hour record by skating 337.773 miles (543.594 km) on June 11–12, 2004.

LONGEST...

★ PAPER CHAINS

A paper chain measuring 54.33 miles (87.44 km) long was made by 60 people, in 24 hours, at Paul D. Camp Community College in Franklin, Virginia, USA, on June 4–5, 2005.

The ★ **longest paper chain by an individual** was made on February 13–14, 2006, by Christopher Potts (UK), whose chain measured 1,073 ft 2 in (327.1 m) long.

★ FRENCH KNITTING

Edward Peter Hannaford (UK) has produced a piece of French knitting 12.26 miles (19.73 km) long. He embarked upon his marathon feat in April 1989 – which means he has been knitting for more than 17 years!

★ MOVIE MARATHON

Claudia Wavra (Germany) watched 40 full-length feature films for a record 114 hr 6 min at the Kinopolis theater, Sulzbach im Taunus, Germany, from August 28 to September 1, 2005. The record-breaking event was organized by Kinopolis Main-Taunus (Germany).

★ DISTANCE BY A MODEL SAILING SHIP IN 24 HOURS

Claudio Vigada-Filiberto (Italy) sailed his 6-ft 6-in-long (2-m) radio-controlled yacht *Urca Delta Colori* a total of 85.12 nautical miles (97.96 miles; 157.65 km) from Imperia, Italy, to Calvi on the French island of Corsica, in 23 hours 42 min on September 25–26, 2004.

FASTEST...

★ HAND-KNITTED "SHEEP TO SWEATER"

Following International Association rules for the International "Back to Back" Wool Challenge, the fastest time to turn wool on a sheep into a hand-knitted sweater is 4 hr 51 min 14 sec, a record set by the Merriwa Jumbucks in New South Wales, Australia, in 2004.

★ TIME TO SHEAR A SHEEP

Dwayne Black (Australia) set the fastest time to shear a single sheep – 45.41 seconds – on the set of *Guinness World Records* at Seven Network Studios, Sydney, Australia, on April 17, 2005.

★ TIME TO POP 100 BALLOONS

Vernon Kay and Alan Connelly (both UK) burst 100 balloons in 47 seconds on *The Paul O'Grady Show*, ITV Studios, London, UK, on December 6, 2005, without using any sharp objects.

★ TIME TO MAKE 100 ORIGAMI CRANES

Akie Morita (Japan) set the record for the fastest time to create 100 origami paper cranes (as below) with a time of 1 hr 38 min 36 sec at Bukyo Gakuin University, Saitama, Japan, on October 23, 2004.

⬅ LARGEST CARD TOWERS

The world's leading builder of structures made entirely from regular playing cards is Bryan Berg (USA). The **largest card structure** was built at Walt Disney World in Florida, USA, on December 12, 2004; it measured 13 ft 10 in x 11 ft 10 in x 8 ft 7 in (4.22 x 3.6 x 2.61 m) and used 162,000 cards. Brian also built the **card structure with the most storys** – his 131-story house of cards, built on November 6, 1999, reached 25 ft 3 in (7.71 m) high.

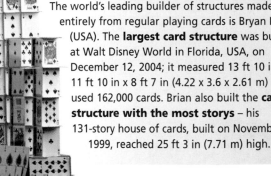

STAMP-COLLECTING ORGANIZATION

With more than 55,000 members in more than 110 countries, the American Philatelic Society (APS) is the largest nonprofit society in the world for stamp collectors and postal historians. It is supported entirely by membership dues, gifts, and the sale of its publications and services. The APS was founded in 1886.

★ SPHERICAL PUZZLE

Unima Industrial (HK) Ltd of Hong Kong, China, created a spherical jigsaw puzzle with a circumference of 15 ft 7 in (4.77 m). The puzzle was unveiled on January 10, 2005, at the Hong Kong Convention and Exhibition Center, where it was officially measured.

JIGSAWS

The **largest commercially available jigsaw puzzle** is produced by Ravensburger of Ravensburg, Germany, and measures 9 ft 0.6 in x 6 ft 3.4 in (2.76 x 1.92 m). The puzzle, which depicts four world maps, consists of 18,000 pieces – which is also a record for the **most pieces in a commercially available jigsaw puzzle**.

The **largest jigsaw ever** measured 58,4351 ft² (5,428.8 m²) – larger than a football field – and consisted of 21,600 pieces, each piece twice as large as this book! It was assembled by 777 people in Hong Kong, China, on November 3, 2002.

The ★ **smallest commercially available 1,000-piece jigsaw puzzle** is made by Standard Project Limited, which produces Tomax puzzles in Hong Kong. It measures 11 x 16 in (29.7 x 42 cm). The miniature puzzles were launched in 2003 and depict images ranging from landmarks to famous works of art.

★ FASTEST COMPLETION OF THE GWR-HASBRO PUZZLE

To *really* put puzzle fans to the test, Guinness World Records has teamed up with Hasbro to create the official GWR Timed Puzzle. So far, the fastest time to complete the puzzle is 34 min 4 sec by Stephane Cornut (UK) at the Hasbro Office in Middlesex, UK, on January 13, 2006.

AVERAGE TIME TO SOLVE A RUBIK'S CUBE

Set by Shotaro Makisumi (Japan), the record for the fastest average time to solve a Rubik's Cube in competition is 14.52 seconds. It took place at the Caltech fall tournament in Pasadena, California, USA, on October 16, 2004.

★ TIME TO SOLVE A RUBIK'S CUBE (ABSOLUTE)

Hosted by the California Institute of Technology's Rubik's Cube Club at the Exploratorium Museum, California, USA, on January 14, 2006, the world record for the fastest time to solve a Rubik's Cube is 11.13 seconds by Leyan Lo (USA).

The ★**most Rubik's Cubes solved in one hour** is 42, set by Mitchell Brom (South Africa) in Johannesburg, South Africa, on December 17, 2004.

★ TIDDLYWINKS MILE

Ashrita Furman (USA) covered a mile – while sticking to Tiddlywinks rules – in 26 min 26 sec at Kuala Lumpur International Airport Building in Kuala Lumpur, Malaysia, on December 15, 2005.

JENGA BUILDING (30 LEVELS)

The fastest time to build a Jenga tower 30 levels high within the rules of the game is 4 min 4 sec by Americans Dan Mogan and Anastasia Carpanzano at Tower Bridge in London, UK, on April 1, 2005.

★ MOST PUBS VISITED IN 24 HOURS

A group of 19 students belonging to St. Andrew's College, University of Sydney, Australia, set a new team record by visiting and drinking at 82 drinking establishments throughout Sydney on June 9–10, 2005.

The individual record for ★ **the most pubs visited** is held by Bruce Masters (UK), who had visited 38,000 pubs and bars since 1960 as of February 27, 2005.

LARGEST...

★ HULA HOOP SPUN

The largest hula hoop ever to be successfully rotated around a person's waist had a diameter of 15 ft 8 in (4.8 m). Ashrita Furman (USA) managed to rotate the enormous hula hoop three times around his waist on the set of *Richard and Judy*, London, UK, on September 24, 2005.

The ★ **most rotations of a giant hula hoop in a minute** was by Laura Rico Rodriguez (Spain). She rotated a giant hula hoop, measuring 11 ft 6 in (3.5 m), around her body 62 times. The record was set on *Lo Show Dei Record* in Milan, Italy, on January 5, 2006.

GAMES & GAMBLING

★LARGEST CARD-GAME TOURNAMENT

On May 20, 2004, in Penela, Coimbra, Portugal, 320 players paired up into 160 teams to play quadrille in the world's largest card-game tournament. The winning pair was Fernando and Antonio Tavares (Portugal).

★ LONGEST PÉTANQUE (BOULES) MARATHON

Members of "Operation Boule" took part in a pétanque marathon of 36 hr 2 min in Marl, Germany, from April 29 to May 1, 2005.

POKER

★MOST ENTRANTS AT A WORLD SERIES OF POKER

The World Series of Poker (WSOP) competition held at Harrah's Rio Casino in Las Vegas, Nevada, USA, in July 2005, attracted a record 5,619 participants.

★MOST PLAYERS AT AN INTERNET POKER ROOM

The most players to simultaneously take part in a poker game online at the same internet poker room is 100,000 at PokerStars.com in February 2006. To date, PokerStars has dealt nearly 5 billion hands,

★LARGEST PRIZE IN THE WORLD SERIES OF POKER

The most prize money awarded to the winner of the Main Event at the World Series of Poker – a $10,000 buy-in, no-limit, Texas Hold 'Em tournament – is $7.5 million, won by Joe Hachem (Australia) at the Rio Casino, Las Vegas, Nevada, USA, on July 16, 2005.

FASTEST GAME OF OPERATION

At an event held by the British Association of Urological Surgeons on June 28, 2001, in Dublin, Ireland, Dr. Isa Massaud Issa, from Tripoli, Libya, completed a game of Operation in 1 min 2 sec.

★LONGEST ➡ CROUPIER MARATHON

Intan Pragi (Estonia) managed a table at the Olympic Casino in Tallin, Estonia, nonstop from February 18 to 20, 2005, the world's longest croupier marathon.

The ★oldest croupier, Robert Jarvis (Canada, b. November 14, 1925), was still employed as a croupier at Niagara Fallsview Casino Resort, Ontario, Canada, on December 19, 2004, aged 79 years 35 days.

run more than 20 million poker tournaments, and made payouts of well over $4 billion in prize money.

★MOST WINS OF THE WORLD SERIES OF POKER MAIN EVENT

Stu "The Kid" Ungar (USA) has won the Main Event at the World Series of Poker three times, in 1980, 1981,

and 1997. The Main Event is a $10,000 buy-in, no-limit, Texas Hold 'Em tournament.

★MOST WORLD SERIES POKER WINNER'S BRACELETS

Doyle "Texas Dolly" Brunson and Johnny "Oriental Express" Chan (both USA) have both won 10 World Series of Poker (WSOP) bracelets. Gold bracelets are awarded to individual event winners at each WSOP competition.

GAMBLING

LARGEST BOOKMAKER

With more than 2,000 betting shops in Great Britain and the Republic of Ireland, as well as outlets in the USA, Argentina, Belgium, Egypt, Peru, and Puerto Rico, Ladbrokes is the world's largest bookmaker. In 1998, it had a peak turnover from gambling of £2.85 billion ($4.72 billion).

LARGEST GAMING VESSEL

Glory of Rome, owned by Caesars (USA) and based in Bridgeport, Indiana, USA, is the world's largest riverboat casino, with a gaming space of 93,000 ft² (8,640 m²) and space for 5,324 passengers.

★ LONGEST MAH-JONG MARATHON

The Sea Trail Dragon Ladies set the record for the longest Mah-Jong marathon on November 10–11, 2005, at the Sea Trail Plantation, Sunset Beach, North Carolina, USA. Organized into two groups of four people, they played simultaneously for 28 hours.

★ MOST SIMULTANEOUS GAMES OF CHESS

On June 25, 2005, 12,388 simultaneous games of chess were played at the Ben Gurion Cultural Park in Pachuca, Hidalgo, Mexico.

★ MOST SIMULTANEOUS OPPONENTS FOR SCRABBLE

In an attempt that took a total of two hours to complete at Sheffield Workstation, Yorkshire, UK, on November 13, 2004, Stewart Holden (UK) took on a record 18 Scrabble challengers simultaneously. Of the 18 games that Stewart played, he lost only two!

LARGEST PRIZE FOR SCRABBLE

The world's largest prize awarded for winning a Scrabble tournament is $50,000. It was won by David Gibson (USA), who had an impressive win-loss record of 21–3. The event was the Las Vegas Superstars held in August 1995.

MOST ⬆ EXPENSIVE MONOPOLY BOARD

A Monopoly set costing $2 million was created by the jeweler Sidney Mobell, of San Francisco, California, USA, in 1988. The board itself is made from 23-carat gold, there are rubies and sapphires topping the chimneys of the solid gold houses and hotels, and the dice have been constructed using 42 full-cut diamonds for spots.

LARGEST SLOT-MACHINE WIN

On March 21, 2003, an unnamed 25-year-old software engineer from Los Angeles, California, USA, invested $100 in the Megabucks slot machine at the Excalibur Hotel-Casino in Las Vegas, Nevada, USA, and won a staggering $39,713,982.25.

BOARD GAMES

★ LARGEST TOURNAMENT

On October 23, 2004, 215 participants played 58 games of Cootie to set the record for the largest board-game tournament. The event took place at the Bob Bullock Texas State History Museum in Austin, Texas, USA. The overall tournament winner was Tara Landschoot (USA).

★ LARGEST TWISTER BOARD

The largest single Twister sheet measured 88 ft 11 in x 27 ft 7 in (27.1 x 8.43 m) and was made by members of the Scouting Kardinaal Mindszenty Groep, Limburg, Netherlands. A giant game of Twister was then played using the sheet on April 24, 2005.

MOST PLAYED GAME

As of 1999, Monopoly has been played by 500 million people worldwide.

SMALLEST ⬆ CHESS SET

The smallest handmade chess set was created by Jaspal Singh Kalsi (India) in Putlighar, Amritsar, India. The board measures 1.2 in x 1.2 in (32 x 32 mm), the largest piece (the king) measures 0.5 in (13 mm) in height, and the smallest (the pawn) 0.27 in (7 mm). All the pieces have a base diameter of 0.1 in (3 mm).

★ NEW RECORD
★ UPDATED RECORD

★ LARGEST CHESS SET

The world's largest chess board measures 17 ft 3 in (5.28 m) square. The king is 47 in (119 cm) tall and 14.5 in (36.8 cm) wide at the base. The set was made by MegaChess, and a full game was played by Denny North and Peter Shikli (both USA) in San Clemente, California, USA, on September 5, 2005.

The world's **largest chess piece** is a king, made by Mats Allanson (Sweden), that measures 13 ft 1 in (4 m) high and 4 ft 7 in (1.4 m) in diameter across the base.

SCIENCE & TECHNOLOGY

CONTENTS

BRIGHTEST NEBULA

The Orion Nebula (Messier 42), a vast diffuse cloud of gas and dust, is the brightest nebula in the night sky. Located in the "sword" of the constellation of Orion, the nebula is the nearest star-formation region to the Earth and is visible to the naked eye as a fuzzy patch of light. It is around 1,500 light-years away.

Between 2004 and 2005, the Advance Camera for Surveys (ACS) on board NASA's Hubble Space Telescope took a series of images of the nebula that, pieced together, represent the most detailed view of the Orion Nebula seen by human eyes. Containing a billion pixels, the new image shown on these pages reveals intricate structures in the gas and dust, and protoplanetary discs surrounding extremely young star systems.

STAR GAZING

LARGEST
DISH RADIO TELESCOPE

Completed in November 1963, this partially steerable ionospheric assembly – built over a natural bowl at Arecibo, Puerto Rico – has a 1,000-ft-diameter (305-m) dish. It covers 18.5 acres (7.48 ha) – comparable to 14 football fields.

On November 16, 1974, scientists at Arecibo sent the **most powerful radio signal deliberately sent into space** – a binary radio signal to the M13 globular cluster in the constellation of Hercules. The signal, featuring basic data about humanity, lasted for 169 seconds at 2,380 MHz.

NEW RECORD
★ UPDATED RECORD

HOTTEST WHITE DWARF

A white dwarf is the compact glowing remnant of a dead star. The white dwarf star H1504+65 has a surface temperature of around 360,000°F (200,000°C) – roughly 30 times the surface temperature of the Sun.

BRIGHTEST PLANET IN THE SKY

Viewed from Earth, the brightest of the five planets normally visible to the naked eye (Jupiter, Mars, Mercury, Saturn, and Venus) is Venus, with a maximum magnitude of -4.4.

CLOSEST APPROACH TO EARTH BY A SPACE ROCK

The closest a space rock has ever been observed to pass by the Earth is around 4,000 miles (6,500 km), by 2004 FU162 on March 31, 2004. The rock, which measures around 19 ft (6 m) across, is too small to be classed as an asteroid (which must be at least 160 ft, or around 50 m, across) and would probably have burned up in Earth's atmosphere had it been on a collision course with our planet.

★ PLANET WITH THE MOST MOONS

As of January 2006, the planet in the Solar System with the most satellites is Jupiter, with 63. Saturn comes second with 47, and Uranus and Neptune have 27 and 13 respectively.

FASTEST STAR IN THE GALAXY

On February 8, 2005, astronomers at the Harvard-Smithsonian Center for Astrophysics, Cambridge, Massachusetts, USA, announced their discovery of a star traveling at over 1.5 million mph (2.4 million km/h). Known as SDSS J090745.0+24507, the star was probably accelerated by an encounter with the supermassive black hole at the center of our Milky Way galaxy nearly 80 million years ago.

The star will eventually speed out of the Milky Way altogether. It is the first star discovered that will travel into intergalactic space.

OLDEST STAR IN THE MILKY WAY

Scientists believe that HE0107-5240, a giant star around 36,000 light-years from Earth, could date back to the very beginning of the universe, around 13.7 billion years ago.

MOST DETAILED IMAGE OF A SPIRAL GALAXY

A mosaic digitally stitched together from 51 separate Hubble Space Telescope images of the galaxy M101 measures 16,000 x 12,000 pixels.

M101 is around 170,000 light-years across, lies around 25 million light-years from our own galaxy, and is estimated to hold a trillion stars. The image was released in March 2006.

★ MOST POWERFUL VOLCANIC ERUPTION RECORDED IN THE SOLAR SYSTEM

In February 2001, a volcanic eruption occurred on Io, a satellite of Jupiter, that generated an estimated output of 78,000 gigawatts. The observations were made with the WM Keck II Telescope, in Hawaii, USA.

GREATEST OBSERVED PLANETARY DESTRUCTION

In January 2002, the star V838 Monocerotis flared up to 600,000 times its normal brightness.

This was probably due to the energy released when the star engulfed and destroyed three orbiting giant gas planets.

NEAR AND FAR

★ MOST DISTANT OBJECT IN THE UNIVERSE

Observations with the European Southern Observatory's Very Large Telescope (VLT), in Chile, show that the galaxy Abell 1835 IR1916 has a redshift of 10, corresponding to a distance from Earth of around 13,230 million light-years.

LARGEST INFRARED SPACE TELESCOPE

NASA's Spitzer Space Telescope was launched into Earth orbit on August 25, 2003. With a mass of 2,094 lb (950 kg), and a primary mirror 2 ft 9 in (0.85 m) across, it is the best tool astronomers have had, to date, for observing heat emissions from objects in deep space as well as from those in our own Solar System.

The picture above, showing the Sombrero Galaxy, combines infrared views from Spitzer with optical views from Hubble to reveal details within the galaxy's dust ring.

★ NEAREST STAR VISIBLE TO THE NAKED EYE

The southern-hemisphere binary Alpha Centauri, visible without a telescope, is 4.40 light-years away.

OUTERMOST PLANET

Since the first Kuiper Belt Object was discovered in the outer Solar System in 1992, astronomers have debated whether or not Pluto should lose its planet status and be reclassified as the largest of the Kuiper Belt Objects – small icy worlds orbiting the Sun beyond Neptune. Observations of 2003 UB313 show that, at around 1,860 miles (3,000 km) across, it is larger than Pluto and also has its own tiny moon. 2003 UB313 has an elliptical orbit, which takes it as far as 10 billion miles (16 billion km) from the Sun.

The discovery of large objects in the Kuiper Belt is challenging both the criteria for defining a "planet" and Pluto's status as a planet, rather than as a Kuiper Belt Object.

PLANET WITH THE SHORTEST ORBITAL PERIOD

A Jupiter-sized gas giant orbiting the star OGLE-TR-3 has an orbital period of only 28 hr 33 min. It orbits just 2.1 million miles (3.5 million km) from its parent star.

LARGEST PLANET IN THE SOLAR SYSTEM

Jupiter, which has an equatorial diameter of 89,405 miles (143,884 km) and a polar diameter of 83,082 miles (133,708 km), is the largest of the nine major planets, with a mass 317 times (and a volume 1,323 times) that of the Earth. It also has the shortest period of rotation, resulting in a Jovian day of 9 hr 55 min 29.69 sec.

EXTRASOLAR PLANET

Announced in January 2001, the discovery of the planet HD168443 orbiting a star 123 light-years away challenges conventional definitions of planets. Jupiter, the largest planet in our Solar System, weighs more than all the other planets and moons combined. But HD168443 is 17 times more massive than even Jupiter.

STARS IN THE GALAXY

The largest diameter for any known star in our galaxy is in excess of 900 million miles (1.5 billion km). Astronomers have identified three stars of this size in an international study of red supergiants – KW Sagitarii, V354 Cephei, and KY Cygni – are at distances of 9,800 light-years, 9,000 light-years and 5,200 light-years from Earth respectively.

TELESCOPES

The twin Keck Telescopes, on the summit of Hawaii's dormant Mauna Kea volcano, are the **largest optical and infrared telescopes**. Each is eight stories tall and weighs 600,000 lb (300 tonnes). Both Kecks have a 32-ft (10-m) mirror made up of 36 hexagonal segments that act as a single reflective surface.

The **largest space telescope** is the NASA Edwin P. Hubble Space Telescope, which weighs 24,250 lb (11 tonnes) and is 43 ft (13.1 m) in overall length, with a 94.8-in (240-cm) reflector. It was launched into space, at an altitude of 381 miles (613 km), by the US space shuttle *Discovery* on April 24, 1990.

At a cost of $2.1 billion, the Hubble Space Telescope is also the **most expensive telescope** ever made.

STAR VISIBLE TO THE NAKED EYE

Eta Carinae is a rare supergiant, some 9,000 light-years from Earth. With a mass estimated at between 100 and 200 times that of the Sun, it is one of the most massive stars in the galaxy. Along with its surrounding gas, it is just visible to the naked eye, with a magnitude of 6.21.

CLEAREST IMAGE OF MARS FROM EARTH

On August 26, 2003, the Hubble Space Telescope imaged Mars just 11 hours before the planet made its closest approach to Earth in 60,000 years – a distance of 34,648,840 miles (55,760,220 km). This color image has a resolution of just 8 miles (12 km) per pixel.

? DID YOU KNOW?

Black holes are born when massive stars collapse at the end of their lives. They exert a gravitational pull so strong that not even light can escape. The **closest black hole to Earth** *is V4641 Sgr – only 1,600 light-years away – discovered on January 14, 2000.*

YOUNGEST EXTRASOLAR PLANET

Infrared observations of the young star CoKu Tau 4 by NASA's (USA) Spitzer Space Telescope reveal a gap in the circumstellar disc of dust and gas that is likely to be a newly formed planet (artist's impression, left).

The star, along with its possible planet, located some 420 light-years from Earth in the constellation of Taurus, is no more than 1 million years old.

SPACE EXPLORATION

LARGEST
SHUTTLE CREW

Two shuttles have had a crew of eight: the *Challenger STS 61A*, which was launched on October 30, 1985, and *STS 71 Atlantis* (pictured), which docked with the *Mir* space station on July 7, 1995.

★ **NEW RECORD**
★ **UPDATED RECORD**

FIRST ARTIFICIAL SATELLITE

The first artificial satellite was successfully put into orbit by an intercontinental ballistic missile from the Baikonur Cosmodrome at Tyuratam, Kazakhstan, on October 4, 1957. It reached an altitude of between 142 miles (228 km) – the perigee, or nearest point to Earth – and 588 miles (946 km) – the apogee, or farthest point from Earth – and had a velocity of more than 17,750 mph (28,565 km/h).

★ REMOTEST MAN-MADE OBJECT

Voyager 1, launched from Cape Canaveral, Florida, USA, on September 5, 1977, is now the farthest man-made object from the Earth. As of February 2006, *Voyager 1* is over 9.12 billion miles (14.68 billion km) from the Sun.

★ LONGEST LASER COMMUNICATIONS LINK

In May 2005, NASA's *Messenger* spacecraft successfully communicated with Earth using a laser beam from a distance of around 15 million miles (24 million km). This experimental form of long-distance communication is designed to allow a higher rate of data return from interplanetary space than current methods of microwave communication.

LONGEST MANNED PERIOD ORBITING THE MOON

Astronauts Eugene Cernan, Harrison Schmitt, and Ronald Evans (all USA) took part in the *Apollo 17* mission, the last one to land on the Moon, from December 7 to 19, 1972. The command module orbited the Moon for 147 hr 41 min 13 sec. Ronald Evans remained on board for the whole mission (while Cernan and Schmitt spent 74 hr 59 min 40 sec on the lunar surface), achieving the **longest stay in orbit for a human around a celestial body**.

LONGEST
SPACEFLIGHT BY A WOMAN

Shannon Lucid (USA) was launched to the Russian *Mir 1* space station aboard the US space shuttle *STS 76 Atlantis* on March 22, 1996, and landed aboard *STS 79 Atlantis* on September 26 after a spaceflight of 188 days 4 hr 14 sec.

★ THINNEST MANNED SPACECRAFT HULL

The lunar modules of the US Apollo program were the only true spacecraft designed solely for flight in space. For landing on and leaving the Moon, no aerodynamic qualities were necessary in their design. The "skin" of the crew compartment was 0.012 in (0.3 mm) thick – equivalent to several layers of aluminum kitchen foil. However, this was sufficient to maintain the integrity of the hull when pressurized.

★ FASTEST ENTRY
INTO EARTH'S ATMOSPHERE

On January 15, 2006, NASA's *Stardust* spacecraft returned to Earth after a seven-year mission to collect samples of comet Wild 2. It entered Earth's atmosphere at a velocity of 29,000 mph (46,660 km/h) and was visible to some people in the USA as a streak of light in the sky before touching down, with the help of a parachute, in Utah, USA. Pictured are *Stardust* scientists getting their first look at the priceless and fragile comet samples collected.

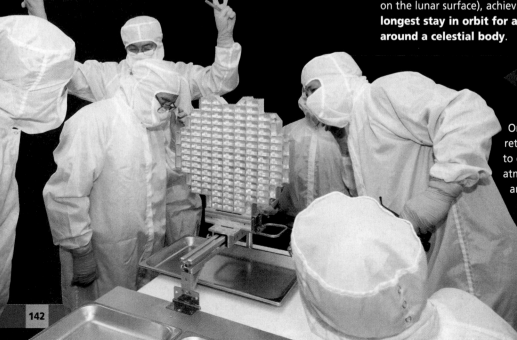

SERGEI KRIKALEV

Sergei Krikalev (Russia) has spent more time in space than any other human being – a total of 803 days 9 hr 39 min. We asked him what most amazed him about his record-breaking experience.

For me, it was seeing that the Earth is actually round! We're all taught that it's not flat, but it means nothing until you've seen it for yourself.

How has your flight affected your physical condition?
Spending so long in space, you have to cope with changes in blood volume and content, reduced bone density, and radiation. My last mission ended four months ago, but I'm still not 100%. It generally takes the same length of time as the mission to fully recover.

What do you miss the most about Earth when you're in space?
I really miss not having my friends and family around me. We're only allowed to take up to 3.3 lb (1.5 kg) of personal belongings with us on any mission, so I try to include photographs and small objects of personal value to me.

How does the International Space Station compare with Mir?
The ISS is now much the same volume as Mir was, but there was more scientific material on Mir. There's more on its way to the ISS, but everything's been delayed by the shuttle disasters.

What's the food like on board the ISS?
It's designed for eating in space, so it's mostly dehydrated and canned. There's actually quite a good variety, and we have more than enough on board because we have to cater for the worst-case scenario.

Which is?
Being stuck up there, on board the space station, with no means of getting back to Earth again until the next shuttle arrives!

Is it true that the toilets are the most sophisticated pieces of equipment?
On the space shuttle, they are. But the toilets on Mir were best – reliable, simple… and better than those on the ISS!

★ FASTEST EARTH DEPARTURE SPEED

NASA's New Horizons spacecraft launched from Cape Canaveral on January 19, 2006, departing from Earth at a speed of 36,250 mph (58,338 km/h). New Horizons was beginning a nine-year flight to the planet Pluto and its moons.

Pluto is the only planet in the Solar System yet to be surveyed by a spacecraft.

FASTEST ATMOSPHERIC ENTRY

On December 7, 1995, a small probe released by the Galileo spacecraft began a fiery descent into the atmosphere of the giant planet Jupiter. During this most difficult atmospheric entry ever, the Galileo probe reached a speed of 106,000 mph (170,000 km/h), the **fastest atmospheric entry**.

★ HEAVIEST INTERPLANETARY SPACECRAFT TO LAND USING AIRBAGS

The twin Mars Exploration Rovers, Spirit and Opportunity, landed successfully on Mars using airbags at touchdown on January 4 and 25, 2004, respectively. Each had a mass of almost 396 lb (180 kg).

The twin Rovers also hold the ★ **land-speed record on Mars**. Each is capable of a maximum velocity of 1.9 in/sec (5 cm/sec).

MOST PEOPLE IN SPACE AT ONCE

On March 14, 1995, 13 people were in space at the same time: seven Americans aboard the US STS 67 Endeavour, three CIS cosmonauts aboard the Russian Mir space station and two CIS cosmonauts and a US astronaut aboard the Soyuz TM-21.

MOST PLANETS VISITED BY ONE SPACECRAFT

NASA's Voyager 2 spacecraft, launched in 1977, visited all four of the outer gas giants, Jupiter, Saturn, Uranus, and Neptune, between 1979 and 1989.

MOST SPACE FLIGHTS BY AN INDIVIDUAL

To date, two US astronauts have accomplished seven spaceflights. Jerry Ross (USA) flew his seventh mission (STS 110) on board the space shuttle Atlantis between April 8 and 19, 2002. Franklin Chang-Diaz (USA) flew his seventh mission on board the space shuttle Endeavour between June 5 and 19, 2002.

★ SMALLEST GEOLOGICALLY ACTIVE BODY IN THE SOLAR SYSTEM

In December 2005, the Cassini team announced their discovery of plumes of icy matter erupting into space from the surface of Saturn's frozen moon, Enceladus. This moon, of which the axes of radii measure 159.2 x 153.6 x 152 miles (256.3 x 247.3 x 244.6 km), joins a small club of worlds in the Solar System known to be geologically active: Earth, Jupiter's moon Io and Neptune's moon Triton.

★ SMALLEST BODY LANDED ON

On November 20, 2005, the Japanese spacecraft Hayabusa made the first of two touchdowns on asteroid Itokawa in an attempt to collect samples for return to Earth. Itokawa measures just 1,600 ft (500 m) across its longest axis.

ROCKET SCIENCE

★ 1986: MOST POWERFUL ICBM

With a price tag of $70 million each, the *Peacekeeper* Intercontinental Ballistic Missile (ICBM) produces 500,000 lb (226,800 kg) of thrust at takeoff. It can deliver 10 independently targeted nuclear warheads over a range of more than 5,000 miles (9,650 km).

★ NEW RECORD
★ UPDATED RECORD

1926: FIRST LIQUID-FUEL ROCKET LAUNCH

The first launch of a liquid-fueled rocket (patented July 14, 1914) was by Dr. Robert Hutchings Goddard (USA, 1882–1945) at Aunt Effie's farm in Auburn, Massachusetts, USA, on March 16, 1926. His rocket reached an altitude of 41 ft (12.5 m) and traveled a distance of 184 ft (56 m) into a neighbor's cabbage patch.

1947: FIRST SUPERSONIC FLIGHT

On October 14, 1947, Capt. (later Brig. Gen.) Charles "Chuck" Elwood Yeager (USA) reached Mach 1.015 (670 mph; 1,078 km/h) – breaking the sound barrier – at an altitude of 42,000 ft (12,800 m) over Lake Muroc, California, USA, in a Bell XS-1 rocket aircraft.

1957: FIRST DOG IN SPACE

On November 3, 1957, Laika became the first dog – and first living thing from Earth – to enter Earth's orbit. Laika (which means "Barker" in Russian) was the only passenger of *Sputnik 2* (Satellite 2), the second spacecraft sent into orbit. Sadly, Laika – dubbed "Muttnik" by the West – had only a one-way ticket, and her food was treated in such a way that she would be poisoned after her 10th day in orbit. However, a few hours after launch, a problem with thermal insulation meant that the cabin temperature inside *Sputnik*

2 rapidly rose to 104°F (40°C). Laika died from overheating – a fact not released by the Russians until October 2002.

1961: FIRST MANNED SPACE FLIGHT

Cosmonaut Flight Major (later Col.) Yuri Alekseyevich Gagarin (1934–68) became the first man in space on April 12, 1961. He took off in *Vostok 1* from the Baikonur Cosmodrome, Kazakhstan, at 6:07 a.m. GMT. *Vostok 1* landed near Smelovka, in the Saratov region of Russia, 115 minutes later. Gagarin ejected 108 minutes into the flight as planned, landing separately from his spacecraft 118 minutes after launch.

1967: FASTEST ROCKET AIRCRAFT

On October 3, 1967, test pilot Pete Knight (USA) reached 4,520 mph (7,274 km/h), or Mach 6.7, over California, USA, in the X-15A-2, the greatest speed ever reached by an air-launched manned aircraft.

1969: MOST POWERFUL ROCKET

The N-1 booster was launched from the Baikonur Cosmodrome, Kazakhstan, on February 21, 1969, but exploded 70 seconds after takeoff. It was to be the rocket that took Russia to the Moon, but the project was abandoned after three failed launch attempts.

2000: HEAVIEST ROCKET PAYLOAD ➡️ (COMMERCIAL)

On October 21, 2000, the 11,260-lb (5,108-kg) *Thuraya-1* satellite was launched by a Zenit-3SL rocket from Sea Launch's *Odyssey*, the **largest ocean-based launch platform**. This semi-submersible launch pad – a former North Sea oil platform – measures 436 ft (132.8 m) long and 220 ft (67 m) wide.

1981: LARGEST SOLID-FUEL ROCKET BOOSTERS

The two re-usable boosters that assist the launch of the US space shuttle – the first, *Columbia*, took off on April 12, 1981 – use solid rather than liquid fuel, and are the largest solid rocket boosters ever flown. Each is 149 ft (45.4 m) long and 12 ft (3.6 m) wide and contains 1 million lb (450,000 kg) of propellant, providing a total thrust of 3.3 million lb (1.49 million kg).

1990: SMALLEST SATELLITE LAUNCH ROCKET

The smallest satellite launch vehicle was *Pegasus* – the **first privately developed space launch vehicle** – which had a three-stage booster just 50 ft 10 in (15.5 m) long. *Pegasus* has now been succeeded by *Pegasus XL*. The original, first sent forth in 1990, was air-launched from an aircraft.

THIS *IS* ROCKET SCIENCE

"Flying fireworks" set off by gunpowder (a mixture of charcoal, saltpeter, and sulfur) were first described in 1042 by Tseng-Kung Liang in China. A rocket is an open-ended, fuel-filled chamber that operates like fireworks. Unlike a jet engine, which extracts atmospheric oxygen, a rocket's oxidizer lets fuel burn on ignition. As it is expelled from the engine, it expands at an incredible rate and accelerates the rocket in the opposite direction.

Although the most basic rocket design resembles a bomb with one end cut off, chemical energy in its fuel is released in a controlled, directional manner rather than all at once. To achieve Earth orbit, space rockets need enough fuel to accelerate their payloads to the incredible speeds required – some 18,020 mph (29,000 km/h).

VOSTOK 1
Length: 101 ft (30.8 m)
Thrust: 875,400 lb (3,894 kN)
Nationality: USSR

SPUTNIK 2
Length: 112 ft (34.2 m)
Thrust: 877,600 lb (3,904 kN)
Nationality: USSR

X-15A-2
Length: 51 ft (15.5 m)
Thrust: 51,090 lb (227 kN)
Nationality: USA (USAF)

PEGASUS
Length: 51 ft (15.5 m)
Thrust: 109,400 lb (487 kN)
Nationality: USA (Orbital Sciences Corporation)

GODDARD'S ROCKET
Length: 11 ft (3.4 m)
Thrust: 9 lb (40 N) est.
Nationality: USA

SPACESHIPONE
Length: 16 ft (5 m)
Thrust: 16,600 lb (74 kN)
Nationality: USA (Scaled Composites)

1967: LARGEST ➡ ROCKET

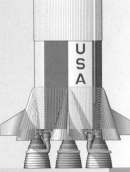

Saturn 5 (USA), which took man to the Moon in 1969 (and was first tested two years prior), was not the most powerful rocket ever built, but it was the largest at 363 ft (110.6 m) tall with the *Apollo* spacecraft on top. It weighed 6,400,000 lb (2,903 tonnes) on the launch pad and had a liftoff thrust of 7,584,000 lb (3,440 tonnes).

1998: MOST POWERFUL ION ENGINE USED IN SPACE

NASA's *Deep Space 1*, launched on October 24, 1998, was powered by an ion engine. A beam of ionized xenon atoms was fired from the engine at 21 miles/second (35 km/s), providing a thrust of 0.02 lb (0.09 N), equivalent to the force exerted by a sheet of paper resting on the palm of a hand. The ion engine was 10 times more efficient than a chemical rocket.

1999: MOST POWERFUL ROCKET LAUNCHER

Ariane 5-ESCA made its first operational flight in December 1999. The rocket launcher is capable of placing a 22,000-lb (10-tonne) payload into geosynchronous orbit 22,000 miles (36,000 km) above the Earth's surface.

2004: FIRST PRIVATELY FUNDED SPACE FLIGHT

The first privately funded manned space flight was achieved on June 21, 2004. *SpaceShipOne* – built and operated by Scaled Composites (USA), funded by Paul G. Allen (USA) and piloted by Mike Melvill (USA) – reached an altitude of 328,492 ft (100,124 m). The spacecraft took off from and landed at Mojave Airport, California, USA.

N-1
Length: 345 ft (105 m)
Thrust: 9,666,000 lb (43,000 kN)
Nationality: USSR

SATURN 5
Length: 363 ft (110.6 m)
Thrust: 7,584,000 lb (33,738 kN)
Nationality: USA (NASA)

ZENIT-3SL
Length: 196 ft (59.6 m)
Thrust: 1,641,000 lb (7,300 kN)
Nationality: Ukraine

ARIANE 5-ESCA
Length: 194 ft (59 m)
Thrust: 3,453,000 lb (15,360 kN)
Nationality: Europe (ESA)

SPACE SHUTTLE
Length: 184 ft (56 m)
Thrust: 5,789,000 lb (25,752 kN)
Nationality: USA (NASA)

INTERNET

★ FIRST PERSON JAILED FOR FILE SHARING

In November 2005, Chan Nai-Ming (China) was jailed for three months for uploading the movies *Daredevil* (USA, 2003), *Miss Congeniality* (USA, 2003), and *Red Planet* (USA, 2000) onto the internet using BitTorrent P2P file-sharing technology. The case against Chan, who adopted the online alias "Big Crook," is the first in the world to lead to a prison sentence.

★ NEW RECORD
★ UPDATED RECORD

⚠ EMOTICONS

Generally used to convey emotions in digital messages, some "smileys" represent things other than feelings...

:-o	bored
:_(	crying
:*)	drunk
@=)	Elvis
:0=/--	gag me
>:0===Q<	giraffe
=)	happy
:-|	indifferent
:-D	laughing out loud
:-#	lips are sealed
:(|)	monkey
(_i_)	mooning
@)->-	rose
:-\	undecided
=(	unhappy
|-O	yawn

★ COUNTRY WITH THE MOST INTERNET USERS

According to the International Telecommunication Union (part of the United Nations), the USA has 161,632,400 internet users. The ★ **country with the most internet users per capita** is New Zealand, with 7,931 people online for every 10,000 in the population.

★ COUNTRY WITH THE MOST WEBSITES PER CAPITA

According to the Organization for Economic Cooperation and Development's (OECD) report *Communications Outlook 2003*, Germany has the most websites per person, with 84.7 per 1,000 people.

★ GREATEST BROADBAND PENETRATION

According to the OECD (see above), the United States has the greatest broadband coverage, with 40,876,000 users connected to a broadband service. The ★**highest broadband coverage per capita** is in South Korea, where 24.66 per 100 people have broadband access.

★ COUNTRY WITH THE MOST INTERNET HOSTS

The USA has 195,138,696 web hosts, or one for every 65 people.

★ FIRST EMOTICON

The very first "smiley" was used by Scott Fahlman (USA) of Carnegie Mellon University, Pittsburgh, USA, on September 19, 1982. In a message on a bulletin-board system, he proposed the use of :-) and :-(in emails to signify the emotional context of the message and so prevent misunderstandings in communication.

DEEPEST LIVE INTERNET BROADCAST

On July 24, 2001, live footage of HMS *Hood* was broadcast over the internet from a depth of 9,200 ft (2,800 m) at the bottom of the Denmark Strait, where it sank in 1941. The broadcast, from an ROV (remotely operated vehicle), followed the discovery of the wreck by David Mearns (UK) of Blue Water Recoveries Ltd (UK).

LARGEST INTERNET TRADING SITE

Founded by Pierre M. Omidyar (USA, b. France) in 1995, eBay (USA) is a website that allows individuals around the world to buy and sell practically anything using a system of real-time, online auction bids. In 2004, 56.1 million users bought, sold, or bidded for an item on eBay sites. At the end of that year, eBay had amassed 135.5 million registered global users.

MOST MONEY DONATED ONLINE IN 24 HOURS

The greatest amount of money ever donated online via a website in a 24-hour period is £10,676,836 ($19,863,186). From 6:16 p.m. (GMT) on December 30, to 6:16 p.m. on December 31, 2004, the Disasters Emergency Committee website received 166,936 donations for the Tsunami Earthquake Appeal following the devastation in southeast Asia on December 26, 2004.

★ LARGEST ONLINE STORE

Amazon.com, founded in 1994 by Jeff Bezos (USA), opened its virtual doors in July 1995 – principally as an online bookstore – and has now sold products to more than 13 million customers in over 160 countries. Its catalog of 4.7 million books, CDs, videos, and more makes it the largest online store in the world.

★ FIRST WEBLOG ➡

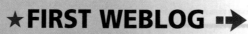

The **first website**, created by Tim Berners-Lee (UK, right) in 1991, would be described as a weblog if it were published online today. It was essentially a website containing news of what was being added to the World Wide Web, also created by Berners-Lee, who was knighted for his achievements in December 2003.

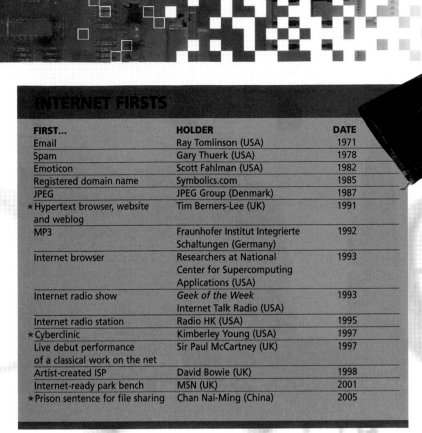

INTERNET FIRSTS

FIRST...	HOLDER	DATE
Email	Ray Tomlinson (USA)	1971
Spam	Gary Thuerk (USA)	1978
Emoticon	Scott Fahlman (USA)	1982
Registered domain name	Symbolics.com	1985
JPEG	JPEG Group (Denmark)	1987
★Hypertext browser, website and weblog	Tim Berners-Lee (UK)	1991
MP3	Fraunhofer Institut Integrierte Schaltungen (Germany)	1992
Internet browser	Researchers at National Center for Supercomputing Applications (USA)	1993
Internet radio show	*Geek of the Week* Internet Talk Radio (USA)	1993
Internet radio station	Radio HK (USA)	1995
★Cyberclinic	Kimberley Young (USA)	1997
Live debut performance of a classical work on the net	Sir Paul McCartney (UK)	1997
Artist-created ISP	David Bowie (UK)	1998
Internet-ready park bench	MSN (UK)	2001
★Prison sentence for file sharing	Chan Nai-Ming (China)	2005

HIGHEST ZOMBIE PC POPULATION

"Zombie PCs" are ordinary home computers that have become infected with viruses or worms in order for criminals to use thousands of them at once to attack websites. These attacks involve the home computers overwhelming a target website with data, causing that site to go offline, without the computer owners being aware of it. According to internet security firm CipherTrust, in 2005 the USA had more zombie PCs than any other country, with an estimated 964,020 infected computers available for criminals to use remotely.

★MOST VALUABLE PAIR OF JEANS (SOLD ON INTERNET)

An original pair of 115-year-old Levi Strauss & Co. (USA) 501 jeans were sold by Randy Knight (USA) to an anonymous collector from Japan for $60,000 through internet auction site eBay on June 15, 2005.

FASTEST INTERNET 2 LAND DATA DELIVERY

On November 9, 2004, a team from the University of Tokyo, Fujitsu Computer Technologies, and the WIDE Project (all Japan) transmitted a total of 541 gigabytes of data across 12,828 miles (20,645 km) of network in 10 minutes.

LARGEST INDEPENDENT INTERNET HUB

The London Exchange (Linx) handles 76 gigabits per second during peak times. Linx consists of eight high-capacity internet routing sites providing internet connections to users in and around the Docklands area of London, UK.

★LARGEST SPAMMING FINE

In December 2004, three companies – AMP Dollar Savings, Cash Link Systems, and TEI Marketing Group (all USA) – were together ordered to pay $1.08 billion to Robert Kramer (USA), owner of CIS Internet Services, an internet service provider based in Iowa, USA. Kramer had accused these companies of spamming his customers with millions of pieces of junk mail in 2003.

★COUNTRY WITH THE HIGHEST NUMBER OF INTERNET SUICIDES

Japan has the highest number of recorded suicides by individuals who have met in online chat rooms and arranged to kill themselves. A total of 91 people – 54 men and 37 women – died in internet suicide pacts (also known as "cybercide") in 2005. In October of that year, a further 11 people were prevented from committing suicide after the introduction of regulations to help police intercept death pacts.

★MOST DOWNLOADED PODCAST

The Ricky Gervais Show podcast on *Guardian Unlimited* (extract left) had an average of 261,670 downloads per episode during its first month (starting December 5, 2005). The podcast features random discussions between Gervais (right), Stephen Merchant (center) and Karl Pilkington (all UK).

RICKY GERVAIS

Below is a transcript of part of the 12th podcast of the *Ricky Gervais Show*. The show, which had been free to access, attracted over 3 million downloads overall during the series. Listen in as Ricky's efforts to convince Karl of his enthusiasm at featuring in *Guinness World Records 2007* are dented by Karl's disappointment at not having charged £1 a time...

Ricky: Karl needs a little bit of money... look at his round little head... he's like little Tiny Tim over there.
Stephen: Exactly.
Ricky: Look at him sitting there. Karl, have you had a good week?
Karl: It's been alright, yeah.
Ricky: Brilliant. Well, more of that next week, only you'll have to pay for it now. I'm surprised you're not buzzing because we've just had our photograph taken to enter the *Guinness World Records* book

for the greatest downloaded podcast of all time. We went along to *The Guardian*, and the press were there and they took a little picture of his round head, didn't they?
Karl: Yeah. I don't know why I should be excited about it when it's just...
Ricky: Haven't you always wanted to be in *Guinness World Records*?
Karl: Not really, no.
Ricky: They presented us with this year's book and I've been looking through it... and there's some fascinating ones... I used to get this as a kid...
Karl: tThere's loads of things in there I used to go to. I looked at it online the other day... you click on it... and there's a fella with the most ear hair! Looks amazing!

UNUSUAL EXPERIMENTS

★ LONGEST MISSION BY A SPACE SUIT

On February 3, 2006, Russian cosmonaut Valery Tokarev and US astronaut Bill McArthur jettisoned an old Russian Orlan-M spacesuit from the International Space Station. Equipped with a transmitter, "SuitSat-1" broadcast nearly 3,500 radio messages and data on the temperature inside the suit, which were picked up by amateur radio operators on Earth. The last transmission from SuitSat-1 was received on February 18, 2006, shortly before its onboard battery died.

★ LONGEST CARBON NANOTUBE MODEL

A model of a carbon nanotube containing 65,000 carbon atoms was constructed on April 22, 2005, from Molecular Visions chemistry building blocks by students and staff at Rice University's Center for Nanoscale Science and Technology in Houston, Texas, USA. It measured 1,181 ft (360 m) long. The model demonstrates how carbon atoms can be arranged to form molecular-scale tubes.

★ LONGEST MEASURED TIME DILATION

In October 1971, four cesium atomic clocks were flown around the world after being synchronized with reference clocks at the US Naval Observatory, Washington, D.C., USA, in order to measure the effects predicted by Einstein's Theory of Special Relativity. When flown westward, the clocks gained 273 +/- 7 nanoseconds, and when flown eastward, the clocks lost 59 +/- 10 nanoseconds. The difference between the two is owing to the Earth's rotation.

HOTTEST FLAME

The hottest flame so far created in a laboratory is produced by carbon subnitride (C_4N_2) which, at 1 atmosphere pressure, burns naturally with a flame calculated to reach 9,010°F (4,988°C).

LOWEST MAN-MADE TEMPERATURE

The lowest man-made temperature achieved so far is 450 picokelvin (0.00000000045° above absolute zero, the lowest possible temperature) by a team of scientists led by Aaron Leanhardt at the Massachusetts Institute of Technology in Cambridge, Massachusetts (MIT), USA. At such low temperatures, matter takes on a new state called a Bose-Einstein condensate. In this state, atoms behave as one "superatom." Scientists can then use magnetic fields to isolate and cool the atoms further.

★ MOST LETHAL MAN-MADE CHEMICAL

The compound 2, 3, 7, 8-tetrachloro-dibenzo-p-dioxin, or TCDD, is the most deadly of the 75 known dioxins – the carcinogenic byproducts of many industrial processes. It is 150,000 times more deadly than cyanide.

In 2004, the Ukrainian presidential candidate Viktor Yushchenko was poisoned with an estimated 100 parts per billion pure TCDD – the equivalent of a single drop in a large gasoline tanker truck and the second

★ FIRST ↑ SPIDER WEB IN SPACE

Arabella and Anita, two female cross spiders (*Araneus diadematus*), were sent into space in 1973 on the *Skylab 3* mission to the US *Skylab* space station. They were chosen for an experiment to see how spiders would spin webs in weightlessness, an idea suggested by student Judy Miles (USA). While the spiders did, indeed, construct normal-looking webs, the silk was finer than on Earth and had variable thickness – unlike terrestrial spiders' silk, which has uniform thickness.

largest ever measured in a human. He survived, though he still suffers from damage to his internal organs and chloracne, a highly disfiguring skin condition.

SMELLIEST SUBSTANCE

The smelliest substances on Earth are the man-made "Who-Me?" and "US Government Standard Bathroom Malodor," which have five and eight chemical ingredients respectively.

←▪ ★ LARGEST "RUBE GOLDBERG"

A Rube Goldberg is a machine inspired by the US cartoonist and Pulitzer Prize winner of the same name, who devised and sketched overly complex inventions to achieve the simplest of tasks. The largest ever Rube Goldberg consisted of 125 different steps and was made by members from the Purdue Society of Professional Engineers (USA, pictured in 2006) on April 9, 2005, as part of an annual Rube Goldberg competition. The winning machine was designed to change the batteries in a flashlight but using a wide variety of everyday items such as a vacuum cleaner, billiard balls, and bicycle wheels.

"Bathroom Malodor" smells primarily of human waste and becomes incredibly repellent to people at just two parts per million. It was originally created to test the power of deodorizing products.

"Who-Me?" is a sulfur-based substance that smells of rotting food and carcasses. It was originally developed during World War II when it was hoped French Resistance fighters would be able to humiliate and embarrass German soldiers by making them smell horrible. The idea failed, since it was impossible to properly target the smell. Instead, it ended up polluting large areas.

★ HIGHEST JUMP BY A STOAT

Animal behavior scientists at Victoria University in New Zealand have discovered that stoats can jump to heights of 6 ft 3 in (1.9 m). The experiment was initially carried out to decide the optimum height and width of a barrier fence for a bird sanctuary, and involved local predators such as rats, ferrets, possums, feral cats, and mice.

★ FASTEST CORK

The fastest speed to which a champagne cork has been subjected is 7.1 miles/sec (11.5 km/sec) in an X2 expansion tube at the University of Queensland, Brisbane, Australia. Like a wind tunnel, the X2 tube replicates the conditions faced by a spacecraft re-entering Earth's atmosphere. At this speed, the cork could fly from London to Paris in 30 seconds!

★ LONGEST ➡ MAN-MADE LIGHTNING

In 1899, Nikola Tesla (Croatia) created a 130-ft-long (40-m) bolt of lightning at his lab in Colorado, USA. The thunderclap was said to have been heard 22 miles (35 km) away. Pictured are members of the Tesla Coil Builders Association of Richmond, Virginia, USA, replicating Tesla's experiments.

LONGEST-RUNNING LABORATORY EXPERIMENT

The Pitch Drop Experiment has been running since 1930 at the University of Queensland, Australia, to measure the viscosity of pitch (tar). It consists of black pitch contained in a glass funnel, with the entire apparatus enclosed in a container. Once the stem of the funnel was cut, the tar slowly began to drip. In late 2000, the eighth drop fell. From this experiment, it has been possible to show that the viscosity of pitch is about 100 billion times that of water.

GREATEST HEIGHT FROM WHICH AN EGG HAS BEEN DROPPED AND REMAINED INTACT

On August 22, 1994, David Donoghue (UK) dropped an egg 700 ft (213 m) from a helicopter onto a golf course in Blackpool, Lancashire, UK, and the egg remained unbroken. "You have

to get the forward velocity equal to the downward velocity, then get the egg to land nearly perpendicular on a steep slope," explains David.

MOST LEAD TURNED INTO GOLD

In 1980, the renowned scientist Glenn Seaborg (USA) transmuted several thousand atoms of lead into gold at the Lawrence Berkeley Laboratory, USA. His technique borrowed from nuclear physics and involved the removal of protons and neutrons from the lead atoms. Seaborg's technique would have been far too expensive to enable routine manufacturing of gold from lead, but his work is the closest thing yet to the concept of the alchemists' fabled "Philosopher's Stone."

★ NEW RECORD
★ UPDATED RECORD

★ LONGEST-RUNNING BODY FARM

The "Body Farm" in Knoxville, Tennessee, USA, was founded in 1971 by forensic anthropologist William Bass (USA, below), as part of the University of Tennessee. The farm is a 3-acre (1.2-hectares) plot of land where human bodies are left to decay under varied conditions; there are about 40 rotting cadavers present at any one time. This gives scientists a chance to study how the decay happens. Tests with the bodies provide valuable data for murder crimes and post-mortems.

SCIENCE FRONTIERS

★ SMALLEST CALCULATOR

James Gimzewski (UK) and a team of scientists at IBM Research Division's laboratory in Zurich, Switzerland, created a calculator with a diameter of less than one-millionth of a millimeter.

The molecular abacus consists of 10 molecules of carbon 60 that can be moved along a microscopic groove on a copper surface with the tip of a scanning tunneling microscope.

★ NEW RECORD
★ UPDATED RECORD

SMALLEST RULER

A ruler used for measuring very small lengths in an electron microscope was developed in 1994 by John McCaffrey and Jean-Marc Baribeau (both Canada) of the Institute for Microstructural Sciences at the National Research Council of Canada. The smallest division on the ruler is 18 atoms thick and individual atoms are visible. It is so small that 10 of the rulers stacked end to end would equal the diameter of a human hair.

DARKEST MAN-MADE SUBSTANCE

The darkest man-made substance is a black coating composed of a nickel-phosphorus alloy. It reflects just 0.16% of visible light – making it around 25 times less reflective than conventional black paint. The principle was first developed by researchers in the USA and India in 1980. In 1990, Anritsu (Japan) further refined this method to produce the darkest version so far.

★ LARGEST KNOWN PRIME NUMBER

A prime number is a number that can be divided only by itself and the number one – such as the number 13.

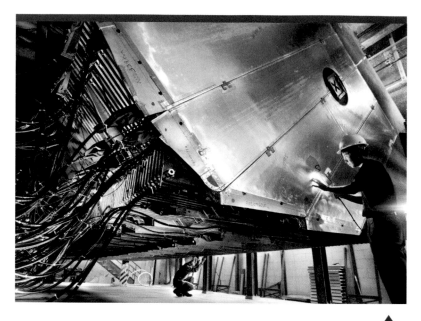

In March 2005, German eye surgeon and mathematics buff Martin Nowak generated a prime number that is composed of 7,816,230 digits, making it the largest prime number ever recorded and beating the previous record by over half a million digits.

QUIETEST PLACE ON EARTH

The quietest place on Earth is the Anechoic Test Chamber at Orfield Laboratories, Minneapolis, Minnesota, USA. Ultra-sensitive tests performed on January 21, 2004, gave a background noise reading of -9.4 dBA (decibels A-weighted).

★ HIGHEST MAN-MADE TEMPERATURE

Scientists using the Z-Machine at the Sandia National Laboratories, Albuquerque, New Mexico, USA, have achieved temperatures that were in excess of 3.6 billion°F (2 billion Kelvin). The temperatures generated by the experiment – which produced superheated gas, or plasma, by inputting

★ MOST POWERFUL NEUTRINO BEAM

The most powerful beam of neutrinos in the world is that produced by the Neutrinos at the Main Injector (NuMI) Beamline at Fermi National Accelerator Laboratory, Batavia, Illinois, USA.

With an output of 200 kilowatts, this beam is fired below ground to a detector in Minnesota, USA, approximately 450 miles (720 km) away, as an experiment to learn more about the nature of these elusive subatomic particles.

This experiment, known as MINOS (Main Injector Neutrino Oscillation Search), was initiated in March 2005.

20 million amps of electricity into steel wires – were far hotter than expected. It is hoped that this discovery may one day contribute toward more efficient nuclear fusion plants. The achievement was announced in February 2006.

◄ ★ LARGEST KUGEL

A kugel is a perfectly balanced, polished stone sphere that fits into a base carved to match its curvature; the sphere floats on a film of water and revolves 360° in all directions. The world's largest kugel by both diameter and weight is *Mary Morton Parsons Earth-Moon Sculpture* (pictured), which was unveiled on January 8, 2003, at the Science Museum of Virginia, Richmond, USA. It is a single piece of South African black granite polished into a sphere that is 8 ft 8 in (2.65 m) in diameter.

★ MOST POWERFUL RESISTIVE MAGNET

The world's strongest resistive (as opposed to superconducting) magnet is the 35 Tesla magnet at the National High Magnetic Field Laboratory, Tallahassee, Florida, USA.

Upgraded from a 30 Tesla magnet in December 2005, the 35 Tesla has a magnetic field some 700,000 times stronger than the Earth's own.

★ SMALLEST NANOTUBE BRUSHES

Dr. Pulickel M. Ajayan (USA) – at Rensselaer Polytechnic Institute, Troy, New York, USA – and Vinod P. Veedu, Dr. Anyuan Cao, and Dr. Mehrdad N. Ghasomi-Nejhad (all USA) – at the University of Hawaii at Manoa, Honolulu, Hawaii, USA – have created the smallest nanotube brushes, with bristles over a thousand times finer than a human hair.

The bristles are composed of carbon nanotubes, tiny straw-like molecules just 30 billionths of a meter across.

★ LONGEST SUSTAINED NUCLEAR FUSION REACTION

In 2002, scientists at the experimental Tore Supra reactor, Cadarache, France, were able to sustain a nuclear fusion reaction of 3 megawatts for 210 seconds.

★ MOST GENETICALLY STREAMLINED BACTERIUM

Most of the human genome, the code required to "build" human beings, is carried by just one or two per cent of our DNA; the rest is thought to be "junk." In extremely hostile environments, however, evolution reduces this junk to a bare minimum. This has created an oceanic bacterium called *Pelagibacter ubique*, which, with only 1,354 genes, is the most streamlined bacterium in existence.

★ LONGEST-BURNING LIGHT BULB

The Livermore Centennial Light Bulb, at Firestation No.6, Livermore, California, USA, has been burning since it was installed in 1901. It is a hand-blown bulb operating at about 4 watts, and is left on 24 hours a day in order to provide night illumination of the fire engines. There has been only one break in its operation, when it was removed from one fire station and installed in another.

★ LARGEST ➡ MICROPHONE ARRAY

The largest microphone array is LOUD (Large acOUstic Data array project). It consists of 1,020 microphones gathered in a single array, allowing operators to pinpoint, track, and amplify individual voices in a crowd.

The array was built by a team of scientists at the Massachusetts Institute of Technology, Cambridge, Massachusetts, USA, and led by Professor Anant Agarwal (India). It became operational in January 2004.

★ SMALLEST HOLE DRILLED

On November 29, 2005, scientists at Cardiff University, UK, announced the development of machinery that can drill holes just 22 microns (0.022 mm) across. The technique uses a process called electro-discharge machining, and will eventually allow for improvements in the miniaturization of electronic systems. By way of comparison, a human hair is 50–80 microns wide.

SMALLEST HOMINID

The smallest known member of the hominid family is *Homo floresiensis*, who stood 3 ft 3 in (1 m) tall. Remains of the species were discovered in a cave (below) on the island of Flores, Indonesia; *H. floresiensis* lived here 13,000 years ago and probably interacted with modern humans. The discovery of this new species was announced on October 28, 2004.

ACTUAL SIZE

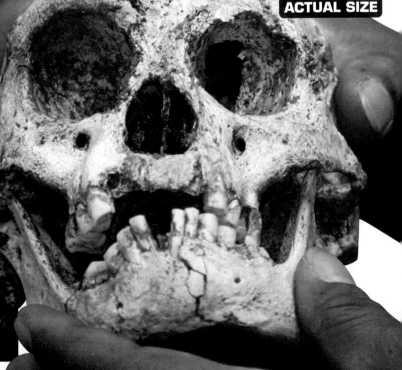

COMPUTER GAMES

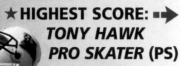

★ HIGHEST SCORE: ➡
TONY HAWK PRO SKATER (PS)

Though skateboarding is an American invention and *Tony Hawk Pro Skater* (1999) for the Playstation is one of the biggest games in US history, the world record holder is not an American but Domagoj Broj of Zagreb, Croatia, who scored 1,943,543 points on the Warehouse track on August 9, 2002.

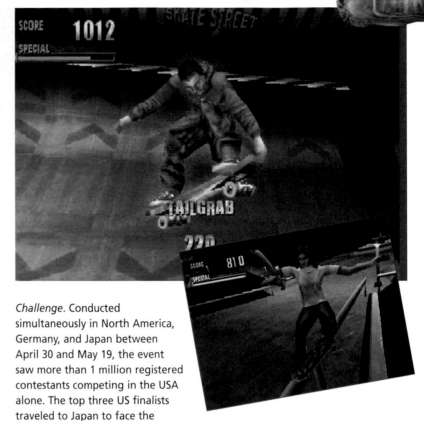

★ MOST SUCCESSFUL VIDEO-GAME HERO

Mario, a computer-generated carpenter created by Shigeru Miyamoto (Japan), first made an appearance under that name in Nintendo's "Game & Watch" version of *Donkey Kong* in 1982. (He was otherwise known as "Jumpman" in the original 1981 arcade version of the game). To date, Mario has featured in at least 125 video games that, combined, have sold nearly 200 million copies worldwide.

★ LARGEST VIDEO-GAME CONTEST

In 1984, the children's charity March of Dimes International and video-game manufacturer Konami/Centuri sponsored the *Track & Field*

Challenge. Conducted simultaneously in North America, Germany, and Japan between April 30 and May 19, the event saw more than 1 million registered contestants competing in the USA alone. The top three US finalists traveled to Japan to face the Japanese and German champions in the finals on June 12, and the final world champion was 18-year-old accordion player John Phillip Britt of Riverside, California, USA.

★ FIRST NATIONAL PINBALL CHAMPIONSHIP

A "Big Whiffle Tournament" – whiffle being considered the first

pinball machine – was held between May 24 and 26,1935, in the Futuristic Ballroom in Milwaukee, Wisconsin, USA, and attracted hundreds of pinball players from all across the USA. It featured 200 whiffle pinball tables and promised $1,000 in prizes (including a "fine bedroom suite"). The event was conducted as a charity fundraiser for the Badger State

---

Got an Xbox? Then play your way into the record books with Madden 2005:

1. *Choose the mini game "Two Minute Drill;" set level to "All Madden"*
2. *Only default settings are allowed, so you may NOT use profile info*
3. *Pick two teams (must both be NFL)*
4. *You MUST beat the computer for your high score submission*

GUINNESS WORLD RECORDS PINBALL HIGH SCORES

"TOURNAMENT" MODE
Disallows certain bonus features

EXACT INCLINE
Each gamefield needs to be measured with an inclinometer, to insure that the incline is correct to .001, in order to comply with competition standards.

FRESH, NEW, WAXED GAMEFIELD
This is very important because the game becomes easier if the gamefield is worn.

WHITE BUMPERS/ RED FLIPPERS
Generally required for tournament play, though many machines don't automatically carry them.

PLUNGER
This must always be in perfect condition so that it works uniformly in every game.

LEG UNIFORMITY
If legs are not uniform, it biases the incline, causing a jittery gamefield.

On April 28–30, 2006, Guinness World Records and Twin Galaxies hosted a pinball championship at the Pinball Hall of Fame in Las Vegas, Nevada, USA. Machines were set to tournament standard (see left) to find the ultimate high scorers. Since no two pinball machines are alike, players must play on the same game machine, with the serial numbers logged to ensure this happens.

GAME	SCORE	PLAYER	SERIAL NO.
Kings and Queens	2,243	Michael Frankovich (USA)	05376
Captain Fantastic	245,240	Tom Neighbors (USA)	13428
Lawman*	159,530	Brian Weilbacher (USA)	7522
Wizard*	190,240	Tom Neighbors (USA)	11207
Scared Stiff*	69,895,370	Craig Sengstock (USA)	51048103373
Taxi*	19,507,390	Tony Moore (USA)	162553
Creature from the Black Lagoon	1,015,433,710	Jim Belsito (USA)	835280
Twilight Zone*	1,726,330,320	Jim Belsito (USA)	183171
Addams Family	1,591,573,470	Jim Belsito (USA)	20017-590681
South Park	456,968,070	Tony Moore (USA)	E-148449

Extra balls received; going forward, no extra balls allowed

★ MOST SUCCESSFUL VIDEO-GAME HEROINE

The *Tomb Raider* computer game character Lara Croft has transcended the boundary of the videogame and become a recognizable figure in mainstream society, making her more successful in terms of global recognition than the likes of Chun Li (*Street Fighter*), Pauline (*Donkey Kong*), Daphne (*Dragon's Lair*), and Jill Valentine and Claire Redfield (*Resident Evil* series).

The ★**most successful non-human videogame heroine** is Ms. PAC-MAN.

Advancement Association of the Blind, and certain whiffles were adapted to allow blind teams to compete in the event.

★ LARGEST VIRTUAL FUNERAL

In October 2005, an avid computer gamer known only as Snowly (China) indulged in a three-day nonstop marathon of the MMORPG (Massively Multiplayer Online Role-Playing Game) *World of Warcraft* (Blizzard Entertainment, USA) and died of fatigue. Over 100 gamers visited a virtual cathedral inside the game, where a service was held for her.

MMORPG manufacturers are now being urged to add three-hour "anti-obsession" breaks into their games.

LARGEST JOYPAD

A video-game joypad (controller) measuring 8 ft (2.43 m) wide and weighing around 150 lb (68 kg) was built by a team led by David Randolph and David Ledger (both USA). It was unveiled on March 28, 2005, on the TV show *Attack of the Show* (G4, USA) as a fully-functional, scaled-up replica of an original Nintendo Entertainment System (NES) joypad.

HIGH SCORES

★ BERZERK (ARC)

Attaining a high score on this classic arcade game is still considered a major achievement, despite the game's 26-year history.

On March 27–28, 2005 – more than 11 years since the record was last broken – former *Ms. PAC-MAN* world champion Chris Ayra (USA) took 4 hr 26 min to amass 325,270 points. He did so in "Fast Bullets" mode, which is widely considered the more difficult version of the game.

★ DOOM 3 (PC)

With the skill level set at "Marine," 19-year-old engineering student Jérôme Bouzillard (France) set a time of 1 hr 30 min 52 sec to complete *Doom 3* on his laptop. (Timing stops after each fade-to-black at the end of a level and resumes after the loading screen disappears.)

This record was verified by Twin Galaxies reviewing an AVI (Audio Video Interleave) computer file; however, it was not checked for "concatenation" (that is, it cannot be guaranteed that the game was played in one continuous attempt).

! STOP PRESS

Remember Activision's 1982 jungle-based Atari game Pitfall!? On April 24, 2006, Rodrigo Lopes (Brazil) achieved the fastest "perfect completion" – which requires the player to score the maximum of 114,000 points without losing a single life – with only 1 min 6 sec remaining.

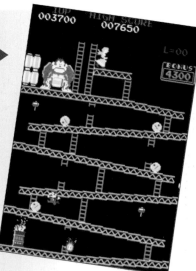

★ DONKEY KONG: "NO HAMMER" CHALLENGE (ARC)

Shawn Cram (USA) achieved a world record score of 317,000 points playing the original *Donkey Kong* coin-operated machine – without using the hammer (which usually allows Jumpman (Mario) to smash oncoming barrels thrown at him by Kong)! Cram achieved this gaming milestone on May 5, 2006.

COMPUTER GAMES

◄━ DANCE DANCE REVOLUTION EXTREME (ARC)

After 18 months' practice, Jason Gilleece (USA) danced his way to a record 97.72% for his timing, missing only four (0.12%) of his steps, to break a record that had stood for six months. He was just 1.3% away from the perfect score of 690 million points.

★ DRAGON'S LAIR (ARC)

Greg Sakundiak (Canada) is the world record high-scorer on the arcade videogame *Dragon's Lair*, with a score of 374,954. He also holds arcade game records for ★ **Tag Team Wrestling**, with 3,795,500 points and ★ **Twin Cobra** (1,900,450). Greg also happened to be ranked by the World

Armwrestling Federation (WAF) as the world No.4 best professional arm wrestler in 2003!

★ FROGGER (ARC)

On March 25, 2005, at the Funspot Family Entertainment Center in Weirs Beach, New Hampshire, USA, Donald Hayes (USA) – holder of seven classic arcade world records – claimed his seventh record with a final score on *Frogger* of 589,350. Hayes is still the only player to score over 500,000, an achievement that earned him a $250 "bounty" placed by senior referee Robert Mruczek of Twin Galaxies. It took him 2 hr 55 min to reach the 148th stage, crossing his frog to its lily pad more than 735 times.

★ GRAND THEFT AUTO: VICE CITY (PS2)

In a single session lasting 3 hr 59 min 3 sec on June 25, 2003, Matthew J. Baker (Canada) achieved the fastest completion of the controversial driving adventure game set in Miami, USA. The rules allow unessential tasks to be ignored; saving and loading can be done only within the game.

★ HALO 2 (XB)

In August 2005, Cody Miller (USA) completed *Halo 2* – with the difficulty level set to "Legendary" – in a time of 3 hr 17 min 50 sec, without game-death. Miller is the first Twin Galaxies-verified champion to finish the game without losing a life. Twin Galaxies senior referee Robert T Mruczek noted: "There are a variety of ultra-cheesy tactics that Cody specifically did not employ… It was a clean run and one that should be respected by his fellow gamers on the title." ➡

★ NEW RECORD
☆ UPDATED RECORD

The following represents a selection of the 30 greatest video arcade game scores of all time, as chosen by Twin Galaxies:

GAME	SCORE	PLAYER	FROM	DATE
★Asteroids	41,336,440	Scott Safran	USA	Nov. 13, 1982
★Battlezone	23,000,000	David Palmer	USA	Aug. 30, 1985
★Carnival	386,750	Fred Pastore	USA	Jun. 1, 2001
★Centipede	7,111,111	Donald Hayes	USA	May 4, 2001
★Congo Bongo	1,506,300	Jason Cram	USA	Jul. 21, 2003
★Crystal Castles	910,722	Frank Seay	USA	Jul. 11, 1988
★Depth Charge	4,660	John Lawton	USA	Nov. 30, 1977
★Dig Dug	4,388,520	Donald Hayes	USA	Dec. 12, 2003
★Donkey Kong	1,047,200	Billy Mitchell	USA	Jun. 1, 2005
★Donkey Kong, Jr.	1,004,000	Steve Wiebe	USA	Sep. 10, 2002
★Frogger	589,350	Donald Hayes	USA	Apr. 2, 2005
★Galaga	15,999,990	Stephen Krogman	USA	Jun. 1, 1989
★Galaxian	399,290	Gary Whelan	UK	Aug. 13, 2004
★Gorf	653,990	Todd Rogers	USA	Nov. 24, 1982
★Joust	1,002,500	Don Morlan	USA	Jun. 30, 1984
★Mappy	1,277,410	Greg R. Bond	USA	Apr. 1, 2004
★Missile Command	1,967,830	Tony Temple	UK	Mar. 9, 2006
★Ms PAC-MAN	933,580	Abdner Ashman	USA	Apr. 6, 2006
★Pengo	1,110,370	Rodney Day	Australia	Aug. 13, 1983
★Pole Position	67,310	Les Lagier	USA	Jun. 30, 1986
★Q*Bert	33,273,520	Bob Gerhardt	Canada	Nov. 28, 1983
★Scramble	1,147,580	Robert Mruczek	USA	Jun. 6, 2001
★Space Harrier	35,774,740	Nick Hutt	UK	Aug. 13, 2005
★Star Wars	31,660,614	David Palmer	USA	Jul. 31, 1986
★Super PAC-MAN	1,045,000	Rick D. Fothergill	Canada	Feb. 2, 2002
★Tapper	3,162,125	Greg Erway	USA	Jun. 5, 2005
★Tetris	1,648,905	Stephen Krogman	USA	Jun. 5, 1999
★Tron	6,768,288	David Cruz	USA	Sep. 7, 2005
★Wizard of Wor	384,200	David S. Yuen	USA	Jan. 1, 2005
★Zookeeper	35,732,870	Shawn Cram	USA	Feb. 8, 2004

★ OLDEST ↑
COMPETITIVE VIDEO GAMER

Doris Self achieved a world record on *Q*Bert* on July 1, 1984, at the age of 58, and still competes for the world title today at the age of 80. She began playing in 1983, after the death of her husband, and regularly plays through the night at her local arcade.

★ JUNIOR PAC-MAN (ARC)

Abdner Ashman (USA) played *Junior PAC-MAN* for six straight hours, starting at 6 p.m. on December 4, 2005, and achieved a new record of 3,330,950 points by midnight. Ashman, without a break, then went on to smash the *Robotron* arcade record with 945,550 points! *(See entry on Robotron for more details.)*

★ LEGEND OF ZELDA: OCARINA OF TIME (N64)

Michael Damiani (USA) completed the fifth game of the *Zelda* series in an impressive 5 hr 4 sec, shaving over seven minutes off his best time. He also holds the record for the Zelda game *The Minish Cap*, with a time of 2 hr 46 min 32 sec.

★ PAC-MAN (ARC)

Since Billy Mitchell (USA) scored the first "perfect" *Pac-Man* game (3,333,360 points) on July 3, 1999, four more players have matched it. The top players now consider it a greater accomplishment to achieve the perfect game in the fastest time:

TOP 5 "PERFECT" *PAC-MAN* RANKINGS:

Chris Ayra (USA)	3:42:04	2/16/2000
Rick Fothergill (Can)	3:58:42	7/31/1999
Tim Baldarramos (USA)	4:45:15	8/8/2004
Donald Hayes (USA)	5:24:46	7/21/2005
Billy Mitchell (USA)	5:30:00	7/3/1999

★ ROBOTRON (ARC)

During a night of marathon gaming on December 4–5, 2005, having just spent six hours smashing the *Junior PAC-MAN* record, Abdner Ashman (USA) immediately began to play *Robotron* for a further six hours (more than 100 games), until 6 a.m. He scored 945,550 points

in total, breaking the former world record of 838,475 held by John Martinez (USA) since July 2, 1985.

★ POKEMON PINBALL (GBC)

On June 25, 2005, Matt O'Rourke (USA) achieved a score of 309,374,900 on *Pokemon Pinball* (Blue) and 322,497,700 (Red).

★ SPYHUNTER (ARC)

Paul Dean (USA) scored 9,512,590 points on this coin-op more than 20 years ago (June 28, 1985) – and his record still remains more than ten times higher than the second best score of 832,620 points.

★ STAR FOX 64 (N64)

Michael Damiani (USA) defeated Andross and the Venomian Army in just 27 min 40 sec. The bill for ending the Galactic War totaled $21,312 (in Star dollars), though Michael killed only 333 Venomians.

★ SUPER MARIO WORLD (SNES)

A record time was more than halved when Jason Baum (USA) completed *Super Mario World* in just 1 hr 31 min 44 sec – smashing the previous record of 3 hr 8 min 34 sec. During his run through nine worlds, he never lost a life.

? DID YOU KNOW?

Guinness World Records now accepts computer-game high scores, but only those that have been submitted and ratified by judges from Twin Galaxies (www.twingalaxies.com), the official body that monitors all computer and pinball high scores. You can still submit your claims to us – find out how on p.7.

Guinness World Records encourages safe gameplay – we do not accept video- or computer-game marathons in this category. Please play safely and responsibly, and take regular screen breaks.

Key

ARC – arcade game
GBC – GameBoy Color
N64 – Nintendo 64
PC – personal computer
PS/2 – PlayStation/2
XB – Xbox
SNES – Super Nintendo

ROBOTS

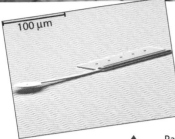

100 μm

★ SMALLEST MOBILE ROBOT

A controlable, untethered robot measuring just 60 x 250 μm (micrometers) was unveiled by a team led by Prof. Bruce Donald (UK) of Dartmouth University, UK, in October 2005. (A micrometer is 1/1,000th of a millimeter.) Two hundred such robots could stand side by side on a single M&M. The microrobot has various applications in fields such as biotechnology and integrated circuitry.

? DID YOU KNOW?

The United Nations predicts that there will be almost 2.5 million "entertainment and leisure" robots in homes in 2007, compared to the 137,000 that there are currently. By the end of 2007, 4.1 million robots will be doing jobs in homes.

★ NEW RECORD
★ UPDATED RECORD

★ FIRST ROBOT OLYMPICS

The First International Robot Olympics was held on September 27–28, 1990, at the University of Strathclyde in Glasgow, UK. An Olympic torch was carried from the Parthenon Greek restaurant through the streets of Glasgow by Trolleyman (a golf-cart-like wheeled robot that eventually suffered power failure) before robot representatives from the USA, Japan, Canada, Europe, and the former Soviet Union participated in events such as collision avoidance, wall climbing, speaking and bipedal walking. Unfortunately, a carpet laid especially for the event proved to be the undoing of most entrants, as they became caught in its pile.

★ LARGEST ROBOT COMPETITION

A total of 646 engineers, 466 robots, and 13 countries took part in the 2005 RoboGames held at San Francisco State University, California, USA. Events included soccer with re-programmed Aibo robot dogs, robo-sumo wrestling in various weight categories, bipedal racing, firefighting, and musical artistry.

The USA topped the medals table, with 28 golds out of a possible 34.

★ FASTEST 25-M SPRINT BY A ROBOT

The fastest 25-m sprint by a robot is 6.5 seconds by Scuttle – built by Mike Franklin (UK) – in Fairford, UK, on July 16, 2005.

★ FIRST ROBOT BABYSITTER

NEC's (Japan) range of "Partner-type Personal Robots," or "PaPeRos," are designed for maximum interaction with humans. The PaPeRo Childcare robot has been specially adapted with two (stereoscopic) camera "eyes" to recognize surroundings and faces, eight microphone "ears" to detect and recognize speech – even from multiple sources – and cell-phone connectivity that allows PaPeRo to stay in touch with the absent parents.

It also can speak with a 3,000-word vocabulary and react to touch via nine sensors. Children in the care of PaPeRo wear an ultrasonic transmitter and wireless microphone, allowing the robot to track their positions at all times.

★ FASTEST ROPE CLIMB BY A ROBOT

ClimbActic, built by John Thorpe (UK) and Highfields School, Matlock, Derbyshire, UK, climbed up a 33-ft (10-m) rope in 5.2 seconds in Fairford, UK, on July 17, 2005.

HIGHEST-JUMPING ROBOT

Sandia National Laboratories, USA, has developed "hopper" robots that use combustion-driven pistons to jump to heights of 30 ft (9 m). They have potential applications in planetary exploration, where hoppers could be released by a lander to survey the surrounding landscape.

LARGEST ROBOT

The Tower Belcon, completed in 1998, is a concrete-conveying robot that is 231 ft (70.5 m) high with a 250-ft (76.5-m) boom. It can deliver around 6,350 ft³ (180 m³) of concrete per hour with its two concrete buckets, which have a combined volume of 105 ft³ (3 m³). The robot was designed and manufactured by Mitsubishi Heavy Industries, Tokyo, Japan.

★ FASTEST COMPLETION OF THE DARPA CHALLENGE

The robot that completed the 2005 DARPA Grand Challenge competition – an unmanned vehicle race – in the fastest time was a Volkswagen Touareg modified by a team from Stanford University (USA). It completed the 131.2-mile (211.1-km) off-road course through the Mojave Desert in just 6 hr 53 min on October 8. The team won a prize of $2 million, awarded by DARPA (Defense Advanced Research Projects Agency), a division of the US Department of Defense.

Artificial lips can change embouchure on instrument's mouthpiece

Moveable joints with 31 degrees of freedom

Two legs capable of walking and dancing

★LARGEST ROBOT EXHIBITION

The International Robot Exhibition, held every two years, is the world's largest gathering of robots and their creators. The 2005 event, at the 183,000-ft^2 (17,020-m^2) Tokyo International Exhibition Center, Japan, attracted 152 companies, 40 industry bodies, and 99,713 visitors over three days from November 30 to December 3.

★LONGEST FLIGHT BY A ROBOTIC ASTRONAUT ASSISTANT

NASA's Sprint AERCam is a free-flying camera designed to provide astronauts with detailed live views of colleagues performing spacewalks. It is a small self-propelled sphere capable of maneuvering in six degrees of freedom. On December 3, 1997, it flew in space for 1 hr 15 min in a highly successful test flight (pictured).

★FASTEST ROBOT JOCKEY

Kamel is a robot jockey designed by K-Team (Switzerland) for racing camels in the Arabian Gulf states. A traditional sport in the region, it has recently attracted human rights groups who fear for the lives of the jockeys, some as young as four years old, who are forced – often after starvation to keep weight down – to race in endurance events. To combat this, the ruling sheiks of Qatar are calling for all camel races to be ridden by robot jockeys by the end of 2007.

Weighing in at 60 lb (27 kg), Kamel comes with in-built GPS and shock absorbers, and can be controlled remotely by joystick. The fastest time recorded to date is 25 mph (40 km/h).

MOST EMOTIONALLY RESPONSIVE ROBOT

Kismet, created by Cynthia Breazeal (USA) at the Massachusetts Institute of Technology (MIT), Massachusetts, USA, is a robotic head powered by 15 networked computers and 21 motors. It is designed to recognize different emotions while interacting with humans, and to respond to them accordingly. Nine of the onboard computers are used to control Kismet's vision alone.

MOST THERAPEUTIC ROBOT

PARO, a robotic seal designed by Takanori Shibata (Intelligent Systems Institute, Japan), is able to respond to human touch and sound. Developed to be a therapeutic robot, it measurably reduces stress levels in patients. During a six-week trial in 2001 at a day-care center for the elderly, tests carried out on patients showed a marked improvement in stress levels after interaction with the white fur-covered robot.

LARGEST ROBOTIC TELESCOPE

The Liverpool Telescope, owned by the Astrophysics Research Institute (ARI) of Liverpool John Moores University on La Palma, Canary Islands, Spain, has a main mirror with a diameter of 6 ft 6 in (2 m). Designed for observing in visible wavelengths and near infrared, it achieved "first light" on July 27, 2003.

MOST WIDELY USED INDUSTRIAL ROBOT

Puma (Programmable Universal Machine for Assembly), designed by Vic Scheinman (Switzerland) in the 1970s and manufactured by Swiss company Staubli Unimation, is the most commonly used robot in university laboratories and automated assembly lines.

★FIRST ROBOT TRUMPETER

Playing a brass instrument requires constant changes to the embouchure (the arrangement of the mouth, lips, and tongue) to reach certain notes. The first robot to achieve this is an as-yet-unnamed bipedal invention designed by Toyota (Japan). In the same "family" are robots with the dexterity to play the tuba and drums.

★FASTEST ROBOTS ➡

The ★**fastest two-wheeled robot** is Emiew (right), capable of moving at 3.7 mph (6 km/h). Built by Hitachi (Japan) and announced in March 2005, the robot uses sensors to measure gradients in order to be able to move and stop in a stable fashion, thus allowing it to keep up with a walking human. Emiew stands for Excellent Mobility and Interactive Existence as Workmate.

The **fastest humanoid robot** is ASIMO, which stands for Advanced Step in Innovative Mobility. Its creator, Honda (Japan), announced in December 2005 that ASIMO can now reach 3.7 mph (6 km/h). Crucially, it does so by lifting both feet off the ground; it can also shift its center of gravity and run in circles.

GADGETS

★ LARGEST LCD SCREEN

In March 2006, LG Philips – a partnership of LG (Korea) and Philips (Netherlands) – announced development of the largest LCD (liquid-crystal display) panel, in Paju, South Korea. The 100-in (254-cm) panel is 7 ft 2 in (2.2 m) wide and 3 ft 11 in (1.2 m) high, and has a picture quality of 6.22 million pixels.

SMALLEST DIGITAL VOICE RECORDER

The EDIC-mini A2M by Telesystems (Russia) is just 1.69 x 1.42 x 0.12 in (43 x 36 x 3 mm) and weighs 10 g (0.35 oz). It can record up to 37 hours of audio.

ACTUAL SIZE

★ WIDEST-RANGING ULTRASONIC YOUTH DETERRENT

"Mosquito" is a speaker that emits a harmless, high-frequency (ultrasonic) tone that can be heard only by people under 20 years old. It was invented by Howard Stapleton (UK), of Compound Security Systems, and takes advantage of presbycusis – the natural loss in hearing that occurs in the 20s, usually in the 18–20 kHz range – to deter groups of teenagers away from areas in which they are not wanted.

The device, which has a range of up to 65 ft (20 m), was first used outside a Spar store in Barry, South Wales, UK, and is now employed by over 100 British retailers.

★ LIGHTEST TENT

The world's lightest commercially available tent is the Laser Competition, by Terra Nova Equipment (UK). Launched in October 2005, this one-man tent weighs just 32 oz (930 g), which includes the inner sheet, flysheet, poles, and the stakes needed to pitch it, as well as the packaging.

★ FASTEST HOVER SCOOTER

In January 2006, Hammacher Schlemmer & Company, Inc. (USA) announced the release of the very first hoverboard. The Levitating Hover Scooter hovers a few inches (around 10 cm) above the ground on a powerful cushion of air and has a top speed of 15 mph (24 km/h). The rider controls the direction by transfering body weight, and modifes the engine/fan speed by levers on the handlebars. The whole package costs $17,000, and the 1-gal (5-liter) engine provides up to one hour's worth of travel.

★ THINNEST CELL PHONE

Cell-phone specifications are improving on a seemingly daily basis, but at the time of going to press (end of May 2006), the thinnest phone available – in the Far East, at least – is Samsung's X828 (right), at just 0.27 in (6.9 mm)! Despite its size, it has a two-megapixel camera, an MP3 player, 80 MB of memory, and a full-color screen.

★ FASTEST TEXT MESSAGE SENT AROUND THE WORLD

On May 22, 2005, on the Isle of Coll, Scotland, UK, members of the organization Project Trust sent a text message around the world by forwarding it to cell phones in six countries in six continents, and finally back to the original phone in Coll. The message was received back in the UK only 2 min 28 sec after the original sender began typing in the message.

ACTUAL SIZE

★ HIGHEST-DEFINITION SCREEN ON A WRISTWATCH TELEVISION

The sharpest picture achieved on a wearable television screen is the NHJ TV Wristwatch, with 130,338 pixels. The 1.5-in (3.8-cm) color TV screen relies on TFT (Thin Film Transistor) technology to deliver such a high-resolution picture. It also displays the time and channel selection, and has a battery time of one hour. The TV watches began shipping in May 2005 for ¥19,800 ($185).

★ ZANIEST ALARM CLOCKS

On March 20, 2006, Newlauches.com announced its top five strangest yet most effective alarm clocks:

5. Sfera alarm: Hangs from ceiling; every time the "snooze" button is hit, it slowly retracts toward the ceiling by 7.8 in (20 cm); after a few more snoozes, it is so high up you need to stand up to turn it off.

4. Anemone: Vibrates violently, throws itself off your nightstand, and rumbles around your bedroom until you get up and stop it. The "off" button is also difficult to find.

3. Clocky: Every time the snooze button is hit, this clock rolls off your nightstand and "hides"; you need to get up to find it and turn it off.

2. Blowfly: This cunning clock takes flight when its alarm rings and buzzes with an irritating insect-like hum, forcing you awake to chase it around the room and slot it back into its base.

1. Puzzle clock (pictured): When the alarm rings, a four-piece jigsaw puzzle is fired into the air, and the alarm will not stop until the pieces are found and slotted into place on top.

★ HIGHEST-CAPACITY MULTIMEDIA JUKEBOX

The Archos AV700 PVP (Personal Video Player) has a 100-gigabyte (GB) memory capable of storing 400 hours of video, and an impressive 16:9-ratio 7-in (18-cm) screen. It can record from any device with a standard video output (TVs, DVDs, set-top cable boxes, etc) without any software or special hardware. It also can schedule and manage your choice of TV programs and play all music file formats. It went on sale in Europe in July 2005 for €850 ($1,027).

LARGEST-CAPACITY DISC STORAGE MEDIA

In March 2006, Sony released its Blu-ray Disc Technology, which has the highest capacity of storage of any portable media. The single-layer Blu-ray Disc Recordable and Blu-ray Disc Rewritable have 25 GB worth of storage – five times more than a regular DVD.

★ LARGEST-CAPACITY PORTABLE MEDIA PLAYER

Wolverine Data Inc., of California, USA, announced the launch of the MVP 9120 – the world's largest-capacity PMP (Portable Media Player), with a 120-GB hard drive and a 2.5-in (6.4-cm) color screen – at the PMA 2006 International Convention and Trade Show in Orlando, Florida, USA.

★ LARGEST PLASMA SCREEN

Panasonic's 103-in (261-cm) Plasma Display measures more than 8 ft 6 in (2.6 m) in width, and has 1,080 p (progressive) High-Definition TV resolution. The prototype for the enormous screen was shown at the 2006 International Consumer Electronics Show in Las Vegas, USA, on January 5–8, 2006.

★ SMALLEST COLOR VIDEO CAMERA

The PC208 Mini CMOS Camera, produced

by Supercircuits (USA), measures 0.3 x 0.3 in (7.5 x 7.5 mm) with an onboard 0.25-in (6.3-mm) color chip and provides full-color video pictures. Smaller than a dime, it requires a viewing hole of only 0.08 in (2 mm). The price for the PC208 in February 2006 was $140.

ACTUAL SIZE

★ **NEW RECORD**
★ **UPDATED RECORD**

★ MOST POWERFUL HANDHELD LASER

The Spyder Green 300 is the most powerful battery-powered handheld laser commercially available. Made by Wicked Lasers (China), the class IIIb device has an average output of 300 mW with peak readings of 420 mW. By way of comparison, a typical laser pointer has an output of around 1 mW.

The Spyder can reportedly project its beam 120 miles (193 km); at close range, it can ignite matches, cut tape, and pop balloons. A 500+mW model, codename MANTIS, is available to military clients.

Sshhh!

THE HOTTEST CELEBRITY GOSSIP

from GUINNESS WORLD RECORDS

Old Dogs... ...New Tricks

Paris Hilton (USA) was voted the **most overexposed celebrity** of 2005, according to E-Poll Market Research (USA). The Hilton hotel heiress made numerous headlines with stories about the breakup with her best friend, Nicole Richie (USA), with fiancé Paris Latsis (Greece), and her apparent abandonment of Tinkerbell, her pet Chihuahua, for a kinkajou – a small raccoon-like mammal – named Baby Luv.

Jeans model Anna Nicole Smith (USA) met her wheelchair-bound oil billionaire husband J. Howard Marshall II (USA) while working at a Texas strip club. He was 89 and she 27 when they married in 1994 – then a record **age difference** of 62 years. Marshall died just over a year after the wedding.

HIGHEST EARNERS

When he took the starring role in his first movie, *The Scorpion King* (USA, 2002), **DWAYNE JOHNSON** (USA) – a.k.a. WWE star The Rock – earned a tidy $5.5 million, making him the **highest-paid debut actor**.

According to the 2005 *Forbes Celebrity 100* list, **the highest annual earnings for an actress** in 2004 was $22 million by **DREW BARRYMORE** (USA).

> I feel physically better now than I did when I was 20.

BRUCE WILLIS (USA) received $100 million for his role in the $55-million film *The Sixth Sense* (USA, 1999), the **highest salary for an actor**.

The **most money paid per minute to an actor** for appearing in a TV advertisement is $928,800. **NICOLE KIDMAN** (Australia) earned $3.71 million for a four-minute commercial for Chanel No.5 perfume in December 2003.

The **highest annual earnings for a pop star ever** is an incredible $125 million by **MICHAEL JACKSON** (USA), who topped the *Forbes* list in 1989 as the highest-paid entertainer of all time.

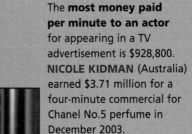

The holder of the record for **highest annual earnings by a female singer** is **MADONNA** (USA), who earned $50 million in 2004, according to the *Forbes Celebrity 100* list released on June 15, 2005.

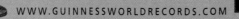

Google – the world's **largest search engine**, with an index of over 8 billion pages – keeps a count of the most searched-for content on the World Wide Web. Known as Google Zeitgeist, the annual summary is effectively a reflection of the world's most wanted people...

In the last year, Britney Spears (USA, left) lost top spot to Janet Jackson (USA, below) as the **most searched-for person** – and the **most searched-for news item** – of 2005. Predictably the **most searched-for man** on Google was Brad Pitt (USA, right).

SCANDALS!

No.1... IN THE POKEY
Which thespian holds the dubious Guinness World Record for the most jailed actor? We look over some of the usual suspects...

◀ **SUSPECT 1**
Could it be Aussie bad boy **Russell Crowe**? Was his first jail sentence handed down for punching a Chinese man who addressed him without the prefix "Mr."?

◀**SUSPECT 2**
What about shock rocker **Courtney Love**? Was she jailed for killing a man before conducting her own defense and being acquitted after the prosecution failed to produce the dead body?

▶ **SUSPECT 3**
Could it be *Chaplin* star **Robert Downey Jr**? Did he spend a night under lock-and-key in the African city Djibouti, capital of French Somaliland (now also known as Djibouti), for punching a customs officer?

▲ **SUSPECT 4**
Or could it be swashbuckler **Errol Flynn**? Did he stamp on a police officer's foot after being asked for an autograph?

☆**Answers below**

No. 2... POPPING OUT
How did Janet Jackson excuse the "mishap" that led to a fine of $550,000, the largest imposed by a broadcaster?

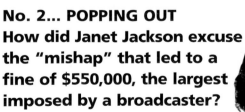

ANSWERS: 1. All of these crimes were attributed to Errol Flynn (USA, 1909–59), who was jailed four times. 2. "Wardrobe malfunction" was the excuse given by Janet Jackson (USA) when her left breast was exposed during a live Super Bowl performance with Justin Timberlake (February 2004).

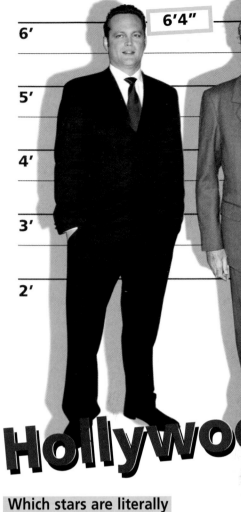

6' 6'4" 5' 4' 3' 2'

Hollywoo

Which stars are literally reaching for the skies? Check out our guide to the tallest (and smallest) talent in Tinseltown

EXCLUSIVE

REALITY TV SUCCESS STORIES

They may be universally panned by the critics, but the stars of reality TV shows are often more successful than their "genuine" celebrity counterparts...

↓ LARGEST PREDATORY FISH

The great white shark (*Carcharodon carcharias*) averages 15 ft (4.6 m) long and weighs up to 1,700 lb (770 kg), although there is plenty of circumstantial evidence to suggest that some grow to more than 20 ft (6 m)! The International Shark Attack File confirmed that great whites were responsible for 55 "unprovoked attacks" on humans in 2005.

NATURAL BORN KILLERS

MOST DANGEROUS MOSQUITO ↑

Malarial parasites carried by mosquitoes of the genus *Anopheles* have probably been responsible for 50% of all human deaths since the Stone Age (excluding wars and accidents). Each year in sub-Saharan Africa alone between 1.4 million and 2.8 million people die from malaria.

Malaria also imposes a huge economic burden. According to the World Health Organization, Africa loses $12 billion per year in lost production... all because of a bug 0.1 in (3 mm) long!

MOST DANGEROUS BIRD

The cassowary (family Casuariidae) lives in New Guinea and Queensland, Australia, and grows up to 6 ft 6 in (2 m) tall. On each foot it has three toes with strong claws, the inner toe having a 5-in-long (12-cm) spike. A cornered bird can be extremely dangerous and will leap into the air and lash out with its spike if it feels threatened. Its kick is powerful enough to rip open a person's stomach and can even cause death.

MOST SUCCESSFUL ←• PREDATOR

African hunting dogs, also called Cape hunting dogs or hyena dogs (*Lycaon pictus*), are successful in 50–70% of their hunts, consistently the highest figure in the mammalian world. Their Latin name translates as "painted wolf," reflecting the dog's coat of red, black, brown, yellow, and white stripes or patches. African hunting dogs live in packs of between 7 and 15 on average, although packs of up to 40 have been observed. An alpha male takes the lead in coordinating hunts, stalking and chasing animals up to twice their size until they tire, at which point they are disembowelled alive. The prey is then torn to shreds and divided equally among the group.

6'0"

... and L WS

2'8"

od Highs ...

Guys, you'll have to stretch yourselves if you're to top the **tallest leading men** currently working in Hollywood. Pictured from left to right are VINCE VAUGHN (USA) and CHRISTOPHER LEE (UK), who – along with Clint Eastwood (USA) – all top out at a whopping 6 ft 4 in (1.94 m)!

But who's the leggiest lady in La La Land? The record for the **tallest leading woman** is shared by an impressive tree-size threesome: SIGOURNEY WEAVER (USA), star of *Ghostbusters* and the *Alien* quadrilogy; former Mrs Stallone BRIGITTE NEILSEN (Denmark), star of, erm, *Celebrity Big Brother*

(UK, 2004) and the aptly named *She's Too Tall* (USA, 1998); and GEENA DAVIS (USA), star of *Beetlejuice* (USA, 1988) and the greatest box-office flop of all time (see above). Each of these leading ladies, pictured from left to right, measure up at an impressive 6 ft (1.82 m).

And finally, let's have a big hand for the **shortest working actor** in Hollywood, VERNE TROYER. Best known for his role in the *Austin Powers* movies, he's a minuscule 2 ft 8 in (81 cm) tall – just 9.4 in (24 cm) taller than the shortest man who ever lived (Gul Mohammed from India).

The **most successful female pop group formed by a TV reality show** is Girls Aloud (UK, below), who had an incredible seven consecutive UK Top 3 singles between December 2002 and September 2004.

"That's My Goal" by Shayne Ward (UK, left), winner of *The X Factor 2005*, was downloaded 71,997 times in the week ending December 24, 2005! "Just 21 years old and I'm a Guinness World Record holder!" he said. "How crazy is *that*?!"

Simon Cowell (UK, right), who has appeared as a judge on TV shows *Pop Idol* (UK), *American Idol* (USA), and *The X Factor* (UK), is currently the world's **highest-paid TV talent show judge**. He earned a whopping £18 million ($34 million) in 2004, according to *Forbes*.

Double A-side "Anything Is Possible"/ "Evergreen," released by *Pop Idol 2002* winner Will Young (UK, above left), sold a record 1,108,269 copies in its first chart week from February 25 to March 2, 2002, with 385,000 on its first day. It went on to

sell an unprecedented 2 million singles in the UK in just 15 weeks.

Kelly Clarkson (USA, above right), winner of *American Idol 2002*, broke a record set by the Beatles (UK) in 1964 when her first single "A Moment Like This" jumped from No.53 to No.1 in October 2002.

HENRY "FATTY" FOULKE

TAKING A KICK

HEAVIEST GOALTENDER ⬆

The largest goaltender in representative soccer was the England international Willie Henry "Fatty" Foulke (1874–1916), who stood 6 ft 3 in (1.9 m) and weighed 311 lb (141 kg). His last games were for Bradford City, by which time he was 364 lb (165 kg). He once stopped a game by snapping the crossbar.

MICHAEL OWEN

YOUNGEST ENGLISH PREMIERSHIP HAT TRICK SCORER

In the Premiership, the youngest hat-trick scorer is Michael Owen (UK), who was aged 18 years 62 days when he scored three goals for Liverpool against Sheffield Wednesday on February 14, 1998.

ANDRIY SHEVCHENKO

MOST CHAMPIONS LEAGUE GOALS

The greatest number of goals in UEFA Champions League matches is 52 by Andriy Shevchenko (Ukraine) playing for Dynamo Kiev and AC Milan from 1994 to the present.

DINO ZOFF

LONGEST INTERNATIONAL CLEAN SHEET

The longest time that any goaltender has succeeded in preventing goals being scored during international matches is 1,142 minutes (nearly 13 matches) by Dino Zoff (Italy), from September 1972 to June 1974.

RIO FERDINAND

MOST EXPENSIVE DEFENDER

Rio Ferdinand (UK) continued to hold the title of the world's most expensive defender in July 2002 when he joined Manchester United from Leeds United in a deal worth £30 million ($46.9 million).

NORMAN WHITESIDE

YOUNGEST WORLD CUP FINALS PLAYER

The youngest ever player in a finals match is Norman Whiteside (UK), who played for Northern Ireland against Yugoslavia aged 17 years 41 days in Zaragoza, Spain, on June 17, 1982.

MIA HAMM

MOST INTERNATIONAL GOALS SCORED BY A WOMAN

The greatest number of international goals scored by a woman is 158 by Mia Hamm (USA), from 1987 to 2004. Widely regarded as the best female soccer player ever, Hamm began her senior international career at the age of just 15.

ALI DAEI

MOST INTERNATIONAL GOALS SCORED BY A MAN

The most international goals scored by a man is 109 by Ali Daei (Iran) between 1993 and 2005.

WORLD CUP STATS AT A GLANCE

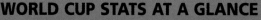

Fastest expulsion	56 seconds	José Batista (Uruguay) vs. Scotland	Jun. 13, 1986
Fastest goal	11 seconds	Hakan Sukur (Turkey) vs. Korea	Jun. 29, 2002
Oldest scorer	42 years 39 days	Albert Roger Milla (Cameroon) vs. Russia	Jun. 28, 1994
Youngest scorer	17 years 239 days	Pelé (Brazil) vs. Wales	Jun. 19, 1958
Youngest player	13 years 310 days	Souleymane Mamam (Togo) vs. Zambia	May 9, 2001*
Largest attendance	199,854	Maracanã Stadium (Brazil) vs. Uruguay	Jul. 16, 1950
Most goals (individual)	5	Oleg Salenko (Russia) vs. Cameroon	Jun. 28, 1994
Most goals (team)	27	Hungary	1954
Most appearances in World Cup finals (individual)	5	Antonio Carbajal (Mexico)	1950–1966
		Lothar Matthäus (Germany)	1982–1998
Most appearances in World Cup finals (team)	17	Brazil	1930–2002
Most World Cup wins	5	Brazil	1958, 1962, 1970, 1994, 2002
Most women's World Cup wins	2	USA	1991, 1999

*Preliminary qualifying game; all other figures are for the 32-team finals matches

MOST DANGEROUS ANT ⬆

The bulldog ant (*Myrmecia pyriformis*) of Australia has been the cause of at least three human fatalities since 1936, the latest a farmer in 1988. In an attack, the ant holds onto its victim with long, toothed mandibles, and thrusts its long, barbless sting into the skin. This sting is powerful enough to kill an adult human within 15 minutes.

MOST FATALITIES IN ➡ A CROCODILE ATTACK

On February 19, 1945, a Japanese Army unit was forced to cross 10 miles (16 km) of mangrove swamps on the Burmese (now Myanmar) island of Ramree. The swamps were home to many saltwater crocodiles (*Crocodylus porosus*), which can grow to 15 ft (4.5 m). By the morning, of the 10,000 soldiers that entered the swamp, only 20 had survived.

LARGEST FELINE CARNIVORE

The male Siberian tiger (*Panthera tigris altaica*) averages 10 ft 4 in (3.15 m) from the nose to the tip of the tail, stands 3 ft 3 in–3 ft 6 in (99–107 cm) at the shoulder and weighs about 580 lb (265 kg).

The **most human fatalities from a tiger attack** is 436 by a tigress, eventually shot by Col. Jim Corbett (UK), in the Champawat district of India between 1902 and 1907.

MOST DANGEROUS LIZARD ⬆

The Gila monster (*Heloderma suspectum*) is a heavy-built, brightly colored lizard that lives in the arid parts of Mexico and the southwestern USA. It has eight well-developed venom glands in its lower jaws that carry enough venom to kill two adult humans. The venom is not injected but seeps into the wound caused when the gila monster bites its victim. To make sure that it kills its prey, the lizard may hang on after it has bitten and actively chew for several minutes.

LARGEST LAND ➡ CARNIVORE

Polar bears (*Ursus maritimus*) typically weigh 880–1,320 lb (400–600 kg) and have a nose-to-tail length of up to 8 ft 6 in (2 m). The **heaviest land carnivore ever** was a polar bear shot on a frozen ice pack in the Chukchi Sea, west of Kotzebue, Alaska, USA. The bear was said to measure 11 ft 5 in (3.5 m) from nose to tail over the contours of the body.

SOCCER LEGENDS

RECORD-BREAKING SOCCER STARS

The Fédération Internationale de Football Association (FIFA) World Cup is the most important competition in the soccer calendar, and is contested every four years. The first official tournament was organized by FIFA President Jules Rimet – after whom the trophy is now named – in 1930 in Uruguay; since then over 200 countries have competed. Despite the international popularity of soccer, only 11 national teams have reached the final, and just seven have won it (see World Cup History, right).

To celebrate the 2006 World Cup in Germany, Guinness World Records has brought together a selection of the sport's greatest legends, from league heroes to international superstars, and from the women's game to the World Cup – every one of them a record breaker in his or her own right...

MOST ↑ VALUABLE SOCCER SHIRT

The most valuable soccer shirt in the world is the No.10 shirt worn by Pelé in the 1970 World Cup final. It was sold at Christie's, London, UK, on March 27, 2002, for £157,750 ($225,109) – over three times the estimated price. It was sold by Italian international Roberto Rosato, who exchanged shirts with the star after Brazil's 4–1 victory in Mexico City. Pelé scored the first goal of the game.

PELÉ

MOST CAREER GOALS
The greatest number of goals scored in a specified period is 1,279 by Edson Arantes do Nascimento (Brazil, b. October 23, 1940), known as Pelé, between September 7, 1956 and October 1, 1977, during which he played 1,363 games. His best year was 1959, when he scored 126 goals. The Milésimo (1,000th) came from a penalty for his club Santos at the Maracanã Stadium, Rio de Janeiro, Brazil, on November 19, 1969, when he played his 900th first-class match.

JUST FONTAINE

MOST WORLD CUP FINALS GOALS
The most goals scored by one player in a World Cup finals tournament is 13 by Just Fontaine (France) in 1958, in Sweden.

GERD MÜLLER

MOST GOALS SCORED IN WORLD CUP FINALS TOURNAMENTS
Gerd Müller scored a total of 14 goals for West Germany in World Cup finals tournaments. Müller scored 10 goals in Mexico (1970) and four in West Germany (1974), when the host nation went on to lift the trophy.

ALAN SHEARER

MOST ENGLISH PREMIERSHIP GOALS
The greatest number of goals scored in the English Premiership is 260 by Alan Shearer (UK). He began his soccer

ZINEDINE ZIDANE

MOST EXPENSIVE PLAYER
The highest transfer fee for a player is a reported 13,033,000,000 Spanish pesetas ($66 million) for Zinedine Zidane (France) from Juventus to Real Madrid on July 9, 2001. Zidane's unprecedented deal was for a four-year contract, with a buy-out clause of $195 million.

career with Southampton before moving to Blackburn Rovers and finally to Newcastle United in July 1996 for a then record fee of £15.6 million ($22.4 million). In January 2006, Shearer scored his 200th goal for Newcastle United, equaling a club record set nearly 50 years previously. He scored 206 goals for the club in total before retiring on 20 April 2006.

DAVID BECKHAM

HIGHEST ANNUAL EARNINGS
According to *Forbes*, England captain and Real Madrid player David Beckham (UK) earned $32.5 million in 2005.

DID YOU KNOW? ?

Pelé was the youngest scorer in a World Cup finals match, aged 17 years 239 days.

WORLD CUP HISTORY

DATE	HOST	WINNER	SCORE	RUNNER-UP
1930	Uruguay	Uruguay	4–2	Argentina
1934	Italy	Italy	2–1	Czechoslovakia
1938	France	Italy	4–2	Hungary
1942		No tournament		
1946				
1950	Brazil	Uruguay	2–1	Brazil
1954	Switzerland	W. Germany	3–2	Hungary
1958	Sweden	Brazil	5–2	Sweden
1962	Chile	Brazil	3–1	Czechoslovakia
1966	England	England	4–2*	W. Germany
1970	Mexico	Brazil	4–1	Italy
1974	W. Germany	W. Germany	2–1	Netherlands
1978	Argentina	Argentina	3–1*	Netherlands
1982	Spain	Italy	3–1	W. Germany
1986	Mexico	Argentina	3–2	W. Germany
1990	Italy	W. Germany	1–0	Argentina
1994	USA	Brazil	0–0; 3–2**	Italy
1998	France	France	3–0	Brazil
2002	South Korea and Japan	Brazil	2–0	Germany
2006	Germany			
2010	South Africa			

*after extra time; ** after penalties

RUUD VAN NISTELROOY

MOST CONSECUTIVE PREMIERSHIP GOALS

Ruud Van Nistelrooy (Holland) scored goals in eight consecutive English Premiership matches for Manchester United in the 2001/02 season. He surpassed the previous achievements of Mark Stein (England), Thierry Henry (France), and Alan Shearer (England), who had all been halted at seven matches.

PETER SHILTON

MOST WORLD CUP CLEAN SHEETS

Peter Shilton (England) played in 10 World Cup finals matches without conceding a goal. He played in 17 World Cup ties, in three tournaments, between 1982 and 1990. He also holds the record for **most soccer matches played**, with 1,390 senior appearances. These included a record 1,005 League appearances – 286 for Leicester City (1966–74), 110 for Stoke City (1974–77), 202 for Nottingham Forest (1977–82), 188 for Southampton (1982–87), 175 for Derby County (1987–92), 34 for Plymouth Argyle (1992–94), 1 for Bolton Wanderers (1995), and 9 for Leyton Orient (1996–97).

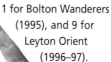

WALTER ZENGA

LONGEST WORLD CUP FINALS CLEAN SHEET

The longest time played in World Cup finals matches by a goaltender without conceding a goal is 518 minutes by Walter Zenga (Italy) in the 1990 tournament.

WORLD CUP WINNERS

1. Brazil (right) — 5 — 1958, 1962, 1970, 1994, 2002
2. W. Germany — 3 — 1954, 1974, 1990
   Italy — 3 — 1934, 1938, 1982
3. Argentina — 2 — 1978, 1986
   Uruguay — 2 — 1930, 1950
4. England — 1 — 1966
   France — 1 — 1998

JOSÉ MOURINHO

★ HIGHEST PAID SOCCER MANAGER

Chelsea FC's José Mourinho (Portugal) signed an extended five-year deal worth £5.2 million ($9.8 million) a year in May 2005, with a bonus package per season equating to the potential of an additional year's salary.

ARTS & MEDIA

CONTENTS

★ MOST EXPENSIVE MOVIE EVER MADE

King Kong (New Zealand/USA, 2005) had an estimated budget of $207 million. This puts the film ahead of both *Titanic* (USA, 1997) and *Spider-Man 2* (USA, 2004) – both of which cost $200 million – as the most expensive movie ever made.

Director Peter Jackson (New Zealand), who also filmed *The Lord of the Rings*, was paid $20 million to direct the movie. This represents the ★**highest salary ever paid to a film director prior to production**.

ART & SCULPTURE

MOST...

★ INTERNATIONAL PHOTOGRAPHY AWARDS

Minoru Daigaku (Japan) has received 1,302 awards for his work at 46 international photographic exhibitions since 1967.

★ EXPENSIVE PAINTING SOLD ONLINE

The Misses Stewart Hodgson by Lord Frederic Leighton (UK) sold on www.sothebys.com for $550,750 on November 29, 2001.

EXPENSIVE ELEPHANT ART

Cold Wind, Swirling Mist, Charming Lanna I, which sold for 1.5 million baht ($39,000) to Panit Warin (Thailand) on February 19, 2005, at Maesa Elephant Camp, Chiang Mai, Thailand, was painted by the sanctuary's elephants.

★ FINGERPRINTS IN ONE ARTWORK (NO REPEATS)

Beginning in 1999, an oil painting entitled *The Tree of Peace* was created using 42,515 unduplicated, children's fingerprints upon a single canvas measuring 5.5 x 9.1 ft (1.7 x 2.8 m) and was organized by the Foundation for the Defense of Our Values, Santiago de Cali, Colombia.

LARGEST COTTON SCULPTURE

In April 1999, after working on it for 11 months – for four hours a day – Anant Narayan Khairnar (India) completed a 7-ft 6-in-tall (2.28-m) sculpture of Mahatma Gandhi made entirely from cotton. Once soaked in a chemical hardener for protection, it weighed 44 lb (20 kg).

★ NEW RECORD
★ UPDATED RECORD

LARGEST...

★ BATIK

The world's largest batik painting measured 340 ft x 21 in (103.9 m x 55 cm) and was created by Sarkasi Said (Singapore) on May 20, 2003, at the Singapore Expo Hall. Batik is a method of dyeing fabric using wax to protect areas that are to be left untouched by the dye.

★ BOTTLE-CAP MOSAIC

On June 19, 2005, a mosaic created from 2,280,000 bottle caps was laid out to celebrate the 950th anniversary of the founding of the German town of Landesbergen. The completed mosaic covered 325 x 209 ft (99 x 64 m).

★ CANNED FOOD STRUCTURE

On April 27, 2006, in Durbanville, South Africa, eXtreme Connection (Durbanville

LARGEST TOOTHPICK SCULPTURE

Alley, an alligator made by Michael Smith (USA) from more than 3 million toothpicks, measured 15 ft (4.5 m) long and weighed 292 lb (132 kg) when examined at Galvez Middle School, Prairieville, Louisiana, USA, on March 22, 2005. It took three years to complete.

★ LARGEST HANDPRINT PAINTING

Green Power is a giant handprint painting created by 3,138 participants at Discovery Park, Tsuen Wan, Hong Kong, China, on April 22, 2005. The painting – created to spread the message of environmental protection – measures 3,636 ft² (337.8 m²).

Youth Transformation) built a structure using 16,276 cans. After the record attempt, the food was donated to less privileged members of the Durbanville community.

★ CHALK SIDEWALK ART

A huge piece of sidewalk art measuring 53,456 ft² (4,966 m²) was made by 1,564 children at an event organized by the Casa del Tercer Mundo, the Child and Adolescent Commission of Estelí, FUNARTE, and the local government in Estelí, Nicaragua, on May 27, 2005.

★ CHOCOLATE SCULPTURE

A chocolate egg measuring 27 ft 3 in (8.32 m) high and 20 ft 11 in (6.39 m) wide was created by Guylian (Belgium) at the Grote Markt, Sint-Niklaas, Belgium, on March 23, 2005.

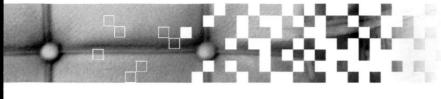

★ LARGEST CITYSCAPE CREATED FROM KITCHEN UTENSILS

Zhan Wang (China) made a model of London, UK, using more than 1,000 pots, pans, and kitchen utensils – the London Eye wheel is a ball of stainless-steel wire and St. Paul's Cathedral a large oven dish. From October 6 to December 11, 2005, it was part of the *Universal Experience* exhibition at the Hayward Gallery, London, UK.

★ FINGER PAINTING

A finger painting covering 10,840 ft² (1,007 m²) was created by 187 people at the University of Tulsa, Oklahoma, USA, on September 1, 2005, to celebrate the university's first home soccer game of the season.

★ INDOOR MURAL

From February 27 to March 5, 2005, six artists contributed to an indoor mural covering 9,731 ft² (904 m²) at Shyam Vatika, Saraswati Estate, Cimmco Tiraha, Gwalior, India.

★ PHOTO EXHIBITION

A photographic exhibition showing 33,670 shots of smiling individuals was held at the Royal College of Art in London, UK, on August 29, 2005. It was organized by Hewlett Packard and NCH, a children's charity.

★ SAND PAINTING

On September 18, 2005, the Art in the Frame Foundation of Jersey in the Channel Islands, UK, organized the creation of a sand painting measuring 2,604 ft² (241.92 m²).

★ STAMP MOSAIC

From May 6, 2004 to July 19, 2005, Andrey Andreev (Bulgaria) created a 546.8-ft² (50.8-m²) mosaic containing 102,153 stamps. It depicted historic scenes and emblems of Bulgaria.

★ TEMPORARY COIN MURAL

On October 10, 2004, a coin mural using 2,546,270 one-yen coins and measuring 98 x 131 ft (30 x 40 m) was created as part of the Saitama Festival in Saitama, Japan.

★ TV SCULPTURE

Gintaras Karosas created a sculpture titled *LNK Infotree* using 2,903 individual television sets, spanning 33,744.85 ft² (3,135 m²) at the Open-Air Museum in Vilnius, Lithuania.

★ WOODBLOCK PRINT

A woodblock print created by 334 children had a total area of 3,720 ft² (345.6 m²) when displayed in Lich, Germany, on September 19, 2004.

★ FASTEST BALLOON MODELING

On November 21, 2005, John Cassidy (USA) blew up and tied 654 balloon sculptures in one hour in New York City, USA. Cassidy – whose lips are insured against cracking – repeatedly tied 30 different shapes, including: a dog, elephant, fish, poodle, crocodile, sword, Viking helmet, basic hat, horse, dragonfly, giraffe, moose, camel, airplane, and mouse.

★ LARGEST KNITTED SCULPTURE

On a hillside near the village of Artesina in north Italy lies an enormous 200-ft-long (60-m) stuffed rabbit knitted from "toilet-paper pink" wool. Titled *Rabbit*, it took five years to knit and is to remain in place for 20 years, decomposing naturally. Its spilled entrails provide a nesting ground for local wild animals. Visitors are encouraged to clamber over the giant body, say its creators, Gelitin (Italy).

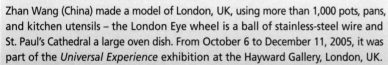

COMICS & GRAPHIC NOVELS

★ LONGEST COMIC STRIP

The world's longest continuous comic strip, created by 35 Disney artists (all Italy) and entitled *Ciccio e il compleanno sottosopra* ("Ciccio and the Topsy-Turvy Birthday"), measured 795 ft 5 in (242.45 m) long and 3 ft (0.9 m) high on Guinness World Records Day 2005 (see p.8), in Lucca, Italy. The strip consisted of 242 panels and was completed in 8 hr 30 min.

and drawn by Todd McFarlane (Canada) and edited by Jim Salicrup (USA). The record-breaking edition was sold with a variety of differently colored covers and several reprints were ordered to keep up with high public demand.

★ BIGGEST-SELLING SINGLE-EDITION COMIC

Spider-Man No.1, first published in August 1990, had an initial print run of 2.35 million. It was written

LONGEST-RUNNING COMIC

The Dandy has been produced continuously by DC Thomson & Co. of Dundee, UK, since its first edition appeared on December 4, 1937. The weekly comic's best-known character is an unshaven cowboy named Desperate Dan, pictured here with other major characters who have appeared in *The Dandy* over the years.

LARGEST AUCTION OF COMIC BOOKS

The world's largest auction of comic books, comic art, movie posters and other related memorabilia took place on October 13, 2002. The four-day auction was conducted by Heritage Comic Auctions of Dallas, Texas, USA, and realized $5,207,430.

★ MOST EISNER COMIC AWARD WINS IN ONE CATEGORY

Todd Klein (USA) has won 12 out of a possible 13 awards at the Eisner Comic Awards for Best Lettering. The Will Eisner Comic Industry Awards are named after cartoonist Will Eisner, creator of comic-book character The Spirit, and were first awarded in 1988.

MOST VALUABLE COMIC

The world's most valuable comic is a 1939 "pay copy" of *Marvel Comics* No.1, which was sold to Jay Parrino (USA) for $350,000 in November 2001.

MOST EDITIONS OF A COMIC

The first edition of Mexican comic *Pepin* printed on March 4, 1936, as a weekly anthology of comics that eventually became a daily, and ran until October 23, 1956. There were a total of 7,561 issues.

GUINNESS WORLD RECORDS 2007

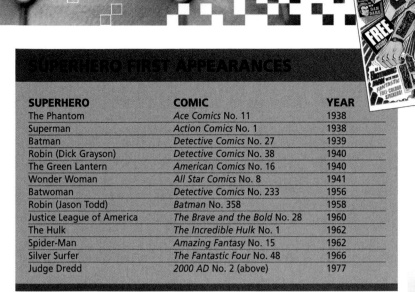

SUPERHERO FIRST APPEARANCES

SUPERHERO	COMIC	YEAR
The Phantom	*Ace Comics* No. 11	1938
Superman	*Action Comics* No. 1	1938
Batman	*Detective Comics* No. 27	1939
Robin (Dick Grayson)	*Detective Comics* No. 38	1940
The Green Lantern	*American Comics* No. 16	1940
Wonder Woman	*All Star Comics* No. 8	1941
Batwoman	*Detective Comics* No. 233	1956
Robin (Jason Todd)	*Batman* No. 358	1958
Justice League of America	*The Brave and the Bold* No. 28	1960
The Hulk	*The Incredible Hulk* No. 1	1962
Spider-Man	*Amazing Fantasy* No. 15	1962
Silver Surfer	*The Fantastic Four* No. 48	1966
Judge Dredd	*2000 AD* No. 2 (above)	1977

★ MOST SUCCESSFUL COMIC-BOOK MOVIES

Spider-Man (USA, 2002) took a record-breaking $403,706,375 at the US box office. It passed the $200-million mark in 10 days – taking $223.04 million by May 12, 2002 – faster than any other movie. *Spider-Man 2* grossed $373,377,893, resulting in an overall gross for the two movies of $777,084,268. The third movie in this franchise is out in 2007.

GRAPHIC NOVELS

★ FIRST GRAPHIC NOVEL

Graphic novels are book-length comics – printed stories told visually. Creators of these "graphic stories" or "graphic literature" often argue that they represent an artistic movement, not just a publishing format.

The word "graphic novel" first appeared in 1976 on the jacket of *Bloodstar* by Richard Corben (USA, illustrator) and Robert E. Howard (USA, author). In the same year, George Metzger's (USA) comic book *Beyond Time and Again* was subtitled *A Graphic Novel*, and *Red Tide* by Jim Steranko (USA) was labeled both a "visual novel" and a "graphic novel."

★ LARGEST GRAPHIC NOVEL (EXTENT)

Craig Thompson's (USA) multi-award winning *Blankets: An Illustrated Novel* is a single-volume graphic novel with a record extent of 592 pages. It tells the story of two brothers as they pass through childhood and into their teens.

★ MOST "BEST COVER ARTIST" AWARDS

Ian Bolland (USA) has won five Eisner Comic Awards for Best Cover Artist: *Animal Man* (1992–94), *Wonder Woman* (1993–94), *Batman: Gothic Knights* (2001), *The Invisibles* (1999, 2001), and *The Flash* (2001).

★ MOST "BEST WRITER" AWARDS

Alan Moore (UK) has been voted Best Writer eight times at the Eisner Comic Awards for: *Watchmen* (1988), *Batman: The Killing Joke* (1989), *From Hell* (1995–97), *Supreme* (1997), *The League of Extraordinary Gentlemen* (2000–01) and *The League of Extraordinary Gentlemen*, *Promothea*, *Smax*, *Tom Strong*, and *Tom Strong's Terrific Tales* (all 2004).

★ MOST "BEST GRAPHIC ALBUM" AWARDS

Alan Moore (UK) collected four awards in the Best Graphic Album (new and reprinted) categories at the Eisner Comic Awards. He won for *Watchmen* (1988, with Dave Gibbons), *Batman: The Killing Joke* (1989, with Brian Bolland), *A Small Killing* (1994, with Oscar Zarate), and *From Hell* (2000, with Eddie Campbell).

★ NEW RECORD
★ UPDATED RECORD

GREATEST COMIC-READING NATION

Manga makes up 40% of the printed material sold in Japan, with 13 weekly magazines, 10 biweeklies, and around 20 monthlies! In the 1990s, manga sales averaged 600 billion yen ($5.5 billion) yearly – around 60% for magazines, the rest for paperbacks.

ACTUAL SIZE

★ NEW RECORD
☆ UPDATED RECORD

BESTSELLING BOOK
Excluding non-copyright works, such as the Bible (with an estimated 6 billion copies sold) and the Koran, the world's all-time bestselling book is *Guinness World Records* (formerly *The Guinness Book of Records*). Since it was first published in 1955, global sales, in 37 languages, have exceeded 100 million.

BESTSELLING FICTION AUTHOR
The world's bestselling fiction writer is the late Dame Agatha Christie (UK, née Miller, later Lady Mallowan), whose 78 crime novels have sold an estimated 2 billion copies in 44 languages. She also wrote 19 plays and, under the pseudonym Mary Westmacott, six romantic novels. Royalty earnings from her works are worth millions of pounds per year.

FASTEST-SELLING NONFICTION BOOK
Living History, Hillary Rodham Clinton's (USA) memoir of her life with US president Bill Clinton, including his relationship with

SMALLEST REPRODUCTION OF A PRINTED BOOK
In 2001, using a process known as microlithography, similar to that used to make computer chips, scientists at Massachusetts Institute of Technology (MIT), USA, printed the New Testament text of the King James Version of the Bible in 24-carat gold on a silicon tablet measuring just 0.196 x 0.196 in (5 x 5 mm).

Monica Lewinsky, is the fastest-selling nonfiction book ever, with 200,000 copies sold on its first day of sales in the USA in June 2003.

☆ HIGHEST ANNUAL EARNINGS FOR A CHILDREN'S AUTHOR
J. K. Rowling's (UK) annual earnings in 2004 were estimated to be $59.1 million according to the 2005 *Forbes Celebrity 100* list released on June 15, 2005.

☆ HIGHEST ANNUAL EARNINGS FOR AN AUTHOR
According to Forbes, *The Da Vinci Code* author Dan Brown (USA) earned around $76.5 million in 2005.

HIGHEST PRICE PAID FOR A FIRST NOVEL
In 1999, *Sunday Times* journalist Paul Eddy (UK) was reported to have been paid $2.8 million by British and American publishers for his first novel *Flint* and its unwritten (at that time) sequel. The crime thriller is about an undercover policewoman called Grace Flint, and the novel was the investigative reporter's first venture into fiction.

LARGEST ADVANCE FOR A NONFICTION BOOK
Former US president Bill Clinton agreed to sell the worldwide publishing rights for his memoirs to Alfred A. Knopf Inc. for an advance of more than $10 million – the largest-ever advance for a nonfiction book.

L-O-N-G-E-S-T collaged novel **WOMAN'S** world : *a* Novel (2005) by Graham Rawle (UK) contains **437** pages of PROSE cut and pasted from 1,208 **different** women's magazines from the 1960s. The **76,768** word story is pieced together from an estimated **40,000** fragments of text, making it the longest Novel ever ASSEMBLED from **magazine** or newspaper clippings. It took the **author** five years, 37 **glue** pens and **three** pairs of scissors to **COMPLETE THE** monumental work.

← LARGEST PUBLISHED BOOK
Unveiled on December 15, 2003, in New York City, USA, the largest published book is titled *BHUTAN*. It weighs 133 lb (60.3 kg), contains 114 full-color pages, and measures 5 ft high by 7 ft wide (1.52 x 2.13 m) when opened.

JIM DALE

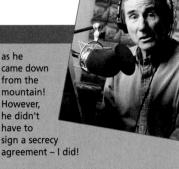

Jim Dale (UK) is the performer who brings J. K. Rowling's creations to life in the *Harry Potter* audiobooks. He secured a Guinness World Record for creating an incredible 134 voices for *The Order of the Phoenix*. He talks to us about his achievements.

How difficult is it to keep up with so many different characters?
The technique I use to remind myself of the various voices I've created is to use a small tape recorder and list them as I invent them. So, I record the words "Page 2, Uncle Vernon...," then his first line of dialog. I had a tape containing a total of 134 voices by the time the recording session was over.

How much collaboration did you have with J. K. Rowling?
Not much this time for *Order of the Phoenix* – just some help with a few pronunciations for the words she'd invented herself. She must trust me by now, after six books! I do rely a great deal on J. K.'s description of the characters and of their attitude and temperament and so on, to give me some idea of what she'd be happy with.

You must have been one of the first to read the new book – how did that feel?
It's an amazing thing to have in your possession the only manuscript of the latest *Harry Potter* story! I felt like Moses as he came down from the mountain! However, he didn't have to sign a secrecy agreement – I did!

Security must have been an issue throughout the recording?
I promised not to tell a soul about the book, the recording session, or where we were working. Everything relating to *Harry Potter* was done in absolute secrecy. I still have the scars from biting my lip so often!

LARGEST RETAINED ADVANCE

In February 1996, the New York State Supreme Court ruled that the actress Joan Collins (UK) could retain a $1.2-million advance for her unpublished novel *A Ruling Passion*. Publishers Random House found her first draft unsatisfactory and tried (unsuccessfully) to sue her.

★ MOST POSITIONS IN AN AUDIOBOOK CHART

Narrator Jim Dale (UK, see box above) occupied six positions in an audiobook chart when his readings of the Harry Potter books held the top six places in Amazon's "Best-Selling Audiobooks of America" in August 2005.

LARGEST POP-UP BOOK ↓

A revised edition of *Aesop's Fables* measuring 48 x 30 in (122 x 76 cm) and weighing 28 lb (13 kg) is the world's largest pop-up book. It was designed by Roger Culbertson (USA) using illustrations by Peter de Sève (USA).

The TORTOISE and the HARE

The tortoise and the hare were running a race. The hare was so far ahead of the tortoise that she decided to stop for lunch and a nap. The determined tortoise plodded along, passed the hare while she was busy dreaming of victory, and won.

Slow and steady wins the race.

★ MOST LETTERS PUBLISHED IN ONE NATIONAL PAPER

During 2001, Pooran Chandra Pande (India) had 118 of his letters published in the *Dainik Jagran* newspaper.

LONGEST NOVEL

À la récherche du temps perdu (*Remembrance of Things Past*) by Marcel Proust (France) contains an estimated 9,609,000 characters.

LARGEST MAGAZINE SALES

In 1974, the US *TV Guide,* with a weekly circulation of 11.8 million copies, became the first weekly to sell a billion copies in a year.

★ MOST TRANSLATED AUTHOR

The books of L. Ron Hubbard (USA) had been translated into 65 languages as of October 2005.

★ YOUNGEST AUTHORS

The **youngest commercially published female author** is Dorothy Straight (b. May 25, 1958), of Washington, D.C., USA, who wrote *How the World Began* in 1962, aged four. It was published in August 1964 by Pantheon Books.

The ★ **youngest commercially published male author** is Matheus de Souza Barra Teixeira (Brazil, b. May 5, 1997), who had his book *A Ilha dos Dragões* (*The Dragon's Island*) published on October 12, 2003, when he was aged 6 years 160 days.

At age 11, Emily Rosa (USA) was the **youngest person to have research published in a scientific journal** when an article she co-authored appeared in the *Journal of the American Medical Association* in April 1998. The fourth-grader's article questioned the use of "touch therapy," causing an uproar at the time as the therapy was being used in over 80 hospitals throughout the USA.

★ OLDEST AUTHOR TO HAVE A FIRST BOOK PUBLISHED

Bertha Wood (UK, b. June 20, 1905) had her first book, *Fresh Air and Fun: The Story of a Blackpool Holiday Camp*, published on her 100th birthday on June 20, 2005.

OLDEST ➡ MECHANICALLY PRINTED BOOK

It is widely accepted that the first mechanically printed, full-length book was the Gutenberg Bible. It was printed in Mainz, Germany, *ca.* 1455 by Johann Henne zum Gensfleisch zur Laden, commonly known as zu Gutenberg (*ca.* 1398–1468).

TV & ADVERTISING

★ COUNTRY WITH THE HIGHEST RATE OF TV VIEWING

Americans watch more hours of television per week than any other country in the world, at 28 hours per individual per week – or 4 hr 32 min per individual per day – according to Nielsen Media. In fact, Americans watched more TV in 2005 than in any other year since Nielsen Media research started tracking viewing habits in the 1950s.

★ HIGHEST FINE IMPOSED ON A BROADCASTER

In March 2006, the US Federal Communications Commission (FCC) levied its highest-ever fine against a single TV show when it charged CBS and its affiliates $3.6 million for broadcasting an episode of *Without a Trace* (pictured) that featured scenes suggestive of a teenage orgy.

★ MOST TV CHANNELS OWNED BY A POLITICIAN

In the run-up to Italy's elections on April 9, 2006, former Prime Minister Silvio Berlusconi (Italy) made an unprecedented number of appearances on Italian TV to get his message across and woo voters. It was not hard for Mr. Berlusconi to do so: his company, Mediaset, owns three TV stations – Canale Cinque, Italia Uno, and Rete Quattro. Two of the three publicly run

stations, Rai Uno and Rai Due, were also run by his supporters since, traditionally, they are controlled by the government. Despite these advantages, Mr. Berlusconi lost the election by a narrow margin.

★ MOST SUCCESSFUL US IMPORT ON UK TV

UK broadcaster Channel 4 posted its best-ever ratings for a US series launch after the first episode of *Lost* (ABC, USA) on August 10, 2005. With an estimated 6.4 million viewers, *Lost* comfortably beat the previous record – that of 4.6 million – which had been held by *Desperate Housewives* (ABC, USA).

★ LARGEST STANDING SET

Rome, an epic historical drama produced by HBO (USA) and the BBC (UK), boasts a set comprising 5 acres (2 hectares) of backlot and six soundstages at Cinecittà Studios in Rome, Italy. The Forum set is 60% of the size of the original, and the olive trees in the Sacred Grove are over 200 years old.

★ MOST EMMYS FOR A TV SERIES

The Emmy awards are US television's equivalent to the Oscars. As of May 2005, the most Emmys won by the same show is 101 by *Sesame Street* (PBS, USA). Pictured is Oscar the Grouch, who will no doubt be unimpressed with his show's record!

★ MOST EXPENSIVE MINISERIES

The 10-part World War II miniseries *Band of Brothers*, produced by HBO in association with Steven Spielberg and Tom Hanks (both USA), cost $125 million to make and took nine months to shoot in Hertfordshire, UK, from March 2000. Of the total budget, $17 million was construction costs.

The show also holds the record for the ★ **most artificial snow made for TV**: 330,000 lb (150 tonnes) of recycled paper were used to create the snow for a forest scene. It took four weeks to dress the entire set.

DAVID TENNANT (DOCTOR WHO)

Doctor Who (BBC, UK) is the longest-running science-fiction TV series. From the day it first aired on November 23, 1963, to the time of going to press, there have been 709 episodes documenting 173 storylines. We spoke to David Tennant (UK), the 10th and latest incarnation of the Doctor, about how he prepared for such a daunting role:

I've been a *Doctor Who* fan for a very long time. My grandma knitted me a cricket sweater when Peter Davison was the

Doctor. She'd already knitted me a Tom Baker scarf when I was nine. In fact, Tom Baker was responsible for my becoming an actor. I took one look at his Doctor Who and decided it was the job for me. I was convinced that when I was old enough I was going to play the part of the Doctor on TV.

What's it like to have your dream come true?
Fantastic! I've got my own Tardis, not to mention the sonic screwdriver and a fun companion [Billie Piper (UK), pictured left]!

★ MOST ➡
PROPS IN A TV COMMERCIAL

An astonishing 250,000 multi-colored balls were used in a TV commercial for a new line of Sony LCD televisions. No computer graphics were used to produce the striking visuals. The ad, first shown in 2005, was filmed on Russian Hill in San Francisco, California, USA, and was directed by Nicolai Fuglsig (Denmark).

★ GREATEST GAMESHOW DEATH TOLL

On February 4, 2006, at least 74 people died during a stampede for tickets for the Filipino gameshow *Wowowee* (ABS-CBN). The chance to win 1 million pesos ($19,300) led to 30,000 people vying to be at the front of the line into the Ultra Stadium in Manila. When the gates finally gave way, hundreds were crushed by the desperate mob.

★ LONGEST UNINTERRUPTED LIVE BROADCAST

Big Brother V (Endemol Germany) was broadcast for 8,763 hours on the Premiere Fernsehen channel from March 2, 2004 to March 1, 2005.

ADVERTISING

★ LONGEST TIME PROMOTING ONE BRAND

Since 1991, Thomas Gottschalk (Germany) has been in every advertising promotion for candy manufacturer Haribo. In 14 years, he has appeared in 206 TV and 118 radio commercials for the company.

HIGHEST AD RATE (TV SERIES)

An average of $2 million per 30 seconds was paid by advertisers for slots during the hour-long, last-ever episode of *Friends* (NBC, USA). The show aired in the USA on May 6, 2004, and was seen by an estimated 51.1 million Americans.

The **highest TV advertising rate ever** was $2.4 million per 30 seconds for the NBC network during the transmission of Super Bowl XXXV on January 28, 2001.

★ LONGEST TV COMMERCIAL

A commercial advertising Lipton Ice Tea Green lasted for 24 minutes and was broadcast by the Yorin television channel across the Netherlands in March 2005.

The **shortest TV commercial** is half a frame (one field) and lasts for just 1/60 of a second. Advertising MuchMusic (Canada), 12 versions of the commercial were produced, the first of which was aired on January 2, 2002.

❓ DID YOU KNOW?

The crashed aircraft fuselage on the beach in TV series Lost *is not a prop but a genuine retired Lockheed Tristar L-1011. Its cost, estimated at $200,000, made a significant contribution to the pilot episode's record-breaking budget (see below).*

★ MOST EXPENSIVE PILOT ⬇

The two-hour pilot of *Lost* (ABC, USA), which first aired on September 22, 2004, had a $12-million budget. Disney fired ABC's Lloyd Braun (USA) for green-lighting such an expensive show; *Lost* then went on to become ABC's most successful show ever!

TV PERSONALITIES

⬅ ## LONGEST
RUNNING SCI-FI TV SHOW (CONSECUTIVE)

Stargate SG-1 (1997–current) is in its 10th series, having run without a break since its first episode, "Children of the Gods," on July 27, 1997. In 2006, with episode 203 entitled "Company of Thieves," it beat the *The X Files*, which ran to 202 episodes (September 10, 1993, to May 9, 2002). Pictured is the current cast, together with the executive producers, Brad Wright (front left) and Robert C. Cooper (front right, both USA).

★ LONGEST RUNNING TV VARIETY SHOW

Sábado Gigante (Univision Television Network, USA) is a Spanish-language TV variety show that has been broadcast every Saturday evening since August 8, 1962. It was created – and has been continually hosted – by Mario Kreutzberger (Chile, below), or "Don Francisco" as he is known.

★ FIRST REALITY TV MARRIAGE

In February 2000, Darva Conger (USA), a former emergency room nurse, was selected by Rick Rockwell (USA) to be his bride on Fox's pioneering reality-competition show *Who Wants to Marry a Multimillionaire?* (Fox, USA). Although Fox later canceled any reruns of the show – and the marriage was quickly annulled after it was discovered that Rick had been accused of beating a former girlfriend and the fact that Darva did not even like him – the show drew huge ratings and is actually credited with launching the reality TV boom that has been the mainstay of television for over half a decade.

★ MOST POPULAR DECEASED TV CELEBRITY IN THE USA

According to a poll by Marketing Evaluations Inc. (USA), the most popular dead celebrity in the USA is comedian and actress Lucille Ball (USA). Perhaps most famous for the character she played in her television program *I Love Lucy* (CBS, USA), she also appeared in more than 70 films, including *Yours, Mine, and Ours* (USA, 1968) with Henry Fonda (USA) and *Fancy Pants* (USA, 1950) with actor Bob Hope (USA).

HIGHEST EARNING TV WRITER ➡

Larry David (USA), co-writer and co-creator of hit US comedy *Seinfeld*, earned an estimated $242 million in 1998. David left the show in 1996, returning to pen the final episode in 1998. More recently, he has written and acted in the TV comedy *Curb Your Enthusiasm*.

★ LONGEST TIME IN SAME TV SERIES ROLE

Helen Wagner (USA) has played Nancy Hughes McClosky in *As The World Turns* (CBS, USA) since it premiered on April 2 1956, the longest an actor or actress has portrayed the same role in a television series (she also spoke the very first line in the debut episode). Helen celebrated the 50th anniversary of Nancy's – and the show's – debut in April 2006.

★ MOST FREQUENT CLAPPER

It has been estimated that *Wheel of Fortune* hostess Vanna White (USA) claps 720 times per show. This works out at 28,080 times in a year – or approximately 393,120 claps since her first show in 1982!

AWARDS

★ MOST BAFTA TV AWARDS FOR BEST ACTRESS

Four actresses have won three times: Dame Judi Dench (UK) for *Talking to a Stranger* (1968), *A Fine Romance* (1982), and *Last of the Blonde Bombshells* (2001); Thora Hird (UK) for *Talking Heads* (1989), *Talking Heads 2* (1999), and *Lost for Words* (2000); Dame Helen Mirren for *Prime Suspect 1, 2,* and *3* (1991–93); and Julie Walters (UK) for *My Beautiful Son* (2002), *Murder* (2003), and *The Canterbury Tales* (2004).

Mirren and Walters also share a record with three ★ **consecutive Best Actress wins**.

YOUNGEST EMMY AWARD NOMINEE

At age 15, Frankie Muniz (USA, b. December 5, 1985) was the youngest actor nominated for an Emmy award, in the Outstanding Actor in a Comedy Series category, for his role of Malcolm in *Malcolm in the Middle* (Fox, USA) at the 53rd annual Primetime Emmy awards, 2001.

★ MOST BAFTA TV AWARDS FOR BEST ACTOR

Sir Michael Gambon (Ireland) has won a record four BAFTAs in the Best Actor category: *The Singing Detective* (1987), *Wives and Daughters* (2000), *Longitude* (2001), and *Perfect Strangers* (2002).

His three **consecutive Best Actor** wins is also a record that he shares with Robbie Coltrane (UK). Coltrane won three consecutive BAFTA Best Television Actor awards for his role as forensic psychiatrist Gerry "Fitz" Fitzgerald in Granada Television's award-winning series *Cracker* between 1994 and 1996.

MOST EMMYS WON BY A LEAD ACTOR (SAME ROLE)

Actor Don Knotts (USA) won the Emmy award for Outstanding Performance by an Actor in a supporting role, a record five times, as Barney Fife in *The Andy Griffith Show* in 1961–63 and 1966–67.

The **most Emmys won by a lead actress in the same role** is also five, by Candice Bergen (USA), who won the Outstanding Lead Actress in a Comedy Series in the title role *Murphy Brown* in 1989–90, 1992, and 1994–95.

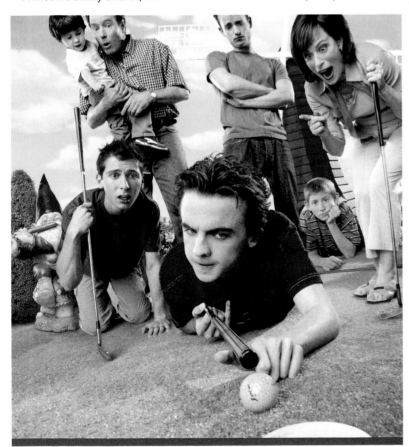

HIGHEST PAID MEDIA STARS

★ **NEW RECORD**
★ **UPDATED RECORD**

OPRAH WINFREY
The world's **highest paid person on TV** and **highest paid TV chat show** is Oprah Winfrey (USA), who earned $225 million in 2005 according to the *Forbes Celebrity 100* list.

HOWARD STERN
The **highest earning radio host** in 2005 was "shock jock" Howard Stern who earned $31 million.

RAY ROMANO
The **highest paid TV actor** per episode continues to be Ray Romano (USA), who received $1.94 million per episode of *Everybody Loves Raymond* (CBS, USA) for the ninth and final series in 2004–05.

TERI HATCHER
The world's **highest paid TV actress** is Teri Hatcher (USA), who plays Susan Mayer in *Desperate Housewives* (ABC, USA). Although she was paid a reported $70,000 for the first season, the second season earned her $285,000 per episode (ahead of the $250,000 paid per episode to the other "housewives"), taking her salary to over $6 million.

DAVID LETTERMAN
Perhaps one of America's most famous chat-show hosts, and often described as a "night-time legend," David Letterman is the **highest paid male TV personality**, with annual earnings of $40 million according to *Forbes*.

MOVIES

HIGHEST GROSSING...

3-D MOVIE
Spy Kids 3-D: Game Over
(USA, 2003)

Budget: $39 million
Gross: $189 million

MOCKUMENTARY
Best in Show
(USA, 2000)

Budget: $6 million
US Gross: $18.6 million

RAP MOVIE
8 Mile
(USA/Germany, 2002)

Budget: $41 million
Gross $242 million

SPORTS MOVIE
Rocky IV
(USA, 1985)

Budget: $31 million
Gross: $300 million

TEEN MOVIE
American Pie
(USA, 1999)

Budget: $11 million
US Gross: $101 million

MOST OSCARS FOR A MOVIE

At the 2004 Academy Awards ceremony, the third instalment of Peter Jackson's (New Zealand) *The Lord of the Rings* trilogy, *The Return of the King* (NZ/USA, 2003), won all 11 of its nominations. *The Return of the King* shares this record with only two other movies: *Ben-Hur* (USA, 1959) and *Titanic* (USA, 1997).

★ HIGHEST PER-SCREEN GROSS FOR A LIVE ACTION MOVIE (OPENING WEEKEND)

During its opening weekend, Ang Lee's (Taiwan) *Brokeback Mountain* (USA, 2005) played in only five theaters in the USA, yet still grossed $547,425. This is an average of $109,485 per screen and the highest gross per screen of any non-animated movie in history.

The **highest per-screen gross of all time** is an incredible $793,376 from just two screens showing *The Lion King* (USA, 1994).

★ FASTEST-SELLING LIVE-ACTION DVD

The DVD of *Harry Potter and the Goblet of Fire* (UK/USA, 2005) sold more than six copies a second on the day of release in the UK (March 20, 2006), and has continued to sell over three copies per second since then. It also sold more than 5 million copies on March 7, 2006, the first day of the DVD release in America.

★ LARGEST MOVIE STUDIO

The largest movie studio in the world is Ramoji Film City, Hyderabad, India, which opened in 1996. It measures 1,666 acres (674 ha), with 47 sound stages and permanent sets ranging from railroad stations to temples.

★ LARGEST SIMULTANEOUS PREMIERE

Star Wars: Episode III – Revenge of the Sith (USA, 2005) was simultaneously released in a record 115 territories around the world by 20th Century Fox on May 19, 2005. The movie subsequently went on to gross $303 million internationally.

★ MOST PROLIFIC SCREENWRITER

During the course of his screenwriting career, Safa Önal (Turkey) wrote scripts for 395 films made between 1969 and 2004.

★ MOST VERSATILE FILMMAKER

Robert Rodriguez (USA) wrote the screenplay for *El Mariachi* (USA, 1992) while employed in medical research as a human guinea pig, and used his fee to produce the film. He also directed and edited the movie, recorded and edited the sound and music, handled the cinematography and special effects, and operated the camera.

MOST VALUABLE FILM SCRIPT

Marlon Brando's (USA, 1924–2004) personal 173-page film script from *The Godfather* (USA, 1972) sold for $312,800 to an anonymous bidder at Christie's auction house, New York City, USA, on June 30, 2005.

VAMPIRE MOVIE
Van Helsing
(USA/Czech Republic, 2004)

Budget: $160 million
Gross: $275 million

COMPUTER GAME SPINOFF
Lara Croft: Tomb Raider
(UK/Germany/ USA/Japan, 2001)

Budget: $80 million
Gross: $252 million

CROSS-DRESSING MOVIE
Mrs. Doubtfire
(USA, 1993)

Budget: $25 million
Gross: $423 million

CHRISTMAS MOVIE
How the Grinch Stole Christmas
(USA/Germany, 2000)

Budget: $123 million
Gross: $340 million

ZOMBIE MOVIE
Dawn of the Dead
(USA, 2004)

Budget: $28 million
US Gross: $58.8 million

★ HIGHEST BOX OFFICE ↑ FILM GROSS – OPENING DAY

Star Wars: Episode III – Revenge of the Sith (USA, 2005) took a record $50,013,859 on its opening day in the USA on May 19, 2005. It was screened in a total of 3,661 US theaters.

★ MOST PLASTICINE USED IN A FEATURE FILM

During the filming of Aardman Animation's (UK) full-length animated feature *Wallace & Gromit: Curse of the Were-Rabbit* (UK, 2005), 6,272 lb (2,844 kg) of plasticine was used to make and animate the characters. The movie took five years to make and was first released on September 4, 2005, in Australia.

★ OLDEST MOVIE THEATER IN OPERATION

The Pionier theater, which opened as the Helios on September 26, 1909, at 138 Flkenwalderstrasse, Stettin, Germany (now Szczecin, Poland), is still in operation. In December 1945, with the town changing its national status, the theater became known as the Ordra. In 1950, it changed its name back to the Pionier.

★ SHORTEST CLASSIFIED FEATURE FILM

Soldier Boy (USA, 2004), directed by Les Sholes (USA) and awarded a certificate G, runs for only seven seconds, making it the shortest classified feature film. The story, about a couple separated during World War II, premiered on March 18, 2005 at the Empire Arts Center, Grand Forks, North Dakota, USA.

★ NEW RECORD
★ UPDATED RECORD

★ HOLLYWOOD FIRSTS...

The ★ **first movie shot in Hollywood**, *In Old California* (USA, 1910), was filmed in 1907 when a Chicago production moved to California looking for good weather to finish the movie.

The ★ **first Hollywood studio** was the Nestor Film Company, established in 1910. In 1919, Nestor became part of a merger that produced Universal.

The iconic Hollywood sign went up in 1923 as a real estate advertisement and originally read "Hollywoodland." It was bought and renovated by the Chamber of Commerce in 1949 and had the LAND letters removed.

MOVIES

← ★ MOST POWERFUL ACTOR

According to the 2005 *Forbes Celebrity 100* list, the most powerful actor in Hollywood is Johnny Depp (USA), who achieved an all-celebrity power rating of seven, but headed the list for actors and actresses.

The *Forbes* annual power rating is based on a combination of factors, comprising the stars' earnings and their exposure on TV, radio, the press, and online.

international box office – an average of $24.5 million per movie, according to Box Office Mojo.

King's highest-grossing story is *The Green Mile* (1999), taking $287 million worldwide.

★ HIGHEST-GROSSING MOVIE STUDIO

Warner Bros. (USA) grossed a total of $1.37 billion in 2005, an unprecedented achievement that gave the company a market share of 15.6%. Their three highest-grossing movies of 2005 were *Harry Potter and the Goblet of Fire* ($290 million), *Charlie and the Chocolate Factory* ($206 million), and *Batman Begins* ($205 million).

★ HIGHEST ANNUAL EARNINGS BY AN ACTOR

Star of *Elf* (USA, 2003), John William Ferrell (USA) – known as Will Ferrell – earned $40 million in 2004.

★ HIGHEST ANNUAL EARNINGS BY AN ACTRESS

Drew Barrymore (USA) earned a total of $22 million in 2004, according to the 2005 *Forbes Celebrity 100* list.

★ ACTOR WITH THE HIGHEST AVERAGE BOX-OFFICE GROSS

Orlando Bloom (UK) has appeared in 14 movies that have grossed over $4.61 billion, according to the-movie-times.com, taking his box-office gross per movie to $328 million.

The ★ **leading man with the highest average gross** is Mark Hamill (USA), who has starred in 14 movies with average box-office receipts of $181 million.

Overall, the ★ **highest-grossing actor** is Samuel L Jackson, whose 68 movies have grossed a total of $7.42 billion.

HIGHEST ANNUAL EARNINGS (FILM PRODUCER)

Star Wars producer-director George Lucas (USA) topped the 2005 *Forbes Celebrity 100* list having earned an estimated $290 million in 2004.

★ MOST POWERFUL ACTRESS

According to the 2005 *Forbes Celebrity 100* list, Jennifer Lopez (USA) is Hollywood's most powerful actress. She achieved an all-celebrity power rating of 24, and was sixth in the list of most powerful actors ahead of all other actresses.

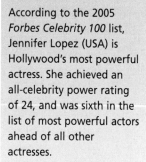

★ MOST CONSECUTIVE $100-MILLION-GROSSING MOVIES (ACTOR)

Tom Hanks (USA) has appeared in 14 movies with a domestic gross of over $100 million, seven of which were consecutive: *Catch Me If You Can* (2002), *The Road to Perdition* (2002), *Cast Away* (2000), *Toy Story 2* (1999), *The Green Mile* (1999), *You've Got Mail* (1998), and *Saving Private Ryan* (1998). The record would have been 10 had it not been for *That Thing You Do!* (1996), which only grossed $25.8 million.

★ MOST CONSECUTIVE $100-MILLION-GROSSING MOVIES (ACTRESS)

Jada Pinkett Smith (USA) has starred in six movies with a domestic gross of over $100 million, four of them back to back: *The Matrix Reloaded* (2003), *The Matrix Revolutions* (2003), *Collateral* (2004) and *Madagascar* (2005). Her other two $100-million movies were *Scream 2* (1997) and *The Nutty Professor* (1996).

★ HIGHEST-GROSSING LIVING NOVELIST AT THE MOVIES

There have been 34 movies from the writings of Stephen King (USA), grossing $835.9 million at the

★ NEW RECORD
★ UPDATED RECORD

DANIEL RADCLIFFE

The DVD of *Harry Potter and the Goblet of Fire* (UK/USA, 2005) is the fastest-selling live-action DVD of all time, selling at a rate of six copies a second in the UK, and over 5 million on its first day in the USA. It's considered the scariest Harry Potter movie to date and was given a US 12/UK PG-13 rating. The 17-year-old star of the movie, Daniel Radcliffe (pictured with costars Emma Watson and Rupert Grint), tells us what scared him most during the filming of the movie.

Well, there were lots of really exciting moments that could be described as scary. There's a scene where Harry gets knocked off his broom and I have to fall about 30 ft (9 m). Though I was suspended on a wire and knew we had the best stunt and safety professionals in the business, the first time I had to free-fall was absolutely terrifying.

What's the best part about being in the Harry Potter movies?
Really? Everything! It's great to get back to work with all my friends. I've made some really good ones, not just within the cast but within the production team too. It's really exciting getting each new script and seeing what challenges lie ahead. I'm learning so much about acting and movie-making. It really is one of the greatest experiences of my life.

What do you think of the world record for the DVD?
It's amazing. I'm so grateful to everyone for buying it. All I can say is a great big, "Thank you." It's wonderful!

! X-REF

*Movie stars regularly appear in our newspapers and on TV too. But the person who is regarded as the **most overexposed celebrity** in the world today isn't a movie star. Can you guess who it might be? Find out the answer on p.160.*

★ HIGHEST AVERAGE BOX-OFFICE GROSS (ACTRESS)

The average domestic receipts for a movie featuring actress Natalie Portman (USA) is $113.6 million. She is also the ★ **leading actress with the highest average gross**, at $155.74 million, starring in 8 of her 14 movies.

Julia Roberts remains the **highest-grossing actress**, with 33 movies taking $2.10 billion.

★ MOST PROFANITIES IN A MOVIE

According to the Family Media Guide, there are 534 uses of profane language in Martin Scorsese's *Casino* (USA, 1995): almost three per minute.

The record for the **most profanities in an animated film** is held by *South Park: Bigger, Longer and Uncut* (USA, 1999). Rated an "R" in the USA and a "15" in the UK, it included 336 profanities.

AT THE OSCARS

★ MOST NOMINATIONS FOR BEST ORIGINAL SCREENPLAY

Woody Allen (USA) has received 14 nominations for Best Original Screenplay. His first was for *Annie Hall* (USA, 1977), which he won in addition to Best Actor in a Leading Role and Best Director; his 14th nomination was for *Match Point* (USA, 2005) in January 2006 – his 21st Oscar nomination overall.

MOST "BEST DIRECTOR" NOMINATIONS FOR AN ACTOR IN THE SAME MOVIE

Woody Allen (USA) has been nominated for Best Director on five occasions for movies in which he also had a leading role: *Annie Hall* (USA, 1977) in 1978; *Interiors* (USA, 1978) in 1979; *Broadway Danny Rose* (USA, 1984) in 1985; *Hannah and her Sisters* (USA, 1986) in 1987; and *Crimes and Misdemeanors* (USA, 1989) in 1990. His sixth Best Director nomination was for *Bullets over Broadway* (USA, 1993), in which he did not act.

MOST "BEST DIRECTOR" OSCARS WON BY AN ACTOR IN THE SAME MOVIE

Clint Eastwood (USA) has won the Oscar for Best Director twice for movies in which he has also starred. The first was on March 29 1993 for *Unforgiven* (USA, 1992), followed by *Million Dollar Baby* (USA, 2004) on February 27, 2005. In all, he has been nominated in this category three times, the second occasion was in 2004 with *Mystic River* (USA, 2003), a movie in which he did not act.

★ MOST NOMINATIONS FOR A LIVING PERSON

Composer John Williams (USA) has had 45 Oscar nominations from 1968 to 2006. He was nominated twice in 2006 – for *Munich* and *Memoirs of a Geisha* – although the statue went to *Brokeback Mountain's* Gustavo Santaolalla (Argentina). Williams has won five of his 45 nominations.

HIGHEST SALARY PER MOVIE FOR AN ACTRESS

On February 28, 2006, it was revealed that actress Reese Witherspoon (USA) negotiated a pay deal worth $29 million to both star in and produce the horror movie *Our Family Trouble*. The deal is based on her wage as an actress, plus a percentage of box-office receipts depending upon the movie's success.

MUSIC – CHART-TOPPERS

★ FASTEST-SELLING ➜ UK DEBUT ALBUM

Whatever People Say I Am, That's What I'm Not by the Arctic Monkeys (pictured is lead singer Alex Turner, UK) sold an unprecedented 363,735 copies in its first week of sales, from January 21 to 28, 2006. This band beat the previous record of 306,361 copies held by Hear'Say (UK), which was set in 2001.

? DID YOU KNOW?

In 2005, downloaded tracks accounted for 98% of single sales in the USA, the ★ highest percentage of music singles sold as paid downloads. Global download sales for 2005 were around $420 million.

FASTEST-SELLING DOWNLOAD IN A WEEK (USA)

D4L's single "Laffy Taffy" registered higher sales in one week than any other download in the USA. At its peak, 175,000 downloads of the single were selling in a week.

★ HIGHEST-EARNING MUSIC ARTIST

A survey (the first of its kind) carried out by *Billboard* and Nielsen revealed U2 (Ireland) to be the top-earning act in the world in 2005 with an income of $255,022,633.

★ FASTEST RAP MC

Ricky Brown (USA) rapped 723 syllables in 51.27 seconds on his track "No Clue" at B&G Studios, Seattle, Washington, USA, on January 15, 2005.

★ MOST SUCCESSFUL R&B PRODUCER

Jermaine Dupri (USA) became the first to produce the top three singles on the US R&B chart on September 3, 2005. However, the ★ producer with the most No.1 hits on the R&B chart is Babyface (Kenneth Edmonds, USA), with 19.

★ HIGHEST SIMULTANEOUS CHART POSITIONS FOR THE SAME SONG

On July 9, 2005, the same song appeared twice in the top three for the first time in the rock era. The song was "Inside Your Heaven," and the two recordings were by Carrie Underwood and Bo Bice (both USA) – the winner and runner-up, respectively, on *American Idol 4*.

★ YOUNGEST GROUP TO BE BANNED FROM RADIO

The recording "I Like Fat Chicks," by Who's Ya Daddy? of Ballina, New South Wales, Australia, was banned from ZZZ FM in Lismore, New South Wales, Australia, on December 23, 2004. The group has an average age of 12 years 26 days.

CHARTS

★ BEST UK CHART START

On March 4, 2006, Irish vocal group Westlife became the first act to see their initial 20 releases all reach the UK top five (and 13 of them reached No.1 – a total not matched by any act launched in the last 40 years).

★ LONGEST TIME TO RETURN TO NO.1

In the UK, Elvis Presley's "Jailhouse Rock" reached No.1 on January 15, 2005 (after first reaching No.1 on January 24, 1958). In the USA, Presley's "Heartbreak Hotel" topped the US charts on January 21, 2006 (having first reached No.1 on April 21, 1956).

Presley's 18 No.1 records have occupied the top of the charts for a total of 80 weeks, the **most weeks at No.1 for any artist in the US**.

★ MOST US NO.1 SINGLES BY A FEMALE ARTIST

Mariah Carey (USA) has had a record 17 different singles reach No.1 in the US charts up to the end of 2005.

Whitney Houston (USA) had seven chart-toppers from 1985 to 1988, the **most consecutive US No.1 singles**.

★ ARTIST WITH THE MOST SIMULTANEOUS US TOP FIVE HITS

US rapper 50 Cent (Curtis Jackson) had three singles in the US top five on March 12, 2005 – "Candy Shop," "How We Do," and "Disco Inferno."

BESTSELLING MUSIC VIDEO

The Making of Michael Jackson's Thriller, released in December 1983, has sold more than 900,000 units to date.

★ MOST CONSISTENT CHART ARTIST (UK)
Daniel O'Donnell (Ireland) has had at least one new UK Top 40 album every year between 1991 and 2006.

☆ MOST CHARTS TOPPED WORLDWIDE BY AN ALBUM
Confessions on a Dance Floor by Madonna (USA) has topped the charts in 40 countries. The lead single, "Hung Up," has also reached No.1 in the singles charts of 41 countries.

On November 19, 2005, "Hung Up" became her 11th UK chart topper, the ★ most UK no.1 singles by a female artist. It also made her the ★ oldest artist to simultaneously top the UK singles and album charts – a feat she accomplished for a record third time.

★ LOWEST-SELLING CHART TOPPER
Irish band U2's recording of "All Because of You" topped the Canadian chart with physical sales of only 85 copies in April 2005.

The ☆ lowest weekly sale for a UK No.1 is now 17,694, achieved by American rock band Orson's single "No Tomorrow" on the week's chart dated March 25, 2006. Of these sales, only 6,249 were physical records or CDs.

DOWNLOADS

★ FIRST DIGITAL MILLION SELLER
In October 2005, Gwen Stefani's (USA) "Hollaback Girl" became the first track to achieve 1 million paid downloads in the USA.

☆ MOST SALES IN A WEEK
In the week ending April 8, 2006, sales of paid download singles in the UK passed 1 million for the first time, with a total of 1,076,986. Weekly sales in the USA peaked at 19,906,000 in the week following Christmas 2005.

☆ BIGGEST-SELLING TRACK (UK)
"(Is This The Way To) Amarillo" by Tony Christie featuring Peter Kay (both UK), released March 14, 2005, registered sales of 57,804.

☆ LARGEST ONLINE MUSIC STORE
The largest online collection of legally downloadable music is Apple's iTunes, which launched in May 2003. Since then, its catalog of songs has grown to over 1 million individual tracks. On February 23, 2006, Alex Ostrovsky of Michigan, USA, downloaded the billionth song, Coldplay's (UK) "Speed of Sound."

★ HIGHEST-GROSSING MUSIC TOUR BY A FEMALE ARTIST
In April 2005, Cher (USA) completed her "Farewell Tour" with a show at the Hollywood Bowl in Los Angeles, California, USA. After 605 shows around the world, Cher had been seen by a total of 5.88 million fans and the tour had grossed a record $394 million.

★ NEW RECORD
☆ UPDATED RECORD

★ MOST ALBUMS SOLD IN A YEAR (UK)
James Blunt's (UK) debut album *Back to Bedlam* sold an unprecedented 2,368,000 copies in 2005 – more than any other album in a calendar year in the UK.

CHART-BUSTERS

RECORD	HOLDER	COPIES SOLD
Bestselling LP worldwide	*Thriller* (1982) by Michael Jackson	46–52 million (estimated)
Bestselling LP in UK	*Sgt. Pepper's Lonely Hearts Club Band* (1967) by The Beatles	4.5 million
Bestselling debut LP in USA (shared)	*Boston* (1976) by Boston & *Cracked Rear View* (1994) by Hootie & the Blowfish	16 million to date
Bestselling debut LP in UK	*Back to Bedlam* (2005) by James Blunt	2.8 million to date
Fastest-selling LP worldwide	*1* by The Beatles (2000)	13.5 million in its first month
Fastest-selling debut LP in UK	*Whatever People Say I Am, That's What I'm Not* (2006) by Arctic Monkeys	363,735 in its first week
Bestselling single worldwide	"White Christmas" (1942) by Bing Crosby	50 million (estimated)
Bestselling single worldwide since charts began	"Candle in the Wind 1997"/ "Something About the Way You Look Tonight" (1997) by Elton John	33 million

MUSIC – AWARDS

★ NEW RECORD
★ UPDATED RECORD

★ LARGEST SIMULTANEOUS ROCK CONCERT ATTENDANCE

The largest live audience for a simultaneous rock concert is an estimated 1 million people for Live 8 held at concert venues around the world in 10 cities, including London (UK), Philadelphia (USA), Paris (France), Berlin (Germany), Johannesburg (South Africa), Rome (Italy), and Moscow (Russia) on July 2, 2005.

The UK event also led to the ★ **largest text message lottery**, as 2,060,285 SMS applications were sent for the 150,000 available tickets.

AWARDS

BIGGEST PRIZE FOR WRITING

The University of Louisville Grawemeyer Award for Music Composition is the world's largest single prize for music writing, with a value of $200,000. The most recent recipient was György Kurtág (Hungary) for his Concertante Op. 42 for violin, viola, and orchestra.

FIRST GOLDEN DISC AWARD

The first golden disc was presented on February 10, 1942, to the trombonist and bandleader Alton "Glenn" Miller (USA) for his song "Chattanooga Choo Choo."

MOST SONGS NOMINATED FOR AN OSCAR IN A SINGLE YEAR

The 18th Academy Awards, held on March 7, 1946, saw a record 14 songs from movies released in 1945 being nominated for the Best Original Song category. The following year, the Academy changed the rules so that only five songs are nominated each year.

★ MOST SUCCESSFUL ◄■ ARTISTS IN THE UK RINGTONE CHARTS

Gorillaz (UK) held the three top positions in the UK ringtones chart during the week of December 24, 2005. The **most successful virtual band**, Gorillaz had global album sales of nearly 10 million, as of April 2006, for their eponymous debut album and its follow-up, *Demon Days*.

LEAST SONGS NOMINATED FOR AN OSCAR IN ONE YEAR

There have been three years in Oscar history where only three songs have been nominated: at the 7th Academy Awards held in 1935, the 8th in 1936, and the 61st held in 1988.

★ MOST DIAMOND ALBUMS

In May 2005, The Beatles were awarded a diamond album for *1* – making them the only act to have received six of these awards, which are presented for sales of over 10 million copies of an album in the USA alone.

GRAMMYS

MOST WINS BY A SOLO POP PERFORMER

Stevie Wonder (USA) has won an unprecedented 20 Grammys – including six wins in the Best Male R&B Vocal Performance category – since 1973. Wonder is also the youngest solo artist to reach No.1 on the US album charts – he was just 13 years 3 months old when his album *Little Stevie Wonder: The Twelve-Year-Old Genius* (1963) topped the US charts.

MOST WINS BY A FEMALE

Aretha Franklin (USA) has won 15 Grammys since receiving her first in 1967 for Best R&B Vocal Performance with "Respect."

MOST WINS IN A SINGLE YEAR BY AN INDIVIDUAL

The record for the most Grammy Awards won in a year is eight by Michael Jackson (USA) in 1984.

★ MOST NOMINATIONS IN DIFFERENT CATEGORIES

Banjoist Béla Fleck (USA) has been nominated in more categories than any other musician, namely country, pop, jazz, bluegrass, classical, folk, spoken word and composition, and arranging. He has won eight of his 20 nominations.

★ MOST WINS BY A GROUP

U2 (Ireland) have won a record 22 Grammys, the most for a group. The **most Grammy Awards won in a single year by a group** is eight by US rock group Santana on February 23, 2000.

★ FASTEST CONCERT RECORDING TO DIGITAL DOWNLOAD RELEASE

At the Live 8 event of July 2, 2005, Sir Paul McCartney (UK, above right) and Bono (Ireland, above left) sang The Beatles' (UK) classic "Sgt. Pepper's Lonely Hearts Club Band," which became available for download just 44 min 39 sec after the performance ended. This also gives them the absolute record for ★ fastest available download.

★ FIRST RAP AWARDS

In 1998, DJ Jazzy Jeff & The Fresh Prince (the latter a.k.a. Will Smith; both USA) won the first Grammy for Best Rap Performance with "Parents Just Don't Understand." They boycotted the show, however, after learning that their award presentation would not be shown on TV.

★ FIRST WINNER OF THE "BIG FOUR" IN SAME YEAR

Christopher Cross (USA) was the first artist to win in the "big four" categories in the same year. His debut album *Christopher Cross* (1980) won Album of the Year, "Sailing" won Record of the Year and Song of the Year, and he also picked up the Best New Artist award.

★ FIRST ARTIST TO BE STRIPPED OF THEIR AWARD

In 1990, pop duo Milli Vanilli – a.k.a. Fabrice Morvan (France) and Rob Pilatus (USA) – won Best New Artist for their album *Girl You Know It's True*. However, when it was revealed that the only roles the two men had played in the creation of the album were appearing on its cover and lip-synching along to professional singers in the video – they were exposed during a "live" performance on MTV when a song they were miming to began skipping – they were stripped of their Grammy.

BRITS

MOST WINS BY AN INDIVIDUAL

Robbie Williams (UK) has won 14 BRIT (British Record Industry Trust) Awards during his career – more than any other artist or act. His most recent win was for Best Song (of the last 25 years) Award, received for "Angels" at the ceremony held on February 10, 2005.

★ MOST WINS BY A FEMALE ARTIST

Annie Lennox (UK) has won seven BRIT Awards – including one as a member of Eurythmics in 1999.

★ MOST WINS BY A GROUP

U2 (Ireland) have won seven BRIT Awards, the most for a group.

MOST WINS IN A YEAR BY A GROUP

British band Blur hold the record for the most BRIT Awards won in a year, with four presented to them in 1995.

★ YOUNGEST SOLO WINNER

Joss Stone (UK, b. April 11, 1987) became the youngest recipient of a BRIT Award by winning Best Female Solo Artist and Best Urban Artist in 2005 at the age of 18.

★ OLDEST SOLO WINNER

At the age of 62, Tom Jones (UK) became the oldest BRIT Award recipient after picking up the Outstanding Contribution award in 2003.

★ LONGEST TIME AT NO.1 OF THE US TOP LATIN SONG CHART

"La Tortura," a duet by Shakira (Colombia, above) and Alejandro Sanz (Spain), completed a record-breaking 25 weeks at the top of the US Top Latin Song chart on December 3, 2005.

Shakira also holds the record for ★ fastest-selling Spanish language album, when *Fijacion Oral Vol 1* sold 157,000 copies in its first week in June 2005.

MUSIC MISCELLANY

◀ YOUNGEST RECORDED VIOLINIST

Vanessa-Mae (UK) recorded both the Tchaikovsky and Beethoven violin concertos at the age of 13.

The recording of Tchaikovsky's violin concerto in D (Opus 35) and Beethoven's violin concerto in D (Opus 61), in 1991, was released on the Trittico label, with proceeds of the sales pledged to charity.

services – one cantata every Sunday for a year – 78 services for special occasions, 40 operas, 600–700 orchestral suites, and 44 passions, plus concertos, sonatas, and other pieces of chamber music.

LONGEST VIOLIN PLAYING MARATHON

L. Athira Krishna (India) played violin for 32 hours on November 10–11, 2003, at the Soorya Dance and Music Festival, Trivandrum, Kerala, India.

CONCERT PERFORMED AT THE HIGHEST ALTITUDE

On October 24, 1998, pianist Gianni Bergamelli and flutist Ombretta Maffeis (both Italy) gave a concert to mark the 150th anniversary of the death of Italian opera composer Gaetano Donizetti. It took place at a height of 16,568 ft (5,050 m) above sea level, at the Laboratory-Observatory Pyramid in Mount Everest's Khumba Valley, Nepal.

★ MOST DIFFICULT MUSICAL INSTRUMENTS TO PLAY

The American Music Conference announced in September 1977 that the most difficult musical instruments to play are the French horn (below) and the oboe. (The latter has been described as the "ill woodwind that no one blows good.")

HIGHEST VOCAL NOTE BY A MALE

Adam Lopez Costa (Australia) hit C sharp in the eighth octave (C#8) on the set of *Guinness World Records*, Seven Network Studios, Sydney, New South Wales, Australia, on June 4, 2005.

MOST PROLIFIC COMPOSER

Georg Philipp Telemann (Germany, 1681–1767) wrote 12 complete sets of

★ FASTEST BASSOON PLAYER

Bassoonist Carmelo Crucitti (Italy) played "The Flight of the Bumble-Bee" in 33.8 seconds in Cosenza, Calabria, Italy, on October 1, 2003.

★ LONGEST SUSTAINED NOTE ON A WIND OR BRASS INSTRUMENT

Dominic Barth (Germany) sustained one continuous note on a tenorhorn for 49.2 seconds during a music festival in Melchingen, Germany, on August 10, 2005. He wore a nose plug to prevent circular breathing.

LONGEST OPERA

The Sadler's Wells company (UK) performed an uncut version of *Die Meistersinger von Nürnberg* by Richard Wagner (Germany) between August 24 and September 19, 1968. Each performance comprised 5 hr 15 min of music.

YOUNGEST OPERA SINGER

Ginetta Gloria La Bianca (USA) sang Gilda in *Rigoletto* at Velletri, Italy, on March 24, 1950, aged 15 years 316 days. She appeared as Rosina in *The Barber of Seville* at the Teatro dell'Opera, Rome, Italy, on May 8, 1950, 45 days later.

MOST VALUABLE...

ITEM	VALUE	SOLD	DETAILS
Cello	£682,000 ($1,217,711)	Jun. 22, 1988 Sotheby's, London, UK	Stradivarius known as The Cholmondeley, made in Cremona, Italy, *ca.* 1698
Double bass	£155,500 ($252,283)	Mar. 16, 1999 Sotheby's, London, UK	Domenico Montagnana double bass made in Venice in 1750
★Drum kit	£139,650 ($252,487)	Sep. 29, 2004 Christie's, London, UK	Five-piece Premier drum kit played by The Who's drummer Keith Moon from 1968 to 1970
Guitar	$2.7 million (£1.57 million)	Nov. 17, 2005 Ritz-Carlton Hotel, Doha, Qatar	Fender Stratocaster guitar signed by various rock stars, sold in aid of Reach Out to Asia charity
Piano	£1.45 million ($2.1 million)	Oct. 17, 2000 Hard Rock Café, London, UK	Steinway model Z upright piano, owned by John Lennon, on which he wrote the song "Imagine"
Violin	Undisclosed sum (reported by the dealer to be $1.25 million [£762,707] more than previous record price for a violin, which was £947,500 [$1,360,927] in 1998	Oct. 29, 1999 Zurich, Switzerland	Violin made by Guarneri del Gesù in Venice, in 1742, and once owned by Yehudi Menuhin

All values and conversions are accurate to date of auction

★ NEW RECORD
UPDATED RECORD

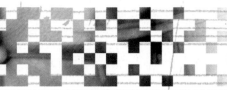

OLDEST ORCHESTRA

The first modern symphony orchestra – four sections consisting of brass, woodwind, percussion, and bowed string instruments – was founded at the court of Duke Karl Theodor at Mannheim, Germany, in 1743.

The **oldest existing symphony orchestra**, the Gewandhaus Orchestra of Leipzig, Germany, was also established in 1743. Originally known as the Grosses Concert and later as the Musikbende Gesellschaft, its current name dates from 1781.

LARGEST...

★ DOUBLE BASS

In 1924, Arthur K. Ferris (USA) built a double bass 14 ft (4.26 m) tall in Ironia, New Jersey, USA. It weighed 1,301 lb (590 kg), with a sound box 8 ft (2.43 m) across, and had leather strings 104 ft (31.7 m) long in total. Its low notes could be felt rather than heard.

★ LARGEST VIOLIN

Erick Furlan, Emil Furlan, and Elmer De Bona (all Italy) completed a 13-ft 8-in-long (4.2-m), 4-ft 6-in-wide (1.4-m) violin, and 13-ft 1-in-long (4-m) bow, in Belluno, Italy, on October 10, 2004.

LARGEST MUSICAL INSTRUMENT ENSEMBLES

INSTRUMENT	NUMBER	PLACE	DATE
★ Accordion	625	Vila Verde, Portugal	Oct. 16, 2005
Bell (campanology)	10,000	Gdańsk, Poland	Dec. 31, 2000
Bicycle bell	503	Leipzig, Germany	Nov. 23, 2003
★ Bugle	674	New York City, USA	May 21, 2005
Cello (middle, right)	1,013	Kobe, Japan	Nov. 29, 1998
★ Dhol	314	Oldbury, UK	Jul. 3, 1999
Didgeridoo	219	Tragoess, Steiermark, Austria	Aug. 30, 2003
Drum	7,727	Hong Kong, China	Feb. 20, 2005
Electronic keyboard	107	Florissant, Missouri, USA	Sep. 25, 2004
Erhu (top)	1,490	Jiangsu, China	Oct. 17, 2004
Flute	556	Hong Kong, China	Jul. 3, 2005
Full drum kit	502	Tacoma, Washington, USA	Feb. 16, 2004
Guitar	1,322	Vancouver, BC, Canada	May 7, 1994
★ Gu zheng	1,008	Guangxi, China	Oct. 15, 2005
Harmonica	1,706	Seattle, Washington, USA	May 27, 2005
Human beat box	106	Maidenhead, Berkshire, UK	Jun. 3, 2002
Japanese drum	1,899	Tainan, Taiwan	Aug. 7, 2004
Kazoo	1,791	Quincy, Illinois, USA	Jun. 30, 2004
★ Mandolin	383	Bürgstadt, Germany	Sep. 25, 2005
★ Marimba	78	Cape Town, South Africa	Oct. 29, 2004
★ Melodica	126	Oschatz/Riesa, Germany	Jun. 15, 2003
★ Panpipes	2,317	La Paz, Bolivia	Oct. 24, 2004
Piano (bottom, right)	301	Shenyang City, China	Aug. 26, 2005
★ Recorder	6,243	Wanchai, Hong Kong, China	Dec. 27, 2004
★ Saxophone	900	Toronto, Ontario, Canada	May 30, 2004
★ Shamisen	815	Tokyo, Japan	Nov. 27, 1999
Shofar	400	Elkins Park, Pennsylvania, USA	Sep. 25, 2005
★ Taishogoto	1,034	Nagoya City, Japan	Apr. 21, 2005
★ Trombone	289	Broekhuizen, Netherlands	Jun. 8, 1997
★ Tuba	134	Olpe, Germany	May 23, 2004
★ Ukulele	125	Coronado Island, San Diego, California, USA	Aug. 27, 2005
Violin	4,000	London, UK	Jun. 15, 1925
★ Wobble board	230	Ashfield Reserve, Western Australia	Nov. 3, 2002
★ Xun	11,551	Kaohsiung City, Taiwan	Dec. 18, 2004

★ BRASS INSTRUMENT

The world's largest contrabass tuba stands 7 ft 6 in (2.28 m) tall, with 39 ft (11.8 m) of tubing and a bell measuring 3 ft 4 in (1 m) across. It was constructed for a world tour by the band of American composer John Philip Sousa ca. 1896–98, and is now owned by a circus promoter in South Africa.

ORCHESTRA

A total of 6,452 musicians from the Vancouver Symphony Orchestra and music students from across British Columbia played "Ten Minutes of Nine" – an arrangement of Beethoven's "Ode to Joy" – for 9 min 44 sec at BC Place Stadium, Vancouver, Canada, on May 15, 2000. It was conducted by Maestro Bramwell Tovey (UK).

CHOIR

A 60,000-strong choir sang as the finale to a choral contest in Breslau, Germany (now Wroclaw, Poland), on August 2, 1937.

CLASSICAL CONCERT ATTENDANCE

An estimated 800,000 attended a free open-air concert by the New York Philharmonic, conducted by Zubin Mehta (India), on the Great Lawn of Central Park in New York City, USA, on July 5, 1986, as part of the Statue of Liberty Weekend.

★ RECORDING SERIES BY A SOLO ARTIST

From 1985 to 1999, Leslie Howard (Australia) recorded all Franz Liszt's piano works on 94 CDs (95, including the "Sophie Menter Concerto," which may not have been by Liszt). The playing time exceeds 117 hours and includes 9–10 million notes of music.

? DID YOU KNOW?

• A bound volume of nine complete symphonies in Mozart's hand sold for the sum of £2,585,000 ($4,340,215) at Sotheby's, London, UK, on May 22, 1987 – more than any other music manuscript.

• The earliest known draft of Beethoven's Ninth Symphony sold for £1,326,650 ($1,932,398), at Sotheby's, London, UK, on May 17, 2002 – a record for a single-page music manuscript. (We've used it as the background to these pages.)

AT THE CIRCUS

★LARGEST BIG CAT ➡ CIRCUS ACT

Clyde Raymond Beatty (USA) handled 43 "mixed cats" (lions and tigers) simultaneously in 1938. For 40 years, he was the star attraction at every single show in which he appeared.

★ NEW RECORD
★ UPDATED RECORD

CLYDE BEATTY TRAINED WILD ANIMAL CIRCUS (IN PERSON)

GIGANTIC RAILROAD CIRCUS

VENUES & SHOWS

LARGEST AUDIENCES

An audience of 52,385 attended Ringling Bros. and Barnum & Bailey Circus at the Superdome, New Orleans, Louisiana, USA, on September 14, 1975. The **largest circus audience in a tent** was 16,702 (15,686 paid), for Ringling Bros. and Barnum & Bailey at Concordia, Kansas, USA, on September 13, 1924.

★COUNTRY WITH THE MOST CIRCUS ARTISTS

Russia has about 15,000 circus artists. It is also the ★**country with the most permanent circus buildings**, with 72.

OLDEST PERMANENT CIRCUS

The Cirque d'Hiver (originally known as Cirque Napoléon) opened in Paris, France, on December 11, 1852. It was built by Jacques-Ignace Hittorf, designer of Paris's Gare du Nord railroad station.

LARGEST ANIMAL ACTS

The **most lions mastered** and fed in a cage by an unaided lion tamer was 70, by "Captain" Alfred Schneider (UK) at Bertram Mills' Circus, Olympia, London, UK, in 1925.

The **largest polar bear act** involved 70 bears worked by Willy Hagenbeck (Germany) at the Paul Busch Circus, Berlin, Germany, in 1904.

The **largest elephant act** was a Ringling Bros. and Barnum & Bailey Circus (USA) tour during the 1920s and 1930s with 55 elephants trained by Hugo Schmitt (Germany).

LARGEST CIRCUS ACT

The greatest number of performers in a circus act was 263 – plus around 175 animals – in the 1890 Barnum & Bailey Circus (USA) tour of the USA.

CIRCUS SKILLS

★TALLEST STILT TRIPLE SALTO WITH TRIPLE TWIST FROM TEETER BOARD

Balancing on a single stilt measuring 5 ft 1 in (1.55 m) in height, Sergey Cherkasov (Russia) achieved a triple salto and triple twist off a teeter board at the 27th International Circus Festival of Monte Carlo, Monaco, in January 2003.

★LONGEST TIME STANDING ON HANDLEBARS

In the discipline of artistic cycling, the record for the longest time standing on the handlebars of a moving bicycle is 37.5 seconds, achieved by Ivan Doduc (France) on the set of *L'Été De Tous Les Records* at La Tranche Sur Mer, France, on July 26, 2005.

★YOUNGEST RINGMASTER

On December 26, 2005, at the age of three, Cranston Chipperfield (UK) became the youngest person to take the stage as master of ceremonies at a circus. He is the eighth generation of ringmasters in the Chipperfield family.

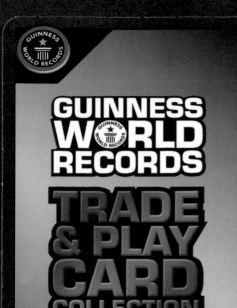

GUINNESS WORLD RECORDS
TRADE & PLAY CARD COLLECTION

NARROWEST WAIST

15

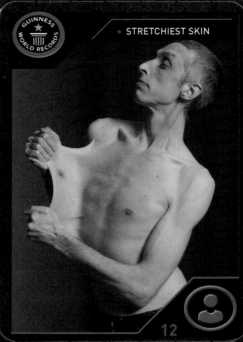

★ STRETCHIEST SKIN

12

MOST POISONOUS EDIBLE FISH

45

MOST TENNIS BALLS HELD IN THE MOUTH

50

FASTEST MONOWHEEL

59

MOST OLYMPIC MEDALS WON BY A MAN IN A SINGLE GAMES

85

HIGHEST AIR ON A SKATEBOARD

79

LARGEST SKATEBOARD

70

Card 1 — Stretchiest Skin

WHAT'S THE RECORD?
Fiendishly flexible, exceptionally elastic, and super stretchy. He's the UK's Garry Turner – the man with the world's Stretchiest Skin. Garry is able to stretch the skin of his stomach an amazing 6.25 in (15.8 cm) away from his body. The British record-breaker has a rare skin condition called Ehlers-Danlos Syndrome, which means his skin is very loose.

TEST YOUR BUDDIES
TRUE OR FALSE? Garry's rare skin disorder, Ehlers-Danlos Syndrome, affects one in every 100 people. FALSE! Around one in every 5,000–10,000 people suffer from the condition.
KILLER QUESTION: What was Garry's job before he became a professional circus performer? A: He was a pub landlord.

FACTFILE
WHO: Garry Turner
WHAT: 6.25 in (15.8 cm)
WHERE: UK
WEBCODE: GHOPCM

X-RATINGS
WOW: 7
GROSS FACTOR: 7
BREAKABILITY: 5
SKILL: 1.5
XTREME: 8

X-REFER
Card 11: Most Clothespegs Pinned to Face
Card 13: Hairiest Family
Card 21: Longest Necks
Card 25: Most Gurning World Championship Wins

www.guinnessworldrecords.com/cards

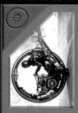

Card 2 — Smallest Waist

X-RATINGS
WOW: 7
GROSS FACTOR: 5.5
BREAKABILITY: 1.5
SKILL: 8.5

FACTFILE
WHO: Cathie Jung
WHAT: 38.1 cm (15 in)
WHERE: USA
WEBCODE: PCMDNS

WHAT'S THE RECORD?
What a waist! Inside a tight corset, Cathie Jung (USA) can shrink her waist down to gut-wrenchingly tiny proportions. Wearing the outfit, her waist measures just 15 in (38.1 cm), making Cathie the woman with the world's Smallest Waist. Without the corset her waist measurement is 21 in (53.34 cm).

TEST YOUR BUDDIES
TRUE OR FALSE? Corsets are just for women. FALSE! In ancient times, men from the European island of Crete wore corsets. They, too, developed smaller waists!
KILLER QUESTION: For how long each day does Cathie wear her corset? A: 23 hours a day, only taking it off to shower!

"THERE'S A SLIM CHANCE THAT ANYONE WILL BEAT THIS RECORD. I'VE GOT JARS OF MAYO AT HOME BIGGER THAN THIS!" – THE EDITOR, GUINNESS WORLD RECORDS

X-REFER
Card 9: Most Pierced Woman
Card 14: Largest Waist
Card 16: Tallest Man Ever

www.guinnessworldrecords.com/cards

Intro Card

EXPERIENCE THE THRILLS, EXCITEMENT, AND AMAZEMENT OF YOUR FAVORITE GUINNESS WORLD RECORDS IN THESE NEW TRADE & PLAY CARDS!

COLLECT
Build your *Guinness World Records* **Trade & Play Card Collection** with these **eight exclusive cards.** Collect your unique card series from the record-breaking worlds of Extreme Bodies, Sporting Legends, Incredible Creatures, and Awesome Vehicles. Check out our official website www.guinnessworldrecords.com/cards to learn more about where to get cards and how to collect them.

TRADE
Swap and trade your cards with your friends to complete the set. Visit the website to see a sneak preview of the other cards, keep track of your collection, and much more.

PLAY
Challenge your friends to an exciting memory game based on your knowledge of *Guinness World Records.*

GUINNESS WORLD RECORDS TRADE & PLAY CARD COLLECTION

www.guinnessworldrecords.com/cards

Card — Highest Speed on a Monowheel

X-RATINGS
WOW: 7
GROSS FACTOR: 0
BREAKABILITY: 6
SKILL: 7.5
XTREME: 8.5

FACTFILE
WHO: Monowheel
WHAT: 48 in (1.22 m)
WHERE: USA
WEBCODE: WDISLC

WHAT'S THE RECORD?
Take one wheel, one racetrack, and one determined biker. Put them together and you're looking at a new world record for the Highest Speed on a Monowheel. The record was set by America's Kerry McLean, who reached a speed of 57 mph (91.7 km/h) at the Irwindale Speedway in California in 2001.

TEST YOUR BUDDIES
TRUE OR FALSE? The monowheel is powered by a lawnmower engine. FALSE! It's powered by a 340-cc snowmobile engine.
KILLER QUESTION: How big is the monowheel? A: It has a diameter of 48 in (1.22 m).

"THIS IS THE PERFECT WAY TO GET AROUND TOWN... BUT IT'S DIFFICULT TO STEER WITH AN ARM-LOAD OF SHOPPING!" – THE EDITOR, GUINNESS WORLD RECORDS

X-REFER
Card 52: Fastest Furniture
Card 64: Fastest Electric Car
Card 61: Tallest Limo

www.guinnessworldrecords.com/cards

Card 37 — Most Tennis Balls Held in the Mouth by a Dog

WHAT'S THE RECORD?
Mega-mouthed mutt Augie served up an ace with this record: the Most Tennis Balls Held in the Mouth by a Dog. The super-pooch was able to fetch and gobble up FIVE regulation-sized tennis balls in one barking-mad bite... all by himself! And this is no shaggy dog story – we've got the evidence on video!

TEST YOUR BUDDIES
TRUE OR FALSE? Augie is a cross between a Rottweiler and a Chihuahua. FALSE! Augie's a golden retriever.
KILLER QUESTION: On which TV show did Augie get to showcase this record-breaking trick? A: Augie appeared in Animal Planet's *Pet Star*.

FACTFILE
WHO: Augie
WHAT: Five tennis balls in the mouth
WHERE: USA
WEBCODE: PZPAKL

X-RATINGS
WOW: 7
GROSS FACTOR: 0
BREAKABILITY: 8.
SKILL: 5
XTREME: 8

X-REFER
Card 33: Highest Jump by a Dog
Card 37: Largest Gape
Card 43: Laziest Mammal
Card 77: Fastest Tennis Serve (Female)

www.guinnessworldrecords.com/cards

Card — Puffer Fish

X-RATINGS
WOW: 8
GROSS FACTOR: 7
BREAKABILITY: 8
SKILL: 2
XTREME: 4

FACTFILE
WHO: Puffer fish
WHAT: Contains poison more lethal than cyanide
WHERE: Japan
WEBCODE: PODPOA

WHAT'S THE RECORD?
For Japan-ese diners, the puffer fish is a tasty but potentially deadly dish. The fish is packed with a poison that's around 1,250 times more lethal than cyanide. Although puffer fish is a delicacy in Japanese restaurants, only two small strips of its flesh are edible.

TEST YOUR BUDDIES
TRUE OR FALSE? In Japan, you need a special license to prepare puffer fish. TRUE! And it takes years of training before you can qualify. **KILLER QUESTION:** How many people die each year from puffer-fish food poisoning? A: Between 70 and 100 people.

"EATING PUFFER FISH CAN BE A RISKY OCCUPATION, BUT IF PROPERLY PREPARED IT SHOULD BE SAFE" – THE EDITOR, GUINNESS WORLD RECORDS

X-REFER
Card 56: Largest Passenger Liner
Card 62: Longest Car
Card 66: Largest Monster Truck

www.guinnessworldrecords.com/cards

Card — Largest Skateboard

X-RATINGS
WOW: 7
GROSS FACTOR: 0
BREAKABILITY: 5
SKILL: 5
XTREME: 8

FACTFILE
WHO: Foundation Skateboards WBS
WHAT: 12 ft (3.66 m) long, 4 ft (1.2 m) wide
WEBCODE: BGHQWE

WHAT'S THE RECORD?
Good luck trying to ollie with this board! The Foundation Skateboards WBS is a whopping 12 ft (3.66 m) long, 4 ft (1.2 m) wide, and 2 ft 6 in (0.76 m) high. It's the world's Largest Skateboard and is about as long as a small car! It was made in San Diego, California, USA, in October 2004.

TEST YOUR BUDDIES
TRUE OR FALSE? The skateboard uses wheels taken from motorbikes. FALSE! But the skateboard does use car tires.
KILLER QUESTION: How much does the skateboard weigh? A: It weighs around 500 lb (200 kg).

"WITH A SKATEBOARD THIS BIG, YOU'D BE HARD-PUSHED TO WIN AT THE X GAMES!" – THE EDITOR, GUINNESS WORLD RECORDS

X-REFER
Card 56: Largest Passenger Liner
Card 62: Longest Car
Card 66: Largest Monster Truck

www.guinnessworldrecords.com/cards

Card — Highest Air on a Skateboard

WHAT'S THE RECORD?
Where there's a will there's a way, and where there's a daredevil stunt you're likely to find American ace Danny Way. The high-flying skater holds the record for the Highest Air on a Skateboard. Way completed a 23-ft 6-in (7.1-m) leap from a quarterpipe ramp on June 19, 2003. No way, dude!

TEST YOUR BUDDIES
TRUE OR FALSE? Danny once broke his neck. TRUE! He broke his neck in a freak surfing accident in 1994.
KILLER QUESTION: Which famous monument did Danny leap over on his skateboard in 2005? A: He jumped over the Great Wall of China.

FACTFILE
WHO: Danny Way
WHAT: 23 ft 6 in (7.1 m)
WHERE: USA
WEBCODE: TDFHGD

X-RATINGS
WOW: 8
GROSS FACTOR: 1
BREAKABILITY: 4
SKILL: 9
XTREME: 6

X-REFER
Card 33: Highest Jump by a Dog
Card 68: Largest Surfboard
Card 76: Most Skateboard X Games Medals

www.guinnessworldrecords.com/cards

Card — Michael Phelps

X-RATINGS
WOW: 7
GROSS FACTOR: 0
BREAKABILITY: 7
SKILL: 9
XTREME: 5.5

FACTFILE
WHO: Michael Phelps
WHAT: Most Individual Medals Won at an Olympics
WHERE: Worldwide
WEBCODE: CDSCKT

WHAT'S THE RECORD?
America's Michael Phelps holds the record for the most Individual Medals Won in a Single Olympic Games. At the 2004 Games in Athens, Greece, Phelps scooped six golds by winning the 100 m and 200 m butterfly, the 200 m and 400 m medley, the 4 x 200 m freestyle, and the 4 x 100 m medley.

TEST YOUR BUDDIES
TRUE OR FALSE? The Athens Olympics was Phelps's first Olympic Games. FALSE! Phelps took part in the 2000 Olympics in Sydney, Australia, at the age of just 15!
KILLER QUESTION: What interesting anatomical feature helps Michael swim so fast? A: He's double-jointed!

"I HAVE BEEN SUCCESSFUL BECAUSE OF MY HARD WORK, MY COACH, AND THE SUP-PORT FROM MY FRIENDS FAMILY, AND FANS" – MICHAEL PHELPS

X-REFER
Card 85: Most X Games Medals Won
Card 81: Most Formula One World Championships

www.guinnessworldrecords.com/cards

★JUGGLING DURATION (THREE BALLS, SUSPENDED)

Mark Easson (Australia) juggled three balls for 55.9 seconds while suspended by gravity boots on the set of *Guinness World Records*, Seven Network Studios, Sydney, New South Wales, Australia, on June 19, 2005.

★TALLEST UNICYCLE SKIPPING

Chaz Marquette (USA) successfully jumped over a skipping rope while balancing on a 9-ft 2-in-tall (2.79-m) unicycle at Venice Beach, California, USA, on August 17, 2003.

★HIGHEST FLAME BLOWN BY A FIRE BREATHER

Tim Black (Australia) blew a flame to a height of 17 ft 8.5 in (5.4 m) on the set of *Guinness World Records* at Seven Network Studios, Sydney, New South Wales, Australia, on June 19, 2005.

★HIGHEST UNICYCLE PLATFORM DROP

Alex Toms (Australia) successfully rode a unicycle off a 8-ft 2-in (2.5-m) platform in the studios of *Guinness World Records* in Epping, Sydney, New South Wales, Australia, on June 4, 2005.

FASTEST...

★MOTORCYCLE WHEELIE ON A TIGHTROPE

Johann Traber (Germany) performed a motorcycle wheelie on a tightrope while traveling at a speed of 32 mph (53 km/h) during the Tummelum Festival, Flensburg, Germany, on August 13, 2005.

★STRAITJACKET ESCAPES

Ben Bradshaw (Australia) escaped from a regulation straitjacket in a time of 50.08 seconds on the set of *Guinness World Records* at Seven Network Studios, Sydney, New South Wales, Australia, on June 19, 2005.

On April 17, 2005, he was fully submerged in a tank of water and was able to escape from a regulation straitjacket in a time of 38.59 seconds, earning him the world record for the ★**fastest underwater straitjacket escape**.

MOST...

HULA HOOPS HULA'D SIMULTANEOUSLY

Kareena Oates (Australia) was able to hula 100 hoops at once on the set of *Guinness World Records* at Seven Network Studios, Sydney, New South Wales, Australia, on June 4, 2005. As per the official Guinness World Records guidelines, she sustained three full revolutions of the standard size and weight hula hoops between her shoulders and her hips.

★HULA HOOPS HULA'D (SUSPENDED FROM WRISTS)

Kareena Oates (Australia) spun 41 hula hoops around her waist – sustaining three full revolutions between her shoulders and hips – while suspended by the wrists on the set of *Guinness World Records* in Sydney, New South Wales, Australia, on June 4, 2005.

BODY TURNS WITH THREE CIGAR BOXES

Kristian Kristof (Hungary) completed a quadruple turn, with three cigar boxes, releasing all three in the air and catching them in their original position, at the Hungarian State Circus practice halls in Budapest, Hungary, on March 13, 1994.

★TIGHTROPE SKIPS (ONE MINUTE)

Henry Ayala (Venezuela) completed 211 skips on a tightrope in a minute at Billy Smart's Circus, Durdham Down, Bristol, UK, on September 30, 2003.

★JUGGLING – GREATEST COMBINED WEIGHT

Milan Roskopf (Slovakia) juggled a total weight of 57 lb (25.8 kg) using three 19-lb (8.6-kg) shot puts for 40.44 seconds at the Impossibility Challenger Games, Starnberg, Germany, on November 7, 2004.

★TALLEST UNICYCLE (HARNESSED)

Sem Abrahams (USA) rode a 114-ft 9-in-tall (35-m) unicycle for a distance of 28 ft (8.5 m) at the Silverdome in Pontiac, Michigan, USA, on January 29, 2004.

ENGINEERING

CONTENTS

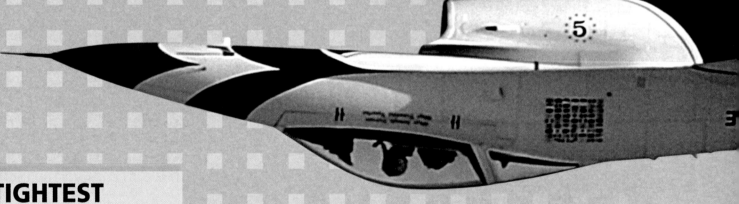

★ TIGHTEST CALYPSO PASS

On November 13, 2005, two Lockheed-Martin F-16 Falcons belonging to the USAF Thunderbirds display team carried out a "Calypso Pass" with only 18 in (45.7 cm) between them – just under the width of this open book – at the Aviation Nation Air Show 2005 in Nellis, Las Vegas, Nevada, USA. Major Scottie Zamzow flew *Thunderbird 5*; *Thunderbird 6* was flown by Major Brian Farrar (both USA). They performed the stunt at close to the speed of sound (760 mph; 1,223 km/h), although the fighter planes have the ability to reach speeds of up to 1,319 mph (2,122.7 km/h).

ARCHITECTURE

HIGHEST MOSQUE (ABOVE GROUND LEVEL)

The King Abdullah Mosque on the 77th floor of the Kingdom Center building in Riyadh, Saudi Arabia, is 600 ft (183 m) above ground level and was completed on July 5, 2004.

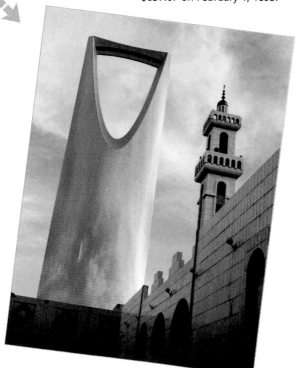

★ LONGEST LAUNDRY CHUTE

The Grand Hyatt Shanghai (China) has a laundry chute running from the 87th floor to the basement of the Jin Mao Tower, a distance of around 1,083 ft (330 m) – longer than the height of the Eiffel Tower!

★ FIRST ESCALATOR

The first inclined moving stairway was installed by Jesse W. Reno (USA) in 1891 as a pleasure ride at Coney Island in Brooklyn, New York City, USA. This device had a vertical rise of 7 ft (2.1 m), an inclination of 25 degrees and a speed of 75 ft (22.8 m) per minute.

★ MOST EXPENSIVE AIRPORT

The Hong Kong International Airport at Chek Lap Kok, China, opened on July 6, 1998, at a cost of $20 billion. The bill included the terminal building – which at 0.8 miles (1.3 km) long is the **largest airport terminal building** in the world – as well as infrastructure improvements such as reclaiming the 3,083-acre (1,248-ha) island on which it is built.

★ FIRST MOVIE STUDIO

Thomas Edison's "Black Maria" – a frame building covered in black roofing-paper – was built at the Edison Laboratories in New Jersey, USA, and completed at a cost of $637.67 on February 1, 1893.

TALLEST...

★ UNREINFORCED MASONRY STRUCTURE

At 555 ft 5 in (169.3 m), the Washington Monument in Washington D.C., USA, is the tallest stone structure in the world that is constructed entirely without any steel reinforcement. Most modern buildings of any substantial height are built around a framework of steel-reinforced concrete to give them the necessary structural strength.

★ ATRIUM

The atrium of the Burj Al Arab Hotel in Dubai, United Arab Emirates, is 590 ft (180 m) high. It forms a vast central cavity around which the hotel is built, and extends upward from the ground floor. The Burj Al Arab is also the world's **tallest building used solely as a hotel**.

OPERA HOUSE

The Civic Opera Building on Wacker Drive in Chicago, Illinois, USA, is a 45-story, 555-ft-tall (169-m) limestone skyscraper that houses a 3,563-seater theater.

The Teatro della Scala in Milan, Italy, and the Bolshoi Theater in Moscow, Russia, share the distinction of being the **opera house with the most tiers**: each has six.

LARGEST CHURCH BUILT BY ONE PERSON

At Mejorada del Campo, 20 miles (32 km) from Madrid, Spain, Justo Gallego Martínez (Spain) has single-handedly been building a "cathedral" on a site measuring 164 x 65 ft (50 x 20 m) since 1962.

Justo has constructed his church without architectural or engineering training and has worked out the plans in his head. It has an exterior resembling a Castilian castle and the interior of a Romanesque church.

HIGHEST...

RESIDENTIAL APARTMENTS

The John Hancock Center in Chicago, Illinois, USA, stands 1,127 ft (343.5 m) and 100 storys high. It was completed in 1970 and remodeled in 1995, and although the building is mixed-use, floors 44 to 92 are residential, making them the highest in the world.

CLOCK
The world's highest two-sided clock is 580 ft (177 m) above street level, on top of the Morton International Building in Chicago, Illinois, USA.

HOTEL
The Grand Hyatt Shanghai in Pudong, China, is the highest hotel in the world. It occupies floors 53 to 87 of the 88-story Jin Mao Tower, the tallest building in China and at 1,377 ft 10 in (420 m) one of the tallest buildings in the world. The hotel offers spectacular views over the adjacent Huang Pu River.

LARGEST...

★ ICE HOTEL
The Ice Hotel in Jukkasjärvi, Sweden, has a total floor area of 43,000–54,000 ft^2 (4,000–5,000 m^2), and in the winter of 2004–05 featured 85 rooms. The hotel also boasts an ice theater – based on the design of Shakespeare's famous Globe playhouse in London, UK – an ice bar, and an ice church. The first hotel was built in 1990 and was a mere 164 ft^2 (50 m^2); it has been re-created every December since then.

★ NEW RECORD
☆ UPDATED RECORD

★ PAPER BUILDING
The largest building constructed entirely of paper had a base measuring 49 ft 9.5 in x 58 ft 8.4 in (15.2 x 17.9 m), and was 21 ft (6.4 m) tall. The construction, unveiled at the APEC Investment Mart Thailand in Bangkok in October 2003, took the form of a traditional Thai house.

★ IGLOO
The largest self-supporting domed igloo had an internal diameter of 24 ft 2 in (7.36 m) and an internal height of 12 ft 6 in (3.81 m). It was constructed at the power station in Québec, Canada, and was completed on February 22, 2005, after 18 days of work by a team of 29.

HOTEL LOBBY
The lobby at the Hyatt Regency in San Francisco, California, USA, is 350 ft (107 m) long, 160 ft (49 m) wide, and, at 170 ft (52 m) tall, is the height of a 15-story building.

OBSERVATION WHEEL
The *British Airways London Eye*, designed by David Marks and Julia Barfield (both UK), is 443 ft (135 m) tall. Constructed at Jubilee Gardens on London's South Bank, UK, it made its first "flight" on February 1, 2000, with regular service commencing the following month.

! X-REF

How many of the Seven Wonders of the Ancient World can you name? Try to come up with as many as you can, then turn to p.109 for the full list.

SEVEN WONDERS OF THE MODERN WORLD

EMPIRE STATE BUILDING
When it opened on May 1, 1931, the 1,472-ft-tall (448-m) icon at 350 Fifth Avenue, New York City, USA, was the world's tallest building.

ITAIPÚ DAM
The Itaipú hydroelectric power plant linking Brazil and Paraguay has 4.7 miles (7.7 km) of dam and generates 75 million megawatt-hours of electricity a year.

CN TOWER
Completed in 1975, the world's **tallest tower** in Toronto, Canada, rises to 1,815 ft 5 in (553.34 m). Enjoy the view from the observation deck at 1,465 ft (446.5 m).

PANAMA CANAL
The 51-mile-long (82-km) canal connecting the Caribbean Sea and Pacific Ocean was opened in August 1914. Over 27,000 workers are believed to have died during its construction.

CHANNEL TUNNEL
Two 31-mile-long (50-km) train "chunnels," each 25 ft (7.6 m) wide, opened in 1994 to connect England and France under the English Channel.

NORTH SEA PROTECTION WORKS
Begun in 1923, this huge series of floodgates, dams, and storm barriers was built to combat the forces of nature faced by the Netherlands.

GOLDEN GATE BRIDGE
Formerly the world's longest and tallest suspension bridge, the 746-ft-high (227-m) towers – and their 80,000 miles (128,000 km) of wire – still strike an imposing view over San Francisco Bay, California, USA.

MONUMENTS

★ TALLEST
STONE BUDDHA

The Leshan Giant Buddha in the Sichuan province of China was carved out of a hillside in the 8th century. Its height of 233 ft (71 m) makes it the tallest statue of Buddha to be carved entirely out of stone. The statue and surrounding area have been designated a World Heritage Site by the United Nations Educational, Scientific, and Cultural Organization (UNESCO).

★ LONGEST
ANCIENT CITY WALL

The ancient city wall of Nanjing in China's Jiangsu province was 22.7 miles (33.6 km) when first constructed during the Ming Dynasty (1368–1644), and around two-thirds of it remains. It has an average height of around 40 ft (12 m) and contains 13 gates.

LARGEST...

★ MONOLITHIC BUILDING

The largest building carved out of a single piece of rock is the Kailasa temple at the Ellora cave complex in the Maharashtra province of India.

★ NEW RECORD
★ UPDATED RECORD

It is approximately 164 ft (50 m) long, 108 ft (33 m) wide, and 100 ft (30 m) high at its tallest point. Construction of the temple started in the 8th century. The Ellora complex is a UNESCO World Heritage Site.

★ GILDED BUILDING

The cone-shaped Shwedagon Pagoda in Rangoon, Myanmar, stands 325 ft (99 m) tall, measures 450 ft (137 m) across its base, and is covered in gold leaf. The Buddhist shrine has been rebuilt many times, but there is thought to have been a *stupa* (dome-shaped Buddhist monument) on the site for over 2,000 years.

STONE SCULPTURE

The statue of the God of Longevity stands on the northwest side of the peak Guimeng, in the Meng Shan Mountains near Pingyi, Shandong, China. It measures 656 ft (200 m) wide and 715 ft (218 m) high.

WOODEN SCULPTURE

Between January and August 1999, G. P. Reichelt (Germany), assisted by Ida Bagus Jiwartem (Bali), carved a Noah's Ark from a single piece of wood.

The sculpture measures 4 ft 11 in (1.5 m) long, 2 ft 1 in (0.64 m) wide, and 7 in (0.18 m) high. It contained 71 pairs of carved wooden animals.

★ TRIUMPHAL ARCH

The Arc de Triomphe in Paris, France, stands 164 ft (50 m) high and 148 ft (45 m) wide. It was commissioned by Napoleon Bonaparte (France) in 1806 and completed in 1836.

TALLEST...

STATUE

A bronze statue of Buddha measuring 393 ft 8 in (120 m) high was completed in Tokyo, Japan, in January 1993. A joint Japanese-Taiwanese project that took seven years to complete, it is 115 ft (35 m) wide and weighs 2,204,620 lb (1,000 tonnes).

★ WOODEN PAGODA

The Sakyamuni Pagoda in the Yingxian county of China's central Shanxi province stands 216 ft (65 m) high and was built in 1056. The structure, which stands on a stone base and has five levels, is currently undergoing repairs after withstanding extreme weather, earthquakes, and artillery fire.

Sways
Apex sways
1 in (2.5 cm)
in high
winds

Apex
Narrows to 17 ft
(5.2 m) wide at the top

**Average
male height**
6 ft (1.8 m)

"Catenary" curve
Arch forms a natural
curve – the upside-
down version of the
curve formed by
a heavy chain
hanging freely
between two
supports

TALLEST ➡
COMMEMORATIVE
MONUMENT

The Gateway Arch in St. Louis, Missouri, USA,
is a sweeping stainless-steel construction
spanning 630 ft (192 m) and rising to the same
height. It cost $29 million and was designed in
1947 by Finnish-American architect Eero Saarinen
to commemorate the westward expansion after
the Louisiana Purchase of 1803. The arch was
completed on October 28, 1965.

★ LARGEST
GROUPING OF
STANDING STONES

The village of Carnac in France is the
site of more than 3,000 prehistoric
stone monuments, consisting of
menhirs (single standing stones) and
dolmens (structures consisting of
multiple stones). The stones were
erected in the Early, Middle, and
Late Neolithic (Stone Age) periods.

TOTEM POLE

On August 4, 1994, a totem pole
180 ft 3 in (54.94 m) tall, known as
the Spirit of Lekwammen ("land of
the winds"), was raised in Victoria,
British Columbia, Canada, for the
staging of the Commonwealth Games.

OBELISK

The Washington Monument, in
Washington D.C., USA, stands 555 ft
(169 m) tall – over 65 ft (20 m)
higher than the Great Pyramid at
Giza, Egypt – and was completed in
1884 to honor George Washington,
the first president of the USA. An
obelisk is a tapered four-sided
column, usually with a pointed top.

MONUMENTAL COLUMN

The tapering column on the bank of
the San Jacinto River near Houston,
Texas, USA, stands 570 ft (173.7 m)
tall, 150 ft^2 (14 m^2) at the base, and
96 ft^2 (9 m^2) at the observation
tower. Built between 1836 and 1939,
the column commemorates the
Battle of San Jacinto (April 21, 1836).

STATUES

MOST STATUES RAISED
TO AN INDIVIDUAL

Although precise figures cannot be
documented, Buddha is believed
to be the figure to whom the
greatest number of statues have
been raised worldwide.

The record for the **greatest number
of statues raised to oneself** was
set by Joseph Vissarionovich
Dzhugashvili, alias Stalin (1879–1953),
the leader of the Soviet Union from
1924 to 1953. It is estimated that at
the time of his death there were
approximately 6,000 statues to Stalin
throughout the USSR and in many
cities in eastern Europe.

LARGEST JADE BUDDHA

The largest statue of Buddha
constructed from a single piece
of jade weighs 574,876 lb (over
260.76 tonnes) and measures 26 ft
(7.9 m) high, 22 ft 6.8 in (6.8 m)
wide, and 13 ft 5.4 in (4.1 m) deep.
The statue stands in a temple at the
Jade Buddha Garden, Anshan,
Liaoning province, China.

LARGEST STATUE
OF THE VIRGIN MARY

A statue of the Virgin Mary
holding the infant Jesus,
on the Hill of Youth
overlooking the city
of Haskovo in southern
Bulgaria, measures 46 ft
(14 m) high and stands on a
55-ft 9-in-tall (17-m) base. It was
unveiled on September 8, 2003.

Cladding
Covered in 14-in-
thick (35-cm)
panels of polished
stainless steel

"Legs"
Hollowed legs of
double-layered
steel (filled with
concrete between
the steel)

Base
Triangular cross-section
widens to 54 feet
(16.45 m) at the base

LARGEST
RELIGIOUS
STRUCTURE

Angkor Wat (City Temple)
in Cambodia covers a
401-acre (162.6-ha) site.
It was built to the Hindu
god Vishnu by the Khmer
king Suryavarman II in
the period 1113–50. Its
curtain wall measures
4,200 ft (1,280 m), and
its population, before it
was abandoned in 1432,
was 80,000. The temple,
begun *ca.* AD 900, forms
part of a complex of
72 major monuments that
extends over 15.4 miles
(24.8 km).

★ HEAVIEST
VEHICLE PULLED BY A TRACTION KITE

A 750-ft^2 (70-m^2) traction kite manufactured by KiteShip Corporation (USA) pulled a 55,115-lb (25-tonne) Americas Cup-Class yacht at a speed of around 7 knots (8 mph; 13 km/h) for 45 minutes in Auckland Harbor, New Zealand, on December 17, 2004.

A traction kite is similar to the aerofoil kites flown by kite enthusiasts, but is far larger.

★ NEW RECORD
☆ UPDATED RECORD

HIGHEST EARNINGS FROM TOURISM

According to the United Nations World Trade Organization (UNWTO), a specialized agency of the United Nations, the USA has the ☆ **world's highest earnings from tourism**.

In the USA, tourism was worth $74.5 billion in 2004, accounting for 12% of international tourism revenue.

TRANSPORTATION

★ BUSIEST NATIONAL RAIL SYSTEM FOR FREIGHT

China's national rail network carried 2.178 billion tonnes of freight during 2004, making it the world's busiest for cargo, according to the International Union of Railways (UIC).

★ FIRST COMMERCIAL JET AIRCRAFT

The British De Havilland Comet was the first jet-powered commercial aircraft. It was powered by four De Havilland Ghost 50 engines mounted within its wings and took its first flight in 1949. Its first scheduled passenger-carrying flight was also the ★ **first jet-passenger service**, between London, UK, and Johannesburg, South Africa, on May 2, 1952, operated by BOAC. On October 4, 1958, it began the ★ **first transatlantic jet service** between the UK and the USA, also operated by BOAC.

☆ BUSIEST INTERNATIONAL AIRLINE

In 2004, 34.407 million people were carried to and from destinations outside Germany by German airline Lufthansa, according to the International Air Transport Association (IATA).

In 2004, Delta Air Lines carried 79.289 million passengers within the USA, making it the ★ **busiest airline for domestic passengers**, according to the IATA. Reflecting the size of the internal US aviation industry, its nearest rivals – American Airlines (72.729 million) and United Airlines (61.868 million) – are also US-based.

★ LARGEST AIR CARGO CARRIER

In 2004, FedEx (USA) flew a total of 14.579 billion freight tonne km, according to the IATA. Korean Air Lines is second with 8.264 billion freight tonne km, and Lufthansa (Germany) is third with a total of 8.040 billion freight tonne km.

LONGEST BUS

The articulated DAF Super CityTrain buses of the Democratic Republic of the Congo are 105.6 ft (32.2 m) long and can carry 350 passengers comfortably. They weigh 61,729 lb (28 tonnes) unladen.

The **longest regularly scheduled bus route**, the "Liberator's Route," is 6,003 miles (9,660 km) long and is operated by Expreso Internacional Ormeño SA of Lima, Peru. It links Caracas (Venezuela) and Buenos Aires (Argentina), and passes through the capitals of six South American countries.

☆ HIGHEST RAILROAD LINE

The Qinghai-Tibet railroad in China, completed in October 2005, is the world's highest railroad. Most of the 1,215-mile-long (1,956-km) line lies at 13,123 ft (4,000 m) above sea level, with the highest point reaching an altitude of 16,640 ft (5,072 m). The service is due to open to the public in 2007.

★LONGEST
NONSTOP COMMERCIAL AIRCRAFT FLIGHT

The longest nonstop commercial aircraft flight was one of 11,664 nautical miles (13,422 miles; 21,600 km) from Hong Kong Airport (China) to London Heathrow (UK), eastward over North America by a Boeing 777-200LR. It took place on November 9–10, 2005 and the total journey time was 22 hr 42 min.

LEAST EXTENSIVE METRO

The shortest operating subway system is the Carmelit in Haifa, Israel. Opened in 1959, the Carmelit is just 1 mile 626 ft (1,800 m) long.

TOURISM

★MOST POPULAR FORM OF INTERNATIONAL TRAVEL

According to the UNWTO, 49.3% of tourists who visited foreign countries in 2004 arrived by land, compared with 43% who traveled by air.

MOST EXPENSIVE TRIP BY A TOURIST

Businessman Dennis Tito (USA) and internet millionaire Mark Shuttleworth (South Africa) each paid a reported $20 million to Russia for their trips to the International Space Station (ISS). Tito's trip lasted from April 28 to May 6, 2001, and Shuttleworth's from April 25 to May 5, 2002.

Both men can be called the first "space tourists," because their trips were paid for entirely out of their own pockets. Shuttleworth returned to South Africa a national hero.

★MOST VISITED TOURISM REGION

According to the UNWTO, the region that received the most international tourists in 2004 was Europe, with 763 million arrivals. Although its market share is gradually shrinking, the continent still attracts 54.5% of all international travelers.

Within the region, southern and western Europe attracted the most tourists, accounting for 19.8% and 18.2% of world market share respectively.

★MOST POPULAR TOURIST DESTINATION

In 2004, France attracted a total of 75.1 million international visitors, making it the most popular tourist destination, according to the UNWTO.

The country accounts for nearly 10% of the world international tourism market.

The next most popular tourist destinations are Spain, with 53.6 million visitors, and the USA, with 46.1 million.

★BIGGEST TOURISM SPENDERS

The country whose citizens spend the greatest amount on vacations abroad is Germany.

In 2004, Germans spent $71 billion while on vacation (excluding airfares). The USA was second, with $65.6 billion, and the UK third with $55.9 billion.

LONGEST BUS TRIP

Between November 6, 1988 and December 3, 1989, Hughie Thompson, John Weston, and Richard Steel (all UK) covered 54,289 miles (87,367 km) through 18 countries in the *World Bus*, a red London Routemaster double-decker bus.

★MOST COUNTRIES VISITED BY BICYCLE

Since leaving his home in November 1962, Heinz Stücke (Germany) has traveled 335,000 miles (539,130 km) and visited 211 countries and territories. In total, he has used 15 passports and his bike has been stolen five times, although he has always managed to recover it.

★BUSIEST NATIONAL RAILROAD SYSTEM

In terms of passenger numbers carried, Japan's railroad network is the world's busiest, with 8.617 billion passenger journeys in 2004, according to the International Union of Railways (UIC). India is second, with 5.112 billion, and Germany third, with 1.694 billion.

In Japan, during busy periods, guards cram passengers into carriages to make sure the doors can close!

? DID YOU KNOW?

According to International Civil Aviation Organization data, 2001 was the safest year in modern times for travel on scheduled air services. In this year there was, on average, one fatality for each 3.1 billion miles (5 billion km) flown.

★BUSIEST AIRPORT

According to the Airports Council International (ACI), Hartsfield International Airport – which serves Atlanta, Georgia, USA – handled 83.6 million passengers in 2004, making it the world's busiest airport.

WEAPONS

FIRST TANK

The earliest tank was "No.1 Lincoln," built by William Foster & Co., Ltd., of Lincoln, UK. After modification, it was dubbed "Little Willie" and first ran on September 6, 1915. It saw action with the Heavy Section, Machine Gun Corps, later the Tank Corps, at the Battle of Flers-Courcelette, France, on September 15, 1916. The Mark I "Male" tank weighed 62,600 lb (28.4 tonnes) and was powered by a 105-hp (78-kW) engine, giving a maximum road speed of 3–4 mph (5–6 km/h).

FIRST ⬆ UNMANNED AERIAL VEHICLE (UAV) OFFENSIVE

On November 3, 2002, in Yemen, an AGM-114 Hellfire missile was fired from a CIA-operated General Atomics RQ-1 Predator (pictured) at six Al-Qaeda operatives in a car. Before this attack, the Predator had been used only for reconnaissance and surveillance.

★ NEW RECORD
✰ UPDATED RECORD

FIRST ATOMIC BOMB USED IN BATTLE

At 8:16 a.m. on August 6, 1945, the crew of the US Air Force B-29 bomber *Enola Gay* dropped an atom bomb on the city of Hiroshima, Japan. The bomb had an explosive power equivalent to that of approximately 15 kilotons of trinitrotoluene ($C_7H_5O_6N_3$), better known as TNT.

The resulting explosion claimed the lives of of 155,200 people, the **greatest death toll from an atomic bomb raid**. This figure includes radiation deaths that occurred within the following year.

OLDEST MILITARY MANUFACTURERS

The earliest recorded mention of the arms company Beretta (Italy), the ★**oldest weapons manufacturer in the world**, came in 1526. The business has been passed down through 16 generations, but its headquarters is still based in the village of Gardone Val Trompia near Brescia, Italy.

The N. P. Ames Company, which was founded in 1791 in Chelmsford, Massachusetts, USA, is the ★**oldest sword-manufacturing company in the USA**. It operates today as the Ames Sword Company.

The origins of Wilkinson Sword, the ★**oldest sword-manufacturing company in the UK**, can be traced back to 1772, when it was founded by Henry Nock. Wilkinson Sword was appointed as Royal Gun Maker to King George III in 1804.

John Brooke & Sons (UK) was founded in 1541, making it the ★**oldest manufacturer of uniforms**. Based in Huddersfield, UK, the company provided uniforms for a diverse range of clients, including British troops in the Battle of Trafalgar, British and French troops in both World Wars, and the Russian military. Manufacturing ceased in 1987.

★ MOST SUCCESSFUL SUBMARINE COMMANDER

Lothar von Arnaud de la Perière fought in the German Imperial Navy in World War I, during which he sank an astounding 194 ships with a total capacity of 454,000 gross tonnage. Even though he was operating in the very early days of practical submarine warfare, de la Perière's achievement remains unmatched to this day.

MOST ACCURATE BOMB ⇒

The Joint Direct Attack Munition, co-funded by the United States Air Force and US Navy, is the world's most precise air-drop bomb. Accurate to +/- 6 ft 6 in (2 m) upon impact, its location is continually checked by satellite fixes after release. This bomb was apparently accidentally dropped on the Chinese Embassy in Belgrade in May 1999.

★ LONGEST-RANGE ARTILLERY PIECE

The South African G6 is a 155-mm (6.1-in) gun produced by the LIW division of Denel, mounted on a chassis made by Alvis OMC. As well as being employed by the South African Army, the G6 also has been exported to the United Arab Emirates and Oman. In September 2001, the G6 achieved a range of 33.3 miles (53.6 km) using the Velocity-enhanced Long-range Artillery Projectile (V-LAP) and the new M64 bi-modular charge system.

FLYING ACES – MOST KILLS

FLYING ACE	WAR	KILLS (PLANES)
Erich Hartmann (Germany)	WWII	352
Baron Manfred Freiherr von Richthofen (Germany)	WWI	80
★Joaquin Morato (Spain)	Spanish Civil War	40
Nikolai V Sutyagin (USSR)	Korean War	21
Lydia Litvak (USSR)*	WWII	12
★Nguyen Van Coc (North Vietnam)	Vietnam War	9

*Lydia Litvak has the distinction of being the **top-scoring WWII female flying ace**

★LONGEST-RANGE COMBAT MISSION

Two US Air Force Barksdale B-52Hs – the first of that model to fly in combat – struck Iraqi targets with 13 conventional air-launched cruise missiles on September 2, 1996, as part of Operation Desert Strike. The 34-hour, 16,000-mile (26,000-km) round trip from Andersen Air Force Base, Guam, was the longest distance ever flown for a combat mission. The planes' high cruising speed meant that the feat took an hour less to complete than the similar mission carried out by B-52Gs during Operation Desert Storm five years earlier.

LARGEST...

WARSHIPS

The warships with the largest full-load displacement are the US Navy Nimitz-class aircraft carriers USS *Nimitz, Dwight D Eisenhower, Carl Vinson, Theodore Roosevelt, Abraham Lincoln, George Washington, John C Stennis, Harry S Truman* and *Ronald Reagan*, the last five of which displace approximately 217 million lb (98,550 tonnes). The ships are 1,092 ft (333 m) long, have a 4.49-acre (1.82-hectare) flight deck and are driven by four nuclear-powered 260,000-hp (194,000-kW) geared steam turbines. They can reach speeds in excess of 30 knots (34.5 mph; 56 km/h).

SUBMARINES

On September 23, 1980, NATO announced the launch of the first Russian 941 Akula (aka "Typhoon") at the secret covered shipyard in Severodvinsk on the White Sea, Russia. The vessels are thought to have a dive displacement of 58.4 million lb (26,500 tonnes), measure 562 ft 7 in (171.5 m) overall and be armed with 20 multiple warhead SS-N-20 missiles with a range of around 4,480 nautical miles (8,300 km; 5,160 miles). It is thought that fewer than five remain in service.

GUN EVER BUILT

At the siege of Sevastopol, USSR (now Ukraine), in July 1942, the Germans used the *Schwerer Gustav*, a railroad gun with a caliber of 31.5 in (80 cm) and a barrel 106 ft (32.5 m) long, built by Krupp (Germany). The gun was 141 ft (42.9 m) long and weighed 2.963 million lb (1,344 tonnes). The range for an 17,857.4-lb (8.1-tonne) projectile was 13 miles (20.9 km); a 10,582.1-lb (4.8-tonne) projectile had a range of 29 miles (46.7 km).

It is believed that the **first guns** were constructed in both China and northern Africa *ca.* 1250.

! X-REF

Which war was history's bloodiest? Discover records about ancient battles, air and marine warfare and the biggest causes of genocide on p.118–19.

★MOST ACCURATE CORNER GUN

The Corner Shot APR™ (Assault Pistol Rifle), devised by two former senior officers from elite units of the Israel Defense Forces, is a weapons system that allows the user to shoot around corners using a video screen to aim and a swiveling gun-mount that can rotate up to 90°. The Corner Shot can accurately engage targets up to 330 ft (100 m) away with a 9-mm handgun and up to 656 ft (200 m) with a 5.7-mm rifle.

Laser sight

Light source
Equipped with a retractable filter that prevents camera-blinding when used at short range

Monitor
A 2.5-in (6.3-cm) color video screen with aiming cross in center; detachable hood and shading sleeve protect against direct sunlight

Video camera
Detachable color video camera

Main body
Moulded from polyamide, fiberglass and glass globules; mount accommodates most models of handgun such as Glock or Beretta

Quick-change battery housing

Pistol grip
Ergonomic grip with housing for two spare lithium batteries

Trigger system
Pulls with a weight of 4.6 lb (2.1 kg); comes with safety mechanism

LARGEST...

★ RIDEABLE MOTORCYCLE

Gregory Dunham (USA) has constructed a rideable motorcycle that is 11 ft 3 in (3.42 m) tall to the top of the handlebars, 20 ft 4 in (6.18 m) long, and weighs 6,500 lb (2.94 tonnes). It is powered by an 502-cu-in (8.2-liter) V8 engine and has tires that are 6 ft 2 in (1.88 m) tall.

suspended between two platforms. As the cable was pulled backward and forward between the platforms, it sliced through the sunken ship and its cargo of nearly 3,000 luxury cars.

★ NEW RECORD
  UPDATED RECORD

★ PERMANENT LIGHT & SOUND SHOW

The "Symphony of Lights" – myriad colored lights set to music – takes place nightly in Victoria Harbor, Hong Kong, China, and involves 33 buildings. The show was developed by the Tourism Commission of the Government of the Hong Kong Special Administrative Region and launched on January 17, 2004.

★ BAR OF SOAP

The largest bar of soap measured 13 ft 4 in x 8 ft 2 in x 4 ft 6 in (4.1 x 2.5 x 1.4 m) and weighed 27,557 lb (12.5 tonnes). It was made by Unilever South Africa Home & Personal Care in Durban, South Africa, and completed on August 12, 2005.

★ PILLOW

On 16 August 2004, Charbel Barooky of Wadi Chahrour, Beirut, Lebanon, created a pillow that measured 17 ft 2 in x 24 ft 4 in (5.2 x 7.4 m).

The pillow was made from fabric and sponge filling and weighed 716.5 lb (325 kg).

★ CARDBOARD-BOX PYRAMID

The largest cardboard-box pyramid consisted of 5,250 empty detergent boxes that were stacked into 24 layers, measuring 18 ft 3 in (5.57 m) long x 18 ft (5.50 m) wide x 18 ft 10 in (5.76 m) high. It was built by six members of staff from the Ismail Ali Abudawood Trading Company (IATCO) at the HyperPanda Store, Riyadh, Saudi Arabia, on January 12, 2005.

★ SAW

The largest saw had a blade 230 ft (70 m) long and was used to cut the wrecked car-carrier *Tricolor* into pieces at the bottom of the English Channel in 2004. The saw consisted of an armored cutting cable

★ BOAT LIFT

The Strepy-Thieu boat lift in Belgium has a vertical travel of 240 ft (73.15 m) and can lift barges weighing up to 2.9 million lb (1,350 tonnes). The boat lift, which opened in November 2001, has a total height of 384 ft (117 m) and forms part of the Canal de Centre, a man-made waterway linking the rivers Meuse and Scheldt.

DOOR

Each of the four doors in the NASA Vehicle Assembly Building near Cape Canaveral, Florida, USA, is 460 ft (140 m) high – as tall as a 35-story building. The doors were originally constructed to such a huge size in order to allow fully assembled *Saturn* and *Apollo* rockets to pass through them. In more recent times, the building has been employed in space-shuttle operations.

★ CENTERLESS FERRIS WHEEL

Big-O is the world's first centerless Ferris wheel. It is 196 ft 9 in (60 m) in diameter and is located in LaQua, an amusement park in Tokyo, Japan. To add to the thrill level, the Thunder Dolphin mega-coaster – at 262 ft (80 m) in height, Tokyo's largest coaster – shoots through the center of Big-O with maximum speeds of 80 mph (130 km/h). LaQua opened in May 2003.

★ ICE-BREAKING PASSENGER SHIP

The ro-ro ferries MV *Caribou* and MV *Joseph & Clara Smallwood* are 587 ft (179 m) long, with a displacement of 35.7 million lb (16,203 tonnes). They are rated as ice-class "A1 Super," the highest possible ice rating for commercial vessels. Operated by Marine Atlantic between the Canadian mainland and the Canadian island of Newfoundland, they are capable of carrying 1,200 passengers and 370 cars.

★ DOUBLE-ACTING (REVERSIBLE) SHIP

The sister ships *Tempera* and *Mastera*, both oil tankers in the service of Finnish company Fortum, are the world's largest ships designed to travel both forward and backward. The vessels, which are 755 ft (230 m) long, have been designed with ice-breaking capabilities. Instead of the bow of the ships being strengthened for this purpose, however, it is their sterns that have been designed to cut through the ice, meaning that the ships travels backward in icy waters.

★ SHIP SUNK INTENTIONALLY

The largest ship ever sunk by its owners was the aircraft carrier USS *America* (CV 66), which was 1,047 ft 6 in (319.2 m) long and had a displacement of 167 million lb (75,800 tonnes). It was sunk in a live-fire exercise off the coast of Virginia, USA, on May 14, 2005.

★ CONTAINER SHIP

The two sister ships MSC *Pamela* and MSC *Susanna* each have a declared capacity of 9,200 TEU (Twenty-Foot Equivalent Unit – a unit of measurement used to assess container ship capacity). They were built by Samsung Heavy Industries for the Mediterranean Shipping Company and are 1,106 ft (337 m) long and 151 ft (46 m) wide. The two ships entered service in 2005.

★ AQUARIUM

In terms of water volume, the Georgia Aquarium in Atlanta, Georgia, USA, is the world's largest, with 63.99 million pints (7.9 million gal) of fresh- and saltwater. The attraction, which opened in November 2005, covers 500,000 ft² (46,450 m²) and contains 100,000 aquatic creatures from more than 500 different species.

★ TILTING SHIP

The Floating Instrument Platform, or FLIP, is a 355-ft-long (108-m) oceanic research barge that is able to rotate through 90°, with 55 ft (17 m) of its length above the water and 300 ft (91 m) below, by flooding ballast tanks. As the flooded end sinks, FLIP's buoyant end – containing accommodation for the 16 crew and their research equipment – rises.

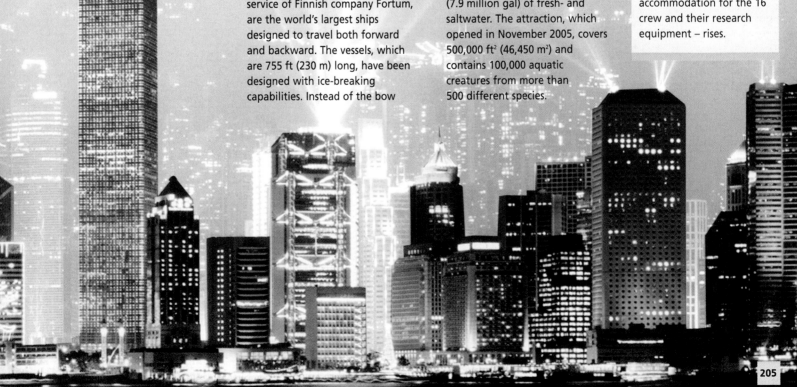

LONGEST...

← BRIDGE

At 23.8 miles (38.4 km), the longest bridge in the world is the Second Lake Pontchartrain Causeway that joins Mandeville and Metairie, Louisiana, USA. Completed in 1969, the causeway is so long that it is possible to stand in the middle of it and be unable to see land in either direction.

★ GARBAGE TRUCK RAMP JUMP

Alfred Sleep (USA) jumped a garbage truck a distance of 77 ft 4 in (23.57 m) at Lebanon Valley Speedway, New York, USA, on June 22, 2004.

★ DRAWBRIDGE

The longest drawbridge is the Charles Berry Bridge across the Black River in Lorain, Ohio, USA, with a span of 333 ft (101.5 m). Like Tower Bridge, its more famous counterpart in London, UK, the bridge has two "leaves" that can be raised to enable ships to pass underneath.

★ MODEL TRAIN

An H0 (1:87.1) scale model train 361 ft 10 in (110.3 m) long, made up of three locomotives of type "lore" and 887 carriages, was completed by Miniatur Wunderland in Hamburg, Germany, on November 27, 2005. If the model had been a full-scale train it would have measured 5.969 miles (9.607 km) in length.

★ LIFT BRIDGE

A lift bridge is a type of drawbridge where the moveable sections are lifted directly upward – rather than being "leaves" that swing on hinges. A 558-ft (170-m) section of the railroad bridge across the Arthur Kill Channel between New Jersey and Staten Island, New York, USA, can be raised vertically to allow ships to pass beneath it. The moveable section is suspended between two 215-ft 6-in-high (66-m) towers. The bridge was completed in 1959.

TRANSPORTER BRIDGE

The Newport Transporter Bridge across the Usk River in Wales, UK, spans 594 ft (181 m) and stands 246 ft (75 m) high.

CYCLEWAY BRIDGE

A cycleway bridge 779 ft 6 in (237.6 m) in length spans the 17 tracks at Cambridge Railway Station, Cambridge, in the UK.

SWING BRIDGE

El Ferdan Railroad Bridge across the Suez Canal near Ismailia, Egypt, has a central span of 1,115 ft (340 m) that rotates 90 degrees in order to allow ships to pass. The bridge, which has a total length of 2,100 ft (640 m), was opened in 2001. The rotation section weighs 29 million lb (13,200 tonnes).

BOARD
CUT FROM ONE TREE

The world's longest piece of wood cut from one tree measured 120 ft 10 in (36.83 m) on June 12, 2002. It was cut traditionally by hand-saws over nine days in an event organized by Daniel Czapiewski (Poland) and his company, Danmar, in Szymbark, Gdañsk, Poland.

★ ABACUS

An abacus constructed by Phyilly Wong and Amanda Yen Chiu Jung (both Singapore) in October 2004 measures 31 ft 4 in (9.55 m).

★ MOTORCYCLE

Rogov Oleg (Russia) built a motorcycle measuring 31 ft 6 in (9.6 m) in Tver, Russia, on December 19, 2005.

TRIKE ⬆

Swiss carnival band Guggä Rugger Buus constructed a trike 26 ft 7 in (8.1 m) long and weighing 13,300 lb (6,030 kg) to serve as a mobile grandstand for 21 members of the band. The machine has a 732-cu-in (12-liter) engine and the chassis of a Saurer truck.

★ RUBBER DAM

The Xiaobudong rubber dam on the Yihe River, China, measures 3,723 ft (1,135 m) and consists of 16 sections, with each section 229 ft (70 m) long.

CAKE

Chefs from 28 leading hotels in Dubai made a date-and-banana cake measuring 8,303 ft (2,530 m) in length, which they assembled along the seafront in Dubai, United Arab Emirates, on December 2, 1996.

REVERSAL OF A TRACTOR-TRAILER

Hans Frei (Switzerland) reversed a tractor-trailer for 21.49 miles (34.6 km) nonstop in 6 hr 25 min in Germany on July 8, 2004.

BRIDGE SPANNING AN AREA OF OPEN OCEAN

The 22.4-mile-long (36-km) Hangzhou Bay Bridge links the cities of Cixi and Zhapu in the Zhejiang province of China. Construction of the $1.4-billion bridge, which spans part of the East China Sea, began in June 2003; it is expected to open in 2008.

BRA CHAIN

A bra chain measuring 37.29 miles (60.01 km) long, and comprising 79,001 bras, was created on Sentosa Island, Singapore, on December 21, 2002. The feat was organized by Class 95FM, Wacoal, and the Breast Cancer Foundation (Singapore) for Breast Cancer Awareness.

CABLEWAY

A 59.6-mile (96-km) cableway was constructed in Sweden in the 1940s to transport lead sulfide ore from a mine in Kristineberg to a processing plant at Boliden. Although the cableway is no longer used for its original purpose, tourists can now take a two-hour ride along a 8.5-mile (13.6-km) stretch of it between Orträsk and Mensträsk.

BIG-SHIP CANAL

The world's longest big-ship canal is the Suez Canal, which opened on November 17, 1869, linking the Red Sea and the Mediterranean Sea. It took 10 years to build, and required a workforce of 1.5 million people, 120,000 of whom perished during the construction. The canal is 100.8 miles (162.2 km) in length and has a minimum width of 984 ft (300 m) and a maximum width of 1,198 ft (365 m).

ESCALATOR RIDE

Australian Suresh Joachim traveled an overall distance of 140 miles (225 km) on escalators at Westfield Shopping Center, Burwood, New South Wales, Australia, for 145 hr 57 min from May 25 to 31, 1998.

☆ DRIVEN JOURNEY

Emil and Liliana Schmid (both Switzerland) have covered more than 364,745 miles (587,000 km) in their Toyota Land Cruiser since October 16, 1984, crossing 150 countries and territories in the process.

! X-REF

You'll find plenty of records to do with size in GWR 2007. How tall do you think the world's tallest residential building is? Find out on p.209.

GOLF CART

Peter Nee (USA) has created a golf cart "limo" that measures 19 ft 1 in (5.81 m) from bumper to bumper. It boasts a bar, stereo, DVD player, cigar humidor, and wine rack to help keep its occupants entertained.

☆ ROAD TRAIN ➡

The record for the longest road train is 4,836 ft 11 in (1,474.3 m). A single Mack Titan prime mover, driven by John Atkinson (Australia), towed 113 trailers for a distance of approximately 490 ft (150 m). The event was sponsored by Hogs Breath Café in Clifton, Australia, on February 18, 2006.

TALLEST...

TALLEST
BUILDING DEMOLISHED

Controlled Demolition Incorporated, of Maryland, USA, used explosives to demolish the 25-story, 439-ft-tall (133-m) Hudson Building in Detroit, Michigan, USA, on October 24, 1998. The building had a capacity of 2.2 million ft³ (62,297 m³), and it took 2,278 lb (1,033 kg) of explosives detonating over a period of 9.5 seconds to reduce the venerable old department store to 595 million lb (270 million kg) of rubble.

ENCLOSED ELEVATOR

The large-scale elevator installed in the New National Theater, Tokyo, Japan, in 1997 has a ceiling 36 ft (11 m) high. With a width of 9 ft 9 in (3 m) and a depth of 19 ft 8 in (6 m), it is designed to carry stage scenery.

★ WORKING WINDMILL

The tallest traditional windmill, powered by sails, is de Noord Molen in Schiedam, Netherlands, at 109 ft 4 in (33.33 m), though there are some other traditional derelict Dutch windmills taller than this one.

CEMETERY

The permanently illuminated Memorial Necrópole Ecumônica, in Santos, near São Paulo, Brazil, is 10 storys high and occupies an area of 4.4 acres (1.8 ha). Its construction started in March 1983 and the first burial here was on July 28, 1984.

★ STADIUM LIGHTING TOWERS

The six lighting towers at Sydney Cricket Ground (Australia) stand 265 ft (81 m) tall. Erected in 1979, they are 16 ft (5 m) taller than the previous record holder – the cricket ground in Melbourne, Australia.

AMUSEMENT PARK BIG WHEEL

The Dai-Kanransha big wheel, which opened to the public at Pallet Town grounds, Tokyo, Japan, on March 17, 1999, stands 394 ft (120 m) tall from the base of the pedestal to the top of the wheel. It has a passenger capacity of 384.

UNSUPPORTED FLAGPOLE

The world's tallest unsupported flagpole stands 416 ft (126.8 m) tall and is located in Amman, the capital of Jordan. It was erected by the Trident Support Corporation in May 2003.

FULL-CIRCUIT ROLLER COASTER

Kingda Ka at Six Flags Great Adventure near Jackson, New Jersey, USA, reaches a maximum height of 418 ft (127.4 m), making it the world's tallest roller coaster. It opened in spring 2005 and is also the world's **fastest roller coaster**, with riders reaching 128 mph (206 km/h) just seconds after launch.

AIRPORT CONTROL TOWER

The 425-ft (130-m) tower at Kuala Lumpur International Airport (KLIA), Malaysia, is the tallest air-traffic control tower in the world. The work of a local architect, it looks like a giant Olympic torch.

HOSPITAL BUILDING

The world's tallest hospital building is Guy's Tower at Guy's Hospital in London, UK, which is 468 ft (142.6 m) tall. It was completed in 1974 and has 34 floors.

MOBILE CRANE

The Demag CC 12600 made by Mannesmann Dematic is 650 ft (198 m) high in its tallest configuration, which consists of a 394-ft-long (120-m)

"fixed jib" attached to a 374-ft-high (114-m) near-vertical boom. It has a maximum lifting capacity of 3,527,000 lb (1,600 tonnes) and is so large that it requires 100 trucks to transport all of its different parts to a site.

MINARET

The tallest minaret in the world is that of the Great Hassan II Mosque, Casablanca, Morocco, measuring 656 ft (200 m). The cost of construction of the mosque was 5 billion dirhams ($513.5 million). Among minarets of earlier centuries the tallest is the Qutab Minar, south of New Delhi, India, built in 1194 to a height of 238 ft (72.54 m).

★ RESIDENTIAL BUILDING

The world's tallest building designed for purely residential purposes is Q1 on the Gold Coast in Queensland, Australia, which has a height to the roof of 902 ft (275 m) and a structural height of 1,060 ft (323 m). It opened in October 2005 and its 80 levels accommodate 527 apartments.

BRIDGE

The 8,070-ft-long (2,460-m) Millau Viaduct (France) is supported by seven concrete piers, the tallest of which measures 1,095 ft 4 in (333.88 m) from the ground to its highest point. The maximum total height from the highest point to the deepest part of the valley below is 1,125 ft (343 m). Though in France, it was designed by Foster and Partners

★ TALLEST
← TWIN TOWERS

Although no longer the world's tallest buildings, the 1,482-ft 7-in (451.9-m) Petronas Towers in Kuala Lumpur, Malaysia, remain noteworthy as the world's tallest matching pair of buildings. The 88-story towers opened in March 1996.

(UK). Opened in December 2004, it provides a vital road link between central and southern France.

FREE-STANDING STRUCTURE

The tallest free-standing structure on earth is the Petronius oil and gas drilling platform, which stands 1,870 ft (570 m) above the ocean floor in the Gulf of Mexico. Operated by Texaco, it began commercial production on July 21, 2000. The highest point on the platform, the vent boom, stands more than 2,000 ft (610 m) above the ocean floor, making it more than 165 ft (50 m) taller than the CN Tower in Toronto, Canada, the **tallest free-standing building** on land.

★ TALLEST STRUCTURE

The tallest structure on Earth is the Ursa tension leg platform, a floating oil production facility operated by Shell in the Gulf of Mexico. The top of its drilling rig is 4,285 ft (1,306 m) above the ocean floor. The platform is connected to the sea floor by oil pipelines and four massive steel tethers at each corner, giving a total weight of approximately 35 million lb (16,000 tonnes).

TALLEST
BUILDING

Taipei 101 (also known as the Taipei Financial Center) in Taiwan is the world's tallest building at 1,666 ft (508 m). It topped the Petronas Towers (pictured left) during its construction in mid-August 2003. It then achieved its maximum height in October 2003, several months ahead of its planned completion date in the summer of 2004.

★ NEW RECORD
★ UPDATED RECORD

> **!** **X-REF**
>
> *Some monuments are bigger than many buildings. The tallest stone statue of Buddha was actually carved directly out of a hillside. Find out more on p.198.*

Find out more on p.198.

FASTEST...

COMBAT JET

The fastest combat jet is the Russian Mikoyan MiG-25 fighter (NATO code name "Foxbat"). The reconnaissance "Foxbat-B" has been tracked by radar at about Mach 3.2 (2,110 mph or 3,395 km/h).

★ FASTEST SPEED ON A CONVENTIONAL MOTORCYCLE

John Noonan (USA) reached 252.66 mph (406.62 km/h) on a modified 1,350-cc Suzuki Hayabusa at Bonneville Salt Flats, Utah, USA, on September 7, 2005. This is the average of two timed runs over 1 mile (1.6 km) in opposite directions.

SOLAR-POWERED VEHICLE

Molly Brennan (USA) achieved a speed of 48.71 mph (78.39 km/h) driving the solely solar-powered *General Motors Sunraycer* at Mesa, Arizona, USA, on June 24, 1988.

HOVERCRAFT (ON WATER)

Bob Windt (USA) achieved a speed of 85.3 mph (137.4 km/h) on the Douro River, Peso de Regua, Portugal, at the 1995 World Hovercraft Championships. Windt was driving a streamlined 19-ft (5.8-m) Universal UH19P hovercraft called *Jenny II*, with a 110-hp (82-kW) V6 car engine driving its two fans (one at the rear to provide propulsion, and one underneath to provide lift).

BICYCLE WHEELIE (REAR WHEEL)

Bobby Root (USA) achieved a speed of 86 mph (138 km/h) while riding his bicycle on the rear wheel at Palmdale, California, USA, on January 31, 2001, for *Guinness World Records: Primetime*. He traveled in the slipstream of another vehicle for a distance of 328 ft (100 m) prior to the stunt to build up speed.

DIESEL TRAIN

The former British Rail inaugurated its HST (High-Speed Train) daily service between London, Bristol, and South Wales, UK, on October 4, 1976, using InterCity 125 trains. One of these holds the world speed record for diesel trains, at 148 mph (238 km/h), set on a test run between Darlington, County Durham, and York, North Yorkshire, UK, on November 1, 1987.

HELICOPTER

The official Féderation Aéronautique Internationale (FAI) speed record for helicopters is 249.09 mph (400.87 km/h). It was set by John Trevor Eggington with co-pilot Derek J. Clews (both UK), over Somerset, UK, on August 11, 1986, in a Westland Lynx demonstrator.

MOTORCYCLE

Riding a 23-ft-long (7-m) streamliner named *Easyriders* powered by two 1,500-cc Ruxton Harley-Davidson engines, Dave Campos (USA) set American Motorcyclist Association (AMA) and Féderation Internationale de Motocyclisme (FIM) absolute records with an overall average of 322.158 mph (518.450 km/h) at Bonneville Salt Flats, Utah, USA, on July 14, 1990. He did the faster run at an average of 322.870 mph (519.609 km/h).

WHEEL-DRIVEN VEHICLE

Don Vesco (USA) achieved a speed of 458.456 mph (737.794 km/h) in the turbine-powered *Vesco Turbinator* at Bonneville Salt Flats, Utah, USA, on October 18, 2001. (The term "wheel-driven" refers to the fact that the power of the engine is directed to the wheels, and it is these that then power the car forward.)

HISTORY'S FASTEST...

Each entry in this timeline was once the quickest way to travel. We've provided a top speed, place, and (where possible) name for each. Amazingly, for more than 5,000 years, sleds were the fastest way to get around...

SLED
25 mph (40 km/h)
Heinola, Finland

ca. 6500 BC

HORSE
35 mph (56 km/h)
Anatolia, Turkey

ca. 1400 BC

ICE YACHT
50 mph (80 km/h)
Netherlands

AD 1600

DOWNHILL SKIER
87.8 mph (141.3 km/h)
La Porte, California, USA
Tommy Todd (USA)

March 1873

MIDLAND RAILWAY 4-2-2
90 mph (144.8 km/h)
Ampthill, Bedford, UK

March 1897

CAR

The official land-speed record (over one mile) is 763.055 mph (1,227.985 km/h or Mach 1.002) set by Andy Green (UK) on October 15, 1997, in the Black Rock Desert, Nevada, USA, in *Thrust SSC*. The car was jet powered – unlike the record for the fastest wheel-driven vehicle, in this case the wheels were "passive."

AIRLINER

The Tupolev Tu-144, first flown on December 31, 1968, in the former USSR, was reported to have reached Mach 2.4 (1,607 mph or 2,587 km/h), but normal cruising speed was Mach 2.2 (1,674 mph or 2,695 km/h). It was taken out of service in 1978.

The BAC/Aerospatiale Concorde, first flown on March 2, 1969, cruised at up to Mach 2.02 (1,450 mph or 2,333 km/h) and became the first supersonic airliner used on passenger services on January 21, 1976. The New York–London record for the fastest time by a commercial aircraft is 2 hr 54 min 30 sec, set on April 14, 1990. The last Concorde was removed from service on October 24, 2003.

SPEED BY HUMANS

The command module of *Apollo 10*, carrying Col (now Brig. Gen.) Thomas Patten Stafford (USAF), Cdr (now Capt.) Eugene Andrew Cernan, and Cdr (now Capt.) John Watts Young (USN) reached a maximum speed of 24,790 mph (39,897 km/h) at the 75.7-mile (121.9-km) altitude interface on its trans-Earth return flight on May 26, 1969, traveling at 6.88 miles/sec (11.08 km/sec).

SPACECRAFT

The highest speed reached by a spacecraft is 157,000 mph (252,800 km/h), believed to have been attained by the unmanned NASA–German *Helios 1* (launched December 10, 1974) and *Helios 2* (launched January 15, 1976) solar probes each time they reach the perihelion (the point in their solar orbits when they came nearest to the Sun). On April 16, 1976, *Helios 2* came within 27 million miles (43.5 million km) of the Sun, meaning that this probe also holds the record for the ★ **closest approach to the Sun by a spacecraft**.

★ HEARSE

Joe Gosschalk (Australia) covered a quarter of a mile in his 1979 Ford LTD P6 hearse in 13.7 seconds at 98 mph (158 km/h) at Willowbank Raceway, Queensland, Australia, on June 10, 2005. The hearse has a 351-in³ (5.7-liter) engine with nitrous oxide boost.

[?] DID YOU KNOW?

The fastest speed possible is the speed of light. It achieves its maximum velocity – 983,571,056 ft/sec (299,792,458 m/sec) when traveling in a vacuum.

★ PRODUCTION CAR

A Bugatti Veyron achieved two-way timed speeds in excess of 248 mph (400 km/h) at the Volkswagen proving grounds in Wolfsburg, Germany, on May 20, 2005.

★ NEW RECORD
★ UPDATED RECORD

MESSERSCHMITT 163V-1
623.87 mph (1,004 km/h)
Peenemunde, Germany
Heinz Dittmar (Germany)

October 2, 1941

USAF BELL XS-1
670 mph (1,078 km/h)
Murdoc Dry Lake, California, USA
Capt. C. E. Yeager (USA)

October 14, 1947

NORTH AMERICAN X-15
2,905 mph (4,675.1 km/h)
Murdoc Dry Lake, California, USA
Maj. R. M. White (USA)

March 7, 1961

VOSTOK 1
ca. 17,560 mph (ca. 28,260 km/h)
Earth orbit
Gen. Y. A. Gagarin (USSR)

April 12, 1961

APOLLO 10
24,790 mph (39,897 km/h)
Re-entry into Earth's atmosphere
Crew of Apollo 10 (USA)

May 26, 1969

SPORTS & GAMES

CONTENTS

★ FIRST NON-US SNOWBOARDER
TO EARN SUPERPIPE GOLD – WINTER X GAMES

Antii Autti (Finland, pictured above in time-lapse photography) became the first snowboarder from outside the USA to earn a gold medal in SuperPipe. He landed back-to-back 1080s (three full 360° rotations) in Aspen, Colorado, USA, in 2005, at Winter X Games Nine to take the top spot over Danny Kass and Shaun White (both USA).

ACTION SPORTS

★ NEW RECORD
☆ UPDATED RECORD

★ LARGEST PAINTBALL TOURNAMENT

The Paintball Sports Promotions World Cup held at Disney's Wide World of Sports Complex in Orlando, Florida, USA, from October 24 to 30, 2005, featured a total of 370 teams playing on 11 paintball fields.

★ MOST POPULAR EXTREME SPORT

According to a survey conducted in the USA in 2004 by the Sporting Goods Manufacturing Association, inline skating is the most popular extreme sport, with 17.3 million participants. In second place is skateboarding with 11.6 million, and paintballing is third with 9.6 million participants per year.

★ LARGEST SIMULTANEOUS BASE JUMP

The largest ever simultaneous BASE (Building, Antenna, Span, Earth) jump involved 15 participants from five countries, who jumped from different points on the Petronas Towers, Kuala Lumpur, Malaysia, seconds before midnight on December 31, 1999. The jump was timed so that the participants would be in the air at midnight as a celebration of the new millennium.

★ MOST RACE WINS IN A RED BULL AIR RACE SEASON

Mike "Mungo" Mangold (USA) won the Rotterdam, Zletweg, Longleat, Budapest, and San Francisco events in 2005. During the same season, Mangold secured 36 points, the ★ most points scored in a Red Bull Air Race Season by an individual.

☆ LONGEST MOTORCYCLE RAMP JUMP

Trigger Gumm (USA), a member of the Crusty Demons freestyle motocross team, jumped 277 ft 4 in (84.5 m) on a Honda CR500 at the Queensland Raceway, Ipswich, Queensland, Australia, on May 14, 2005, for Seven Network's *Guinness World Records* TV show.

CLIMBING

★ MOST WORLD CUP VICTORIES

François Legrand (France) took five individual men's World Cup titles, from 1990 to 1993 and in 1997.

The ★ most climbing World Cup titles won by a woman is also five, set by Muriel Sarkany (Belgium) in 1997, 1999, 2001–02, and 2004.

★ MOST BOULDERING WORLD CUP VICTORIES

The greatest number of World Cup titles won by an individual in the men's bouldering competition is two by Christian Core in 1999 and 2002 and Jerome Meyer in 2001 and 2003 (both France).

The ★ most bouldering climbing World Cup victories by a woman is three, by Sandrine Levet (France) in 2000–01 and 2003.

★ INLINE SKATES – MOST CONSECUTIVE FLATSPINS

Stephane Alfano (France) performed an unprecedented 16 consecutive flatspins on inline skates on the set of *L'Été De Tous Les Records*, Port Medoc, France, on July 18, 2005.

FASTEST FREE CLIMBER

Dan Osman (USA) climbed a 400-ft (121-m) rock face at Lake Tahoe, California, USA, without the use of ropes or harnesses of any kind, in a time of 5 min 52 sec on May 29, 1997.

GLIDING

☆ GREATEST DISTANCE FLOWN – FREE

Terence Delore (New Zealand) flew 1,362 miles (2,192.9 km) at El Calafate, Argentina, on December 4, 2004.

The **greatest out and return distance** is 1,396.6 miles (2,247.6 km) by Klaus Ohlmann (Germany) from Chapelco, Argentina, on December 2, 2003.

The **greatest overall distance for a Fédération Aéronautique Internationale (FAI) world record** is 1,869.7 miles (3,009 km) for three turn points Free distance by Klaus Ohlmann (Germany) from Chapelco, Argentina, on January 21, 2003.

★ HIGHEST MOTORCYCLE JUMP ⬆

The highest ramp jump performed on a trials motorcycle is 16 ft 8 in (5.11 m) by Graham Jarvis (UK) on the set of *L'Été De Tous Les Records*, Port Medoc, France, on July 18, 2005.

★ GREATEST DISTANCE FLOWN – FREE (WOMEN)

The greatest free distance flown in a glider by a woman is 669.9 miles (1,078.2 km), achieved by Pamela Kurstjens-Hawkins (UK) from Kingaroy, Queensland, Australia, on January 5, 2003.

The **greatest out and return distance in a glider by a woman** is 647.8 miles (1,042.55 km), by Hana Zejdova (Czech Republic), from Tocumwal, New South Wales, Australia, on December 25, 1998.

The **greatest overall distance for an FAI world record by a woman** is 789.4 miles (1,270.5 km) for three turn points Free distance, by Reiko Morinaka (Japan) from Chapelco, Argentina, on December 30, 2004.

BOARDING & BMX

MOST BMX GYRATOR SPINS IN ONE MINUTE

Sam Foakes (UK) executed 33 gyrator spins in one minute at the offices of Guinness World Records in London, UK, on July 20 2004. The record was set as part of filming a DVD game.

HIGHEST BMX VERTICAL AIR

Mat Hoffman (USA) achieved a BMX air of 26 ft 6 in (8.07 m) from a 24-ft-tall (7.3-m) quarterpipe on March 20, 2001, in Oklahoma, USA. Hoffman was towed by a motorcycle in the run-up to the jump. The highest unassisted air is 19 ft (5.8 m) by Dave Mirra (USA) off an 18-ft-tall (5.4 m) ramp in California, USA, in January 2001.

★ HIGHEST SKATEBOARD AIR (HALFPIPE)

Jocke Olsson (Sweden) achieved a halfpipe skateboard air of 7 ft 8 in (2.35 m) at Argelès-Gazost, France, on July 6, 2005; Terence Bougdour (France) did the same at La Tranche Sur Mer, France, on July 27, 2005.

★ HIGHEST SKATEBOARD AIR (QUARTERPIPE)

Danny Way (USA) reached 23 ft 6 in (7.1 m) off a 27-ft (8.2-m) ramp at Point X Camp in California, USA, on June 19, 2003.

★ MOST CONSECUTIVE FRONTSIDE OLLIES (HALFPIPE)

Sascha Müller (Germany) performed a total of 34 skateboard frontside ollies off a halfpipe ramp on the set of *L'Été De Tous Les Records* in Argelès-Gazost, France, on July 5, 2005.

? DID YOU KNOW?

BMX legend Mat Hoffman's (USA) contribution to action sports is unparalleled. Not only has he invented hundreds of bike tricks but, in 1991, he was the first person to build an oversized ("Big") ramp. In 2002, at the Summer X Games, he also became the first person to successfully pull off a no-handed 900!

★ HIGHEST ➡ McTWIST (HALFPIPE)

Terence Bougdour (France) achieved a 4-ft 10-in-high (1.5-m) skateboard 540 McTwist off a halfpipe on the set of *L'Été De Tous Les Records*, La Tranche Sur Mer, France, on July 27, 2005.

FOOTBALL

★ MOST → CONSECUTIVE POST-SEASON VICTORIES

The New England Patriots won a record 10 consecutive NFL post-season games from 2001 to 2006. During this time, they captured three Super Bowls in four seasons.

Patriots coach Bill Belichick (USA) also holds the record for the **most post-season wins by an NFL head coach**. His 11–2 record is one better than Vince Lombardi (USA), who had a post-season record of 10 wins and two losses as coach of the Green Bay Packers.

★ NEW RECORD
☆ UPDATED RECORD

LONGEST FIELD GOAL, CLAIMED (NON-NFL)

The longest claimed kick is one of 78 yards by a barefooted Ching Do Kim (USA) at Honolulu Stadium, Hawaii, USA, on November 23, 1944.

★ MOST CAREER TOUCHDOWNS THROWN BY A QUARTERBACK AT ONE STADIUM

Brett Favre (USA), playing for the Green Bay Packers from 1992 to 2005, has thrown for a career total of 189 touchdowns at Lambeau Field in Green Bay, Wisconsin, USA – the most touchdown passes ever by a quarterback at one stadium.

★ LONGEST ← PLAY

On November 13, 2005, Nathan Vasher (USA), playing for the Chicago Bears, returned a missed field goal attempt 108 yards for a touchdown against the San Francisco 49ers at Soldier Field, Chicago, Illinois, USA. This record play – the longest ever – also represents the **longest return of a missed field goal**.

☆ MOST CONSECUTIVE NFL GAMES PLAYED

Punter Jeff Feagles (USA) played in a record 288 consecutive games (New England Patriots 1988–89, Philadelphia Eagles 1990–93, Arizona Cardinals 1994–97, Seattle Seahawks 1998–2002, and New York Giants 2002–05). Feagles has also kicked the ★**most punts by an individual in a career** with a record of 1,437 punts during his 18-year NFL career.

★ MOST CONSECUTIVE NFL GAMES WITH A RUSHING TOUCHDOWN

LaDainian Tomlinson (USA), playing for the San Diego Chargers, established an NFL record by scoring at least one rushing touchdown in 18 consecutive games during the 2004 and 2005 seasons. The streak ties Lenny Moore (USA, Baltimore Colts), who scored a rushing or receiving touchdown in 18 straight games from 1963 to 1965.

★ MOST CONSECUTIVE NFL SEASONS THROWING A TOUCHDOWN PASS

Vinny Testaverde (USA) has accomplished an achievement unprecedented in NFL history by throwing a touchdown pass in 19 consecutive seasons (1987–2005).

☆ HIGHEST ↑ NFL ATTENDANCE

The largest crowd for a regular season NFL game is 103,467 for the Arizona Cardinals against the San Francisco 49ers at Azteca Stadium in Mexico City, Mexico, on October 2, 2005.

MOST POINTS IN A SUPER BOWL CAREER

Jerry Rice (USA) scored 48 points over his four-game Super Bowl career in 1989, 1990, 1995, and 2003, playing for the San Francisco 49ers and the Oakland Raiders.

MOST POINTS IN A CAREER

Gary Anderson (USA, Pittsburgh Steelers, Philadelphia Eagles, San Francisco 49ers, Minnesota Vikings) has scored a record 2,080 points in his NFL career (1982–2001).

MOST → TOUCHDOWNS
IN AN NFL SEASON

Shaun Alexander (USA) scored 28 touchdowns for the Seattle Seahawks during the 2005 NFL season. Alexander scored 27 rushing touchdowns and one receiving touchdown.

MOST POINTS IN ONE GAME

Ernie Nevers (USA) scored 40 points for the Chicago Cardinals against the Chicago Bears on November 28, 1929.

★MOST RECEIVING YARDS BY A RUNNING BACK IN AN NFL CAREER

Marshall Faulk (USA, Indianapolis Colts 1994–98, St. Louis Rams 1999–2005) is the career leader in receiving yards among NFL running backs, gaining an all-time record of 6,875.

★MOST QUARTERBACK SACKS (POST-SEASON)

Willie McGinest (USA, below, wearing 55) recorded 16 quarterback sacks during his post-season career with the New England Patriots (1994–2006). He also recorded the ★most quarterback sacks in an NFL post-season game, with 4½ sacks in a divisional game against the Jacksonville Jaguars on January 7, 2006.

★FIRST QUARTERBACK AND WIDE RECEIVER TANDEM TO COMBINE FOR 10,000 YARDS

Indianapolis Colts quarterback Peyton Manning (USA) and wide receiver Marvin Harrison (USA) are the first quarterback and wide receiver tandem to combine for 10,000 yards, gaining 10,542 yards through the 2005 NFL season.

★MOST TOUCHDOWNS BY AN NFL QUARTERBACK AND WIDE RECEIVER DUO IN A CAREER

In the 2005 season, Indianapolis Colts quarterback Peyton Manning (USA) threw a record 94th touchdown pass to wide receiver Marvin Harrison (USA).

The Manning-to-Harrison pairing has also set an NFL record for ★most pass completions (783).

★YOUNGEST NFL COACH

Harland Svare (USA, b. November 25, 1930) was 31 years 11 months when he was signed on to coach the Los Angeles Rams, midway through the 1962 season. Under Savre, the Rams finished the 1962 season 0–5–1. He compiled a record of 14–31–3 before being dismissed after the 1965 season.

★OLDEST ROOKIE

Ola Kimrin (Sweden), a placekicker, played in five games at the age of 32 years old for the Washington Redskins during the 2004 season.

★OLDEST ROOKIE TO START AN NFL SEASON ON THE ACTIVE ROSTER

Ben Graham (USA), playing for the New York Jets, was 31 years old at the start of the 2005 season.

★MOST FIELD GOALS IN A SEASON

Neil Rackers (USA, Arizona Cardinals) scored a record 40 field goals in the 2005 NFL season. He also established records for the ★most consecutive games kicking 50-yard field goals – by kicking at least one field goal in four consecutive games during the 2005 season – and for the ★most consecutive games kicking two field goals, achieving at least two in 11 games of the 2005 season.

TRACK & FIELD

FASTEST
100 M (MEN)

Justin Gatlin (USA) ran a time of 9.77 seconds at the IAAF Grand Prix in Doha, Qatar, on May 12, 2006. His time equalled the 100 m record set by Asafa Powell (Jamaica) at the IAAF Super Grand Prix in Athens, Greece, on June 14, 2005.

Florence Griffith-Joyner (USA) recorded the **fastest women's 100 m** with a time of 10.49 seconds in Indianapolis, Indiana, USA, on July 16, 1988.

MEDALS AND WINS

MOST OLYMPIC GOLD MEDALS (MEN)

Three people have won nine gold medals each. Paavo Nurmi (Finland) won three in 1920, five in 1924, and one in 1928 for track and field; Mark Spitz (USA) won two in 1968 and seven in 1972 for swimming; Carl Lewis (USA) won four in 1984, two in 1988, two in 1992, and one in 1996 for track and field.

If the Intercalated Games of 1906 are included, the record is 10 by Raymond Clarence Ewry (USA), for three in 1900, three in 1904, two in 1906, and two in 1908. He competed in standing high, standing long, and standing triple jumps, but all were dropped from the Olympics after 1912.

MOST OLYMPIC GOLD MEDALS (WOMEN)

Four women have won four track and field gold medals: Francina Elsje Blankers-Koen (Netherlands), for the 100 m, 200 m, 80 m hurdles, and 4 x 100 m relay, all 1948; Elizabeth Cuthbert (Australia), for the 100 m, 200 m, 4 x 100 m relay, 1956, and 400 m, 1964; Bärbel Wöckel (née Eckert, GDR), for the 200 m and 4 x 100 m relay in both 1976 and 1980; and Evelyn Ashford (USA), for the 100 m in 1984, and 4 x 100 m relay in 1984, 1988, and 1992.

FIELD EVENTS

☆ MOST POINTS SCORED IN THE DECATHLON (WOMEN)

Austa Skujyte (Lithuania) scored a total of 8,358 points in the decathlon in Columbia, Missouri, USA, on April 14–15, 2005. *For her results per event, see p.268.*

☆ HIGH JUMP

On February 4, 2006, Kjasa Bergqvist (Sweden) jumped to a height of 6 ft 9.8 in (2.08 m), breaking Heike Henkel's (Germany) indoor record that had been standing since 1992. Javier Sotomayor's (Cuba) record in the men's indoor high jump at 7 ft 11.66 in (2.43 m) has been standing since March 4, 1989. He also holds the record for **highest outdoor jump by a man** at a height of 8 ft 0.45 in (2.45 m), achieved in Salamanca, Spain, on July 27, 1993.

The **highest outdoor jump by a woman** is 6 ft 10.28 in (2.09 m), achieved by Stefka Kostadinova (Bulgaria) on August 30, 1987, in Rome, Italy.

FARTHEST JAVELIN THROW

The **men's javelin** record belongs to Jan Zelezný (Czech Republic). He threw 323 ft 1 in (98.48 m) in Jena, Germany, on May 25, 1996.

On August 14, 2005, Osleidys Menéndez (Cuba) threw a distance of 235 ft 2.8 in (71.7 m) in Helsinki, Finland, the ☆ **farthest javelin throw by a woman**.

☆ FARTHEST HAMMER THROW (WOMEN)

Tatyana Lysenko (Russia) threw a distance of 252 ft 9.8 in (77.06 m) at the Vladimir Kuts Memorial meeting in Moscow, Russia, on July 15, 2005.

☆ HIGHEST ➡
POLE VAULT (WOMEN)

Yelena Isinbayeva (Russia) recorded the highest outdoor pole vault by a woman with a height of 16 ft 5.24 in (5.01 m) at the IAAF World Outdoor Championships in Helsinki, Finland, on August 12, 2005. On February 12, 2006, she also broke her own indoor record with a vault at a height of 16 ft 1.3 in (4.91 m) in Donetsk, Ukraine.

FASTEST 3,000 M STEEPLECHASE

Saif Saaeed Shaheen (Qatar, above center) ran the 3,000 m steeplechase in a time of 7 min 53.63 sec at the TDK Golden League Meeting staged in Brussels, Belgium, on September 3, 2004.

Gulnara Samitova (Russia) recorded the **fastest 3,000 m steeplechase by a woman** with a time of 9 min 1.59 sec at the Super Grand Prix in Iráklio, Greece, on July 4, 2004.

TRACK EVENTS

★ FASTEST INDOOR 400 M

Kerron Clement (USA) attained a time of 44.57 seconds in the indoor 400 m competition in Fayetteville, Arkansas, USA, on March 12, 2005.

On March 7, 1982, Jarmila Kratochvílová (Czechoslovakia) ran the **fastest indoor 400 m by a woman**, with a time of 46.59 seconds in Milan, Italy.

FASTEST INDOOR 4 X 200 M RELAY

Great Britain's team (Linford Christie, Darren Braithwaite, Ade Mafe, and John Regis) set a time of 1 min 22.11 sec in Glasgow, UK, on March 3, 1991.

The ★ **fastest time set for the 4 x 200 m relay by a women's team** is 1 min 32.41 sec, recorded by the Russian team (Yekaterina Kondratyeva, Irina Khabarova, Yuliva Pechonkina, and Julia Gushchina) at the IAAF World Indoor Championships in Glasgow, UK, on January 29, 2005.

FASTEST INDOOR 5,000 M

Kenenisa Bekele (Ethiopia) ran the indoor event in a time of 12 min 49.6 sec in Birmingham, UK, on February 20, 2004. Bekele also holds the outdoor record of 12 min 37.35 sec, run in Hengelo, Netherlands, on May 31, 2004.

Tirunesh Dibaba (Ethiopa) ran the ★ **fastest indoor 5,000 m by a woman** with a time of 14 min 32.93 sec at the IAAF World Indoor Championships in Boston, Massachusetts, USA, on January 29, 2005.

★ FASTEST 10,000 M

Kenenisa Bekele (Ethiopia) ran the 10,000 m in a record time of 26 min 17.53 sec at the IAAF World Outdoor Championships in Brussels, Belgium, on August 26, 2005.

The record for **fastest 10,000 m by a woman** has been held since September 8, 1993, by Junxia Wang (China), with a time of 29 min 31.78 sec run in Beijing, China.

★ FASTEST 25 KM ROAD RACE

On September 25, 2005, Mizuki Noguchi (Japan) won the Berlin Marathon in Germany. During this race she set two new world records: for **fastest 25 km**, in a time of 1 hr 22 min 13 sec, as well as ★ **fastest 30 km road race by a woman**, in a time of 1 hr 38 min 49 sec.

The **fastest 30 km road race by a man** was run by Paul Kosgei (Kenya) in Berlin, Germany, on May 9, 2004, in a record-breaking time of 1 hr 12 min 45 sec.

FASTEST OUTDOOR 5,000 M (WOMEN)

Elvan Abeylegesse (Turkey) ran the fastest outdoor 5,000 m by a woman, with a time of 14 min 24.68 sec, in Bergen, Norway, on June 11, 2004.

? DID YOU KNOW?

The International Association of Athletics Federations (IAAF) is the worldwide governing body for track and field; its headquarters are in Monaco. The IAAF is responsible for standardizing time-keeping methods as well as monitoring world records.

Founded in 1912 in Stockholm, Sweden, by 17 national athletics federations, the IAAF was first known as the International Amateur Athletic Federation. In 1982, the IAAF began to amend some of its rules, allowing athletes to be paid for their participation in international athletics competitions, but it retained the word "amateur" in its name. It was only in 2001 that the IAAF's title was changed to its current form.

! X-REF

There's a full run-down of track and field records in the Sports Reference tables at the end of this book. You'll find track events listed on pp.266–67; field events are listed on pp.268–69.

SIR RANULPH FIENNES

Sir Ranulph Fiennes and Michael Stroud (both UK) were the first to complete seven marathons on seven continents in seven days. Between October 27 and November 2, 2003, they ran in Chile's Tierra del Fuego, Falkland Islands, Sydney, Singapore, London, Cairo, and New York City. We asked how they came up with the idea.

In January 2003, I spoke to Mike Stroud about doing a three-month expedition. But he could only get one week off work, so it had to be seven days! After sorting out a route, I started training.

You had a few obstacles along the way, didn't you?

In June I had a massive heart attack, and was in a coma for three days; I had a double heart bypass and 13 jump-starts to try to get the heart going again. We risked losing the sponsorship by Land Rover if we delayed the challenge, so I started to walk a bit, then after a week I could walk for five minutes, then eventually jog for 10 minutes. We did two trial marathons before we were due to leave.

What did you think about or focus on while you were running?

I was thinking I mustn't exhaust myself, because I have another one the next day!

Which of the seven was the hardest?

Everything was fine until the Singapore one where it was very hot, very humid – we hadn't recovered from the Australian one and it was a real rush to get to the European one.

Of all your expeditions, which one are you most proud of?

The one that took the longest – trying to find the lost city of Ubar in Arabia, which took about 26 years.

What is next for you – or is it a secret?

Vertical challenges. All my expeditions have been horizontal ones – I'm now under instruction for ice- and rock-climbing. I'd like to move to a mountaineering field.

★ NEW RECORD
☆ UPDATED RECORD

STROLLER-PUSHING MARATHONS

The **fastest time to run a marathon while pushing a stroller** is 2 hr 49 min 43 sec by Michal Kapral (Canada, pictured) at the Toronto Waterfront Marathon, Canada, on September 26, 2004.

Neil Davison (UK) ran the City of Norwich Half Marathon, in Norfolk, UK, while pushing a stroller, in 1 hr 15 min 8 sec on June 12, 2005.

MARATHONS

OLDEST MARATHON FINISHER

At the age of 98, Dimitrion Yordanidis (Greece) completed a 26-mile (41.8-km) marathon in Athens, Greece, on October 10, 1976, in 7 hr 33 min.

Jenny Wood-Allen (UK, b. 1911) is the **oldest female marathon finisher**. She completed the 2002 London Marathon, which she has said will be her last, aged 90 years 145 days, in a time of 11 hr 34 min on April 14, 2002.

OLDEST MARATHON

The Boston Marathon was first held on April 19, 1897, when it was run over a distance of 24 miles (39 km).

John A. Kelley (USA) finished the Boston Marathon (USA) 61 times between 1928 and 1992.

☆ FASTEST MARATHON

Paul Tergat (Kenya) ran a time of 2 hr 4 min 55 sec in Berlin, Germany, on September 28, 2003. Paula Radcliffe (UK) has run the **fastest marathon by a woman**, with a time of 2 hr 15 min 25 sec in London, UK, on April 13, 2003.

★ FASTEST MARATHON DISTANCE RELAY

A team of 211 runners completed the marathon distance in 1 hr 38 min 50.97 sec by the Kanagawa Prefecture High School Sport Federation at Hiratsuka Stadium, Kanagawa, Japan, on May 5, 1998.

FASTEST AGGREGATE TIME FOR THREE MARATHONS IN THREE DAYS

Raymond Hubbard (UK) ran three marathons in three days with an aggregate time of 8 hr 22 min 31 sec from April 16 to 18, 1988. They took place in Belfast, UK (2 hr 45 min 55 sec), London, UK (2 hr 48 min 45 sec), and Boston, USA (2 hr 47 min 51 sec).

★ SHORTEST DURATION TO COMPLETE A MARATHON ON EACH CONTINENT (WOMEN)

Amie Dworecki (USA) is the fastest woman to have completed a marathon on each continent, in 523 days, from February 25, 2002, to August 2, 2003.

The ★**youngest person to have completed a marathon on each continent** is Mark Sinclair (UK). He completed the feat on March 26, 2005, at the age of 24 years 356 days.

MOST MARATHONS RUN

From 1974 to December 31, 2004, Horst Preisler (Germany) ran 1,305 races of 26 miles 385 yd (42.195 km) or longer.

MOST MARATHON RUNNERS

A total of 36,562 runners finished out of 37,257 starters in the New York Marathon (USA) on November 7, 2004.

HIGHEST MARATHON

The Everest Marathon begins at Gorak Shep (17,100 ft; 5,212 m) and ends at Namche Bazar (11,300 ft; 3,444 m). The fastest times to complete this race are: (men) 3 hr 50 min 23 sec by Hari Roka (Nepal) in 2000, and (women) 5 hr 16 min 3 sec by Anne Stentiford (UK) in 1997.

MARATHON ACHIEVEMENTS

WAYS TO RUN MARATHON	TIME	NAME/COUNTRY	DATE
Three-legged	3:40:16	Nick and Alastair Benbow (UK)	Apr. 26, 1998
Backwards	3:43:39	Xu Zhenjun (China)	Oct. 17, 2004
Carrying a 112-lb (50.8-kg) coalbag	8:26:00	Brian Newton (UK)	May 27, 1983
Joggling three objects	3:07:48	Michal Kapral (Canada)	Sep. 25, 2005
Flipping a pancake	3:02:27	Mike Cuzzacrea (USA)	Oct. 24, 1999
Dressed as a waiter (with open bottle of mineral water on tray)	2:47:00	Roger Bourban (Switzerland)	May 9, 1982
Skipping (without a rope)	5:55:13	Ashrita Furman (USA)	Aug. 31, 2003

SYDNEY 97

2:00:32

← ★ MOST TRIATHLONS WON (WOMEN)

The most wins in the women's triathlon World Championships is two by Michellie Jones (Australia) in 1992 and 1993, Karen Smyers (USA) in 1990 and 1995, and Emma Carney (Australia, pictured in each discipline) in 1994 and 1997. Michellie Jones has won the most medals: two gold medals, two silver, and three bronze.

HALF MARATHONS

★ FASTEST HALF MARATHON

Haile Gebrselassie (Ethiopia) ran the world's fastest half marathon in a time of 58 min 55 sec at the Arizona Marathon and Half Marathon in Phoenix, Arizona, USA, on January 15, 2006. During this race he also broke the world record for the ★ **fastest 20 km road race**, with a time of 55 min 48 sec.

MOST INDIVIDUAL MEDALS AT THE HALF MARATHON WORLD CHAMPIONSHIPS

Between 1996 and 2000, Lidia Simon-Slavuteanu (Romania) won eight medals at the IAAF Half Marathon World Championships: three team gold, one team silver, one individual silver, and three individual bronze. The men's record is held by Jifar Tesfaye (Ethiopia), who won seven medals from 1999 to 2002: one team gold, two team silver, one individual silver, one team bronze, and two individual bronze.

MOST INDIVIDUAL WINS AT THE HALF MARATHON WORLD CHAMPIONSHIPS

The greatest number of individual wins at the IAAF Half Marathon World Championships is three. The record is shared by Tegla Loroupe (Kenya) for wins in 1997, 1998, and 1999, and Paula Radcliffe (UK), for wins in 2000, 2001, and 2003.

MOST TEAM WINS AT THE HALF MARATHON WORLD CHAMPIONSHIPS

Kenya's men's team have recorded eight wins at the IAAF Half Marathon World Championships in 1992–95, 1997, 2000, 2002, and 2004. The women's record is six, held by Romania for wins in 1993–97 and 2000.

LARGEST HALF MARATHON

On October 22, 2000, the BUPA Great North Run, between Newcastle-upon-Tyne and South Shields, Tyne and Wear, UK, had 36,822 finishers out of 50,173 entries.

★ FASTEST BACKWARDS-RUN HALF MARATHON (WOMEN)

Paula Mairer (Austria) ran a half marathon backwards in a time of 2 hr 49 min 48 sec in Austria on October 10, 2004.

? DID YOU KNOW?

Why do you think the marathon distance is set at 26 miles 385 yd? This distance was first run at the 1908 Olympic Games, based in London, and was calculated so that the race could begin at Windsor Castle and end in front of the Royal Box in the Olympic arena. This was not accepted as the official distance for marathons by the International Association of Athletics Federations (IAAF) until 1921, however.

FASTEST ➡
20 KM RACE WALK (WOMEN)

Olimpiada Ivanova (Russia) holds the world record for the women's 20 km road race walk, achieved in a time of 1 hr 25 min 41 sec at the 10th IAAF World Athletics Championships in Helsinki, Finland, on August 7, 2005.

AUTO SPORTS

FIRST ↑ INDY 500 WINNER

On May 30, 1911, Ray Harroun (USA), driving the *Marmon Wasp*, won the inaugural Indianapolis 500 race (a.k.a. the Indy 500) – initially known as the "International Sweepstakes" – at an average speed of 74.6 mph (120 km/h).

★ HIGHEST SEASON EARNINGS (NASCAR)

Tony Stewart (USA) set a record for the most money won in a single season with over $13 million in winnings for 2005.

DRAG RACING

★ FIRST FEMALE DRIVER IN FINAL ROUND (PRO STOCK)

Erica Enders (USA) became the first female Pro Stock driver in National Hot Rod Association (NHRA) history to advance to a final round, which she did at the Ameriquest Mortgage Nationals in Chicago, Illinois, USA, in October 2005. She lost in the final round to Jason Line (USA).

★ FIRST TOP FUEL DRAGSTER TO BREAK 300 MPH

Kenny Bernstein (USA) made history in his Budweiser King Top Fuel dragster by breaking the 300 mph (482.8 km/h) barrier – with a speed of 301.70 mph (485.5 km/h) – while competing in a qualifying heat at the NHRA's Gatornationals on March 20, 1992.

★ OLDEST WINNING PRO STOCK DRIVER

Warren Johnson (USA, b. July 7, 1943) became the oldest driver to win a POWERade Series event. He won three events in 2005, the last at the Mopar Mile-High Nationals in Denver, Colorado, USA, aged 62 years 9 days.

LOWEST ELAPSED TIME IN A TOP FUEL DRAGSTER

The ★ lowest elapsed time to cover 440 yd in a Top Fuel dragster by a man is 4.437 seconds by Anthony Schumacher (USA) in Chicago, Illinois, USA, on October 1, 2005.

The ★ lowest elapsed time to cover 440 yd in a Top Fuel dragster by a woman is 4.458 seconds by Melanie Troxel (USA) at the Texas Motorplex in Dallas, Texas, USA, in October 2005.

★ MOST CONSECUTIVE TOP FUEL DRAG-RACING WINS

Anthony Schumacher (USA), who drives the US Army dragster (see p.225), set an NHRA record by winning five consecutive races.

Schumacher also holds the record for reaching the ★ most consecutive final rounds (7) and for ★ winning the most consecutive rounds (20) in Top Fuel drag racing. All of his records were set in the 2005 season, and his winning streaks are active entering the 2006 season.

★ MOST FUNNY CAR DRAG-RACING CHAMPIONSHIPS ↑

The most National Hot Rod Association championships won in the Funny Car category is 13 by John Force (USA) in 1990–91, 1993–2002, and 2004. At Yorba Linda, California, USA, on March 10, 2004, Force reached a terminal velocity of 333.58 mph (536.84 km/h) from a standing start, the **fastest speed in a Funny Car**.

FORMULA ONE

★ MOST "FASTEST LAPS" IN A CAREER

The most "fastest laps" by one driver in a Formula One career is 69 by Michael Schumacher (Germany) between 1991 and 2005. He also holds the record for ★ **most grand prix wins by a driver**, with 84 between 1991 and 2005, as well as the ★ **most points scored in an F1 career**, with 1,248.

For more Schumacher records, see Formula One – At A Glance on p.223.

★ FIRST WOMAN TO LEAD THE INDIANAPOLIS 500

Danica Patrick (USA) made history by becoming the first woman to lead the Indianapolis 500, leading three times for 19 laps in May 2005. Patrick, the fourth woman to compete in the Indianapolis 500, started the race fourth and finished fourth – the highest start and finish by any woman in the history of the event.

YOUNGEST DRIVER TO CLAIM A WORLD CHAMPIONSHIP POINT

Jenson Button (UK, b. January 19, 1980) was aged 20 years 67 days when he finished in sixth place in the Brazilian Grand Prix on March 26, 2000.

★ MOST GRAND PRIX WINS BY A MANUFACTURER

Ferrari (Italy) had 183 wins between 1961 and 2005.

MOST GRAND PRIX RACES WITHOUT A VICTORY

Between 1980 and 1994, Andrea de Cesaris (Italy) competed in 208 Formula One races without a win.

MOST SUCCESSFUL GRAND PRIX FAMILY

Graham Hill (UK) was World Drivers Champion in 1962 and 1968 and runner-up three times. His son Damon became World Drivers Champion on October 13, 1996.

DRIFTING

★ MOST D1 DRIFT SERIES IRL CHAMPIONSHIPS WON

The drifting D1 Drift Series IRL Championship has been contested on two occasions, both won by Damian Mulvey (Ireland) in 2004 and 2005.

★ MOST SUCCESSFUL CAR IN D1 GRANDS PRIX

The drifting D1 Grand Prix has been held every year since 2001 and has been won by five different drivers. Three drivers – Nobuteru Taniguchi in 2001, Miki Ryuji in 2004, and Kazama Yasuyuki in 2005 (all Japan) – drove the Nissan S15 Silvia.

INDYCAR

★ MOST INDY 500 WINS BY AN OWNER

Roger Penske (USA) is the team owner of 13 Indianapolis 500 winners, entering the 2006 season. His most recent triumph was on May 25, 2003, when Gil de Ferran (Brazil) won the 87th Indy 500 race by 0.2990 of a second – the third-closest finish in 500 history – over Team Penske team mate Helio Castroneves (Brazil). With Tony Kanaan (Brazil) finishing third only 1.2475 seconds behind, it was the closest 1-2-3 finish in the race's history.

★ MOST INDY 500 POLE POSITION WINS

Rick Mears (USA) has had six pole position wins, in 1979, 1982, 1986, 1988, 1989, and 1991.

★ CLOSEST MARGIN OF VICTORY IN THE INDY 500

Al Unser Jr. beat Scott Goodyear (both USA) in the closest finish in the history of the Indy 500 race on May 24, 1992. The margin was 0.043 of a second.

★ OLDEST INDY 500 WINNER

Al Unser (USA) was 47 years 360 days old when he won the 71st Indianapolis 500 on May 24, 1987.

The ★ **youngest winner** is Troy Ruttman (USA), who was 22 years 80 days old when he won the 36th Indianapolis 500 on May 30, 1952.

FORMULA ONE – AT A GLANCE

RECORD	NO.	WHO	DATES
Most wins (constructor)	183	Ferrari (Italy)	1961–2005
Most wins (driver)	84	Michael Schumacher (Germany)	1991–2005
Most wins in a season (driver)	13	Michael Schumacher	2004
Most points in a season (driver)	148	Michael Schumacher	2004
Most points in a season (const.)	262	Ferrari (Italy)	2004
Most starts in a career	256	Riccardo Patrese (Italy)	1977–93
Most consecutive victories	9	Alberto Ascari (Italy)	1952–53
Most consecutive victories of the same Grand Prix	5	Ayrton Senna (Brazil)	1989–93
Most races without a victory	208	Andrea de Cesaris (Italy)	1991–2004

★ NEW RECORD
★ UPDATED RECORD

★ YOUNGEST FORMULA ONE WORLD CHAMPION

The youngest driver to win a Formula One World Championship is Fernando Alonso (Spain, b. July 29, 1981), who won his first title on September 25, 2005, in Interlagos, Brazil, aged 24 years and 59 days.

Alonso also became the **youngest driver to win a Formula One World Championship race**, at the age of 22 years 26 days, when he won the Hungarian Grand Prix on August 24, 2003, driving for Renault.

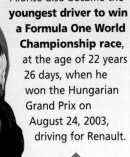

AUTO SPORTS

★ YOUNGEST
WORLD CHAMPIONSHIP RALLY DRIVER

The youngest driver to compete in a Fédération Internationale de l'Automobile (FIA) World Championship Rally is Jari-Matti Latvala (Finland), who was 18 years 61 days old when he drove in the 50th Rally Acropolis, Athens, Greece, from June 6 to 8, 2003.

★ NEW RECORD
★ UPDATED RECORD

★ YOUNGEST DRIVER TO WIN A NASCAR RACE

On September 4, 2005, Kyle Busch (USA, b. May 2, 1985) became the youngest driver to win a NASCAR NEXTEL Cup Series event.

Aged 20 years 125 days, Busch only just beat the record set by Donald Thomas (USA), who was four days older when he won at Atlanta in November 1952.

★ FIRST DRIVER TO WIN THE INDYCAR CHAMPIONSHIP AND THE INDY 500 IN THE SAME SEASON

In an unprecedented feat in 2005, Dan Wheldon (UK) won the Indy Racing League IndyCar Series Championship and the Indianapolis 500 in the same season.

MOST CHAMPIONSHIP TITLES

The most wins in the national championship – currently the FedEx Series Championship; formerly the AAA (American Automobile Association, 1909–55), USAC (US Auto Club, 1956–78), CART (Championship Auto Racing Teams, 1979–91), and IndyCar (1992–97) – is seven by A. J. Foyt (USA) in 1960–61, 1963–64, 1967, 1975, and 1979.

★ FIRST CHAMPIONSHIP WIN BY A ROOKIE

Nigel Mansell (UK) made history in 1993 by becoming the first rookie to win the IndyCar Championship.

Mansell was also the 1992 Formula One World Driving Champion, making him the **★ first driver to win both titles in consecutive seasons**.

★ MOST LEAGUE CHAMPIONSHIP WINS

Sam Hornish Jr. (USA) won the IRL Championship twice, in 2001–02.

NASCAR

★ CLOSEST MARGIN OF VICTORY

NASCAR is the National Association for Stock Car Auto Racing. Ricky Craven beat Kurt Busch (both USA) by 0.002 seconds to win the closest finish in a NASCAR race, at Darlington Raceway, in Darlington, South Carolina, USA, on March 16, 2003.

★ FIRST DRIVER TO WIN THREE SERIES RACES AT THE SAME TRACK

Bobby Labonte (USA) won his first career NASCAR Craftsman Series race at Martinsville Speedway in Virginia, USA, on April 11, 2005. With that victory, Labonte became the first driver to win all three major NASCAR series (truck, Busch, and Nextel Cup series races) at the same speedway.

Bobby and Terry Labonte (also USA) became the **first siblings to win the NASCAR Winston Cup Championship**. Bobby won in 2000, while his brother Terry had won in 1984 and 1996.

Bobby Labonte is also the **first driver to win the NASCAR Busch Series and NASCAR Winston Cup titles** during his career.

★ MOST INDYCAR VICTORIES IN A CAREER

A. J. Foyt (USA) won a total of 67 IndyCar races during his career, from 1960 to 1994.

Foyt also won the **★ most IndyCar driving championships in a career**, with seven, and holds the world record for the **★ most Indianapolis 500 starts**, with 35 between 1958 and 1992.

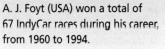

FASTEST SPEED TOP FUEL NHRA DRAG RACING

The highest terminal velocity at the end of a 440-yard run by a Top Fuel drag racer is 336.15 mph (540.98 km/h). The record was set by Anthony Schumacher (USA) in Hebron, Ohio, USA, on May 25, 2005, in a Hadman RED dragster.

★ MOST SOUTHERN 500 RACE VICTORIES

The most wins at the Southern 500, the oldest race in the NASCAR series, is five, a record shared by Cale Yarborough (USA) in 1968, 1973–74, 1978, and 1982; and Jeff Gordon (USA) in 1995–98 and 2002.

RALLYING

★ MOST INDIVIDUAL MONTE CARLO RALLY WINS BY A DRIVER

Three drivers have won the Monte Carlo Rally four times. The record is shared by: Sandro Munari (Italy), winner in 1972, 1975, 1976, and 1977 driving a Lancia; Walter Röhrl (with co-driver Christian Geistdorfer, both West Germany), winner in 1980, 1982–84, each time in a different car; and Tommi Mäkinen (with co-driver Risto Mannisenmäki, both Finland) winner in 1999–2001 (in a Mitsubishi) and 2002 (in a Subaru).

MOST DAKAR RALLY WINS

Ari Vatanen (Finland) has won the Dakar Rally four times, the **most**

Dakar Rally wins by an individual. His first victory was in 1987 and he went on to win in three consecutive years, 1989–91.

The ★**most wins of the Dakar Rally car category by a manufacturer** is 10 by Mitsubishi (Japan) between 1985 and 2005.

MOST DAKAR RALLY BIKE CATEGORY WINS

The greatest number of wins in the bike category of the Dakar Rally is six by Stéphane Peterhansel (France) in 1991–93, 1995, and 1997–98.

MOST CONSECUTIVE WORLD RALLY CHAMPIONSHIP TITLES

Tommi Mäkinen (Finland) won four consecutive World Rally Championship titles from 1996 to 1999.

YOUNGEST WORLD RALLY CHAMPION

Colin McRae (UK, b. August 5, 1968) was 27 years 89 days old when he won the title of World Rally Champion in 1995.

★ MOST WINS IN THE GUMBALL 3000

The greatest number of times the Gumball 3000 rally has been won by an individual is twice by Kim Schmitz (Germany) in 2001, driving a Mercedes Brabus EV12 Megacar, and 2004, driving a Mercedes CL3000. First staged in 1999, the Gumball 3000 rally is a private race that takes place each year on public roads.

★ CLOSEST CHAMPIONSHIP CHASE (FUNNY CAR, NHRA DRAG RACING)

Gary Scelzi (USA) won the 2005 POWERade world championship title by eight points over Ron Capps (USA) in the closest margin of victory for a Funny Car world champion in NHRA history.

LONGEST RALLY

The longest ever rally was the Singapore Airlines London–Sydney Rally over 19,329 miles (31,107 km) starting from Covent Garden, London, UK, on August 14, 1977, and finishing at Sydney Opera House, Australia, on September 28, 1977. The winning team comprised Andrew Cowan, Colin Malkin, and Michael Broad (all UK), who drove a Mercedes 280E.

Pictured is the German team driving its Trabant 601R in Kenya's Ulu region on December 17, 2003.

BALL SPORTS

← ★ MOST AFL MATCHES AS CAPTAIN

The most consecutive Australian Football League matches played as captain is 226 by Stephen Kernahan (Australia), playing for Carlton from 1986 to 1997. Stephen is pictured holding the 1995 AFL Premiership Cup – one of 16 cups Carlton has won – during the Farewell Game Breakfast Launch on May 16, 2005, in Melbourne, Australia.

★ MOST TIMES AS A LEADING GOAL-KICKER IN A SEASON

Dick Lee (Australia) was the leading goal-kicker in an AFL season a total of 10 times, playing for Collingwood between 1907 and 1921.

★ MOST FINALS GAMES WON

Essendon has played in 126 finals games (only Collingwood has played in more, with a record 157) and won 69 of them; however, the team to win the ★ **most grand finals** is Carlton, with 16 wins out of 29.

★ NEW RECORD
★ UPDATED RECORD

★ TALLEST AFL PLAYER

The tallest player to feature in the Australian Football League is Aaron Sandilands (Australia) at 6 ft 9 in (2.11 m) tall, playing for Fremantle from 2003 to 2005.

★ FASTEST WOMEN'S SOFTBALL PITCH

The fastest softball pitch is 68.9 mph (111 km/h) achieved by Zara Mee (Australia) on the set of *Guinness World Records* at Seven Network Studios, Sydney, New South Wales, Australia, on May 8, 2005.

★ MOST INTERNATIONAL NETBALL APPEARANCES

Irene van Dyk (New Zealand) made a record 129 appearances at international level playing for South Africa and New Zealand between 1994 and 2005.

★ MOST CONSECUTIVE WATER POLO PASSES

The record for the most consecutive passes between two water polo players is 42. It was set by Maxime Lepinoy and Nicholas Britto (both France) on the set of *L'Été De Tous Les Records* in Soulac, France, on August 16, 2005.

★ MOST KORFBALL WORLD GAMES TITLES WON

First held as part of the World Games in 1985, the most titles won is six (every occasion the event has been held) by the Netherlands, in 1985, 1989, 1993, 1997, 2001, and 2005.

AUSTRALIAN FOOTBALL (AFL)

★ MOST CONSECUTIVE MATCHES KICKING GOALS

Peter McKenna (Australia) kicked at least one goal in each of 120 consecutive matches playing for Collingwood from 1968 to 1974.

★ MOST GOALS IN A CAREER

Tony Lockett (Australia) scored 1,360 goals playing for St. Kilda and the Sydney Swans from 1983 to 1999.

★ MOST INTERNATIONAL RULES SERIES WINS ➡

The International Rules Series has been contested every year since 1998 and has been won on four occasions by both Australia (2000, 2002, 2003, and 2005) and Ireland (1998, 1999, 2001, and 2004). The teams play each other over two matches in a hybrid game featuring elements of Australian rules and Gaelic soccer; the team with the highest aggregate score wins.

★MOST WOMEN'S HANDBALL EUROPEAN LEAGUE WINS

Norway has won three European league titles, in 1994, 1996, and 2002. Pictured are Norway's Karoline Breivang (left), Randi Gustad (center), and Gro Hammerseng (right), with Russia's Ludmyla Bodnieva (kneeling) during the sixth Women's European Handball Championships on December 14, 2004.

CANADIAN FOOTBALL (CFL)

★LONGEST KICKOFF RETURN IN A GREY CUP FINAL

The longest kickoff return in a Grey Cup final is 96 yd (288 ft; 87.7 m) by Tony Tompkins (USA) playing for the Edmonton Eskimos against the Montreal Alouettes on November 27, 2005. The Eskimos went on to win the match 38–35.

★MOST CONSECUTIVE GREY CUP FINAL DEFEATS

Between 1928 and 1932, the Saskatchewan Roughriders (then known as Regina) lost five consecutive Grey Cup finals. Overall, they were outscored 102–15 during the course of these finals.

FIELD HOCKEY

★MOST MEN'S WORLD CUP WINS

The Pakistan men's team has won the field hockey World Cup a record four times, in 1971, 1978, 1982, and 1994.

★MOST WOMEN'S WORLD CUP WINS

The most wins of the field hockey World Cup by a women's team is five by the Netherlands, in 1974, 1978, 1983, 1986, and 1990.

MOST INTERNATIONAL GOALS SCORED BY AN INDIVIDUAL

The greatest number of goals scored in international field hockey is 274 by Sohail Abbas (Pakistan) between 1998 and 2004.

FOOTBAG

★MOST CONSECUTIVE DIVING BUTTERFLIES

The record for the most consecutive "diving butterfly" moves with a footbag is 35. The feat was achieved by Vasek Klouda (Czech Republic) on the set of *L'Été De Tous Les Records* at Argelès-Gazost, France, on July 6, 2005.

★MOST CONSECUTIVE ECLIPSES

The record for the most consecutive eclipses completed with a footbag is 26, set by Alex Zerbe (USA) on the set of *L'Été De Tous Les Records* in Biscarrosse, France, on June 30, 2004.

HANDBALL

★MOST EUROPEAN CUP TITLES WON (MEN)

The most wins of the Champions League is seven by Barcelona (Spain) in 1991, from 1996 to 2000, and again in 2005.

★MOST MEN'S EUROPEAN CHAMPIONSHIPS

The most handball European Championships won by a men's team is four by Sweden in 1994, 1998, 2000, and 2002.

★ MOST OLYMPIC TITLES (WOMEN)

Denmark has won three Olympic women's handball gold medals, in 1996, 2000, and 2004.

MOST ALL-IRELAND FINAL HURLING WINS

The greatest number of All-Ireland Championships won by one team is 30 by Cork between 1890 and 2005. Pictured is Cork goal scorer Ben O'Connor (Ireland) celebrating his side's victory over Galway in the All-Ireland Hurling final on September 11, 2005.

BALL SPORTS

★ MOST →
POINTS SCORED IN A SINGLE LACROSSE GAME

The most points scored by a winning team in a single Major League Lacrosse (MLL) game is 31 when, on June 12, 2005, the Baltimore Bayhawks (pictured) beat the Philadelphia Barrage by 22 goals. The final score was 31–9 in favor of the Baltimore team.

? DID YOU KNOW?

The Major League Lacrosse (MLL) is a professional US lacrosse organization formed in 2001. It has six teams: Baltimore Bayhawks, Boston Cannons, Long Island Lizards, New Jersey Pride, Rochester Rattlers, and Philadelphia Barrage.

★ MOST NETBALL COMMONWEALTH BANK TROPHY WINS

The most wins of the Commonwealth Bank Trophy is five by the Melbourne Phoenix (Australia), in 1997, 1999, 2002–03, and 2005. This competition is the elite national tournament in Australian netball. Pictured are Melbourne's Liz Boniello (left) and Eloise Sothby.

HURLING
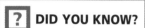

★ MOST ALL-IRELAND FINAL REPLAYS

In 1931, Cork took three games to beat Kilkenny in the All-Ireland Hurling final.

★ MOST ALL-IRELAND FINAL DEFEATS

The greatest number of All-Ireland Championships lost by one team is 24 by Kilkenny, between 1893 and 2004.

LONGEST HIT

The greatest distance for a "lift-and-stroke" hit is 387 ft 2 in (118 m), credited to Tom Murphy of Three Castles, Kilkenny, Ireland, in 1906.

LARGEST ATTENDANCE

A crowd of 84,865 watched the final between Wexford and Cork at Croke Park, Dublin, Ireland, in 1954.

LACROSSE

★ MOST MAJOR LEAGUE LACROSSE TITLES

The most MLL titles won by a team is two, by the Long Island Lizards (USA) in 2001 and 2003 and the Baltimore Bayhawks (USA) in 2002 and 2005.

★ MOST MANN CUP WINS

The Mann Cup is awarded to the senior men's lacrosse champions of Canada. The New Westminster Salmonbellies won the cup 24 times between 1908 and 1991.

★ MOST POINTS SCORED IN A MAJOR LEAGUE CAREER

Two players have scored 305 points in an MLL career: Mark Millon (USA) playing for the Baltimore Bayhawks and the Boston Cannons; and Casey Powell (USA) playing for the Long Island Lizards and the Rochester Rattlers, both in 2001–05.

★ MOST GOALS SCORED IN A MAJOR LEAGUE CAREER

The most goals scored in an MLL career is 206 by Mark Millon (USA) of the Baltimore Bayhawks and the Boston Cannons in 2001–05.

★ MOST WOMEN'S WORLD CUP WINS

The USA has won the International Federation of Women's Lacrosse Associations World Cup five times – 1982, 1989, 1993, 1997, and 2001.

LONGEST THROW

The longest recorded lacrosse throw is 162.86 yd by Barnet Quinn of Ottawa, Canada, on September 10, 1892.

HIGHEST SCORE (MEN)

Scotland beat Germany 34–3 in Manchester, UK, on July 25, 1994. In the World Cup Premier Division, the record score is the USA's 33–2 win over Japan in Manchester, UK, on July 21, 1994.

HIGHEST SCORE (WOMEN)

The highest score by an international team was by Great Britain and Ireland with a 40–0 defeat of Long Island (USA) on a 1967 tour of the USA.

MOST INDOOR WORLD CHAMPIONSHIP WINS

The inaugural indoor lacrosse World Championships held in Ontario, Canada, in 2003 were won by Canada, who were undefeated.

★ MOST MEN'S CHAMPIONS LEAGUE TITLES

The most volleyball Champions League titles won by a single team is 13 by CSKA Moscow (USSR) between 1959 and 1991. The volleyball Champions League features the best club teams in Europe and is played yearly.

★ MOST SPIKES IN ONE MINUTE

The most volleyball spikes in one minute completed by a team of four is nine and was set by Stephane Mathurin, Denis Damel, Sebastien Le Bosse, and Stephane Faure (all France) on the set of *L'Été De Tous Les Records* in Soulac, France, on August 15, 2005.

MOST OLYMPIC GAMES MEDALS (MEN)

Three men share this record: Yuriy Mikhailovich Poyarkov (USSR), who won gold medals in 1964 and 1968 and a bronze in 1972; Katsutoshi Nekoda (Japan), who won gold in 1972, silver in 1968, and bronze in 1964; and Steve Timmons (USA), who won gold in 1984 and 1988 and bronze in 1992.

★ MOST VOLLEYBALL WORLD LEAGUE TITLES (MEN)

The most World League gold medals won by a national team is eight by Italy (pictured in white) between 1990 and 2000.

★ MOST BEACH VOLLEYBALL TITLES (WOMEN)

The most beach volleyball tournament titles won by an individual female player is 72 by Holly McPeak (USA) between 1993 and 2005. McPeak won the titles with different partners: Angela Rock, Cammy Ciarelli, Linda Chisholm, Nancy Reno, Lisa Arce, Misty May, and Elaine Youngs. Her current playing partner is Nicole Branagh.

★ HIGHEST ⬆ BEACH VOLLEYBALL CAREER EARNINGS

Karch Kiraly (USA) has won a record $3,076,023 in official AVP Tour earnings through to the end of the 2005 season. Karch also holds the **most AVP tour titles**, with 144 between 1979 and 2005.

VOLLEYBALL (BEACH)

★ MOST CONSECUTIVE PASSES

A total of 49 consecutive passes, one pass per person, were performed on the set of *L'Été De Tous Les Records* in Soulac, France, on August 18, 2005.

★ MOST OLYMPIC WINS (MEN)

Beach volleyball has been part of the Olympic Games since 1996, and the USA has won the men's competition on two occasions: by Karch Kiraly and Kent Steffes in Atlanta in 1996; and Dain Balanton and Eric Fonoimoana in Sydney 2000. The Brazilian pair of Ricardo Alex Santos and Emanuel Rego won the gold medal in 2004.

★ MOST MEN'S WORLD CHAMPIONSHIPS

The World Championships were first staged for both men and women in 1997. The Brazil men's pair has won the title four times, in 1997, 1999, 2003, and 2005.

★ MOST PRIZE MONEY FOR A WORLD TOUR

The most prize money for a Federation Internationale de Volleyball beach volleyball World Tour was $7.28 million in 2005.

VOLLEYBALL

★ MOST NATIONAL CHAMPIONSHIPS

The Changos de Naranjito team in the Puerto Rico Men's Volleyball National League won 20 titles between 1958 and 2004.

★ MOST MEN'S EUROPEAN CHAMPIONSHIPS WINS

The most wins of the volleyball European Championships by a men's team is 12 by the USSR between 1950 and 1992.

★ NEW RECORD
UPDATED RECORD

BASKETBALL

★ NEW RECORD
★ UPDATED RECORD

★ MOST GAMES PLAYED BY A WOMAN (CAREER)

Vickie Johnson (USA) played 282 games for New York Liberty during her Women's National Basketball Association (WNBA) career between 1997 and 2005.

! X-REF

Baseball is affectionately known as "America's national pastime." For record-breaking stats and facts from this much-loved sport, simply turn the page.

NBA

★ MOST FIELD GOALS IN A CAREER

The greatest number of field goals scored by an individual player in a National Basketball Association (NBA) career is 15,837 by Kareem Abdul-Jabbar (USA) playing for the Milwaukee Bucks and the Los Angeles Lakers, from 1969 to 1989.

★ FIRST ROOKIE TO WIN A SIXTH MAN AWARD

Ben Gordon (USA) of the Chicago Bulls is the first-ever rookie to win the NBA Sixth Man Award, honoring the league's top player in a reserve role. Gordon appeared in all 82 regular season games of the 2004/05 season, coming off the bench in 79 of them to average 15.1 points, 2.6 rebounds, and 2.0 assists per game.

★ FEWEST POINTS SCORED BY A TEAM IN A HALF

The New Orleans Hornets scored just 16 points in the second half of a 89–67 loss to the Los Angeles Clippers in Los Angeles, California, USA, on March 1, 2006. The Hornets missed 21 shots in a row during one stretch and converted only 5 field goals in 34 attempts overall.

★ MOST FATHER VS. SON MATCHES

Up to and including January 2006, Mike Dunleavy Sr. (USA), coaching the Los Angeles Clippers, had faced his son Mike Dunleavy Jr. (USA), of the Golden State Warriors, in a total of 11 games, the greatest number of times in NBA history that a father coaching one team has faced his son playing for another team.

★ MOST PLAYOFF GAMES WON BY A COACH

Phil Jackson (USA) has won 175 playoff games as coach of the Chicago Bulls (1989–97) and Los Angeles Lakers (1999–2003, 2005 to present). Pat Riley (USA) is second with 155 post-season wins as coach of the Lakers (1981–89), New York Knicks (1991–94), and Miami Heat (1995–2002, 2005 to present).

★ MOST ➡ THREE-POINT FIELD GOALS IN AN NBA CAREER

Reggie Miller (USA) scored a total of 2,560 three-point field goals for the Indiana Pacers between 1987 and 2005, a career record for an NBA player.

★ MOST POINTS SCORED BY AN INDIVIDUAL IN AN OVERTIME PERIOD

Earl Boykins (USA) of the Denver Nuggets scored 15 points in a 5-minute overtime period on January 19, 2005, against the Seattle Supersonics in Seattle, Washington, USA. His feat topped the previous best of 14 points set by Butch Carter (USA) of the Indiana Pacers against the Boston Celtics on March 20, 1984.

★ YOUNGEST INDIVIDUAL TO WIN MOST VALUABLE PLAYER AWARD OF THE ALL-STAR GAME

Aged 21 years 51 days, LeBron James (USA) became the youngest Most Valuable Player award winner in the NBA All-Star Game. He scored 29 points and sparked a second-half comeback as the Eastern Conference rallied for a 122–120 victory over the Western Conference, in Houston, Texas, USA, on February 19, 2006.

RECORD-BREAKING BASKETBALL ACHIEVEMENTS

RECORD	DISTANCE	NAME/COUNTRY
Highest slam dunk	12 ft (3.65 m)	Michael Wilson (USA)
★ Farthest front flip slam dunk (trampoline)	15 ft 1 in (4.6 m)	Matej Tomšic (Slovenia)
Farthest slam dunk (trampoline)	20 ft 4 in (6.2 m)	Jonathon Thibout (France)
Farthest shot made with head	25 ft (7.62 m)	Eyal Horn (Israel)
Longest goal shot by a man (game)	90 ft 2 in (27.49 m)	Christopher Eddy (USA)
Longest goal shot by a woman (game)	81 ft 6 in (24.85 m)	Allyson Fasnacht (USA)
Longest goal shot (exhibition)	90 ft 6 in (27.6 m)	Ian McKinney (UK)
Farthest distance dribbled (24 hours)	108.41 miles (174.46 km)	Tyler Curiel (USA)

★ MOST DEFENSIVE PLAYER OF THE YEAR AWARDS

The 7-ft 2-in (2.18-m) shot-blocker extraordinaire Dikembe Mutombo (Democratic Republic of the Congo) won the NBA Defensive Player of the Year award four times, playing for the Atlanta Hawks (1995, 1997–98) and Philadelphia 76ers (2001).

★ MOST REGULAR SEASON GAMES BY A REFEREE

Dick Bavetta (USA) refereed 2,035 regular-season games (up to February 8, 2006), surpassing Jake O'Donnell's (USA) record for the most regular-season games in NBA history. Bavetta has never missed a day of work in his 31 years in the NBA.

★ YOUNGEST INDIVIDUAL TO SCORE 15,000 POINTS

Kobe Bryant (USA, b. August 23, 1978) scored his 15,000th point aged 27 years 136 days while playing for the Los Angeles Lakers against the Philadelphia 76ers on January 6, 2006.

← ★ YOUNGEST PLAYER TO SCORE 5,000 POINTS IN AN NBA CAREER

Aged 21 years 22 days, LeBron James (USA, b. December 30, 1984) scored 5,000 points while playing for the Cleveland Cavaliers (USA), including a 51-point tally against the Utah Jazz in Salt Lake City, Utah, USA, on January 21, 2006.

WNBA

★ HIGHEST POINT-SCORING AVERAGE

Cynthia Cooper (USA) scored 2,061 points in 124 games for the Houston Comets between 1997 and 2003, giving her a record point-scoring average of 21.0.

★ MOST ASSISTS

Ticha Penicheiro (USA) provided 1,591 assists in 240 games playing for the Sacramento Monarchs between 1998 and 2005.

★ MOST BLOCKS

Margo Dydeck (USA) achieved 726 blocks in 255 games playing for the Utah Starzz (1998–2002), the San Antonio Silver Stars (2003–04), and the Connecticut Sun (2005).

★ MOST CHAMPIONSHIP TITLES

The greatest number of championship titles won is four by the Houston Comets between 1997 and 2000.

★ MOST FIELD GOALS

Lisa Leslie (USA) scored 1,743 field goals playing for the Los Angeles Sparks between 1997 and 2005.

The ★ **most free throws in a WNBA career** is 1,137 in 273 games, also by Lisa Leslie playing for the Los Angeles Sparks from 1997 to 2005.

With an average of 17.3 points per game, Leslie scored 4,732 points playing for the Los Angeles Sparks – the ★ **most points scored in a WNBA career**.

Finally, the same player also won an unprecedented 2,540 rebounds playing for the same team between 1997 and 2005, giving her the record for the ★ **most rebounds in a WNBA career**.

★ MOST STEALS

The greatest number of steals in a WNBA career by an individual player is 520 in 228 games by Sheryl Swoopes (USA) playing for the Houston Comets between 1998 and 2005.

★ MOST THREE-POINT FIELD GOALS

Katie Smith (USA) scored 478 three-point field goals playing for the Minnesota Lynx from 1995 to 2005 and the Detroit Shock in 2005.

? DID YOU KNOW?

In the official leagues, men and women use basketballs of different sizes. The ball used by the NBA is 30 in (76 cm) in circumference. The WNBA use a smaller ball, with a circumference of 28.5 in (72.4 cm). Both leagues play on the same size court, however, which is 92 ft (28 m) long and 50 ft (15 m) wide.

★ MOST CHAMPIONSHIP TITLES WON BY A COACH

Two coaches have each won nine NBA championships: Red Auerbach (USA) with the Boston Celtics (1957, 1959–66), and Phil Jackson (USA, below) with the Chicago Bulls (1990–92, 1995–97) and Los Angeles Lakers (1999–2001).

BASEBALL

HIGHEST CUMULATIVE ATTENDANCE FOR A FRANCHISE ➡

The highest cumulative attendance for a baseball franchise is 169,374,364, a record held by the Los Angeles (formerly Brooklyn) Dodgers (USA) between 1901 and 2005. Pictured is Cezar Izturis (USA) of the Los Angeles Dodgers, autographing memorabilia.

★ MOST STRIKEOUTS BY A BATTER IN A MAJOR LEAGUE CAREER

Reggie Jackson (USA, below) struck out 2,597 during his MLB career, the most by an individual batter. He set the record between 1967 and 1987 playing for the Kansas City Chiefs, New York Yankees, Oakland Athletics, Baltimore Orioles, and California Angels.

★ FASTEST TIME TO VISIT ALL MAJOR LEAGUE STADIUMS
Michael Wenz and Jacob Lindhorst (both USA) visited every Major League Baseball stadium in just 29 days, from June 12 to July 10, 2005, and watched a complete game of baseball at all the grounds visited.

FASTEST PITCHER
Lynn Nolan Ryan (USA) pitched a ball at a speed of 100.9 mph (162.3 km/h) while playing for the California Angels at Anaheim Stadium, California, USA, on August 20, 1974.

He also pitched 5,714 strikeouts over his career from 1966 to 1993, the **most strikeouts in an MLB career**.

★ HIGHEST ATTENDANCE FOR A MAJOR LEAGUE SEASON
In 2005, Major League Baseball (MLB) saw an overall attendance of 73,070,631, the highest ever recorded for a single season. The average per game was 30,936.

HIGHEST BATTING AVERAGE IN A MAJOR LEAGUE SEASON
Playing for the San Francisco Giants in 2001, Barry Bonds (USA) recorded a batting average of .863 – the highest average for one player in a single season.

LARGEST CONTRACT FOR A CATCHER
In 1998, Mike Piazza (USA) signed a contract with the New York Mets that made him the world's most valuable catcher, earning a total salary of $91 million payable over a period of seven years. As well as his substantial income, Piazza also benefited from the use of a luxury box for all home games and luxury hotel suites while on the road playing away games.

LONGEST THROW BY A MAN
Glen Edward Gorbous (Canada) threw a distance of 445 ft 10 in (135.88 m) on August 1, 1957.

The **longest throw by a woman** is 295 ft 11 in (90.2 m) by Mildred Ella "Babe" Didrikson (USA) in Jersey City, New Jersey, USA, on July 25, 1931.

MOST...

★ AMERICAN LEAGUE PENNANTS
The New York Yankees won the American League pennant 39 times between 1921 and 2005.

★ BATTERS HIT BY A PITCHER IN A SEASON
Joe McGinnity (USA) hit a total of 40 batters while playing for the Brooklyn Dodgers in 1900, a Major League Baseball season record.

★ CONSECUTIVE WORLD SERIES VICTORIES
The New York Yankees won the World Series five times from 1949 to 1953, the most consecutive World Series wins by a single team.

★ CY YOUNG AWARDS
Awarded annually since 1956 to the most outstanding pitcher in the major leagues, the greatest number of Cy Young awards to one player is seven. The record is held by Roger Clemens (USA) playing for the Boston Red Sox (1986, 1987, 1991), Toronto Blue Jays (1997–98), New York Yankees (2001), and Houston Astros (2004).

★ WILD PITCHES IN A MAJOR LEAGUE SEASON
Playing for the Boston Braves in 1886, Bill Stemmeyer (USA) pitched 63 wild pitches, the most ever thrown by a pitcher in a Major League Baseball season.

★ MOST TEAM WINS IN THE WORLD CUP

Set up in 1938, the baseball World Cup is a tournament played by teams from countries as diverse as Spain, Puerto Rico, and South Korea. It has been won a record 24 times by Cuba (above): 1939–40, 1942–43, 1950, 1952–53, 1961, 1969–73, 1976, 1978, 1980, 1984, 1986, 1988, 1990, 1994, 1998, 2001, 2003, and 2005.

DURABLE ANNOUNCER

Ernest "Ernie" Harwell's (USA, b. January 25, 1918) 55-year career began in 1948 with the Brooklyn Dodgers, followed by the New York Giants (1951–53), Baltimore Orioles (1954–59), and Detroit Tigers (1960–2002). During his career, Harwell announced more than 8,300 Major League Baseball games.

NO-HIT GAMES

Lynn Nolan Ryan (USA) pitched seven no-hit games between 1973 and 1991.

STOLEN BASES IN A MAJOR LEAGUE SEASON

The most stolen bases in a season is 138 by Hugh Nicol (USA) playing for the Cincinnatti Reds in 1897.

GAMES PLAYED IN A CAREER

During his career, Peter Edward "Pete" Rose (USA) played an unprecedented 3,562 games for Cincinnati Reds (1963–78 and 1984–86), Philadelphia Phillies (1979–83), and Montreal Expos (1984).

GAMES PLAYED IN A SEASON

In 1962, Maury Wills (USA) played an unparalleled 165 games for the Los Angeles Dodgers.

★ GAMES LOST BY A PITCHER IN A SEASON

John Coleman (USA) lost a total of 48 games as a pitcher playing for the Philadelphia Phillies in 1883, a record for a Major League Baseball season.

★ GAMES SAVED BY A PITCHER IN A MAJOR LEAGUE SEASON

Playing for the Boston Braves in 1875, Al Spalding (USA) set a record of 54 games for the most games saved by a pitcher in a Major League Baseball season.

★ HOME RUNS ALLOWED BY A PITCHER IN A MAJOR LEAGUE CAREER

Playing for the Philadelphia Phillies, Baltimore Orioles, Houston Astros, and Chicago Cubs, Robin Roberts (USA) allowed 505 home runs, the most by an individual pitcher, in the course of his MLB career between 1948 and 1966.

★ MAJOR LEAGUE COMPLETE GAMES PITCHED

The pitcher with the most complete games pitched in a career is Denton True "Cy" Young (USA). From 1890 to 1911, he played 749 games for the Cleveland Spiders, St. Louis Cardinals, Boston Red Sox, Cleveland Indians, and Boston Braves.

MAJOR LEAGUE DOUBLES IN A CAREER

From 1907 to 1928, Tris Speaker (Philadelphia Phillies, Boston Red Sox, Washington Nationals, and Cleveland Indians) hit 792 doubles, the most in an MLB career.

MAJOR LEAGUE TRIPLES IN CAREER

From 1899 to 1917, Sam Crawford (Cincinnati Reds and Detroit Tigers) hit 309 triples.

★ MOST AT-BATS IN A MAJOR LEAGUE CAREER

Playing for the Cincinnati Reds, Philadelphia Phillies, and Montreal Expos between 1963 and 1986, Pete Rose (USA) was at-bat 14,053 times, the most at-bats in an MLB career by an individual player.

★ MOST JAPAN SERIES WINS

Played annually between the winners of the Central League and the Pacific League in Japan, the Japan Series was first staged in 1950 and has been won on 20 occasions by the Yomiuri Giants between 1951 and 2005. Koji Uehara (Japan) is pictured here pitching for the Giants.

★ NEW RECORD
★ UPDATED RECORD

COMBAT SPORTS

BOXING

LONGEST FIGHT

The longest world title fight (under Queensberry Rules) was between the lightweights Joe Gans (USA) and Oscar Matthew "Battling" Nelson (Denmark) in Goldfield, Nevada, USA, on September 3, 1906. It ended in the 42nd round when Gans was declared the winner on a foul.

LONGEST UNBEATEN RUN

Ricardo "Finito" López (Mexico) remained unbeaten throughout his professional career, with 50 wins and 1 draw from 51 fights over 17 years to March 2002.

MOST KNOCKDOWNS

Vic Toweel (South Africa) knocked down Danny O'Sullivan (UK) 14 times in 10 rounds in their world bantamweight fight in Johannesburg, South Africa, on December 2, 1950, before the latter retired.

★ MOST ⬆ WWE MEN'S CHAMPIONSHIPS

The most World Wrestling Entertainment (WWE) men's championships won by an individual is six by "Stone Cold" Steve Austin (USA) between 1998 and 2001. Stone Cold is pictured above, celebrating his defeat of The Rock (USA) on March 28, 1999.

YOUNGEST WORLD CHAMPION

Wilfred Benitez (USA, b. September 12, 1958) of Puerto Rico was 17 years 176 days old when he won the WBA light welterweight title in San Juan, Puerto Rico, on March 6, 1976.

★ MOST CONSECUTIVE WORLD SUPER-MIDDLEWEIGHT TITLE DEFENSES

The most consecutive successful defenses of this title is nine by Nigel Benn (UK) between 1992 and 1995.

★ MOST CONSECUTIVE WORLD FEATHERWEIGHT TITLE DEFENSES

Eusebio Pedroza (Panama) successfully defended his title 19 times between 1978 and 1985.

★ MOST CONSECUTIVE WORLD LIGHTWEIGHT TITLE DEFENSES

Roberto Duran (Panama) defended his title 12 times between 1972 and 1979.

MOST ROUNDS IN A FIGHT

Before the Queensberry Rules were introduced in 1867, Jack Jones defeated Patsy Tunney (both UK) in a boxing match that comprised 276 rounds in Cheshire, UK, in 1825. The fight lasted 4 hr 30 min.

⬅ ★ MOST WWE WOMEN'S CHAMPIONSHIPS

The most World Wrestling Entertainment women's championships won by an individual is six, by Trish Stratus (Canada) between 2001 and 2005.

★ TALLEST HEAVYWEIGHT CHAMPION EVER ⬆

The tallest World Boxing Association Heavyweight Champion is Nicolay Valuev (Russia), who measures 7 ft (2.13 m) tall and weighs 330 lb (150 kg). Nicknamed the "Beast of the East," Valuev fought 12 rounds to defeat 6-ft 2-in (1.8-m) John Ruiz (USA, above right) and claim the title on December 17, 2005, in Berlin, Germany.

MARTIAL ARTS

MOST THROWS IN AN HOUR

Dale Moore and Nigel Townsend (both UK) did 3,786 judo throws in an hour in London, UK, on February 23, 2002.

MOST PUNCHES IN AN HOUR

On October 22, 2005, Anthony Kelly (Australia) threw 11,557 martial-arts punches in one hour in Armidale, New South Wales, Australia. The feat was in aid of fellow GWR holder Danny Higginbotham, whose home was destroyed by Hurricane Katrina.

HIGHEST KICK

Jessie Frankson (USA) kicked a target with a pin attached, which in turn burst a balloon, at a height of 9 ft 8 in (2.94 m) on December 21, 2000.

MOST THROWS IN 10 HOURS

Csaba Mezei and Zoltán Farkas (both Hungary) completed 57,603 judo throws in a 10-hour period in Szany, Hungary, on May 1, 2003.

WRESTLING

LARGEST MONGOLIAN WRESTLING TOURNAMENT
A tournament held in Bayanwula, Xiwuzhumuqinqi, Inner Mongolia, China, between July 28 and August 1, 2004, featured 2,048 competitors.

★ MOST YUSHO WINS BY A SUMO WRESTLER
The most Yusho or Makuuchi Tournament wins by an individual sumo wrestler is 32 by Yokozuna Taiho (Japan) between 1961 and 1971.

MOST SUCCESSFUL SUMO BROTHERS
Ozeki Wakanohana was promoted to the rank of *yokozuna*, a rank held by his younger brother Takanohana (both Japan) since 1994, after winning the *Natsu* (summer) *Basho* in 1998.

LARGEST ATTENDANCE
The largest wrestling attendance was 190,000 at the Pyongyang Stadium, Pyongyang, North Korea, on April 29, 1995.

LONGEST REIGN
AS A WORLD HEAVYWEIGHT CHAMPION
Joe Louis (USA) was champion for 11 years 252 days from June 22, 1937, when he knocked out James Joseph Braddock (USA, a.k.a. "The Cinderella Man") in the eighth round in Chicago, Illinois, USA, until announcing his retirement on March 1, 1949. He defended his title a record 25 times.

★ NEW RECORD
☆ UPDATED RECORD

★ MOST ⬆
UFC WELTERWEIGHT CHAMPIONSHIPS
The greatest number of Ultimate Fighting Championship (UFC) welterweight titles won by an individual fighter is eight by Matt Hughes (USA, pictured above right) between 2001 and 2005.

ULTIMATE FIGHTING

★ LIGHTEST FIGHTER
The lightest fighter currently participating in the Ultimate Fighting Championship is Thiago "Pitbull" Alves (Brazil), whose lowest recorded fighting weight was 145 lb (65 kg).

★ HEAVIEST FIGHTER
The record for the heaviest UFC contestant is shared by three individuals – Sean Gannon, Gan McGee and Tim Sylvia (all USA). The three fighters each weigh in at 265 lb (120 kg).

★ MOST HEAVYWEIGHT CHAMPIONSHIPS
The most UFC heavyweight championship titles won by an individual fighter is five, by Randy Couture (USA) between 1997 and 2001. He has also won three light heavyweight championships.

★ MOST MIDDLEWEIGHT CHAMPIONSHIPS
The greatest number of Ultimate Fighting Championship middleweight championship titles won by an individual is five by mixed martial-arts fighter Frank Shamrock (USA) between 1997 and 1999.

★ TALLEST FIGHTER
The tallest fighter participating in the UFC is Gan McGee (USA), who measures 6 ft 8 in (2.04 m).

★ MOST UFC WINS ➡
Light heavyweights Randy "The Natural" Couture (USA) and Chuck "The Iceman" Liddell (USA, pictured right in blue shorts, fighting Brazilian Tito Ortiz) have both won 11 Ultimate Fighting Championships. Mixed martial artist Liddell has only ever lost two Ultimate Fighting Championships, while wrestler Couture has lost three.

CRICKET

? DID YOU KNOW?

After England's first defeat on home soil by Australia, in August 1882, a mock obituary appeared in The Sporting Times: "In Affectionate Remembrance of English Cricket, which died at the Oval on 29th August, 1882 [...] The body will be cremated and the ashes taken to Australia." Later, some bails – or a cricket ball – were burned, and the ashes placed in a small urn. This trophy – "The Ashes" – is still contested by the two sides.

★ MOST ONE-DAY INTERNATIONAL RUNS (CAREER)

Sachin Tendulkar (India) scored 14,146 runs (average 44.20) in 362 one-day international matches from 1989 to 2006.

TEST MATCHES

★ MOST RUNS SCORED
Brian Lara (Trinidad and Tobago) scored 11,124 runs in 294 Tests (at an average of 53.02) for the West Indies between 1990 and 2006.

★ FASTEST CENTURY
Viv Richards (Antigua) scored a century in 56 balls playing for the West Indies vs. England at St. John's, Antigua, from April 11 to 16, 1986.

★ MOST CENTURIES
Sachin Tendulkar (India) scored 35 centuries between 1989 and 2005.

★ MOST DOUBLE CENTURIES
The greatest number of innings of 200 runs or more is 12 by Sir Don Bradman (Australia) playing for Australia in 52 matches from 1928 to 1948. He also holds the record for the **highest batting average in Test cricket**, with an average of 99.94 in 52 Tests (6,996 runs in 80 innings) between 1928 and 1948.

★ MOST RUNS WITHOUT SCORING A CENTURY
Shane Warne (Australia) has scored a total of 2,908 runs

★ FASTEST ➡ TEST MATCH HALF-CENTURY

Jacques Kallis (South Africa) made a half-century from 24 balls by playing for South Africa against Zimbabwe at Newlands, Cape Town, South Africa, on March 4–5, 2005.

without making a century, from 1992 to the present. Warne has scored 11 half-centuries in that run total.

★ HIGHEST BATTING AVERAGE IN A LAST INNINGS
The highest batting average in the fourth innings of a Test match is 73.40 by Sir Don Bradman (Australia) in 52 matches from 1928 to 1948.

★ BEST BOWLING AVERAGE IN A LAST INNINGS
The best bowling average in the fourth innings of a Test match is 14.46 by Bishan Bedi (India), in 26 matches between 1966 and 1979.

★ MOST WICKETS
Shane Warne (Australia) is the leading Test match wicket-taker, with 670 wickets (average 25.16 runs per wicket) in 137 matches from August 1992 to March 2006.

★ BEST BOWLING AVERAGE
From 1886 to 1896, George Lohman (UK) averaged a strike rate of 10.75 for England, from at least 2,000 balls.

MOST MATCHES UMPIRED
Steve Bucknor (Jamaica) has officiated at a total of 110 Test matches between 1989 and 2006.

★ MOST INTERNATIONAL WICKETS
Muttiah Muralitharan (Sri Lanka) has taken over 1,000 international wickets. The off-spinner became the first to reach a four-figure aggregate from Test matches and one-dayers when he took his 1,000th wicket – that of Khaled Mashud (Bangladesh) – in a Test match held at Chittagong, Bangladesh, on March 2, 2006.

★ MOST THREE-FIGURE INNINGS IN A TEST MATCH

The most three-figure innings recorded by individual batsmen in a single cricket Test match is eight, in the game between the West Indies and South Africa at the Antigua Recreation Ground, St. John's, Antigua, between April 29 and May 3, 2005. The South African team is pictured.

ONE-DAY INTERNATIONALS

★ MOST CENTURIES (CAREER)

Sachin Tendulkar (India) scored 39 centuries in the course of 362 matches from 1989 to 2006.

Tendulkar and Rahul Dravid scored 331 runs against New Zealand in Hyderabad, India, on November 8, 1999, setting a record for the **highest one-day international partnership**.

★ HIGHEST TEAM SCORE

South Africa scored 438–9 in the second innings of a one-day international against Australia, staged in Johannesburg, South Africa, on March 12, 2006. Australia had actually set a new record for the highest team score themselves in the first innings of the match, with 434–4.

The **★ lowest completed innings total** is 35 by Zimbabwe against Sri Lanka at Harare, Zimbabwe, on April 25, 2004.

★ MOST MATCHES PLAYED (CAREER)

Sachin Tendulkar played 362 matches for India between 1989 and 2006.

★ MOST WICKETS IN A MATCH

The best bowling analysis is 8–19 by Chaminda Vass (Sri Lanka) against Zimbabwe at Colombo, Sri Lanka, on December 8, 2001.

BEST INTERNATIONAL BOWLING START

The best bowling start to a match was made in a World Cup game by

★ MOST TRIPLE ➡ CENTURIES IN TEST CRICKET

Only two batsmen in the history of Test match cricket have scored two innings of more than 300 runs: Sir Don Bradman (Australia) in 52 matches, between 1928 and 1948; and Brian Lara (Trinidad and Tobago, pictured right) for the West Indies, between 1990 and 2005.

Chaminda Vass playing for Sri Lanka against Bangladesh in Pietermaritzburg, South Africa, on February 14, 2003. He took a hat-trick with the first three balls of the game and then claimed a fourth victim in his opening over before finishing with 6–25. Sri Lanka won the match by 10 wickets.

★ MOST TIMES DISMISSED BY THE SAME BOWLER

Sanath Jayasuriya (Sri Lanka) was dismissed by Waqar Younis (Pakistan) 13 times in 45 matches between Sri Lanka and Pakistan between 1989 and 2002, a record for one-day international cricket matches.

★ WICKET-KEEPING – MOST DISMISSALS (CAREER)

Adam Gilchrist (Australia) secured a total of 384 dismissals (342 catches, 42 stumpings) in 239 matches between 1996 and 2006.

MOST CATCHES BY A FIELDER (CAREER)

Mohammad Azharuddin (India) took 156 catches in 334 matches between 1985 and 2000.

★ MOST TIMES DISMISSED BY THE SAME BOWLER IN TEST CRICKET

Between 1994 and 2001, Michael Atherton (UK, above left) was dismissed by Glen McGrath (Australia, above right) 19 times in 17 matches between England and Australia.

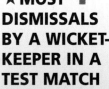

★ MOST ⬆ DISMISSALS BY A WICKET-KEEPER IN A TEST MATCH

Jack Russell (UK) made 11 dismissals for England against South Africa in Johannesburg, South Africa, in the Test match staged between November 30 and December 4, 1995. The match was drawn.

★ NEW RECORD
★ UPDATED RECORD

CYCLING

★ LONGEST ⇥
DISTANCE BACKWARD IN 24 HOURS

Darl Bonnema (USA) cycled a distance of 111.956 miles (180.177 km) backward – on an ordinary front-facing bicycle – at Disney's Wide World of Sports Complex, Florida, USA, on November 19–20, 2004.

MAJOR TOURS

MOST TOUR DE FRANCE "KING OF THE MOUNTAINS" TITLES

The "best climber" in the Tour de France is traditionally awarded a polka-dot jersey and the title "King of the Mountains." Richard Virenque (France) won the polka-dot jersey seven times between 1994 and 2004.

MOST TOUR OF ITALY WINS

Three people share the record for the most wins of the Giro d'Italia (Tour of Italy): Alfredo Binda (Italy) in 1925, 1927–29, and 1933; Fausto Coppi (Italy) in 1940, 1947, 1949, and 1952–53; and Eddy Merckx (Belgium) in 1968, 1970, and 1972–74. All have won five times. The first Giro d'Italia started on May 13, 1909, in Milan, with eight stages totaling 1,521 miles (2,448 km).

★ FASTEST
500 M UNPACED STANDING START (WOMEN)

The 500 m standing start world record belongs to Anna Meares (Australia), who completed the distance in 33.952 seconds at the Olympic Games in Athens, Greece, on August 20, 2004.

★ MOST TOUR OF SPAIN MOUNTAIN STAGE WINS

Roberto Heras Hernández (Spain) – riding for teams Kelme (1996–2000), US Postal (2001–03), and Liberty (2004–05) – has won nine mountain stage victories (out of 10 stage wins) during his nine Vuelta a España (Tour of Spain) races. Considered to be one of the best "mountain climbers" in the world – he shepherded multiple Tour de France winner Lance Armstrong (see facing page) through the mountains for three years – Heras last donned the famous gold leader's jersey on September 18, 2005, in Spain's capital, Madrid.

LONGEST TOUR DE FRANCE SOLO ESCAPE

The longest solo escape in the Tour de France was 157 miles (253 km) by Albert Bourlon (France) to win 14th stage, Carcassonne to Luchon, in 1947.

FASTEST...

500 M UNPACED FLYING START (WOMEN)

Erika Salumäe (USSR, now Estonia) holds the 500 m flying start world record. She achieved the distance in 29.655 seconds in Moscow, USSR, on August 6, 1987.

★ 3 KM UNPACED STANDING START (WOMEN)

The women's world record for the unpaced 3 km race from a standing start, better known as the women's individual cycling pursuit, is held by Sarah Ulmer (New Zealand), who finished in a time of 3 min 24.537 sec at the Olympic Games in Athens, Greece, on August 22, 2004.

★ MOST OLYMPIC GOLD MEDALS (WOMEN)

Leontien Zijlaard-Van Moorsel (Netherlands) has won a record total of four individual gold medals, plus a silver and bronze, at two recent Olympic Games: for the road race, time trial, and pursuit at the Sydney, Australia, games in 2000, and for the time trial at the Athens, Greece, games in 2004. Her overall tally of six medals is also a world record.

← MOST TOUR DE FRANCE WINS

Lance Armstrong (USA) holds the record for the greatest number of wins in the Tour de France. From 1999 to 2005, he won the famous cycle race seven times. He also holds the record for ★ **fastest average speed in the Tour de France**, finishing first in the 2005 Tour de France – his final Tour – with an average speed of 25.882 mph (41.654 km/h). Armstrong finished the 2,241-mile-long (3,607-km) Tour in a time of 86 hr 15 min 2 sec.

★ PERTH TO SYDNEY TRANS-AUSTRALIA CYCLE RIDE (MEN)

Tristan Barnes (Australia) cycled from Perth, Western Australia, to Sydney, New South Wales, Australia, in only 9 days 9 hr 17 min. He started out from Perth on September 27, and arrived in Sydney on October 6, 2005.

★ 4 KM TEAM PURSUIT (MEN)

The Australian men's team, consisting of Luke Roberts, Brett Lancaster, Brad McGee, and Graeme Brown, completed the 4 km pursuit (unpaced and front standing start) in 3 min 56 sec at the Olympic Games in Athens, Greece, on August 22, 2004.

GREATEST DISTANCE...

★ ONE HOUR UNPACED STANDING START (WOMEN)

The UCI one-hour women's distance record from a standing start is 28.62 miles (46.065 km) by Leontien Zijlaard-Van Moorsel (Netherlands) in Mexico City, Mexico, on October 1, 2003.

The one-hour "best performance" distance is 29.92 miles (48.15 km) by Jeannie Longo-Ciprelli (France) on October 26, 1996, also in Mexico City.

★ CYCLED WITH NO HANDS IN ONE HOUR

Scott Koons (USA) cycled 13.15 miles (21.16 km) in one hour without touching the handlebars. He set his record on a track at Northern Michigan University, Michigan, USA, on September 12, 2004.

MOST...

★ COMPETITORS IN THE BMX WORLD CHAMPIONSHIPS

The 2005 UCI BMX World Championships held at the Palais Omnisport de Paris-Bercy, France, drew 2,560 competitors from 39 countries on July 29–31, 2005.

★ VERTICAL DISTANCE CYCLED IN 24 HOURS

Marcel Knaus (Switzerland) cycled 59,362 ft (18,093 vertical meters) in a 24-hour period on July 16–17, 2005 in Wildhaus, Switzerland.

MOUNTAIN BIKE DOWNHILL WORLD CUPS

The **most downhill World Cup titles won by a man** is five, by Nicolas Vouilloz (France) in 1995–96 and 1998–2000.

The **most downhill World Cup titles by a woman** is also five, set by Anne-Caroline Chausson (France) from 1998 to 2002.

Chausson has also recorded the **most downhill World Championships won by a woman**, with 11 victories: three in the junior championship from 1993 to 1995 and eight in the senior class from 1996 to 2003.

★ LONGEST DISTANCE ONE-HOUR UNPACED STANDING START (MEN)

Ondrej Sosenka of the Czech Republic covered 30.8 miles (49.7 km) in one hour in Moscow, Russia, on July 19, 2005.

★ NEW RECORD
★ UPDATED RECORD

MOST TOUR → OF SPAIN WINS

Roberto Heras Hernández (Spain, far right) has secured four wins in the Vuelta a España in 2000 and 2003–05, as well as 10 stage victories. However, his 2005 title was handed to overall runner-up Denis Menchov (Russia, right) following Heras's two-year suspension by the Spanish Cycling Federation (Real Federación Española de Ciclism) for testing positive to the banned substance erythropoietin (EPO) – a hormone also produced by the kidneys. If the ban is upheld, Heras will hold a joint record of three wins with Tony Rominger (Switzerland), who won in 1992–94.

SOCCER

! X-REF

Which soccer player do you think earns the most money? You can find out on p.167, where you'll also discover some fantastic facts and stats about the world's soccer legends.

★ BEST START TO A PREMIERSHIP SEASON

Chelsea FC began the 2005/06 season with seven wins. Chelsea's Joe Cole (UK) is pictured below left, celebrating a goal with teammate Eider Gudjohnsen (Iceland).

167

★ MOST BEACH SOCCER WORLD CUPS

The inaugural FIFA Beach Soccer World Cup was held in Rio de Janeiro, Brazil, in August 2005, and was won by France. The French team is pictured left, proudly displaying the trophy after beating Portugal in the World Cup final. After a 3–3 draw, France went on to win 1–0 on penalties.

CLUBS – DOMESTIC

★ FASTEST GOAL ON PREMIERSHIP DEBUT

Ledley King (UK) scored in just nine seconds playing for Tottenham Hotspur in their 3–3 draw against Bradford City on December 9, 2000.

★ FEWEST GOALS CONCEDED IN AN ENGLISH PREMIERSHIP SEASON

Chelsea FC (UK) conceded only 14 goals in the 2004/05 season.

FASTEST TIME TO SCORE A HAT TRICK

The fastest time to score three goals is 90 seconds by Tommy Ross (UK) for Ross County against Nairn County at Dingwall, Ross-shire, UK, on November 28, 1964.

★ RICHEST SOCCER CLUB

Real Madrid (Spain) had a total income of €273.5 million ($324.3 million) for the 2004/05 season, according to the Deloitte Football Money League. It was the first time in eight years that the team had overtaken Manchester United (UK), whose revenue for the same period was £166.4 million ($289.8 million; €244.4 million).

MOST GOALS SCORED BY A GOALTENDER IN ONE GAME

Paraguayan goaltender José Luis Chilavert scored a hat trick of penalties for Vélez Sarsfield in a 6–1 defeat of Ferro Carril Oeste in the Argentine professional league on November 28, 1999.

Chilavert, who also played for Real Zaragoza (Spain) and Strasbourg (France), also holds the record for the **most goals scored by a goaltender**, with 56 official league and international goals between July 1992 and October 2001.

★ MOST ➡ CHAMPIONS LEAGUE VICTORIES

Real Madrid (Spain) won 65 UEFA Champions League matches between 1992 and 2005, scoring a record 228 goals in the process. Pictured is David Beckham (UK) of Real Madrid celebrating with Robinho (Brazil) after a goal against Rosenborg during a UEFA Champions League game on October 19, 2005, in Madrid, Spain.

MOST CONSECUTIVE LEAGUE APPEARANCES FOR THE SAME TEAM

Harold Bell (UK) played in 401 consecutive soccer league games for the English soccer team Tranmere Rovers from 1946 to 1955.

★ MOST FA CUP FINAL APPEARANCES

Lord Arthur Kinnaird (UK) appeared in nine finals between 1873 and 1883. He played for Wanderers, Old Etonians, and Newton Heath, the team that became Manchester United.

★ SHORTEST REIGN AS A TOP DIVISION MANAGER

Brian Clough (UK) lasted 44 days in charge of Leeds United in 1975.

★ YOUNGEST PREMIERSHIP GOAL-SCORER

James Vaughan (UK) was just 16 years 271 days old when he scored for Everton against Crystal Palace on April 10, 2005.

← ★ **MOST CONSECUTIVE**
PREMIER LEAGUE SOCCER APPEARANCES

Frank Lampard (UK) played in 160 consecutive English Premier League games for Chelsea FC, between October 13, 2001 and November 26, 2005. Lampard is pictured left scoring a penalty during the FA Cup fourth round replay match between Chelsea and Everton at Stamford Bridge, London, UK, on February 8, 2006.

★ MOST CONSECUTIVE SEASONS IN ENGLISH TOP DIVISION

Arsenal has been in the top flight of English soccer for 80 consecutive seasons from 1920 to 2006 (excluding 1939–45, during World War II).

Arsenal also holds the record for the ★**longest unbeaten Premiership run**. They remained undefeated in the English Premier League for a 49-game run between May 7, 2003 and October 16, 2004.

★ MOST GAMES PLAYED IN THE ENGLISH TOP DIVISION (TEAM)

Everton has played over 4,000 games in the top flight of English soccer – more matches than any other English soccer team.

MOST GOALS SCORED IN A SOCCER LEAGUE SEASON (INDIVIDUAL)

Soccer legend William Ralph "Dixie" Dean (UK) scored a total of 60 goals in 39 games for Everton (First Division) in 1927/28; James Smith (UK) scored 66 goals in 38 games for Ayr United (Scottish Second Division) in the same season. With three more goals in Cup ties and 19 in representative matches, Dean's overall total was 82.

TEAMS – EUROPEAN

★ MOST CHAMPIONS LEAGUE APPEARANCES

The greatest number of UEFA Champions League appearances by an individual player is 118 by Paolo Maldini (Italy) playing for AC Milan from 1992 to 2005.

★ MOST GOALS IN A CHAMPIONS LEAGUE MATCH

In the Group C match between Monaco (France) and Deportivo La Coruña (Spain), 11 goals were scored, with the French hosts winning 8–3 on November 5, 2003.

★ MOST EUROPEAN CUPS WON BY A COACH

The greatest number of European Cups won by a coach is three by Bob Paisley (UK) with Liverpool FC (1977–78 and 1981).

★ MOST CONSECUTIVE APPEARANCES IN EUROPEAN CUP COMPETITIONS

The most consecutive appearances in European Cup competitions by a team is 15 by Real Madrid (Spain) from 1955 to 1970.

★ MOST EUROPEAN CUPS WON BY A PLAYER

Francisco Gento Llorente (Spain) won six European Cups with Real Madrid (Spain) between 1956 and 1960 and, again, in 1966.

★ MOST GAMES PLAYED IN A SINGLE CHAMPIONS LEAGUE TOURNAMENT

AC Milan (Italy) played 19 games in the 2002/03 competition.

★ MOST CHAMPIONS LEAGUE WINNERS MEDALS WITH DIFFERENT TEAMS

Clarence Seedorf (Netherlands) has won the Champions League with a record three teams: Ajax (Netherlands), Real Madrid (Spain), and AC Milan (Italy).

★ FASTEST CHAMPIONS LEAGUE FINAL GOAL

Paolo Maldini (Italy) scored in just 53 seconds playing for AC Milan against Liverpool on May 25, 2005.

He was 36 years 333 days old when he scored the goal, which also makes him the ★**oldest player to score in a Champions League final**.

★ NEW RECORD
★ UPDATED RECORD

BALL CONTROL

TITLE	RECORD	NAME/NATIONALITY
Most touches – men (30 sec)	147	Tim Crowe (USA)
Most touches – women (30 sec)	137	Tasha-Nicole Terani (USA)
Most touches with head (1 min)	319	Erick Hernández (Cuba)
★Most headers, team of 11 (2 min)	54	Energie Cottbus under-17s (Germany)
Heading (duration)	8 hr 32 min 3 sec	Tomas Lundman (Sweden)
Head (seated)	3 hr 59 min	Andrzej Kukla (Poland)
Chest	30.29 sec	Amadou Gueye (France)
Feet, legs, head (men)	19 hr 30 min	Martinho E Orige (Brazil)
Feet, legs, head (women)	7 hr 5 min 25 sec	Cláudia Martini (Brazil)
Lying down	8 min 27 sec	Tomas Lundman (Sweden)
Fastest marathon distance	7 hr 18 min 55 sec	J. Skorkovsky (Czech Rep.)

SOCCER

★ MOST EUROPEAN PLAYER OF THE YEAR AWARDS

The European Player of the Year award, also known as "Ballon d'Or," has been awarded every year since 1956 by the French soccer magazine *France Football*. The award has been won on a record three occasions by three soccer players: Johan Cruyff (Netherlands) in 1971 and 1973–74; Michel Platini (France) in 1983–85; and Marco van Basten (Netherlands) in 1988–89 and 1992.

★ MOST AFRICAN CUP OF NATIONS VICTORIES

Egypt has won the Confédération Africaine de Football (CAF) African Cup of Nations five times, in 1957, 1959, 1986, 1998, and 2006. The tournament is held every two years.

★ MOST GOALS IN A WORLD CUP FINALS MATCH

A total of 12 goals were scored in a single game in the 1954 finals in Switzerland, when Austria beat the host nation 7–5.

★ MOST ↑ DOMESTIC LEAGUE TITLES

Rangers FC (UK) has won 51 titles in the Scottish Division One and Premier Division championships between 1891 and 2005.

Rangers FC also holds the record for the **most Scottish league titles**, having won it 51 times (including one shared title in 1891) between 1891 and 2005.

★ OLDEST SOCCER BALL

During an excavation project at Stirling Castle, UK, in the mid-1970s, a gray leather ball was discovered behind oak paneling in a bedroom once used by Mary, Queen of Scots, during her reign in the 16th century. Tests confirmed that it was more than 430 years old, and made between 1540 and 1570.

★ MOST VALUABLE SOCCER MEMORABILIA

The most valuable piece of soccer history is an original FA Cup, one of four made for the first competition held in 1871 and presented to the winning team between 1896 and 1910. An anonymous telephone bidder bought the cup for £420,000 ($771,387) from Christie's (UK) auction house on May 19, 2005.

★ LARGEST SOCCER SHIRT

The world's largest soccer shirt measures 168 ft 4 in x 168 ft 10 in (51.32 x 51.46 m) and is in the national colours of Mexico. It was made by The Coca-Cola Company of Mexico and displayed at the Azteca Stadium, Mexico City, Mexico, on May 10, 2006.

★ MOST ASIAN FOOTBALLER OF THE YEAR AWARDS

The Asian Footballer of the Year has been awarded by the Asian Football Confederation since 1993. Hidetoshi Nakata (Japan) has won the award twice, in 1997 and 1998.

★ MOST AFRICAN FOOTBALLER OF THE YEAR AWARDS

The African Footballer of the Year has been awarded by the Confederation of African Football since 1992. Samuel Eto'o (Cameroon) won the award three times, from 2003 to 2005.

? DID YOU KNOW?

*Everyone feels fed up when their team loses a game. But spare a thought for American Samoa. On April 11, 2001, it was defeated 31–0 by Australia in a World Cup-qualifying match at Coffs Harbor, New South Wales, Australia. This represents the **highest score in an international match**.*

★ MOST GOALS SCORED IN A WOMEN'S OLYMPIC ⇒ SOCCER TOURNAMENT

Cristiane (Brazil, full name Cristiane Rozeira de Souza Silva) and Birgit Prinz (Germany) both scored five goals at the 2004 Olympics in Athens, Greece. Cristiane is pictured right, in yellow, with Brandi Chastain (USA), in an Olympic match on August 26, 2004.

★ MOST MAJOR LEAGUE SOCCER GOALS

The greatest number of goals scored in Major League Soccer is 100 by Jason Kreis (USA) in 271 games, playing for FC Dallas from 1996 to 2004, and for Real Salt Lake (both USA) in 2005.

★ MOST GOALS SCORED IN A SINGLE WORLD CUP FINALS

A record 171 goals were scored during the finals of the 1998 World Cup tournament in France, over the course of 64 games.

★ MOST COUNTRIES SCORED FOR IN WORLD CUP FINALS

Robert Prosinecki scored for Yugoslavia in 1990 against the United Arab Emirates. He went on to score for Croatia in 1998 against Jamaica.

FASTEST EXPULSION FROM A WORLD CUP MATCH

José Batista (Uruguay) received a red card after one minute playing for Uruguay against Scotland on June 13, 1986, at the Estadio Neza '86, Nezahualcoyotl, Mexico.

★ MOST EXPULSIONS IN WORLD CUP FINALS (PLAYER)

Rigobert Song (Cameroon) is the only player to have been sent off more than once in the World Cup finals. He received his marching orders against Brazil in 1994 and again playing against Chile in 1998.

★ MOST EXPULSIONS IN A SINGLE WORLD CUP FINALS

The finals of the 1998 World Cup tournament in France yielded an unprecedented 22 red cards over the course of 64 games.

INTERNATIONAL (WOMEN)

★ MOST GOALS SCORED IN A WOMEN'S WORLD CUP TOURNAMENT

Michelle Akers (USA) scored 10 goals in the 1991 Women's World Cup tournament held in China.

MOST WORLD CUP WINS (WOMEN)

This competition was initiated in 1991 and is held quadrennially. Of the four occasions the event has been held, the USA has won twice, in 1991 and 1999.

★ MOST FIFA WORLD PLAYER OF THE YEAR AWARDS

Ronaldo (Brazil, full name Luiz Nazario de Lima Ronaldo, pictured right) has won three Fédération Internationale de Football Association (FIFA) World Player of the Year awards, in 1996–97 and 2002. This feat was matched by Zinedine Zidane (France) in 1998, 2000, and 2003.

★ MOST WOMEN'S OLYMPIC TITLES

Women's soccer was introduced to the Olympic Games in 1996. The USA has won the gold medal twice, in 1996 and 2004.

FUTSAL

★ MOST GOALS IN A WORLD CHAMPIONSHIPS MATCH (INDIVIDUAL)

Konstantin Eremenko (Russia) scored seven goals for Russia against China in the 1992 tournament held in Hong Kong (now China).

★ MOST GOALS IN A WORLD CHAMPIONSHIPS MATCH (TEAM)

The greatest number of goals scored in a Futsal World Cup match is 31, when Brazil beat Guatemala 29–2 on November 23, 2000.

★ MOST HAT TRICKS IN A WORLD CHAMPIONSHIPS MATCH

Manoel Tobias (Brazil) scored four hat tricks – against Kazakhstan, Egypt, Guatemala, and Russia – in the 2000 tournament held in Guatemala.

★ MOST GOALS IN A WORLD CHAMPIONSHIPS TOURNAMENT

Manoel Tobias (Brazil) scored 19 goals in the 2000 tournament in Guatemala.

★ MOST GOALS IN FUTSAL WORLD CHAMPIONSHIPS BY A TEAM

The greatest number of goals scored in Futsal World Championships is 258 by Brazil in the five stagings of the tournament in 1989, 1992, 1996, 2000, and 2004.

★ NEW RECORD
☆ UPDATED RECORD

GOLF

! **X–REF**

The **youngest female to score a hole in one** was Katy Langley (UK), on a 134-yard par-three golf course. How old do you think she was at the time? Find out on p.99.

★ HIGHEST EUROPEAN TOUR EARNINGS IN A CAREER

Between 1986 and 2001, Colin Stuart Montgomerie (UK) earned a record $12,008,908 on the European Tour.

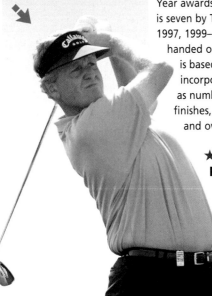

AWARDS

★ MOST PGA PLAYER OF THE YEAR AWARDS

The greatest number of Professional Golfers' Association Player of the Year awards won by an individual is seven by Tiger Woods (USA) in 1997, 1999–2003, and 2005. First handed out in 1948, the award is based on a points system incorporating variables such as number of wins, top 10 finishes, scoring average, and overall performance.

★ MOST LPGA PLAYER OF THE YEAR AWARDS

The greatest number of Ladies Professional Golfers' Association Player of the Year awards won is eight by Annika Sorenstam (Sweden) in 1995, 1997–98, and 2001–05.

★ MOST PGA TOUR PLAYER OF THE YEAR AWARDS

Inaugurated in 1992 – and also known as the Jack Nicklaus award – this award is voted for by PGA Tour members, and has been won an unprecedented seven times by Tiger Woods (USA), in 1997, 1999–2003, and 2005.

MAJOR VICTORIES

★ MOST MAJOR TOURNAMENT VICTORIES BY A MAN

Jack Nicklaus (USA) recorded a total of 18 major tournament wins between 1962 and 1986.

★ MOST PGA TOUR TOURNAMENT VICTORIES

The most tournament wins on the PGA Tour is 82 by Sam Snead (USA) between 1937 and 1979.

★ MOST CONSECUTIVE US OPENS STARTED

The greatest number of consecutive US Open tournaments started by an individual golfer is 44, recorded by Jack Nicklaus between 1957 and 2000.

★ MOST WOMEN'S BRITISH OPEN WINS

Karrie Webb (Australia) won the women's British Open golf tournament a record three times, in 1995, 1997, and 2002.

MOST ➡ TIMES A GOLFER HAS SCORED THEIR AGE

The most times for a golfer to score their age and below – that is, to complete 18 holes using the same or less number of strokes than their age in years – is 930 by Kermit Dannehl (USA, b. August 31, 1919), mostly at Ahwatukee Country Club, Phoenix, Arizona, USA, between 1992 and 2005.

★ FASTEST HOLE BY AN INDIVIDUAL

The fastest single hole of golf played by an individual golfer is 1 min 52 sec by Phil Naylor (UK) on the first hole of the Devlin course at St. Andrews Bay Golf Resort and Spa, St. Andrews, Scotland, UK, on June 18, 2005.

◄-■

MOST RYDER CUP WINS

The biennial Ryder Cup professional match between the USA and Europe (British Isles or Great Britain prior to 1979) was instituted in 1927. Up to 2004, the USA had won 24 matches and lost 9; there have been 2 ties.

★ MOST SOLHEIM CUP WINS

The female equivalent of the Ryder Cup is contested biennially between the top professional players of Europe and the USA and was first held in 1990. The USA has won six times, with Europe winning just three times (1992, 2000, and 2003).

★ MOST WALKER CUP WINS

The Walker Cup – contested between the USA and Great Britain and the Republic of Ireland since 1921 and held biennially since 1924 – has been won on 32 occasions by the USA, and seven times by Great Britain and Ireland. The 1965 match was tied.

MOST HOLES ⬆
PLAYED IN 24 HOURS

With the aid of a golf cart, Robb James (Canada) played 851 holes at Victoria Golf Course at Edmonton, Alberta, Canada, on June 21–22, 2004. During the attempt, James hit 45 birdies and 430 pars, four low rounds of 68 and a high of 87.

The **most holes played in 24 hours (walking)** is 401, a feat achieved by Ian Colston (Australia) at Bendigo Golf Club, Victoria, Australia, on November 27–28, 1971.

EARNINGS

★ HIGHEST US PGA CAREER EARNINGS
The all-time career earnings record on the US PGA circuit is held by Tiger Woods (USA) with $55,770,760 between August 1996 and December 2005.

★ HIGHEST US LPGA CAREER EARNINGS
Annika Sorenstam (Sweden) won a total of $18,332,764 on the US LPGA Tour between 1993 and 2005.

MISCELLANEOUS

★ LONGEST ONE-HANDED GOLF SHOT
The longest golf shot with one hand is 282 yd (843 ft 2 in; 257 m) by Cristian Sterning (Sweden) at the St. Andrews Bay Golf Resort and Spa, St. Andrews, Scotland, UK, on June 18, 2005.

★ LONGEST GOLF SHOT CAUGHT
Ian Cahill (UK) caught a golf shot of 200 yd (597 ft; 182 m) at St. Andrews Bay Golf Resort and Spa, St. Andrews, Scotland, UK, on June 18, 2005. The ball was hit by Phil Naylor (UK) with a Callaway X3.

★ LONGEST TIME TO SPIN A GOLF BALL ON A PUTTER
The longest time for an individual to spin a golf ball on the face of a putter is 2 min 22 sec by Henry Epstein (Australia) on the set of *Guinness World Records* at Seven Network Studios, Sydney, New South Wales, Australia, on June 18, 2005.

★ LONGEST SERVING GOLF CLUB EMPLOYEE
Raymundo Coelho (Brazil) began work at the Gavea Golf and Country Club in Rio de Janeiro, Brazil, in January 1935 to provide upkeep and maintenance of the course. He continues at the club, now as an instructional professional, more than 70 years later.

★ FASTEST HOLE OF GOLF (FOURBALL)
A fourball organized by Paul Coffey (UK) and consisting of caddies Michael Armitt, John Calcutt, Tom Greaves, and Gordon Archibald (all UK) completed 18 holes in 1 hr 13 min 49 sec on the Torrance Course at St. Andrews Bay Golf Resort & Spa, St. Andrews, Scotland, UK, on June 18, 2005.

★ MOST HOLES PLAYED IN 12 HOURS
The **most holes of golf played in 12 hours using a cart** is 476 by Brennan F. Robertson (USA) at Foxfire Golf Club in Sarasota, Florida, USA, on August 19, 2000.

The **most holes played in 12 hours by a walking golfer** is 221 by Scott Holland (Canada) at the Fairmont Banff Springs Golf Course in Banff, Alberta, Canada, on May 5, 2005. Holland played the entire time using only one club, a seven iron.

★ MOST GOLF BALLS HELD IN THE HAND
The most golf balls held in one hand for 10 seconds is 17 by Simon Wake (UK) during the Kimby Cup Challenge 2005 at Puckrup Hall, Gloucestershire, UK, on August 20, 2005.

★ MOST ⬆
TOURNAMENT VICTORIES BY A WOMAN

The most major golf tournament wins by a woman is 15 by Patty Berg (USA) between 1937 and 1962. A leading force in the women's game, she helped establish the Ladies Pro Golf Association (LPGA).

★ NEW RECORD
⭒ UPDATED RECORD

★ FASTEST
TIME TO PLAY A ROUND OF GOLF ON EACH CONTINENT

The fastest time to play a complete 18-hole round of golf on six continents is 5 days 9 hr 15 min (January 26–31, 2005) by Basil Bielich (South Africa), Brian Kelly, Adrian Cleevley, and David Dean (all UK).

⬅▪

ICE HOCKEY

★ MOST ➡ CAREER WINS BY A GOALTENDER

Patrick Roy (Canada) of the Montreal Canadiens (1984–95) and Colorado Avalanche (1995–2003) secured a record 551 NHL career wins as a goaltender.

Roy has also won the ★**most Conn Smythe Trophies** with three, playing for the Canadiens in 1986 (pictured with the Stanley Cup) and 1993, and in 2001 for Colorado. *For more NHL trophy records, see box on p.247.*

★ NEW RECORD
☆ UPDATED RECORD

[?] DID YOU KNOW?

*The **most durable ice hockey player** is John Burnosky (USA), who began playing at Kelvin Technical High School, Winnipeg, Manitoba, Canada, in 1929 and still plays, 76 years on!*

★ FASTEST GOAL SCORED IN AN NHL DEBUT

The fastest goal from the start of a game by a player making his NHL debut was scored by Alexander Mogilny (USSR) just 20 seconds into his debut with the Buffalo Sabres on October 5, 1989.

The ★**fastest goal scored in any ice hockey game** occurred after just 2 seconds, when Per Olsen (Denmark) scored for Rungsted against Odense in the Danish First Division at Horsholm, Denmark, on January 14, 1990.

The ★**fastest hat trick** took just 10 seconds and was achieved by Jorgen Palmgren Erichsen for Frisk v. Holmen in a junior league match in Norway on March 17, 1991.

NATIONAL HOCKEY LEAGUE (NHL)

★ FEWEST LOSSES BY A TEAM IN ONE SEASON

The Montreal Canadiens recorded just eight losses during a season of at least 70 games in the 1976–77 season. The ★**fewest wins by a team in one season** is just eight by the Washington Capitals in 1974–75.

★ MOST WINS – ONE ROAD TRIP

The Philadelphia Flyers finished their franchise road trip during December 2005 and January 2006 with an 8-2-1 record, setting a new NHL mark for the most wins on a single stretch of games away from home.

Their 17 points on the trip is also a new league record, far surpassing the old mark of 13 points set by the Montreal Canadiens in 1968–69.

★ MOST NHL GAMES PLAYED BY A ⬅ DEFENSEMAN

Scott Stevens (Canada) played in 1,635 games. He played for 22 seasons with the Washington Capitals, St. Louis Blues, and New Jersey Devils (1982–04), captained the Devils to three Stanley Cup wins (1995, 2000, and 2003) and on February 4, 2006, became the first Devils player to have his number (No.4) retired. Stevens also played in 223 career playoff games – a record for a defenseman.

★ MOST CONSECUTIVE ONE-GOAL GAME WINS

The Buffalo Sabres won six consecutive games by a one-goal margin (including two overtime victories and one shoot-out win), between December 8 and 19, 2005. Buffalo's six straight one-goal wins are a league record.

MOST STANLEY CUP WINS (TEAM)

The greatest number of Stanley Cup wins by a team is 24 by the Montreal Canadiens, who won the cup in 1916, 1924, 1930–31, 1944, 1946, 1953, 1956–60, 1965–66, 1968–69, 1971, 1973, 1976–79, 1986, and 1993, from a record 32 finals.

The Stanley Cup – a silver bowl – was first presented in 1893 by Lord Stanley of Preston, then Governor-General of Canada, who originally bought it for $48.67. From 1894, it was contested by amateur teams for the Canadian Championship. After 1910, it became the award for the winners of the professional league playoffs.

★ MOST CONSECUTIVE YEARS IN STANLEY CUP PLAYOFFS

The most appearances in Stanley Cup playoffs in consecutive years is 21 by Larry Robinson (Canada) playing for the Montreal Canadiens in 1972–89 and Los Angeles Kings in 1989–92.

GUINNESS WORLD RECORDS

NHL TROPHIES – MOST WINS

TROPHY	AWARDED FOR	TO	WINS
★Art Ross	Most points scored in regular season play	Wayne Gretzky (Canada)	10
★Hart Memorial	Most valuable player of the year	Wayne Gretzky (Canada)	8
★Lady Byng	Most sportsman-like behavior and highest standards of play	Frank Boucher (Canada)	7
★Vezina	Best goalkeeper of the year	Jacques Plante (Canada)	7
★Jack Adams	Biggest contribution by a coach in a season	Pat Burns (Canada)	3
★Conn Smythe	Most valuable player in Stanley Cup playoffs	Patrick Roy (Canada)	3
★Maurice Richard	Leading goal scorer in the year	Pavel Bure (Russia)	2
		Jarome Iginla (Canada)	2

★MOST VEZINA TROPHIES WON

The most Vezina trophies won by an individual is seven by Jacques Plante (Canada) playing for the Montreal Canadiens in 1956–60 and 1962, and jointly with his St. Louis Blues team mate Glenn Hall (Canada) in 1969. The Vezina Trophy is awarded each year to the best goalkeeper in the NHL.

★MOST GAMES COACHED

Scotty Bowman (Canada) was behind the bench for an NHL record 2,141 games during his 35-year coaching career with the St. Louis Blues, Montreal Canadiens, Buffalo Sabres, Pittsburgh Penguins, and Detroit Red Wings, from 1967 to 2002. He also holds the record for the ★most playoff wins by a coach, with 223, and the ★most regular season wins by a coach, with a total of 1,244 NHL games.

Bowman also recorded nine Stanley Cups at the helm with the Montreal Canadiens (1973, 1976–79), Pittsburgh Penguins (1992), and Detroit Red Wings (1997–98, 2002), the ★most Stanley Cup wins by a coach.

MOST GAMES PLAYED

From 1946 to 1979, Gordon "Gordie" Howe (Canada) played in 2,421 ice hockey games, a career record. He also holds the record for the **most NHL All-Star selections**, being picked 21 times while playing for the Detroit Red Wings (1946–79).

OLYMPICS & WORLD CHAMPIONSHIPS

★OLDEST OLYMPIANS

Bela Ordody (Hungary) and Alfred Steinka (Germany) were 48 years old at the 1928 Olympic Winter Games in St. Moritz, Switzerland.

★LONGEST CAREER

The longest Olympic ice hockey career is that of Richard Torriani (Switzerland), from 1928 to 1948.

★MOST INTERNATIONAL GOALS SCORED

Chris Bourque (USA) scored five goals to help power the USA past Norway (11–2) during the International Ice Hockey Federation World Junior Championship in Vancouver, British Columbia, Canada, on December 26, 2005.

Bourque equaled the record set by Wally Chapman (USA), who scored five goals in a 12–3 victory against Switzerland on January 3, 1984.

YOUNGEST US PLAYER (WOMEN)

On December 27, 2005, Sarah Parsons (USA, b. July 27, 1987) became the youngest woman ever named to a US Women's Olympic Ice Hockey Team, aged 18 years 153 days.

★MOST WOMEN'S WORLD CHAMPIONSHIP WINS

Canada won the World Championships eight times in a row, in 1990, 1992, 1994, 1997, 1999, 2000, 2001, and 2004. The USA, who won in 2005, are the only other winners.

★FIRST SHOOT-OUT GOAL

The first shoot-out goal in NHL history was scored – on the first ever shot – by Daniel Alfredsson (Sweden, below, wearing No.11), playing for the Ottawa Senators, against the Toronto Maple Leafs and goaltender Ed Belfour on October 5, 2005. Also pictured is Toronto's No.88, Eric Lindros.

OLYMPICS

◀ LONGEST CAREERS

The following have sustained Olympic careers for 40 years: Paul Elvstrom (Denmark, pictured far left and center), yachting (1948–60, 1968–72, 1984–88); Dr. Ivan Osiier (Denmark), fencing (1908–32, 1948); and Magnus Konow (Norway), yachting (1908–20, 1928, 1936–48). The **longest Olympic career by a woman** is 28 years, a record shared by Anne Ransehouse (USA, 1960, 1964, 1988) and Christilot Hanson-Boylen (Canada, 1964–76, 1984, 1992), both in dressage.

★ NEW RECORD
☆ UPDATED RECORD

MOST MEDALS WON AT THE WINTER GAMES (INDIVIDUAL)

The most medals won by an individual at the Winter Olympic Games is 12 by Bjorn Daehlie (Norway) in the men's Nordic skiing event, from 1992 to 1998. The greatest number of Winter Games medals won by a woman is 10 by Raisa Smetanina (USSR/ Russia), also in Nordic skiing, from 1976 to 1992.

MOST PARTICIPANTS AT A SUMMER OLYMPIC GAMES

The Summer Games in Sydney, Australia, in 2000, featured 10,651 athletes, of which 4,069 were women.

★ MOST NOCs AT A WINTER GAMES

A total of 80 National Olympic Committees (NOCs) entered athletes at the 2006 Winter Olympic Games. This was an increase of three from the 77 represented at the 2002 Olympic Winter Games.

★ FIRST WINTER SPORT IN THE OLYMPIC GAMES

Figure skating was the first winter sport to be included in the Olympics. It appeared in the program of the Summer Olympics in 1908 and 1920, before the Winter Olympics themselves were established.

★ LARGEST CITY TO HOST A WINTER GAMES

With a population of 1.7 million and an area of 50.2 miles^2 (130 km^2), Turin in the Piedmont region of Italy is the largest city to host a Winter Olympics (in 2006). The title will go to Vancouver, Canada, the host of the XXI Winter Olympiad, in 2010.

LARGEST STADIUM ROOF

The acrylic glass "tent" of the Munich Olympic Stadium, Germany, measures 915,000 ft^2 (85,000 m^2). It sits on top of a steel net supported by masts.

★ LONGEST TORCH RELAY

The longest Olympic torch relay in one country was for the 1988 Winter Olympic Games in Canada. The relay arrived at St. John's, Newfoundland, from Greece on November 17, 1987, and was transported 11,222 miles (18,060 km) – 5,088 miles (8,188 km) by foot, 4,419 miles (7,111 km) by aircraft/ferry, 1,712 miles (2,756 km) by snowmobile, and 3 miles (5 km) by dogsled – to arrive in Calgary on February 13, 1988.

MOST EVENTS FEATURED AT AN OLYMPIC GAMES

An unprecedented 301 sporting events took place at the Summer Olympic Games staged in Athens, Greece, in 2004.

INDIVIDUALS

YOUNGEST GOLD MEDALIST

The youngest-ever female champion to win a gold medal was Kim Yun-Mi (South Korea, b. December 1, 1980), who was aged 13 years 85 days when she took part in the women's 3,000 m short track speed skating relay event held at Lillehammer, Norway, in 1994.

YOUNGEST GOLD MEDALIST (INDIVIDUAL DISCIPLINE)

The youngest individual Olympic champion was Marjorie Gestring (USA, b. November 18, 1922) who won the springboard diving title at the Olympic Games in Berlin, Germany, on August 12, 1936, aged just 13 years 268 days.

OLDEST GOLD MEDALIST

Oscar Swahn (Sweden) competed with the winning Running Deer shooting team at the 1912 Olympics in Stockholm, Sweden, aged 64 years 258 days. In 1920, at the Antwerp Olympics, Belgium, he also took the silver medal for this event aged 72 years 280 days.

★ OLDEST GOLD MEDALIST AT A WINTER GAMES

Duff Gibson (Canada, b. August 11, 1966) was aged 39 years 190 days when he won the gold medal for the skeleton event, on February 17, 2006, at the XX Winter Olympiad, held in Turin, Italy.

YOUNGEST COMPETITOR AT A WINTER GAMES

The youngest-ever competitor at the Winter Olympic Games was Magdalena Cecilia Colledge (GB, b. November 28, 1920). She was only 11 years 74 days old when she participated in the figure skating event in Lake Placid, New York, USA, in 1932.

★ FIRST WINTER OLYMPIC MEDALIST FROM THE SOUTHERN HEMISPHERE

In 1992, at the XVI Olympiad in Albertville, France, skier Annelise Coberger (New Zealand) made history with a silver medal in the women's slalom, becoming the first Winter Olympic medalist from the southern hemisphere.

★ FIRST BLACK ATHLETE TO WIN GOLD AT A WINTER GAMES

Shani Davis (USA) became the first black person to win an individual gold medal in the history of the Winter Olympics after winning the 1,000 m speed skating with a time of 1 min 08.89 sec on February 18, 2006.

★ HIGHEST SCORE IN FIGURE SKATING

Figure skater Evgeni Plushenko's (Russia) short-program score of 90.66, achieved on February 15, 2006, at the Winter Olympic Games, Turin, Italy, was the highest free skate score since the new scoring system was adopted in 2003. He opened by landing his big jump combination – a quadruple

←■ OLDEST WINTER GAMES COMPETITOR

The oldest-ever competitor at the Winter Olympic Games is James Coates (GB), who competed in the skeleton in St. Moritz, Switzerland, in 1948 aged 53 years 328 days. The **oldest female competitor to take part in the Winter Olympics** is Anne Abernathy (US Virgin Islands, pictured) who took part in the luge in Salt Lake City in 2002, aged 48 years 307 days.

toe loop and a triple toe loop – for a total of 13.86 points. He added a triple axel for 9.36 points and a triple Lutz for 7.43 points.

COUNTRIES

MOST COUNTRIES PRESENT

Five countries attended 24 Summer Games from 1896 to 2000: Australia, France, Great Britain, Greece, and Switzerland (who, for Melbourne in 1956, contested only the Equestrian events in Stockholm, Sweden).

MOST MEDAL-WINNING COUNTRIES AT A WINTER GAMES

The greatest number of countries to take home a medal at a single Winter Olympic Games is 25, at the 2002 Winter Olympics, Salt Lake City, Utah, USA.

MOST MEDAL-WINNING COUNTRIES AT A SUMMER GAMES

A total of 80 different countries won at least one medal at the 2000 Summer Olympic Games, which were held in Sydney, Australia.

? DID YOU KNOW

The ceremony of the Olympic torch as we know it today has taken place only since 1936. It was in this year, at the Berlin Olympics in Germany, that the first ever official Olympic torch relay was organized. The tradition of the Olympic torch is central to the ideas underpinning the games, and plays an important role in reminding us of the importance of fire in human endeavor. The Olympic Museum, at Lausanne in Switzerland, houses a collection of torches from both the Winter and Summer Games.

! X-REF

Who is the world's fastest man? Turn to p.266 to find out the answer and to discover a host of other fascinating sports records.

GREATEST ATTENDANCE AT THE OLYMPICS

An astonishing 5,797,923 spectators attended the Summer Olympic Games in Los Angeles, California, USA, in 1984. This was the XXIII Olympiad.

PROFESSIONAL BULL RIDING

★ HIGHEST MARKED RIDE ➡

Three riders have achieved a highest marked ride of 96.5 points: Bubba Dunn (USA) riding Promise Land in 1999; Chris Shivers (USA) riding Jim Jam in 2000 and Dillinger in 2001; and, most recently, Michael Gaffney (USA, pictured) – a.k.a. "G-Man" – riding Little Yellow Jacket in 2004.

★ **NEW RECORD**
★ **UPDATED RECORD**

★ GREATEST ATTENDANCE AT A PROFESSIONAL BULL RIDING WORLD FINALS

An unprecedented 76,936 spectators attended the Professional Bull Riding (PBR) World Finals in Las Vegas, Nevada, USA, in 2005.

★ HEAVIEST RIDER

Three competitors share the distinction of being the heaviest riders to participate in Professional Bull Riding: Ross Coleman (USA) and brothers Allan and Adriano Moraes (both Brazil). All three riders weigh 185 lb (84 kg). By contrast, the bulls they ride weigh an average of 1,800 lb (820 kg).

Adriano Moraes (Brazil, b. April 10, 1970) was 35 years old when he took part in the 2005 World Finals, which also makes him the ★ **oldest professional bull rider still competing**.

Adriano is also the holder of a third record – the ★ **greatest number of career wins in Professional Bull Riding**. To date he has won 25 times.

★ LIGHTEST RIDER

Brian Canter (USA) started his professional bull-riding career in 2005 weighing just 110 lb (50 kg). By way of comparison, the lightest bulls in competition weigh no less than 1,700 lb (770 kg).

Brian (b. June 25, 1987) also holds the record for the ★ **youngest professional bull rider ever to feature in competition**. He was just 18 years old when he first appeared in the 2005 Professional Bull Riding World Finals.

★ MOST 90-POINT RIDES IN A SEASON

In 1999, the year that he won the Professional Bull Riding World Championships, Cody Hart (USA) achieved 16 90-point rides.

★ MOST ⬅ SCORED RIDES IN A CAREER

Justin McBride (USA) achieved 276 scored rides in his Professional Bull Riding career. McBride's six wins in 2005 matched Cody Hart's (USA) score in 1999 – they share the record for ★**most wins in one season**. In 2005, McBride's earnings totaled $1,529,630, the ★ **most money won in a season**. He is pictured winning the World Championships at the PBR World Finals in Las Vegas on November 6, 2005, his first world title after eight years as a professional.

The ★**most consecutive wins in a season** is three by Chris Shivers (USA) in 2000.

★ MOST WORLD CHAMPIONSHIPS WON ➡

Two riders have each won two Professional Bull Riding World Championships and claimed the PBR trophy (right): Adriano Moraes (Brazil) in 1994 and 2001, and Chris Shivers (USA) in 2000 and 2003. Shivers has also recorded the ★ **most rides in a career**, with 514 in 1997–2006, and PBR's ★ **highest career earnings**: $2,702,447 as of 2005.

Another trophy, the PBR Ring of Honor (below) is awarded each year to the rider judged to have contributed most to the sport.

EARNINGS

★ HIGHEST ANNUAL EARNINGS FROM A WORLD FINALS

In 2004, Team Army's Mike Lee (USA) set a record for the highest annual earnings from a World Finals, netting a total of $303,300. In the same year, he also won the PBR World Championships.

HIGHEST ANNUAL EARNINGS FOR A ROOKIE

"Cool Hand" Luke Snyder (USA) earned $348,561 in 2001 – a record, and a feat for which he was voted PBR Rookie of the Year. His career earnings so far total $730,907.

BULLS

★ MOST RIDDEN BULL

Promise Land, owned by Terry Williams Bucking Bulls (USA), has been ridden a total of 39 times.

Promise Land also holds the record for the ★ **bull with the most 90-point rides** – his riders achieved this feat 34 times.

★ HEAVIEST BULL

Nile, owned by Jerry Nelson (USA), weighed 2,400 lb (1,088 kg). This is more than twice the weight of the ★ **lightest bull ever in PBR competition**, Blueberry Wine – owned by the Herrington Cattle Company (USA) – who tipped the scales at only 1,100 lb (500 kg).

Blueberry Wine – a black-and-white speckled Plummer/ Brahma cross – also holds the record for the ★ **bull responsible for the most buck-offs**, with 86. Blueberry Wine's career-average buck-off time is just 3.71 seconds!

★ OLDEST BULL

Professional Bull Riding bulls start competing when they are three years old, and typically buck for between five and seven years. Red Wolf, from the Herrington Cattle Company (USA), however, bucked until the 2000 World Finals, retiring at the age of 13.

★ MOST BUCK-OFFS FOR A BULL

The greatest number of buck-outs a bull has participated in is 111, by Western Wishes owned by Page & Teague Bucking Bulls (USA).

★ MOST WORLD CHAMPION BULL TITLES

Little Yellow Jacket, a red Brangus bull owned in partnership by Joe and Nevada Berger, Tom Teague and Bernie Taupin, won three World Champion bull titles. He was born in 1996 and weighs 1,750 lb (794 kg).

⚠ PROFESSIONAL BULL RIDING

Professional Bull Riders, Inc., was founded in 1992 by 20 bull riders who wanted to make bull riding – the most popular event in traditional rodeo – in to a stand-alone sport.

Each rider chipped in $1,000 to help launch their dream of seeing bull riders recognized as mainstream professional athletes. Since that time, the PBR has been owned and operated by its athletes, and more than 700 riders from the USA, Canada, Brazil, and Australia hold PBR memberships.

When the first world champion was crowned in 1994, the PBR's major tour consisted of eight events offering a combined pot of $250,000. Today, the Built Ford Tough Series is a $10-million tour that has 100 million viewers tuning in to watch on NBC Sports and the Outdoor Life Network (OLN).

★ MOST EVENTS ATTENDED

J. W. "Ironman" Hart (USA) has attended a total of 220 Professional Bull Riding events. His record also encompasses the ★ **most consecutive events competed in**, with 197 between 1994 and 2003 – a feat that earned him the "Ironman" nickname – as well as the ★ **most times to qualify for the World Finals** (12) and the ★ **most buck-offs in a career** (316).

RUGBY

MOST ⬆ WORLD CUP TITLES (WOMEN)

The Women's World Cup has been contested four times (1991, 1994, 1998, and 2002). New Zealand has won the title twice, in 1998 and 2002; the USA and England have one win each. The fifth tournament takes place from August 31 to September 17, 2006.

★ NEW RECORD
★ UPDATED RECORD

★ MOST TRIES IN A SUPER LEAGUE MATCH

The greatest number of tries scored by an individual player in a Super League match is five by Lesley Vainikolo (New Zealand) playing for the Bradford Bulls against Hull FC on September 2, 2005. The Super League, in its current format, has been in existence since 1996.

LEAGUE

★ MOST AUSTRALIAN PREMIERSHIP WINS

South Sydney (Australia) won 20 titles between 1908 and 2005. The competition has had three titles: the New South Wales Rugby League (1908–94); the Australian Rugby League (1995–97); and the National Rugby League (1998–present).

YOUNGEST INTERNATIONAL PLAYER

The youngest rugby league international is Gavin Gordon, who played for Ireland v. Moldova on October 16, 1995, at Spotland, Rochdale, UK, aged 17 years 229 days.

★ MOST WORLD CLUB TROPHY WINS

The most World Club Trophy victories is three by Wigan (UK) in 1987, 1991, and 1994. The World Club trophy is contested each year by the winners of the Great British and Australian Grand Finals.

HIGHEST SCORE

The highest score in an international match is France's 120–0 defeat of Serbia and Montenegro during the Mediterranean Cup in Beirut, Lebanon, on October 22, 2003.

★ MOST TRI-NATIONS TITLES

The rugby league Tri-Nations was inaugurated in 1999 and contested by Australia, Great Britain, and New Zealand. It has been won a record three times by Australia in 1999, 2004, and 2005.

LONGEST DROP KICK (LEAGUE)

Joseph Paul "Joe" Lydon (b. November 22, 1963) scored a drop goal of 61 yd (56 m) for Wigan against Warrington (both UK) in a Challenge Cup semifinal at Maine Road, Manchester, UK, on March 25, 1989.

HIGHEST ATTENDANCE

A crowd of 107,558 spectators watched the National Rugby League Grand Final at Stadium Australia, Sydney, New South Wales, Australia, on September 26, 1999, when Melbourne defeated St. George Illawarra 20–18.

★ MOST MAN OF STEEL AWARDS

Ellery Hanley (UK) won three Man of Steel trophies in 1985, 1987, and 1989. The trophy is awarded to the best player each season.

UNION

★ MOST SIX NATIONS GRAND SLAMS

France has won two Grand Slams in the Six Nations Championship, in 2002 and 2004. A Grand Slam is recorded when a team wins all of its matches.

★ MOST SUPER 12 TITLES

The greatest number of Super 12 tournament victories by a team is five by the Canterbury Crusaders (New Zealand) in 1998–2000, 2002, and 2005.

HIGHEST ⬆ ATTENDANCE (RUGBY UNION)

All Black Byron Kelleher passes away from Todd Blackadder (both New Zealand) against the Wallabies in the Tri-Nations match in Sydney, Australia, on July 15, 2000. The game was watched by 109,874 paying spectators, the highest attendance for a rugby union match. New Zealand went on to win with a 39–35 victory over Australia.

★ MOST HEINEKEN CUP TITLES

Inaugurated in 1995, the Heineken Cup – European club rugby's premier competition – has been won three times by Toulouse (France), in 1996, 2003, and 2005.

OLDEST COMPETITION

The United Hospitals Cup, played between teams representing hospitals in England, was first contested in 1875.

MOST POINTS SCORED BY AN INDIVIDUAL AT A WORLD CUP MATCH

Simon Culhane (New Zealand) scored 45 points for his country against Japan in Bloemfontein, South Africa, on June 4, 1995.

★ MOST TRIES SCORED IN WORLD CUP TOURNAMENTS

Jonah Lomu (New Zealand) scored an unprecedented 15 tries in the 1995 and 1999 competitions.

★ MOST INTERNATIONAL APPEARANCES

George Gregan played 117 times for Australia between 1990 and 2005.

★ MOST POINTS IN A FIVE/SIX NATIONS CHAMPIONSHIP CAREER

The most points scored by an individual in a Five/Six Nations career is 409 by Neil Jenkins (Wales) in matches between 1991 and 2001.

★ MOST TRIES IN A FIVE/SIX NATIONS CHAMPIONSHIP MATCH

George Lindsay (Scotland) scored five tries against Wales in Edinburgh, Scotland, UK, on February 26, 1887.

★ MOST TRIES IN A FIVE/SIX NATIONS CHAMPIONSHIP CAREER

Ian Smith (Scotland) scored 24 tries in matches between 1924 and 1933.

LONGEST DROP KICK

The longest drop goal was one of 90 yd (82 m) scored by Gerald

MOST POINTS (IRB SEVENS)

Ben Gollings (UK), pictured right with Johnnny Weston (UK), scored 1,225 points playing in tournaments from 1999 to 2005 for England.

★ MOST → RUGBY TACKLES IN ONE HOUR

Cranleigh RFC under-13s made 1,979 tackles on February 6, 2005, in Surrey, UK. They reclaimed the record after the under-11s team (who originally set the record in April 2001) had their total of 1,644 tackles beaten.

Hamilton Brand for South Africa v. England at Twickenham, London, UK, on January 2, 1932. It was taken 7 yd (6 m) inside the England half, 55 yd (50 m) from the posts, and dropped over the dead-ball line.

HIGHEST POSTS

The highest rugby union goal posts measure 110 ft (33.54 m) – equivalent to the height of 12 buses stacked on top of each other. The record-breaking posts stand at the Roan Antelope Rugby Union Club, Luanshya, Zambia.

IRB SEVENS

★ MOST SERIES TITLES

The IRB Sevens Series, which began in 1999, has been won six times, and every year, by New Zealand between 1999 and 2005. The series is a competition consisting of between seven and 11 separate Sevens tournaments, played around the world each season.

★ MOST INDIVIDUAL GOALS

The greatest number of kicks at goal scored by an individual player in IRB Sevens tournaments is 385 by Waisale Serevi (Fiji), playing for his country between 1999 and 2005.

★ MOST INDIVIDUAL APPEARANCES

Amasio Raoma Valence (New Zealand) made 50 appearances in IRB sevens tournaments between 1999 and 2005.

★ MOST TRIES SCORED

The record for the greatest number of tries in IRB Sevens events is jointly held by Ben Gollings (England) and Fabian Juries (South Africa). Each has scored 128 tries.

? DID YOU KNOW?

The main difference between rugby league and rugby union is the number of players in each team. League features 13 players per team while union has 15. More emphasis is placed on scrums and line-outs in union, while league is considered a more free-flowing and -running game. Historically, there are lots of differences between the two disciplines, one of the main ones being that league began as a professional sport, and union as an amateur one.

TARGET SPORTS

! X-REF

Turn to p.271 for a comprehensive list of individual events and disciplines that the International Shooting Sport Federation (ISSF) monitors at Olympic level.

★ NEW RECORD
★ UPDATED RECORD

SHOOTING – RUNNING TARGET 10 M (MEN)

On August 19, 2004, Manfred Kurzer (Germany) set a new world record score of 590 points in the men's 10 m running target at the Olympic Games in Athens, Greece.

He also holds the world record for the **10 m running target mixed**, with a score of 391 at Pontevedra, Spain, on March 14, 2001.

ARCHERY

★ HIGHEST SCORE IN AN OUTDOOR RECURVE FITA ROUND (WOMEN – TEAM)

On November 10, 2005, Park Sung-Hyun, Yun Mi-Jin, and Yun Ok Hee (all South Korea) scored 4,129 points from a possible 4,320 in the single FITA round (3 x 144), women's team category, in New Delhi, India.

MOST BULL'S-EYES IN 90 SECONDS

Jeremie Masson (France) hit three bull's-eyes in 90 seconds on the set of *L'Été De Tous Les Records* in Argelès-Gazost, France, on July 15, 2004, while standing at a distance of 59 ft (18 m) from the targets.

OLDEST ORGANIZATION

The Ancient Society of Kilwinning Archers in Scotland, UK, recorded its first Papingo shoot in 1483.

DARTS

★ HIGHEST SCORE IN 24 HOURS (MEN)

Kenny Fellowes (UK) scored 567,145 in 24 hours at The Prince of Wales, Cashes Green, Gloucestershire, UK, on September 28–29, 1996.

The ★**highest darts score in 24 hours, hitting only bull's-eyes and 25s**, is 526,750 by a team of eight players at the George Inn, Morden, Surrey, UK, on July 1–2, 1994.

★ HIGHEST DARTS SCORE IN SIX HOURS

Russell Locke (UK) scored 210,172 at the Hugglescote Working

Men's Club, Coalville, Leicestershire, UK, on September 10, 1989.

Karen Knightly (UK) scored 99,725 in six hours at the Lord Clyde, Leyton, UK, on March 17, 1991, the ★**highest darts score in six hours by a woman**.

★ HIGHEST DARTS SCORE IN 10 HOURS BY A PAIR

Jon Archer and Neil Rankin (both UK) scored 465,919 in 10 hours at the Royal Oak, Cossington, Leicestershire, UK, on November 17, 1990.

POOL

MOST POCKET BILLIARDS WORLD CHAMPIONSHIPS

Pool, or championship pocket billiards, with numbered balls, began to be standardized around 1890. One of its greatest exponents was Ralph Greenleaf (USA), who won the world professional title a total of 19 times between 1919 and 1937.

OLDEST COMPETITIVE PLAYER

Wesley Walker (USA, b. April 24, 1916) plays for Southern Vending in the Valley National Eight-ball Association league in Oklahoma, USA.

MOST BALLS POCKETED IN 24 HOURS

The **most balls pocketed in 24 hours on a US table** is 16,723 by Nick Nikolaidis (Canada) at the Unison Bar, Montreal, Canada, on August 13–14, 2001.

During the attempt, he also broke the record for **fastest pool pocketing (two tables)**, when he cleared two consecutive racks in 1 min 33 sec.

Paul Sullivan (UK) pocketed a total of 16,511 balls at the Royal Oak,

Hirst Courtney, North Yorkshire, UK, on April 17–18, 1998, the **most balls pocketed in 24 hours on a UK table**.

FASTEST TIME TO POCKET ALL BALLS

Dave Pearson (UK) pocketed all 15 pool balls in 26.5 seconds at Pepper's Bar And Grill, Windsor, Ontario, Canada, on April 4, 1997, the **fastest time to pocket all balls on a US table**.

Susan Thompson (UK) pocketed all 15 pool balls in 37.07 seconds at the Phoenix Pool & Snooker Club, Wallasey, Merseyside, UK, on December 1, 1996, the **fastest time to pocket all balls on a UK table**.

SHOOTING

★ MOST CLAY-PIGEON TARGETS BROKEN IN 12 HOURS (TEAM)

A team of five – David Billingsby, Bob Barrett, Matt Kendall, Ken Newman, and Bernard Walshe (all UK) – shot 4,602 targets in the Down the Line discipline, in 12 hours, at Kent Gun Club, Dartford, Kent, UK, on March 27, 2005.

CLAY-PIGEON SHOOTING – FASTEST 25 TARGETS

Jose Lopes (France) shot 25 clay pigeons in 1 min 11 sec on the set of *L'Été De Tous Les Records* in Argelès-Gazost, France, on July 12, 2004.

MOST WINS IN THE CLAY-PIGEON SHOOTING WORLD CHAMPIONSHIPS

Susan Nattrass (Canada) has won six world championships, in 1974–75, 1977–79, and 1981.

★ YOUNGEST BDO DARTS WORLD CHAMPION

Jelle Klaasen beat Raymond Van Barneveld (both Netherlands) 7–5 in the final of the British Darts Organization (BDO) World Professional Darts Championships at Lakeside, Frimley Green, UK, on January 15, 2006, at the age of 21 years 121 days.

MOST CONSECUTIVE BULL'S-EYES

Leonard Proteau (Canada) scored 1,530 consecutive bull's-eyes in target shooting over a period of six months, from 1967 to 1968, at the Canadian Forces Station at Mont Apica, Quebec, Canada. He used a Dominion Marksman Model 190 S rifle in the prone position over a distance of 25 yd (22.8 m).

HIGHEST SCORE WITH AN AIR PISTOL OVER 10 M

Sergey Pyzhyanov (USSR) achieved a score of 695.1 (prelim. 593 + 102.1) in the men's 10 m air pistol competition in Munich, Germany, on October 13, 1989.

The women's record over this distance is 493.0 (393+100.0) and was set by Svetlana Smirnova (Russia) in Munich, Germany, on May 23, 1998.

HIGHEST SCORE WITH AN AIR RIFLE OVER 10 M

Artem Khadjibekov (Russia) scored 700.7 (597 + 103.7) at the men's 10 m air rifle competition in Munich, Germany, on November 18, 2000.

Gaby Buehlmann (Switzerland) set a world record for the women's air rifle 10 m competition (40 shots) in Munich, Germany, on May 24, 1998, with a score of 503.5 (398+105.5).

★ MOST PISTOL-SHOOTING TARGETS HIT IN ONE MINUTE

Manuel Alexandre-Augrand (France) hit 19 targets in one minute on the set of *L'Été De Tous Les Records*, Benodet, France, on August 25, 2005. He used an air pistol and shot from a distance of 10 m.

SNOOKER

FASTEST 147

The only way to score a 147 clearance is to pot the black ball after every red, then clear the colored balls in order: yellow, green, brown, blue, pink, and black. The fastest 147 snooker break in a professional tournament was achieved in 5 min 20 sec by Ronnie O'Sullivan (UK) during the World Championships held at Sheffield, South Yorkshire, UK, on April 21, 1997.

O'Sullivan (b. December 5, 1975) also holds the record for **the youngest person to score a break of 147**, a feat that he achieved at the age of 15 years 98 days during the English Amateur Championship (Southern Area) at Aldershot, Hants, UK, on March 13, 1991.

★ FASTEST COLORS CLEARANCE

James Popplewell, a.k.a. "The Mayor of Flair" (UK), potted all of the colored balls, in sequence, in 23 seconds at the studios of Sky Sports Soccer AM's *All Sports Show*, Isleworth, Middlesex, UK, on May 12, 2005.

MOST CENTURY BREAKS IN A SEASON

Stephen Hendry (UK) scored a total of 53 century breaks in 1994–95.

MOST "MISSES" CALLED

During the 1997 Benson and Hedges Masters Snooker Tournament at Wembley Arena, London, UK, Mark King (UK) played 12 consecutive foul shots that were called "misses" and replaced by the match referee.

? DID YOU KNOW?

The first Olympic Games of modern times took place in 1896 in Athens. Of the nine different sports featured, shooting drew the second-highest number of participants.

In 1907, eight national shooting federations formed the Union International des Fédérations et Associations Nationales de Tir (UIT), which standardized rules of conduct for shooting competitions for the first time. These rules still form the basis for ISSF-recognized competitions.

In pistol, rifle, and running target contests, shooters fire at round black aiming areas set against white backgrounds. The targets are divided into 10 concentric scoring zones, and are electronic; a computer system scores each shot.

For shotgun events, a hit is scored (resulting in one point) whenever the shooter fires and hits the target so that at least one piece of it is visibly broken.

ARCHERY
OUTDOOR RECURVE, FITA ROUND (WOMEN)
Park Sung-Hyun (South Korea) scored a record 1,405 (out of a possible 1,440) at Cheongju, South Korea, on October 10, 2004.

TENNIS & RACKET SPORTS

HIGHEST ↑ EARNINGS (TENNIS)

Between 1982 and 1999, Steffi Graf (Germany, above) earned $21,807,509. For the men, Pete Sampras (USA) holds the record with earnings of $41,314,315 up to March 2001.

Turn to p.125 to find out which tennis star earned the most money in 2005.

★ **NEW RECORD**
☆ **UPDATED RECORD**

BADMINTON

LONGEST RALLY IN A COMPETITION

In the men's singles final of the 1987 All-England Championships between Morten Frost (Denmark) and Icuk Sugiarto (Indonesia), there were two successive rallies of more than 90 strokes.

WORLD CHAMPIONSHIPS – MOST TITLES OVERALL

Park Joo-bong (South Korea) has won a record five World Championship badminton titles. He triumphed in the men's doubles in 1985 and 1991, and in the mixed doubles in 1985, 1989, and 1991.

SHORTEST MATCH

Ra Kyung-min (South Korea) tasted badminton victory in the fastest time ever when she beat Julia Mann (UK) 11–2, 11–1 in six minutes during the 1996 Uber Cup in Hong Kong, China, on May 19, 1996.

TABLE TENNIS

LONGEST RALLY

Brian and Steve Seibel (USA) maintained a rally for 8 hr 15 min 1 sec at the Christown YMCA, Phoenix, Arizona, USA, on August 14, 2004.

LONGEST MARATHON (DOUBLES)

Bill Weir and Lance, Phil and Mark Warren (all USA) played for 101 hr 1 min 11 sec in Sacramento, California, USA, between April 9 and 13, 1979.

★ MOST MEN'S OLYMPICS GOLD MEDALS

China won six men's Olympic golds between 1988 and 2004.

TENNIS

YOUNGEST WORLD NUMBER ONE (WOMEN)

Martina Hingis (Switzerland, b. September 30, 1980) was aged 16 yr 182 days when she achieved top ranking on March 31, 1997.

★ YOUNGEST SEEDED WIMBLEDON MEN'S SINGLES PLAYER

The youngest seeded Wimbledon men's singles competitor is Björn Borg (Sweden), who was aged 17 yr 19 days old when he completed his first match in the 1973 tournament.

The **youngest seeded Wimbledon ladies singles player** is Jennifer Capriati (USA), who was aged 14 yr 89 days when she played her first match on June 26, 1990.

←▪ FASTEST TENNIS SERVE

Andy Roddick (USA) served an ace measured at an unprecedented speed of 153 mph (246.2 km/h) during a match at the Queen's Club, London, UK, on June 11, 2004.

The **fastest serve by a woman** is 127.4 mph (205 km/h) by Venus Williams (USA) at a match in Zurich, Switzerland, on October 16, 1998.

OLDEST WIMBLEDON CHAMPION

Martina Navratilova (USA, b. October 18, 1956) was aged 46 yr 261 days when she won the mixed doubles at Wimbledon with Leander Paes (India) on July 6, 2003.

Navratilova also holds the record for the **greatest number of women's singles tournament titles**, with 167 victories between 1974 and 1994.

★ MOST WIMBLEDON MEN'S SINGLES TITLES

W. C. Renshaw (UK) won a total of seven Wimbledon men's singles titles in 1881–86 and 1889. Pete Sampras (USA) equaled this feat with title wins in 1993–95 and 1997–2000.

YOUNGEST WINNER OF A FEDERATION CUP MATCH

Anna Kournikova (Russia, b. June 7, 1981) beat Anna-Karin Svensson 6–0, 6–3 on April 25, 1996, aged 14 yr 323 days. Her performance helped Russia defeat Sweden 3–0 in the Federation Cup.

★MOST
WOMEN'S TEAM TABLE TENNIS OLYMPIC GOLDS

The most gold medals won in Olympic competitions by a women's team is seven by China between 1988 and 2004. Pictured is Yining Zhang (China) at the Athens 2004 Summer Olympic Games. She is serving during the women's singles table tennis semifinal match on August 21, 2004.

★MOST TOURNAMENT TITLES BY A MAN

Jimmy Connors (USA) accumulated 109 men's singles tournament victories between 1972 and 1989.

Connors (USA) won a total of 1,222 matches in 1972–89, the **most tournament match wins by a man**.

MOST TOURNAMENT MATCH WINS

Martina Navratilova (USA) achieved 1,440 tournament match wins between 1974 and 1994.

★MOST CONSECUTIVE ➡
TENNIS FINAL VICTORIES

The most consecutive wins of tennis tournament finals in the Open era is 24 by Roger Federer (Switzerland) between October 2003 and September 2005. Federer is pictured winning the men's singles final match at Wimbledon on July 4, 2004. A location list of all his final victories can be found in the box, above right.

★LOWEST-RANKED PLAYER TO WIN A GRAND SLAM TOURNAMENT

The lowest-ranked individual player to win a Grand Slam tournament is Mark Edmonson (Australia), who was ranked No.212 in the world when he won the Australian Open in 1976.

LONGEST TENNIS MARATHON (DOUBLES)

The longest competitive doubles tennis match lasted 48 hr 6 min and was contested between Jaroslaw Kadzielewski and Rafal Siupka, and Mateusz Zatorski and Kamil Milian (all Poland), from August 30 to September 1, 2002, at Gliwice Sports Hall, Gliwice, Poland.

★MOST CLUB MEN'S DOUBLES CHAMPIONSHIPS (MULTIPLE PARTNERS)

The greatest number of club men's doubles championships won by an individual at the same club is 20 by Stuart Foster (UK) between 1985 and 2005, playing with various partners at Leverstock Green Lawn Tennis Club in Hertfordshire, UK.

★LONGEST RALLY

Steven Worrallo and Allen Benbow (both UK) played a contrived rally consisting of 24,696 strokes at the Droitwich Spa Lawn Tennis Club, Droitwich Spa, Worcestershire, UK, on April 23, 2005. The feat lasted just over seven hours.

★MOST ACES SERVED IN A GRAND SLAM TOURNAMENT MATCH

The greatest number of aces served by an individual player in a Grand Slam tournament match is 49 by Richard Krajicek (Netherlands)

WORLD MIXED TEAM BADMINTON CHAMPIONSHIPS (SUDIRMAN CUP) ➡

The most wins of the Sudirman Cup is five by China in 1995, 1997, 1999, 2001, and 2005. Zhang Jun (top) and Gao Ling of China are pictured right.

against Yevgeny Kafelnikov (Russia) in a quarter-final match of the US Open on September 8, 1999.

★MOST ATP TOUR DOUBLES TITLES

Todd Woodbridge (Australia) secured an unprecedented 81 Association of Tennis Professionals (ATP) Tour doubles tennis titles between 1990 and 2005.

★MOST WINS IN THE SINGLES COMPETITION AT THE ATP TOUR CHAMPIONSHIPS

The greatest number of wins in the singles competition of the ATP Tour Championships is five. The record is shared by two players: Ivan Lendl (USA), who won in 1982–83, twice in 1986, and once in 1987; and Pete Sampras (USA), who won in 1991, 1994, 1996–97, and 1999.

> **[!] ROGER FEDERER'S TENNIS FINAL VICTORIES**
>
> **Vienna** (Oct. 2003)
> **Houston Masters Cup** (Nov. 2003)
> **Australian Open** (Jan. 2004)
> **Dubai** (Mar. 2004)
> **Indian Wells Masters** (Mar. 2004)
> **Hamburg Masters** (May 2004)
> **Halle Open** (Jun. 2004)
> **Wimbledon** (Jul. 2004)
> **Gstaad** (Jul 2004)
> **Canadian Masters** (Jul. 2004)
> **US Open** (Sep. 2004)
> **Bangkok** (Oct. 2004)
> **Houston Masters Cup** (Nov. 2004)
> **Qatar Open** (Jan. 2005)
> **Rotterdam** (Feb. 2005)
> **Dubai Open** (Feb. 2005)
> **Indian Wells Masters** (Mar. 2005)
> **Miami Nasdaq-100 Open** (April 2005)
> **Hamburg Masters** (May 2005)
> **Halle Open** (Jun. 2005)
> **Wimbledon** (Jul. 2005)
> **Cincinnati Masters** (Aug. 2005)
> **US Open** (Sep. 2005)
> **Bangkok** (Oct. 2005)

W@CKy WOR[d Ch&mplonsHips

the five-minute contest is 21 by Henri Pellonpää (Finland) in 1995. The insects must be killed by hand.

★ PILLOW FIGHTING

The World Pillow Fighting Championships in Kenwood, California, USA, is the ★ **longest-running annual pillow-fighting competition**, with its 40th event held on July 4, 2006. Each year, about 100 pillow fighters battle it out with wet, muddy pillows while sitting on a steel pole above a mud-filled creek!

★ PIPE SMOKING

Dr. Lubomir Cinka (Czech Republic) smoked for 3 hr 4 min 35 sec at the 2001 World Cup in Pipesmoking Championship at Ascot racecourse, Berkshire, UK, on October 14, 2001, the ★ **longest time to smoke a pipe without relighting**.

★ AIR GUITAR

The Oulu Music Video Festival's Air Guitar World Championships are held annually in Oulu, Finland. Zac "The Magnet" Monro (UK) has won the championships a record two times, in 2001 and 2002 – the first time a champion has won more than once since it was first contested in 1996.

"Air guitar is the purest art form there is left," said Monro, an architect, whose 60-second performance of "Fell In Love With A Girl" by The White Stripes in 2002 also earned him a *real* handmade guitar!

★ CONKERING

The ★ **most World Conker Championships won in the men's category** is three by P. Midlane (UK), who won in 1969, 1973, and 1985, and J. Marsh (UK), who took the 1974, 1975, and 1994 titles.

The ★ **greatest number of wins in the women's category** is two by Shelia Doubleday (UK), who won in 1988 and 1993. The annual contest has been held in Ashton, UK, since 1965.

HAGGIS HURLING

Alan Pettigrew (UK) threw a haggis – with a minimum weight of

1 lb 8 oz (680 g) – a distance of 180 ft 10 in (55.11 m) in Inchmurrin, Argyll, UK, on May 24, 1984.

★ CELL-PHONE THROWING

Mikko Lampi (Finland) beat 60 other international competitors when he threw his cellular phone a record 311 ft 7 in (94.97 m) in the Sixth Mobile Phone Throwing World Championships, held in Savonnlina, Finland, on August 27, 2005.

MOSQUITO KILLING

The World Mosquito Killing Championships are held annually in Pelkosenniemi, Finland. The **most mosquitoes killed** in

★ BEARD & MUSTACHE SCULPTING

Karl-Heinz Hille (Germany, below) is the only person to win the overall title twice at the World Beard and Mustache Championships. He won in 1999 and 2003, both times in the Imperial Cheek Beard category.

In the 2005 event, held in Berlin, Germany, there was no clear winner (in accordance with Berlin rules), but Elmar Weisser (Germany, below left) of the Swabian Beard Club was the clear favorite thanks to his hirsute representation of his country's famous Brandenburg Gate.

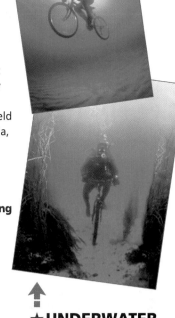

GURNING

The only gurner to have won the World Gurning Championships – held at the Egremont Crab Fair and Sports event in Cumbria, UK – 10 times is Gordon Mattinson (UK), in 1967–72 and in 1974–77.

To gurn means "to snarl like a dog and distort the countenance" – a tradition dating back to days when "village idiots" were persuaded to make faces for ale. The competition is not limited to toothless old men, although they do make up a large proportion of the contestants.

Another traditional event at the fair is competitive pipe smoking.

★ SANTA CLAUS EVENTING

Of the many Santa Claus contests, the ★ Santa Claus competition with the most disciplines is the ClauWau Santa Claus Championships, held in Samnau, Switzerland. Each entry is judged on five disciplines in the qualifying rounds: chimney-climbing, costume beauty, snowball-dueling, "tangerines and donkey" (an event that includes donkey-trekking), and gingerbread decorating. Qualifiers then compete in three more disciplines before

a winner is selected: a horn-sledging race, ski-racing, and performing in a Santa show.

★ SHEEP COUNTING

The ★ first Sheep Counting World Championships were held in Hay, New South Wales, Australia, on September 14–15, 2002. In this contest, hundreds of sheep run past competitors, who then attempt to come up with a precise figure. Peter Desailly (Australia) took the inaugural title by correctly counting 277 sheep.

★ SHIN KICKING

The ★ longest-running shin-kicking competition has taken place since 1636, as part of Robert Dover's (UK) Cotswold Olimpicks, held in England, UK, since 1612.

TOBACCO SPITTING

The **farthest tobacco-spit** is 53 ft 3 in (16.23 m) and was achieved by David O'Dell (USA) at the World Tobacco Spitting Championships held at the Calico Ghost Town, California, USA, on March 22, 1997.

★ TESTICLE COOKING

The world's ★ largest and ★ longest-running testicle-cooking world championship is the World Ball Cup, held each year in Gornji Milanovac, Serbia. The 2005 championship attracted 1,000 visitors to watch teams cook 44 lb (20 kg) of bull, boar, camel, ostrich, and kangaroo testicles!

TOE WRESTLING

The **most men's Toe Wrestling World Championships victories** is five by Alan "Nasty" Nash (UK) in 1994, 1996–97, 2000, and 2002. The **most ladies' wins** is four by Karen Davies (UK), from 1999 to 2002.

WIFE CARRYING

The fastest time to complete the 771-ft (235-m) course of the World Wife-Carrying Championships – held annually in Sonkajärvi, Finland – is 55.5 seconds by Margo Uusorg and Birgit Ulricht (both Estonia) on July 1, 2000.

★ UNDERWATER CYCLING

The ★ largest underwater cycle race involved 19 scuba divers who competed in the 196-ft (60-m) SeaGuernsey Cycle Soumarine, in Havelet Bay, Guernsey, UK, on September 4, 2005. The first of its kind, the event was part of celebrations commemorating the 200th anniversary of the Battle of Trafalgar and will be held each year. The 2005 winner was Simon Bradbury from Guernsey, UK.

★ UGLIEST DOGS

The greatest number of times that the same dog has won the World's Ugliest Dog Contest at the Sonoma-Marin Fair in Petaluma, California, USA, is seven, by Chi Chi (left), a rare African sand dog. The most recent multiple-title holder was Sam (right), a 14-year-old pedigree Chinese crested dog who made judges recoil in horror between 2003 and 2005.

★ NEW RECORD
UPDATED RECORD

WATER SPORTS

★ MOST AQUABIKE BARREL ROLLS IN 2 MIN

Romain Stampers (France) achieved a total of 12 barrel rolls in 2 minutes on his aquabike. The record was set on *L'Été De Tous Les Records* at Argelès-Gazost, France, on July 6, 2005.

★ FASTEST 100 M WATERSKI TOW BY A ROWING BOAT

Set by Iris Cambray (France), who was only 12 years old at the time, the record for the fastest time for a waterskier towed by a rowing boat to travel 100 m (328 ft) is 19.9 seconds. Iris was towed by a team of eight from the rowing club Ligue Midi Pyrénées des Sociétés d'Aviron on the set of *L'Été De Tous Les Records* at Argelès-Gazost, France, on July 4, 2005.

FASTEST 2,000 M ROW (MEN'S EIGHT)

The record time to cover 2,000 m (6,562 ft) on non-tidal water is 5 min 22.80 sec (13.85 mph; 22.30 km/h), set by the Netherlands at the World Championships at St. Catharines, Ontario, Canada, on August 28, 1999.

FASTEST 2,000 M ROW (WOMEN'S EIGHT)

The women's record time to cover 2,000 m (6,562 ft) on non-tidal water is 5 min 57.02 sec (12.52 mph; 20.16 km/h), set by Romania in Lucerne, Switzerland, on July 9, 1999.

★ DEEPEST FREEDIVE – MEN (FINS)

On July 10, 2005, in Loutraki, Greece, Tom Sietas (Germany) set a new world record for men's freediving. Diving in the dynamic apnea with fins category, he managed to reach a remarkable depth of 695 ft 6 in (212 m), beating his own 2004 record of 610 ft 3 in (186 m).

★ NEW RECORD
★ UPDATED RECORD

★ LARGEST DRAGON BOAT REGATTA

A dragon boat regatta for 154 boats took place from June 17 to 19, 2005, in the city of Duisburg, Germany. A total of 121 races were staged, involving 3,224 athletes. The event was organized by Wanheimer Kanu-Gilde eV.

★ LONGEST DISTANCE BY A DRAGON BOAT IN 24 HOURS

Set by the Pickering Dragon Boat Club at Frenchman's Bay, Pickering, Ontario, Canada, on July 24–25, 2004, the record for the longest distance achieved in a dragon boat in 24 hours is 94.13 miles (151.5 km).

★ LONGEST RIVER BORE RIDE ON A SURFBOARD

The longest recorded surf ride on a river bore is 6.27 miles (10.1 km) by

★ DEEPEST FREEDIVE – WOMEN

On September 3, 2005, in Nice, France, Natalia Molchanova (Russia) set the record for women's freedive constant weight category, descending to a depth of 282 ft 1 in (86 m). She also holds the **women's dynamic apnea with fins** record of 584 ft (178 m).

Sergio Laus (Brazil). He surfed the Pororoca bore on the Araguari River, Amapa, Brazil, continuously for 33 min 15 sec on June 24, 2005.

MOST PEOPLE RIDING A SURFBOARD

Set at Snapper Rocks, Queensland, Australia, on March 5, 2005, the record for the greatest number of surfers riding a single surfboard at once is 47. This was achieved by the surfers climbing aboard and simultaneously riding a huge, scaled-up surfboard measuring 39 ft 4 in (12 m) in length.

★ DEEPEST FREEDIVE – MEN

The men's freedive constant weight record is held by Carlos Coste (Venezuela). On September 4, 2005, at the world championships in Villefrance-sur-Mer, France, he completed a dive of 344 ft 5 in (105 m).

MOST ➡ SURFERS
TO RIDE THE SAME WAVE SIMULTANEOUSLY

The world record for the greatest number of surfers to ride the same wave simultaneously is 42 and was set at Rico Point, Macumba Beach, Rio de Janeiro, Brazil, on November 18, 2005.

★ MOST WATERSKI FLIPS IN 30 SECONDS (WOMEN)

Clementine Lucine (France) completed seven full 360-degree flips on one waterski in 30 seconds. The record took place on the set of *L'Été De Tous Les Records* at Biscarrosse, France, on July 13, 2005.

★ MOST PARTICIPANTS IN A SWIMMING RELAY IN ONE HOUR

The record for the greatest number of swimmers to take part in a continuous relay to complete a lap in one hour is 137. It was set by members of the public at the "Big Splash" event at Horsham War Memorial Pool, Victoria, Australia, on February 25, 2005.

★ FASTEST LIFEGUARD DRILL RELAY (TEAM OF THREE)

Guillem Riand, Gregory Pratlong, and Marie Passebosc (all France) set a record of 45 seconds for the fastest time to complete the lifeguard drill relay. The record took place on the set of *L'Été De Tous Les Records* at Benodet, France, on August 23, 2005.

★ FASTEST TIME TO SWIM 50 M UNDERWATER

The fastest time to swim 50 m (164 ft) underwater in a 33-ft (10-m) pool is 24.6 seconds by Cédric Genin (France). The record took place on the set of *L'Été De Tous Les Records* at Cabourg, France, on August 1, 2005.

★ FASTEST 100 M BACKSTROKE (MEN)

On April 2, 2005, in Indianapolis, Indiana, USA, Aaron Peirsol (USA) set a new record for the fastest 100 m (164 ft) men's backstroke, in a time of 53.17 seconds.

★ FASTEST 50 M BACKSTROKE (WOMEN)

With a time of 28.19 seconds, Janine Pietsch (Germany) set a new record for the fastest 50 m women's backstroke. The time was completed on May 25, 2005, in Berlin, Germany.

FARTHEST DISTANCE SWUM BY A RELAY TEAM UNDERWATER IN 24 HOURS

A relay team of six members swam a distance of 94.44 miles (151.987 km) underwater in a swimming pool in Olomouc, Czechoslovakia (now Czech Republic), on October 17–18, 1987.

MOST PEOPLE
SCUBA DIVING AT ONE TIME

A total of 722 scuba divers were submerged simultaneously at Koh Tao, Thailand, on February 12, 2005, at the Koh Tao Underwater World Festival 2005. The event was organized by the Koh Tao Dive Operators Club and was the second festival of its kind, aimed at promoting awareness of the environment and related marine issues.

WINTER SPORTS

FASTEST ➡
1,000 M SHORT TRACK SPEED SKATING

Jiajun Li (China) recorded a time of 1 min 24.674 sec in the men's 1,000 m short track speed skating event in Bormio, Italy, on February 2, 2004. He is pictured during the semifinals of this event at the XIX Winter Olympics, in Salt Lake City, Utah, USA, in 2002.

FASTEST 500 M SPEED SKATING

Joji Kato (Japan) achieved a record-breaking time of 34.3 seconds in the men's 500 m speed skating event at the Second World Cup in Salt Lake City, Utah, USA, on November 19, 2005.

WINTER OLYMPICS

YOUNGEST OLYMPIC BOBSLED CHAMPION

William Guy Fiske (USA) was aged just 16 years 260 days when he won the gold medal with the five-man bobsled team during the 1928 Winter Games held in St. Moritz, Switzerland.

MOST PARTICIPANTS

In all, 2,550 competitors – from 77 countries – took part in the 2002 Winter Games in Salt Lake City, USA.

GREATEST PRESENCE AT THE WINTER OLYMPIC GAMES

Of the five countries represented at every Summer Games since 1896 (see p.249), only France, Great Britain, and Switzerland also have sent athletes to every Winter Games.

The Winter Games were first held in 1924, and the ★ **most medals won by a country** is 280, by Norway, followed by the USA with 216.

FIGURE-SKATING

HIGHEST MARKS

Donald George Jackson (Canada) achieved the **highest marks by a man in a figure-skating competition** with seven perfect 6.0s in the men's World Championship in Prague, Czechoslovakia, in 1962.

The **highest marks achieved by a woman in a figure-skating competition** is seven perfect 6.0s by Midori Ito (Japan) at the 1989 World Championships held in Paris, France.

MOST FIGURE-SKATING GRAND SLAMS

The **most men's figure-skating Grand Slams won** is two by Karl Schäfer (Austria) in 1932 and 1936. The Grand Slam comprises the European, World, and Olympic titles.

The **most figure-skating Grand Slams won by a woman** is also two, a record shared by Sonja Henie (Norway) in 1932 and 1936, and Katarina Witt (Germany) in 1984 and 1988.

BIATHLON

★ FIRST BIATHLETE TO WIN THE "BIG FOUR" IN THE SAME GAMES

Ole Einar Bjørndalen (Norway) became the first biathlete to win the sprint, pursuit, individual, and relay events in a single Winter Games, when he competed in the Salt Lake City Games, Utah, USA, in 2002.

Bjørndalen also holds the record for the ★ **most biathlon World Cup wins**. He had secured 61 victories as of March 23, 2006.

★ MOST WORLD CUP SPRINT MEDALS BY A COUNTRY (MEN)

The history of the men's 10 km sprint has been dominated by Germany, which has won a record 20 medals (12 as GDR): eight gold, eight silver, and four bronze.

MOST OLYMPIC BIATHLON ⬇ MEDALS (MEN)

The greatest number of men's biathlon medals won to date is seven by Ricco Gross (Germany): three golds (4 x 7.5 km in 1992, 1994, and 1998), three silver (10 km in 1992 and 1994; 4 x 7.5 km in 2002), and a bronze (pursuit in 2002).

★ MOST OLYMPIC BOBSLED GOLD MEDALS WON ➡

Three athletes have won three Olympic golds: Meinhard Nehmer and Bernhard Germeshausen (both GDR, now Germany) in the two-man (1976) and four-man (1976, 1980) events, and Andre Lange (Germany, pictured right, arms raised) who won gold in the two-man (2006), and four-man (2002, 2006) races.

★ MOST BIATHLON WORLD CUP 4 X 6 KM MIXED RELAY MEDALS ⬆

Since its introduction in 2005, the mixed 4 x 6 km relay has been won by Russia both times. The Russian team also has won a record three medals in total, taking silver and gold in 2005 (above) and gold in 2006.

★ MOST WORLD CUP SPRINT MEDALS BY A COUNTRY (WOMEN)

The women's sprint event (3.1 miles; 5 km until 1988, then 4.6 miles; 7.5 km) has seen the Russian team win 17 medals: five gold, eight silver, and four bronze. Russia also holds the overall record, with 35 medals in the men's and women's events.

CURLING

★ MOST WORLD CUP WINS BY A TEAM (MEN)

Canada has won 29 gold medals in the curling World Cup from the cup's inception in 1959. Canadians David Nedohin, Randy Ferbey, Scott Pfeifer, Marcel Rocque, and Dan Holowaychuk took gold most recently in the 2005 World Cup.

★ MOST WORLD CUP WINS BY A TEAM (WOMEN)

Canada has won 13 golds in the curling World Cup from the cup's inception in the women's game in 1979 to the present.

★ MOST MEDALS IN WORLD CHAMPIONSHIPS (WOMEN)

Dordi Nordby (Norway) won a total of 11 medals (two gold, three silver, and six bronze) in 1989–2005.

★ MOST CURLING APPEARANCES

Peter Lindholm, Tomas Nordin, Magnus Swartling, and Peter Narup (all Norway) have appeared at the last three Winter Olympics (1998, 2002, and 2006), the ★ most men's curling appearances.

The ★ most curling appearances by a woman is also three, shared by Marianne Haslum and Dordi Nordby (both Norway) who both appeared in the 1998, 2002 and 2006 Games.

MOST CURLING OLYMPIC MEDALS WON (WOMEN)

Mirjam Ott (Switzerland) took home a silver medal in 2002 and 2006.

OLDEST CURLER

Carl Riley (USA, b. October 14, 1904) was still playing on a regular basis on July 22, 2004, at Assiniboia Curling Club, Saskatchewan, Canada, aged 99 years 281 days.

★ NEW RECORD
★ UPDATED RECORD

★ HIGHEST SPEED ON AN AIRBOARD

The highest speed recorded on an Airboard Classic snow bodyboard is 88.1 mph (141.7 km/h) and was achieved by Laurent Matthey (Switzerland) at the Open Glis 2005 in Les Arcs, France, in 2005. The Airboard is an inflated snow bodyboard, made from a tough, plastic-coated textile, on which riders lie, chest-down, and steer by shifting their weight.

X GAMES

MOST → SNOCROSS MEDALS

Blair Morgan (Canada) has won eight medals for SnoCross: gold in 2001–03 and 2005–06, silver in 1999 and 2000, and bronze in 2004.

★ **NEW RECORD**

UPDATED RECORD

MOST X GAMES GOLD MEDALS WON BY AN INDIVIDUAL

As of August 2005, the most X Games gold medals won by an individual is 14 by Dave Mirra (USA), who competes in BMX Park and Vert.

★ LONGEST RAMP-TO-RAMP MOTORCYCLE BACK FLIP

Mike Metzger (USA) did a ramp-to-ramp back flip measuring 125 ft (38.1 m) over the fountains in front of Caesars Palace in Las Vegas, Nevada, USA, on May 4, 2006. "The Impossible Jump," as it was called, was part of the launch of the movie *Mission: Impossible III* starring Tom Cruise.

HIGHEST MOTO X STEP UP JUMP

The greatest height achieved in the X Games Moto X Step Up event is 35 ft (10.67 m) by Tommy Clowers (USA) on August 18, 2000. Essentially "high-jump" on motorcycles, riders must try to clear a bar placed at the top of a steep take-off ramp.

★ LONGEST BMX 360° RAMP JUMP

Mike "Rooftop" Escamilla (USA) performed a 50-ft 6-in (15.39-m) BMX 360° ramp jump on the Mega Ramp at X Games 11 in Los Angeles, California, USA, on August 3, 2005.

YOUNGEST MEDALIST

Ayumi Kawasaki (Japan) was 12 years old in 1997 when she earned the X Games bronze medal in the women's Aggressive In-line Vert.

The **oldest medalist** was Angelika Casteneda (USA), who was 53 years old in 1996 when she earned the X Venture Race gold medal.

OLDEST ATHLETE

Angelika Casteneda (USA) was 53 years old when she competed in the X Venture Race in 1996.

YOUNGEST GOLD MEDALISTS

Ryan Sheckler (USA, b. December 30, 1989) became the youngest person to win a gold medal at the X Games in any discipline when he won the Skateboard Park gold medal at the age of 13 years 230 days at X Games 9 in Los Angeles, California, USA, on August 17, 2003.

Lindsey Adams Hawkins (USA, b. September 21, 1989) is the ★ **youngest female gold medalist** at X Games. She won the Skateboard Vert competition aged 14 years 321 days at X Games 10, Los Angeles, California, USA, on August 7, 2004.

SUMMER MEDALS

AGGRESSIVE IN-LINE SKATING

The most medals won for Aggressive In-line Skating (AIS) is eight by Fabiola da Silva (Brazil), seven of which are gold. In 2000, the "Fabiola Rule" was introduced to allow women to qualify for the finals of the men's Vert, a discipline of AIS.

MOTO X

Brian Deegan (USA) has won a total of eight X Games medals during his career in the discipline of Moto X, one of them gold.

SKATEBOARD

Andy Macdonald and Tony Hawk (both USA) have each won 16 X Games medals during their careers.

MOST ↑ SNOWBOARD SLOPESTYLE MEDALS (MEN)

Shaun White (USA) has earned five Snowboard Slopestyle medals: gold in 2003, 2004, 2005, and 2006, and silver in 2002.

★LONGEST
BMX BACK FLIP

Mike "Rooftop" Escamilla (USA) completed a 62-ft 2-in (18.94-m) BMX back flip off the Mega Ramp at X Games 11 in Los Angeles, California, USA, on August 3, 2005.

WINTER MEDALS

★ MOST GOLD MEDALS

Shaun Palmer (USA) and Shaun White (USA) have both won six Winter X Games gold medals each. Palmer earned his gold in four different sport disciplines: Skier X in 2000, Snowboarder X (1997–99), Snow Mountain Biking in 1997, and UltraCross in 2001. White won his golds in Snowboard SuperPipe (2003 and 2006) and Slopestyle (2003–06).

★ SNOWBOARD SUPERPIPE (WOMEN)

Kelly Clark (USA) won four Snowboard SuperPipe medals: gold in 2002 and 2006, and silver in 2003 and 2004.

★ SKIER X (MEN)

Skier X is a race over a course that features tabletop jumps, banked turns, rollers, and gaps. Enak Gavaggio (France) has won five medals: he took gold in 1999 and bronze in 2001–04.

★ SKIER X (WOMEN)

Aleisha Cline (Canada) won five medals for Skier X, taking gold in 1999 and 2001–03, and silver in 2004.

★ SKIING SUPERPIPE (MEN)

Jon Olsson (Sweden) has won four medals for Skiing SuperPipe by taking the gold in 2002, silver in 2004, and bronze in 2003 and 2005.

★ SKIING SLOPESTYLE

Tanner Hall (USA) and Jon Olsson (Sweden) have each won four medals for Skiing Slopestyle. Hall took gold in 2002–04 and silver in 2005. Olsson took bronze in 2002–05.

SKIING

Jon Olsson (Sweden) and Tanner Hall (USA) have both won a total of eight Winter X Games medals for skiing. Olsson won four medals in Slopestyle and four in SuperPipe. Hall earned one medal in Big Air, four in Slopestyle, and three in SuperPipe.

★ SNOWBOARDER X (MEN)

Seth Wescott (USA) has won a record five medals for Snowboarder X. He took silver in 2002, 2004, and 2005, and bronze in 1998 and 2001.

★ SNOWBOARDER X (WOMEN)

Two women have won three medals each: Lindsey Jacobellis (USA) won

gold in 2003, 2004, and 2005; Erin Simmons (Canada) took silver in 2001, 2002, and 2005.

★ SNOWBOARD SLOPESTYLE (WOMEN)

Barrett Christy (USA) has won five medals for Snowboard Slopestyle: gold in 1997, silver in 1998 and 1999, and bronze in 2000 and 2002. Janna Meyen (USA) equaled this feat with silver in 2002 and gold in 2003–06.

SNOWBOARD SUPERPIPE (MEN)

Danny Kass (USA) has won four medals: gold in 2001, silver in 2003 and 2004, and bronze in 2005.

★ MOTO X BEST TRICK

Brian Deegan has won two gold medals in Winter X Moto X Best Trick, in 2002 and 2005.

MOST WINTER X GAMES INDIVIDUAL MEDALS

The most Winter X Games medals won by an individual is 10 by Barrett Christy (USA), between 1997 and 2001 for snowboard disciplines.

★LONGEST MOTO X DIRT-TO-DIRT BACK FLIP

Jeremy Stenberg (pictured) and Nate Adams (both USA) did a dirt-to-dirt back flip measuring 100 ft (30.48 m) in the Moto X Freestyle finals at X Games 11 in Los Angeles, California, USA, on August 6, 2005.

SPORTS REFERENCE

MEN'S 10,000 M

Kenenisa Bekele (Ethiopia) on his way to breaking his own record in the men's 10,000 m in Brussels, Belgium, on August 26, 2005, with a winning time of 26 min 17.53 sec.

OUTDOOR TRACK EVENTS

MEN	TIME/DISTANCE	NAME & NATIONALITY	PLACE	DATE
100 m	9.77	Asafa Powell (Jamaica)	Athens, Greece	Jun 14, 2005
	9.77	Justin Gatlin (USA)	Doha, Qatar	May 12, 2006
200 m	19.32	Michael Johnson (USA)	Atlanta, USA	Aug. 1, 1996
400 m	43.18	Michael Johnson (USA)	Seville, Spain	Aug. 26, 1999
800 m	1:41.11	Wilson Kipketer (Denmark)	Cologne, Germany	Aug. 24, 1997
1,000 m	2:11.96	Noah Ngeny (Kenya)	Rieti, Italy	Sep. 5, 1999
1,500 m	3:26.00	Hicham El Guerrouj (Morocco)	Rome, Italy	Jul. 14, 1998
1 mile	3:43.13	Hicham El Guerrouj (Morocco)	Rome, Italy	Jul. 7, 1999
2,000 m	4:44.79	Hicham El Guerrouj (Morocco)	Berlin, Germany	Sep. 7, 1999
3,000 m	7:20.67	Daniel Komen (Kenya)	Rieti, Italy	Sep. 1, 1996
5,000 m	12:37.35	Kenenisa Bekele (Ethiopia)	Hengelo, Netherlands	May 31, 2004
10,000 m	26:17.53	Kenenisa Bekele (Ethiopia)	Brussels, Belgium	Aug. 26, 2005
20,000 m	56:55.60	Arturo Barrios (Mexico)	La Flèche, France	Mar. 30, 1991
1 hour	21,101 m	Arturo Barrios (Mexico)	La Flèche, France	Mar. 30, 1991
25,000 m	1:13:55.80	Toshihiko Seko (Japan)	Christchurch, New Zealand	Mar. 22, 1981
30,000 m	1:29:18.80	Toshihiko Seko (Japan)	Christchurch, New Zealand	Mar. 22, 1981
3,000 m steeplechase	7:53.63	Saif Saaeed Shaheen (Qatar)	Brussels, Belgium	Sep. 3, 2004
110 m hurdles	12.91	Colin Jackson (GB)	Stuttgart, Germany	Aug. 20, 1993
	12.91	Xiang Liu (China)	Athens, Greece	Aug. 27, 2004
400 m hurdles	46.78	Kevin Young (USA)	Barcelona, Spain	Aug. 6, 1992
4 x 100 m relay	37.40	USA (Michael Marsh, Leroy Burrell, Dennis Mitchell, Carl Lewis)	Barcelona, Spain	Aug. 8, 1992
	37.40 USA	(John Drummond Jr., Andre Cason, Dennis Mitchell, Leroy Burrell)	Stuttgart, Germany	Aug. 21, 1993
4 x 200 m relay	1:18.68	Santa Monica Track Club, USA (Michael Marsh, Leroy Burrell, Floyd Heard, Carl Lewis)	Walnut, USA	Apr. 17, 1994
4 x 400 m relay	2:54.20	USA (Jerome Young, Antonio Pettigrew, Tyree Washington, Michael Johnson)	New York City, USA	Jul. 22, 1998
4 x 800 m relay	7:03.89	Great Britain (Peter Elliott, Garry Cook, Steve Cram, Sebastian Coe)	London, UK	Aug. 30, 1982
4 x 1,500 m relay	14:38.80	West Germany (Thomas Wessinghage, Harald Hudak, Michael Lederer, Karl Fleschen)	Cologne, Germany	Aug. 17, 1977

WOMEN	TIME/DISTANCE	NAME & NATIONALITY	PLACE	DATE
100 m	10.49	Florence Griffith-Joyner (USA)	Indianapolis, USA	Jul. 16, 1988
200 m	21.34	Florence Griffith-Joyner (USA)	Seoul, South Korea	Sep. 29, 1988
400 m	47.60	Marita Koch (GDR)	Canberra, Australia	Oct. 6, 1985
800 m	1:53.28	Jarmila Kratochvílová (Czechoslovakia)	Munich, Germany	Jul. 26, 1983
1,000 m	2:28.98	Svetlana Masterkova (Russia)	Brussels, Belgium	Aug. 23, 1996
1,500 m	3:50.46	Qu Yunxia (China)	Beijing, China	Sep. 11, 1993
1 mile	4:12.56	Svetlana Masterkova (Russia)	Zurich, Switzerland	Aug. 14, 1996
2,000 m	5:25.36	Sonia O'Sullivan (Ireland)	Edinburgh, UK	Jul. 8, 1994
3,000 m	8:06.11	Wang Junxia (China)	Beijing, China	Sep. 13, 1993
5,000 m	14:24.68	Elvan Abeylegesse (Turkey)	Bergen, Norway	Jun. 11, 2004
10,000 m	29:31.78	Wang Junxia (China)	Beijing, China	Sep. 8, 1993
1 hour	18,340 m	Tegla Loroupe (Kenya)	Borgholzhausen, Germany	Aug. 7, 1998
20,000 m	1:05:26.60	Tegla Loroupe (Kenya)	Borgholzhausen, Germany	Sep. 3, 2000
25,000 m	1:27:05.90	Tegla Loroupe (Kenya)	Mengerskirchen, Germany	Sep. 21, 2002
30,000 m	1:45:50.00	Tegla Loroupe (Kenya)	Warstein, Germany	Jun. 6, 2003
3,000 m steeplechase	9:01.59	Gulnara Samitova (Russia)	Iráklio, Greece	Jul. 4, 2004
100 m hurdles	12.21	Yordanka Donkova (Bulgaria)	Stara Zagora, Bulgaria	Aug. 20, 1988
400 m hurdles	52.34	Yuliya Pechonkina (Russia)	Tula, Russia	Aug. 8, 2003
4 x 100 m relay	41.37	GDR (Silke Gladisch, Sabine Rieger, Ingrid Auerswald, Marlies Göhr)	Canberra, Australia	Oct. 6, 1985
4 x 200 m relay	1:27.46	United States "Blue" (LaTasha Jenkins, LaTasha Colander-Richardson, Nanceen Perry, Marion Jones)	Philadelphia, USA	Apr. 29, 2000
4 x 400 m relay	3:15.17	USSR (Tatyana Ledovskaya, Olga Nazarova, Maria Pinigina, Olga Bryzgina)	Seoul, South Korea	Oct. 1, 1988
4 x 800 m relay	7:50.17	USSR (Nadezhda Olizarenko, Lyubov Gurina, Lyudmila Borisova, Irina Podyalovskaya)	Moscow, Russia	Aug. 5, 1984

WOMEN'S 25 & 30 KM

Mizuki Noguchi (Japan), women's 25 and 30 km record holder, competes at the 9th IAAF World Athletics Championships, Saint Denis, Paris, France, on August 31, 2003.

INDOOR TRACK EVENTS

MEN	TIME	NAME & NATIONALITY	PLACE	DATE
50 m	5.56	Donovan Bailey (Canada)	Reno, USA	Feb. 9, 1996
60 m	6.39	Maurice Greene (USA)	Madrid, Spain	Feb. 3, 1998
	6.39	Maurice Greene (USA)	Atlanta, USA	Mar. 3, 2001
200 m	19.92	Frank Fredericks (Namibia)	Liévin, France,	Feb. 18, 1996
400 m	44.57	Kerron Clement (USA)	Fayetteville, USA	Mar. 12, 2005
800 m	1:42.67	Wilson Kipketer (Denmark)	Paris, France	Mar. 9, 1997
1,000 m	2:14.96	Wilson Kipketer (Denmark)	Birmingham, UK	Feb. 20, 2000
1,500 m	3:31.18	Hicham El Guerrouj (Morocco)	Stuttgart, Germany	Feb. 2, 1997
1 mile	3:48.45	Hicham El Guerrouj (Morocco)	Ghent, Belgium	Feb. 12, 1997
3,000 m	7:24.90	Daniel Komen (Kenya)	Budapest, Hungary	Feb. 6, 1998
5,000 m	12:49.60	Kenenisa Bekele (Ethiopia)	Birmingham, UK	Feb. 20, 2004
50 m hurdles	6.25	Mark McKoy (Canada)	Kobe, Japan	Mar. 5, 1986
60 m hurdles	7.30	Colin Jackson (GB)	Sindelfingen, Germany	Mar. 6, 1994
4 x 200 m relay	1:22.11	Great Britain (Linford Christie, Darren Braithwaite, Ade Mafe, John Regis)	Glasgow, UK	Mar. 3, 1991
4 x 400 m relay	3:01.96	USA (Wallace Spearmon, Kerron Clement Darold Williamson, Jeremy Wariner)	Fayetteville, USA	Feb. 11, 2006
4 x 800 m relay	7:13.94	Global Athletics & Marketing, USA (Joey Woody, Karl Paranya, Rich Kenah, David Krummenacker)	Boston, USA	Feb. 6, 2000
5,000 m walk	18:07.08	Mikhail Shchennikov (Russia)	Moscow, Russia	Feb. 14, 1995

WOMEN	TIME	NAME & NATIONALITY	PLACE	DATE
50 m	5.96	Irina Privalova (Russia)	Madrid, Spain	Feb. 9, 1995
60 m	6.92	Irina Privalova (Russia)	Madrid, Spain	Feb. 11, 1993
	6.92	Irina Privalova (Russia)	Madrid, Spain	Feb. 9, 1995
200 m	21.87	Merlene Ottey (Jamaica)	Liévin, France	Feb. 13, 1993
400 m	49.59	Jarmila Kratochvílová (Czechoslovakia)	Milan, Italy	Mar. 7, 1982
800 m	1:55.82	Jolanda Ceplak (Slovenia)	Vienna, Austria	Mar. 3, 2002
1,000 m	2:30.94	Maria de Lurdes Mutola (Mozambique)	Stockholm, Sweden	Feb. 25, 1999
1,500 m	3:58.28	Yelena Soboleva (Russia)	Moscow, Russia	Feb. 18, 2006
1 mile	4:17.14	Doina Melinte (Romania)	East Rutherford, USA	Feb. 9, 1990
3,000 m	8:27.86	Liliya Shobukhova (Russia)	Moscow, Russia	Feb. 17, 2006
5,000 m	14:32.93	Tirunesh Dibaba (Ethiopia)	Boston, USA	Jan. 29, 2005
50 m hurdles	6.58	Cornelia Oschkenat (GDR)	Berlin, Germany	Feb. 20, 1988
60 m hurdles	7.69	Ludmila Engquist (Russia)	Chelyabinsk, Russia	Feb. 4, 1990
4 x 200 m relay	1:32.41	Russia (Yekaterina Kondratyeva, Irina Khabarova, Yuliva Pechonkina, Julia Gushchina)	Glasgow, UK	Jan. 29, 2005
4 x 400 m relay	3:23.37	Russia (Yulia Gushchina, Olga Kotlyarova, Olga Zaytseva, Olesya Krasnomovets)	Glasgow, UK	Jan. 28, 2006
4 x 800 m relay	8:18.71	Russia (Olga Kuznetsova, Yelena Afanasyeva, Yelena Zaytseva, Yekaterina Podkopayeva)	Moscow, Russia	Feb. 4, 1994
3,000 m walk	11:40.33	Claudia Iovan (Romania)	Bucharest, Romania	Jan. 30, 1999

★ NEW RECORD
☆ UPDATED RECORD

WOMEN'S HALF MARATHON

Elana Meyer (South Africa) in the 10,000 m trials for the 2002 Commonwealth Games in Manchester, UK, on June 16, 2002. She has held the half marathon world record since 1999.

? DID YOU KNOW?

The word "marathon" comes from a legend about the Greek soldier Pheidippides. In 490 BC he ran the 21.4 miles (34.5 km) from the town of Marathon to Athens, both in Greece, to announce that the Persians had been defeated in the Battle of Marathon, but he died shortly afterward.

ROAD RACE

MEN	TIME	NAME & NATIONALITY	PLACE	DATE
10 km	27:02	Haile Gebrselassie (Ethiopia)	Doha, Qatar	Dec. 11, 2002
15 km	41:29	Felix Limo (Kenya)	Nijmegen, Netherlands	Nov. 11, 2001
20 km	55:48	Haile Gebrselassie (Ethiopia)	Phoenix, USA	Jan. 15, 2006
Half marathon	58:55	Haile Gebrselassie (Ethiopia)	Phoenix, USA	Jan. 15, 2006
25 km	1:11:37	Haile Gebrselassie (Ethiopia)	Alphen-aan-den-Rijn, Netherlands	Mar. 12, 2006
30 km	1:28:00	Takayuki Matsumiya (Japan)	Kumamoto, Japan	Feb. 27, 2005
Marathon	2:04:55	Paul Tergat (Kenya)	Berlin, Germany	Sep. 28, 2003
100 km	6:13:33	Takahiro Sunada (Japan)	Tokoro, Japan	Jun. 21, 1998

WOMEN	TIME	NAME & NATIONALITY	PLACE	DATE
10 km	30:21	Paula Radcliffe (GB)	San Juan, Puerto Rico	Feb. 23, 2003
15 km	46:55	Kayoko Fukushi (Japan)	Marugame, Japan	Feb. 5, 2006
20 km	1:03:26	Paula Radcliffe (GB)	Bristol, UK	Oct. 6, 2001
Half marathon	1:06:44	Elana Meyer (South Africa)	Tokyo, Japan	Jan. 15, 1999
25 km	1:22:13	Mizuki Noguchi (Japan)	Berlin, Germany	Sep. 25, 2005
30 km	1:38:49	Mizuki Noguchi (Japan)	Berlin, Germany	Sep. 25, 2005
Marathon	2:15:25	Paula Radcliffe (GB)	London, UK	Apr. 13, 2003
100 km	6:33:11	Tomoe Abe (Japan)	Tokoro, Japan	Jun. 25, 2000

SPORTS REFERENCE

WOMEN'S 20,000 M RACE WALK

Olimpiada Ivanova (Russia) holds the 20,000 m race walking record with a time of 1 hr 26 min 52.3 sec. She also holds the 20 km road race walking record of 1 hr 25 min 41 sec, achieved in Helsinki, Finland, on August 7, 2005 (pictured).

WOMEN'S JAVELIN

Osleidys Menéndez (Cuba) throws for gold at the 10th IAAF World Athletics Championships on August 14, 2005, in Helsinki, Finland.

ULTRA-LONG DISTANCE

MEN	TIME/DISTANCE	NAME & NATIONALITY	PLACE	DATE
100 km	6:10:20	Don Ritchie (GB)	London, UK	Oct. 28, 1978
100 miles	11:28:03	Oleg Kharitonov (Russia)	London, UK	Oct. 2, 2002
1,000 miles	11 days 13:54:58	Piotr Silikin (Lithuania)	Nanango, Australia	Mar. 11–23, 1998
24 hours	303.306 km (188.46 miles)	Yiannis Kouros (Greece)	Adelaide, Australia	Oct. 4–5, 1997
6 days	1,023.200 km (635.78 miles)	Yiannis Kouros (Greece)	Colac, Australia	Nov. 26–Dec. 2, 1984

WOMEN	TIME/DISTANCE	NAME & NATIONALITY	PLACE	DATE
100 km	7:14:06	Norimi Sakurai (Japan)	Verona, Italy	Sep. 27, 2003
100 miles	14:25:45	Edit Berces (Hungary)	Verona, Italy	Sep. 21–22, 2002
1,000 miles	13 days 01:54:02	Eleanor Robinson (GB)	Nanango, Australia	Mar. 11–23, 1998
24 hours	250.106 km (155.40 miles)	Edit Berces (Hungary)	Verona, Italy	Sep. 21–22, 2002
6 days	883.631 km (549.06 miles)	Sandra Barwick (New Zealand)	Campbelltown, Australia	Nov. 18–24, 1990

RACE WALKING

MEN	TIME/DISTANCE	NAME & NATIONALITY	PLACE	DATE
20,000 m	1:17:25.6	Bernardo Segura (Mexico)	Bergen, Norway	May 7, 1994
20 km (road)	1:17:21	Jefferson Pérez (Ecuador)	Paris Saint-Denis, France	Aug. 23, 2003
2 hours	29,572 m	Maurizio Damilano (Italy)	Cuneo, Italy	Oct. 3, 1992
30,000 m	2:01:44.1	Maurizio Damilano (Italy)	Cuneo, Italy	Oct. 3, 1992
50,000 m	3:40:57.9	Thierry Toutain (France)	Héricourt, France	Sep. 29, 1996
50 km (road)	3:36:03	Robert Korzeniowski (Poland)	Paris Saint-Denis, France	Aug. 27, 2003

WOMEN	TIME/DISTANCE	NAME & NATIONALITY	PLACE	DATE
10,000 m	41:56.23	Nadezhda Ryashkina (USSR)	Seattle, USA	Jul. 24, 1990
20,000 m	1:26:52.3	Olimpiada Ivanova (Russia)	Brisbane, Australia	Sep. 6, 2001
20 km (road)	1:25:41	Olimpiada Ivanova (Russia)	Helsinki, Finland	Aug. 7, 2005

OUTDOOR FIELD EVENTS

MEN	RECORD	NAME & NATIONALITY	PLACE	DATE
High jump	8 ft 0.45 in (2.45 m)	Javier Sotomayor (Cuba)	Salamanca, Spain	Jul. 27, 1993
Pole vault	20 ft 1.73 in (6.14 m)	Sergei Bubka (Ukraine)	Sestriere, Italy	Jul. 31, 1994
Long jump	29 ft 4.36 in (8.95 m)	Mike Powell (USA)	Tokyo, Japan	Aug. 30, 1991
Triple jump	60 ft 0.78 in (18.29 m)	Jonathan Edwards (GB)	Gothenburg, Sweden	Aug. 7, 1995
Shot	75 ft 10.23 in (23.12 m)	Randy Barnes (USA)	Los Angeles, USA	May 20, 1990
Discus	243 ft 0.53 in (74.08 m)	Jürgen Schult (GDR)	Neubrandenburg, Germany	Jun. 6, 1986
Hammer	284 ft 7 in (86.74 m)	Yuriy Sedykh (USSR)	Stuttgart, Germany	Aug. 30, 1986
Javelin	323 ft 1.16 in (98.48 m)	Jan Zělezný (Czech Republic)	Jena, Germany	May 25, 1996
Decathlon*	9,026 points	Roman Šebrle (Czech Republic)	Götzis, Austria	May 27, 2001

*100 m 10.64 sec; long jump 8.11 m; shot 15.33 m; high jump 2.12 m; 400 m 47.79 sec; 110 m hurdles 13.92 sec; discus 47.92 m; pole vault 4.80 m; javelin 70.16 m; 1,500 m 4 min 21.98 sec

WOMEN	RECORD	NAME & NATIONALITY	PLACE	DATE
High jump	6 ft 10.28 in (2.09 m)	Stefka Kostadinova (Bulgaria)	Rome, Italy	Aug. 30, 1987
Pole vault	16 ft 5.24 in (5.01 m)	Yelena Isinbayeva (Russia)	Helsinki, Finland	Aug. 12, 2005
Long jump	24 ft 8.06 in (7.52 m)	Galina Chistyakova (USSR)	St. Petersburg, Russia	Jun. 11, 1988
Triple jump	50 ft 10.23 in (15.50 m)	Inessa Kravets (Ukraine)	Gothenburg, Sweden	Aug. 10, 1995
Shot	74 ft 2.94 in (22.63 m)	Natalya Lisovskaya (USSR)	Moscow, Russia	Jun. 7, 1987
Discus	252 ft (76.80 m)	Gabriele Reinsch (GDR)	Neubrandenburg, Germany	Jul. 9, 1988
Hammer	252 ft 9.85 in (77.06 m)	Tatyana Lysenko (Russia)	Moscow, Russia	Jul. 15, 2005
Javelin	235 ft 2.83 in (71.70 m)	Osleidys Menéndez (Cuba)	Helsinki, Finland	Aug. 14 2005
Heptathlon†	7,291 points	Jacqueline Joyner-Kersee (USA)	Seoul, South Korea	Sep. 24, 1988
Decathlon**	8,358 points	Austra Skujyte (Lithuania)	Columbia, USA	Apr. 14–15, 2005

†100 m hurdles 12.69 sec; high jump 1.86 m; shot 15.80 m; 200 m 22.56 sec; long jump 7.27 m; javelin 45.66 m; 800 m 2 min 8.51 sec;
**100 m 12.49 sec; long jump 6.12 m; shot 16.42 m; high jump 1.78 m; 400 m 57.19 sec; 100 m hurdles 14.22 sec; discus 46.19 m; pole vault 3.10 m; javelin 48.78 m; 1,500 m 5 min 15.86 sec

INDOOR FIELD EVENTS

MEN	RECORD	NAME & NATIONALITY	PLACE	DATE
High jump	7 ft 11.66 in (2.43 m)	Javier Sotomayor (Cuba)	Budapest, Hungary	Mar. 4, 1989
Pole vault	20 ft 2.12 in (6.15 m)	Sergei Bubka (Ukraine)	Donetsk, Ukraine	Feb. 21, 1993
Long jump	28 ft 10.06 in (8.79 m)	Carl Lewis (USA)	New York City, USA	Jan. 27, 1984
Triple jump	58 ft 5.96 in (17.83 m)	Aliecer Urrutia (Cuba)	Sindelfingen, Germany	Mar. 1, 1997
	58 ft 5.96 in (17.83 m)	Christian Olsson (Sweden)	Budapest, Hungary	Mar. 7, 2004
Shot	74 ft 4.12 in (22.66 m)	Randy Barnes (USA)	Los Angeles, USA	Jan. 20, 1989
Heptathlon*	6,476 points	Dan O'Brien (USA)	Toronto, Canada	Mar. 14, 1993

*60 m 6.67 sec; long jump 7.84 m; shot 16.02 m; high jump 2.13 m; 60 m hurdles 7.85 sec; pole vault 5.20 m; 1,000 m 2 min 57.96 sec

WOMEN	RECORD	NAME & NATIONALITY	PLACE	DATE
High jump	6 ft 9.8 in (2.08 m)	Kajsa Bergqvist (Sweden)	Arnstadt, Germany	Feb. 4, 2006
Pole vault	16 ft 1.3 in (4.91 m)	Yelena Isinbayeva (Russia)	Donetsk, Ukraine	Feb. 12, 2006
Long jump	24 ft 2.15 in (7.37 m)	Heike Drechsler (GDR)	Vienna, Austria	Feb. 13, 1988
Triple jump	50 ft 4.72 in (15.36 m)	Tatyana Lebedeva (Russia)	Budapest, Hungary	Mar. 6, 2004
Shot	73 ft 9.82 in (22.50 m)	Helena Fibingerová (Czechoslovakia)	Jablonec, Czechoslovakia	Feb. 19, 1977
Pentathlon†	4,991 points	Irina Belova (Russia)	Berlin, Germany	Feb. 15, 1992

†60 m hurdles 8.22 sec; high jump 1.93 m; shot 13.25 m; long jump 6.67 m; 800 m 2 min 10.26 sec

WOMEN'S POLE VAULT

Yelena Isinbayeva (Russia) competes in the women's pole-vault final at the 10th IAAF World Athletics Championships on August 12, 2005, in Helsinki, Finland.

FREEDIVING

MEN'S DEPTH DISCIPLINES	DEPTH	NAME & NATIONALITY	PLACE	DATE
Constant weight with fins	354 ft 4 in (108 m)	Martin Stepanek (Czech Republic)	Grand Cayman, Cayman Islands	Apr. 5, 2006
Constant weight without fins	262 ft 5 in (80 m)	Martin Stepanek (Czech Republic)	Grand Cayman, Cayman Islands	Apr. 9, 2005
Variable weight	459 ft 4 in (140 m)	Carlos Coste (Venezuela)	Sharm, Egtypt	May 9, 2006
No limit	564 ft 3 in (172 m)	Herbert Nitsch (Austria)	Zirje, Croatia	Oct. 2, 2005
Free immersion	347 ft 9 in (106 m)	Martin Stepanek (Czech Republic)	Grand Cayman, Cayman Islands	Mar. 3, 2006

MEN'S DYNAMIC APNEA	DEPTH	NAME & NATIONALITY	PLACE	DATE
With fins	695 ft 6 in (212 m)	Tom Sietas (Germany)	Loutraki, Greece	Jul. 10, 2005
Without fins	590 ft 6 in (180 m)	Tom Sietas (Germany)	Tokyo, Japan	Mar. 14, 2006

MEN'S STATIC APNEA	TIME	NAME & NATIONALITY	PLACE	DATE
Without fins, duration	8 min 58 sec	Tom Sietas (Germany)	Eindhoven, Netherlands	Dec. 12, 2004

WOMEN'S DEPTH DISCIPLINES	DEPTH	NAME & NATIONALITY	PLACE	DATE
Constant weight with fins	282 ft 1 in (86 m)	Natalia Molchanova (Russia)	Nice, France	Sep. 3, 2005
Constant weight without fins	108 ft 5 in (55 m)	Natalia Molchanova (Russia)	Dahab, Egypt	Nov. 7, 2005
Variable weight	400 ft 3 in (122 m)	Tanya Streeter (USA)	Turks and Caicos	Jul. 21, 2003
No limit	524 ft 11 in (160 m)	Tanya Streeter (USA)	Turks and Caicos	Aug. 17, 2002
Free immersion	255 ft 10 in (78 m)	Natalia Molchanova (Russia)	Dahab, Egypt	Nov. 5, 2005

WOMEN'S DYNAMIC APNEA	DEPTH	NAME & NATIONALITY	PLACE	DATE
With fins	656 ft 2 in (200 m)	Natalia Molchanova (Russia)	Moscow, Russia	Apr. 23, 2006
Without fins	429 ft 9 in (131 m)	Natalia Molchanova (Russia)	Tokyo, Japan	Dec. 20, 2005

WOMEN'S STATIC APNEA	TIME	NAME & NATIONALITY	PLACE	DATE
Without fins, duration	7 min 30 sec	Natalia Molchanova (Russia)	Moscow, Russia	Apr. 22, 2006

★ NEW RECORD
☆ UPDATED RECORD

WOMEN'S ➡ FREEDIVING

Natalia Molchanova (Russia) won the "constant weight without fins" category with an 86-m dive at the World Championships on September 3, 2005. She holds a further three diving world records.

⬅ MEN'S FREEDIVING

Carlos Coste (Venezuela) is congratulated by Natalia Molchanova (Russia) after diving 105 m in the men's individual freediving World Championships on September 4, 2005, in Villefranche-sur-Mer, France.

SPORTS REFERENCE

MEN'S ↑ COXLESS FOURS (LIGHTWEIGHT)

Thomas Poulsen, Thomas Ebert, Eskild Ebbesen, and Victor Feddersen (all Denmark) on the podium after winning the coxless fours in the lightweight men's event at the rowing World Cup held in Lucerne, Switzerland, in 1999.

WOMEN'S QUADRUPLE SCULLS (LIGHTWEIGHT)

Zita van der Walle, Marguerite Houston, Miranda Bennett, and Hannah Every (all Australia) win gold in the lightweight quadruple sculls during the Fédération Internationale des Sociétés d'Aviron (FISA) World Rowing Championships in Seville, Spain, on September 2, 2002.

ROWING (FISA)

MEN	TIME	ROWER(S)/COUNTRY	REGATTA	YEAR
Single sculls	6:36.33	Marcel Hacker (Germany)	Seville, Spain	2002
Double sculls	6:04.37	Luka Spik, Iztok Cop (both Slovenia)	St. Catharines, Canada	1999
Quadruple sculls	5:37.68	Italy (Paradiso, Sartori, Galtarossa, Corona)	Indianapolis, USA	1994
Coxless pairs	6:14.27	Matthew Pinsent, James Cracknell (both GB)	Seville, Spain	2002
Coxless fours	5:41.35	Germany (Thormann, Dienstbach, Stueer, Heidicker)	Seville, Spain	2002
Coxed pairs*	6:42.16	Igor Boraska, Tihomir Frankovic, Milan Razov (all Croatia)	Indianapolis, USA	1994
Coxed fours*	5:58.96	Germany (Ungmach, Eicholz, Weyrauch, Rabe, Dedering)	Vienna, Austria	1991
Coxed eights	5:19.85	USA (Deakin, Beery, Hoopman, Volpenheim, Cipollone, Read, Allen, Ahrens, Hansen)	Athens, Greece	2004

WOMEN	TIME	ROWER(S)/COUNTRY	REGATTA	YEAR
Single sculls	7:07.71	Roumiana Neykova (Bulgaria)	Seville, Spain	2002
Double sculls	6:38.78	Georgina and Caroline Evers-Swindell (both New Zealand)	Seville, Spain	2002
Quadruple sculls	6:10.80	Germany (Baron, Ruschaw, Sagers, Koeppen)	Duisburg, Germany	1996
Coxless pairs	6:53.80	Georgeta Andrunache, Viorica Susanu (both Romania)	Seville, Spain	2002
Coxless fours*	6:25.47	Canada (Barnes, Taylor, Monroe, Doey)	Vienna, Austria	1991
Coxed eights	5:56.55	USA (Johnson, Magee, Dirkmaat, Cox, Davies, Korholz, Mickelson, Nelson, Whipple)	Athens, Greece	2004

MEN (LIGHTWEIGHT)	TIME	ROWER(S)/COUNTRY	REGATTA	YEAR
Single sculls*	6:47.97	Karsten Nielsen (Denmark)	St. Catharines, Canada	1999
Double sculls	6:10.80	Elia Luini, Leonardo Pettinari (both Italy)	Seville, Spain	2002
Quadruple sculls*	5:45.18	Italy (Esposito, Lana, Crispi, Guiglielmi)	Montreal, Canada	1992
Coxless pairs*	6:26.61	Tony O'Connor, Neville Maxwell (both Ireland)	Paris, France	1994
Coxless fours	5:45.60	Denmark (Poulsen, Ebert, Ebbesen, Feddersen)	Lucerne, Switzerland	1999
Coxed eights*	5:30.24	Germany (Altena, Dahlke, Kobor, Stomporowski, Melges, Mearz, Buchheit, Von Warburg, Kaska)	Montreal, Canada	1992

WOMEN (LIGHTWEIGHT)	TIME	ROWER(S)/COUNTRY	REGATTA	YEAR
Single sculls*	7:15.88	Marit van Eupen (Netherlands)	Lucerne, Switzerland	1999
Double sculls	6:49.90	Sally Newmarch, Amber Halliday (both Australia)	Athens, Greece	2004
Quadruple sculls*	6:29.55	Australia (van der Walle, Houston, Bennett, Every)	Seville, Spain	2002
Coxless pairs*	7:18.32	Eliza Blair, Justine Joyce (both Australia)	Aiguebelette, France	1997

Denotes non-Olympic boat classes

SHOOTING (ISSF)

MEN	SCORE	NAME & NATIONALITY	PLACE	DATE
300 m rifle three positions	1,178	Thomas Jerabek (Czech Republic)	Lahti, Finland	Jul. 13, 2002
300 m rifle prone	600	Harald Stenvaag (Norway)	Moscow, USSR	Aug. 15, 1990
	600	Bernd Ruecker (Germany)	Tolmezzo, Italy	Jul. 31, 1994
300 m standard rifle 3 x 20	589	Trond Kjoell (Norway)	Boden, Sweden	Jul. 7, 1995
	589	Marcel Buerge (Switzerland)	Lahti, Finland	Jul. 16, 2002
50 m rifle three positions	1,186	Rajmond Debevec (Slovenia)	Munich, West Germany	Aug. 29, 1992
50 m rifle prone	600	11 men have achieved this score; most times: Sergei Martynov (Belarus) with 5		
10 m air rifle	600	Tevarit Majchacheeap (Thailand)	Langkawi, Thailand	Jan. 27, 2000
50 m pistol	581	Alexsander Melentiev (USSR)	Moscow, USSR	Jul. 20, 1980
25 m rapid fire pistol	589	Sergei Alifirenko (Russia)	Munich, Germany	Aug. 26, 2005
25 m center fire pistol	590	Afanasijs Kuzmins (USSR)	Zagreb, Yugoslavia	Jul. 15, 1989
	590	Sergei Pyzhianov (USSR)	Moscow, USSR	Aug. 5, 1990
	590	Mikhail Nestruev (Russia)	Kouvola, Finland	Jul. 1, 1997
	590	Park Byung-Taek (South Korea)	Lahti, Finland	Jul. 14, 2002
	590	Mikhail Nestruev (Russia)	Belgrade, Czech Republic	Jul. 10, 2005
25 m standard pistol	584	Erich Buljung (USA)	Caracas, Venezuela	Aug. 20, 1983
10 m air pistol	593	Sergei Pyzhianov (USSR)	Munich, West Germany	Oct. 13, 1989
50 m running target	596	Nicolai Lapin (USSR)	Lahti, Finland	Jul. 25, 1987
50 m running target mixed	398	Lubos Racansky (Czech Republic)	Milan, Italy	Aug. 4, 1994
10 m running target	590	Manfred Kurzer (Germany)	Athens, Greece	Aug. 18, 2004
10 m running target mixed	391	Manfred Kurzer (Germany)	Pontevedra, Spain	Mar. 14, 2001
Trap	125	Giovanni Pellielo (Italy)	Nicosia, Sicily, Italy	Apr. 1, 1994
	125	Ray Ycong (USA)	Lahti, Finland	Jun. 9, 1995
	125	Marcello Tittarelli (Italy)	Suhl, Germany	Jun. 11, 1996
	125	Lance Bade (USA)	Barcelona, Spain	Jul. 23, 1998
	125	Pavel Gurkin (Russia)	Americana, Brazil	Aug. 10, 2005
Double trap	147	Michael Diamond (Australia)	Barcelona, Spain	Jul. 19, 1998
Skeet	124	Vincent Hancock (USA)	Changwon, South Korea	Apr. 16, 2005
	124	Vincent Hancock (USA)	Rome, Italy	May 22, 2005
	124	Ennio Falco (Italy)	Rome, Italy	May 22, 2005
	124	Mario Nunez (Spain)	Belgrade, Czech Republic	Jul. 18, 2005
	124	Tino Wenzel (Germany)	Belgrade, Czech Republic	Jul. 18, 2005
	124	Vincent Hancock (USA)	Americana, Brazil	Aug. 13, 2005
	124	Erik Watndal (Norway)	Americana, Brazil	Aug. 13, 2005
	124	Antonis Nicolaides (Cyprus)	Dubai, UAE	Nov. 22, 2005
	124	George Achilleos (Cyprus)	Dubai, UAE	Nov. 22, 2005

WOMEN	SCORE	NAME & NATIONALITY	PLACE	DATE
300 m rifle three positions	588	Charlotte Jakobsen (Denmark)	Lahti, Finland	Jul. 12, 2002
300 m rifle prone	597	Marie Enqvist (Sweden)	Plzen, Czech Republic	Jul. 22, 2003
50 m rifle three positions	592	Vesela Letcheva (Bulgaria)	Munich, Germany	Jun. 15, 1995
	592	Shan Hong (China)	Milan, Italy	May 28, 1999
	592	Barbara Lechner (Germany)	Munich, Germany	Jun. 10, 2005
	592	Sonja Pfeilschifter (Germany)	Munich, Germany	Jun. 15, 2005
50 m rifle prone	597	Marina Bobkova (Russia)	Barcelona, Spain	Jul. 1, 1998
	597	Olga Dovgun (Kazakhstan)	Lahti, Finland	Jul. 4, 2002
	597	Olga Dovgun (Kazakhstan)	Busan, Philippines	Oct. 4, 2002
10 m air rifle	400	9 women have achieved this score; most wins: Lioubov Galkina (Russia) with 3		
25 m pistol	594	Diana Iorgova (Bulgaria)	Milan, Italy	May 31, 1994
	594	Tao Luna (China)	Munich, Germany	Aug. 23, 2002
10 m air pistol	393	Svetlana Smirnova (Russia)	Munich, Germany	May 23, 1998
10 m running target	391	Xu Xuan (China)	Lahti, Finland	Jul. 6, 2002
10 m running target mixed	390	Audrey Soquet (France)	Lahti, Finland	Jul. 9, 2002
Trap	74	Victoria Chuyko (Ukraine)	Nicosia, Sicily, Italy	Jun. 13, 1998
Double trap	115	Yafei Zhang (China)	Nicosia, Sicily, Italy	Oct. 20, 2000
Skeet	74	Elena Little (GB)	Belgrade, Czech Republic	Jul. 17, 2005

★ **NEW RECORD**
☆ **UPDATED RECORD**

MEN'S SKEET SHOOTING ➡

Eric Watndal (Norway) – one of the seven men who jointly hold the men's skeet world record of 124 – competes in the ISSF World Cup Skeet and Trap shooting on September 7, 2003, in Lonato, Italy.

↗

WOMEN'S 50 M RIFLE THREE POSITIONS

Sonja Pfeilschifter (Germany) is one of four women who jointly hold the world record in the women's 50 m rifle three positions event.

? **DID YOU KNOW?**

Shooting sports are governed globally by the International Shooting Sport Federation (ISSF). Shooting competitions in one form or another have taken place since the 11th century, but the modern sport took shape in the 19th century with the inclusion of shooting in the first modern Olympic Games (1896). Competing that year were 61 shooters from seven countries – making it the second largest sport after track and field (which had 63 entrants from nine countries).

SPORTS REFERENCE

★ MEN'S 500 M LONG TRACK

Joji Kato (Japan) skates in the first race of the men's 500 m speed skating competition at the 2006 Winter Olympics in the Lingotto Oval, Turin, Italy, on February 13, 2006.

SPEED SKATING – LONG TRACK

MEN	TIME/POINTS	NAME & NATIONALITY	PLACE	DATE
500 m	34.30	Joji Kato (Japan)	Salt Lake City, USA	Nov. 19, 2005
1,000 m	1:07.03	Shani Davis (USA)	Calgary, Canada	Nov. 20, 2005
1,500 m	1:42.68	Shani Davis (USA)	Calgary, Canada	Mar. 19, 2006
3,000 m	3:37.28	Eskil Ervik (Norway)	Calgary, Canada	Nov. 5, 2005
5,000 m	6:08.78	Sven Kramer (Netherlands)	Salt Lake City, USA	Nov. 19, 2005
10,000 m	12:51.60	Sven Kramer (Netherlands)	Calgary, Canada	Mar. 19, 2006
500/1,000/500/1,000 m	137,230 points	Jeremy Wotherspoon (Canada)	Calgary, Canada	Jan. 18–19, 2003
500/3,000/1,500/5,000 m	146,365 points	Erben Wennemars (Netherlands)	Calgary, Canada	Aug. 12–13, 2005
500/5,000/1,500/10,000 m	145,742 points	Shani Davis (USA)	Calgary, Canada	Mar. 18–19, 2006
Team pursuit (8 laps)	3:39.69	Canada (Arne Dankers, Steven Elm, Denny Morrison)	Calgary, Canada	Nov. 12, 2005

WOMEN	TIME/POINTS	NAME & NATIONALITY	PLACE	DATE
500 m	37.22	Catriona LeMay Doan (Canada)	Calgary, Canada	Dec. 9, 2001
1,000 m	1:13.11	Cindy Klassen (Canada)	Calgary, Canada	Mar. 25, 2006
1,500 m	1:51.79	Cindy Klassen (Canada)	Salt Lake City, USA	Nov. 20, 2005
3,000 m	3:55.75	Cindy Klassen (Canada)	Calgary, Canada	Mar. 18, 2006
5,000 m	6:46.91	Claudia Pechstein (Germany)	Salt Lake City, USA	Feb. 23, 2002
500/1,000/500/1,000 m	149,305 points	Monique Garbrecht-Enfeldt (Germany)	Salt Lake City, USA	Jan. 11–12, 2003
		Cindy Klassen (Canada)	Calgary, Canada	Mar. 24–25 2006
500/1,500/1,000/3,000 m	155,576 points	Cindy Klassen (Canada)	Calgary, Canada	Mar. 15–17, 2001
500/3,000/1,500/5,000 m	154,580 points	Cindy Klassen (Canada)	Calgary, Canada	Mar. 18–19, 2006
Team pursuit (6 laps)	2:56.04	Germany (Daniela Anschütz, Anni Friesinger, Claudia Pechstein)	Calgary, Canada	Nov. 13, 2005

SPEED SKATING – SHORT TRACK

MEN	TIME	NAME & NATIONALITY	PLACE	DATE
500 m	41.184	Jean-François Monette (Canada)	Calgary, Canada	Oct. 18, 2003
1,000 m	1:24.674	Jiajun Li (China)	Bormio, Italy	Feb. 14, 2004
1,500 m	2:10.639	Ahn Hyun-Soo (South Korea)	Marquette, USA	Oct. 24, 2003
3,000 m	4:32.646	Ahn Hyun-Soo (South Korea)	Beijing, China	Dec. 7, 2003
5,000 m relay	6:39.990	Canada (Charles Hamelin, Steve Robillard, Francois-Louis Tremblay, Mathieu Turcotte)	Beijing, China	Mar. 13, 2005

WOMEN	TIME	NAME & NATIONALITY	PLACE	DATE
500 m	43.671	Evgenia Radanova (Bulgaria)	Calgary, Canada	Oct. 19, 2001
1,000 m	1:30.037	Jin Sun-Yu (South Korea)	Bormio, Italy	Nov. 13, 2005
1,500 m	2:18.861	Jung Eun-Ju (South Korea)	Beijing, China	Jan. 11, 2004
3,000 m	5:01.976	Choi Eun-Kyung (South Korea)	Calgary, Canada	Oct. 22, 2000
3,000 m relay	4:11.742	South Korea (Choi Eun-Kyung, Kim Min-Jee, Byun Chun-Sa, and Ko Gi-Hyun)	Calgary, Canada	Oct. 19, 2003

★ WOMEN'S 1,000 M AND 1,500 M SHORT TRACK

Jin Sun-Yu (South Korea) skates in the 1,500 m semifinal during the short track competition at the 2006 Winter Olympics in Turin, Italy, on February 18, 2006.

★ WOMEN'S 1,500 M AND 3,000 M LONG TRACK ➡

Cindy Klassen (Canada) competes in the women's 1,500 m race at the World Speed Skating Single Distance Championships at the Utah Olympic Oval in Kearns, Utah, USA, on March 11, 2001.

In addition to the 1,500 m and 3,000 m long track world records (in 1 min 51.79 sec and 3 min 55.75 sec respectively), she also holds the world records for the mini combination (500 m/1,500 m/1,000 m/3,000 m) with 155,576 points, and small combination (500 m/3,000 m/1,500 m/5,000 m) with 154,580 points.

★ NEW RECORD
☆ UPDATED RECORD

SWIMMING – LONG COURSE (50-M POOL)

MEN	TIME	NAME & NATIONALITY	PLACE	DATE
50 m freestyle	21.64	Alexander Popov (Russia)	Moscow, Russia	Jun. 16, 2000
100 m freestyle	47.84	Pieter van den Hoogenband (Netherlands)	Sydney, Australia	Sep. 19, 2000
200 m freestyle	1:44.06	Ian Thorpe (Australia)	Fukuoka, Japan	Jul. 25, 2001
400 m freestyle	3:40.08	Ian Thorpe (Australia)	Manchester, UK	Jul. 30, 2002
800 m freestyle	7:38.65	Grant Hackett (Australia)	Montreal, Canada	Jul. 27, 2005
1,500 m freestyle	14:34.56	Grant Hackett (Australia)	Fukuoka, Japan	Jul. 29, 2001
4 x 100 m freestyle relay	3:13.17	South Africa (Roland Schoeman, Lyndon Ferns, Darian Townsend, Ryk Neethling)	Athens, Greece	Aug. 15, 2004
4 x 200 m freestyle relay	7:04.66	Australia (Grant Hackett, Michael Klim, William Kirby, Ian Thorpe)	Fukuoka, Japan	Jul. 27, 2001
50 m butterfly	22.96	Roland Schoeman (South Africa)	Montreal, Canada	Jul. 25, 2005
100 m butterfly	50.40	Ian Crocker (USA)	Montreal, Canada	Jul. 30, 2005
200 m butterfly	1:53.93	Michael Phelps (USA)	Barcelona, Spain	Jul. 22, 2003
50 m backstroke	24.80	Thomas Rupprath (Germany)	Barcelona, Spain	Jul. 27, 2003
100 m backstroke	53.17	Aaron Peirsol (USA)	Indianapolis, USA	Apr. 2, 2005
200 m backstroke	1:54.66	Aaron Peirsol (USA)	Montreal, Canada	Jul. 29, 2005
50 m breaststroke	27.18	Oleg Lisogor (Ukraine)	Berlin, Germany	Aug. 2, 2002
100 m breaststroke	59.30	Brendan Hansen (USA)	Long Beach, USA	Jul. 8, 2004
200 m breaststroke	2:09.04	Brendan Hansen (USA)	Long Beach, USA	Jul. 11, 2004
200 m medley	1:55.94	Michael Phelps (USA)	Maryland, USA	Aug. 9, 2003
400 m medley	4:08.26	Michael Phelps (USA)	Athens, Greece	Aug. 14, 2004
4 x 100 m medley relay	3:30.68	USA (Aaron Peirsol, Brendan Hanson, Ian Crocker, Jason Lezak)	Athens, Greece	Aug. 21, 2004

WOMEN	TIME	NAME & NATIONALITY	PLACE	DATE
50 m freestyle	24.13	Inge de Bruijn (Netherlands)	Sydney, Australia	Sep. 22, 2000
100 m freestyle	53.52	Jodie Henry (Australia)	Athens, Greece	Aug. 18, 2004
200 m freestyle	1:56.64	Franziska van Almsick (Germany)	Berlin, Germany	Aug. 3, 2002
400 m freestyle	4:03.85	Janet Evans (USA)	Seoul, South Korea	Sep. 22, 1988
800 m freestyle	8:16.22	Janet Evans (USA)	Tokyo, Japan	Aug. 20, 1989
1,500 m freestyle	15:52.10	Janet Evans (USA)	Orlando, USA	Mar. 26, 1988
4 x 100 m freestyle relay	3:35.94	Australia (Alice Mills, Lisbeth Lenton, Petria Thomas, Jodie Henry)	Athens, Greece	Aug. 14, 2004
4 x 200 m freestyle relay	7:53.42	USA (Natalie Coughlin, Carly Piper, Dana Vollmer, Kaitlin Sandeno)	Athens, Greece	Aug. 18, 2004
50 m butterfly	25.57	Anna-Karin Kammerling (Sweden)	Berlin, Germany	Jul. 31, 2000
100 m butterfly	56.61	Inge de Bruijn (Netherlands)	Sydney, Australia	Sep. 17, 2000
200 m butterfly	2:05.61	Otylia Jedrzejczak (Poland)	Montreal, Canada	Jul. 28, 2005
50 m backstroke	28.19	Janine Pietsch (Germany)	Berlin, Germany	May 25, 2005
100 m backstroke	59.58	Natalie Coughlin (USA)	Fort Lauderdale, USA	Aug. 13, 2002
200 m backstroke	2:06.62	Krisztina Egerszegi (Hungary)	Athens, Greece	Aug. 25, 1991
50 m breaststroke	30.45	Jade Edmistone (Australia)	Montreal, Canada	Jul. 31, 2005
100 m breaststroke	1:06.20	Jessica Hardy (USA)	Montreal, Canada	Jul. 25, 2005
200 m breaststroke	2:21.72	Leisel Jones (Australia)	Montreal, Canada	Jul. 29, 2005
200 m medley	2:09.72	Wu Yanyan (China)	Shanghai, China	Oct. 17, 1997
400 m medley	4:33.59	Yana Klochkova (Ukraine)	Sydney, Australia	Sep. 16, 2000
4 x 100 m medley relay	3:57.32	Australia (Giaan Rooney, Leisel Jones, Petria Thomas, Jodie Henry)	Athens, Greece	Aug. 21, 2004

WOMEN'S 100 M BREASTSTROKE

Jessica Hardy (USA) swims in the 100 m breaststroke semifinal on July 25, 2005, at the XI FINA Swimming World Championships at Parc Jean-Drapeau, Montreal, Canada, setting a new world record with a time of 1 min 6.2 sec.

MEN'S 100 M BUTTERFLY

Ian Crocker (USA) in the XI FINA World Championships, on his way to winning the gold medal and setting a new world record of 50.4 seconds in the 100 m butterfly final on July 30, 2005, in Montreal, Canada.

SPORTS REFERENCE

★ MEN'S 200 M BACKSTROKE

A triumphant Markus Rogan (Austria) celebrates winning the men's 200 m backstroke during the European Swimming Short Course Championships in Trieste, Italy, on December 8, 2005. Rogan set a new world record of 1 min 50.43 sec.

[!] X-REF

In August 2005, Cédric Genin (France) set the world record for swimming 50 m underwater. What do you think his time was? To find out, go to page 261.

★ MEN'S 100 M FREESTYLE

Roland Schoeman (South Africa) waves before taking part in the World Cup in Berlin, Germany, on January 22, 2005. During this race, he equaled Ian Crocker's (USA) shortcourse world record of 46.25 seconds for 100 m freestyle.

SWIMMING – SHORT COURSE (25-M POOL)

MEN	TIME	NAME & NATIONALITY	PLACE	DATE
50 m freestyle	21.10	Fred Bousquet (France)	New York City, USA	Mar. 25, 2004
100 m freestyle	46.25	Ian Crocker (USA)	New York City, USA	Mar. 27, 2004
	46.25	Roland Schoeman (South Africa)	Berlin, Germany	Jan. 22, 2005
200 m freestyle	1:41.10	Ian Thorpe (Australia)	Berlin, Germany	Feb. 6, 2000
400 m freestyle	3:34.58	Grant Hackett (Australia)	Sydney, Australia	Jul. 18, 2002
800 m freestyle	7:25.28	Grant Hackett (Australia)	Perth, Australia	Aug. 3, 2001
1,500 m freestyle	14:10.10	Grant Hackett (Australia)	Perth, Australia	Aug. 7, 2001
4 x 50 m freestyle	1:25.55	Netherlands (Mark Veens, Johan Kenkhuis, Gijs Damen, Pieter van den Hoogenband)	Dublin, Ireland	Dec. 14, 2003
4 x 100 m freestyle	3:09.57	Sweden (Johan Nyström, Lars Frolander, Mattias Ohlin, Stefan Nystrand)	Athens, Greece	Mar. 16, 2000
4 x 200 m freestyle	6:56.41	Australia (William Kirby, Ian Thorpe, Michael Klim, Grant Hackett)	Perth, Australia	Aug. 7, 2001
50 m butterfly	22.60	Kaio Almeida (Brazil)	Santos, Brazil	Dec. 17, 2005
100 m butterfly	49.07	Ian Crocker (USA)	New York City, USA	Mar. 26, 2004
200 m butterfly	1:50.73	Franck Esposito (France)	Antibes, France	Dec. 8, 2002
50 m backstroke	23.27	Thomas Rupprath (Germany)	Vienna, Austria	Dec. 10, 2004
100 m backstroke	50.32	Peter Marshall (USA)	New York City, USA	Mar. 26, 2004
200 m backstroke	1:50.43	Markus Rogan (Austria)	Trieste, Italy	Dec. 8, 2005
50 m breaststroke	26.17	Oleg Lisogor (Ukraine)	Berlin, Germany	Jan. 21, 2006
100 m breaststroke	57.47	Ed Moses (USA)	Stockholm, Sweden	Jan. 23, 2002
200 m breaststroke	2:02.92	Ed Moses (USA)	Berlin, Germany	Jan. 17, 2004
100 m medley	51.52	Ryk Neethling (South Africa)	New York City, USA	Feb. 11, 2005
200 m medley	1:53.46	Laszlo Csen (Hungary)	Trieste, Italy	Dec. 8, 2005
400 m medley	4:00.37	Laszlo Csen (Hungary)	Trieste, Italy	Dec. 9, 2005
4 x 50 m medley	1:34.46	Germany (Thomas Rupprath, Mark Warnecke, Fabian Freidrich, Carstein Dehmlow)	Dublin, Ireland	Dec. 11, 2003
4 x 100 m medley	3:25.09	USA (Aaron Peirsol, Brendan Hansen, Ian Crocker, Jason Lezak)	Indianapolis, USA	Oct. 11, 2004

WOMEN	TIME	NAME & NATIONALITY	PLACE	DATE
50 m freestyle	23.59	Therese Alshammar (Sweden)	Athens, Greece	Mar. 18, 2000
100 m freestyle	51.70	Lisbeth Lenton (Australia)	Melbourne, Australia	Aug. 9, 2005
200 m freestyle	1:53.29	Lisbeth Lenton (Australia)	Sydney, Australia	Nov. 19, 2005
400 m freestyle	3:56.79	Laure Manaudou (France)	Trieste, Italy	Dec. 10, 2005
800 m freestyle	8:11.25	Laure Manaudou (France)	Trieste, Italy	Dec. 9, 2005
1,500 m freestyle	15:42.39	Laure Manaudou (France)	La Roche sur Yon, France	Nov. 20, 2004
4 x 50 m freestyle	1:37.27	USA (Kara Lynn Joyce, Neka Mabry, Paige Kearns, Andrea Georoff)	College Station, USA	Mar. 18, 2004
4 x 100 m freestyle	3:34.55	China (Le Jingyi, Na Chao, Shan Ying, Nian Yin)	Gothenburg, Sweden	Apr. 19, 1997
4 x 200 m freestyle	7:46.30	China (Xu Yanvei, Zhu Yingven, Tang Jingzhi, Yang Yu)	Moscow, Russia	Apr. 3, 2002
50 m butterfly	25.33	Anne-Karin Kammerling (Sweden)	Gothenburg, Sweden	Mar. 12, 2005
100 m butterfly	56.34	Natalie Coughlin (USA)	New York City, USA	Nov. 22, 2002
200 m butterfly	2:04.04	Yang Yu (China)	Berlin, Germany	Jan. 18, 2004
50 m backstroke	26.83	Li Hui (China)	Shanghai, China	Dec. 2, 2001
100 m backstroke	56.71	Natalie Coughlin (USA)	New York City, USA	Nov. 23, 2002
200 m backstroke	2:03.62	Natalie Coughlin (USA)	New York City, USA	Nov. 27, 2001
50 m breaststroke	29.90	Jade Edmistone (Australia)	Brisbane, Australia	Sep. 26, 2004
100 m breaststroke	1:04.79	Tara Kirk (USA)	College Station, USA	Mar. 19, 2004
200 m breaststroke	2:17.75	Leisel Jones (Australia)	Melbourne, Australia	Nov. 29, 2003
100 m medley	58.80	Natalie Coughlin (USA)	New York City, USA	Nov. 23, 2003
200 m medley	2:07.79	Allison Wagner (USA)	Palma de Mallorca, Spain	Dec. 5, 1993
400 m medley	4:27.83	Yana Klochkova (Ukraine)	Paris, France	Jan. 19, 2002
4 x 50 m medley	1:48.31	Sweden (Therese Alshammar, Emma Igelström, Anna-Karin Kammerling, Johanna Sjöberg)	Valencia, Spain	Dec. 16, 2000
4 x 100 m medley	3:54.95	Australia (Sophie Edington, Brooke Hanson, Jessica Schipper, Lisbeth Lenton)	Indianapolis, USA	Oct. 9, 2004

★ WOMEN'S 100 AND 200 M FREESTYLE ⇒

Lisbeth Lenton (Australia), member of the Australian 4 x 100 m medley team, swims butterfly during the Australian Swim Team Media Day in Melbourne, Australia, on March 9, 2006.

TRACK CYCLING – ABSOLUTE

MEN	TIME/DISTANCE	NAME & NATIONALITY	PLACE	DATE
200 m	9.865	Curt Harnett (Canada)	Bogotá, Colombia	Sep. 28, 1995
500 m	25.850	Arnaud Duble (France)	La Paz, Bolivia	Oct. 10, 2001
1 km	58.875	Arnaud Tournant (France)	La Paz, Bolivia	Oct. 10, 2001
4 km	4:11.114	Christopher Boardman (UK)	Manchester, UK	Aug. 29, 1996
Team 4 km	3:56.610	Australia (Graeme Brown, Brett Lancaster, Bradley McGee, Luke Roberts)	Athens, Greece	Aug. 22, 2004
1 hour	*49 km 700 m	Ondrej Sosenka (Czech Republic)	Moscow, Russia	Jul. 19, 2005

WOMEN	TIME/DISTANCE	NAME & NATIONALITY	PLACE	DATE
200 m	10.831	Olga Slioussareva (Russia)	Moscow, Russia	Apr. 25, 1993
500 m	29.655	Erika Saloumiaee (USSR)	Moscow, USSR	Aug. 6, 1987
3 km	3:24.537	Sarah Ulmer (New Zealand)	Athens, Greece	Aug. 22, 2004
1 hour	*46 km 65 m	Leontien Ziljaard-Van Moorsel (Netherlands)	Mexico City, Mexico	Oct. 1, 2003

Some athletes achieved better distances within an hour with bicycles that are no longer allowed by Union Cycliste Internationale (UCI). The 1-hour records given here are in accordance with the new UCI rules.

WOMEN'S 3 KM TRACK CYCLING

Sarah Ulmer (New Zealand) does her victory lap after winning the gold medal and setting a new world record in the final of the women's individual pursuit at the Olympic Games in Athens, Greece, on August 22, 2004.

WATER-SKIING

MEN	RECORD	NAME & NATIONALITY	PLACE	DATE
Slalom	1.5 buoy/9.75-m line	Chris Parrish (USA)	Trophy Lakes, USA	Aug. 28, 2005
Barefoot slalom	20.6 crossings of wake in 15 sec	Keith St. Onge (USA)	Bronkhorstspruit, South Africa	Jan. 6, 2006
Tricks	12,400 points	Nicolas Le Forestier (France)	Lac de Joux, Switzerland	Sep. 4, 2005
Barefoot tricks	9,730 points	Andre de Villiers (South Africa)	Carmond, South Africa	Mar. 5, 2005
Jump	239 ft 6 in (73 m)	Freddy Krueger (USA)	Polk City, USA	May 29, 2005
Barefoot jump	8 ft 12 in (27.4 m)	David Small (GB)	Mulwala, Australia	Feb. 8, 2004
Ski fly	298 ft 10 in (91.1 m)	Jaret Llewellyn (Canada)	Orlando, USA	May 14, 2000
Overall	2,818.01 points	Jaret Llewelyn (Canada)	Seffner, USA	Sep. 29, 2002

WOMEN	RECORD	NAME & NATIONALITY	PLACE	DATE
Slalom	1 buoy/10.25-m line	Kristi Overton Johnson (USA)	West Palm Beach, USA	Sep. 14, 1996
Barefoot slalom	17.0 crossings of wake in 15 sec	Nadine de Villiers (South Africa)	Witbank, South Africa	Jan. 5, 2001
Tricks	8,630 points	Tawn Larsen Hahn (USA)	Wilmington, USA	Jul. 11, 1999
Barefoot tricks	4,400 points	Nadine de Villiers (South Africa)	Witbank, South Africa	Jan. 5, 2001
Jump	186 ft (56.6 m)	Elena Milakova (Russia)	Rio Linda, USA	Jul. 21, 2002
Barefoot jump	67 ft 7 in (20.6 m)	Nadine de Villiers (South Africa)	Pretoria, South Africa	Mar. 4, 2000
Ski fly	227 ft 8.2 in (69.4 m)	Elena Milakova (Russia)	Pine Mountain, USA	May 26, 2002
Overall	2,903.43 points	Clementine Lucine (France)	Mauzac, France	Aug. 8, 2004

★ NEW RECORD
⭐ UPDATED RECORD

MEN'S WATER-SKIING – ⇨ TRICKS

Nicolas Le Forestier (France) is officially the world's best-scoring trick-skier, having achieved a record 12,400 points on September 4, 2005. The International Water Ski Federation appointed Le Forestier as 2005 male skier of the year – the first time that this award was presented to an athlete in a specialized area such as trick-skiing.

Le Forestier also holds the Guinness World Record for **most waterski flips in 30 seconds**. He completed 16 full 360° flips on one waterski in 30 seconds on the set of *L'Été De Tous Les Records*, Biscarrosse Lac, France, on August 5, 2003, and again on July 13, 2005.

WOMEN'S 63 KG

Pawina Thongsuk (Thailand) takes part in the weightlifting World Championships in Doha, Qatar, on November 12, 2005. At this event, she broke three world records in the 63 kg category when she lifted 116 kg for snatch, 140 kg for clean and jerk, and 256 kg total.

⚠ X-REF

On September 24, 2005, Franz Müllner (Austria) supported the greatest weight ever on two human shoulders when a helicopter landed on the frame he was supporting on his back. Find out how heavy this was on p.82.

★ **NEW RECORD**
☆ **UPDATED RECORD**

WEIGHTLIFTING

MEN	CATEGORY	WEIGHT LIFTED	NAME & NATIONALITY	PLACE	DATE
56 kg	Snatch	138 kg	Halil Mutlu (Turkey)	Antalya, Turkey	Nov. 4, 2001
	Clean & jerk	168 kg	Halil Mutlu (Turkey)	Trencín, Slovakia	Apr. 24, 2001
	Total	305 kg	Halil Mutlu (Turkey)	Sydney, Australia	Sep. 16, 2000
62 kg	Snatch	153 kg	Zhiyong Shi (China)	Izmir, Turkey	Jun. 28, 2002
	Clean & jerk	182 kg	Maosheng Le (China)	Busan, South Korea	Oct. 2, 2002
	Total	325 kg	World Standard*		
69 kg	Snatch	165 kg	Georgi Markov (Bulgaria)	Sydney, Australia	Sep. 20, 2000
	Clean & jerk	197 kg	Guozheng Zhang (China)	Qinhuangdao, China	Sep. 11, 2003
	Total	357 kg	Galabin Boevski (Bulgaria)	Athens, Greece	Nov. 24, 1999
77 kg	Snatch	173 kg	Sergey Filimonov (Kazakhstan)	Almaty, Kazakhstan	Apr. 9, 2004
	Clean & jerk	210 kg	Oleg Perepetchenov (Russia)	Trencín, Slovakia	Apr. 27, 2001
	Total	377 kg	Plamen Zhelyazkov (Bulgaria)	Doha, Qatar	Mar. 27, 2002
85 kg	Snatch	186 kg	Andrei Ribakov (Bulgaria)	Wladyslawowo, Poland	May 6, 2006
	Clean & jerk	218 kg	Zhang Yong (China)	Tel Aviv, Israel	Apr. 25, 1998
	Total	395 kg	World Standard*		
94 kg	Snatch	188 kg	Akakios Kakiasvilis (Greece)	Athens, Greece	Nov. 27, 1999
	Clean & jerk	232 kg	Szymon Kolecki (Poland)	Sofia, Bulgaria	Apr. 29, 2000
	Total	417 kg	World Standard*		
105 kg	Snatch	199 kg	Marcin Dolega (Poland)	Wladyslawowo, Poland	May 7, 2006
	Clean & jerk	242 kg	World Standard*		
	Total	440 kg	World Standard*		
+105 kg	Snatch	213 kg	Hossein Rezazadeh (Iran)	Qinhuangdao, China	Sep. 14, 2003
	Clean & jerk	263 kg	Hossein Rezazadeh (Iran)	Athens, Greece	Aug. 25, 2004
	Total	472 kg	Hossein Rezazadeh (Iran)	Sydney, Australia	Sep. 26, 2000

WOMEN	CATEGORY	WEIGHT LIFTED	NAME & NATIONALITY	PLACE	DATE
48 kg	Snatch	97 kg	Nurcan Taylan (Turkey)	Athens, Greece	Aug. 14, 2004
	Clean & jerk	118 kg	Mingjuan Wang (China)	Doha, Qatar	Nov. 9, 2005
	Total	213 kg	Mingjuan Wang (China)	Doha, Qatar	Nov. 9, 2005
53 kg	Snatch	102 kg	Ri Song Hui (North Korea)	Busan, South Korea	Oct. 1, 2002
	Clean & jerk	127 kg	Xueju Li (China)	Warsaw, Poland	Nov. 20, 2002
	Total	225 kg	Yang Xia (China)	Sydney, Australia	Sep. 18, 2000
58 kg	Snatch	110 kg	Li Wang (China)	Bali, Indonesia	Aug. 10, 2003
	Clean & jerk	139 kg	Wei Gu (China)	Doha, Qatar	Nov. 10, 2005
	Total	41 kg	Wei Gu (China)	Bali, Indonesia	Nov. 10, 2005
63 kg	Snatch	116 kg	Pawina Thongsuk (Thailand)	Doha, Qatar	Nov. 12, 2005
	Clean & jerk	141 kg	Svetlana Shimkova (Russia)	Wladyslawowo, Poland	May 3, 2006
	Total	256 kg	Pawina Thongsuk (Thailand)	Doha, Qatar	Nov. 12, 2005
69 kg	Snatch	122 kg	Chunhong Liu (China)	Athens, Greece	Aug. 19, 2004
	Clean & jerk	157 kg	Zarema Kasaeva (Russia)	Doha, Qatar	Nov. 13, 2005
	Total	275 kg	Chunhong Liu (China)	Athens, Greece	Aug. 19, 2004
75 kg	Snatch	130 kg	Natalia Zabolotnaia (Russia)	Doha, Qatar	Nov. 13, 2005
	Clean & jerk	159 kg	Chunhong Liu (China)	Doha, Qatar	Nov. 13, 2005
	Total	285 kg	Natalia Zabolotnaia (Russia)	Doha, Qatar	Nov. 13, 2005
+75 kg	Snatch	137 kg	Meiyuan Ding (China)	Vancouver, Canada	Nov. 21, 2003
	Clean & jerk	182 kg	Gonghong Tang (China)	Athens, Greece	Aug. 21, 2004
	Total	305 kg	Gonghong Tang (China)	Athens, Greece	Aug. 21, 2004

* From January 1, 1998, the International Weightlifting Federation (IWF) introduced modified bodyweight categories, thereby making the then world records invalid. This is the new listing with the world standards for the new bodyweight categories. Results achieved at IWF-approved competitions exceeding the world standards by 0.5 kg for snatch or clean and jerk, or by 2.5 kg for the total, will be recognized as world records.

☆ WOMEN'S 58 KG ➡ CLEAN & JERK AND TOTAL

Wei Gu (China) competes in the women's 58 kg category at the weightlifting World Championships held in Doha, Qatar, on November 11, 2005. She had a lift of 139 kg in the clean and jerk, and a total of 241 kg.

WINTER X GAMES

DISCIPLINE	MEDALS	HOLDER & NATIONALITY
Overall	10	Barrett Christy (USA)
Skiing	8	Jon Olsson (Sweden), Tanner Hall (USA)
Snowboard	10	Barrett Christy (USA)
MEN		
SnoCross	8	Blair Morgan (Canada)
Moto X	2	Tommy Clowers, Mike Jones, Mike Metzger, Caleb Wyatt, Brian Deegan (all USA)
★ Skier X	5	Enak Gavaggio (France)
★ Skiing Slopestyle	4	Jon Olsson (Sweden), Tanner Hall (USA)
★ Skiing SuperPipe	4	Jon Olsson (Sweden)
★ Snowboarder X	5	Seth Wescott (USA)
★ Snowboard Slopestyle	5	Shaun White (USA)
★ Snowboard SuperPipe	4	Danny Kass (USA)
WOMEN		
★ Skier X	5	Aleisha Cline (Canada)
★ Snowboarder X	3	Erin Simmons (Canada), Lindsey Jocobellis (USA)
★ Snowboard Slopestyle	5	Barrett Christy, Janna Meyen (both USA)
★ Snowboard SuperPipe	4	Kelly Clark (USA)

← ★ WOMEN'S SNOWBOARD SUPERPIPE

Kelly Clark (USA) competes in the women's Snowboard SuperPipe finals at Winter X Games 10 on January 28, 2006. During her career, Clark has won a record four Winter X Games SuperPipe medals.

X GAMES (SUMMER)

DISCIPLINE	MEDALS	HOLDER & NATIONALITY
Overall	20	Dave Mirra (USA)
BMX Freestyle	20	Dave Mirra (USA)
Moto X	9	Travis Pastrana (USA)
Skateboard	16	Tony Hawk, Andy Macdonald (both USA)
Aggressive In-line skate	8	Fabiola da Silva (Brazil)
Wakeboard	6	Darin Shapiro, Tara Hamilton, Dallas Friday (all USA)

X GAMES ➡ SKATEBOARD

Professional skateboarder Andy Macdonald (USA) has the record for most skateboarding medals at the X Games, with a total of 16. He shares this record with Tony Hawk (USA).

LONGEST SPORTS MARATHONS

SPORT	TIME	NAME & NATIONALITY	PLACE	DATE
Basketball	40 hr 3 min	Titans Basketball Club (Ireland)	Galway, Ireland	Sep. 23–24, 2005
Billiards (singles match)	45 hr 10 min	Arie Hermans and Jeff Fijneman (Netherlands)	Oosterhout, Netherlands	Feb. 12–14, 2004
Bowling	100 hours	Suresh Joachim (Australia)	Toronto, Canada	Jun. 8–12, 2005
Bowling (lawn)	36 hours	Arnos Bowling Club (UK)	Southgate, UK	Apr. 20–21, 2002
Bowls (lawn)	80 hr 25 min	South Grafton Bowling, Sport & Recreation Club (Australia)	South Grafton, Australia	Oct. 1–4, 2004
Cricket	26 hr 13 min	Cricket Club des Ormes (France)	Dol de Bretagne, France	Jun. 21–22, 2003
Curling	33 hr 10 min	Rotary Club of Ayr/Ayr Curling Club (UK)	Ayr, UK	Mar. 24–25, 2005
Football	26 hr 24 min	Tyson and Snickers teams, Ingram Futbol Club (USA)	Centerton, USA	Aug. 19–20, 2005
Futsal	30 hours	Max Cosi/Quinny and Christos Michael Keo teams (Cyprus)	Limassol, Cyprus	Nov. 19–20, 2005
Handball	70 hours	HV Mighty/Stevo (Netherlands)	Tubbergen, Netherlands	Aug. 30–Sep. 2, 2001
Hockey	240 hours	Brent Saik and friends (Canada)	Strathcona, Canada	Feb. 11–21, 2005
Hockey (indoor)	24 hours	Mandel Bloomfield AZA (Canada)	Edmonton, Canada	Feb. 28–29, 2004
Hockey (inline)	24 hours	8K Roller Hockey League (USA)	Eastpointe, USA	Sep. 13–14, 2002
Hockey (street)	30 hours	Conroy Ross Partners (Canada)	Edmonton, Canada	Sep. 17–18, 2004
Korfball	26 hr 2 min	Korfball Club de Vinken (Netherlands)	Vinkeveen, Netherlands	May 23–24, 2001
Netball	55 hours	Capital NUNS Netball Club (UK)	London, UK	Jul. 22–24, 2005
Parasailing	24 hr 10 min	Berne Persson (Sweden)	Lake Graningesjön, Sweden	Jul. 19–20, 2002
Pétanque (boules)	36 hr 2 min	Operation Boule (Germany)	Marl, Germany	Apr. 29–May 1, 2005
Punch-bag	36 hr 3 min	Ron Sarchian (USA)	Encino, USA	Jun. 15–17, 2004
Rifle shooting	26 hours	St. Sebastianus Schützenbruderchaft (Germany)	Ettringen, Germany	Sep. 20–21, 2003
Skiing	202 hr 1 min	Nick Willey (Australia)	Thredbo, Australia	Sep. 2–10, 2005
Snowboarding	180 hr 34 min	Bernhard Mair (Austria)	Bad Kleinkirchheim, Austria	Jan. 9–16, 2004
Softball	95 hr 23 min	Delmar and Renmark/Drive for 95 (Canada)	Dollard-des-Ormeaux, Canada	Jun. 29–Jul. 3, 2005
Tennis (singles match)	25 hr 25 min	Christian Barschel and Hauke Daene (Germany)	Mölln, Germany	Sep. 12–13, 2003
Tennis (doubles match)	48 hr 6 min	Kadzielewski, Siupka, Zatorski, Milian (Poland)	Giliwice, Poland	Aug. 30–Sep. 1, 2002
Volleyball (indoor)	51 hours	Bunbury Indoor Beach Volleyball (Australia)	Bunbury, Australia	Nov. 18–20, 2005
Water polo	24 hours	Rapido 82 Haarlem (Netherlands)	Haarlem, Netherlands	Apr 30–May 1, 1999
Windsurfing	71 hr 30 min	Sergiy Naidych (Ukraine)	Simerferopol, Ukraine	Jun. 6–9, 2003

GWR marathon guidelines are constantly updated – please contact us for information before you attempt a record.

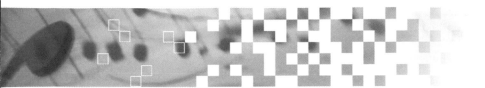

SUPERLATIVES

eye 39
ferris wheel (centerless) 205
fish 41, 164
fish market 130
floating reed islands 25
foods 130, 131
forehead inflation 72
foreign object left in a patient 68
forestation project 16
forests 16
frog 42
fruit pie 129
fruit salad 129
fruit and vegetables 128, 129
gaming vessel 136
geode 15, 16
gun ever built 203
heart 47
hot spring 25
hotel lobby 197
hula hoop spun 135
ice hotel 197
iceberg 27
igloo 197
insectivore 48
jellyfish 34
jigsaw puzzle 135
joypad 153
kangaroo 48
kugel 150
lagomorph 48
lakes 24
land gorge 12
lava lake 16
LCD screen 158
lemur 49
light and sound show 204
liquid body on Earth 17
lizard 43
M&M mosaic 96
mammal 47; land 50
marine animal structure 27
meromictic basin 27
monkey 49
motorcycle (rideable) 204
movie studio 182
musical instrument 191
natural ice rink 25
newspaper 9
oasis 22
object to be removed from a
    human skull 69
observation wheel 197
ocean 27
ocean-based launch platform
    144
ocean landfill site 27
pancake ice 27
paper building 197
parasites 34
pearl 39
plants and flowers 32–33
plasma screen 159
playing card structure 204
political constituency 113
primate 48, 49
pyramid 109
rabbit 126
religious structure 199
reservoirs 24
river basin 25
river to dry up 25
robot 156
rockets 144, 145
rodent 51
Rube Goldberg 148
salt flats 15
sand island 23
saw 204
sculptures 198
sea to dry up 14
ships 205
snowflake 29
soccer shirt 242
spider webs 37
standing set 178
stars and planets 141
statues 199
stealth ship 119
submarines 203
supermarket cart 9

telescopes 140, 141, 157
ticks 37
tornado 29
triumphal arch 198
Twister board 137
underpants 9
venom glands 37
war hospital 71
warships 203
wasp 36
waterfall 17
weasel 47
wing-span (bird's) 45

Least
corrupt country 122
extensive metro 201
Oscar nominations 188

Lightest
birth weight 65
tent 158

Longest (distance)
back flip: BMX 265; Moto X 265
bus trip 201
catches: flying disc by dog 126;
    golf shot 245
cycling: backward 238; no hands
    239
dive by a pig 127
drop kick (rugby) 252, 253
escalator ride 207
fire walk/rides 94
flight: airship 81; nonstop 81,
    201; paper plane 97
hurling hit 228
journeys 78–81, 207
jumps: bungee (tandem) 8;
    kangaroo 49
inline skating 134
lacrosse throw 228
laser communications link 142
lawnmower ride 78
lightning flash 29
mission by a space suit 148
Olympic torch relay 248
one-handed golf carry 245
pilgrimage 79
play (football) 216
polar sled journey 77
rally 225
ramp jumps: BMX 264; garbage
    truck 206; motorcycle 214
range: artillery piece 202;
    combat mission 203
reversal of tractor-trailer 207
surf ride on river bore 260
terrestrial animal migration 51
underwater cave traverse 18
voyage by model sailing ship 134
on water slide 8

Longest (length) 206–207
abacus 206
ancient canal 109
animal 34
bill (bird's) 44
body parts 61
bra chain 207
bridges 206, 207
bus 200
cableway 207
cake 207
canal (big-ship) 207
carbon nanotube model 148
cat 127
cat whiskers 127
city wall (ancient) 198
comic strip 8, 174
dam (rubber) 207
drawbridge 206
ear hair 58
earthquake fault rupture 17
estuary 25
family tree 65
fingernails 55
fjord 27
flowstone cascade 19
foods 131
French knitting 134

goat horns 126
goldfish 127
golf cart 207
hot dog 131
ice tongue 16
laundry chute 196
lightning (man-made) 149
model train 206
motorcycle 206
mountain range 16
nose, primate 49
novel 177; graphic novel 175
paper chains 134
rabbit ears 126
river 22, 25
root 33
salami 131
stalactite 18
subduction zone 20
toenails 57
tongue, mammal 51
tributory 25
trike 207
vegetables 128, 129
whale tooth 47
worm species 35

Longest running
body farm 149
comic 174
horticultural show 128
laboratory experiment 149
TV shows 180

Longest (time)
banzai skydive 95
boxing match 234
cock-crow 45
coma 69
court hearing 123
day on Earth 20
drought 2
earthquake 20
fasts 36
fire burning 20
full-body burn 74
gap between test-tube births 65
holding breath 95
hospital stay 71
ice age 14
in an attic 95
interval between twins 64
juggling (suspended) 193
light bulb burning 151
living mammal 50
living with scorpions 94
manned lunar orbit 142
marriages 65
medical operation 69
memory of a cell 59
note on wind or brass
    instrument 190
nuclear fusion reaction 151
Olympic careers 248
opera 190
pétanque match 136
rally in: badminton 256; table
    tennis 256; tennis 257
reign 111; World Heavyweight
    boxer 235
rodeo ride 82
serving golf club employee 245
spaceflights 142, 143
spinning: frying pan on finger
    96; golf ball on putter 245
standing on handlebars 192
surviving: with no pulse 69;
    with one lung 69; without
    food/water 94; transplantee 69
tattoo session 72
time dilation 148
time at No.1 in music charts 186,
    189
time in same TV role 180
time to return to No.1 186
TV commercial 179
underwater 77
uninterrupted live broadcast 179
volcanic eruption 20
wall of death ride 95
wars 118

Lowest
car ownership 112
cost of living 113
desert 23
food consumption 114
life expectancy 113
selling music chart-topper 187
temperature: body 50; endured
    45; man-made 148

Most
accurate weapons 202, 203
active: muscle 59; volcano 21
beneficial parasite to humans 34
bloodthirsty bird 45; parasite 35
bright: bioluminescent bay 26;
    dolphin 46
compulsive swallower 71
consistent chart artist 187
consumed fruit 115
corrupt country 122
deadly magic trick 95; man-made
    chemical 148
destructive insect 23
detailed image of a spiral galaxy
    140
difficult musical instrument to
    play 190
distant object in universe 140
durable announcer (baseball)
    233
emotionally responsive robot 157
energetic animal brain 40
fearless mammal 46
fertile fish 40; parasite 35
flexible man 57
forested country 16
frequent clapper 180
furry frog 42
genetically streamlined
    bacterium 151
heat-tolerant animal 23;
    organism 34
honest nation 122
hydrophobic seal 47
jailed actor 161
Jell-o eaten with chopsticks 96
lead turned into gold 149
light-sensitive eyes 38
mobile joint 59
northerly primates 30
overexposed celebrity 160
played game 137
popular: extreme sport 214;
    form of international travel
    201; non-surgical aesthetic
    procedure 73; tourist
    destination 201
prolific cat 127; composer 190;
    murderer 122; screenwriter 182
resistant insect 36
salty lake 24
sandy desert 23
scent-dependent robberies 122
sleepy mammal 51
stolen painting 122
Tabasco sauce drunk 132
therapeutic robot 157
versatile film maker 182
visited tourism region 201

Most common
blood group 59
elements 15
language 112

Most dangerous
ant 165; bird 163; insectivore 48;
    lizard 166; mosquito 163; sea
    urchin 27

Most expensive
airport 196
caviar 125
chocolate 124
cocktail 133
cup of tea 133
elephant art 172
hair cut 72
inauguration 113
Monopoly board 137

movie ever made 170
music manuscript 191
painting sold online 172
pair of jeans 125
production car 125
residence 124
sandwich 130
skin beauty treatment 124
soccer players 167, 168
soup 132
toasted sandwich 125
tourist trip 201
TV mini-series 178
whisky purchase 133

Most (number)
360 kickflips in 1 minute 215
abundant bird 44; seal 47
AIDS-related deaths 70
anvil lifts 83
apples bobbed 90
aquabike barrel rolls 260
arrows caught 95
artificial joints 69
ascents of Everest (woman) 76
bee stings removed 69
beer bottles opened with teeth 90
bees in mouth 95
birds ringed 44
blood donated 68
body turns with three cigar
    boxes 193
bone marrow donors 70
bones broken in a lifetime 59
bras unhooked 90
bull's-eyes in 90 seconds 254
bullwhip cracks 90
bungee jumps 93
cartwheels 90, 91
catches by a fielder (cricket) 237
centuries in cricket 236, 237
century breaks in a season
    (snooker) 255
chainsaw-juggling catches 95
chart hits (music) 186, 187
chess games played
    simultaneously 137
children to survive a single birth 64
chilli peppers eaten 132
chin-ups 83, 91
chromosomes 32
circus artists in country 192
clean sheets (soccer World Cup)
    169
clothespins: clipped on face 97;
    held in hand 97
cockroaches eaten 90
cockroaches in a coffin 95
coin rolls 91
concerts performed in a day 93
conquests of Mount Everest 78
consecutive bull's-eyes in
    shooting 255; flatspins 214;
    footbag moves 227; frontside
    ollies 215; haircuts 93; passes
    in beach volleyball 229;
    US Opens started 244; water
    polo passes 226
cosmetic makeovers 72, 93
countries visited by bicycle 201
cows killed by lightning 28
crash-test collisions 95
cricket matches played 237
cricket matches umpired 236
custard pies thrown 91
debt per capita 113
defensive features on a truck 121
diamond albums 188
dismissals (cricket) 237
dogs walked simultaneously 126
downloaded podcast 147
editions of a comic 174
eggs held in hand 97
elastic bands stretched over the
    face 91
entrants at a World Series of
    Poker 136
explosives detonated on a
    person 95
eyes on a fish 40
fatalities in a crocodile attack 165

ACKNOWLEDGMENTS

For Guinness World Records:

Chief Operating Officer Alistair Richards
Financial Controller Nicola Savage
Assistant Accountant Evan Williams
Contracts Administration Lisa Gibbs
Vice President, Sales & Marketing Sam Fay
Senior Marketing Manager Laura Plunkett
Senior Sales & Distribution Manager Nadine Causey
Sales & Marketing Executive Beatriz Fernandez
International Rights Manager Mary Hill
Senior Brand Manager Kate White
Communications Officer Sam Knights
Sales Coordinator Jack Brockbank
Records Management (remote) Amanda Sprague
TV Sales Manager Rob Molloy
Development Producer/A&R Manager Simon Gold
TV Production Executive Pam Schoenhofer
Software Engineer Katie Forde, Anthony Liu
IT Support Paul Bentley, Paul Rouse, Ryan Tunstall, James Herbert
Legal Nicky Boxall, Nick Hanbidge, Barry Kyle, Julia Lawrence
Human Resources Kelly Garrett
Facilities Manager Fiona Ross
GWR overseas Chris Sheedy (Australia), Angela Wu (China), Hiroko Yoshida (Japan), Olaf Kuchenbecker (Germany)

Index Christine Bernstein
Trading cards Yeung Poon, Matt Purkiss-Webb (55 Design)

Special thanks to

Jennifer Banks, James Bradley, Nick Minter, Iain Reid, Christopher Reinke, David Roberts, Nicola Shanks, Dan Stott, Nick Watson, Jimmy Weight

The 2007 book team would also like to acknowledge the following people and organizations for their help during the production of this year's edition:

Aardman Animations (Yalda Armian, Gabrielle Stackpool); Ernest Adams; Pedro Adrega, FINA; Dr Leslie Aiello; Mark S Allen; Stan Allen; Roy Allon; Americon Homes, Chagrin Falls, OH; Dr Martyn Amos; Jorgen Vaaben Andersen; David Anderson; Anritsu; Areotrend; Ed Asmus; Aussie Man & Van; Ron Baalke; Ballistic Marketing; Bank of England; Dr Peter Barham; BBC; BBC Wildlife Magazine; Oliver Basciano, Royal Botanic Gardens; Ted Batchelor and crew; Dane Andrew Beezley; David Billington; Jake and Amanda Birrell; Richard Boatfield; Body Worlds (Lauren Rose, The Franklin Institute Science Museum); Dr Richard Bourgerie; boxoffice mojo.com; Sir Richard Branson; Gail Bridgeman (Hasbro); Professor John Brown; BP; British Academy of Film & Television Arts; British Antarctic Survey; BBFC; British Museum; British National Space Centre; Tim Brostom; Dan Broughton (4W Web Design Ltd); BT; Dr Robert Angus Buchanan; Alasdair Busby, St Andrews Associates Ltd.; Terry Burrows; Pierre Butty (Alimentarium Food Museum); Caida; Caltech; Dr Robert Carney; Casella Group, Bedford, UK; Alan Cassidy; Peter Cassidy, RWA; Dr Kenneth Catania; Rose Catt; CERN; Deborah Chan; Dr Hubert Chanson; Professor Phil Charles; Tom, Robert, Rosie and Charles; Franklin Chang-Diaz; Edd China; Christie's; CIA World Fact Book; Isabelle Clark; Admiral Roy Clare; Richard Clark; Paul Coffey; CMR/TNS Media Intelligence; Competitive Media Reporting/TNS Media; Kathleen Conroy; Dr Mike Coughlan; Coutts UK (Greg Lawson, Iain Johnstone, Jo Underwood); Warren Cowan; Dr Paul Craddock; Neil Cresswell; Professor Mike Cruise; Jim Dale;

Dr Pam Dalton; Louise Danton (Academy of Television Arts & Sciences); Ceri Davies and Davies Media; Davy's at Regent's Place; Professor Kris Davidson; Dr Ashley Davies; Jim DeMerritt; Dr David Dilcher; Discovery News; Martin Dodge; Paddy Doyle; Gregory Dunham; Gary Duschl; Dylan's Candy Store, NY, Tracy Eberts; *The Economist*; Lourdes Edlin; Dr Joan Edwards; Ken Edwards; EETimes; Dr Farouk El-Baz; Dr Cynan Ellis-Evans; Elysium; Dr John Emsley; Louis Epstein; Europroducciones, Spain (Carmen Bodega, Maria Ligues); Europroduzione, Italy (Stefano Torrisi); Xiaohui Fan; Chad Fell; Adam Fenton; Sir Ranulph Fiennes; Keo Films; Sarah Finney; Forbes; Brian Ford; Steve Fossett; Jason French; Arran Frood; Funspot Family Fun Ctr., Weirs Beach, NH (Bob Lawton and Gary Vincent); Ashrita Furman; Tim Furniss; Michael Galbe; Marion Gallimore, FISA; Sarah Garcia (Lucasfilm); Martin Gedny; Geographical Magazine; Geological Society of London; Ricky Gervais; Dr Richard Ghail; Ryan Gibson-Judge; Gibson the Dog; Rosemary, Morris and Grant Gibson; Mauricio Giuliani; Stephanie Gordon; Granada Productions, Australia (Lauren Rudd, Sarah Roberts, Cameron Hammond, Toby Searles, Jason Moody); Mike Green and the Royal International Air Tattoo Show; Professor John Guest; Janine Guiseley; Dr Jim Gunson; Sandy Hall, Mary Hanson; Andy Harris, IWSF; Colin Hart; Fiona Hartley; Russell Harrington; Jed Harris, Harvard-Smithsonian Center for Astrophysics; Julia Hague, GABIT; Joanne Harris; Tony Hawk; Annie Hawkins Turner; Jeff Hecht; Stuart Hendry; Charles Hicks & Family;

Mark Higgins; Dr Paul Hillyard; Mat Hoffman; Hollywood Foreign Press Association; Shannon Holt; Dr David Horne; Graham Hudson; Paul Hughes; Amanda Hunter; imdb.com; Imperial College London; Intel; *Intelligence*; International Energy Agency; International Jugglers' Association; International Shark Attack File; Suresh Joachim; Professor Steve Jones; Iggy Jovanovic; JoAnn Kaeding; Emily Kao; David Keys; Dr Nichol Keith; Paul Kieve; Professor Joseph Kirschvink; Jamie & Ryan Knowles; Jaap Koomen; Sir John Kreb; Sergei Krikalev; Panama J. Kubecka; Dr Rolf Landua; Orla & Thea Langton; LaunchPad Productions (Ed Cunningham, Seth Gordon); Dr Roger Launius; Alain Leger; John Lee; Martin Lindsay; Tony Lloyd; Kate Long; Los Alamos National Laboratories; Robert Loss; Dr Karl Lyons; ReefQuest Centre for Shark Research; Klaus Madengruber; Paul Maisner; Ludivine Maitre; Li Malmberg; Simone Mangaroo; Professor Giles Marion; Lockheed Martin; Brian Marsden; Jenny Marshall; Dr Jim Marshall; Dave Masters, *The Sun Online*; Imre Matrahazi, IAAF, Max Entertainment, Malaysia (Alex, Belle, Marcus, Jeff, Faisal, Janice, Geetha and all); Paul McKain; Dr Alan McNaught; Stephen Merchant; The Met Office; Erin Mick; Microsoft; Angela Miller; Daniel Miller; Lauren Miller; Lucy Millington; Andy Milroy; Robert Milton; Edgar Mitchell; Phil Molloy; Paul Mole NYC, Dr Sir Patrick Moore; Professor Jon Morse; Derek Musso; Munich Re; Martin Munt; Michael Murphy; Derek Musso; nationmaster.com; National Academy of Sciences; National Adventure Sports Show; National Federation of Window Cleaners; *National Geographic*; *National Geographic Kids* (Rachel Buchholz, Eleanor Hannah); Natural History Museum; National Physical Laboratory; National Maritime Museum; National Science Foundation; NASA; the Nelson; NetNames; Ted Nield; NOAA; Amy Noble, NBPR; Natalie Nogueira; Norddeich Film & TV, Germany (Oliver Geissen, Ollie Wieberg, Sandra Milden); Barry Norman; NT gaming clan; Nua.com; Ben Foakes and Jasmine O'Brien; Oracle; Aniko Nemeth-Mora, IWF; Niamh O'Shea, Scottish Rugby; Gerald Overbeck, Amazon.com; Oxford University; Alan Paige; Ed Parsons; Stephen & Morag Paskins; Sheila Patek, Department of Integrative Biology, University of California, Berkeley; Kate Perkins; Conoco Phillips; Professor T. W. Pietsch, University of Washington; Karl Pilkington; Pinball Hall of Fame in Las Vegas, NV ("Airman First Class Hippie", Tim & Charlotte Arnold); Positive-Internet (Jake Jellinek, Jason Johns); PPARC; Fabrice Prahin, ISU; Joshua Prebble; Jeff Probst; Professional Bull Riding Association (Denise Abbott, Megan Buchwald, Megan Darnell, Boyd Moon); Qantas; Qinetiq; Giovanna Quattro, Disney Publishing Italia; Daniel Radcliffe; R&G Productions, France (Stephane Gateau, Jerome

Revon, Olivia Vandenhende, Jeff Peralta); John Reed, WSSR; Professor Sir Martin Rees; Victoria Reeves (Jelly Belly); Regional Planetary Image Facility, University College London; Brian Reinert; Martyn Richards; Ian Ridpath; Dr Mervyn Rose; Cory Ross; Sally Roth; Royal Astronomical Society; Royal Caribbean International; Royal Geographical Society; Royal Horticultural Society; The Royal Institution; Royal Society of Chemistry; Michael Rummery; Michael Russell; Judy Russo; Rutherford Appleton Laboratory; Ryan Sampson; Franz Schreiber, ISSF; The Science Museum, London; Search Engine Watch; Dr Paul Selden; Professor Dick Selley; Jordi Serra; SETI Institute; Kit Shah; Kiran Shah; Shell Fuel Economy Challenge (Zoe Corbett, Mike Evans, Amanda Glaiser, Nick Laffan); Xi Shun; Dr Martin Siegert; Siemens; Sotheby's; Spaces Antiques, Chagrin Falls, OH; Lara Speicher; *Stargate SG-1* (Carole Appleby, Claudia Black, Beau Bridges, Ben Browder, Robert C. Cooper, Christopher Judge, Brigitte Prochaska, Michael Shanks, Michele Sturdivant, Amanda Tapping, Brad Wright, Sony Pictures Home Entertainment, April Brock, Lindsay Colker); Julien Stauffer, UCI; Chantal Steiner, FITA; Dirk Steiner; Natalie Stormer; Stretch Communications; Aaron Studham, Adam Studham; Danny Sullivan; Alexei Svistunov; Greg Swift; Carolyn Syangbo; Mr Tang; Charlie Taylor; Dr Maisie Taylor; Taylor Herring (Bryony Watts, Hayley Hamburg, James Herring, Justin Jeffries, Jo Stapleton); Telegeography; Vincent Teissier (Cogent Communications); David Tennant; the-movie-times.com; Thumbs Up Productions, UK (Martyn Redman, T. J. Sherbrooke); Heather Tinsley; Trafik, Hoxton Square, London; Garry Turner; Twin Galaxies referees: Robert Mruczek, Tim Stodden, Stephen Knox, Tom Duncan, Troy Whelan, Greg Erway, David Nelson, Brien King, Tom Votava, Todd Rogers, Christian F. Cram, Shawn Cram, Mike Morrow, Mike Mahaffey, Wolff King Morrow, Jennifer M. Moore, Rick Carter, Andrew Peter Mee, Pablo Bert, Graham Dingsdale, Rodrigo Lopes, Cristiano T. Assumpcao, Valter A. Treib, Carlos C. Krueger, Perry Rodgers, Kelly Tharp, Joe LeVan, Dwayne Richard, Greg Sakundiak, Rick Fothergill, Paul Drury, Chris and Christine Millard, Mark Alpiger, Mark Longridge and Billy Mitchell; UK Planetary Forum; Professor Martin Uman; United Nations; Universities of Bath, Birmingham, Boston, Cambridge, Colorado, Dundee, Exeter, Florida, Greenwich, Hertfordshire, Lancaster, Louisiana State, Oklahoma, and Southampton; Professor Martin Uman; Niek Vermeulen; Emily Voigt; Juhani Virola; Ryan Wallace; Dr David Wark; Professor Kevin Warwick; Danny Way; Jessica & Isabel Way; Andy Weintraub; James Withers; Richard Winter; Dr Richard Wiseman; Matt Win; Woodreed Creative Consultancy (Nikki Kent, Charlotte Dahl, Jo Moffatt, George Campbell, Paul Austin); Daniel Woods; World Footbag

Association; World Met Organization; Professor Joshua Wurman; Dr David Wynn-Williams; X Games (Kelly Robshaw, Danny Chi, Debbie McKinnis, Katie Moses, Scott Hanley); York House, Twickenham.

In memoriam...
This year's edition is dedicated to Ann Collins, GWR's tireless Customer Relationship Manager. Goodbye also to Michel Lotito (Mr Mangetout, **strangest diet**), Matthew McGrory (**largest feet**), George (**oldest living sheep**), Fred Hale (**oldest man and oldest driver**), John Prestwich MBE (**longest surviving iron-lung patient**), John Rice (brother of Greg, **shortest identical twins**), Bouncer (**oldest chinchilla**), Sam (**ugliest dog**), Dan Ross (**most passes received in a Super Bowl game**), Sniffles (**oldest living rabbit**), Percy Arrowsmith (husband of Florence, **oldest married couple**) and Herbert Brown (husband of Magda Fritz, the **oldest living married couple, aggregate age**).

Endpapers (left to right)
Front: Largest pillow, largest hot cross bun, most people shaving, hairiest family, largest TV sculpture, fastest mile pushing an orange with nose, fastest henna artist, most siblings to celebrate their golden anniversary, largest hora dance, highest bicycle bunny hop, largest water pistol fight, longest spring roll, most dogs walked (solo), most sherries available, largest display of rice dumplings, largest box of chocolate bars, hula hooping the most hoops, largest display of rice dumplings, most people rolling car tyres, largest custard pie fight (most pies), largest chocolate sculpture, tallest Texas bluebonnet, heaviest building moved intact, longest time to hold breath voluntarily, sign language-mass participation, largest rangoli pattern, most couples kissing simultaneously, most consecutive generations of twins, tallest wild cactus.

Back: Largest first aid lesson, longest painting by numbers, most sit-ups (24 hr, abdominal frame), largest finger painting, largest mass jump-rope, largest ice cream boat, largest stamp mosaic, largest dance class, speed gift wrapping, most explosives (squibs) on an individual, longest guitar marathon, oldest author to have first book published, fastest missile in service, fastest typing on a smartphone, most legs waxed in an hour, most siblings to complete the same triathlon, largest focaccia, largest aquarium, largest CPR training session, longest wheel-chair basketball marathon, largest wine bottle, longest reading-aloud marathon (team), most challenging Father Christmas world championships, tallest doughnut stack, largest pillow fight, longest table football marathon, tallest wig, most Smarties eaten (3 min), largest quiz, largest whoopee cushion sit, deepest seawater scuba dive.

STOP PRESS

★ LONGEST CONCERT BY A GROUP

The record for the longest concert by a group is 48 hours and was achieved by the band Sziami (Hungary) in Budapest, Hungary, between March 17 and 19, 2006.

★ MOST EXPENSIVE STAGE SHOW

The musical *The Lord of the Rings*, directed by Matthew Warchus (UK) and produced by Kevin Wallace Ltd, has a budget in excess of $22.3 million. The world premiere was on March 23, 2006, at the Princess of Wales Theatre in Toronto, Canada.

★ LARGEST PASSENGER LINER (CRUISE SHIP)

At 154,407 gross tonnes, the *Freedom of the Seas* is over three times the size of *Titanic* (46,328 gross tonnes). The record-breaking ship is 209 ft (63.7 m) high, 1,112 ft (339 m) long – 52 ft 6 in (16 m) longer than the Eiffel Tower is high – has a beam (width) of 183 ft 9 in (56 m), and space for 4,328 passengers and 1,412 crew. It cost $947 million and made its maiden voyage on May 3, 2006.

★ MOST EXPENSIVE RESIDENCE

La Maison de L'Amite is a beachfront estate in Florida, USA, owned by American billionaire Donald Trump. In May 2006, the sale price of the 33,000-ft² (3,065-m²) house was listed as $125 million.

☆ Longest nonstop international train journey

On May 16, 2006, a Eurostar train traveled the 883 miles (1,421 km) from London, UK, to Cannes, France, without a stop. The train was a special service to promote the big-screen launch of *The Da Vinci Code* (USA, 2006).

★ BIGGEST-SELLING DOWNLOAD IN A WEEK (UK)

Gnarls Barkley's single "Crazy" sold 73,102 units in the UK in the week ending April 15, 2006. This is the first time a song has reached the No.1 spot in the UK charts based exclusively on download sales.

★ LONGEST PEARL NECKLACE

The longest single-strand pearl necklace measured 492 ft 1 in (150 m) and was created and exhibited in Milan, Italy. Roberto Moschetto De Wan (Italy) used over 12,000 pearls to complete the necklace as part of the inauguration of the Fashion Week in Milan, Italy, on February 17, 2006.

★ FISH WITH LARGEST REPERTOIRE OF TRICKS

Albert Einstein, a three-year-old calico fantail goldfish, can perform six tricks, including playing soccer (pictured) and performing the limbo. He was trained by his owner Dean Pomerleau (USA) at the "Fish School" in Gibsonia, Pennsylvania, USA.

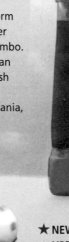

★ TALLEST ICE SCULPTURE

The tallest ice sculpture is 40 ft 3.5 in (12.28 m) high and was carved by Michel Amann (France) in Ski Dubai, Dubai, United Arab Emirates, on April 20, 2006. Michel worked with 10 carvers for 10 days on the sculpture, using 99,200 lb (45 tonnes) of ice in total.

★ NEW RECORD
☆ UPDATED RECORD